ADJUSTMENT
Pathways to Personal Growth

STEPHEN WORCHEL
Texas A & M University

GEORGE R. GOETHALS
Williams College

PRENTICE-HALL, INC., Englewood Cliffs, New Jersey 07632

Library of Congress Cataloging in Publication Data

WORCHEL, STEPHEN.
  Adjustment: pathways to personal growth.

  Bibliography: p.
  Includes index.
  1. Adjustment (Psychology)   I. Goethals, George R.
II. Title.
BF335.W64 1985   155.2   84–18330
ISBN 0–13–004136–X

Production editor: Linda Benson
Cover and interior design: Christine Gehring-Wolf
Page layout: Gail Collis
Photo research: Rhoda Sidney
Cover art: David Attie, ALPHA
Manufacturing buyer: Barbara Kelly Kittle

Portions of this book were previously published by Random House
under the title of *Adjustment and Human Relations*.

Printed in the United States of America
10   9   8   7   6   5   4   3   2   1

ISBN   0-13-004136-X   01

Prentice-Hall International, Inc., *London*
Prentice-Hall of Australia Pty. Limited, *Sydney*
Editora Prentice-Hall de Brazil, LTDA, *Rio de Janeiro*
Prentice-Hall of Canada, Ltd., *Toronto*
Prentice-Hall of India Private Limited, *New Delhi*
Prentice-Hall of Japan, Inc., *Tokyo*
Prentice-Hall of Southeast Asia Pte. Ltd., *Singapore*
Whitehall Books Limited, *Wellington, New Zealand*

For our wives Frances and BB
and our brothers and sisters
Harvey and Jason and
Pook, Bo, Kate, Barry, Sally,
Sam, Jem, Robby, and Ann
for all that you contribute to
our own personal adjustment

OVERVIEW

CONTENTS

SELF-DISCOVERY
IN ADOLESCENCE AND ADULTHOOD, 46

EMOTIONS, 76

PART 3
Interpersonal Relations

RELATING TO OTHERS, 222

AFFILIATION AND ATTRACTION, 256

11

LOVE AND INTIMACY, 280

12

HUMAN SEXUALITY, 312

ENVIRONMENT AND BEHAVIOR, 404

PREFACE

Shortly after we decided to write this text, we spent an evening reminiscing over our days as college students. Our aim was to compare that time with the present day in order to get a better perspective over the task faced in adjusting to today's world. While our memories surely have dulled with time, we were struck with the changes that have occurred over the last twenty years. Our lives as college students seemed so much simpler and more sheltered than those of students today. We rarely heard talk about unemployment; people were only beginning to be concerned about protecting the environment; it was unusual for a woman to consider a career such as medicine, accounting, or business; the possibility of a nuclear war seemed so remote that it was hardly worth talking about.

While we spoke fondly of the simplicity of the past, neither of us desired to return to the "good old days." Change has created a more complex world today, but it has also created one that is potentially more exciting, challenging, and fulfilling. Our world today is characterized by variety: variety in job opportunities, life styles, means of interpersonal communication, and technological advancements designed to make life easier. People today are faced with more choices than we faced as college students; life is more guided by personal choice than by rules and roles of society, some of which were well outdated and counterproductive. The potential to control one's own destiny seems much greater today.

This new freedom, however, can be either a blessing or a nightmare. People must be aware of their choices and know how to use their freedom or they may become lost and confused. Technology can be the spice of life only to the extent that people know how to use it productively. For example, advances in health care have prolonged life. But these additional years can turn into lonely prisons if society is not able to offer fulfilling opportunities to the aged. In short, today's world places great demands on individual adjustment; it can be a wonderland of excitement and fulfillment to the extent that the individual can grasp the new opportunities.

The rapidity of change in the modern world has raised new issues and challenges for personal and interpersonal adjustment. One of the earliest lessons of psychology was that individuals are most comfortable with the familiar and fearful of strangeness or change. Recent studies have shown that the greatest stress in one's life arises from change; both positive and negative changes are stressful. Thus, now, more than ever before, it is important to examine the adjustment process. How are we affected by changes in our environment? How can we best cope with new and different situations? When we have trouble adapting to stress, how and where can we seek help? Finding answers to these and other similar questions is important if we are to live a happy and emotionally healthy life.

The rapid evolution of our world has raised another challenge to our adjustment; this challenge is related to the issue of change but it has a unique complexion of its own. In their efforts to adapt to a changing world, people seem to have grown emotionally more separated from each other. An irony of the times is that as more efficient modes of transmitting news and conversation are developed, individuals increasingly complain that they feel isolated from others. A common complaint is that people have trouble making and keeping close friends. Communication between individuals is often superficial and meaningless. So much effort and attention must be directed to keeping up with changes in our environment that we have paid less and less attention to basic interpersonal interaction and to learning about ourselves.

It can hardly be argued that the study of personal adjustment and human relations is not important. Still, some question can be raised about the best way to approach these topics. For many years both of us have searched for suitable texts for our classes. The psychology of adjustment means different things to different people, and while there are many texts, none has provided exactly what we think is most clearly needed. In short, we felt students need to be aware of the knowledge that has been accumulated in various areas of psychology, and to see the implications of this knowledge in their own lives, as individuals and as human beings who relate to others. We believe contributions in personality, clinical, developmental, and social psychology are all important for a full understanding of the adjustment process. We have tried to present the most important ideas in these areas in a form that is most useful for students.

We believe that concepts and theories come alive for readers when they can see them operating in real lives. Thus we have started each chapter in this book with a biographical sketch of a person or people whose lives illustrate many of the ideas presented in the chapter. For example, Chapter 10, Affiliation and Attraction, presents a sketch of country singer Johnny Cash and his wife June Carter. Many of the concepts and studies discussed in the chapter are related to the lives of these two people. We hope that the application of the concepts to these lives makes the people more real and the concepts clearer and more applicable for you. The lives may also serve as examples by which you can test some of your own theories of human adjustment.

We have tried to select concepts that are useful and to present them in the clearest way we can. As noted, we want to include as much as possible from the various areas of psychology that speaks to our main concerns of adjustment and human relations. Although we have included many relevant theories, we have avoided excessive discussion of research and experiments. We are less concerned with evaluating theories than showing how they might be useful for you to think about. Where theories are controversial or where they con-

flict we have made you aware of it, but we have stood by our commitment to present ideas that can give you valuable insight into your own life and the lives of those around you.

We have also tried to help the reader identify the important points by including review questions within each chapter. These questions should help highlight major ideas. Also as an aid to learning, we have included an identification exercise at the end of each chapter, so the reader will be able to test his or her understanding of the main concepts. In an effort to bring the material to life, we have avoided using excessive jargon. However, we have not shrunk from our responsibility to teach; at times it was necessary to discuss important concepts from the field of psychology. These concepts are carefully defined in the body of the text and in the glossary section at the end of the book. Finally, we strongly believe that adjustment cannot be taught unless it is applied to each individual's own life. To help in this task, we have included exercises in each chapter that are aimed at getting you to reflect on your own life and adjustment process.

While only our names appear as authors, there were many people who played major roles in this project. We would like to thank Angie Giusti for her encouraging comments on the manuscript, especially on the case studies, her superb organization, and her perceptive comments on author stress. We would also like to thank Laura Holmes, Therese Ausems, Vicky Corrington, and Mary Koralewski for their help in preparing the manuscript, bolstering our often flagging spirits, and providing insightful comments on the text. A special note of thanks to John Isley of Prentice-Hall, who bravely captained our ship and gently guided the project from its inception. We are also indebted to Linda Benson, the Production Editor; she managed to keep her cool and wonderful sense of humor as deadline after deadline passed unmet and the authors promised to send her that vital section "tomorrow."

Our reviewers did a very special job. We often had mental pictures of them scratching their heads in wonderment about how we could have written this or that. Their comments were insightful and helpful and their style of gentle encouragement was greatly appreciated. We hope we have done justice to the hours you put into making this book one we can all be proud of. We would like to thank the following people for their reviews: Robert S. Anwyl, Miami-Dade College; Patricia A. Cote, Community College of Rhode Island; and Jeanne Keefer Cunningham.

Finally, we'd like to thank our families, Frances, Leah, and Jessica, and Marion, Jefferson, and Andrew who endured the constant clack of the typewriter, put off that much deserved vacation, suffered the ups and downs of weary authors, and always were there with a word of encouragement.

1
ADJUSTING TO OUR WORLD

E ach morning, Leo Beuerman wakes up, dresses, eats a quick breakfast, and heads off to work in the community near his home. These activities seem routine and hardly worth mentioning, since millions of other Americans go through the same procedure. But Leo's actions assume a new significance when we learn more about him.

Leo Beuerman was born shortly after the turn of the century. His birth was not a happy occasion, however, because Leo was born deformed. His limbs were mere stubs that barely supported his tiny feet and hands. Later it was learned that Leo was also deaf. While other children were growing tall and straight, Leo's body remained twisted and small; he would never be taller than an average three-year-old child.

In time, Leo became a captive of other people's fears. His mother, afraid some accident might befall this helpless creature, always kept Leo at home. She tended to his every need: cooking his food, washing and mending his clothes, and even moving him around the house.

All this aid, though given with the greatest love and good intentions, could have further crippled Leo by adding to his dependency and helplessness. But Leo was determined that this wouldn't happen; he wanted to be useful and to control his own life. He couldn't hear, but he could see. His arms were not long, but he could control his hands and fingers. His body was small, but his determination was great.

Leo learned to read and spent endless hours studying in an effort to gain a greater understanding of life. He felt not only that it was important to learn, but that communicating thoughts and feelings was crucial to a fulfilling life. Few people visited Leo, but he taught himself to use a typewriter and laboriously tapped out his thoughts and beliefs. He also learned to repair clocks and watches and supplemented the meager family income through this activity. His clock repair business gave him a sense of purpose and a feeling that he was making a contribution to his family and society.

The death of Leo's mother had an important effect on his life. He was now alone. There was no one to ensure that he was clothed and fed or that he could move from place to place. He could enter an institution where others would take care of his daily needs. Certainly no one would blame him for this decision; nature had treated Leo cruelly and he had a right to request help.

Leo thought otherwise, however. He refused to look at his misfortune, choosing instead to look at his fortune. He would use his talents and learn to compensate for his limitations. He was determined to be useful and happy.

He built a small cart to serve as his legs and give him mobility. By turning the wheels of the cart with his hands he could scoot from place to place. He designed a series of pulleys and chains that, when hooked to his ancient tractor, could hoist his cart and himself onto the tractor seat. This contraption freed him from the confines of home and allowed him to go into the neighboring community.

Leo was determined not to remain isolated. He felt that an individual can live a fulfilling life only if he or she learns to interact with and adjust to other people, although the adjustment process must stop short of the individual becoming totally dependent on others. So Leo decided to become a merchant; through this activity he

Leo Beuerman was determined to control his own life despite his physical limitations.

Courtesy, Centron Films, Lawrence, Kansas.

could support himself and remain a free and independent individual among others. His size, deafness, and lack of capital prevented his owning a large store with a large inventory. Leo reacted to these limitations by building a business that was suited to his situation; he sold pencils, pens, and other writing material from his little cart.

A common sight in the community near Leo's home is an ancient tractor slowly making its way down Main Street with a shriveled little man perched high on the seat. The tractor pulls into a parking space that, by custom, has become reserved for Leo Beuerman. Leo then goes through the long and tedious process of lowering himself and his cart onto the sidewalk. After securing his display case on the cart, Leo navigates to a shady spot on the sidewalk and opens for business. Proudly written in bold letters across the front of the display case is Leo's business code: "I GUARANTEE IT."

Leo Beuerman leads a useful, productive, and happy life. He is quick to supply the credo that has guided his own life: "I never did believe in being a quitter. Let nothing stop you until you get what you set out for or see your own mistakes." Leo also advises people to see the futility of self-pity and focus instead on the abundance of opportunities and abilities that they do have. Above all, he expresses the philosophy that people should concentrate on understanding themselves and mobilizing their forces for the supremely important endeavor of enjoying life. To accentuate this point, Leo proudly reports that he "is enjoying life very well."

WHAT IS ADJUSTMENT?

Leo Beuerman is different from most of us in many ways. Most of us are not forced to live in silence with a misshapen body. Most of us didn't spend childhood confined inside. Most of us have had far more formal education than Leo did. Yet despite all these differences, we all share something important with Leo Beuerman: We are all faced daily with the task of **adjustment.**

Adjusting to our world today is no simple task. It is probably fair to say that at no time in history has the process of personal adjustment been as complex or as difficult. Our world is a rapidly changing place, and each change—in technology, in social customs—makes new demands on our ability to adapt. On one hand, our world is becoming a more exciting and comfortable place to live; but, on the other hand, we constantly face new questions and challenges. Advances in medicine have added years to our life expectancy, but we must now deal with questions about how to make our additional years fruitful and happy ones. These days we can travel to almost any part of the world in a matter of hours or communicate with people anywhere, but these new freedoms force us to examine how we will handle conflicts that may arise from interactions with different people and cultures. The automobile increases our mobility but also creates the problem of pollution. Unlike our ancestors, we have an incredible array of choices about the type of job we'll hold, the part of the country we'll live in, and the type of social relationships we'll have. While our options are almost unlimited, we are now faced with more choices than earlier generations could've imagined. The prospect of having to make so many important decisions about our lives can be frightening and overwhelming. Thus progress and change add both bitter and sweet seasoning to our process of adjusting to the world around us.

The concept of personal adjustment has been given many definitions. In general, personal adjustment involves the everyday task of coping with ourselves, our environment, and the people we encounter. Adjustment is a com-

The computer allows us to solve problems and access information that was once out of our reach. But the modern invention has also created some problems: The computer does the work that once employed people; there is concern about how to protect individuals' privacy; there is even fear that people will use interaction with the computer in place of social interaction.

Hugh Rogers, Monkmeyer.

plex process. It involves (1) learning about and understanding ourselves and our social and physical environment, (2) using our understanding to set *realistic* goals for ourselves, (3) using our abilities to control our environment and destiny so that we can attain our goals, and (4) being sensitive to the needs and concerns of others so that we can also make positive contributions to the lives of others. In defining adjustment, we may well want to remember Leo Beuerman's life philosophy; in Leo's terms, personal adjustment involves the striving to enjoy life and to help others enjoy their lives. While the specific demands faced by each individual differ, we all face the necessity of adjusting to the world.

While our tasks are similar, it is clear that some of us do a better job of adjusting than others do. The well-adjusted individual is one who copes successfully and effectively with personal and situational demands. Achieving positive personal adjustment doesn't mean that we'll no longer experience problems, obstacles, or depressions. Everyone experiences all of these conditions; they are a normal part of everyday living. In fact, we measure adjustment by the way we handle such experiences. We can't determine the degree of our adjustment by our status in the social world or the size of our bank accounts. Rather, the test of adjustment is how we'll cope with the conditions of our lives.

Leo Beuerman will never be a "success story" in terms of the amount of money he makes or the type of occupation he holds; his daily income is barely sufficient to meet his most basic needs, and he will never enter a profession such as medicine, law, engineering, or teaching. His twisted body excludes him from many social events; in fact, many people turn away or even cross the street to avoid having to stare at the little man. Thus, by many standards, Leo's existence is not enviable. But on another scale Leo is a success. He has coped with his situation. He has learned to compensate for his physical deformities. He has developed friendships with people, many of them children, who are willing to stop and talk to him. Leo leads an independent and free life, and he has developed a sense of purpose and self-esteem. Above all, in spite of feeling lonely and depressed at times, Leo enjoys life and strives to live it to the fullest extent allowed by his capabilities. Leo has adjusted positively to the demands of his life and his environment.

THE PROCESS OF ADJUSTMENT

The beauty of human life is its diversity. Each of us is a unique person. Our experiences are different from other people's; the situations we face each day are unique to us; our attitudes, abilities, and values—however similar to those of others—are expressed in ways that are ours alone. So the requirements for, and the process of, adjustment are slightly different for each of us. This difference makes life exciting and chal-

lenging. It also makes it impossible for any book to lay out a plan of personal adjustment for everyone. No book or expert can tell you exactly what you should do to adjust to your world. Despite our wonderful differences, however, we all have experiences and life requirements in common. We all belong to groups; we all love and are loved; we all face situations that lead to conflict and anger; we all achieve successes and experience failures. Thus, while we can't describe a sure formula for every person's success and happiness, we can examine some of the basic questions and processes involved in our adjustment to our special worlds.

Knowing and Accepting Ourselves

A recent newspaper story told of an elderly woman who, dying of cancer, lamented: "I have spent so much of my life worrying about other people and other things that I have never taken the time to know myself." This statement probably characterizes many of us. Our world is changing at a very rapid pace, and we are constantly bombarded with new objects to possess, new places to go, and new ways to get there. Our increased mobility has brought us into contact with increasing numbers of people, and we spend a great deal of our time working to be accepted and liked by them. With all these environmental and social demands, we seem to spend very little time learning to know ourselves. Who are we? Why do we think, feel, and behave as we do?

Being out of touch with ourselves is unfortunate because it is the self that supplies us with the basic tools of personal adjustment. The self guides and, to some degree, sets the limits on our adjustment. Thus learning about ourselves is vitally important. Knowledge of ourselves may open the door to better understanding of our needs and behaviors and of the world we live in. For example, a clear understanding of our values and attitudes may help explain why we feel uncomfortable in some situations or why we choose the friends we do.

While learning about ourselves may open new avenues for personal adjustment, it may also reveal that we have some characteristics or limitations we aren't happy about. We may be able to change some aspects of ourselves, but there may be others we can't change. It's important to make this distinction in a realistic manner. Having done so, we can mobilize our efforts to alter the changeable characteristics and avoid wasting energy struggling with insurmountable obstacles. Instead, we can focus on compensating for those unyielding aspects of ourselves.

There are two important points to remember as we attempt to answer the question "Who am I?" The first is that our **self-appraisals** must be realistic. While we must be willing to accept that certain characteristics will be a part of us forever, we must avoid classifying a characteristic as unchangeable simply because it might take a great deal of effort to change. The second important point is that once we have made a realistic self-appraisal, we must be accepting of ourselves. To wallow in self-pity or despair because we aren't who we would like to be will destroy our ability to adjust and lead happy and fulfilling lives.

The example of Leo Beuerman clearly illustrates these points. When Leo's mother died, he was faced with deciding whether to enter an institution where others would take care of him or to live as an independent person who would take care of himself. In order to make this decision, he had to make a realistic appraisal of himself and his capabilities. If he indeed lacked the capabilities for self-sufficiency, a decision to remain on his own would be sheer folly and would have serious negative consequences. On the other hand, if he did have the capacity to care for himself, he would waste his life by deciding to become institutionalized simply because it would have required too much work to compensate for his limitations.

Leo learned about himself and made his self-appraisal. He acknowledged his physical deformities and his lack of education. There was nothing he could do to change his stubby limbs or deafness. He didn't like his deformed appendages, but he was willing to accept them.

He would have to compensate for them. He could build a cart to increase his mobility, but his physical condition would always place certain activities out of his reach. Rather than dwell on what he couldn't have, however, he focused on the opportunities that were available despite his impairments. His lack of education was a different story. He could overcome this deficiency. He could learn from books and he could communicate his thoughts by typing them out on his small typewriter.

One of the aims of this book is to present information that will aid you in your search for self-understanding and self-acceptance. We will examine how environmental conditions and social relationships during infancy and childhood play a major role in determining the personality of the adult. We will discuss the way in which individuals experience emotions and why the same condition may lead different individuals to experience different emotions. We will also focus on the factors that influence the development and change of attitudes and values. These discussions should provide further insights into why human beings think, feel, and behave as they do. Addressing these questions will help you to know and accept yourself, and in doing this you will be taking an important step toward positive personal adjustment.

Taking Control of Our Lives

One of the most depressing and frightening things we can experience is the feeling that we don't have any control over our own lives. Unfortunately, many people believe they are the pawns of their physical and social environment. They fail to perceive the choices that are open to them, and, instead of acting to control their situation, they simply react as external conditions dictate. Such people never experience the joys of positive personal adjustment.

In order to be well-adjusted, a person must make decisions about his or her own behavior. Healthy personal adjustment is an active process that requires decisions and independent actions. A state of positive adjust-

KNOWING YOURSELF

An important part of adjustment is knowing yourself and knowing what type of person you would like to be. We often take ourselves for granted and do not examine our strengths, weaknesses, and desires. The items below will help you look at yourself and identify the type of person you would like to be. It should also be interesting to compare how close you are to being the type of person you want to be. In order to get a measure of your Self–Self Ideal Discrepancy, add the numbers up in each column and subtract Column I from Column II. The greater this difference, the greater the Self–Self Ideal Discrepancy.

	I am a person who:					II I would like to be a person who:				
	never	seldom	sometimes	often	very often	never	seldom	sometimes	often	very often
1. feels he/she must win an argument.	1	2	3	4	5	1	2	3	4	5
2. plays up to others in order to advance his/her position.	1	2	3	4	5	1	2	3	4	5
3. refuses to do things because he/she is not good at them.	1	2	3	4	5	1	2	3	4	5
4. avoids telling the truth to prevent unpleasant consequences.	1	2	3	4	5	1	2	3	4	5
5. tries hard to impress people with his/her ability.	1	2	3	4	5	1	2	3	4	5
6. does dangerous things for the thrill of it.	1	2	3	4	5	1	2	3	4	5
7. relies on his/her parents to help make decisions.	1	2	3	4	5	1	2	3	4	5
8. has periods of great restlessness when he/she must be on the go.	1	2	3	4	5	1	2	3	4	5
9. seeks out others so they can listen to his/her troubles.	1	2	3	4	5	1	2	3	4	5
10. gets angry when criticized by his/her friends.	1	2	3	4	5	1	2	3	4	5
11. feels inferior to his/her friends.	1	2	3	4	5	1	2	3	4	5
12. is afraid to try something new.	1	2	3	4	5	1	2	3	4	5
13. gets confused when working under pressure.	1	2	3	4	5	1	2	3	4	5
14. worries about his/her health.	1	2	3	4	5	1	2	3	4	5
15. has difficulty in starting to get down to work.	1	2	3	4	5	1	2	3	4	5

	I am a person who:					II I would like to be a person who:				
	never	seldom	sometimes	often	very often	never	seldom	sometimes	often	very often
16. is dissatisfied with his/her sex life.	1	2	3	4	5	1	2	3	4	5
17. bluffs to get ahead.	1	2	3	4	5	1	2	3	4	5
18. goes out of his/her way to avoid an argument.	1	2	3	4	5	1	2	3	4	5
19. makes quick judgments about other people.	1	2	3	4	5	1	2	3	4	5
20. wonders whether parents will approve of his/her actions.	1	2	3	4	5	1	2	3	4	5
21. is afraid to disagree with another person.	1	2	3	4	5	1	2	3	4	5
22. ignores the feelings of others.	1	2	3	4	5	1	2	3	4	5
23. feels angry when his/her parents try to tell him/her what to do.	1	2	3	4	5	1	2	3	4	5
24. likes to gossip about the misfortunes and embarassments of his/her friends.	1	2	3	4	5	1	2	3	4	5
25. takes disappointment so keenly that he/she can't put it out of his/her mind.	1	2	3	4	5	1	2	3	4	5
26. suppresses or "bottles up" his/her feelings when angry with someone.	1	2	3	4	5	1	2	3	4	5
27. worries about saying things that will hurt other people's feelings.	1	2	3	4	5	1	2	3	4	5
28. feels resentful when bossed.	1	2	3	4	5	1	2	3	4	5
29. feels hurt when ignored by superiors.	1	2	3	4	5	1	2	3	4	5
30. holds grudges against those who have "hurt" him/her.	1	2	3	4	5	1	2	3	4	5
31. dislikes lending things to his/her friends.	1	2	3	4	5	1	2	3	4	5
32. worries about whether other people like him/her.	1	2	3	4	5	1	2	3	4	5
33. is critical of the behavior of most of his/her associates.	1	2	3	4	5	1	2	3	4	5
34. feels jealous when others get ahead of him/her.	1	2	3	4	5	1	2	3	4	5
35. makes excuses for his/her behavior.	1	2	3	4	5	1	2	3	4	5

An important part of controlling our lives involves deciding which groups we wish to join and seeking out friends.

Ken Karp.

ment isn't something that happens to us; it's something we make happen.

Fortunately, human life is filled with both the freedom and the opportunity to make choices. Unlike many animals who possess **instincts** that program them to act in a predetermined manner, humans have few, if any, instincts. As we will see later in this book, humans are influenced by various social and environmental situations. In spite of these influences, however, human beings have great potential to determine their own behaviors and attitudes toward life. It is important that we perceive this freedom and realize that we do control our own behavior. We must avoid the trap of feeling that we don't have freedom of choice in our lives.

One of the best ways to identify and preserve our freedom is to understand how and why specific experiences and situations tend to influence us. Nowhere is the saying, ''Knowledge is freedom,'' more applicable than in the area of personal adjustment. For example, we can know ourselves better by understanding the factors that have shaped our attitudes and values. This understanding will help us see why we choose to pursue certain occupations or why we feel guilty when performing certain actions. This understanding of our attitudes and values also helps us change or reshape those values with which we're uncomfortable. A case in point is Leo's childhood fear of leaving the

house, which kept him confined indoors much of the time. Then Leo realized how he had developed his fear: It was based on his mother's overprotective concern about him getting hurt, not on the fact of real dangers lurking outside the house. Understanding the basis for his fear allowed Leo to change his attitude and venture outside with self-confidence.

Control is one of the major themes of this book. We will examine how we can control our **social interactions** and actively seek out friends. We will discuss the pitfalls of giving up our control and relying on crutches such as alcohol and drugs to mask problems and conflicts. We will examine positive ways of dealing with our life situations, rather than hiding from our problems. By properly understanding the options we have to control our own destiny, we can make great strides in personal growth and adjustment. In a real sense, control is one of the keys to making our lives live up to their potential.

Setting Personal Goals

Leo Beuerman had a purpose in life; his goal was to own his own business and live a life free of dependency on others. This goal not only guided him in his day-to-day activities; it also gave him the strength to carry on when his life became particularly trying.

Positive personal adjustment is aided

when we have life **goals.** These goals give a sense of purpose to living and a direction in which we can focus our energies. For example, the decision to become a nurse not only gives a person a future goal, but also dictates present action. A person who has made such a decision will focus his or her school curriculum on science courses; he or she may wish to choose medically related summer jobs; such a person may also choose friends who have the same goal or who already practice the profession. Goals should be set in many areas. We can have professional goals, social goals, and spiritual goals. By setting many types of goals we can avoid becoming too preoccupied with any one aspect of our lives.

While setting personal goals is important for forming a healthy personality, several points should be remembered in choosing these goals.

First, goals must be realistic. We must carefully evaluate our capabilities and potentials and set goals that, while challenging, are within our abilities. If we set unrealistically high goals, we will encounter frustration and disillusionment. If our goals are too low, we will suffer boredom. Thus we must choose our goals carefully. In order to set realistic goals we must first learn about ourselves. We must also remember that the goal-setting process is a continuous one; we will be setting goals for ourselves throughout our lives. The attainment of one goal fosters the setting of a new one. The self-evaluation process must also be continuous.

The second point to remember about goal setting is that, while goals give a direction to our behavior, we shouldn't become so obsessed with them that we fail to enjoy the present. Some people become so concerned with their future they fail to adjust to the present. College students who feel they can't spend time participating in sports or social activities because they must constantly prepare for a profession are not showing positive adjustment. In cases such as these, the obsession with the future goal may be the result of a lack of self-confidence. These people have either failed to accurately assess their abilities or their goals are unrealistically high. Another trap that some people fall into is the use of a future goal to excuse present behavior. People may hide behind a future goal because they have no confidence in their ability to handle present situations. Students may use preparing for a profession as an excuse to avoid sports because they lack athletic skill. In that case the future goal will keep them from ever developing athletic skill. The well-known author Boris Pasternak once stated, ''Life is for living; not for preparing to live.'' Thus future goals are important, but they should facilitate rather than hinder personal adjustment and enjoyment of the present.

Finally, some attention should be given to

The more skills we learn and the more experiences we have, the better able we will be to set realistic goals for ourselves.
Rhoda Sidney.

choosing goals whose attainment will result in personal satisfaction. Our goals should represent a challenge, but achieving them should also be a source of pleasure. If your goal is to learn to play tennis, you should enjoy not only the learning process, but also the game itself, once you've become a good tennis player. Unfortunately, some people are unable to experience satisfaction from their goals; their lives revolve around challenge only, and they fail to experience the joy of their past achievements. This problem often results when we allow others to set our goals, rather than carefully choosing them ourselves based on our own desires and abilities. A person is unlikely to enjoy being a lawyer if she or he chose that profession simply because of pressure from parents or friends.

Many of the topics discussed in this book will help you in setting realistic personal goals. We will examine human motives and how they guide and focus the individual's attention. We will also examine how people make decisions and what effects these decisions have on thoughts and behavior. In addition, we will examine some of the factors that prevent us from making decisions and setting goals. By understanding these, we should be better able to avoid the paralysis that some people experience when trying to set goals. Finally, much of the information covered in this text is aimed at helping you learn about yourself. The better you know yourself, the more able you will be to set personal goals that are within reach.

Interacting with Others

The human is a social animal; we are born into a social group (the family) and spend our lives interacting with others. As illustrated by John Donne's meditation, written in the seventeenth century, individuals live in a social network and are interdependent:

No man is an island, entire of itself; every man is a piece of the Continent, a part of the main; if a clod be washed away by the sea, Europe is the less, as well as if a manor of thy friends or of thine own were; any man's death diminishes me, because I am involved in mankind; and therefore never send to know for whom the bell tolls; it tolls for thee.

Leo Beuerman clearly realized that the individual can't survive alone. One of his strongest impulses was to avoid a life of isolation. He longed for social interaction, and this longing motivated him to increase his mobility and venture into the world. While it's clear that Leo wanted to be part of society, it's also clear that he realized that social interaction didn't mean social dependency. Leo felt that a satisfying social relationship must be based on give-and-take. Each individual must be able to participate in social relationships without becoming totally dependent on those relationships and without giving up his or her identity and personal freedom.

Clearly, an important part of personal development involves adjusting to the social world. We interact with a large number of people every day. In fact, it may be eye-opening to count the number of people with whom you interact in a single day. All these people affect you to a greater or lesser degree, and in turn you have some influence on them. Because of this, it's crucial that we understand the areas of our lives influenced by social interaction.

In this book we will examine how others influence our attitudes and our behavior. We will discover some of the factors that motivate us to choose certain people as friends and to reject others. We will see how people influence the type of clothes we wear, the decisions we make, and the life styles we choose. We will also examine how our physical environment guides many of our social interactions. This information illustrates both how others influence us and how we influence others.

An understanding of social influences is important for a number of reasons. First, we are often unaware of numerous factors that affect our behavior. We react unwittingly to social and situational influences. A greater awareness of the existence and effect of these factors will not only allow us to better understand our be-

A dilemma in social interactions involves how to be an accepted part of social groups while retaining our independence and individual identity.

Ken Karp.

havior but also give us greater ability to control our own actions. For example, a knowledge of how groups produce pressures for conformity will enable us to better prepare for group membership and to resist those pressures when necessary. To be forewarned is to be prepared.

A second reason to study the process of social interaction is that it will allow us to be better able to relate to others. We can become more aware of how our behavior affects others and more sensitive to the feelings of others.

A third reason for understanding our social world centers on a dilemma that most of us face every day of our lives: On the one hand, we want to be liked and accepted by other people and to help make their lives happier; on the other hand, we want freedom to explore our world and learn about ourselves, free from social pressures and concerns about what others will think of us. In a sense, personal adjustment involves finding the right formula that

will allow us both to have satisfying social interactions without becoming consumed by them and to "do our own thing" without becoming socially isolated. A better understanding of social interactions will help us develop the proper recipe for adjustment to the world of other people.

Thus an understanding of the factors that

REVIEW QUESTIONS

1. How successfully we cope with our environment, others, and ourselves is a measure of our _____ _____.
2. Which of the following is *not* an important aspect of personal adjustment?
   a. knowing and accepting our strengths and weaknesses
   b. realizing that we have control over our life
   c. setting goals and striving to reach them regardless of the costs
   d. understanding the influences of social interaction
3. Unlike animals whose behavior is mostly predetermined by _____, humans have more freedom and ability to _____ their own behavior.
4. _____ _____ are an important aspect of adjustment, as they guide our actions and give us a sense of purpose.
5. A better understanding of _____ _____ helps us to be better able to relate to others, and understand the pressures that affect our behavior.
6. The factors influencing personal adjustment are complex. In order to study these factors in an orderly way, social scientists make systematic statements that attempt to explain why events occur. These statements are called _____.
7. Positive personal adjustment involves not only understanding yourself and others, but also _____ that knowledge.

influence social interactions will give you greater ability to determine your own behavior and to experience more satisfying relationships. Such understanding can be used to allow you to actively participate in relationships without becoming so dependent on those interactions that you sacrifice your individuality. In essence, understanding the factors involved in social interactions will aid you in winning friends, influencing people, and making a valuable contribution to your own development as a person and to your social world.

LEARNING ABOUT ADJUSTMENT

As we pointed out earlier, the path to adjustment is different for each of us. No two people have the same personal histories, nor do they face the same obstacles. The demands you face are different from those faced by the student seated next to you, and the demands on each of you will certainly be different from those faced by Leo Beuerman. Thus no book can supply a program of adjustment to be followed by everyone; neither life nor adjustment is that simple.

However, you can facilitate your adjustment by understanding the factors that infleunce both your feelings and behavior and the feelings and behavior of others. One important way of achieving this understanding is through careful reflection on the past and accurate observation of events and people in the present. These activities provide invaluable knowledge with which to guide personal adjustment.

Another important source of knowledge is the research and theory developed by social scientists. Their work aims to discover the factors that influence human behavior and emotion and to explain the process through which these factors work. A **theory** is a systematic statement that explains why events occur. Much of the research in psychology and other social sciences is aimed at developing theories of human behavior and testing the validity of these theories.

The work of the psychologist is aimed at understanding why people act, feel, think, and react as they do. The psychologist attempts to discover and explain how and why certain factors affect most of the people most of the time. This knowledge is invaluable from the standpoint of personal adjustment because it suggests why you become a particular type of person and why others behave as they do. Psychological theory and research point up the important events and factors to focus on when trying to understand ourselves and others. They also serve as a guide to how our behavior is likely to affect others.

Moving toward Adjustment

The achievement of positive personal adjustment is a two-part process. The first part involves developing a clear and accurate understanding of yourself and others and of the physical and social factors that influence human behavior. This can be achieved by examining the psychological literature presented in this book and supplementing it with observations of your own behavior and surroundings. The psychological literature should serve as a guide to basic processes and to identifying those factors in your personal life that deserve special attention. Your own observations can supplement the literature by pinpointing specific cases where these psychological principles are relevant.

Once you have developed a more complete understanding of yourself and others, it is important to take the second step, applying your knowledge. The road to healthy personal adjustment is paved with trials and errors. You must experiment with new behaviors and new ways of handling problems. The specific nature of these behaviors should be guided by your understanding of social and psychological processes. Even with this guide, however, some of the new attempts at adjustment you make will not be satisfactory, while others will prove very satisfying. It's important not to be discouraged by your mistakes; add the lessons learned from the mistakes to your store of knowledge. The more you understand yourself and others, the more capable you will be of making wise choices. The adjustment process is a lifelong activity, and it is important to have the courage to attempt new behaviors, to have the wisdom to accept and learn from successes and failures, and to have the flexibility to meet the demands of changing personal, social, and physical environments.

ORGANIZATION OF THIS BOOK

The process of adjustment involves knowing yourself, coping with the stresses of everyday life, understanding others, and being aware of the influence of the environment on social behavior. While these endeavors are interrelated, we have attempted to examine each of them in order.

Thus the first set of chapters is organized around the theme of knowing the self. In these chapters we look at how the personality develops from birth to adulthood and what factors influence this development. We also discuss how we can learn about ourselves and form self-concepts. We discuss the emotional process and how we learn to experience and express emotions. In a sense, these chapters discuss the basic tools each person has for meeting the challenges of everyday life. These "tools" include personality, self-concept, attitudes, beliefs, and emotions.

Having the tools is still a long way from getting the house built. As we discussed, our world is filled with choices and challenges that face us each day. The pathway to adjustment is paved by difficult decisions and stress. Understanding the types of stresses that we face and learning how to control our lives to effectively deal with these stresses is the topic of the second set of chapters. These chapters examine how stress arises; you may be quite surprised to learn that some of the joys of life, such as getting a promotion or taking a vacation, create stress. These chapters will also examine a wide variety of responses to stress. Some of

these responses are maladaptive, such as alcohol or drug addiction and emotional disorders. Other responses that involve taking control of the situation and meeting the problem head-on are quite adaptive and can lead to positive personal growth. In some cases the stress may be of a nature that requires us to seek the help of others in order to cope; knowing when and how to seek help increases our options in adjusting to our world. The last chapter of this group examines the wide range of opportunities we have in seeking the help of others in our quest for adjustment.

The next group of chapters focuses on interpersonal relationships. As we have pointed out, a major portion of the adjustment process involves interacting and relating to others. The chapters in this section deal with the factors that influence the relationships between two people. The opening chapter focuses on the variety of ways we communicate with others and how we perceive and interpret the behavior of another person. This is important because our response to others is based on how we perceive their actions, not necessarily on how they intended their actions to be. The next three chapters of this section focus on developing interpersonal relationships. We examine how individuals get to know each other, how norms and unwritten rules guide the acquaintance process, and the factors that determine to whom we will be attracted and with whom we will fall in love. We also discuss intimate relationships, sexual behavior, and marriage in these chapters.

The concluding section contains chapters on how our social and physical environments affect our behavior. The first chapter examines how belonging to a group can affect behavior. Issues such as conformity, dehumanization, and decision making in groups are addressed. The last chapter focuses on the physical environment. The effects of too few people and too many people are covered. We also look at how physical features such as temperature, noise, and building design influence behavior. The chapter concludes with a discussion of how living in a large city can influence our feelings and responses to other people.

We believe that learning about others will also allow you to better understand yourself. Because of this belief we open each chapter with a brief account of events in the life of some person or persons. Throughout the chapter we attempt to illustrate how a particular theory or research finding can lead to a greater understanding of this person or event. In this way we hope to broaden the perspective of human adjustment to include an understanding of both the self and other people.

A final note involves the philosophy of this book. As you can surmise from our earlier remarks, we don't believe that anyone or any book can tell you "how to adjust." We feel that the purpose of a book like this should be to supply the basic knowledge with which you can choose your own pattern of adjustment. So we refrain from saying "you must do this or that

to adjust." Rather, we have tried to draw on the principles of psychology that should give you the greatest insight into human behavior. These principles are not just educated guesses; they have, in most cases, been tested through careful observation and experimentation. We have tried not only to present theories of human behavior but also to discuss the major findings that support them. The research we cite should give you an understanding of how we learn about human behavior; it may also serve as a guide for your own experiments and observations.

Let's turn now to the study of human behavior and adjustment. We hope the information presented in this text will help you follow Leo Beuerman's advice: "Let nothing stop you until you get what you set out for or see your own mistakes."

SUMMARY

1. Adjusting to our world today is no simple task. The fast pace and rapid change that we face pose great challenges and create a number of choices for the individual. Adjustment involves the everyday task of coping with ourselves, our environment, and the people we encounter.

2. One step to personal adjustment involves knowing and accepting ourselves. Realistic appraisal of ourselves involves not only seeing our good and bad points but also knowing those things that we can change and those we can't.

3. A second step in personal adjustment involves taking control of our lives. Adjustment is an active process of understanding the choices that face us and being able to make those choices.

4. Positive personal adjustment is aided when we have goals, which help us organize our lives and guide our behavior. In setting goals, it is important to evaluate our abilities and understand our desires. Our goals should be realistic and likely to be satisfying to us once achieved.

5. Much of the adjustment process involves interacting with others. We are influenced by other people and influence them in turn. Adjusting to our social world includes forming close relationships and helping others lead more satisfying lives. As important as our social relationships are to our adjustment process, we must not lose our personal identity and autonomy.

6. Personal adjustment is a process of constant learning and doing. You can learn about yourself by carefully observing your own behavior and studying the behavior of others in your surroundings. Another important part of learning involves examining the psychological literature. Psychologists develop and test theories to explain why people

act, feel, think, and react in certain ways. These theories may enable you to predict your own behavior and that of others.

7. While it is important to develop a broad understanding of human behavior, it is also important to utilize this understanding. Personal adjustment involves experimenting with new behavior and learning from failures as well as successes.

8. This text is organized to examine how the self develops, how we cope with every-day stresses, how people are influenced and influence others, and how the environment affects personal and social behavior. Psychological theory and research are presented in order to develop a better understanding of these processes.

KEY TERMS

a. ADJUSTMENT d. SELF-APPRAISAL
b. GOAL e. SOCIAL INTERACTION
c. INSTINCT f. THEORY

1. Innate program that determines an organism's behavior in a given situation
2. Relating or interacting with other people
3. Object or condition that a person desires to obtain
4. Complex personal process that involves learning about one's self, setting goals, and coping with social and situational demands
5. Systematic statement that explains why events occur
6. Self-examination aimed at identifying one's abilities, values, and goals

ANSWERS TO REVIEW QUESTIONS

1. Personal adjustment. 2. c. 3. Instincts; control. 4. Personal goals. 5. Social interactions. 6. Theories. 7. Applying.

PERSONALITY DEVELOPMENT

T he newspaper headlines screamed. "JANE FONDA ARRESTED: ACCUSED OF SMUGGLING DRUGS, ASSAULTING OFFICER."

Jane Fonda was already a media celebrity at the time of her arrest in Cleveland in November 1970. The talented and beautiful daughter of one of Hollywood's most revered stars, she had launched a glamorous movie career of her own and had been gaining a reputation as a fine actor. Her work in the film *They Shoot Horses, Don't They?* had recently brought her an Academy Award nomination, and her next film, *Klute,* would win her the coveted Oscar. But for the time being Jane's brilliant career would be overshadowed by her politics.

A dramatic confrontation between Jane and government authority had appeared almost inevitable. Seemingly overnight, this privileged daughter of the conservative Hollywood establishment had become a radical anti–Vietnam War activist. Not long before, she had been one of *Playboy* magazine's sex symbols. Now she was pictured on the nightly news in battle fatigues, making speeches against "U.S. imperialism" and hugging enemy soldiers in Hanoi. For several years during the Vietnam era and afterward, Jane was one of "the system's" most outspoken and visible, if not always persuasive, critics. In time, her acting career would regain top priority and she would make several important films, but for the present she was faced with a series of charges that could result in a ten-year prison sentence and more than $10,000 in fines.

Jane Fonda was born in 1937 to wealth and social prominence. Her mother was Frances Seymour, a descendant of the family of Jane Seymour, the third of King Henry the Eighth of England's six wives. Her father was Henry Fonda, a famous actor whose roles on screen and stage reflected the traditional "All-American" values, and who would finally win an Oscar himself, in 1982, for his performance in *On Golden Pond,* costarring Jane Fonda.

In her early years, "Lady Jane," as she was called by her parents, spent much more time with her mother than with her father. Henry Fonda was in the midst of a demanding career, playing the Dust Bowl refugee Tom Joad in *The Grapes of Wrath,* his most famous role, and then serving in the navy in World War II. During these years Frances Fonda tried to raise Jane, and Jane's younger brother, Peter, in a manner consistent with her own elite New England background. Jane was trained to be a "proper young lady"—polite, refined, and well-disciplined. Frances placed very little emphasis on the expression of feelings and in fact seemed to regard feelings as somewhat unseemly. Jane was sent to parties dressed as "Lady Jane," but she rebelled against that role, and her behavior seldom conformed to her mother's expectations.

When Jane was eight, Henry returned home from the war, but Jane still saw little of her father. His relationship with Frances was deteriorating, and he kept some distance from the family. Nevertheless, Jane found him an attractive and engaging figure. He was interested in farming, and Jane liked to dress in the casual outdoor fashion of blue jeans and cowboy shirts he adopted, rather than in the more formal dress her mother preferred. But Jane's times of closeness to her father were few. She experienced a growing sense of inadequacy, both because she couldn't seem to meet her mother's demanding expectations and because Henry, a loving but emotionally reserved person himself, was preoccupied with other things.

When Jane was ten years old, the Fondas moved from California to Connecticut, a close commute to Henry's hit Broadway play, *Mister Roberts*. This move was hard on Jane, who loved the casual outdoor California life style. She had some difficulties adjusting to a private school in the East and was reported to be something of a hellion. Parents of her peers weren't eager to have their children play with Jane. Jane's mother reprimanded her, but the only result was that Jane's behavior deteriorated to the point that she was thrown out of Girl Scouts.

These relatively minor problems of adjustment faded when Jane, at age 12, faced a much more serious problem. Her parents still weren't getting along, and Frances was suffering from severe depression. While divorce proceedings were in progress, Frances entered a private mental hospital. In March of 1950 she was found in the bathroom next to her room, having bled to death from a self-inflicted throat wound. At first Jane wasn't told that her mother had committed suicide. She eventually found out when she read a story in a friend's movie magazine describing the death of Henry Fonda's wife.

Jane was despondent for several months after she learned the truth about her mother's death. She worried that her own behavior might have caused Frances's depression. One result of these feelings was that Jane tried harder than ever to please her father.

A happier time in Jane's life began when Henry remarried. Jane felt very close to her stepmother, Susan Fonda. She liked her new school, the prestigious girls' academy Emma Willard in upstate New York. At Emma Willard she began to express her talents and consider her future. She decided that she was interested in painting and dance. She also had a role in a school play, and one of the teachers said her performance was memorable.

Jane felt new confidence in herself and enthusiasm about her potential future in the arts when she entered Vassar College in 1955. Jane's experience at Vassar was a disappointment, however. She quickly grew tired of the rather strict social rules governing the all-women's school and neglected her studies. This and other misbehavior led to intense conflict with Henry. He insisted that Jane stay at Vassar and do well. Jane wanted to leave school and spend some time in Paris working on being an artist. Eventually Jane and Henry struck a bargain, and when Jane achieved a good academic record in the spring semester of her sophomore year, Henry allowed her to leave Vassar for Paris. While there, Jane tried to prove her artistic ability and please her father, but couldn't really get started in a productive way. She found herself thinking of becoming an actor, but she was too scared to try.

After a year in Paris, Jane returned to the States, having finally decided to take the plunge and attempt acting. She was admitted to the Actors Studio, a drama school in New York known for promoting "the Method," a naturalistic approach to acting that emphasized tapping into your own deepest emotions in order to express a character. Previous graduates of the Actors Studio had included James Dean, Marlon

Brando, and Marilyn Monroe. Jane's work at the Actors Studio showed considerable talent, and within a short period of time she made her first movie. The film itself, released when Jane was 22, wasn't a success, but Jane appeared to have a promising future in the movies.

Jane's personal life was another story. She was worried about her inability to maintain a relationship with a man. She had had affairs with several men, but couldn't seem to establish a deep and lasting intimacy. This changed when she began an affair with a man named Timothy Everett. Everett gave Jane something Henry had not given her: almost continuous positive reinforcement. He supported her feelings and ambitions and encouraged her to go into psychoanalysis. One of the results of the psychoanalysis was that Jane began to explore her anger toward her father and to express it, sometimes publicly. Jane's attempts to assert her own autonomous identity also led her to ridicule social conventions, such as marriage, that had always been important to Henry. Interviewers could usually count on interesting statements from Jane. Her outspokenness about conflicts with Henry often helped sell magazines.

Jane's estrangement from Henry, and from the ideas and conventions of the conservative America Henry represented, accelerated as Jane had an affair with another man and then moved back to Paris. She became lovers with the French film director Roger Vadim, who had had other well-publicized liaisons with beautiful and unconventional women younger than himself, including the ''sex kitten'' of French film in the fifties, Brigitte Bardot. The nude scene Jane did in a movie directed by Vadim was made much of in the American media.

While Jane's relationship with her father, and with American mores, deteriorated, Jane's acting career was finally established with her ninth film, *Cat Ballou,* which was a great popular and financial success by Hollywood standards. Jane's costar, Lee Marvin, won an Oscar, and Jane herself received praise for her comic performance.

The success of *Cat Ballou* was something Henry could appreciate, and led to a temporary improvement in his and Jane's relations. Then as Jane got more and more involved in the movement opposing the war in Vietnam, she and her father again became estranged. Jane married Roger Vadim and had a daughter. By 1969, when she played a down-and-out victim of the Depression in *They Shoot Horses, Don't They?* Jane had begun to feel that her previous roles in the movies had perpetuated traditionally biased stereotypes about women. By then she was also fully converted to ''New Left'' political ideology and activism and was apparently on President Richard Nixon's ''enemies list.''

In 1970 Jane was arrested in Cleveland and charged with illegal possession of drugs and assaulting a police officer. A civil suit for assault the officer brought against her granted her the ''right of discovery''—that is, the right of access to the information the government had against her. Charges were quickly dropped because the Nixon administration didn't want its struggle against dissidents open to the inspection of radical lawyers. Although Jane was out of legal trouble, her war with the government and with Henry continued. After winning an Oscar for *Klute,* she

Jane Fonda's workout has become very popular in the last few years.

S. Schapiro/Sygma.

went through her most politically radical and least professionally successful period. She split up with Vadim, said she wanted no more relationships with men, and visited the capital of North Vietnam, acquiring the nickname "Hanoi Jane."

Some degree of stability and tranquility entered Jane's life in 1973, when she married Tom Hayden, a "radical superstar" of the sixties, and had a baby boy. She and Hayden decided to "work within the system" and undertook many political projects together, including Hayden's unsuccessful campaign in California for the United States Senate. Jane began acting in, and producing, films that expressed her social and political values. In 1978 she made an acclaimed movie about a crippled Vietnam veteran, *Coming Home,* for which Jon Voigt won an Academy Award.

During the making of *Julia,* a movie about the friendship between two ambitious and socially conscious women, Jane apparently felt that her costar Vanessa Redgrave's extreme left-wing political stance was divorcing her from reality. This insight and her new family life seemed to produce further moderation of Jane's political style, if not of her political beliefs. She continued to make socially significant films, but they were also entertaining. These films included the highly successful *China Syndrome,* which dramatized the hazards of nuclear energy, and *Nine to Five,* a comedy dealing with discrimination against women in the workplace.

As her politics moderated and she became more involved with family, Jane's relationship with Henry improved as well. In 1981 Jane and Henry made their first film together, with Katharine Hepburn. *On Golden Pond,* a film about an elderly couple on vacation with their middle-aged daughter, touched on many themes of intergenerational conflict that were a large part of the lives of Jane and Henry. Making this movie with Henry was one of the most important experiences in Jane's life and symbolized the resolution of their long misunderstanding. Henry Fonda died shortly after winning an Academy Award for *On Golden Pond.*

In recent years Jane has continued to concern herself with improving the position of women in American society. *Jane Fonda's Workout Book,* a huge bestseller, is an example of the way Jane has attempted to encourage other women while also advancing her own career. In addition to her other activities, Jane has become quite a businessperson, promoting both her workout plan and a line of body suits and workout clothes.

With her considerable talent, fame, and belief that entertainment should raise people's consciousness about social problems, Jane Fonda will no doubt continue to be an important spokesperson for the causes in which she believes.

UNDERSTANDING PERSONALITY

Jane Fonda's life has been full of ups and downs: confusion and self-assurance, conflict and reconciliation, failure and success. Crises have marked every stage in her growth as a person, in early and late childhood, in adolescence, in early adulthood, and throughout her years of maturity. Her mother and father's unhappy relationship, their emotional reserve and demanding standards for their children, the loss of her mother, the estrangement from her father, her checkered film career, and her series of clashes with parental and governmental authority have all had important impacts on her life. How are we to understand the ways experiences like these, and other influences, shape a life history?

In this chapter we will consider the various influences on the development of personality, from physiological conditions and internal motivations to external events and social pressures. We will do so by outlining the three major approaches to studying personality: the psychodynamic approach, the behavioral approach, and the humanistic approach. After considering these approaches to personality we will consider what they can tell us about one of the most studied questions in psychology today: How does the behavior of men and women differ, and how can we best explain these differences? This is the question of "sex roles." Sex roles have been undergoing major redefinition in recent years, and Jane Fonda's life illustrates these changes particularly well.

PSYCHODYNAMIC APPROACHES TO PERSONALITY DEVELOPMENT

Psychodynamic approaches to personality have grown out of the theories of Sigmund Freud. Two of Freud's major ideas were that personality is shaped by unconscious motives and conflicts and that people are affected by different motives and conflicts at different times, or different stages, of their lives. These two ideas, unconscious motivation/conflict and stages of development, were central to Freud, and remain central in other psychodynamic approaches to personality. After considering Freud's theories of personality, we will consider some helpful additions to psychodynamic theory by Erik Erikson and Harry Stack Sullivan. Each of these psychological theorists discussed motives and conflicts, and each gave us a picture of psychological growth that nicely supplements Freud's.

Freud's Theory of Personality Structure

Sigmund Freud is a giant in the history of psychology. His thinking has had tremendous impact on our culture. His 23 volumes of writings touch on virtually every aspect of human experience. Many of Freud's ideas are highly controversial. However, we consider his view of the development of the major structures of personality during childhood to be useful in thinking about a person's struggle to adjust (Freud, 1940).

THE ID AND THE EMERGENCE OF THE EGO.

According to Freud, the child's personality, or psyche, at birth consists of a single entity. Freud called this entity the **id.** The id instinctively and unconsciously seeks pleasure and satisfaction of bodily needs. Unfortunately, the methods the id uses to gain pleasure are not very effective. It relies heavily on what Freud called **primary process,** the imagining of objects or behaviors that will bring pleasure. We are all familiar with daydreaming—about great achievements, love, food, or sex—but we know that fantasy by itself won't satisfy a person's needs. In order to get the real satisfaction and nurturance we require for survival, said Freud, we develop a second entity within the psyche to help the id cope with reality. This entity is called the **ego.**

The ego is the conscious, reality-oriented component of the personality. It perceives how the world works and devises plans for how best to obtain gratification. The ego may observe that it is useless to cry for a feeding until four hours have passed but that then screaming loudly brings results. Or it may notice that whimpering will lead to being picked up and rocked. Whatever the circumstances, the ego perceives, notices, remembers, plans, and directs action to obtain gratification for the id.

THE OEDIPUS COMPLEX AND THE EMERGENCE OF THE SUPEREGO.

Freud postulated that at about the age of three or four children develop feelings of intense love and hostility toward their parents. He felt that boys develop a desire to completely possess their mothers and sweep their fathers away as rivals for their mothers' affections. He claimed that girls at this age want to eliminate their mothers and have their fathers to themselves. These desires make up Freud's famous "Oedipus complex," named after the Greek king who unknowingly murdered his father and married his mother. The female's Oedipal wishes are sometimes called the "Electra complex," referring to Electra's

love for her father in the *Oresteia,* the Greek trilogy by Aeschylus.

Ideally, the Oedipal complex is resolved in the following way. The child's desire to possess one parent and destroy the other is repressed by the ego, that is, driven back into the unconscious, into the id, because of fears of punishment and loss of love. Because these fears are so intense, the Oedipal wishes are completely destroyed. Then the child begins to identify with, or emulate, the parent of the same sex, the one he or she previously wanted to eliminate. The child tries to be like that parent because of that parent's apparent success in getting the love of the opposite-sex parent, the one whom the girl or boy desired. By being similar to her mother or his father, the child vicariously enjoys the other parent's affections toward that parent.

A central part of identifying with the par-

A young girl who identifies with her mother will try to be as much like her as possible.
Laimute E. Druskis.

Freud proposed that the superego contains moral prohibitions and helps children resist temptation.

Mimi Forsyth, Monkmeyer.

ent of his or her own sex is that the child incorporates that parent's moral standards and ideals. These principles then form a third and separate entity in the psyche called the **superego.** The superego actually contains two parts, the **conscience,** containing prohibitions and restrictions, and the **ego-ideal,** containing aspirations and values to strive for. The superego can be harsh and punitive, causing the ego to feel very guilty if the person behaves inconsistently with its moral dictates.

Freud suggested that at some unconscious level men are still in love with their mothers and women are still in love with their fathers. Thus it might be expected that men would marry or fall in love with women who resemble their mothers, and vice versa. Although we can't know how Jane Fonda resolved her Electra complex, one of her biographers (Kiernan, 1982) has made an interesting observation about her relationships with men that fits this Freudian theory: Jane Fonda's first husband, Roger Vadim, in many ways resembled Henry Fonda. Her loving such a man would be consistent with Freud's theory of the Oedipal/Electra dynamics.

THE EGO AND SOUND ADJUSTMENT. According to Freud, after the Oedipal complex is resolved, the three major structures of the personality—the id, the ego, and the superego—are in place. The role of the conscious, rational ego is undoubtedly the most crucial to a person's healthy adjustment. In the healthy person the ego functions like the executive of the personality. It satisfies to a sufficient, but not complete, degree the desires of the id, the prohibitions and exhortations of the superego, and the constraints of reality. The ego has to coordinate these demands and plan effective behavior. It must hold the demands of the id and the superego in check so that it can respond to reality. This can be difficult and involve many conflicts. The ego's most important functions are to control our desires and express them in appropriate ways, to abide by moral standards, and to face the world realistically.

Erikson's Theory of Childhood Development

Jane Fonda emerged from her difficult childhood years as an independent and productive young woman. Freud's theory of the id, the ego, and the superego doesn't fully explain this outcome. However, one of Freud's most well-known followers, Erik Erikson, has outlined a theory of childhood development that is helpful in understanding how a person with Jane's strengths and weaknesses might emerge from childhood. Erikson (1968), like Freud, discussed three early stages of childhood development—the oral, anal, and phallic stages—but he added later stages of adult development and described in much more detail the challenges and opportunities people face in each of these stages.

We can probably understand Erikson's theory of early development in terms of a famous statement of Freud's. Asked what made a person healthy, Freud defined a healthy person as one who can "love well and work well." Erikson's discussions of the various "psychosocial stages" of development can be understood in terms of how a child develops the capacities to love well and work well.

Erikson believed that the way parents respond to a child's physical needs is of critical importance. If a child's needs are met in a consistent and caring way, the psychological outcome is likely to be a positive adjustment. If these needs are frustrated, or if the child is treated arbitrarily, the outcome is likely to be less than positive. Let us consider Erikson's views of how adjustment is affected by parent-child interaction in the first few years of life.

TRUST VERSUS MISTRUST. A child's needs in the earliest months of life are for nourishment and for the physical comfort that comes from cleanliness and warmth. This period is called the **oral stage.** The child's needs place great demands on the time, energy, and patience of the parents. The critical question for psychological development is how these needs are met. If the child experiences the parents as dependable and caring, he or she will develop a **sense of basic trust.** Basic trust is trust in oneself and in the external world, a sense that "I can rely on the world to provide some satisfaction of my

needs, and I can rely on myself to find satisfaction and safety in the world." A child with basic trust is able to have faith that the ego will survive psychic stress.

If, on the other hand, the parents are neglectful or hostile and do not reliably and warmly meet the child's needs, the child will probably develop a lasting **sense of basic mistrust,** a sense that the world cannot be counted on and that "I may not be adequate to meet its demands."

A child doesn't develop a total sense of trust or a total sense of mistrust, but rather a balance of the two. For the best adjustment, there should probably be a mix of trusting and skepticism. People who sense that the world, other people, and they themselves are generally trustworthy, but that there are definite exceptions and one needs to stay alert, will have optimal adjustment. Both the person who is too much a Pollyanna, who thinks that everything is wonderful and pure, and the person who is deeply cynical and guarded will have difficulty accepting things as they really are and behaving adaptively.

Another important point of Erikson's is that although a sense of basic trust or basic mistrust is established during the first year, later events can substantially modify the balance of trust and mistrust. The mistrusting child can probably develop a greater sense of trust if his or her experiences in later stages show that other people can be relied on. Still, it is unlikely that what the child learns on the basis of these initial experiences can ever be completely reversed.

The mother's handling of the child during the oral stage contributes to the child's sense of basic trust.

David Strickler, Monkmeyer.

AUTONOMY VERSUS SHAME AND DOUBT. At about the age of 18 months, toilet training typically begins. This phase of life, called the **anal stage,** can be marked by great conflict. The crucial question is how the parents respond to the child's needs and in what fashion they teach or impose control. If parents can set clear, reasonable limits, if they can encourage and help the child to do things independently, and if they are consistent in their demands and in their rewards and punishments, the child will develop a **sense of autonomy.** Autonomy be-

During toilet training, children can develop a sense of autonomy, a sense of control over their bodily functions, and a sense of free will.

Ken Karp.

gins as a sense of control over the body and its functions, a sense that one has the freedom to act individually within a set of clear limits. A sense of autonomy is very important because it provides a person with the "courage to be an independent individual who can choose and guide his own future" (Erikson, 1968, p. 114).

Parents who impose impossible limits on their children before the children are able to understand or meet them and parents who are inconsistent in their demands will usually instill in their children a **sense of shame and doubt.** These children will have difficulty learning to control their bodily functions. They will become ashamed of their failures and of themselves in general, and they will question or doubt their abilities to be independent.

Most children will develop a balance between a sense of autonomy and a sense of shame and doubt, and this balance can be altered by later experiences to some degree. Still, the parents' handling of toilet training and their overall guidance and control of children who are developing their own self-control will have a strong and lasting influence on this balance.

INITIATIVE VERSUS GUILT. Erikson believed that at about the age of three, in what he called the **phallic stage,** children develop strong attachments to the opposite-sex parent and hostility toward the same-sex parent. This view is similar to Freud's theory of the Oedipal conflict. More important, Erikson felt that a child's behavior becomes very assertive at this time. At three or four a child can do and get involved in many more things than a younger child. At this point, the parents' treatment of the child's sexual curiosity, aggressive impulses, and overall tendency toward action are critical. Within reasonable limits, parents must encourage and guide children's expanding activities and help children develop and appropriately use their emerging skills. Many of the child's aggressive energies need to be controlled and suitably channeled.

A child who is guided with clarity and caring will develop a **sense of initiative,** a sense of even greater control than the self-control provided by autonomy, a sense of being able to control objects and other people. A sense of initiative includes a sense of power and a sense of imagination and creative potential in dealing with the environment and people and objects in it. Children whose initiative isn't nurtured and channeled, who are constantly told no, or who are treated in a harsh and arbitrary fashion will develop a **sense of guilt** about the many varied wishes and desires they have in this stage. As in earlier stages, there is a balance of the positive and negative senses.

THE IMPORTANCE OF EARLY EXPERIENCE. Although Erikson frequently noted that the balance of trust and mistrust, autonomy and shame, initiative and guilt can be modified by later experience, the importance of early experience should not be overlooked. In general, Erikson's system holds that the outcome in one developmental stage strongly affects what happens in the next. For example, Erikson noted that "for the growth of autonomy a firmly developed early trust is necessary" (Erikson, 1968, p. 110), and it is likewise virtually impossible to have a sense of initiative without having a sense of autonomy. Although later experiences could modify a sense of shame and doubt, for example, it is difficult to imagine a child with shame and doubt engaging in the kind of exuberant, intrusive exploration and testing that is essential to developing a sense of initiative. With caretakers who provide encouragement, guidance, and support, it is possible for earlier handicaps to be overcome, but the point remains that difficulties or poor outcomes in the early stages can greatly impede successful outcomes in the later stages. Each stage builds on the next, and without a firm foundation little of value can develop later on. It is possible to develop trust, autonomy, and initiative at a much later age, and in effect to begin all over again, but a child who is not helped to overcome earlier psychological deficits is likely to fall further and further behind. Thus the treatment of the child in these first three or four years of life has an important bearing on successful adaptation.

Jane Fonda said that when she left Vassar she had thoughts of becoming an actor, but made a lot of excuses about why it would not be wise for her to get involved in acting. "The truth is," she once stated, "I was just afraid to try" (Kiernan, 1982, p. 65). Erikson's theory of psychosocial development helps explain the source of Jane's feelings of anxiety and inadequacy.

As a child, Jane Fonda's mother was very strict with her, but there was a very close nat-ural bond between mother and daughter. Thus it seems that Jane developed a sense of trust more than of mistrust. However, she resented her mother's demanding behavioral standards. Jane was successful in behaving independently of her mother's behavioral demands, especially when she had support from her father and her peers, so she developed a degree of autonomy; but, because of her failure to live up to her mother's demands, she also developed some degree of shame and doubt.

A weakened sense of initiative was especially damaging to Jane's courage when she thought of trying to become an actor. Frances Fonda's emphasis on everything being "just so" was characterized by "uncompromising rigidity about Jane's conduct" (Kiernan, 1982, p. 16). Jane was not encouraged to be spontaneous and assertive, and much of her independent behavior, especially the expression of strong emotion, was reprimanded. This atmosphere, which made Jane very sensitive to rebuff and gave her a lasting sense of inadequacy, seems to have left her with a weak sense of initiative, which only time was able to overcome.

INDUSTRY VERSUS INFERIORITY IN THE LATENCY PERIOD. The **latency period** is a long stage marked by schooling and children's attempts to develop intellectual, athletic, artistic, and social skills. If the increasing demands of authority figures, especially teachers, are accompanied by appropriate care and guidance, children will have a good chance of mastering the tasks that are required of them. Children with inner strength (in terms of favorable psychological balances from the early stages and sufficient physical and intellectual endowments), who also have caring people in the environment to encourage, instruct, and provide needed resources, will develop what Erikson called a **sense of industry:** a feeling of control and power, a sense of being able to do, to finish, to achieve, of being competent and confident. Children who do not meet with success in their efforts to do what they want or what others demand will develop a **sense of inferiority.** This is a feeling of having little worth and of not being a good human being, of being in-

In the early school years, children develop a sense of industry or a sense of inferiority.

Ken Karp.

ferior to others or to the demands of the environment. We all have these feelings at some time in our lives, but in many people they predominate and create further psychological problems.

Jane Fonda developed a good sense of industry as a young child, largely through success with peers, and the establishment of what can be called a sense of interpersonal competence (White, 1976). When Henry came back from the war and took up gardening and other outdoor activities, Jane did too and began to lead her younger brother, Peter, and some neighbor children in outdoor games. She was an inventive leader and developed a sense that she could do things and to them well. Her weak sense of initiative made her reluctant to try some things, but she did feel able to succeed at what she tried to do.

Sullivan's Theory of Developing Interpersonal Relationships

The last three stages of Erikson's theory we have discussed are primarily related to the "working well," rather than "loving well," part of Freud's formula for psychological health. Though we did touch on Jane Fonda's sense of interper-

sonal competence, we have not said much about her relationships with her peers, the interpersonal, or social, side of her personality.

Erikson didn't provide an extensive analysis of developing interpersonal relationships. Harry Stack Sullivan (1953) did. His theory is much more directed to the "loving well" part of Freud's formula and to how this capacity develops during childhood.

Sullivan emphasized that in the preschool years children's main need is for security. They feel secure when there are no threats to them in the environment and when their needs for tenderness from their parents are fulfilled. Sullivan also emphasized that very young children begin to develop self-concepts in the form of **personifications:** vague ideas or feelings that children have about themselves that contain both "good-me" and "bad-me" images. The "good-me" image is usually experienced when children are secure. The "bad-me" image is experienced when children are anxious or insecure. In Jane Fonda's case "bad-me" personifications would have predominated in the early years. When she became aware of the fact that she disappointed her mother, "bad-me" feelings would have become quite pronounced.

In general, Sullivan felt that by the age of five children have developed patterns of relating to their parents and siblings, ways of trying to maintain security and avoid anxiety, and rudimentary images of the self that are experienced at different times as "good-me" or "bad-me." After age five, interaction outside the home starts on a regular basis, and what happens outside the home becomes as important to adjustment as what happens inside the home. The juvenile era of the child's development then begins.

THE JUVENILE ERA. The juvenile era starts when children go to school and begin interacting with two new sets of people: peers and authority figures other than the child's parents, such as teachers, police, and playground directors. The first thing that juveniles need to learn is that there are tremendous differences among their peers. They also must learn that they are going to have to accept and adjust to these differences. This learning process is called **social accommodation.** It involves learning to perceive realistically the ways others differ from oneself and to make whatever accommodations are necessary so that one can interact with these others in ways that are secure and satisfying for both.

Jane Fonda was quite successful at social accommodation. Her neighbors and close friends, Brooke Hayward and her siblings, were the children of Henry Fonda's first wife, Margaret Sullavan, and Margaret's new husband Leland Hayward. These children were raised very differently from Jane and Peter, but Jane saw the ways they were different and managed to adjust her own behavior to get along well with them.

Jane Fonda may have had no trouble with social accommodation, but for others this learning process may be difficult in a number of ways. Children may be anxious about interacting with their peers. One of the consequences of this insecurity may be a rigidity of behavior and an inability to adapt so as to enjoy those who are different. Also, social accommodation is a two-way street; it also involves

others accommodating to you to some degree. Some children are victimized by the cruelty of their peers, who, according to Sullivan can display a "truly shocking insensitivity to feelings of personal worth in others and a degree of crudeness in interpersonal relations very rarely paralleled in later life." Thus one's own anxieties and rigidities and others' teasing and taunting may make learning to interact successfully with one's peers very difficult.

Just as one must learn ways of interacting successfully with peers, one must also learn about relating to authority figures. **Social subordination** is Sullivan's term for this learning. It involves understanding the roles played by authority figures, such as teachers, principals, and safety patrollers, and devising patterns of responding to these roles. Ideally a child will not be overly rebellious or overly submissive, but will learn the powers and privileges of each of these figures and, very important, the limits on their authority and their abilities. One rather painful lesson is that parents, like other authority figures, have limits on their power and ability. They are not gods, and, like all human beings, they have limits. This can be difficult for some children to accept, but learning a more

Children's behavior toward their peers can be very crude in the juvenile era.

Paul Sequeira, Photo Researchers, Inc.

realistic view of parents and other authorities is of great value in learning to deal successfully with people.

Jane Fonda's experience in forming a more realistic view of her father was complicated by the fact that he was a movie star. Many of the films he made when Jane was a young child were Westerns. Jane assumed that Henry was a real cowboy and was initially quite unhappy to learn that he fired his six-guns only in the movies.

MISFORTUNES OF THE JUVENILE ERA. While Sullivan highlighted the positive things that can happen at each stage of development, he also detailed a fairly devastating list of things that can go wrong at each stage. Many of these unpleasant experiences happen to most of us to some degree, but for some people they can have lasting negative effects on the personality. One of the key "misfortunes," as Sullivan called them, of the juvenile era is directly related to the "crudeness" and insensitivity that juveniles can show to each other, especially in regard to personal differences that they do not find acceptable. This is the experience of **ostracism,** of being cast out of the group by others.

Sullivan noted that juvenile society is divided into ingroups and outgroups, according to differences in background, ability, speed of maturation, health, and so forth. These ingroups and outgroups are recognized by authorities, especially teachers, as well as by peers. This division process always results in some being excluded from the ingroup and thus placed in the outgroup, which in some cases can be an isolated "group" of one. People in the outgroup can join together and work out their own relationships, and this "to some extent takes the curse off ostracism." Still, these ostracized youngsters show "pretty durable evidences of having been in an inferior position." They are uncomfortable with other people and have feelings of little worth.

Related to the idea of ostracism are Sullivan's concepts of **stereotypes** and **social judgments.** Stereotypes refer to juvenile tendencies to categorize people and close off interaction

TABLE 2.1

Psychological Stages, and Approximate Ages, in Psychodynamic Theories of Personality

THEORISTS	
Freud and Erikson	Sullivan
STAGES	
Oral stage (0 to 1½ years)	Infancy (0 to 1 year)
Anal stage (1½ to 3 years)	Childhood (1 to 4 years)
Phallic stage (3 to 5 years)	Juvenile Era (5 to 9 years)
Latency period (5 to 12 years)	Preadolescence (9 to 12 years)

with them as a result of the categorization. These stereotypes can be based on ethnicity or a personal characteristic. A child can be rejected because she is, for example, Oriental, or because he is perceived to be "a farm kid" or the teacher's pet. Social judgments are essentially personal stereotypes. They refer to the reputation a particular child gets as popular or unpopular, average, stupid, athletic, competent, ugly, and so forth. Sullivan lamented the juvenile tendency to stereotype and make social judgments, partly because of the damage to self-esteem that results for those who are denigrated, but also because of the limitations on social learning that are imposed by these practices. Stereotyping and then ostracizing someone on the basis of a difference prevents what might be very enlightening and humanizing interaction among different types of people. There are probably lots of ingroup juveniles who could profit immensely from interaction with stereotyped and ostracized juveniles, and vice versa, but ostracism precludes these possibilities.

A closely related development of the juvenile era is the "learning of disparagement." **Disparagement** is a device, usually learned from one's parents, for enhancing one's self-esteem by derogating and criticizing others, almost always behind their backs. Disparagement is psychologically futile in the long run because it does not ultimately succeed in boosting self-esteem: After cutting everyone down, you don't have any positive models to compare yourself with, aspire toward, or emulate. Also, you don't get any evidence of your own worth if noting the unworthiness of everyone around you consumes all your energy. Sullivan suggested that disparagement of others "gradually evolves into 'I am not as bad as the other swine.' " This provides some relief from insecurity, but "to be the best of swine when it would be nice to be a person . . . strikes at the very roots of that which is essentially human" (1953). Here again Sullivan noted both the crudeness of juveniles—a crudeness learned only too well from adults—and the cost to juveniles themselves of limiting their potentially positive contacts and relations with other people.

PREADOLESCENCE AND INTIMACY. Sometime around the age of nine, a child moves into the era Sullivan called **preadolescence.** The key aspect of this era is that one now has the capacity to genuinely care for, and be sensitive to, another person. A strong need for intimacy also develops. The result is that two preadolescents, usually of the same sex, both having the need and capacity for intimacy, form a close bond and become "chums." The intimate chum relationship is marked by a deep and almost idyllic mutual caring and concern. This closeness is extremely important because it permits the validation of one's own personal worth through a process called **collaboration.** Collaboration involves "adjustments of one's own behavior to the expressed needs of the other" and the pursuit of similar satisfactions. It comes from a genuine concern about the other person, a willingness to fully enjoy the other's successes and to help the other in gaining prestige and status, and a freedom from anxiety. When you find that someone else cares for you in this way and appreciates your own caring, your sense of self-worth and security increases.

Jane Fonda established a chum relationship with her friend Brooke Hayward. This relationship was extremely important to her, especially because her mother was so strict and her father was away much of the time when she was growing up. The importance of chums is often clearest when preadolescents lose them, often because one or the other chum

moves away. This happened to Jane Fonda at age ten when she moved from California to Connecticut. For a while she was miserable in the East because at first she had no friends. In her case, though, an unusually fortunate event occurred: Brooke's family also moved to Connecticut, and Jane and Brooke's friendship was resumed.

Although chum relationships don't last forever, they can be of lasting value because of their tremendous therapeutic potentials. The security and positive sense of worth they entail allow preadolescents to become less rigid in their perceptions and behavior and more open to change in adaptive directions. Preadolescents with chum relationships can be relaxed enough to learn successful modes of behavior from other successful preadolescents. They can drop inappropriate or harmful esteem-maintaining devices developed in the past, such as disparagement, bragging, or unrealistic and distorted self-images. These devices are no longer necessary when people are accepted for what they are. Being accepted by another in a deep way and having one's own caring accepted and appreciated provide a sense of worth and security that is unparalleled. The author William Goldman captures some of the good feeling of the chum relationship: "We walked for miles, hours, never once saying a word. Because right then, we didn't have to. We knew all there was to know; ourselves, the world, each other, everything. Those hours are the happiest I have ever had in all my life. . . . Nothing, nothing in this world is every going to take them away from me . . ." (1957, p. 53).

THE EXPERIENCE OF LONELINESS. The experience of intimacy and the chum relationship are among the most important aspects of interpersonal development. They provide as much joy and learning about oneself and others as is possible in human relations, and they can contribute greatly to psychological health. Unfortunately, not everyone has these relations. Sometimes the profound need for intimacy is not satisfied. When it is frustrated, a person experiences loneliness. We all have an intuitive notion of the experience of loneliness from our

REVIEW QUESTIONS

1. The two central ideas underlying Freud's theory of personality are that personality is shaped by _____ _____ and _____, and _____ _____ _____.

2. According to Freud, the aspect of our psyche that instinctively and unconsciously seeks pleasure and satisfaction of bodily needs is called the _____.

3. The resolution of the Oedipal (and Electra) complex results in the formation of the moral component of our psyche. Freud calls this component the _____.

4. The two aspects of the superego are the _____ and the _____.

5. Balancing the instinctual demands of the _____ against the moralistic demands of the _____ is one of the most important functions of the _____.

6. Erikson's theory of psychosocial development parallels Freud's stages of psychosexual development. Match the stage in Freud's theory with the corresponding psychosocial conflict hypothesized by Erikson.

   _____ oral   a. initiative vs. guilt
   _____ anal   b. industry vs. inferiority
   _____ phallic c. trust vs. mistrust
   _____ latency d. autonomy vs. shame and doubt

7. Sullivan's psychodynamic theory of personality emphasizes the development of interpersonal relationships. The first step in this development involves the "good-me" and "bad-me" feelings that young children have about themselves. Sullivan calls these feelings and ideas _____.

8. One of the most important events in the development of interpersonal relationships is the "chum relationship." This occurs, according to Sullivan, in the _____ era.

own lives. But the kind of loneliness Sullivan talked about is a chronic and unrelieved sense of isolation, despair, and meaninglessness stemming from the lack of deep interpersonal contact.

Sullivan considered loneliness to be the worst emotional experience imaginable. He admitted feeling "inadequate to communicate a really clear impression of the experience of loneliness in its quintessential force," but said that it is "so terrible that it practically baffles recall." Because it is even more painful than anxiety, loneliness will force people to attempt interaction and forming a relationship even though they are intensely anxious in doing so. The anxiety about forming a relationship often comes from having no clear notion of how to approach a relationship. As a result, lonely people often behave in awkward, obviously uncertain ways that are likely to make others uncomfortable. The relationship they seek is then almost doomed from the start. The end result is a disastrous state of affairs resulting in even more anxiety and loneliness.

Clearly, preadolescence is a critical time in human development. It offers the greatest potential for learning to accept oneself and to behave in realistic, truthful, and adaptive ways. On the other hand, if the intimate relations that provide these potentials are missed or lost, the resulting emotional trauma of loneliness can be crippling. Preadolescence and idyllic chum relations come to an end when adolescence begins and people start to develop mature sexual capacities and sexual interests. These will be discussed in the next chapter.

BEHAVIORAL APPROACHES TO PERSONALITY DEVELOPMENT

Jane Fonda had a generally undistinguished academic record at Vassar College. In fact, her behavior suggests that because she disliked being there, she tried to provoke the college administration to the point that she would be expelled. She did perform very effectively her last semester at Vassar, however. The reason for that improvement was that her father finally told her she could leave school and study the arts in Paris if she performed well in the spring semester of her sophomore year and proved to him that she was willing and able to work hard to achieve something. The result of this proposal was Jane's one semester of academic success.

This incident in Jane Fonda's life is highly consistent with the fundamental assumption of the behavioral approach to personality, namely, that behavior is under the control of its consequences. That is, we perform behaviors for which we have been rewarded or reinforced, or for which we expect reward/reinforcement, and we do not perform behaviors for which we expect either no reinforcement or punishment. This behavioral approach to personality development is very different from the psychodynamic approach in an important way: The psychodynamic approach views behavior as mainly determined by *internal* events, specifically, unconscious drives and conflicts; the behavioral approach views behavior as determined by *external* events, specifically, rewards and punishments. The behavioral approach has been put forth in an extreme way, called **radical behaviorism** by J. B. Watson and B. F. Skinner. However, the most influential behavioral approach today is called **social learning theory.** We will first look at radical behaviorism and then at social learning theory.

Radical Behaviorism

Radical behaviorism is heavily influenced by a concept known as the "law of effect." This concept, proposed many years ago by Edward Thorndike (1898), states that behavior that is followed by reward will be "stamped in" and behavior that is followed by punishment will be "stamped out." People learn to perform certain actions on the basis of what follows, reward or punishment. Children will learn to clean up their rooms if that's the only way they can get a smile from their mother in the morning.

The famous psychologist J. B. Watson was highly influenced by the law of effect and other research on conditioning and learning when he stated (1926, p. 10),

> Give me a dozen healthy infants, well-formed, and my own specified world to bring them up in and I'll guarantee to take any one of them at random and train him to become any type of specialist I might select—doctor, lawyer, artist, merchant-chief and, yes, even beggar-man and thief, regardless of his talents, penchants, tendencies, abilities, vocations and race of his ancestors.

In making this statement, Watson was arguing that behavior and personality are totally controlled by the environment.

B. F. Skinner, today's most prominent spokesman for radical behaviorism, agrees with Watson. Skinner is famous for his studies of **operant conditioning,** the procedure whereby the chances of an animal's performing a behavior, such as pressing a bar or pecking at a key, are increased by rewarding the animal after it performs that behavior. A behavior that is performed because of operant conditioning is called an *operant*. The behavior "operates" on the environment to obtain a reward. In short, Skinner and other radical behaviorists assume that personality simply reflects the behaviors that people have learned to perform as the result of what they have been reinforced or not reinforced for doing.

Social Learning Theory

Today most behavioral psychologists believe that learning is more complex than "stamping in" or "stamping out." For example, it has been found that punishment is very seldom an effective way to get people or animals to learn (Skinner, 1971). Furthermore, we know that while reinforcement is a crucial determinant of behavior, it works in subtle and complicated ways. Social learning theorists have made their most important contributions by exploring precisely how reinforcement does get people to perform certain actions. For instance, they have

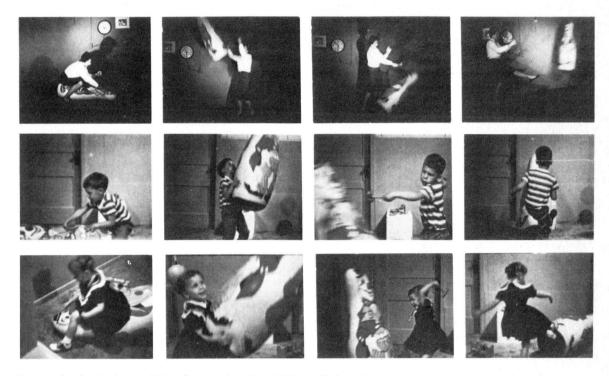

Classic studies by Bandura and his colleagues show that children will closely imitate the aggressive actions of adults. In these pictures, they hit and kick a Bobo doll, just like an adult.

Bandura et al., 1963.

shown that people can learn behaviors even if they are not directly reinforced for performing them. A child can learn aggressive behavior simply by observing another person, a **model,** behaving aggressively. This is called **observational learning.** Reinforcement is still important in this kind of learning because the way we act after observing another person depends in part on whether we see that person rewarded or punished. We are more likely to imitate people if their behavior meets with some kind of success or gratification (Bandura, 1965). Social learning theorists use the term *vicarious reinforcement* when people observe others receive reinforcement for their behavior.

Both direct reinforcement and vicarious reinforcement, based on modeling, were important in Jane Fonda's becoming involved in radical politics. She received direct reinforcement in the form of approval from several of the important men in her life as she began to speak out on social issues, particularly the injustices she perceived in the fabric of American society. Later in her career, as she became more concerned with women's problems, she received a great deal of support from other women who were happy to have such a visible figure (*model*) as Jane Fonda speaking on their behalf (and providing them with vicarious reinforcement). There was also vicarious reinforcement in watching the approval others got, from taking left-wing, anti-American views, particularly from movie people in Europe. In short, Jane had direct reinforcement, modeling, and vicarious reinforcement contributing to her involvement in political issues.

The contribution of social learning theorists to our understanding of how people develop is not limited to the simple concept of observational learning. They have expanded the work of previous behaviorists who argued that people are mechanically influenced by rewards and punishments. Social learning theorists emphasize the importance of cognitive factors such as perceiving, remembering, thinking, and forming expectancies. For example, how much we imitate a model depends on our estimate of exactly what led him or her to be reinforced, how likely we consider it that we would be reinforced for the same behavior, and our impression of whether or not we have the ability to perform that behavior.

Social learning theory also emphasizes the ways people make plans and regulate their own behavior (Mischel, 1973) and ways they can motivate themselves through self-regulation (Bandura, 1982). A specific example of self-regulation would be to allow yourself to do something enjoyable, such as watching a favorite television show, *only after* you have done a complete session of Jane Fonda's workout. This kind of self-management, rather than mere responsiveness to external rewards and punishments, is the kind of psychology emphasized by social learning theory. Jane Fonda's workout also is a good example of the way Jane has tried to outline ways that people, especially women, can improve their self-evaluation and feelings of efficacy through active behavior (Bandura, 1977). Over all, social learning theory provides a much more complete view of how we can learn to behave than does the old law of effect.

Another distinctive feature of social learning theory is that it emphasizes each individual's uniqueness. It maintains that each person is different as a result of his or her learning his-

---

TABLE 2.2

Person Variables in Social Learning Theory

Social learning theorists have shown that certain aspects of the person must be considered in order to fully understand behavior. It is not enough to talk about reinforcement and external factors. Walter Mischel (1973) has identified five key person variables.

1. Competencies: An individual's mental abilities, such as intelligence and creativity; physical abilities, such as athletic prowess; artistic abilities, such as painting, singing, or dancing.

2. Encoding strategies and personal constructs: The ways we categorize information in our environment, especially the groupings or categories we use to classify and judge other people; our concepts about things and people in the world.

3. Expectancies: Our expectancies about the consequences of our own behavior, about the ways others will behave, and the kinds of behaviors that are most likely to lead to reinforcement.

4. Values: What individuals find satisfying or rewarding; the things that matter to us.

5. Self-regulatory systems and plans: Arrangements we make with ourselves to take certain actions and to reward ourselves for doing them. These systems, such as having a snack only after studying for a specified period, are key aspects of self-control.

REVIEW QUESTIONS

9. Unlike the psychodynamic approach to personality that emphasizes internal events such as unconscious drives and psychic conflicts, the behavioral approach views personality as being shaped by external controls, namely _____ and _____ .

10. Radical behaviorism is based on the notion that behavior that is followed by reward will be repeated, while behavior that is followed by punishment will be eliminated. This is the famous Thorndyke formulation known as the "_____ of _____."

11. Personality is not merely shaped by rewards and punishments, but rather is influenced by cognitive factors as well (including self-management and vicarious learning). This is the contention of _____ _____ theorists.

12. Learning that occurs by viewing the actions of a model is called _____ learning.

13. T or F: Social learning theorists reject the importance of reinforcement in shaping personality.

tory. It also holds that a person's character will have a certain continuity, or stability, over time because learned patterns of behavior tend to persist until they are replaced by new ones, which takes time and experience. The approach to personality we will consider next provides a thorough consideration of the way time and experience can lead to major changes in personality, particularly through the experience called self-actualization.

HUMANISTIC APPROACHES TO PERSONALITY DEVELOPMENT

The humanistic approach to personality is in part a reaction against perceived shortcomings in the behavioral and psychodynamic approaches. Both of those approaches stress the fact that behavior is determined: The psychodynamic approach emphasizes the role of unconscious forces in determining behavior; the behavioral approach emphasizes the role of external rewards and punishments. In contrast, the humanistic perspective emphasizes human free will and the capacity of each individual to determine his or her own destiny. Because it is critical of the other two approaches, the humanistic approach is sometimes called "the third force." Two of the major exponents of the humanistic approach have been Carl Rogers and Abraham Maslow.

Rogers's Concept of Self-Actualization

Carl Rogers (1951, 1959) emphasized that each person strives toward **self-actualization,** the development of all his or her potentials and capacities. This tendency is also called self-realization. Rogers believed that children naturally strive to realize all that they are able to become. In addition to the need for self-actualization, humans also have a strong need for approval. As children they are dependent on their parents to meet this need. However, par-

A self-actualized person is one who has developed all his or her human potentials.

Rhoda Sidney.

ents do not approve just any behavior; they only approve certain behaviors, which become a child's **conditions of worth.** Children get approval and feel worthy only when they perform these behaviors. The problem is that the behaviors that meet the conditions of worth may not be the behaviors that lead to self-actualization. As a result of this conflict, children often suppress self-actualizing tendencies in order to get approval from their parents.

The conflict between self-actualizing tendencies and the need for approval must have been very strong when Jane Fonda was growing up. Her mother made very stringent behavioral demands on her. The consequence was that Jane often felt unworthy because she failed to meet these conditions of worth. It also appears that Jane's self-actualization was manifested in troublesome ways when she was a young girl, such as acting up in school and in the Girl Scouts.

Rogers discussed the way people who have lived under stringent parental standards can become more self-actualizing and can build their self-esteem. They must begin to interact with another person, perhaps a psychotherapist, or with other people in general, who will respond to them with unconditional positive regard, caring about them and approving of them as people, even though not necessarily approving of every single behavior they perform. Conditions of worth must be removed.

As a young woman Jane Fonda met someone who satisfied her need for unconditional positive regard. Timothy Everett, the man with whom Jane had a relationship in her early twenties, gave her constant approval, and this dependable approval gave her the inner strength to overcome her fears and begin to try to become the kind of actor she had dreamed of being. Everett helped Jane on the road to becoming what Rogers called a *fully functioning* person, one who accepts all the various self-actualizing tendencies within them, even though many may be inconsistent with the conditions of worth they learned as children.

Maslow's Hierarchy of Motives

Another important humanistic psychologist, Abraham Maslow, also emphasized the concept of self-actualization. In addition, Maslow showed how the need for self-actualization fits in with other important human motives. Maslow did this through his important concept of the hierarchy of motives. Maslow's (1970) hierarchical theory of motivation asserts that many motives drive men and women and that different motives are important at different times and in different situations. People have, "lower" and "higher" motives, and once the lower ones, such as the need to breathe or quench one's thirst, are satisfied, people become concerned with satisfying the higher ones, such as self-actualization.

Five kinds of needs form the motivational hierarchy, according to Maslow. First, there are physiological needs, such as hunger and thirst. Obviously, if physiological needs are not met, they preempt every other drive and become the main focus of concern. After the physiological needs are safety needs. A need for safety is more often seen in children than in adults, although adults show great concern for security

and do many things to ensure their safety. Buying insurance policies and seeking secure occupational positions are examples of adult means of satisfying the safety need. Maslow would have agreed with other theorists that people who have been least secure as children will be most worried about safety and security as adults. Their need for safety will be so strong that it can become neurotic and obsessive. Such people may never get beyond a concern for safety. They will always be frightened and unwilling or unable to turn their attention to deeper and more rewarding activities.

Third up the hierarchical ladder of motives are belongingness and love needs. These are mainly characterized by the need to be included in groups. They also include the need for affection from parents, peers, lovers, and spouses. People experience the need for love mainly when there is an absence of it. People who are included in groups and feel liked by others are satisfied and go on to concern themselves with other needs. Maslow believed that people who have satisfied their lower needs but have been frustrated, especially during their formative years, in their needs for love will be

TABLE 2.3

Maslow's Hierarchy of Motives

| SELF-ACTUALIZATION |
| the need to develop |
| all your potentials and |
| become all you are capable of becoming |

| ESTEEM NEEDS |
| the desire to be |
| competent and to be recognized for your |
| achievements |

| BELONGINGNESS AND LOVE NEEDS |
| the needs to be accepted and loved by others |
| and to be part of groups |

| SAFETY NEEDS |
| the need to feel protected, secure, and out of |
| danger |

| PHYSIOLOGICAL NEEDS |
| hunger, thirst, the need to breathe and other |
| bodily needs |

compulsive in their desire to be approved of and liked by others.

The fourth step up the motivational ladder is esteem needs. The esteem needs include drives to do well, to achieve, to be effective and competent, and to be self-reliant, independent, and autonomous. In addition, esteem needs include the desire to have one's accomplishments recognized, admired, and respected by others so that one can be dominant and important in relation to others. In short, this is the need to have a positive self-image. And, as with any step on the motivational ladder, it is only when the lower physiological, safety, and love needs are met that a person can worry about self-esteem. Also, like the earlier motives, esteem motives are stimulated when there is an absence or deficit of positive self-regard.

The final step in Maslow's hierarchy is the need for self-actualization. As mentioned before, this is essentially a need to develop one's potentials and to do as well as one can. It also includes the need to experience the world and people as deeply and richly as possible. One's own needs and worries fade into the background inasmuch as one wants to appreciate as fully as possible what there is in the world and to grow through this appreciation. Self-actualization is a motive entirely different from the other motives beneath it in the hierarchy. The lower needs are all stimulated by a deficit. They are instigated by some kind of lack, and the person is strongly driven to get what he or she is missing. For these reasons, Maslow called them **deficiency motives.** On the other hand, self-actualization is what Maslow called a growth motive, or a **being motive,** which represents a general need to develop. There is no specific deficit to fill. People are relaxed. They try to do all they can and to grow. The desire for self-actualization is never really satisfied, because more growth is always possible and there is always more experience to appreciate. Being self-actualized is the highest human potential. The impulse toward self-actualization does not avoid negative states, such as hunger or loneliness; it seeks and appreciates positive ones.

Jane Fonda's life illustrates the way Maslow's hierarchy of motives can be applied to understanding a particular person. Jane was raised in a wealthy family. All her basic physiological needs, for food, comfort, and shelter, were met. So were her needs for safety. None of her behavior shows much concern with these needs. In her early life, however, she did have some difficulty satisfying her needs for love and belonging. Her mother was strict and demanding; her father was absent during the war and quite aloof when he returned. Jane's somewhat wild behavior as a girl seems to reflect a need to belong to a peer group where she could get more attention and positive regard than she received at home. Interestingly, after she began to feel close to her stepmother Susan, her behavior in school ceased being a problem. As a young woman, Jane received lots of love from various men in her life, notably Timothy Everett. Then she became more concerned with esteem needs, with acquiring self-respect and respect from others. Jane did this

REVIEW QUESTIONS

14. The approach to personality that emphasizes free will and self-determination is called _____ .

15. An important aspect of the humanistic approach to personality is the idea that people are driven by an innate need to develop themselves to their full potentials and capacities. This is known as the need for _____ .

16. Parents can thwart strivings toward self-actualization by approving only certain behaviors. When this occurs, parents are establishing _____ _____ that can only be counteracted by _____ _____ .

17. In his hiercarchy of needs, Maslow calls physiological, safety, belongingness, and esteem needs _____ motives while the need for self-actualization is called a _____ motive.

by striving to establish an acting career that was both financially successful and respected by the critics. Similarly, her intense involvement in political and social issues, which included public attacks on her father and his life style, seems to reflect an attempt, however ineffective, to get respect from Henry. Now, in the mature years of her late forties Jane seems to have gratified her esteem needs and is exploring routes to self-actualization, including a varied acting career and her whole "workout business," including books, tapes, salons, and her line of workout clothing. Maslow felt that few people are completely self-actualized, but Jane Fonda's behavior reflects self-actualizing needs much more than deficit motivation.

SEX ROLES AND PERSONALITY

As you can see from considering the different perspectives on personality, there are major differences between various theories about the determinants of personality and individuality. Psychodynamic theorists emphasize internal strivings, behavioral theorists emphasize external contingencies, and humanistic theorists emphasize self-determination rather than mere responsiveness to unconscious drives or rewards and punishments. Debate continues about these determinants. One aspect of personality over which the debate rages—particularly about the role of internal, biological determinants, as opposed to external, social determinants—is in the area of sex roles. In this section we will consider the issue of how the behavior of men and women differs, the extent to which these differences are due to biological or social factors, and how traditional concepts of sex roles are changing.

Jane Fonda provides an interesting illustration in considering these questions. Probably most men and women would feel that Jane is a strong, admirable example of what it means to be a woman in our society. What makes her such a good exemplar—biology, social forces, or self-determination? Just as it is impossible to

give a single answer for women and men as a whole, it is hard to give a simple answer for Jane Fonda. However, her life history suggests that self-determination is a very important factor in how one behaves as a woman or a man. Before considering the specific case of Jane Fonda, let us consider various theories about the determinants of sex roles in general.

The Determinants of Sex Roles

There are many differences in the ways men and women behave. In college they dress differently, they tend to take different courses and have different majors, and they often prefer different kinds of parties. These differences among college students have parallels in the ways little boys and girls behave in elementary school. Boys usually play more roughly. Girls seem calmer and are easier to manage by teachers. These differences are by no means uniform. More women than men may major in literature, but many men also select this major. Some women study physics, although this is predominantly a male major. Under some circumstances girls can be just as rowdy as boys.

Interestingly, recent research has shown that some differences that were thought to exist between women and men really do not and that the differences that do exist are narrowing, probably because women and men are attempting to enjoy the freedom inherent in the erosion of traditional strictures on how the sexes should behave. Research in this area is not simply tracking changes in behavior, it is contributing to them as well. For instance, studies by Masters and Johnson (1966) indicate that women have greater sexual capacity than men (see Chapter 12). This research has influenced attitudes about what kind of sexual behaviors are normal and acceptable. Current preferences and practices, within and between the sexes, promise to change more drastically in the future as research tells us more and more about the myths and realities of sex differences. What we need to consider now are what real differences in personality and ability underlie commonly observed differences between men's and women's behavior, interests, and performances, and how both biological and social factors might explain these differences.

BIOLOGICAL INFLUENCES ON SEX DIFFERENCES.

It is possible that some differences between the sexes are caused by purely biological factors. For example, it may be that genes not only determine whether an individual is born male or female, but also cause him or her to act in distinctly "masculine" or "feminine" ways. Research supporting this position has been conducted by John Money (Money & Ehrhardt, 1972). Money has shown that females who, because of drugs administered prenatally, have been exposed to an excess of the male hormone androgen (as opposed to the female hormone estrogen) show distinctly male interests as they grow up. For instance, they prefer boys' toys and are less interested than most girls in child rearing. Money has done other studies which show that environmental factors have a profound influence on sex-related behavior, but his research does suggest that purely biological factors can play some role in determining typically "masculine" or "feminine" behavior.

Goleman (1978) suggests that there are differences in male and female brain organization. For example, for both sexes the left half of the brain has more control over linguistic functioning, while the right half has more control over nonverbal and spatial abilities. However, "right brain" specialization is stronger among men than among women. Recent research suggests that there are prenatal differences in brain development between the sexes as early as four or five weeks after conception (Diamond, 1977).

Other research on animals and humans suggests quite conclusively that there are genetic differences in aggressiveness between males and females. Males are more aggressive than females. Maccoby and Jacklin (1974) conclude that the only other difference between men and women that seems to have a genetic basis is that men have more visual-spatial abilities. They may be better map readers. Still, observed differences between men and women probably owe much more to social learning and training than to genes.

SOCIAL FACTORS AND SEX ROLES.

There have been many studies on the impact of social factors on behavioral differences between women and men. They show that people have strong stereotypes about how females and males do and *should* behave, that girls and boys are consequently treated differently, and that behavior consistent with traditional sex-role conceptions is reinforced and learned. Stereotyped views of how women and men differ abound in our culture. Women are usually thought to be more emotional, sensitive, artistic, talkative, intuitive, and dangerous as drivers. Men are widely viewed as more rational, unfeeling, aggressive, decisive, and inept at running a vacuum cleaner. In fact, very few of these perceived differences exist. As noted before, men are genetically more aggressive and more able to visualize spatial problems. In addition, females in later childhood and adolescence show greater verbal abilities, while males show greater mathematical abilities, although it is not clear what causes these differences (Maccoby & Jacklin, 1974). But that is the complete list of substantial differences! No other differences in behavior or performance have been proven. Still, stereotypes persist and lead frequently, sometimes unconsciously, to strong ideologies about how men and women should behave (Bem & Bem, 1970). Usually these ideologies hold that women should have more responsibility for home and family and that men should earn at least as much income as their spouses.

How do these stereotypes affect treatment of girls and boys in childhood? A study by Rubin, Provenzano, and Luria (1974) showed that parents see distinct differences between male and female newborns, even though the infants are similar in all measurable respects. For example, girls are seen as more refined and more delicate. Moss (1967) has shown that parents treat their infants differently. Boys are apt to be played with more roughly than girls are. These findings suggest that from the very beginning boys and girls are perceived differently and are treated in ways that reinforce typically "masculine" and "feminine" behavior.

What difference does this kind of perception and treatment of girls and boys make in their behavior? One result is that children have a clear idea of what sex they are by the age of two and choose toys that are typically associated with their own sex (Fagot & Patterson, 1969). By the age of three they will even avoid toys that are usually thought of as appropriate for the opposite sex (Hartup, Moore, & Sager, 1963). In other words, children learn quickly what is expected of them in terms of being a boy or a girl and show strong tendencies to live up to these expectations. There is no doubt that both direct and vicarious reinforcement are involved here. Children are reinforced for imitating appropriate models (Grusec & Brinker, 1972) and do so more often as they see adults being rewarded for "masculine" or "feminine" behavior.

Two studies with very different methodologies demonstrate how strongly environment and training can affect the behavior of men and women. The first is a case reported by Money and Ehrdard (1972) of two identical male twins. One of the twins was circumcised at seven months of age. During this surgical procedure the penis was accidentally destroyed, and a sex-change operation was performed on the child. One twin was raised as a boy, the other as a girl. The mother attempted to treat them alike, but recognized that she did not always do so. For example, she let the boy be messier than the girl. By the age of six, one twin had clearly become a little boy and the other a little girl.

A second study is a cross-cultural investigation by Margaret Mead (1935). Mead questioned the universality of the pattern of male aggressiveness and female passivity then prevalent in the United States. She believed that men and women were capable of being equally assertive or submissive and set out to prove her point by finding societies that differed from the United States in the degree of aggressiveness or passivity that they trained into men and women. She reported on the gentle Arapesh, a society where neither men nor women were

TABLE 2.4

Sex and Temperament

Classification of societies according to whether men and women behave passively or assertively.

MEN'S BEHAVIOR	WOMEN'S BEHAVIOR	
	Passive	Assertive
Passive	Arapesh	Tchambuli
Assertive	United States	Mundugumor

Margaret Mead argued that the sex roles that we observe in the United States are not universal but are based on our society's unique history. To back up this claim she has shown that there are other societies where men are passive and women are assertive, and societies where both men and women are either passive or assertive. It is not a cross-cultural universal for men to be dominant and assertive and women to be passive and subordinate.

assertive, the warlike Mundugamors, where both men and women were very aggressive and dominating, and the Tchambuli, where the Western pattern was reversed, the men being passive and submissive, and the women being aggressive. Mead's data clearly indicate the potential of both sexes to be either aggressive or passive. Males may be more naturally aggressive, but learning and training can produce almost any conceivable pattern of assertiveness or passivity among both women and men.

The research we have been discussing suggests quite clearly that there are many determinants of sex roles for each one of us. Jane Fonda's case illustrates this well. It may be that her sex role behavior simply reflects the fact that she is a biological woman. But her life history and the social forces that acted on her as a child reveal a more complicated picture. When Jane was a young girl both her parents, especially her mother, wanted her to become a stereotypically feminine young lady. Her nickname, Lady Jane, underlines this desire. However, Jane's own proclivities took her in a different direction. She enjoyed watching Henry play cowboys in his movies, and she enjoyed following him around as he worked outdoors at their California home. She began to leave her dolls and other feminine toys behind and became something of a tomboy, leading the way in active, outdoor games. Thus she was more influenced by the way she saw Henry behave, and by the way she wanted to behave, than by what her parents directly encouraged. Since those very early years, Jane has remained independent of her mother and father's expectations and has chosen to behave, in the domain of sex roles and other areas, exactly as she pleases.

Sex, Physical Characteristics, and Adjustment

The research we have been discussing should alert us to a fact of interpersonal relations that has important implications for adjustment. In many situations, what others expect of us and how they treat us may be influenced by our gender or by other physical characteristics such as body build or physical appearance. A beautiful women is expected to be happy and competent (Dion, Berscheid, & Walster, 1972). A thin man may be expected to have a submissive manner. Those who violate others' expectations are likely to make others uncomfortable, especially if the expectations also contain a conception of how we ought to behave.

Given that others may have certain expectations about us based on sex or other physical attributes, each of us has to make a decision about how to respond to these expectations. Some people feel that it is easier to go along with others' expectations and behave within those limits. Others feel it is unfairly restrictive to be constrained by cultural biases and casual stereotypes. They insist on defying preconceptions where necessary. In the realm of sex roles, there are some data by Bem (1975) indicating that people who are willing to ignore traditional sex roles and behave in either a tender and nurturant manner or an assertive and independent manner depending on the situation are the most adaptive and have the best chance for good adjustment.

HOW ANDROGYNOUS ARE YOU?

Check off which of the following adjectives describe you:

self-reliant	cheerful
independent	shy
assertive	affectionate
forceful	loyal
analytical	sympathetic
self-sufficient	understanding
dominant	compassionate
individualistic	warm
competitive	gullible
ambitious	gentle

Sandra Bem (1975) has argued that androgynous individuals, people who can behave in both masculine and feminine ways, rather than in strictly sex-typed ways, may be the best adjusted. If you have indicated that the adjectives above on the left fit you but that the ones on the right do not, you have described yourself in a masculine way. If you have indicated that the terms on the right, but not the ones on the left, fit you, you have described yourself in a feminine manner. If you have indicated that several terms from both lists fit you, you have described yourself in an androgynous way.

The data on sex differences indicate that women and men have similar capacities for competence, caring, and self-fulfillment. There is little justification for expecting either women or men to follow archaic norms for acceptable "masculine" and "feminine" behavior. All of us should be aware that other people's beliefs are sometimes different from our own, and each of us should be prepared to cope with prejudice in whatever manner he or she considers to be best. Fortunately, unwarranted expectations are now decreasing and opportunities to live with maximum freedom are increasing.

Changing Sex Roles

Jane Fonda is one of the women in American society who are leading both women and men to view sex roles differently. Her own life and her film portrayals of women who are active, professional, physically fit, and involved in more equitable arrangements in marriage is striking a positive note among millions of Americans. The changing views of men and women about proper sex roles are reflected in a recent study of American couples (Blumstein & Schwartz, 1983) showing that men believe that they should be much more heavily involved in housework and childcare than their fathers were. This changing attitude can be seen in Jane Fonda's life. Her husband, Tom Hay-

REVIEW QUESTIONS

18. Research has shown that at least part of the differences between the sexes can be attributed to genetically determined hormones. The male hormone is called _____ and the female hormone is called _____ .

19. T or F: There are no genetically based differences in aggressiveness between males and females.

20. While it is true that some of the differences between the sexes can be traced to genetic factors, most of the differences between males and females are the result of _____ factors.

21. There is evidence to suggest that children are aware of sex appropriate behaviors (such as how they are expected to act in terms of being a boy or girl) as early as age _____ .

22. T or F: In later childhood and adolescence, females demonstrate higher verbal abilities while males show higher mathematical abilities.

den, spends much more time with Jane's children than Henry spent with Jane. Although men may advocate that men participate equally in doing housework, especially when the wife

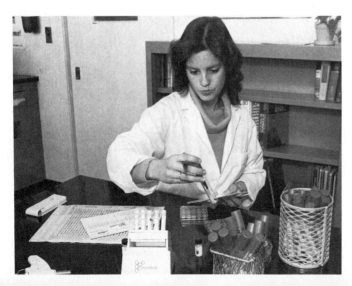

Today, more and more women are successfully entering occupations that were formerly open only to men.

Rhoda Sidney.

works, Blumstein and Schwartz report that women still do most of the chores around the house. There appear to be several reasons for this. Many men find that their intentions are better than their actual performance. Men find it hard to change habits ingrained by male models of a different generation. Also, it appears that many women feel, after sampling their husbands' cooking and housework, that it might be better to take care of these activities themselves. Another restraining factor on changes in sex roles is that while many people have changed their attitudes, if not always their behavior, sizeable numbers of people still don't question the traditional arrangements. Many women responding to a recent survey (New York Times, 1983) had hostile reactions to feminism, and two-thirds of them felt that the women's movement had not improved their lives. Still, the direction of change is clear. People like Jane Fonda are certainly not pushing toward a unisex society, but they are providing models for how men and women can go beyond the limits of traditional expectations to more fully realize their potential.

SUMMARY

1. There are three major approaches to understanding the individual personality: the psychodynamic, the behavioral, and the humanistic.

2. The psychodynamic approach to personality emphasizes internal factors. Behavior is determined by unconscious motives and conflicts related to distinct stages of development.

3. Freud's psychodynamic theory suggests how basic personality structures form in early childhood. The rational ego develops to help the instinctual id satisfy its drives. To resolve intense conflict with the same-sex parent arising from the Oedipal/Electra complex, a child usually forms a strong identification with that parent. The superego develops as a result of a child incorporating the same-sex parent's moral standards and ideals.

4. Erikson's psychodynamic theory points out how interactions with others in early childhood give people positive or negative psychological balances that are important throughout life. In the oral stage, a child learns a sense of trust or mistrust; in the anal stage, a sense of autonomy or shame and doubt; in the phallic stage, a sense of initiative or guilt; and in the latency period, a sense of industry or inferiority.

5. Sullivan's psychodynamic theory outlines the ways interpersonal relations develop in later childhood. During the juvenile era a child learns how to accommodate to peers and how to react to authority figures. Ostracism by peers can lead to long-lasting feelings of inferiority. In preadolescence a child develps a strong need and capacity for intimacy with others. Most people form close chum relationships at this time. If they don't, intense loneliness can contribute to feelings of lack of worth and despair.

6. The behavioral approach to personality emphasizes external factors. Behavior is determined by reinforcement or expectation of reinforcement from the environment.

7. Radical behaviorism holds that personality reflects behaviors directly controlled by reward and punishment.

8. Social learning theory, a behavioral approach, emphasizes vicarious reinforcement and observational learning, where behavior is learned by observing a model. It also stresses the role of cognitive factors, self-regulation of behavior, and individual uniqueness.

9. The humanistic approach to personality emphasizes human free will. Behavior is self-determined and motivated by the individual's desire for self-actualization, the development of full potential.

10. Roger's humanistic theory shows how conditions of worth established by parents can lead to conflict between behavior that will obtain parental approval and behavior that is self-actualizing.

11. Maslow's humanistic hierarchy of motives shows how the need for self-actualization fits in with other important human motives. Physiological needs, safety needs, and love and belongingness needs must be satisfied before people can attempt to actualize their full potential.

12. Research on the differences in the behavior of men and women indicates that some differences, such as in aggressiveness, are biologically based.

13. Most differences in the behavior of men and women are not biologically based, but are the product of learning and training. As people become more conscious of this fact, there is a tendency to break away from traditional conceptions of proper behavior for men and women. Thus sex roles are in a state of change.

KEY TERMS

a.	BEING MOTIVATION	g.	SENSE OF AUTONOMY
b.	DEFICIENCY MOTIVATION	h.	SENSE OF BASIC TRUST
c.	EGO	i.	SENSE OF INDUSTRY
d.	ID	j.	SENSE OF INITIATIVE
e.	OBSERVATIONAL LEARNING	k.	SUPEREGO
f.	SELF-ACTUALIZATION		

1. Learning that takes place when a person observes a model performing a behavior
2. The development or realization of all one's potentials
3. A basic feeling of trust in one's self and the environment, and the feeling of adequacy in meeting external demands
4. A sense of control over one's body and a feeling one is free to act independently
5. The motivation to grow and develop
6. Motivation instigated by some psychological deficit experienced as an inner drive to obtain what is missing
7. The structure of the psyche that notices, perceives, remembers, and helps the individual cope with reality
8. The structure of the psyche that instinctively and unconsciously seeks pleasure and satisfaction of bodily needs
9. The child's sense of having some control over objects and other people, along with the ability to act creatively
10. The child's sense of control, power, and competence in achieving desired goals
11. The structure of the psyche that contains the parents' morals, ideals, and values

ANSWERS TO REVIEW QUESTIONS

1. Unconscious motives; conflicts; stages of development. **2.** Id. **3.** Superego. **4.** Conscience; ego ideal. **5.** Id; superego; ego. **6.** c; d; a; b. **7.** Personifications. **8.** Preadolescent.

9. Rewards; punishments. **10.** Law, effect. **11.** Cognitive learning. **12.** Vicarious or observational. **13.** False (Social learning theorists see reinforcement as an important determinant of behavior when viewed in the context of individual uniqueness and cognitive variables.)

14. Humanistic. **15.** Self-actualization. **16.** Conditions of worth; unconditional positive regard. **17.** Deficiency; being.

18. Androgen; estrogen. **19.** False. **30.** Social. **21.** Two. **22.** True.

SELF-DISCOVERY IN ADOLESCENCE AND ADULTHOOD

T

he crescendo of voices built up to a deafening roar. "Go home, traitor! I hope he kills you, nigger!" The boos and threats greeted Muhammad Ali as he began his seemingly endless walk to the boxing ring in the Atlanta Coliseum. It had been three and half years since Ali had been in the ring. His 28-year-old body showed the effects of this inactivity; small bulges of fat protruded where once only tight muscles had glistened beneath the dark skin. From the opening bell, it was clear that this was not the same Muhammad Ali who had destroyed Zora Folley in Madison Square Garden in 1967. The present Muhammad Ali was slower, his punches lacked crispness, and the graceful rhythm was no longer evident in the famous "Ali shuffle." Ali did beat the clearly out-classed Jerry Quarry that night, but all the experts agreed that Ali's three-and-a-half-year exile from the ring during his prime did damage that no amount of training or conditioning would repair.

The groundwork for Ali's exile from boxing was actually laid in Louisville, Kentucky, in the early 1950s, when a young, sensitive black boy named Cassius Marcellus Clay began to experience discrimination firsthand. Ali recalls becoming very thirsty one day while shopping with his mother in downtown Louisville. There was, however, no place where blacks could get a drink of water; over each water fountain was a sign reading "WHITES ONLY." He was forced to endure his parched throat until they reached the "black section" of town. Incidents such as this tormented young Ali and filled his head with conflicting attitudes. On the one hand, he began to believe that blacks were inferior. He saw that blacks held the poorest, most menial jobs; they were not allowed in "white" restaurants, nor could they go to the "white" theaters. When he began boxing, Ali realized that the crowds always supported the white boxer and were disappointed when he emerged victorious. On the other hand, there were a number of blacks whom Ali admired. He felt that his father was one of the greatest men who had ever lived. The elder Clay was a talented artist who painted many of the billboard signs in Louisville. Ali also idolized Joe Louis, the black heavyweight boxing champion. The existence of these men refuted the idea that blacks were inferior to whites.

By the age of ten, Ali had become fascinated with boxing. He often went to the local gymnasium to watch the boxers work out. By the time he was twelve, he had convinced Joe Martin, a white policeman who managed amateur boxers, to teach him to box. The skinny, 112-pound Ali worked hard at boxing. He trained almost every evening and spent hours on conditioning exercises. In addition, he read about the accomplishments of black boxers such as Joe Louis, Sugar Ray Robinson, Archie Moore, and Floyd Patterson. His pride in black people increased, and his suspicions about black inferiority eroded. He began to feel that blacks were unfairly treated.

Ali's hard work paid off, and he won the Golden Gloves championship in 1959 and 1960. One of the turning points in Ali's career came in the summer of 1960, when he won an Olympic gold medal. He was treated as a hero throughout the United States. Fans greeted him at airports, and people began to root for him to win fights. Despite this reception, Ali's belief that blacks were unfairly treated became more pronounced. In discussing his own treatment after his Olympic victory, Ali

Muhammad Ali.
Rusty Brown/Sygma.

wrote: "One Kentucky newspaper described my medal as 'the biggest prize any black boy every brought back to Louisville.' But if a white had brought back anything better to this city, where only race horses and whiskey were important, I hadn't heard about it" (Ali, 1975, p. 60).

After winning the Olympic gold medal, Ali was approached by William Reynolds and nine other white Louisville millionaires who offered to manage and finance Ali as a professional boxer. They offered him a $10,000 bonus for a six-year contract (1960–1966), under which they would get 50 percent of Ali's earnings both inside and outside the ring. To Ali, the $10,000 seemed like a huge sum; his family had paid only $4,500 for their home. Ali signed the contract but even then felt he was being exploited.

Ali's early professional boxing career was very successful; he achieved an impressive string of victories and his fame grew. In an effort to gain increased recognition, he developed an image as a braggart. He taunted his opponents in the press and boasted, "I am the greatest!" Despite his own personal success, Ali retained his belief that blacks were exploited in the United States. He viewed himself as the champion of blacks in this country, and in each of his fights he felt he was defeating the "Great White Hope" that was promoted against him.

This attitude encouraged him to join the Black Muslims in 1964. He felt that this was a group that held values similar to his. He changed his name from Cassius Clay to Muhammad Ali, which means "one who is worthy of praise." When his contract with the Louisville millionaires expired, Ali hired a fellow Black Muslim, Herbert Muhammad, to manage him. His association with the Black Muslims infuriated people both in and out of boxing who saw the Black Muslims as a "race-hate sect." Everyone around Ali urged him to renounce his association with this group. They told him it would ruin his boxing career. The promoters of the upcoming Ali-Liston fight threatened to cancel the fight. This fight was to be Ali's first opportunity at the world heavyweight title. Though he desperately wanted this chance, he refused to renounce his new religion.

Ali and Sonny Liston did fight, and Ali emerged as the World Heavyweight Champion. But his troubles were not over. The United States had become involved in the Vietnam conflict. Ali was opposed to the war on a number of grounds. He felt that it was a "white man's war," and his religious convictions were clearly at odds with it. He summed up his position in rhyme: "Keep asking me, no matter how long/ On the war in Viet Nam, I sing this song/I ain't got no quarrel with the Viet Cong . . ." (Ali, 1975, p. 124).

The trouble raged on. On April 1, 1967, the champ received his induction notice; he was to report to the induction office in Houston, Texas, on April 28. Failure to accept induction into the army would mean a jail sentence. The newspapers were ablaze with the news: "ARMY TELLS CLAY—PUT UP OR SHUT UP!" Everywhere Ali went, crowds gathered either to jeer him or to cheer him. The turmoil increased. If he didn't change his position, he would lose his title and probably have to spend time in jail.

At 8:30 A.M. on April 28, 1967, Ali stood before the induction board. When his name was called, he walked slowly forward and signed a statement refusing induction into the United States Army. That same day, the World Boxing Association stripped him of his title and the New York Boxing Commission revoked his license to box. Later, he was given the maximum legal sentence for refusing induction: five years in prison and a $10,000 fine.

Ali's forced exile from the ring began. Three and a half years and numerous legal appeals later, Ali's fight with Jerry Quarry was allowed to go forward. In the next year, 1971, two undefeated heavyweight champions, Ali and Joe Frazier, met in Madison Square Garden in New York. Frazier won, but shortly afterwards the United States Supreme Court unanimously overturned Ali's conviction for draft evasion, and for the first time in four years Ali was free of legal problems. For Ali, the decade of the 1970s was marked by fisticuffs in the ring rather than in the headlines. Ali beat Joe Frazier in a return match and in 1974 and regained the World Championship by beating George Foreman in a stunning upset in Zaire. After epic fights with Joe Frazier (the "Thrilla in Manila") and Ken Norton, Ali lost and regained his crown for the third time in 1978 fights with Leon Spinks. He retired as champ but came out of retirement in an unsuccessful attempt to wrest the crown away from the next champion, Larry Holmes.

Since then, Muhammad Ali has put the boxing part of his life behind him. He has become active in politics again, and in various charitable organizations. He is enjoying his third marriage and his five children. In a turbulent life marked by strife in his personal life, in his profession, and in his public image, Ali has always been aided by maintaining an unshakable belief in himself: "I am the greatest!"

SELF-DISCOVERY IN ADOLESCENCE AND ADULTHOOD

A key aspect of becoming a healthy, well-adjusted person is the ability to discover who you are, define yourself, and then begin a lifelong process of developing your potentials and abilities. Most people go through this process of self-discovery most actively during adolescence. Muhammad Ali's development followed this pattern, although his self-definition was strongly affected by early childhood experiences, and his troubles with the Selective Service System led to major changes in his concept of himself during his adulthood and in his concept of the role he wanted to play, and could play, in society.

Self-discovery is a process of defining what is called a **self-concept** and making important decisions about what you will do in life, what attitude you will take toward yourself, and what attitude you will take toward others. The self-concept is a very difficult idea to define simply. We can begin by saying that people's self-concepts are their opinions of themselves—both what they are and how "good" they are. That is, people have perceptions of their abilities, their goals and aspirations, what they value and believe in, how they look, how they will behave in life, and what other people think of them. They also have an overall belief or feeling about how worthy they are and whether they are first-rate or inferior.

We would like to emphasize that a self-concept or identity is not defined only during adolescence. Self-discovery is not a one-time event, as Muhammad Ali's life makes clear. The self is not a single, stable, static entity, like the Rock of Gibraltar or the Pacific Ocean, that is discovered once and for all at a single time during the course of life. The self is more like a plant or tree or even a river that grows and changes its course of development. Usually we have a self-concept that is an important and stable part of our lives for a certain period of time. This is often followed by a time of questioning and change, a time when freshness and redirection are required. Then a slightly different self-concept may emerge, not completely different from the old, yet fresh. In other words, the self develops, grows, and renews itself. Self-discovery is a lifelong process rather than a one-time event.

In this chapter, using as an example the extraordinary life of Muhammad Ali, we will consider how beliefs about the self take root in childhood and how identity is defined in adolescence and reformed again and again throughout life. We want to emphasize the capacity for alteration, improvement, and excitement that is possible at all ages. It is critical for people to realize that they can keep "alive" by doing new things and that they can avoid being old by becoming new.

The process of self-discovery is very active during adolescence, an unusually stormy and difficult period of life. Adolescence begins with puberty, with the first feelings of strong and perhaps frightening sexual drives. During this period young men and women must cope with family conflicts about independence and autonomy, with uncertainty about values and morality, with doubts about their ability to cope in the adult world, and with questions about who they are, what role in society they can fill, and, in general, what they are good for. Most adolescents make it through these years with their egos and their mental health intact. For some the result is exhilarating, as they find their potentials and inner being. For others the experience of adolescence is overwhelming. Our first concern in this chapter will be the many challenging aspects of adolescence and their various outcomes.

Although adolescence is important, those who have passed through it know that challenges, opportunities, and self-discovery continue in adulthood. Psychologists have been slow to consider this fully. Freud emphasized development from birth to age five, and it is only recently, thanks largely to Erikson, that people have begun to consider life-span or "womb-to-tomb" development. In the second portion of this chapter we will consider the important psychological developments of adulthood and especially how the process of self-discovery and renewal continues.

Our goals here are to explain some important aspects of the workings of the self-concept and to discuss adolescence and adulthood in ways that will help you understand the difficult times that some of you may be going through now, and to make you realize the endless possibilities of change and new beginnings that life offers. We don't want to minimize various midlife crises. Rather we want to prepare you for them and help you realize the opportunities, as well as the problems, that they present.

THE SELF-CONCEPT

Our self-concept is the total set of opinions or beliefs we have about ourselves. As we noted before, it includes beliefs about our background; our personal characteristics, such as introversion or extraversion; our abilities, such as being good in the arts, but weak in the sciences; and our values and philosophy, for example, our conviction that society as a whole must take more responsibility for poor people. For every person this set of self-beliefs is differ-

---

ARE YOU A HIGH SELF-MONITOR?

Answer each of the following statements True or False as they apply to you.

T F 1. I can make improtu speeches, even on topics about which I have almost no information.

T F 2. When I am uncertain how to act in a social situation, I look to the behavior of others for cues.

T F 3. I am particularly good at making other people like me.

T F 4. Even if I'm not enjoying myself, I often pretend to be having a good time.

T F 5. I can look anyone in the eye and tell a lie with a straight face (if for a right end).

T F 6. I guess I put on a show to impress or entertain people.

T F 7. I would probably make a good actor.

T F 8. I sometimes appear to others to be experiencing deeper emotions than I actually am.

T F 9. In different situations and with different people, I often act like very different persons.

T F 10. In order to get along and be liked, I tend to be what people expect me to be rather than anything else.

T F 11. I may deceive people by being friendly when I really dislike them.

T F 12. I'm not always the person I appear to be.

People who are high self-monitors tend to present themselves slightly differently in different situations, and they are highly attuned to how other people expect them to behave. They are more adept at reading other people and sensing how they feel or what they want. They are more likely to try to behave as others expect or want, and they are more adept at doing so convincingly. Low self-monitors tend to have a clearer self-concept and a definition of who they are that carries across different situations and makes them behave more consistently. You can get some idea of how much of a self-monitor you are by counting how many statements above you answered as True. In every case a True answer represents high self-monitoring. You might see how your friends answer the questions compared to you, and if their higher or lower self-monitoring score makes sense.

ent. Muhammad Ali's self-concept includes the belief that he is an exceptional athlete, that he is a symbol of great importance for black people, and that he may not be the most intelligent person in the world. When asked once how he could have not passed the Army mental abilities test, which some people believed he failed on purpose, Ali said with a smile, "I never said I was the smartest, just that I was the greatest."

Today psychologists talk about these kinds of beliefs about ourselves as being a **self-schema,** an overall concept about ourselves that affects how we remember the past and how we interpret the present. For example, a person may have the schema that he or she is a generous person. Such a person would be more likely than people who do not possess a generosity schema to remember times when he or she was generous and to perceive present opportunities to behave generously.

In addition to various **schemata** (the plural of **schema**) people have an overall belief about their worth, that is, their overall self-esteem. Our overall sense that we are good people, that we are moral and competent, that we have value and worth, constitutes our self-esteem. Muhammad Ali's self-esteem is quite high.

So we can say that our self-concept is equivalent to our various beliefs about ourselves, including our self-esteem. In order to understand and specify the nature of these beliefs and the ways they work to affect our behavior, feelings, and thoughts about the world, it is very useful to think about our self-concept as our **theory** about the kind of person we are, that is, to regard our self-concept as our own self-theory (Epstein, 1973). Let's consider a few of the ways that our self-concept, or self-theory, is like any other theory.

First, our self-theory is like any other theory in that it consists of a variety of concepts or beliefs that vary in importance and are all logically related. Our most important concept is our self-esteem, our belief about our worth. All our other beliefs about ourselves are usually consistent with our overall belief that we are worthy or unworthy. The self-theory is also like other theories in that we use it to predict future

events. For example, our theory of ourselves predicts whether we are likely to do well if we enter a dance contest and therefore whether it is worth our while to pay the entry fee. Muhammad Ali's self-theory predicted that he would be successful in fighting Sonny Liston for the heavyweight championship. Few others agreed, and people tried to persuade Ali not to attempt the fight; but Ali went ahead, and his self-theory proved correct. Another way the self-theory is like other theories is that it must adapt to new data it may not have predicted and therefore must change to some degree. On the other hand, like any theory, the self-theory has to have some stability. It can collapse if events prove that it is wrong in major ways, and then there may be total disorganization of the self-concept and serious psychological disorder. Thus it is important that our self-concept be relatively accurate and able to make reliable predictions, but that it also be able to change and be updated when surprising new information requires. Muhammad Ali's self-theory did not predict that he would lose his first fight with Joe Frazier. This new contradictory data led to a change in his self-theory, but at the same time Ali's basic stability was maintained. Ali concluded that he had not trained as hard as he needed to and that Frazier was better than he had thought, but he maintained his belief that he was the best fighter of all time and that he could beat Frazier in a rematch. In the rematch his self-theory was proven correct.

Muhammad Ali's extremely positive self-theory is unusual. Most of us have a more modest view of ourselves. Where did Muhammad Ali's very positive self-concept come from, and where do ours come from?

The Processes of Self-Conception

Many factors determine how we feel about ourselves, what we think we are capable of, and what we think of the persons that we have become. These feelings of self-worth and self-image are among the most important of all the conflicts and uncertainties that need to be sorted out during adolescence. We will now consider the processes of self-conception that affect what we think of ourselves throughout life (see Gergen, 1971). There are four major processes of self-conception: reflected appraisal, social comparison, attribution, and identification. None of them is tied to any particular age or stage of development. However, all of them are very much in evidence during adolescence as people strive to define themselves. We will also consider how bias and distortion affect the conclusions we draw about ourselves from these processes.

REFLECTED APPRAISAL. Probably the most powerful determinant of our overall estimate of ourselves is the process of reflected appraisal. Reflected appraisal is simply the assessment or evaluation that someone else has of you. People's opinions of themselves are greatly affected by the evaluations of others, from the time of the most primitive "personifications" (see Chapter 2) through adulthood. One major step in positive adjustment is being able to become independent, to some degree, of what others think of us and to decide for ourselves who we are and what we are worth.

The first person to write systematically about the notion that one's ideas of self derive from what others think was Charles Horton Cooley. In 1902 Cooley discussed how our feelings about ourselves arise from what we imagine others to think of us: We feel "ashamed to seem evasive in the presence of the straightforward man, cowardly in the presence of a brave one, gross in the eyes of a refined one, and so on. We always imagine, and in imagining share the judgments of the other mind" (Cooley, 1902). The result of imagining what others think of us, and sharing or accepting their opinion, is a "looking-glass self," a self-image directly reflecting the appraisals of others.

Another social psychologist to write about the self-concept was George Herbert Mead (1934). Mead emphasized the importance of "significant others"—parents, teachers, and peers—in a child's development. He suggested that as children we begin to base our self-con-

Our parents' appraisal of us, positive or negative, has lasting effects on our self-concepts.
Ken Karp.

ceptions on the view of us that is implied in the behavior of significant others. People imply by the way they treat us what they think of us. Then what we think they think of us affects our opinion of ourselves. For example, if the behavior of your parents implies that you are not to be trusted, you will come to feel that you are not a trustworthy person. If your siblings treat you as if you are very skilled, you will come to believe that you are skilled. Parents, siblings, peers, and other significant others have a vast impact on our self-concept through the view of us that their behavior implies.

The importance of reflected appraisal is very clear in the life of Muhammad Ali. When he returned home to Louisville in 1960 after winning the Olympic gold medal he described himself as the "The Prettiest," the wittiest, the greatest. He would look at his own reflection in store windows and say, "Look at me—I'm beautiful! An' I'm gonna stay pretty cuz there ain't a fighter on earth fast enough t' hit me" (Schulberg, 1971, p. 37). This view of himself as the prettiest or most beautiful came directly from his parents. When Ali was a child his father was always saying that he was "pretty as a picture" and "don't mess up that beauty"

(Ali, 1975, p. 37). His father's appraisal of Ali is reflected in Ali's self-appraisal as he stands in front of a real mirror.

Many studies show that even in later years our opinions of ourselves are affected by the feedback we get from others. One is a study by Videback (1960) in which college students who read poems in a speech class were given feedback from an expert on oral communication about their adequacy in controlling voice and conveying meaning. The appraisals the students received were fixed ahead of time to be either positive or negative. The subjects rated themselves on several traits before and after getting the feedback, and the results showed that those who got positive feedback rated themselves more positively at the end than those who got negative feedback.

One very important aspect of the results of this study was that subjects changed their opinions about characteristics of themselves that had nothing to do with the specific feedback they received. For example, subjects' opinions of their abilities in social conversation went up or down depending on whether they got good or bad feedback about voice control. This happened even though what the evaluator said had nothing to do with social conversation. Why did this happen? What does it mean?

First, it is hard for people to accept feedback about a specific behavior without letting it affect their overall self-evaluation. Even when someone tries to give us feedback about a single trait, it tends to affect our overall feelings of adequacy and our overall emotional state. A second related point is that our opinion of ourselves does have some consistency to it. We do not have isolated sets of opinions about various unrelated aspects of ourselves. If our opinion of one aspect of ourselves is raised or lowered, this affects our opinions about other aspects of ourselves, all of which are connected and contribute to some extent to our total self-concept. These tendencies mean that we are affected by specific feedback from others more than we ought to be, from a rational point of view, and more than is good for us emotionally. We should be alert to this problem.

SOCIAL COMPARISON. A second highly important process involved in forming opinions of ourselves is social comparison (Festinger, 1954). In addition to passively accepting other people's appraisals of us, we also form our own opinion by comparing ourselves to other people. People compare themselves with others in terms of many different traits. When we consider whether we are smart, dull, religious, athletic, lovable, or idealistic, we probably engage in social comparison (Gergen, 1971).

Muhammad Ali used social comparison even as a young 14-year-old to conclude that he was capable of being world heaveyweight champion. He watched the dominant fighters of the time on television, including the fast heavyweight champ, Floyd Patterson. Ali compared his own style with theirs and decided that he could beat them. He could do what none of them, even the swift ones, could do, and that was moving backward, circling, staying away from the heavy punches. In fact, Ali was right. During the early part of his career he was seldom hit, because of an uncanny ability to back away just enough to avoid getting tagged with a punch. For this reason he was able to confound all predictions in beating Liston, who had taken the title away from the supposedly speedy Floyd Patterson.

When we engage in social comparison, we usually don't compare ourselves with just anyone. We usually compare ourselves with others who should be about as good as we are, inasmuch as they have similar standing on characteristics related to the attribute in question. For example, if we were evaluating our swimming ability, we would compare ourselves with others of the same age and sex who had had the same amount of training and recent practice. If they were the same in terms of these characteristics, we would know that any difference between us in swimming performance must reflect ability and we could judge ourselves accordingly.

Comparison with similar others allows very accurate self-appraisal, sometimes too accurate. People don't always like what comparison implies. Muhammad Ali didn't like what comparison implied when he lost to Joe Frazier. As a result, people sometimes compare themselves with others who are slightly different in terms of related attributes or make excuses for themselves by perceiving more or less similarity than actually exists. Ali may have decided that Frazier had the advantage because he had been able to fight and stay sharp during the three years before their fight, whereas Ali had been in forced exile. In short, they were not similar in amount of training. In the same way, a college student might compare his or her tennis ability with that of a friend still in high school or with that of his or her little sister and conclude he or she has more ability. In fact, the performance difference might simply reflect age. Or we might decide that someone who did better than we did had advantages over us.

Even though similarity is very important, we are sometimes affected by social comparison with those who are not very much like us. One clear demonstration of the impact on self-esteem of such social comparison is Morse and Gergen's (1970) "Mr. Clean–Mr. Dirty" study. In this experiment college students answered an ad for a part-time job at a research institute and came to a secretary's office to be interviewed. They were asked to complete some questionnaires, which included a measure of self-esteem and a measure of self-consistency. After the ratings had been completed, another person, posing as an applicant for the same job, entered the room and filled out the same questionnaires. The appearance of this person was varied to make him a "Mr. Clean" or a "Mr. Dirty." When he was Mr. Clean, he wore a dark business suit, carried an attaché case and opened the case to remove several sharpened pencils, a statistics book, a philosophy text, and a calculator. When he was Mr. Dirty he wore a smelly sweatshirt with no socks and seemed dazed by the entire procedure. He carried a worn copy of a trashy novel and had to borrow a pencil. After Mr. Clean or Mr. Dirty had been working on his questionnaires a while, the subject was given some additional questionnaires to complete, which included another form of the self-esteem measure that he or she had completed before.

The results, which were predicted from social comparison theory, were that subjects who encountered Mr. Clean showed a decrease in self-esteem between the two measures, and subjects who found themselves with Mr. Dirty showed an increase in self-esteem. That is, subjects who thought they were competing with the well-organized, well-prepared Mr. Clean felt slightly inferior and outclassed, and their self-esteem dropped, at least temporarily. Those who were up against the seemingly inept Mr. Dirty felt fairly smug and experienced a rise in self-esteem. An additional interesting finding was that the subjects who

We often evaluate our own performances by comparing them to the performances of others.

Maureen Fennell, Photo Researchers, Inc.

scored high on the self-consistency measure were less affected by social comparison with Mr. Clean or Mr. Dirty. Their self-esteem changed less than did that of the subjects who were low in self-consistency. Perhaps the high self-consistency subjects had a clearer self-concept and thus were unlikely to have their self-concept much affected by brief interactions and short-term social comparisons. Their self-esteem was probably less affected by momentary external events and more determined by inner thought and evaluation.

ATTRIBUTION. Research shows that other important determinants of the self-concept are attributions, or inferences, we make from our behavior about our attitudes, emotions, abilities, and motives (see Kleinke, 1978). In many cases the kinds of attributions we make about ourselves are quite simple. We might simply look at our behavior—for example, turning down invitations to parties, avoiding crowded places, and going alone to movies—and infer that we are introverted. Sometimes people make inferences about the strength of their political attitudes by observing whether they are willing to sign a petition, contribute money to a cause, or join a demonstration. Sometimes we know our attitudes fairly well already and guide our behavior according to them; other times we don't have a clear idea of where we stand until something forces us to make a choice. In some cases, we may not like what our behavior implies about us. There is a very effective advertisement for helping poor children in undeveloped countries which says, "You can help this child or you can turn the page." The ad is effective because most people would ordinarily glance at the ad and turn the page, ignoring both the ad and their own behavior and its implications. By calling attention to the act of turning the page, the ad elicits a good deal of guilt and suggests that you are indifferent, lazy, and uncaring. It's interesting to see how people interpret their behavior in this case.

IDENTIFICATION. Closely related to attribution is the process of identification. In the case of attribution people infer specific traits from a be-

havior or behavior pattern. In the case of identification, people adopt an entire pattern of behavior in an attempt to be like someone they admire and then conceive of that behavior pattern as an important aspect of their identity. People may identify with a parent, teacher, charismatic leader, or celebrity, or with a slightly older peer who seems to have been successful. Their identifications govern a great deal of their behavior and self-concept.

Muhammad Ali identified with a number of people during his formative years. First he identified with his father. He wanted to be as skilled and distinguished in his own work, boxing, as his father had been in painting. He also identified with the skilled black boxers he saw on television or heard about as an adolescent, especially the ones who emphasized their pride in being black, such as Jack Johnson. Later his identification with the slain political and religious leader, Malcolm X, who was killed just after Ali became champ, was important in making him stick to his religious convictions even if this meant being exiled from boxing and perhaps even being put in jail.

SELF-ESTEEM MOTIVES. All the self-conception processes we have discussed thus far involve perception and, to some extent, thinking and reasoning. Psychologists know that a great deal of perception and thinking is irrational and biased. People see what they want to see or what they expect to see. They draw conclusions that serve their own needs. In no place is bias more pronounced than in the perception of what we care about most—ourselves. It is easy to observe biased self-concept formation in all the self-perception processes we have mentioned.

In the case of reflected appraisal, we can easily distort what others think of us, since people seldom state a positive or negative opinion of another person directly. In the case of social comparison, there is room for enormous distortion in the meaning of any comparison outcome. If someone sitting next to you in class does better on an exam, there are probably lots of ways that you could convince yourself that his or her performance in no way implies that

TABLE 3.1

Self-Conception Processes

Kenneth Gergen (1970) has outlined four psychological processes that are central in defining yourself. They are important in establishing what characteristics you have such as beliefs, abilities, and interpersonal style and also in evaluating your self-worth.

1. Reflected appraisal: The impact that the evaluation of someone else, especially an important person, such as a parent, has on you.

2. Social comparison: The process of evaluating opinions, abilities, and personal traits by comparing them with the opinions, abilities, and personal traits of other people.

3. Attribution: The process of inferring that you possess certain traits by looking at the causes of your behavior and, where appropriate, seeing that they reflect personal characteristics.

4. Identification: The process of admiring or envying another person and trying to be as much like that other person as possible.

he or she is brighter. You might conclude that he or she spends all his or her time in the library and only does well because he or she works so hard. You might distort the attribution process by deciding that your own performance was poor because of competing demands on your studying time that you couldn't ignore: An old friend from high school came by to visit, and you were stuck. In the case of identification, it is easy to imagine ourselves as closer to the ideal we are striving for than is the case. Aspiring singers often think they sound more like Linda Ronstadt or Paul McCartney than anyone else does.

The Totalitarian Ego and Self-Concept Biases

The various kinds of distortion noted above serve to maintain whatever beliefs we have about ourselves, and the kind of beliefs we have generally tend to be quite positive. One very provocative theory about the self-concept argues that the self, or ego, manages information about the self like a totalitarian state manages information about itself (Greenwald, 1980). Just as totalitarian states manage the news and

other information so that positive information prevails over negative information and traditional claims about the state are supported, so the ego manages information so that people perceive themselves positively rather than negatively and maintain whatever self-theories they have held in the past. The ego does this through three biases in the way it processes information about our behavior. These three biases are called the **egocentricity, beneffectance,** and **cognitive conservatism** bias.

The *egocentricity* bias is the tendency to perceive oneself as the central actor in events where you are involved. For example, when playing a game of softball, you might remember a put-out you made as the key play that turned the tide for your side. In addition, you might perceive yourself as the cause of other people's behavior. When the opposing side changes pitchers, you might attribute their changing to the fact that they feared facing you at the plate. Muhammad Ali often perceived himself as the key figure in boxing history, and as the one indispensable fighter in the profession. He predicted that once he retired a ghostly voice wailing "Aliiii . . ." would haunt boxing and that the sport would die. Most sports fans miss Ali, his talk as much as his fighting, but the sport has been able to continue without him.

In addition to the egocentricity bias, people sometimes fall prey to the *beneffectance* bias, the bias toward taking responsibility for success but denying it for failure. To demonstrate this, ask people to call to mind a specific test they felt they had done less well on than they had hoped, and then ask them whether they felt the test was fair or fairly graded. Then ask them the same fairness questions for an exam they did well on. Chances are good they will feel that the test they did well on was fairer than the test they did poorly on. Similarly, people often embrace the successes of the groups they belong to, but distance themselves from the groups' failures. When our school team wins a game, we have a tendency to say "We won"; when the team loses, it's "They lost."

The final bias attributed to the totalitarian ego is called *cognitive conservatism.* Cognitive

When we are successful, we take credit for it and feel happy. We tend to deny responsibility for failure.

Michael Uffer, Photo Researchers, Inc.

TABLE 3.2

The Biases of the Totalitarian Ego

Psychologist Anthony Greenwald (1980) has argued that the ego controls information in ways that are similar to the way totalitarian states control information. Both the ego and the totalitarian state want to believe that they are central and important, that they are responsible for good things but not bad ones, and that they have not changed and do not need to because they have been correct all along. The ego maintains these beliefs by using three biases.

1. Egocentricity: People tend to recall the role that they have played in a group and the contributions they have made; they tend to see themselves as playing a central role in the events they have taken part in.
2. Beneffectance: People accept responsibility for success but deny blame for failure; when they fail or behave immorally they make excuses, and attribute their actions to external factors.
3. Cognitive conservatism: People tend not to change their beliefs; when they learn new information they believe they knew it all along, so that the information is not new; when they change their attitudes they think that they have held their new attitude all along.

Since these biases are the result of the way we process information, it is hard to recognize them in ourselves, or to be aware of them when we show them. But think of your parents or friends. You probably can recall them showing these biases.

conservatism is the tendency to maintain your beliefs and to perceive the beliefs and thoughts you have as being the ones you have held for a long time. An example of this is how, after you've changed your mind about something, you come to believe that the new opinion you hold is the one you have always held. Ask your parents why they've changed their minds on some issue, perhaps whether the president is doing a good job. Make sure you know they have actually changed. Chances are they will say that they haven't changed, that they've always had high regard for (or doubts about) the president. A similar tendency is the "I knew it all along" effect. Tell one of your friends you just heard that your school is raising tuition by $300 next year. Ask them how long they've known about it. They might well think they've known the information you just told them for several weeks.

These three cognitive biases—egocentricity, beneffectance, and cognitive conservatism—are pervasive. Their primary function is to make us feel that we are important, successful, and stable or consistent.

Self-Concept Biases and Self-Handicapping

How should we evaluate these various biases of the self-concept? Do they help or hurt our overall degree of adjustment? Overall, they are probably helpful because they contribute to positive feelings about ourselves. On the other hand, they distort reality to some degree. The cognitive conservatism bias, for example, leads us to think we've always believed something, when that isn't really true. One unfortunate effect of cognitive conservatism is that we may not be aware of the interesting ways we've changed, because we assume we've always been the way we are now. Still, these biases probably can't be changed very much. They happen automatically, and for the most part they protect us. As long as they just make us feel good, what harm can they be? We should be aware, however, that some of our efforts to maintain a positive self-image can affect our behavior, and not always for the better. We see this happen in the case of something psychologists call *self-handicapping* (Jones & Berlgas, 1978).

When Muhammad Ali wanted to succeed at boxing he worked hard and continuously to meet his goal. For example, in 1973 Ali lost the second fight of his career to Ken Norton, who was then unknown. This defeat was a major upset. Ali knew that if he was to be taken seriously and have a chance at the new champion, George Foreman, he would have to defeat Norton in a rematch. He trained harder than he ever had and succeeded in beating Norton in a very close fight. Does it always happen that when people want to succeed they work their hardest and put out maximum effort? Sometimes the unfortunate answer is no. This is where self-handicapping comes in. Sometimes students, for example, will stay up too late partying, or perhaps even drinking, before the day of an exam. They seem to do things that will clearly handicap themselves and lower the probability of a good performance. Why should they do this? Research shows that people often do things that impede their own performance because they are afraid they might not succeed and they want to have an excuse for failure, so that the failure won't be blamed on low ability. In this way they maintain their image of themselves as having plenty of ability. By handicapping themselves, they never let their true ability be put to the test. Therefore

their ability can never be shown to be inadequate. People may attribute their failures to having drunk too much, to not having studied enough, or to insufficient practice. Jones and Berlgas (1978) argue that one contributor to alcoholism is people's tendency to drink in order to handicap their own performance. In such a case, your self-esteem is being maintained, but at a very high price, one that hardly seems worth paying. You are lowering your own level of performance and developing a dangerous and destructive drug dependency in addition.

The underlying assumption in this discussion is that people care about themselves and want to have a positive opinion of themselves. As a consequence, they perceive their behavior and other people's behavior in ways that allow them to maintain a positive self-concept. While this is undoubtedly true, it should not be taken to imply that people always interpret information about themselves positively. As much as people want to believe that they are

Many people handicap their own performances so that they have an excuse for failure. One way of doing this is by drinking excessively.
Laimute E. Druskis.

good and appreciated by others, they fear that this is not true and often make overly negative interpretations of information about themselves. Just as there are people who wouldn't recognize a putdown if it left them lying on their backsides, others, because of anxiety about their worth, insecurity about other people's opinions, or a poor self-concept, interpret

everything negatively. The most minuscule change in tone of voice, or the most insignificant glance, is taken as a sign of displeasure or rejection. Any failure is taken as a sign of incompetence and unworth. These fears and insecurities can cause as much distortion and psychological trouble as the need for feelings of self-worth. They can contribute greatly to depression and lack of productivity.

In the course of busy and complex lives, we all fall prey to overjustifying ourselves at some times and psychologically burning ourselves at the stake at other times. We all go through periods of feeling good and feeling bad about ourselves. It is important to remember that while we can be more or less accurate in judging how much of a specific ability we have, such as high-jumping, our overall worth is not an objective matter. What we feel about ourselves is affected by others' judgments, real and imagined, and by the comparisons and attributions we make, but what we finally decide about our worth is determined by us alone. We have considerable choice about feeling good or miserable about ourselves. We have only to exercise that choice. Furthermore, if we can choose positive or negative evaluations, why not choose the positive? Why not accept ourselves? Why not assume that we have worth and value and act on that assumption? It's amazing how beneficial that choice and following through on it can be. This may seem like self-deception to a certain extent, but it is an important stance you can take in your own life. (We'll return to this point in Chapter 8.)

ADOLESCENCE

Adolescence begins at sexual maturity, usually around age 11 for girls and age 13 for boys. Physical growth is rapid, feelings are strong, and there is a great deal of energy. There is also a questioning and challenging of parents, and sometimes of the culture or society, plus some fear, uncertainty, and guilt. These are powerful emotions, and adolescents have many such needs and feelings to recognize, understand,

---

REVIEW QUESTIONS

1. Match the following definitions to the appropriate concept.
   _____ a belief or attitude that affects how we remember the past and integrate the present
   _____ adoption of a pattern of behavior of someone admired, and integration of that pattern into our self-identity
   _____ our belief about our worth
   _____ the total set of opinions or beliefs we have about ourselves
   _____ process involving the effect of other's opinions of ourself on our estimate of our worth
   a. reflected appraisal
   b. self-concept
   c. self-esteem
   d. identification
   e. self-schema
2. One theory of the self argues that the self manages information about itself in a totalitarian manner, such that positive information prevails over negative information. This is done through the information processing biases of _____, _____, and _____.
3. T or F: Although biases of the self-concept may distort reality to some degree, they are unlikely to ever negatively affect our behavior.
4. _____ is when a person impedes his/her own performance because he/she is afraid of not succeeding and wants an excuse for failure.

and cope with. Somewhere in this sorting-out process the self is discovered. Let's consider specifically some of the conflicts and emotions that arise during these years.

Conflicts about Independence and Responsibility

With their new-found interests, energies, and strengths, adolescents often expect more freedom and independence from their parents. While they are still very dependent on their parents for satisfying their basic needs for shelter and nourishment, they often feel that they are old enough to decide how late to stay out at night, how often to date, and in general, where to be when. They object to having to notify their parents of their after-school plans and to their parents evaluating their friends. They feel that they should be able to drive the family car or have their own. They feel that parents are too restrictive. Parents usually doubt that their children are able to handle as much freedom as they want or to behave completely responsibly without some monitoring of their behavior. Adolescents feel that adults "cramp their style." These feelings can make home life something of a battleground. Certainly adolescent resentment of adults who have power and privileges that adolescents feel they too deserve contributes to tensions between parents and their adolescent children.

For the young Muhammad Ali many of these adolescent strivings for independence were supported by his parents. When he first decided, at age 12, that he wanted to become a boxer, his parents, after some thought, gave him the go-ahead. They felt it was better for him to do something on his own, even if it was potentially dangerous, than for him to simply conform to a rowdy gang of peers who roamed the streets and got into trouble. Those of you who are, or will be, parents of adolescents, might remember the importance of giving youngsters enough slack so that they can get used to taking on responsibility and independence in productive ways.

Uncertainties about Sex

Adolescence begins with sexual maturity, and one of its major challenges is sorting out confusions about sex. The new sex drives are both powerful and frightening, and there is a great deal of uncertainty about which feelings are normal and moral, which behaviors will be pleasurable and which will lead to guilt or self-respect, and which kinds of sexual expression will lead to adaptive adjustment to the world in the long run. Our culture tantalizes us with ever-increasing amounts of sexuality in movies, advertisements, books, and television. Sex isn't nearly as forbidden as it was in earlier generations. People suffer fewer feelings of guilt and shame over sex now than in the past. Still, adolescents are often taught that premarital sex is dirty and immoral.

How do young people deal with these confusions and contradictions? Probably few adolescents know adults with whom they can easily discuss these matters. Conflicts with parents make it very difficult for parents to be helpful in many cases. As a result, adolescents rely mostly on their peers, who are often no better informed and no more mature than they are, for information and counsel. Norms evolve in adolescent society, and most adolescents abide by them rather than risk rejection. For some these norms lead to satisfaction; for others they do not.

As a child Muhammad Ali relied mostly on peers for his information about sex. Adults seemed to treat the subject as something children shouldn't concern themselves with. Ali and his friends were reprimanded sharply on more than one occasion for peeping through windows at night trying to find out what the forbidden activities behind closed doors were all about. Later, when he began to get into boxing, Ali was confronted with an uncertainty about sex that still concerns him. He was told by most of the men who trained him to fight that sex would sap the strength of a boxer, a boxer who was sexually satisfied was lazy and lacked the sharpness and aggressiveness that were necessary to win. Ali heard that some scientists believed the opposite was true, that sex

Young men and women have to learn to handle sexual feelings. Many people have strong conflicts about sex.

Mimi Forsyth, Monkmeyer.

was good for boxers because the lack of sexual frustration let them concentrate better. He never found out the truth about this, but as a boxer he always hoped the scientists were right.

Value Conflict and Change

Part of the struggle for autonomy and independence that goes on during adolescence is a questioning of values. Adolescents frequently question the religious faith and practice that parents have instilled, or tried to instill, in their children since birth. Adolescents wonder whether they share their parents' beliefs, whether the same ideas make sense to them. Sometimes the questioning of parents' values and beliefs comes from observing that parents do not really live up to the abstract moral principles they have taught their sons and daughters. Bem (1970) notes that the "generation gap" often consists not of children rejecting parental values, but of children becoming disillusioned when they find their parents do not practice what they have preached. During the Vietnam War, for example, many adolescents felt that adults were not following principles of freedom and justice that they had taught their offspring when they were growing up.

Part of the reason that there is so much questioning of beliefs, values, and moral behavior is that adolescence is a time of rapid moral as well as physical development. This aspect of personal growth has been explored most extensively by Lawrence Kohlberg (1976). His ideas, and some classic research by Jean Piaget, provide an overview of the stages of moral development people move through, a process that culminates in profound changes in adolescent conceptions of morality.

STAGES OF MORAL DEVELOPMENT.   The earliest studies of moral development were reported by Piaget in his famous book *The Moral Judgment of the Child* (1932). The ideas in that book were based on Piaget's findings about the way children's intellectual, or cognitive, abilities mature. Erikson proposed that the personality develops through distinct stages; Piaget argued that cognitive functions such as thinking and reasoning develop in the same way. He showed that children are capable of qualitatively different kinds of thinking as they grow older. It's not simply that they are able to handle a greater quantity of information. For example, young children are unable to view things from other people's point of view or understand people's intentions very well. Both Piaget and Kohlberg believe that moral development follows the acquisition of new cognitive capacities.

When Piaget discussed morality he was especially concerned with children's judgments abut how severely to punish other children who had caused damage, such as broken dishes or ripped clothing. He felt that the biggest change in these moral judgments came after the age of nine, when children move from the stage of **moral realism** to the stage of **moral relativism.** During the earlier stage of moral realism, children believe in rules very literally. It's almost as if they think of them as objects. A rule is a rule, and it must be followed. If children break rules or cause harm, they must be punished according to the magnitude of the harm they cause. For example, children listening to a story about a young girl who breaks dishes assign punishment according to how many dishes she breaks. That is, others are punished according to the seriousness of the consequences of their acts. Little thought is given to why someone caused damage or to mitigating circumstances.

During the later stage of moral relativism, or "cooperative morality," children realize that rules have no independent meaning or existence other than that which has been given to them by human beings. They become aware that rules and laws are made by people to serve human purposes. They realize further that rules can be changed if change is needed to better serve human needs, and that rules can sometimes be broken if that is in the best human interest. During this stage, punishment is not mechanically assigned on the basis of how serious the consequences of action are. Instead, the individual's intention is taken into account. If a child broke some dishes while trying to surprise his or her parents by cleaning up the kitchen, the child is not seen as guilty or deserving of punishment. The intention was a good one. In general, moral judgments are made in a more humanistic way. There is less rigid application of rules. The purpose behind behavior is considered, as well as the behavior itself and its consequences.

Kohlberg's (1976) scheme of moral development shows some of the same kind of increased human understanding as Piaget's. Rules instilled in childhood are replaced by more carefully thought-out moral principles. Kohlberg investigated moral development using methods similar to those of Piaget. He presented stories about moral dilemmas to subjects who were asked to say what a person in the situation should do and why. In one story a man needed a drug to save his wife from cancer. The druggist who invented the medicine was charging ten times the cost of making it. The man was unable to borrow more than half the money and could not get the druggist to lower his price. The man got desperate and broke into the store and stole the drug. Subjects were asked whether the man should have done this and why.

On the basis of subjects' responses to this dilemma Kohlberg distinguished three major levels of moral development. Within each level there are two separate stages, giving six stages in all (see Table 3.3). As with stages of personality development, a person must go through the stages in order. They cannot be skipped. However, people vary greatly in how fast they progress through the stages and in how far they eventually get. Many people do not get past Stage 4 in Kohlberg's system. The period of most intense moral development is during adolescence. Between the ages of 10 and 17, some individuals may move all the way from Stage 1 to Stage 6.

The first two stages of moral development make up the "preconventional" level. Here the child really has no internal morals or values, but simply governs his or her behavior on the basis of anticipated rewards and punishments. The first stage, which may last until age 10, is oriented toward the avoidance of punishment. Children may decide not to steal or to interrupt their parents, so that they won't be punished. The second stage of the preconventional level is oriented more toward reward than toward punishment. Children may clean up their rooms in order to earn money or tell of their achievements in school in order to see their parents' delight. During this second stage the idea of reciprocity also begins to take hold. Children realize that if they do something kind to someone else they are likely to be helped or rewarded in the future. Thus children behave

TABLE 3.3

Kohlberg's Six Stages
of Moral Development

Level I: Precon-ventional	Stage 1: Orientation toward obedience and punishment or reward. Deference to superior power. Goodness or badness is determined by the physical consequences of action.
	Stage 2: Actions are motivated by desire for reward or benefit. People share, but in a pragmatic way, not out of a sense of justice or loyalty.
Level II: Conventional	Stage 3: "Good boy, nice girl" orientation. Emphasis on conformity. Behavior that pleases others and is approved by them is good behavior.
	Stage 4: "Law-and-order" orientation. Focus on authority, fixed rules, and the social order. Right behavior consists of maintaining the given social order for its own sake. Respect is earned by performing one's duty.
Level III: Postcon-ventional	Stage 5: Social-contract, legalistic orientation. Standards that have been agreed upon by the whole society define right action. Emphasis upon legal rules for reaching consensus.
	Stage 6: Emphasis on decisions of conscience and self-chosen, abstract ethical principles such as universal principles of justice, of equality of human rights, and of respect for the dignity of human beings as individuals.

in ways that are likely to lead others to reward them. This second stage characterizes children's actions and morality between ages 10 and 13.

The next two stages of moral development make up the "conventional morality" level. In these two stages the major concern is conformity to rules and values that have been learned from authorities. The first of these two stages is the one that most 13-year-olds are in. It is marked by "good girl" or "good boy" morality, where children and adolescents are concerned with the approval of parents and other important adults and adopt moral stances that they know conform to family standards. Values are adopted in order to gain the approval of others. A 14-year-old boy may refuse to smoke because his father or a teacher he admires would be disappointed in him. An adolescent girl may change the way she dresses to gain the approval of an employer she very much respects.

The second stage of the conventional morality level, Stage 4, is marked by what is sometimes called a "law-and-order orientation." This stage is most common among people 16 and older. Many people never grow beyond this kind of conventional morality. In this stage people adopt and follow rules and laws that are set by powerful authorities in the culture, such as churches, government, and society as a whole. They learn the rules of these authorities, such as that it is wrong and illegal to steal, and obey them. They do what they think will be regarded as honorable by those in a position to judge. People who do not engage in sexual relations because their religious leaders say it is wrong or who do not exceed the speed limit because it is the state law are following Stage 4 conventional morality.

Sometime during the latter part of adolescence, perhaps around 17 years of age, some people move beyond conventional morality into Stages 5 and 6 in the Kohlberg scheme. These stages constitute the "postconventional" level of morality, in which people commit themselves to self-accepted moral principles. Few reach this level. Most adults follow one form or another of conventional morality.

In Stage 5, morality is based on what one perceives as good for people as a whole. It is based on consensus or agreement about what is in people's best interest and what seems fair and equitable in general. In this stage people want the respect of others and want to perceive their choices as rational in light of the interests of all. Morality reflects community welfare. This seems to be a highly democratic stage where morals are based on what people can agree on as equals. No authority is allowed to make rules for its followers.

In Stage 6, reached by some individuals during late adolescence or early adulthood, people finally adopt internalized, universal ethical principles. They choose these for themselves on the basis of experience and reason. In this stage, people might protest the persecution of minorities or defend or challenge laws on the basis of their own consciences. No longer is their morality based on gaining rewards, approval, or respect from others. People are only concerned with avoiding self-condemnation and feeling at peace with their own values and their implications.

If their consciences reject values that society seems to have accepted, people in Stage 6 often experience conflict with those who follow conventional morality. They may be condemned by society as they protest society's laws. Thus Henry David Thoreau, who described marching to the beat of a "different drummer," was put in jail for not paying taxes that he considered to be unjust. When he was asked by his friend Ralph Waldo Emerson what he was doing in jail, Thoreau, expecting Emerson to have followed his own conscience as well, replied: "What are you doing out there?"

Muhammad Ali never had to go to jail for his beliefs, but he came close. He definitely heard a "different drummer" with respect to religion and the military, and his case is a good illustration of the stages of moral development. When Ali first asserted that he would not go into the Army, many people cynically felt that he was just trying to escape from military service—that is, operating on the reward-conscious Stage 2 level. Actually, Ali's position, for which he was clearly willing to go to jail, was in part Stage 4 morality: He was doing his duty as told to him by Muslim religious leaders. But to a greater extent his decision to go to jail was an independent choice, based on his own con-

Adolescence is a time of rapid moral development. People at this time of life get actively involved in moral and political issues.

Hugh Rogers, Monkmeyer.

science telling him that he had to abide by his beliefs, no matter what the consequences. This choice represented Stage 6 morality.

Outcomes of Adolescent Conflict and Confusion

As we have noted, adolescence is a time of rapid physical, cognitive, and moral growth. For many, there are great uncertainties about where all this is taking them. We have seen that adolescents experience conflicts about independence, doubts about sex, confusion about values, and uncertainties about self-worth. In short, this is the time of life when people first wonder intensely "Who am I? What am I worth? What shall I do?" This is the period when people have their first *identity crisis*, their first struggles with the question of what they can do and be in the world. What are the outcomes of identity crises? We know most about the answer to this question from Erikson (1968).

IDENTITY VERSUS IDENTITY CONFUSION. For some people the outcome of the identity crisis is a positive balance. They have a greater sense of **ego-identity** than of **identity confusion.** They seem to be able to take hold of themselves and their lives in some way, to gain an overall sense of who they are, what they can do, and how they want to live. Most important, perhaps, they are able to find a place for themselves in society, a job or a career. They feel that they know who they are and that who they are is understood and accepted by others around them. Even more than this, people with a sense of ego-identity feel that there is purpose and meaning in what they have been doing in the past and what they will be doing in the future. They feel that the past and future connect, that this is some coherence in who they are, and that they have things to do in living and becoming. Erikson described this as "an invigorating sense of sameness and continuity" (1968, p. 19).

How do people who have a sense of identity come by it? What makes them so fortunate? Like all other balances, identity rests on what has happened in earlier stages. Erikson proposed that identity has a basis in early childhood (see Chapter 2) in that the sense of basic trust then established forms the foundation for faith, which, in turn, is an important aspect of a sense of identity. Similarly, a sense of autonomy in childhood and the early experiencing of the capacity to act alone provide a basis for the young adult's sense of free will, another important part of identity. This sense of free will is extremely important for functioning in a democratic and essentially capitalistic society. Similarly, a sense of initiative in childhood becomes a sense of creative potential, and the sense of industry developed in the latency period contributes to a feeling of being able to behave effectively in the adult world. All of these psychological strengths provide a foundation for the sense of ego-identity.

These foundations are important, but

identity still must be achieved by an active process of sorting out, pulling together, and choosing. To Erikson, identity is based on an integration of past identifications and roles, life-long motives, needs, and strivings, and the person's skills and modes of coping. From these, a core self is identified, and a place for that self is made within available social roles. In other words, people decide who they are on the basis of what they have been in the past, what they aspire to, and what they are capable of, and then decide what role they will play in society.

For Muhammad Ali, there was little difficulty in establishing a sense of identity. From boyhood on, he had the goal of becoming a boxer and a leader for better treatment of black people. He identified with famous boxers and Muslim religious leaders and attempted successfully to become a champion and a leader. He aspired to be "the greatest," and he was. It is interesting that Erikson emphasizes the dependence of a sense of identity on having others understand and accept your own sense of who you are. When Ali won the heavyweight championship, before he would answer questions from reporters he made them state publicly that, yes, he was the greatest.

Of course not all people are able to achieve a strong sense of ego-identity. If they are unable to integrate their aspirations, needs, and skills into social roles and find a place for themselves within the social structure, they will suffer *identity confusion.* Part of identity confusion is role confusion, uncertainty about what career one is going to follow or, more generally, what one is going to *do* in society. Some people can have identity confusion even if they have jobs or social roles, because the roles they have don't fit well with their personalities. They may feel that their jobs require them to be too assertive or not assertive enough, that their jobs place too much emphasis on unimportant or even disliked values, or that their jobs require too much time away from other valued activities. People can also have careers that they like and are good at, but still have identity confusion in other ways. They may feel that there is not a good match between their definitions of

REVIEW QUESTIONS

5. Piaget felt that moral development occurs in stages. He felt that the biggest changes in moral development came after the age of nine when children move from the stage of _____ ____ to the stage of _____ _____ .

6. Kohlberg distinguished six stages of moral development: three major levels each containing two separate stages. Match each two stages with the major level they occur in.

_____ 1st stage: social-contract, legalistic orientation
_____ 2nd stage: emphasis on conscience and ethical principles
_____ 1st stage: conformity, "good boy/nice girl" orientation
_____ 2nd stage: "law-and-order," authority orientation
_____ 1st stage: obedience/punishment orientation
_____ 2nd stage: actions motivated by desire for reward

  a. preconventional
  b. conventional
  c. postconventional

7. T or F: An identity crisis is most likely to occur during middle age.

8. The outcome of an identity crisis may be positive; a person may feel he/she knows who he/she is and have a good sense of ego-identity. However, some people may experience a conflict between how they see themselves and how others see them. Erikson calls this conflict _____ _____ .

themselves and other people's definitions. People sometimes feel that the world doesn't really understand what is inside them, what they want and what they value, and that they have no way of communicating this. An example might be a homosexual who is afraid to "come out of the closet" or a wife and mother who really doesn't

like house care and child rearing. Without the direction that is provided by having social roles *and* a clear sense of self that is also understood and accepted by others, people will be confused about who they are. They will not have the "invigorating sense of sameness and continuity" that is such an important part of identity.

ADULTHOOD

When the identity crisis is over in late adolescence, people are well on their way to making the transition to adulthood. They face new tasks, challenges, and opportunities in establishing their own independent lives. Like childhood and adolescence, the adult years are filled with different problems and possibilities at different times. We can consider the prospects of adult development by considering the various psychological crises that people face as they grow older, a basic reorientation toward experience that many adults go through at midlife, and a comprehensive study of stages of adult development by Yale psychologist Daniel Levinson.

Psychological Challenge and Crisis in Adult Development

INTIMACY VERSUS ISOLATION IN YOUNG ADULTHOOD. The first specific task of becoming an adult, according to Erikson (1968), is to establish an intimate relationship. This relationship must be consistent with the identity you have established in late adolescence. For many people establishing a relationship of love, respect, and intimacy is not difficult. For others the sexual side of love is a very difficult aspect of an intimate relationship. Integrating the sexual side of love into a total relationship is an important but often problematic part of establishing genuine intimacy.

One reason that this integration may be difficult is that many people have grown up feeling that sex is basically immoral. Feeling sexually aroused and behaving sexually can cause a great deal of guilt and anxiety for such people. This is especially true for women who have been taught that, for them, sex in marriage is normal but before marriage is taboo. It can be very difficult to make the psychological transition from feeling that sex is wrong and dirty to feeling that you now have a green light. So much time has been spent in inhibiting sex and justifying the inhibition that it is hard to make a turnaround. Either the prior inhibitions or the present lack of restraint, or both, seem slightly absurd and confusing. Of course, due to traditional sex roles some women have been taught that even in marriage sexuality for women is basically unacceptable; satisfying men's needs is a duty to be borne, according to this biased viewpoint.

Men can also have difficulty handling the lesson that sex for women is bad before marriage. They often grow up with the stereotype that women who are not virgins are slightly less than moral. They may not overcome this in their own intimate relations in or out of marriage, and may find it difficult to accept and feel at ease with the sexual behavior and sexual interest of their partners.

Muhammad Ali had some difficulty accepting the sexuality of his first wife, Sonji. Ali was married to Sonji when he was 22, but the marriage lasted less than a year and a half. Part of the reason that Ali was attracted to Sonji was that she was a very beautiful and sexually attractive woman, but this became part of the problem. Sonji liked to dress in an attractive and alluring way. Ali felt that this was not the way a woman should behave, especially in the Islamic religion. He had difficulty accepting his own wife's sexuality at this early stage in his adulthood.

Even if both partners feel that being sexually intimate is good in principle, much may be lost in the translation to practice. Many young people have inadequate knowledge of sex. They find it hard to communicate openly about sexual feelings with their partners. They are too insecure and self-conscious about their performance or strong sexual drives to be sensitive to the other person. As a result, awkwardness and failure frequently prevail, instead of the relaxed mutual caring and support that is so central to the intimate relationship.

For some people intimacy is never achieved. They are unable to participate in a "fusing of identities" or deep caring. Instead of a sense of intimacy they develop a **sense of isolation** and feel distant from others. They may feel alienated and cynical about humanity in general. If so, they may avoid others or simply engage in superficial relationships in which they are only concerned with using others to satisfy their own needs. Their sexual relationships may be quite exploitative. They may be reasonably content as individuals, but sharing and caring are absent from their lives.

GENERATIVITY VERSUS STAGNATION IN THE MIDDLE YEARS. Erikson noted that during the early stages of development people are very dependent on others. In middle age, however, they develop a concern for others who are dependent on them. This concern, called **generativity,** takes the form of a "concern for establishing and guiding the next generation" (Erikson, 1968, p. 138). This can mean having children of one's own and nurturing them, or it can mean living a creative and productive life with the aim of leaving something positive behind, something that will enrich others. Generativity involves being unselfish, un-self-centered, and greatly invested in the needs of those who are younger, specific younger people or the younger generation in general. This rich expansion of caring about others does not always develop. The alternative is *stagnation,* a lack of caring except for oneself, accompanied by boredom, cynicism, and pessimism about the future, one's own and that of humankind. Psychological stagnation accompanied by the biological reality of having children of one's own can often lead to the kind of inconsistent and uncaring treatment of children and adolescents that can produce in them the negative balances discussed in Chapter 2.

INTEGRITY VERSUS DESPAIR IN LATE ADULTHOOD. According to Erikson, a person who

Older people with a sense of integrity can help young people face life with trust and optimism.

Mimi Forsyth, Monkmeyer.

has done well in the earlier stages of development, who has adjusted successfully to life, and who has been productive in spite of life's disappointments will be able in old age to fully accept his or her life cycle as it has run its course. This person will accept responsibility for what has happened and not blame parents or society. In general, such people will have a **sense of integrity.** They will be at peace with themselves and with others. They will have a feeling of the oneness of their own existence and of life in general.

The opposite of integrity is despair or a feeling of disgust. A person will realize that it is too late to make any changes. Whatever one is has been decided already. A person who feels that his or her life and work have not been worthwhile does not have integrity and will face this despair. Old age will lack meaning or happiness. Even at this age, one's psychological

balance can affect the younger generation positively or negatively. Erikson suggests that healthy children will not fear life if the elder generation has achieved enough integrity so as not to fear death.

The Midlife Cultural Orientation

Now in his early forties, Muhammad Ali has left boxing behind forever, with the exception of an occasional exhibition. He has become highly involved in charitable causes and with cultural activities, such as the work of black musicians and painters. To some extent these activities represent Erikson's generativity, an attempt to pass something of value on to the next generation. But they can also represent a specific midlife transition described by the famous theorist Carl Jung (1960).

Although Jung did not discuss personality development in any detail, he did make an important observation about a transition in personality orientation during midlife. This transition may take place during middle adulthood, probably during the midforties. Jung believed that during the first part of life a person's orientation is generally *biological*. There is a concern with gratifying the instincts and with the *expansion* of experience. Young people will seek out as many experiences as they can. They will strive to enrich themselves by encountering as many new people, places, ideas, and experiences as possible.

For the mature older person, further expansion and further instinctual gratification is not desirable. Rather, there is an increasing need for simplification, limitation, and intensification. In lieu of seeking more experience, the older person wants life to be simpler and calmer, with each experience enjoyed more deeply and intensely. Older people spend more time reflecting on experiences, rather than having new ones right away. This is the time of *spiritual and* **cultural orientation** as opposed to the earlier biological orientation. The trend is toward discovering the meaning of life rather than frantically living it. Unfortunately, Jung notes, "Not a few are wrecked during the transition from the biological to the cultural sphere. Our collective education makes practically no provision for this transitional period. Concerned solely with the education of the young, we disregard the education of the adult" (Jung, 1960, p. 60). That is, middle adulthood may be the time when men and women are most in need of education and guidance and most receptive to it. Their curiosity about the meaning of life puts them in a position to profit immensely from education. This is an extremely important psychological transition that the culture does nothing to provide for, although people who are aware of it can take their own steps to prepare for it.

Stages of Adult Development

Several years ago Yale psychologist Daniel J. Levinson published a book called *The Seasons of a Man's Life* (1978). This book, which formed the basis for Gail Sheehy's well-known book, *Passages* (1976), represents Levinson's attempt to outline the stages of adult life through which people pass. Although his study was based on male subjects, Levinson believes that women go through the same stages in slightly different ways. His work provides a useful overall picture of how people grow during adulthood.

For Levinson, adult male development is marked by an alternation of two types of stages. First, there are several stages marked by structuring, that is, choices and commitments to certain aspects of living. These structuring stages are interspersed with transition stages, where earlier commitments are questioned and new decisions made. These new decisions modify what has been built in earlier stages, sometimes with minor adjustments, sometimes with major changes.

MOVING INTO ADULTHOOD.

THE EARLY ADULT TRANSITION (AGES 17 TO 22). The first stage in Levinson's view of adult development is one of change rather than of structuring or commitment. It is

TABLE 3.4

Stages of Adult Development

Recently psychologists have begun to focus on the stages that adults move through during the long years of middle life. Daniel Levinson (1978) has suggested that people go through an alternating series of structuring and transition stages. In the structuring stages a life pattern is formed and established, in the transition stages it is modified or altered. Levinson's stages are listed below:

The Early Adult Transition	(Ages 17–22)
Entering the Adult World	(Ages 22–28)
The Age-Thirty Transition	(Ages 28–33)
Settling Down	(Ages 33–40)
The Midlife Transition	(Ages 40–45)
Entering Middle Adulthood	(Ages 45–50)
Middle and Later Adult Eras	(Beyond Age 50)

called the "early adult transition" and its main task is emergence from the preadult world. It takes place during the late teens and early twenties, which for some people are the college years, and involves parting with preadult styles of living and old friends, to some extent, and taking a preliminary step into the adult world. During this stage people start to form an "initial adult identity," to begin to build an idea of what they would like to be as independent persons. This idea is based on what Levinson calls the "**Dream**." The Dream is a vision of what people would like to accomplish in life. It is a "vague sense of self in the world," an "imagined possibility" of adult life that "generates excitement and vitality" (Levinson, 1978).

Muhammad Ali actually moved into the early adult transition stage at a very young age, 14. At that time he committed himself to his Dream, winning the world heavyweight championship. Even though he was a slender youth, he wanted to fight as a heavyweight and gain the prestige that goes with the heavyweight championship. He won his Olympic title as a light heavyweight but never gave up the Dream to move to the top category. He managed to do that shortly after he became a professional.

THE EARLY ADULT YEARS.

ENTERING THE ADULT WORLD (AGES 22 TO 28).   People who have formed their Dream during the early adult transition seem prepared to move into the adult world. During this stage they make decisions that form a provisional structure for adult life. Initial choices can provide a strong sense of identity if they fit a person's overall personality, especially if they fit the Dream. The more that choices are consistent with the Dream and seem to be advancing it, the more the sense of identity will be experienced.

The choices a person makes at this stage are in the very important areas of occupation, love, values, and life style. Most critical perhaps are choosing an occupation and choosing a marriage partner. Both are important in the extent to which they help actualize the Dream. The person whose occupation doesn't fit the Dream will feel a deep sense of alienation from self. A spouse who can share a partner's Dream and help pursue it can contribute greatly to the partner's adjustment. Each must understand and contribute to the other's Dream. After the Dream has been fulfilled, two people can outgrow each other unless there is more to the relationship than one using the other to reach his or her goals.

Another special relationship young people need to establish is with a "mentor." The mentor is usually a somewhat older person who is part parent and part friend and peer. The mentor relationship generally lasts two or three years, during which time the mentor can provide needed guidance about the adult world, especially about one's occupation. Not all relationships with mentors are positive, but they have great emotional intensity. They too help make the Dream more concrete and give the young person a tangible model of how to live as an adult.

A man named Drew "Bundini" Brown served as Muhammad Ali's mentor. He was a constant supporter in Ali's boxing career and a helpful adviser as Ali faced many key life decisions. Brown was most visible as a cornerman during Ali's fights, but Ali relied on him in many of the ways people rely on their mentors.

One of the difficulties of this stage of entry into adulthood is that people want to explore as many possibilities for adult living as possible, but they must make choices to create a stable structure, even if it is a temporary one. Achieving a balance between these opposing tendencies can be difficult. A person who explores too much may end up with a rootless, unsettled life. A person who does not explore enough may have a deep sense of being locking into a structure that may not be the right one. In any case, during this stage the initial provisional structure of adult life is established. During the next stage it can be modified.

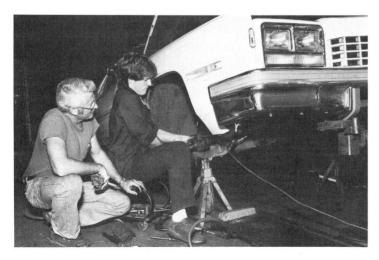

Young adults are often helped by an older mentor who guides the way in a trade or profession.
Rhoda Sidney.

THE AGE-30 TRANSITION (AGES 28 TO 33). The task of the age-30 transition is to modify the life structure that was formed in the previous stage. In making the initial choices required during that stage, one inevitably ignored parts of life that were important. For example, having children may have been overlooked. Now an attempt is made to review the initial choices to see if it is possible to include some of the important things that have been left out. For some this transition is fairly smooth, and most of the choices made upon entering the adult world are reaffirmed. For others there can be major changes in direction—divorce, perhaps, or a complete shift in career. Some people feel a deep sense of frustration and crisis at this stage and profound anxiety about the worth of their lives.

SETTLING DOWN STAGE (AGES 33 TO 40). People eventually complete the age-30 transition period and begin to establish a new life structure. This usually begins at about age 33, as people attempt to form a niche for themselves and become successful. They create their own sense of who they are and what they want to be in the adult world. They define their goals for living, or their "project."

This is the stage at which people do most "climbing the ladder" in their occupations. They move from becoming junior members of their professions to senior partners with more authority and power. At the end of this era is a special substage (ages 36 to 40) in which people make a major effort to achieve eminence in their occupations and to become leading figures in them. People may well become mentors for others younger than themselves. This is the time when individuals most firmly establish themselves and become dominant members of the adult world.

MIDDLE ADULTHOOD. The time of middle-age is of special importance. Major questions, crises, and reorientations take place during these years. Many people go through severe "midlife crises," wondering whether their lives have been worthwhile, whether there is any hope of changing them for the better, and whether there is any potential for freshness and vitality in their later years. We will consider two stages that Levinson has identified as important during these years.

THE MIDLIFE TRANSITION (AGES 40 TO 45). Levinson's studies show that during a stage he calls "the midlife transition," people question more deeply than ever what their lives have been up to that point. They try to discover their lives' meaning, they question the significance and the satisfactions their lives have provided for them. This can be the most traumatic of life stages. After a rather frantic early adulthood during which people have pursued their Dream, formed a family, worked to achieve, and in all these senses "made it," they must now ask, "What have I really got?" If they feel that they haven't got much or that too many needs were unmet in the struggle to get to the top, they may make profound changes in their lives. People will realize that any shifts that are to be made in life style had better be made now. Probably not all our needs are met in any of the choices that we make. In the midlife transition a final opportunity can be taken to try to change the life structure so as to incorporate our unmet needs.

ENTERING MIDDLE ADULTHOOD (AGES 45 TO 50). Levinson also found that the questioning of one's life choices that marks the midlife transition inevitably leads to new choices and thus changes in life. Sometimes these changes are quite radical; in other cases they are minor. The new choices may simply reaffirm the old. But whatever degree of change is caused by the new choices, some kind of new life structure will have to be formed. The task of entering middle adulthood is to build this new life structure. The new structure may involve spending more time with the family and less on the job, or more time in a position of new responsibility at work and less time in community affairs. New interests may be explored. In some cases these new involvements may build on interests, such as artistic pursuits, that were held briefly in the past, perhaps in the college years. In other cases a person may plunge into something entirely new. Wherever energies go in this era, it is again a time of choosing and commitment rather than questioning and exploring.

THE LATER YEARS.   Research on what happens during the later adult years is relatively sparse. Psychologists have considered how people deal with terminal illness and death, but less work has been done on the psychological stages people pass through in later years. However, Levinson has given us some insights into the psychological events of this time.

MIDDLE AND LATER ADULT ERAS.   Although Levinson's subjects had not lived past the "entering middle adulthood" stage, he did speculate about the nature of later eras. Generally he felt that the alternation of transition stages and structuring stages would continue throughout life. People would choose, structure, reevaluate, and choose again. This implies a future of continued psychological activity that has the potential to keep life fresh and satisfying. At the same time there is the potential for deep disillusionment if people discover that their life patterns are not very satisfying but that they are unable to make new commitments. They may feel intensely dissatisfied with their career but unable to begin a new one, or may regret not having children but find that it is too late to begin a family.

REVIEW QUESTIONS

9. T or F: According to Erikson, the first specific task of becoming an adult is to establish an intimate relationship.

10. Erikson noted that in middle age people often develop _____ , a concern for establishing and guiding the next generation. The alternative is _____ , a lack of caring, accompanied by boredom, cynicism, and pessimism.

11. Jung believed that during the first part of life a person's orientation is generally biological and is directed toward expansion of experience. For the mature older person, there is an increasing need for simplification, limitation, and intensification. This is a time of _____ and _____ orientation.

12. Levinson views adult development as occurring through the alternation of two kinds of stages. One stage involves making choices and commitments while the second stage involves questioning those earlier commitments and making new decisions. Levinson calls these processes _____ and transition.

13. T or F: The establishment of a new life structure in which people begin to settle down and define their goals for living usually occurs between ages 28 to 32.

SUMMARY

1. A person goes through many changes, and faces many problems, throughout life. A healthy self-definition, or self-concept, is crucial to dealing with these changes and problems. Most people first form their self-concepts in adolescence.

2. A person's self-concept, or self-theory, is based on reflected appraisal, social comparison, inferences drawn from his or her own behavior, and identification with others.

3. A person maintains a positive self-concept by using several biases that make up the "totalitarian ego": egocentricity, beneffectance, and cognitive conservatism.

4. Sometimes people engage in self-handicapping so as to provide excuses for possible failure.

5. Among the problems and challenges adolescents face are questions about independence, doubts about sex, and value conflicts and changes.

6. Kohlberg identifies changes in morality that adolescents go through. Adolescents move from a preconventional level of morality, where moral behavior is based on anticipated punishments and rewards, to a level of conventional morality, where the emphasis is on conforming to the rules established by authority, and then, in some cases, to a level of postconventional morality, where moral principles are adopted on the basis of one's own experience.

7. People generally resolve the conflicts and confusions of adolescence by forming an ego-identity, a clear sense of who they are and what role they play in society. Some fail to do this and suffer identity confusion, an inability to decide how to live.

8. After identity is formed, a person can develop intimate relationships that include sex. Integrating sexuality into intimate relationships often poses many difficulties.

9. Although identity is first formed during adolescence, it is modified throughout life.

10. Erikson identified generativity and integrity as the positive psychological balances of adulthood, and stagnation and despair as the negative balances.

11. Jung argued that there is a midlife transition during which people become more oriented toward cultural concerns and questions about the meaning of life.

12. Levinson noted several stages of development that adults go through. These stages alternate between structuring and commitment, on the one hand, and questioning and transition, on the other. Levinson emphasized that people redefine themselves at different periods throughout their lives.

KEY TERMS

a.	BENEFFECTANCE	f.	GENERATIVITY
b.	COGNITIVE CONSERVATISM	g.	IDENTITY CONFUSION
c.	CULTURAL ORIENTATION	h.	SELF-CONCEPT
d.	EGOCENTRICITY	i.	SENSE OF INTEGRITY
e.	EGO-IDENTITY		

1. The ego's tendency to maintain its beliefs and to perceive the beliefs it currently holds as the ones that it has held for a long time
2. The ego's tendency to take credit for success but to deny responsibility for failure
3. At midlife, an interest in spiritual and cultural matters as opposed to the gratification of instincts and to gaining more experience
4. The ego's tendency to see oneself as the center of action and as the cause of one's own and other's behavior
5. A positive sense of self and of the role one can play in society
6. A sense of peace with one's self and others and the acceptance of responsibility for one's life

7. One's perceptions of one's abilities, goals, and aspirations and one's overall feeling of worth
8. Lack of a clear sense of self and what one is capable of accomplishing in society
9. A concern for establishing and guiding the next generation

ANSWERS TO REVIEW QUESTIONS

1. e; d; c; b; a. **2.** Egocentricity; beneffectance; cognitive conservatism. **3.** False. **4.** Self-handicapping.

5. Moral realism; moral relativism. **6.** c; b; a. **7.** False. **8.** Identity confusion.

9. True. **10.** Generativity; stagnation. **11.** Spiritual; cultural. **12.** Structuring; transition. **13.** False.

EMOTIONS

I n September 1799 three sportsmen hunting in the French county of Aveyron were surprised by a strange animal that crossed their path. They pursued the animal, and finally treed it. To their utter amazement, the "animal" turned out to be a child of 11 or 12. He was completely naked and his body was badly scarred. He apparently didn't understand a word they said and reacted to them with bared teeth and snarls. The hunters captured the boy and transported him to Rodez, France. He stayed there for almost a year under the care of an elderly man who treated him with great tenderness and affection. However, he remained as wild and restless as he had been when captured, and he repeatedly sought to escape.

The story of the "Wild Boy of Aveyron" was widely reported in the newspapers. These accounts caught the attention of Jean-Marc Gaspard Itard, a 25-year-old physician at a new institution for deaf mutes. Itard requested that the Wild Boy be placed in his institution so that he could be carefully observed and studied. The permission was granted, and in September 1800 the "man-animal" arrived in Paris. The primitiveness of the Wild Boy surprised even Itard, who described him as follows:

> A disgustingly dirty child affected with spasmodic movements and often convulsions who swayed back and forth ceaselessly like certain animals in the menagerie, who bit and scratched those who opposed him, who showed no sort of affection for those who attended him, and who was, in short, indifferent to everything and attentive to nothing (Itard, 1932, p. 4).

Itard found that the Wild Boy's senses were extremely retarded. Neither cold nor heat seemed to affect him. He would sit naked for hours, squatting on the ground in the extreme cold of winter. To Itard's amazement, the Wild Boy would often seize glowing embers from the fire with his bare hands and "replace them without any haste upon the flaming fire." Itard also witnessed the Wild Boy plucking potatoes out of boiling water with his bare hands. The Wild Boy seemed insensible to even the loudest sounds; he showed no reaction when Itard sneaked up behind him and fired a gun. The boy had no ability to communicate with others.

While this dullness of senses was surprising, Itard was most fascinated by the Wild Boy's limited range of emotions. Itard reports that the Wild Boy "passed rapidly and without any apparent motive from apathetic melancholy to the most immoderate peals of laughter." The only emotions the boy expressed with any regularity were anger and joy, although their expression was often unrelated to the situation. To Itard's surprise, the boy showed no emotion when he was separated from the man who had cared for and loved him for a year after his capture. And, Itard reported, during his first six months at the institution, the Wild Boy never wept, regardless of the treatment he received.

Itard was faced with a creature who showed few physical sensations and almost no emotions. Itard embarked on a five-year program to transform this creature into a human. His major goals were to increase the Wild Boy's physical senses, to teach him to communicate, and to develop his emotions. Before beginning this effort, Itard conducted a number of tests to determine the present capabilities of his charge and

The Wild Boy expressed only a limited number of emotions, and those expressions were often unrelated to the situation.

Copyright © 1970, United Artists Corporation.

to ascertain how he had been living. As a result of these tests he concluded that the Wild Boy had been abandoned at the age of four or five. Apparently, whoever had abandoned him had also tried to kill him, as evidenced by the long scar on the boy's throat. The boy had lived in the forest and survived on a diet of acorns, nuts, and potatoes. He ate almost no meat. When Itard began his training of the boy, he noted that "his knowledge was limited to four things, viz. sleeping, eating, doing nothing, and running about the fields."

The boy's training progressed slowly, but he made steady improvement in many areas. Itard's first step was to give the Wild Boy a name, Victor. Itard spent hours subjecting Victor to various experiences. Victor was shown different colors, bathed in a wide variety of water temperatures, given a large range of odors to smell, and served an extremely varied diet. As a result of these stimulations, Victor's senses began to develop. For example, Itard reports that Victor's sense of smell developed to the extent that the least irritation of his nose caused him to sneeze, "and I judged by the fright that seized him the first time this happened, that this was a new experience to him."

Another result of Victor's training was that he became more aware of the activities of his body. He felt pain; he noticed his pounding heart and hurried breathing after he had exercised; he studied his own face in the mirror for hours and felt different muscles tense when he changed his expressions.

Victor eventually learned to do a limited amount of reading and developed a two-word vocabulary.

Of all Victor's achievements, the one that most delighted Itard was Victor's development of emotion. It took more than a year for Victor to develop affection for his governess, Mme. Guerin. Mme. Guerin was responsible for feeding and clothing Victor and taking him for walks. Victor would carefully take Mme. Guerin's hand and at times gently hug her. He had observed others performing these actions to show affection, and he imitated them. Victor also learned to express sadness. At one point he ran from Mme. Guerin; when she reproached him, he wept. This was one of the first times in his life he had ever shed tears. Other emotions also developed. Itard taught Victor the "appropriate times" to feel anger. He purposely frustrated Victor and allowed him to express anger and rage. At other times, when Victor expressed rage for no apparent reason, he was punished.

Through all these lessons, Victor learned to watch others to determine what emotions he "should" feel in a particular situation and how he should express them. For example, one of Victor's chores was to set the dinner table. In Victor's third year with Itard, Mme. Guerin's husband fell ill and died. The night after his death, Victor set the dinner table as usual, including a place for M. Guerin. The sight of the empty seat greatly distressed Mme. Guerin. At first, Victor responded to the scene with confusion; then he expressed signs of grief. He removed the setting he had placed for M. Guerin and never set a place for him again.

During the five years he spend being trained by Itard, Victor's repertoire of emotions expanded greatly. He learned to feel happiness, love, indignation, sadness, fear, moroseness, and anger. He also learned to communicate these emotions to others. Itard felt that learning emotions was what "transformed Victor from a savage into a civilized human being."

EMOTIONS AND PERSONAL ADJUSTMENT

Emotions are extremely important in our lives. Imagine a society in which no one experiences emotions. This would be a society without love, without the laughter of excited children, and without close friendships. It would also be a society where the expressions of anger were absent. Because the inhabitants of this society could not experience pleasure, there would be no amusement parks such as Disneyland, no gourmet cooking, no music, no dancing, and no literature or sports or touching that didn't have strictly utilitarian purposes. Television programs would be intended only for instruction; there would be no comedies or love stories. Death would not be mourned, and birth would not be celebrated. People would be little more than robots who could plan actions and perform them. Gone would be the satisfaction over successful accomplishment and the disappointment that accompanies failure.

Certainly life would be possible without a wide range of emotions. Victor, who experienced only a limited number of emotions, was able to survive. However, as we pointed out in Chapter 1, healthy adjustment to the world involves a great deal more than survival.

Functions of the Emotions

Psychologists have identified three major functions that emotions serve in personal adjustment.

One function of emotions is *enrichment*. The ability to experience a wide range of emotions adds variety and depth to our personal and interpersonal experience. The desirability of this quality can be seen in the fact that humans often go to great lengths to increase their emotional experiences—even to include experiences we would label negative. Some of us willingly seek out the haunted house sideshows at county fairs or ride the giant roller coaster so that we can experience fear and exhilaration. Others seek thrills by participating in dangerous sports such as hang gliding and mountain climbing. And we all look for love, even though we know we may get our hearts broken. In a more negative sense, some people who desperately seek to broaden their emotional experience rely on drugs such as cocaine, marijuana, or LSD.

In order to get an idea of the range and variety of emotions, observe yourself for a few hours. How many emotions do you experience in one afternoon, and how often do you engage in an activity that is designed to give you an emotional experience? You may drive a car fast, look at movies or pictures that are sexually arousing, eat something that tastes good, seek the warmth and comfort of a friend, or participate in a sporting event. Now imagine how dull your afternoon would have been had you not been able to experience the range of emotions associated with these activities. Clearly your emotions—even the unpleasant ones—add variety and ''spice'' to your life.

A second function of emotions is that they *motivate and guide our behavior*. Charles Darwin (1872) noted this function of emotion when he pointed out that emotions are important for the survival of the individual. In general, we tend to avoid things we fear and feel are dangerous, and to approach things we love and feel safe about. For example, some students report that the main reason they study hard for exams is to avoid the bad feelings they get if they receive a poor grade. Thus our actions affect our emotions, while our emotions affect our behavior in turn.

When a person experiences strong emotions, the adrenal gland secretes the hormones adrenaline and noradrenaline into the bloodstream. The effects of these secretions include increases in heart rate, breathing rate, blood pressure, and muscle tension. This state of arousal often leads to increased levels of activity. To illustrate this, think of a time when you experience a strong emotion (anger, happiness, fear); it's likely that you would have difficultly sitting still and performing a task that required complex reasoning at such a time. You would probably engage in a more active behavior, even if only pacing the floor. An even more dramatic example of the increased activity elicited by strong emotions is seen during some emergencies. Newspapers periodically report stories of people performing great feats of strength (such as a mother lifting an automobile off her child) or acts of heroism involving personal risk (such as the case of a man who rushed into a burning gasoline truck, ripped out a door, and pulled the driver to safety). Such behaviors are possible when people are in heightened states of emotional arousal.

A third function of emotions is *interpersonal communication*. Every culture in the world has accepted patterns for the expression of emotion. In Western cultures, for example, we know that laughter and smiling signal happiness and that crying is often a sign of sadness. Because of these familiar patterns, we can communicate with each other by physically expressing our emotions. A mother can quickly convey displeasure to a child with a stern look and a wrinkled brow. We learn that it is safe to approach people who show the outward signs of happiness and to avoid people who show the signs of anger. One of Itard's major difficulties was that Victor didn't properly communicate his emotions. Itard was perplexed by Victor's uncontrollable laughter because he couldn't determine what emotion Victor was communicating. Normally, the physical expression of emotion helps to clarify human interaction.

Because emotions play such an important role in our lives, let us examine them more closely. In doing this, we will identify what an emotion is and why we experience certain emotions in certain situations. Some of the issues surrounding emotions are a bit complex, but fascinating. It is interesting to see that we have been able to develop robots that can perform a variety of activities, store information, and even give logical conclusions. But, we have not developed a machine that can love, feel angry, or experience happiness. In a sense, emotions may be seen as a spark of life. To understand emotions is to understand a great deal about human behavior and interaction. For this reason, let us begin by spending some time examining the concept of emotion and some theories about how we experience emotions.

WHAT IS EMOTION?

Everyone agrees that emotions are a crucial part of being human, but what exactly constitutes an emotion is hard to define. *The Random House Dictionary of the English Language* (1969) gives five different definitions of the word **emotion.** While it may be difficult to achieve complete agreement about a definition, psychologists have identified three components of emotions, which reflect some of the functions of emotion we just discussed (see Berscheid, 1983). The first component of emotion is *physiological arousal,* or bodily changes such as sweating, increased heart rate, quickened breathing, trembling, or variation in brain wave pattern (Strongman, 1973). The second component is feeling, or **affect;** we are aware that we are experiencing an emotion. Feeling has a positive or negative quality; it's usually very easy for us to determine whether our emotional experience is satisfying or unsettling. Finally, emotions generally have an expressive component, including such things as smiles, weeping, or laughter.

Physiological Arousal: The Body's Signal of Emotion

If we carefully examine our emotional experience, we quickly see the importance of physiological arousal. For example, recall your own experience of fear. The fear may have resulted from a near-miss automobile accident or from hearing strange noises in your house when you were alone. In either of these cases, you should have been aware of your heart beating so rapidly you thought it would leap from your chest. Your hands may have become clammy with sweat. You were probably aware that your throat was dry and its muscles were tight.

The extent of such physiological arousal may surprise you. Psychologists have found that emotions may be accompanied by changes in heart rate, blood pressure, breathing, muscle tension, pupil size, skin temperature, and the electrical conductance of the skin. Hormone levels may change, and these effects can be seen in changes in the composition of blood and urine. Almost every function of the body can change when we experience an emotion.

We are often unaware of the physiological arousal that accompanies our emotions. As you examine this picture, pay attention to what you are feeling and how your own body is responding.

Rhoda Sidney.

These changes happen automatically and are not under our control. In some cases, the events that trigger these changes are innate or preprogrammed into our bodies. For example, young infants become physiologically aroused in the presence of sudden loud noises or the loss of support to their bodies. In most cases, however, learning and experience play a major role in determining the events that will cause physiological and emotional arousal in us.

In 1904 the Russian physiologist Ivan Petrovich Pavlov made a startling discovery quite by accident. He was interested in studying the digestive secretions of dogs when they were fed. Each day, his assistant fed dogs meat powder and measured their salivary secretions. In the beginning of the study, the dogs would salivate each time they tasted the meat powder. As the experiment progressed, however, Pavlov found that the dogs began salivating when they saw the meat powder. Later they would salivate when they saw the assistant enter with the food. Finally, late in the study, Pavlov found that the dogs salivated upon hearing the assistant's footsteps coming down the hall. Essentially, the dogs were responding to stimuli associated with the meat powder in much the same way that they responded to the meat powder itself. This phenomenon has been labeled **classical conditioning.**

We can extend the notion of classical conditioning to understand physiological arousal and the experience of emotion. For example, the major goals of young infants are to have their basic needs satisfied; they want to be fed when hungry, have their diapers changed when wet, and be caressed and hugged when cold or lonely. The satisfaction of these needs brings an infant pleasure. In most societies, an infant's parents perform these functions, and simply the sight of the parents produces the feeling of pleasure. Just as Pavlov's dogs responded to the assistant in the same way they responded to the meat powder, so an infant responds to his or her parents in the same way he or she responds to the parents' need-satisfying activities. Thus the arousal of pleasure becomes associated with even the sight of the parents, which causes physiological

Infants learn to associate love and pleasure with their parents through classical conditioning.
Ken Karp.

arousal in the infant (relaxed muscles, widening of pupils) and the experience of pleasure. This process can extend to other stimuli associated with positive feelings about the parents: their names, people who look like them, the type of automobile they drive, and so on.

Such extended emotional arousal can occur with many types of emotions and stimuli. A child who has a bad experience with a dog may learn to fear that dog. Through the conditioning process, the child may feel fear upon seeing any dog. The fear may be conditioned even further, to the point where the sight of any furry animal frightens the child.

Richard Lazarus (1982) pointed out that our physiological arousal may also be influenced by our interpretation of an event. For example, the sight of someone coming toward you with a gun may not arouse you if you believe the person merely intends to show you the gun. But your heart is likely to race and your stomach to tighten if you believe the person with the gun intends to shoot you. Lazarus's observation is particularly interesting because it suggests that our cognitive processes can influence both the amount of physiological arousal evoked by a particular event and the type of emotion we experience.

THE NAKED TRUTH OF AROUSAL: LIE DETECTION.

As we pointed out earlier, we generally have no control over the physiological arousal that results in the face of emotion-producing events. And, unless we grew up in an environment like Victor's, completely isolated from other people, most of us have many experiences in common. One of these experiences was being punished when we lied or tried to hide the truth from our parents and others. Our everyday lives and our religious training taught us that lying was wrong; we learned to expect stern punishment for lying, and most of us were conditioned to experience guilt when we told a falsehood.

If we want to find out if someone is lying, we can ask him or her directly, "Are you lying?" But people have control over what they say, and may not answer the question truthfully. On the other hand, they don't have control over the responses of their bodies. So, instead of asking the individual, we might get a more truthful response by "asking their body."

The ancient Chinese seemed to have drawn this conclusion. History shows that when they expected a person might not answer questions truthfully, they had that individual chew rice powder while being questioned (Rice, 1978). After the questioning period, the powder was carefully examined. If it was found to be dry, the individual was determined to be guilty of lying. The reasoning behind this technique was that the feeling of guilt associated with lying would be accompanied by physiological arousal. One effect of this arousal was to block or slow down the secretion of saliva, which in turn resulted in a dry wad of rice powder—proof of falsehood.

Modern techniques don't rely on rice powder, but they do rely on the same theory: We should measure the body's response to determine the truth. The modern technique for measuring the body's signals about truth or falsehood uses a **polygraph.** The polygraph records changes in heart rate, blood pressure, breathing, and galvanic skin response (GSR). The person being questioned is hooked up to the polygraph and then asked a number of questions. Lies are identified when the individual shows *changes* in physiological arousal.

Now this might lead us to think the polygraph is a fantastic machine that can solve a host of problems. If a crime is committed, we can just round up everyone who's a remote suspect, hook them all up to the polygraph, and find the one true criminal. Employers in retail stores and banks could ensure that they hired only honest people by giving every job applicant a polygraph test. Unfortunately, the situation is not so simple. The polygraph does have a high rate of success; it is accurate over 70 percent of the time, and some estimates have run as high as 90 percent. While these seem to be dazzling figures, an error rate of even 10 percent is high when someone's life, liberty, or livelihood is at stake. For this reason, the results of polygraph tests are not admissible evidence in many courts, and criminal suspects and witnesses can't be forced to take polygraph tests.

This man is hooked up to a polygraph machine which records his breathing rate, blood pressure, heart rate, and GSR while the examiner asks him questions.

David Strickler, Monkmeyer.

The business world has been more willing to accept the margin of error, and some companies require their employees to take lie detector tests.

One of the problems with the polygraph is that people know they are being tested. This makes some people very anxious, and others may try to "fool" the machine by tensing up when they are telling the truth. More recently, investigators (see Rice, 1978) have developed a machine called the **voice stress analyzer.** This machine measures voice tremor. The muscles in the throat control the voice. When a person is physiologically aroused, the throat muscles tighten and a distinct pattern of voice tremor results (see Figure 4.1). The theory behind the voice stress analyzer is the same as that behind the polygraph; the analyzer simply measures physiological arousal by examining voice tremor. But the marvelous, and frightening, feature of the voice stress analyzer is that it can be used to examine recorded voices. Therefore, without your knowing it, someone could tape your voice and then examine it with the voice stress analyzer. In other words, you could be subjected to a lie detector test without your ever knowing it. This raises many legal and ethical questions about the use of lie detectors. The United States Congress and many state legis-

FIGURE 4.1 WATCHING WHAT YOU SAY

The voice stress analyzer measures voice tremor. It has been found that the arousal produced by telling a lie changes the voice tremors. The graph on top is the voice tremor of a relaxed speaker. The graph on the bottom shows the voice tremor of a speaker under stress.

From Holden, C. Lie detectors: PSE gains audience despite critics' doubt. *Science,* 1975, *190,* 359-362. Reproduced by permission.

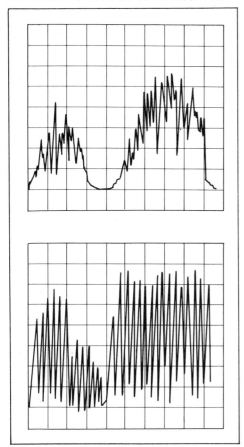

REVIEW QUESTIONS

1. In addition to the richness that emotions add to our lives, they also provide an important energizing function in that they _____ and _____ our behavior.

2. Although psychologists do not completely agree on the definition of an emotion, nearly all agree that an emotion has three components. These components have been identified as the _____ , _____ , and _____ components.

3. During a particularly suspenseful movie, you find hands sweating, your heart beating rapidly, and your throat dry. These bodily reactions are all part of the _____ component of an emotion.

4. Situations the elicit emotional responses in some people may not elicit that response in others. This demonstrates the role of _____ in the experience of emotion.

5. An instrument for detecting deception by measuring changes in physiological response is called a _____ .

latures are currently wrestling with laws designed to govern the use of lie detectors.

While the discussion of lie detection is of interest, the point to be realized is that these methods highlight the important role of physiological arousal in our emotional experiences.

Physiology into Psychology: The Experience of Emotion

Even knowing that physiological arousal is central to the experience of emotion serves as only one step in understanding what emotion is. The next step is to determine how the physical behavior of our bodies is related to feeling, or affect, the psychological component of emotions. This may seem to be a waste of time. You may feel that the process is obvious: We encounter a certain situation, and it arouses a specific emotion in us. The process isn't that simple, however. Does the physiological arousal we experience in a situation determine our emotions, or do our emotions determine how and when we will become physiologically aroused? Why do different people experience very different emotions in the same situation? The Wild Boy showed no sorrow at parting from the old man who had taken care of him for a year. The old man, on the other hand, wept bitterly. How and why does a certain person experience a certain emotion in a given situation?

ANCIENT THEORIES OF EMOTION. The ancient Greeks believed there were four basic, innate emotions and that these emotions were engendered by different body fluids. For example, black bile in one's system caused melancholy, while an overabundance of blood led to a sanguine, or cheerful, feeling.

While rejecting the Greek's connection of emotion to body fluids, eighteenth-century philosophers did view emotions as innate. They argued that a particular situation causes a person to experience a specific emotion. As a result of the emotional experience, the individual becomes physiologically aroused. They also believed that there are different patterns of arousal for each type of emotion. According to

this view, you would feel fear if you saw a bear running toward you. As a result of this fear, your body would become aroused in a specific way: Your heart would beat faster, you would become short of breath, and you might break out in a sweat.

THE JAMES-LANGE THEORY OF EMOTION. In 1890, William James proposed a different theory of emotion. He suggested that emotion occurs *after* physiological arousal and after the person's response to the arousal. The particular emotion is determined by the type of arousal experienced and by the reaction to it. Looking back at the bear example used above, James suggested that upon seeing the bear you would become physiologically aroused and then turn and run. You would survey your arousal and your behavior and *only then* would you feel fear. Another example used by James was that we "are sad because we cry." This is a very different position from the common-sense idea that we cry because we are sad.

James and the Danish physician C. G. Lange offered a number of observations to support this theory. For example, they pointed out that the experiencing of emotions is not instantaneous; it takes some time for an individual to "feel" an emotion. However, it would be maladaptive to wait to feel a specific emotion before experiencing the physiological arousal that leads to action. Think again of the bear example. The bear charges: You wait to react until you feel fear. Then you break out in a sweat and begin to run. The moment of delay could mean the difference between your being able to escape and your making a meal for the bear.

A more common example of this can be seen in the case of a driver who sees another car pulling out in front of him or her. The driver jams on the breaks and swerves to avoid an accident. Finally, upon stopping the car he or she may tremble and *then* experience fear. The emotion comes only after the driver's arousal and behavior. Had the driver waited to experience fear before acting, it is unlikely that the accident would have been avoided. Thus the James-Lange theory argued rather convincingly for an arousal-action-feeling view of emotional experience.

THE COGNITIVE THEORY OF EMOTION. In 1962 Schachter and Singer revised the James-Lange theory. They pointed out that we are able to experience emotions without noticing our own behaviors. Take the Wild Boy, for example. Victor saw Mme. Guerin break into tears upon seeing a place set at the table for her deceased husband. After watching Mme. Guerin's response, Victor experienced grief. In this case, Victor experienced an emotion by watching the reactions of someone else, not by considering his own behavior in the situation.

Schachter and Singer further emphasized that there is not a different type of arousal associated with each emotion. In 1929 W. B. Cannon had shown that it is impossible for the body to produce as many different arousal patterns as there are emotions. Instead, Schachter and Singer hypothesized, physiological arousal does accompany emotions, but people do not distinguish among types of arousal, and the arousal alone does not determine the type of emotion.

In light of these observations, Schachter and Singer (1962) proposed a two-step theory of emotion. They suggested that the first step to feeling an emotion is a general physiological arousal. After we perceive this arousal, we search for an explanation for it. When we do not specifically know the cause of this arousal, we rely on environmental cues to explain it. These cues may be situational (arousal at the circus probably means excitement) or they may be stimuli based on the behavior of others (Mme. Guerin's tears gave Victor a cue that stimulated his own grief reaction). A bear growling at you would be a situational environmental cue; if you heard other people scream because a bear was growling at them, those people's behavior would be your environmental cue that you, too, should experience fear. In either case, the emotion that we "feel" will be determined by the explanation we place on the arousal.

Thus Schachter and Singer argue that an emotion is the result of physiological arousal followed by a cognitive interpretation of the cause of the arousal. The process of combining the arousal and cognition is called **attribution.**

$$\underset{\text{(Emotion)}}{E} = \underset{\text{(Arousal)}}{A} \times \underset{\text{(Cognition)}}{C}$$

The multiplication sign in this equation means that if either the arousal or the cognition is zero, $A \times C$ will equal zero, and the individual will not experience an emotion.

The important point to understand is that our emotions are the result of our attributing a meaning to our arousal; the attribution we make may or may not truly reflect the actual cause of our arousal. An interesting example of the attribution of emotion probably happens hundreds of times each day in the dentist's chair (Valins & Nisbett, 1972). When dentists inject an anesthetic before drilling, they often include a vasoconstrictor in the injection to retard the absorption rate of the anesthetic. This vasoconstrictor is often epinephrine, which causes a state of general physiological arousal. The person's heart rate increases, his or her

---

REVIEW QUESTIONS

6. An early theory of emotion proposing that our emotions occur *after* we observe our behavioral response to some arousing event is the _____ theory of emotion.

7. Schacter and Singer proposed that our emotions are a multiplicative function of _____ and _____ .

8. Advertisers who use emotionally arousing scenes in their commercials are probably taking advantage of the findings that people who are emotionally aroused are more easily _____ .

9. Our memory of highly emotional events is likely to be specific rather than general. This occurs because emotions tend to influence our _____ and _____ .

10. Cognitive theories of emotion suggest that the correct labeling of an emotion depends on the accurate utilization of _____ cues.

breathing speeds up, and there is dryness in the mouth. Imagine the patient who feels somewhat apprehensive about going to the dentist in the first place. He or she sits in the dentist's chair and suddenly becomes aware of a high degree of physiological arousal. Unaware that the arousal is caused by the epinephrine, the patient is likely to interpret it as fear of the dentist. Utilizing Schachter's theory, we can see that it would be nice if the dentist informed the patient of the side effects of the injection so that the patient wouldn't start feeling more afraid than he or she actually is.

Another phenomenon that can be understood within the framework of the attribution of emotion comes from the first-century Roman poet Ovid. In his book *Ars Amatoria* (The Art of Love), Ovid advised men of Ancient Rome that one of the best ways of arousing romantic passion in a woman was to take her to the gladiator matches. Although Ovid didn't supply the rationale behind his suggestion, we can use attribution theory to offer a modern interpretation. Watching the gladiatorial combat would presumably arouse the woman, whereupon the suitor need only manipulate the situation so that she would misattribute her arousal to feelings of love or sexual excitement.

Showing Our Feelings: The Expression of Emotion

As Itard taught Victor to experience a wide range of emotions, he encountered an additional problem: He had to teach Victor how to express those emotions. In the beginning, Victor's behavior didn't necessarily reflect what he was feeling. At times he would laugh uncontrollably when he was frustrated. At other times, when he felt only mildly frustrated, he would thrash around wildly, trying to bite anyone in the vicinity. Thus Itard realized that healthy emotional behavior involves not only experiencing emotions, but also expressing them correctly. How are emotions expressed? Why do people express their emotions as they do?

VARIETIES OF EMOTIONAL EXPRESSION. In order to demonstrate how people express emotions, observe the behavior of some people for a short period of time. How will you determine what they are feeling? One way is to ask them. In most cases, they would gladly tell you. But in other cases, they may be unwilling or unable to tell you what they are feeling. For example, they may become suspicious about why you want to know. Or they may be embarrassed to tell you their feelings. Or they may simply not be able to put their feelings into words. Most of us do very poorly when we try to verbalize our feelings. We have little practice in our daily lives in telling people how we feel.

Given that we cannot completely trust verbal descriptions to identify emotions, how else could we find out what someone is feeling? People who study emotions have found that we use a wide variety of nonverbal channels to express our feelings. The communication of emotions through these channels is often called **body language.** Psychologists have found that we can communicate many feelings by how close we stand to others, how much we look at them, and how often we touch them. Research in these areas has found that people who like each other tend to look at each other, stand close to each other when interacting, and touch each other often. Phenomena such as the "lover's gaze" emphasize the fact that emotion can be transmitted along such nonverbal channels. Even more subtle cues can signify emotions. For example, Hess (1965) noted that Chinese jade dealers would carefully observe the eyes of a prospective buyer. They felt that the pupils of the buyer's eyes would dilate if he or she were looking at a piece of jade that he or she liked. In an experiment, Hess and Polt (1960) found that pupil size did reflect attraction: When subjects were looking at an attractive object, their pupil size increased. Later research has shown that pupils also dilate if an individual is experiencing fear.

Probably the most important mode of nonverbal emotional expression is facial cues. Smiling, wrinkling the forehead, frowning, gazing downward, and gritting the teeth are changes in facial expression that can be utilized to express emotions. Tomkins and Mc-Carter (1964) felt that they could identify eight primary emotions by specifying facial cues. As can be seen from Table 4.1, anger may be communicated by a clenched jaw and narrowed eyes, and joy by a smile and "wide eyes."

While some research shows similarities in the way individuals utilize facial expressions to transmit emotions, there is also evidence of individual differences in the facial expression of emotion (Ekman, Sorenson, & Friesen, 1969; Mortensen, 1972). This suggests that we can't simply use facial expressions to determine the emotions an individual is experiencing. We must also examine the context in which the emotion is being expressed.

Birdwhistle (1952) combines the study of body language and facial cues in what he calls **kinesis.** Birdwhistle suggests that the vocabulary of body language includes such features as tilt of the head, posture, hand and arm movements, and shuffling of the feet. He believes that each movement transmits a message, and he has spent years coding the meaning of these messages. His evidence suggests that the *type* of emotion is communicated through facial cues while its *intensity* is communicated through body language.

This discussion of the nonverbal modes of emotional communication illustrates the complexity of the task facing Itard. To communicate his emotions effectively, Victor had to be

What are these people feeling? We use facial expression and body cues such as posture to express our emotions.

taught to use all these channels simultaneously. We are able to do this largely because we are generally not aware of our use of body language and facial cues. Often we do not know that our brows are wrinkled, that our eyes are open wide, or that we are staring. Others are aware of our nonverbal behavior, however, and they are judging our emotions on the basis of it.

INNATE AND LEARNED EMOTIONAL EXPRESSION. In 1872 Charles Darwin published *The Expression of Emotions in Man and Animals,* in which he took the position that the manner in which humans express emotions is innate and has evolved through a long process over time. Darwin pointed out that animals bare their teeth when preparing to attack. Similarly, humans often grit or bare their teeth when angry. Darwin also pointed out that there is similarity in the way different infants express the same emotions.

Darwin was convinced that the expression of emotions is crucial to the survival of a species. Through emotional expression, he

TABLE 4.1

Facial Cues and Emotional Expression

Interest-excitement: eyebrows down, eyes track, look and listen.
Enjoyment-joy: smile, lips widened up and out, smiling eyes (circular wrinkles).
Surprise-startle: eyebrows up, eyes blink.
Distress-anguish: cry, arched eyebrows, mouth down, tears, rhythmic sobbing.
Fear-terror: eyes frozen open, pale, cold, sweaty face, trembling, hair erect.
Shame-humiliation: eyes down, head up.
Contempt-disgust: sneer, upper lip up.
Anger-rage: frown, clenched jaw, eyes narrowed, red face.

SOURCE: Tomkins and McCarter (1964). Permission granted by S. S. Tomkins.

said, people or animals can communicate to members of their own species what they are feeling and how they intend to act. If emotional expression is so important to survival, it must be innate, thought Darwin, and he conducted a series of ingenious observations of human emotional expression. He watched people who had been blind since birth and found that many of their emotional expressions were similar to those of sighted individuals. This, Darwin felt, showed that emotional expression is in fact innate rather than learned; for if these blind individuals had never observed others expressing emotions, how could their expressions be similar to those of sighted persons unless they were innate reflections of feeling?

Over a hundred years later, Paul Ekman and his colleagues conducted a number of studies whose findings suggest that the expression of some emotions may be innate. In one study, Ekman and Friesen (1971) interviewed natives of New Guinea. They told the natives brief stories such as "A man's child has died and he feels very sad." They then showed the natives three photographs of Americans expressing different emotions and asked them to choose the photograph appropriate for the story. The natives chose the correct photograph over 80 percent of the time.

In another interesting study, Ekman (1973) showed photographs of people expressing six different emotions to college students in five different countries. Subjects were asked to identify what emotion was being expressed by the individual in the photograph. As can be seen from Figure 4.2, there was a high degree of agreement about the emotion across the different cultures.

Overall, research suggests that there may be innate means of expressing some emotions. If so, these innate means don't cover the total spectrum of emotions. The range of emotions we can express is much greater than the six emotions that have been examined in the re-

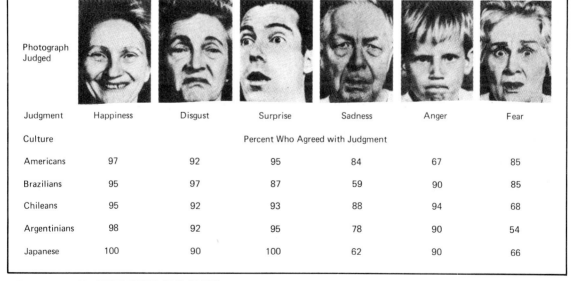

Photograph Judged						
Judgment	Happiness	Disgust	Surprise	Sadness	Anger	Fear
Culture	Percent Who Agreed with Judgment					
Americans	97	92	95	84	67	85
Brazilians	95	97	87	59	90	85
Chileans	95	92	93	88	94	68
Argentinians	98	92	95	78	90	54
Japanese	100	90	100	62	90	66

FIGURE 4.2   SPEAKING WITH OUR FACES
What do these faces say to you? Students from five cultures were asked this question and their responses were generally very much alike. This and similar findings suggest that some aspects of the nonverbal communication of emotions may be innate.

(Adapted from Ekman, P., Friesen, W., & Ellsworth, P. Emotion in the human face: Guidelines for research and an integration of findings. Elmsford, N.Y.: Pergamon Press, 1972. Reproduced with permission of the publisher.)

search. And there is a great deal of evidence suggesting that many of our emotional expressions are learned. For example, many emotional expressions differ from culture to culture. Americans clap to show approval and delight, while in some Oriental cultures clapping is a sign of disapproval. Furthermore, if emotional expression is innate, how can we explain the lack of expression in Victor? Another point arguing against the innateness of emotional expression is the wide range, even in our own culture, of individual differences in emotional expression. Some people cry openly when they are sad, while other do not. Males are taught at a young age that it is not manly to cry or to be too emotionally expressive. Females, on the other hand, are often encouraged to be emotionally expressive. You may be aware of wide differences in emotional expression among your friends.

Thus we can't unequivocally say that emotional expression is innate. We do know, however, that the way in which a person expresses emotion can be affected by the environment and by learning. One of the clearest forms of learning is imitation. Children often imitate the way their parents express emotion. A child whose parents yell and scream when angry is likely to yell and scream when angry. A child whose parents give stern disapproving looks is likely to mimic these expressions. And of course we all learn ways of expressing emotion from other people around us, friends and strangers, in our real lives or on television, for instance. Victor learned many of his emotional expressions simply by watching Dr. Itard and Mme. Guerin. Thus learning plays a major role in determining how we express our emotions.

THE INFLUENCE OF EMOTIONS ON OUR EVERYDAY LIVES

The theories of emotion help us understand why we experience certain feelings. The theories not only allow us to see why people may differ in the feelings they have, but they also show how our environment, behavior, and situation influence our emotions. This understanding is indeed, important because it will help us understand our own feelings and be more accepting of the feelings of others.

There is, however, another important way to study emotions. Instead of looking at how our behavior and experience influence our emotions, we can examine how our emotions influence our behavior and experience.

Our emotions influence our activities in many ways and of course have a great effect on our everyday lives. At the most general level, we have pointed out that people often seek out events that will lead them to experience emotions. A curious aspect of human behavior is that we don't only seek to experience positive emotions such as love and happiness. People also are attracted to events that will cause them to feel more negative emotions such as fear and anger. For example, people often stand in long lines and pay several dollars to watch grisly horror movies. People also attend sporting activities where they can shout and become enraged at the activities of an opposing team or referee. Overall, it seems that the quest for emotional experience drives us to a wide variety of activities and situations.

While some emotional effects on our everyday lives are very obvious, other interesting effects of emotions are more subtle, but equally important in understanding ourselves and others.

Emotions and Persuasion

Spend an evening paying close attention to the advertisements on television. What do many of them have in common? At first glance, this may be a hard question to answer. But after awhile you should begin to notice that many, if not most, commercials are aimed at creating an emotional state in you. On one hand, some commercials try to make you feel happy or sexually excited by playing catchy music and showing pictures of happy people in sentimental situations or showing sensual women or rugged men, often half-dressed, making suggestive gestures toward you. On the other hand, some television advertisements attempt to arouse fear in you by showing frightening scenes of death and destruction. Other advertisements attempt to arouse you by being funny. Often these emotion-arousing events have little, if anything, to do with the product being pushed; their intent is simply to arouse emotion in you.

While this approach to selling merchandise may seem odd, it is strongly grounded in research. A wide range of studies have shown that *people are more easily persuaded when they are emotionally aroused* (Biggers & Pryor, 1982; see Worchel & Cooper, 1983, for a review of the literature). It seems that when we are emotionally aroused, we are less critical of information that is presented to us. We don't question the information as carefully as we would if we weren't aroused. Interestingly, there is evidence that the emotion-persuasion link holds for both positive and negative emotions. Skillful speakers may be able to get crowds of people to commit horrible violent acts by first arousing anger in the people and then suggesting acts of violence. The effect seems to be much like that created by alcohol or other drugs that place us in a state where we don't question information or rationally consider our actions.

This point is very important to understand when you attempt to explain to yourself or a friend why you purchased a particular product or acted in a particular way. It may well be that your emotional state allowed you to be influenced by information that normally wouldn't have had an effect on you. The emotion-per-

suasion factor may also explain why you feel totally convinced by a public speaker who really had little of substance to say. The mood created by the speaker may have played a larger role in influencing you than did the actual words of the speaker.

Emotions and Perception

When Itard first met the Wild Boy, he marveled at how aware Victor was of all that happened around him. Regardless of where Victor's attention seemed to be, if anyone around him moved or even shifted their position, Victor quickly turned toward that movement. After Victor had been with Itard for a period of time, however, this sharp awareness began to dull under some conditions. Itard found that he could sneak up behind Victor when Victor was in a high state of emotional arousal. For example, Victor developed strong affection for Mme. Guerin and would follow her around the house watching her every move. But while he was very aware of Mme. Guerin, he was almost totally unaware of the rest of his environment. Similarly, when Victor was angry, his attention would focus on the person who had angered him, and he would show very little awareness of other things that were going on around him.

A wide variety of research has found that emotions affect our perceptions and attention (Broadbent, 1978; Cohen & Weinstein, 1981). When we experience strong emotions our attention becomes focused on events and stimuli that are important to our state of feeling. While

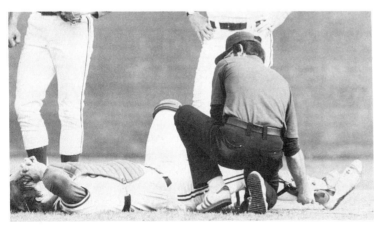

The experience of strong emotion narrows the focus of our attention. This baseball player is probably focusing his attention on his pain; he is unaware of the crowd or other players around him.

Tim Davis, Photo Researchers, Inc.

our attention to these events is heightened, our attention to other events and stimuli decreases. An interesting example of this effect can be observed when we are involved in an arousing sporting event. We may suffer an injury, sometimes severe, during the event, but not be aware of this injury until after the contest is over. In this case, our aroused emotional state caused us to focus our attention on the sporting event and away from our own bodies.

The effect of emotions on perceptions is also seen in eyewitness testimonies about crimes. In many cases, witnesses may be able to give very detailed reports about certain events in a crime (for example, the size, shape, and color of a gun that was held on the witness), while not being able to recall any details of other events (for example, the person who held the gun).

In all such cases, we find that emotions sharpen attention to certain events and perception of certain stimuli while greatly limiting our awareness of other events and stimuli. It is important to understand this point when we are called upon to recount events we may have witnessed when experiencing high emotional arousal.

Emotions and Judgment

There's an old saying, "When you're in love, the whole world is smiling." Most of us might be willing to support this statement when we recall situations where good things happened to us. After we received a promotion at work, fell in love, or got a great grade on an exam, everyone around us seemed a bit more friendly; the sun even shone brighter. It's possible that this was in fact the case. However, it's more likely that the world was the same every day, but on this special day we simply saw it differently.

There is a great deal of evidence showing that our moods affect our judgment (Clark; 1983; Bower & Cohen, 1983). For example, in one study people who were happy, sad, or angry were shown the same picture and asked what was happening in the scene (Bower & Cohen, 1982). The happy people saw happy events, the angry people saw angry events, and the sad people told sad stories about the picture. Our emotions influence almost every aspect of our judgment and memory. Clark (1982) reviewed the effects of positive emotions and concluded that "when we are feeling good, the evidence indicates that we tend to view others more positively, to give more favorable reports about products we have purchased, to rate ambiguous slides as more pleasant, to have more positive expectations about the future, and to give more positive associations to situations in which we imagine ourselves" (p. 264). Similar effects have been reported for other emotions. Leventhal (1982) found that our emotions influence when we will see ourselves as physically sick and how we will respond to our illness. He studied people with cancer and found that depressive emotions caused people to dwell on the pain of their disease and on the brevity of life, while anger encouraged active, coping, cure-oriented behavior. Thus the old saying should be rewritten to read, "When you're in love, you see the whole world as smiling."

The bottom line in this discussion is that our emotions have a strong effect on our thinking, perceptions, judgment, and behavior. Emotions may push us to act in ways in which we would not normally act and to give interpretations of events that may be more in line with our feelings than with what is actually happening. Being aware of these possibilities not only should help us understand ourselves better but also may make us more cautious in insisting that we are unbiased judges of the events and people around us.

HEALTHY EMOTIONAL EXPERIENCE

We have seen some of the factors that determine the quality of our emotions and how our emotions affect us. We can now examine the question of how to utilize this information to promote our own healthy emotional experience. In order to help answer this question let's return to the Wild Boy.

Itard was faced with the task of teaching Victor to experience emotions. Two aspects of Victor's primitive behavior troubled Itard. The first was that Victor did not seem to be aware of his body being aroused. Victor would reach into boiling water with his bare hand to grasp potatoes and show not the slightest awareness of pain or other physiological arousal. The second point that troubled Itard was that the emotional responses Victor began to show were often inappropriate to the situation. More than once, Itard reports administering strenuous punishment to Victor only to have Victor smile and break into laughter.

Itard followed two directions in schooling Victor in emotions. The first was to make Victor more sensitive to his body cues. Itard spent hours each day stimulating Victor's senses and forcing him to attend to his body's responses. For example, Itard would have Victor perform exercises such as running long distances. After the exercises, Itard would force Victor to listen to his own breathing and rapid heartbeat. Through such training, Victor's senses improved and sharpened, and he became more aware of the physiological cues his body used to signal emotional arousal.

A second program instituted by Itard involved coaching Victor to be more aware of his surroundings, especially when he was emotionally aroused. For example, when Victor did something wrong, Itard made sure that Victor looked directly at him when punishment was administered. Itard would exaggerate his expressions so that Victor could see that he was angry. As a result of paying attention to his surroundings, Victor became better able to experience emotions appropriately. The example of how Victor learned to experience grief (by observing Mme. Guerin's tears) shows how he was able to adjust his emotions to the situation.

These examples have important implications for healthy emotional experience. The first lesson to be learned is that *we should be sensitive to our own body responses.* The Schachter and Singer (1962) attribution theory maintains that our body's arousal initiates our emotional experience. As such, we need to be aware of the message when our bodies send the signal "It is time to feel an emotion." This may seem trite; you may feel that you are aware of the changes in your arousal level. If so, you are the exception rather than the rule. Most people take for granted the functioning of their bodies; their heart rates can change significantly and their rates of breathing can vary without them being aware of these changes.

A second lesson to be learned from the Wild Boy is that healthy emotional experience involves *properly identifying our emotions.* Itard labored long to teach Victor to utilize the environment to help define his emotions. Modern theories of emotion also make clear that we must be able to utilize environmental cues effectively in order to label our emotions properly. Thus healthy emotional experience involves using the environment to help determine the specific emotion we are feeling.

The failure to correctly utilize environmental cues may cause problems for the individual. Walster and Berscheid (1971) offer an interesting example of the fact that incorrect labeling of emotions can have troublesome consequences. Adolescent couples are often faced with parents who attempt to interfere with their intimate relationships. The parents, believing that they are doing what is best for their son or daughter, attempt to keep the relationship from becoming too intimate. Their interference may physiologically arouse the couple, who in turn interpret their arousal as love. Thus, instead of "cooling" the relationship, the parents' interference actually brings the couple closer. This is unfortunate for both the parents and the young couple. Having misidentified their emotion as love, the couple may take steps to make their relationship more permanent, only to discover later (when the interfering parents are removed) that they are not as deeply in love as they had previously believed.

Healthy Emotional Expression

Once we've identified an emotion, we must also concern ourselves with *how much emotion to express.* Young children are often spontaneous in their emotional expression; they

REVIEWING EMOTIONAL BEHAVIOR

Because we experience emotions so often, we usually take them for granted. We give little thought to how we experience emotions and to how our emotions affect our interactions with others. Below are five pairs of statements. Read them over carefully and determine which one of the pair best fits you. By doing this, you should become more aware of the way in which you have been dealing with emotions. You may also be able to identify areas in which you could improve your handling of emotions.

1. _____ a. I am fully aware of what I am sensing in the present situation.
   _____ b. I ignore what I am sensing by thinking about the past or the future.

2. _____ a. I understand the interpretations I usually make about other people's actions. I work to be aware of the interpretations I am making.
   _____ b. I deny that I make any interpretations about what I sense. I insist that I do not interpret someone's behavior as being mean. The person is mean.

3. _____ a. I accept my feelings as being part of me. I turn my full awareness on it. I try to feel it fully. I keep asking myself, "What am I feeling now?"
   _____ b. I reject and ignore my feelings. I deny my feelings by telling myself and others, "But I'm not feeling anything at all." I avoid people and situations that might make me more aware of my feelings.

4. _____ a. I decide how I want to express my feelings. I think of what I want to result from the expression of my feelings. I think of what is an appropriate way to express a feeling in the present situation. I review the sending skills in my mind.
   _____ b. Since I've never admitted to having a feeling, I don't need to decide how to express it! When my feelings burst, I am too emotional to remember good sending skills.

5. _____ a. I express my feelings appropriately and clearly. Usually, this means using nonverbal messages to back up my words. My words and my nonverbal messages communicate the same feeling.
   _____ b. I express my feelings inappropriately and in confusing ways. Usually, this means indirectly through commands, accusations, "put downs," and evaluations. I may express feelings physically in destructive ways. I shout at people, push or hit them, avoid people, or refuse to look at them or speak to them. I may hug them, put my arm around them, give them gifts, or try to do favors for them. My words and my nonverbal messages often contradict each other. I sometimes smile and act friendly toward people I'm angry at. Or I may avoid people I care a great deal for.

From D. W. Johnson, *Human Relations and Your Career: A Guide to Interpersonal Skills*, © 1978, pp. 177–178. Reprinted by permission of Prentice-Hall, Inc. Englewood Cliffs, N.J.

may squeal with delight for long periods of time or wail with anguish because of a minor frustration. Victor's behavior was "childish" in this respect; he would sometimes throw a fit in the face of relatively insignificant obstacles. This degree of spontaneity isn't as permissible for healthy adults, however.

Adults are expected to exert control over their emotional expression. This does not mean that adults shouldn't spontaneously express emotion. But healthy emotional expression means that adults are able to feel an emotion, understand it, and decide how intensely to express it. The key is having enough control over the process to be able to determine how strongly to express the emotion. For example, a person may feel sadness over the death of a pet. The person should allow himself or herself to feel the sadness and decide how intensely to express it. Some people may express their sadness in such a situation more intensely than others do. This diversity should be expected. The emotional expression becomes a problem only if the individual loses control over it—for example, cries continuously over the loss of the pet. In such a case, the emotion has taken over the expression, and the individual can no longer control the intensity of the expression.

Another aspect of the control of emotions involves *attention to the particular situation* in which an emotion is expressed. Certain situations may require the dampening of emotional expression, while others may allow exaggerated forms of expression. An example of the former would be the taboo on bursting out laughing in a church or a library. In such a case, the emotional expression infringes on the comfort of others. A football game is an example of a situation in which exaggerated emotional expression is not only proper, but encouraged by the cheerleaders.

Healthy emotional expression involves connecting the expression of emotion to one's feeling and to the environmental context. It does not mean that everyone should express emotions in the same way or with the same intensity. There is considerable variation among people in emotional expression. But it is im-

portant for the individual to be able to control the expression of emotions, rather than have the expression dictated solely by the experience of emotion or by environmental constraints.

On the other hand, it is equally, if not more, important for people to be able to "let themselves go" and express what they are feeling. Perls (1969) and other humanists argue that people often become overconcerned with controlling their emotional expression; they fear ridicule by others if they let their feelings show. As a result they may become rigid and nonexpressive. In doing this, they close off important parts of themselves and important means of communicating with others. Thus the aim in expressing emotions is to achieve a balance between one's feelings and the context, while always remembering that the expression of emotions is an important part of our personal and social being.

A related, and very important, issue has to do with *"proper" and "improper" emotions.* Victor grew up in the wild without anyone to tell him what were the "proper" emotions he should feel. Most people don't live in that type of environment, however; we live in a society that does define "proper" and "improper" ways to feel. It's "proper" to love your parents, and "improper" to hate your brother or sister; you should love family members, but that love should not involve sexual desires. While it is important for the functioning of society that people obey these rules, such rules about emotions may cause problems for individuals in some cases. Sigmund Freud, the founder of modern day clinical psychology, became aware of this dilemma in his discussions with patients. He saw patients suffering a wide variety of physical and psychological symptoms for which, in many cases, there was no apparent reason. Through long discussions and, in some cases, the use of hypnosis, Freud began to see a common thread in the history of his patients. In many cases, these people had experienced events in their childhoods that gave rise to "improper" or unacceptable emotions. In some cases, the root of these emotions was sexual desire for a parent or sibling; in other cases, the emotion was an intense hatred of a family member. However, rather than realize and deal with these feelings, the patients became frightened of them. They *repressed* them and denied that they ever had such "terrible" feelings. According to Freud (1917) it took considerable energy for his patients to repress these feelings; as an individual grew older these feelings threatened to surface, and the ensuing struggle to prevent this gave rise to the physical and psychological symptoms Freud observed.

We have discussed Freud and psychoanalytic theory in Chapter 2, and there is no need to review his work here. The important point for our present discussion is to realize that all of us will experience emotions that we may not like or that we feel are wrong. As we have seen, we can't always control what we feel; we can't turn our emotions on and off whenever we like. Similarly, we will wage a futile fight if we attempt to deny that we experience these unpleasant emotions. To try to deny or run away from our feelings will cost us a great deal of energy, and we may develop the painful symptoms observed by Freud. Certainly we will not be able to hide from ourselves.

Rather than run away from our feelings, it is important to know our feelings and understand from where they come. According to a wide variety of experts, we should acknowledge our feelings and deal with them (see Freud, 1946; Rogers, 1961; Perls, 1969). Knowing how and why we feel will help us better understand ourselves and the world around us. In other words, we need to give ourselves the freedom to feel. We may be troubled or unhappy by some of the emotions we experience, but this shouldn't be cause to deny our feelings. Rather, our concern about troublesome emotions should drive us to more carefully examine those feelings and the events that gave rise to them. One point should be made clear: Allowing ourselves the freedom to feel and observing our emotions does not necessarily mean that we should act on those emotions. To live effectively in our world requires that we be sensitive to situations and adjust our emotional expression accordingly. Still, adjusting our

Healthy emotional expression involves giving vent to our emotions in appropriate situations. Cheering and yelling is fine at a football game but not in a library.
Michael Hayman, Photo Researchers, Inc.

emotional expression to the world we live in should not lead us to deny to ourselves how we feel.

Emotional Problems

Positive personal adjustment requires that we allow ourselves to experience and express our emotions. It is also important that we use situational cues effectively to identify the causes of our emotional arousal and the nature of our emotions. Unfortunately, many people have difficulty doing this. In many cases, they attempt to deny their emotions or keep them "bottled up inside." The most common result of these maladaptive approaches is depression and increased stress. In some cases the results of constricted emotional behavior can be even more visible and more serious. We will examine many of these problems in greater detail in Chapters 6 and 7, but it may be helpful to review briefly here a few of the problems that result from unhealthy approaches to emotions.

One of the possible results of repressing emotions is the development of **psychophysiological disorders** (see Chapter 7), more commonly known as "psychosomatic illnesses." Disorders of this type are manifested in physical symptoms but have psychological causes. The arousal cues are the body's way of telling us that there is energy that needs to be dissipated. Expressing emotion can release this energy. If energy is not released, it builds up in the body much as pressure builds in a balloon after each breath. As the pressure in a balloon increases, greater and greater stress is placed on it, until a tear develops in a weak spot and the balloon explodes. The energy in the body acts similarly if it is not released; it builds up and seeks a "weak spot" in the body. The result is a psychosomatic illness.

Because such disorders are so common, let's examine a few. It may surprise you to find out that **asthma,** a lung condition where breathing becomes difficult, is often considered psychosomatic. Asthma is most common among children and adult males and may result from frustrations of a dependency need or of a desire for close relationships. Migraine headaches occur mostly among females and are often produced by tension and frustration over social and interpersonal relationships. Ulcers, a common psychosomatic illness, affect four times as many males as females. Ulcers are most likely to occur in ambitious, hard-driving individuals who feel insecure or anxious about their responsibilities.

These are just a few examples of illnesses that may be psychosomatic in origin; these types of problems can be caused by tension that was not released in other ways (for further examples, see Chapter 7). While all these illnesses are caused by similar psychological pressures, the particular form they take is partly a result of the individual's constitutional predisposition. That is, just as two balloons may have weaknesses in different places in their walls, so too may individuals vary in terms of

where their weaknesses are located. Hence the type of psychosomatic illness is likely to be different for any two individuals.

Another important step in healthy emotional adjustment is to correctly identify the underlying causes of our emotions. Some people find this hard to do, and they are likely to suffer unpleasant and, in some cases, debilitating consequences. One such consequence is a feeling of **diffuse anxiety.** In this case, a person experiences dread but is unable to identify the reason for it or what he or she is really afraid of. As a result, he or she lives in fear of undertaking any task.

A second example of the importance of utilizing cues and related information to identify emotions involves phobias. A **phobia** is an intense fear of a thing or situation that clearly poses no threat to the individual. The list of possible phobias is almost endless: acrophobia

REVIEW QUESTIONS

11. Two types of nonverbal expressions of emotion are body language and facial cues. In general, _____ communicate the type of emotion while _____ communicates its intensity.

12. T or F: Babies who have been blind since birth have many of the same emotional expressions of babies with normal sight.

13. Repressing emotions may lead to a disorder whereby the individual has physical symptoms that are the result of stress. This type of disorder is called a _____ disorder.

14. The inability to correctly identify the underlying causes of our emotions may lead a person to experience dread and become immobilized with fear without really knowing why. This experience is called _____ _____.

15. T or F: Healthy emotional expression means that people should ignore the demands of the situation and express their true feelings.

(fear of high places), astraphobia (fear of storms), nyctophobia (fear of darkness), monophobia (fear of being alone), pyrophobia (fear of fire). It is believed that many phobias are the result of the classical conditioning process discussed earlier.

An example of a phobia involves the case of an infant named Albert (Watson & Rayner, 1920). Albert was a normal, well-adjusted 11-month-old boy. He was placed in an experimental room and shown a white rat. At first, he showed no fear of the rat. Later, each time Albert was shown the rat, the experimenter sounded a loud frightening noise. The noise made Albert cry, and soon the mere sight of the rat brought tears of fright to Albert's eyes. But Albert was not only conditioned to fear white rats; he also came to fear anything that was white and furry. He cried upon seeing a white dog or a white rabbit; he even cried when he saw the white beard of Santa Claus.

People who experience these emotional problems live uncomfortable and unsatisfying lives. They feel controlled and constrained by their own emotions. They are afraid to act lest they become overwhelmed by their fears. In fact, there are case histories of individuals whose phobias became so strong they couldn't even leave the house. That is certainly a sad state, because, as we pointed out earlier, our emotions should enrich our lives and increase the depth and meaning of our interpersonal relationships.

SUMMARY

1. Emotions are complex states having physiological, affective, and expressive components.

2. The major functions of emotions are to enrich our lives, to motivate and guide our behavior, and to help us in interpersonal communication. Emotions are important to the survival of the individual and the species.

3. Almost every physiological function can be affected by the experience of emotion. In some cases, physiological changes are innately linked to certain stimuli, but many times learning determines what stimuli will cause physiological arousal. A number of lie detection methods, including the polygraph, are designed to measure physiological arousal that is suspected of accompanying lying.

4. There are many theories of emotion. The James-Lange theory argues that emotions result after we perceive our physiological arousal and behavior. Cognitive theories suggest that emotions are the result of our cognitive interpretation of perceived physiological arousal.

5. Emotions are expressed through body language and facial cues, as well as by verbal means. There is some evidence that the way we express some emotions is innate, but the expression of many other emotions is learned and determined by our experiences and the culture in which we live.

6. Emotions affect many aspects of our lives. Research suggests that we are more easily persuaded when in a heightened state of emotional arousal. Emotions affect our attention and perceptions, tending to focus our attention on events central to our feeling and away from events unimportant to our current state. Emotions influence our judgment, causing us to interpret events in line with the emotion we are feeling.

7. Healthy emotional experience involves being sensitive to the body's cues, understanding that our emotions are influenced by cues from our environment, and acknowledging our feelings.

8. People also need to have a good sense of how much emotion to express. Within the demands of the situation, it is important for people to "let themselves go" and express their feelings. Open emotional expression is crucial for a person's sense of well-being and communication with others. Attempting to repress emotions or their expression may result in a host of problems, including psychophysiological disorders, such as asthma and headaches, and psychological symptoms, such as diffuse anxiety and phobias.

KEY TERMS

a. AFFECT
b. ASTHMA
c. ATTRIBUTION
d. BODY LANGUAGE
e. CLASSICAL CONDITIONING
f. DIFFUSE ANXIETY
g. EMOTION

h. KINESIS
i. PHOBIA
j. POLYGRAPH
k. PSYCHOPHYSIOLOGICAL DISORDER
l. VOICE STRESS ANALYZER

1. A complex state of feeling involving conscious experience, internal and overt physical responses, and motivation to action
2. A form of conditioning in which a formerly neutral stimulus is paired with a stimulus that elicits a response, so that the neutral stimulus acquires the capacity to elicit the response
3. A disorder in which the individual shows physical symptoms that have psychological causes
4. A psychological disorder in which breathing becomes difficult
5. Feeling or emotion
6. Nonverbal communication of emotions by posture, positioning, and facial expressions
7. The study of communication through body movements
8. A machine, often called a lie detector, which records changes in heart rate, blood pressure, and galvanic skin responses
9. Records tremors in speech which reflect stress and tension
10. The experience of dread without the ability to identify the reason for the feeling
11. The process labeling physiological arousal as a particular emotional state
12. An intense fear of a particular behavior, object, or place that poses no immediate threat to the individual

ANSWERS TO REVIEW QUESTIONS

1. Motivate; direct. 2. Physiological; affect; expressive. 3. Physiological. 4. Learning. 5. Polygraph.

6. James-Lange. 7. Physiological arousal; cognitive interpretation. 8. Persuaded. 9. Attention; perceptions. 10. Environmental.

11. Facial cues; body language. 12. True. 13. Psychophysiological or psychosomatic. 14. Diffuse anxiety. 15 False.

THE DIMENSIONS OF STRESS

On a hot, humid day in the spring of his senior year in high school, Elvis Presley was scared to go outside. Elvis was hiding inside the dark hallways of Humes High in Memphis, Tennessee. Three boys were waiting outside to beat him up. Red West, a boy Elvis only knew slightly, a year younger than Elvis, but a tough football player, came walking down the corridor. Elvis violated the usual teenage norm of older students waiting until younger students spoke first and said, ''Hi, Red.'' Red immediately sensed that something was wrong and asked Elvis if he could help. Red said he would go outside with Elvis and make sure there was no trouble. In later years, Red West became Elvis Presley's close friend and bodyguard.

Elvis Presley was probably the most successful entertainer in American history. His record sales and box office receipts from movies were astronomical—and still are, years after his death. He made very few films that are regarded as having much artistic value, but he never made one that wasn't a big money-maker. Elvis had the power so many people crave—creative talent and physical magnetism, lots of money, a large retinue of friends and underlings coddling and protecting him, millions of adoring fans all over the world. Yet he was in terrible shape physically and psychologically when he died at the young age of 42. Though the contributors to his death are still shrouded in some mystery, it's clear that years of abusing drugs, mostly uppers and downers, as well as acute problems with weight control, contributed to the heart attack that finally killed him. Despite his fantastic wealth and fame, Elvis felt like a prisoner for most of his adult life, just as he was a prisoner that day in the halls of Humes High School.

Elvis was born on January 8, 1935, in Tupelo, Mississippi. His parents, Gladys and Vernon Presley, were extremely poor. In the midst of the Depression in the South, people like the Presleys were known as ''white trash.'' The most important fact of Elvis's early life was the intense affection showered on him by his mother. Elvis was a twin, but his brother, Jesse, was born dead. As the surviving son and only child, Elvis was worshipped by his mother. She gave him everything he asked for and needed, and even walked to school with him until he was past 12 years old. Elvis adored his mother in return. The unusually strong bond between mother and son remained one of the most important factors in Elvis's life.

All of Gladys's love couldn't break the hold of poverty that grasped Elvis and his family during his early years. In 1948, when Elvis was 13, his father decided to move north to Memphis to find a better life. The family moved into a housing project supported with federal funding. Their economic position showed little improvement. Gladys took on extra work so that Elvis could have a little more than other kids similar to him and feel less like a ''poor boy.'' Elvis worked whenever he could and turned over every cent he earned to his mother.

In high school Elvis wasn't outstanding in any particular way. Earlier, an elementary school teacher had said he was sweet and average. He was still very shy. Nobody much noticed him. Then, late in high school, Elvis's appearance began to distinguish him from the crowd. Most boys in the South in the early 1950s wore crewcuts and modest, conventional clothing. Elvis, who admired the music and style of the black blues singers Memphis was famous for, began sporting long hair in a rakish "ducktail" and loud, "hip" clothing, usually in some combination of pink, silver, and black. This made him noticed, but not in a particularly favorable way. The day Red West rescued him from being beaten up, the other boys were picking on Elvis because they thought his "outrageous" appearance was some kind of claim to being special. They wanted to challenge that claim with their fists. On another occasion Red rescued Elvis from the boys' bathroom, where several students were holding Elvis while the others were trying to cut his long hair.

Elvis's long hair was part of a unique identity he was forming for himself, but wasn't yet ready to reveal completely to anyone else. Memphis was a "music town," and Elvis had been interested in gospel and rhythm-and-blues for a long time. He learned to play a guitar his father bought him when he was a young boy and sang in his church choir with his family. He hung around little clubs in black sections of town, where he learned some licks from "Memphis Soul."

The first time Elvis sang for his peers was in a high school talent show during his senior year. Most of his fellow students were amazed to see Elvis walk shyly onto the stage with his guitar. But his performance surprised them even more. His singing was captivating. He sang a fast song, a ballad, and a sad song about a dying pet, "Old Shep." He got the loudest applause in the show and was asked to do an encore. Once Elvis began to sing, his shyness left him. He seemed confident, commanding, and "cool." At the same time, he projected a lot of feeling. One teacher was moved to tears by "Old Shep," and some of the girls began to squeal at the way Elvis moved his body on stage.

Elvis clearly wanted to become an entertainer, but it seemed that little would come of it. After the talent show, he occasionally sang at high school parties if he was cajoled into it, but his shyness prevented him from actively pursuing a singing career. After high school Elvis got a job as a truck driver. He wasn't singing in public at all. He was still living with his folks and bringing money home to his mother.

Elvis's big break occurred in 1954, two years after he graduated from high school. His truck route in Memphis took him past the Sun Record Company's recording studio. As part of a promotion, and for a fee of four dollars, Sun would let anyone come in and make a record. Elvis decided to record a few of his own songs as a present for his mother. The woman running the studio at the time, Marion Keisker, noticed that there was something special in Elvis's voice. She felt he might be the singer her boss, Sam Phillips, had been looking for, a white man who sang with the strong feeling that seemed more characteristic of black rhythm-and-blues than of white country-and-western. Phillips was interested and had Elvis come back to the studio to play with a group of accomplished musicians. They tried quite a few songs but couldn't seem to come up with one that fit Elvis's style. Finally, during a break, someone noticed Elvis playing around with an upbeat, raunchy tune by the black musician Arthur Cruddup called "That's All Right, Mama." The song was recorded and sold well.

Elvis made more records for Sun, which some connoisseurs now consider the best of his career. He went on tour around the South and slowly began to attract broader attention. He became the lead singer on touring shows, displacing such well-

Elvis in *Loving You:* His movies were not artistic achievements, but they earned him lots of money.

Springer/Bettmann Film Archive.

known and established country singers as Hank Snow. Elvis's performances usually caused a stir. His frankly sexual body language and the debt his style owed to black rhythm-and-blues ("race music") titillated or shocked white audiences, depending on their age group.

In January 1956, when Elvis made the first of several television appearances, singing "Heartbreak Hotel," the network censor insisted that the cameras show him only from the waist up. The next morning, Elvis's performance was big news among kids across the country. His career was really soaring. By the end of 1956 Elvis had a string of Number One Gold Records and had made his first movie, *Love Me Tender.* He had also acquired a manager, one "Colonel" Tom Parker, who began telling the inexperienced Elvis how to run his booming career. From then on, Parker made most of Elvis's artistic and financial decisions.

At that time Elvis wasn't much different from how he'd been in high school. He was daring and commanding on stage—"Elvis the Pelvis"—but polite and shy off stage—strictly "Yes, sir" and "Yes, ma'am." Although many adults argued that his raucous, hip-swinging performances were too sexually suggestive and were corrupting the youth of the land, off stage Elvis seemed too well-mannered and reserved to threaten anyone.

Then, at the height of Elvis's first huge success, two events had a great impact on his career. First, his mother died in 1958, when Elvis was 23. Second, Elvis was drafted and had a two-year hitch in the army from 1958–1960. When Elvis returned from military service in Germany, his fans were more numerous than ever, and his exemplary performance in the military (that greasy ducktail had been shaved off, of course) made him more acceptable to the older generation. But those two years of spinning his wheels in Germany had marked a major transition in Elvis's life and work. Tom Parker now began directing Elvis away from his earlier style, away from live performances, and into making it big in the movies. The songs Elvis recorded were "middle of the road," chosen for appeal to an audience broader than those who had loved "Jailhouse Rock."

Elvis was always mobbed by fans after he became successful. As a result, he had to insulate himself from the public.

The Bettmann Archive, Inc.

During the 1960s, when Elvis "went Hollywood," he made two or three films a year, most with the same plot about a troubled young man with lots of singing ability that rescues him from trouble and gives him the means to succeed at the end. Though the sixties were good to Elvis commercially, they gradually became disastrous to his creative and personal life. One of Elvis's biggest problems was boredom. He was bored because all his films were so similar and required little acting ability. Elvis's main ambition at that time was to be a really fine actor, but his managers, chiefly Tom Parker, never let him attempt a challenging script. They were reluctant to alter the formula that was making Elvis, and them, so rich.

Elvis didn't sing in public for eight years, in part so that people could only see him in the movies and would continue buying tickets to theaters and drive-ins. But Elvis had always been at his best giving live performances. The challenge excited him. He worked hard to do well and invariably presented highly energized and carefully crafted shows. Without the creative demands and excitement of live performances, Elvis began to stagnate. He had few other interests that really kept him occupied. He began to get lazy and spoiled and became dependent on drugs to energize him for his acting.

Another problem was that Elvis's incredible popularity and instant recognizability made it impossible for him to live a normal life. He couldn't go out in public for fear of being mobbed. He could only leave Graceland, his mansion in Memphis, with an entire entourage of bodyguards, advance men, and helpers. Elvis had become a captive of his own fame.

In the late 1960s Elvis began to do live performances again, first on a much-heralded television show, where he seemed to have regained some of his 1950s "spark," and then in Las Vegas hotels. For a while going on the road again rejuvenated him. But Elvis felt that the routine lacked excitement and challenge, and he slipped back into using drugs. A further setback was that in 1973, after six years of marriage and the birth of a daughter, Elvis's wife, Priscilla, began an affair with Mike Stone, a man who had been teaching her karate at Elvis's insistence. The boredom, the confinement, and the loss of the only woman he'd really loved, other than his mother, took their toll. Elvis tried to keep life interesting by studying the martial arts, racing cars, and collecting guns. But he failed to find any sustaining involvement or significance in his life. He was still performing and making phenomenal amounts of money, but the money couldn't buy fulfillment. The combination of irregular eating and sleeping and drug taking ruined his body and distorted his personality. He died at 42, the same age his mother had.

Elvis Presley's records still sell, and his movies are shown frequently on television. His performances still sustain millions of his fans, but his way of living couldn't sustain him.

DEFINING STRESS

Although Elvis Presley's life was highly successful by the conventional standards of fame and fortune, his difficulties with drugs and his untimely death reveal that all was not well with him. His life was filled with stresses that were somewhat different from the ordinary person's, but that took their toll nevertheless. Elvis's stress resulted from too much success rather than too little, and from too little challenge rather than too much. Still, whatever stress is caused by, it is a factor in everyone's life to some extent; the effects of stress on Elvis Presley's life were extreme, but otherwise not so different from what all of us must face in day-to-day living.

The concept of stress is of critical importance in the psychology of personal adjustment. Stress is a pattern of psychological and physiological reactions to demands in the environment that threaten our well-being, self-esteem, or integrity and that cause us to devote a great deal of our resources to coping with the danger and defending ourselves (Cofer & Appley, 1964; Crider, Goethals, Kavanaugh, & Solomon, 1983). Stress always taxes, and sometimes overwhelms, people's energies and abilities to protect themselves (Lazarus, 1976). Sometimes we get confused and think of events and situations in the environment themselves, such as an upcoming exam, as stress. Instead, we should think of such external demands or threats as stressors, the causes of stress. The psychological and physiological reactions to these demands, such as a feeling of fear and an upset stomach, are what constitute stress. We will talk about the stresses of living in general terms first and then try to classify in psychological terms the various kinds of stress we must cope with in today's world.

STRESSES IN THE MODERN WORLD

Most readers probably don't need reminding of the stresses of everyday living. They are obvious, and you would probably like to forget them for awhile. Nevertheless, it is useful to briefly remind ourselves of the various ways that modern life challenges us. Stressors in today's world can be divided for convenience into four categories: complex relations, hard work, tough choices, and rough edges. Let's consider each in turn.

Complex Relations

Throughout our lives we are involved in relationships with other people. While our greatest satisfactions in life often come through interactions with parents, siblings, friends, lovers, spouses, children, and others, relationships also involve considerable stress. Stress is particularly high during the college years when people are actively engaged in the "interpersonal marketplace," trying to find others who are compatible with them and with whom close and perhaps even intimate relations are possible. People often experience conflicts about whether to trust, whether to make a commitment, whether to ask for a commitment, how much to accommodate, and how much to draw back. Many of us get hurt, and it is easy to feel vulnerable.

Sullivan (1953) noted some of the stresses of interpersonal relations in late adolescence and early adulthood when he discussed the collisions between three needs: intimacy, sex, and security. He pointed out how difficult it can be to find a relationship in which each of these needs can be met, and how long it can take to decide how to pattern relationships so that these needs are satisfied.

Elvis Presley faced some of these conflicts when he first started to be successful as a singer. Women were often available to him sexually, but having casual sexual relations with them was against the moral principles he had learned from his mother. Gladys Presley always asked Red West to "take care of my boy." Elvis knew this and felt insecure when he had sexual relationships he knew his mother would disapprove of. Working out relationships so that all one's needs are satisfied can be extremely stressful.

Getting our work done can be highly stressful.
Irene Springer.

Hard Work

One of the foremost realities of life today is that success, whether financial or social, requires hard work. Work today is probably not as physically demanding as it was at the turn of the century, when people worked at least ten hours a day for six days a week, but it is probably more psychologically stressful than ever before. The level of intelligence and responsibility required of college graduates in most occupations is probably at an all-time high.

If we regard stress-filled jobs as the "bad news," the "good news" is that there are not enough to go around. There is fierce competition for those stressful but high-paying jobs. Many people are pessimistic about the long-term economic situation, and when our economy is not growing, only the most talented, hardworking, and lucky will be able to advance. When there are not enough high-paying, high-prestige jobs for all, one person's success occurs only at another person's expense.

This competition for advancement makes work even more pressure-filled.

When one does succeed, that simply means taking on more responsibility and being stretched closer to the limits of one's capacities of energy and talent. People want to achieve and get ahead, but doing so entails a great deal of stress. Even in a college we can see the difficult competitive situation in which people find themselves. When 50 percent of students want to be in the top 20 percent of the class so they can start good careers after school, it's clear that the pressure is intense.

Tough Choices

One of the advantages of modern life is that its complexity and mobility offer people many more options than ever before. On the other hand, people have to make many more important choices than ever before. For instance, most young people today face difficult decisions about sex: How heavily involved with sex should I get in my relationships? How will sex affect my own self-esteem? What will others think of me? How do I feel about birth control? Students also face difficult choices about courses, a field to major in, whether to take some time off from school, and how to pay for their education.

Major decisions about job and career are just a few years away, if they aren't being faced already. Many students want a profession that will give them "high income and low guilt," that is, a good salary and a feeling of doing something significant and helpful. They wonder if they'll find one. They also face major decisions about marriage and children, how to participate in or contribute to community affairs, and how to help older members of the family who have become unable to care for themselves. A great deal more is potentially under your control than before, if you are willing and able to make hard choices. But this doesn't alter the fact that making life decisions involves conflict and causes stress.

Rough Edges

We use the term "rough edges" simply to indicate that the world today can be cold and abrasive in many ways. Elvis Presley found this to be true in the film industry of the 1960s, and it seems to be more true of more parts of the world today than ever before. The environment is overcrowded and polluted in many places. There is too much information. It's hard to escape, even temporarily, from people, ideas, hard-sell advertisements, machines, and noise. Relations with other people tend to be cold and impersonal. We usually don't know the people we encounter in stores, theaters, and banks, and there is often little sense of empathy or community among us and those we run into in such situations. Research has shown that these "rough edges" are stressful and harm the quality of interpersonal relations and personal adjustment (see Chapter 15). They can be

managed, but they make life more difficult than it already is.

When one stops to think about the stresses and challenges of the modern world, the future can seem pretty grim. We wonder if we will be able to meet these challenges. Of course most people do meet them. Most of us are able to assess stressful situations, consider our needs, and select an appropriate course of action. If you are enrolled in a college now and reading this book in a course, the chances are that you have done a good job in meeting life's challenges in the past and will continue to do so in the future. There is no real point in dwelling on the negative except to remind ourselves that we all have significant stresses to cope with. They should be kept in mind when we try to understand people who have not been successful in handling them.

VARIETIES OF STRESS

The various difficulties of modern living cause a variety of stressful reactions in us. Perhaps the most common but least serious reaction is the simple response of frustration when one of our needs is blocked or thwarted. Another kind of stress is caused by conflict about choices. Sometimes two alternatives are equally appealing or unappealing. Sometimes we have ambivalent feelings about one situation or course of action. And of course there are times when all our options have their negative and positive aspects. In general, decision making taxes our resources and abilities and generates stress. Finally, people face various extreme situations that threaten their physical well-being, self-esteem, or personal integrity.

Frustration

Frustration occurs when an important need or motive can't be satisfied. Usually this happens when a person is trying to meet a need or satisfy a drive and his or her behavior is blocked by some barrier. The negative emotional arousal produced by this thwarting of behavior is frustration. In everyday terms, we all know that barriers to behavior are "frustrating." Frustration occurs when you are late for work and your car won't start, when the store sends you the wrong size sweater, or when you drop a part of the outboard motor you are fixing into the lake. In all these cases, behavior designed to meet a need has been blocked and the need is not met. Not all negative experiences involve frustration. Grief and loneliness, for example, involve quite different types of stress. But frustration is a common negative emotional experience, and it occurs whenever a person is unable to do or complete what is necessary to reach a motive-satisfying goal.

Barriers that stand in the way of motive gratification must be coped with in some way. Further action must be taken to overcome the barrier somehow. This could mean calling a service station for help with the car, writing a firm letter to the department store, or putting on your goggles and diving into the lake. In many cases, perhaps most, it's easy for a calm, objective, and rational person to figure out what adaptive behavior is required, plan the behavior, and carry it out expeditiously. The problem, of course, is that the negative emotional arousal of frustration makes it exceedingly difficult to be calm, rational, and objective. Frustration has been shown to produce several responses that are incompatible with adaptive action. We shall consider two of them.

FRUSTRATION AND AGGRESSION. One of the most well-known hypotheses in all of psychology is the frustration-aggression link originally proposed by Dollard, Doob, Miller, Mowrer, and Sears in 1939. This formulation holds that one of the key emotions produced by frustration is anger, which then leads to aggression. This aggression can be directed against people who might be responsible for thwarting a person's desires, against others who are similar, against those who are powerless, or even against the self. For our present purposes, suffice it to say that anger is one of the emotions produced by frustration, and it often produces

destructive behavior in turn. Such behavior usually doesn't lead to gratification of the originally blocked motive.

FRUSTRATION AND REGRESSION. Another line of research explores the relation between frustration and regression (Barker, Dembo, & Lewin, 1941). The essential hypothesis is that when people are frustrated, their behavior often becomes more disorganized and infantile, and they often behave in ways that, although successful in the past, have no adaptive relation to the present situation. For example, a person might become very glum and sulky if this way of behaving had been successful in the past, perhaps in getting parental attention and help.

Closely related to the frustration-regression hypothesis is Maier's (1949) idea that people who are frustrated behave in rigid ways that are not directed toward any goal or solution but simply express agitation and arousal. That is, Maier believes that people can become infantile, undirected, and maladaptive when frustrated. Their aggressiveness is uncontrolled striking out, which relieves tension, but may not do anything to remove a frustrating barrier. A person may kick the dog when highly frustrated by something else. This is the kind of infantile, nondirected behavior to which Maier refers.

HANDLING FRUSTRATION. Frustration can be extremely arousing and upsetting. People respond to upsetting situations in very different ways. Elvis Presley vented his frustrations more and more as he grew older. His shy reserve gave way to fits of anger, and even to regressive behavior, when he was frustrated. Elvis was fascinated with guns and owned a large collection of them. Often when he was frustrated he would start shooting the gun at televisions. On one occasion when he saw an actor on television who was a competitive threat to him, Elvis simply blasted away at his image on the screen. When this happened in hotels, hotel employees would simply clean up the mess and replace the television set, and the hotel management would send Elvis the bill.

There are good arguments in favor of expressing tension, but the most adaptive response to frustration is not to "act out," but to direct one's attention away from the frustrating circumstances. If these circumstances can be put behind you and you can concentrate on the next steps that must be taken to meet your goal, you'll be on the road to controlling frustration and minimizing tension. Then you can let off steam by patting yourself on the back instead of kicking your dog on the backside or shooting at a television set. Elvis Presley increasingly acted out his frustration as he grew older, which was part of the pattern of uncontrolled behavior that led to his early death.

Conflict

In 1973 when Priscilla Presley left Elvis to live with Mike Stone, Elvis faced an extremely stressful conflict and had to make a difficult decision. On the one hand he knew that Priscilla was better off with Mike. Despite the fact that, after his mother, Priscilla was the only person Elvis had deeply loved, their marriage had not worked out. On the other hand, Elvis was deeply hurt and publicly humiliated. He wanted to "get a contract out" on Mike's life and have him killed by a professional assassin. After struggling with the conflict over what to do, he decided to order the execution. He told his bodyguards, Sonny West and Red West, to take care of the assassination. Sonny refused, but Red, who had been close to Elvis since their days in high school, felt he should follow Elvis's orders, even though he knew they were wrong. After agonizing and trying to put Elvis off, Red eventually did call a "hit-man," who said he would await further orders. When Red told Elvis he had done this, Elvis said maybe the whole idea should be forgotten. In the end he decided against it. Red had felt very badly about his own decision, and now he was relieved to hear Elvis tell him to cancel the contract.

Few of us have to resolve conflicts or face decisions of the kind faced by Elvis and Red West in this situation, but conflicts are nevertheless a pervasive part of human existence. They are inevitably difficult. Yet, in making the hard choices necessary to resolve conflicts, people often learn a great deal about themselves. They grow, they accept responsibility for their lives, and they clarify and sharpen their identities. This is most likely to happen when conflicts are met head-on and resolved as they arise, rather than avoided and left to cause problems in the future.

How do conflicts arise? The famous psychologist Kurt Lewin, who came to the United States from Nazi Germany in the 1930s, proposed a useful classification of various conflict situations (1935): approach-approach, avoidance-avoidance, approach-avoidance, and double approach-avoidance conflicts. We will consider approach-approach and avoidance-avoidance conflicts first and then some of the interesting aspects of approach-avoidance conflicts.

APPROACH-APPROACH AND AVOIDANCE-AVOID-ANCE CONFLICTS. In the approach-approach conflict we are attracted to two alternative actions or objects that are both desirable but that we can't do or have at the same time. A child in an ice cream parlor who must decide whether to have a hot fudge sundae or a banana split is in an approach-approach conflict. Either choice would be wonderful, but the child must choose one and give up the other. Approach-approach conflicts can be just as difficult to resolve as other conflicts, but they are clearly the most fun. Maybe ten years later the child in the ice cream parlor will have to decide which of two keenly desired colleges to attend after having been accepted by both. This is another approach-approach conflict.

As you might expect, the least pleasant kind of conflict is the avoidance-avoidance conflict. Here you face two unpleasant alternatives and must choose between them. The student who must choose between studying for a test and doing research for a term paper may be in such a conflict. The person who feels bound to accept an invitation from someone he or she doesn't like or else stay home from a dance is in an avoidance-avoidance conflict. Both alternatives are unappealing, but answering the phone forces the person to choose between them.

APPROACH-AVOIDANCE CONFLICT.   While there are many times when we have to choose between two positive alternatives or two negative ones, probably more often we face situations where we feel conflicting tendencies to approach and to avoid. These occur when we must decide whether to do something that has both positive and negative aspects. Elvis's decision to stop off at Sun Records to record some songs for his mother involved an approach-avoidance conflict. On the one hand, he was anxious to surprise and please his mother, and he thought he could do that. On the other hand, he was shy and intimidated about going into a recording studio.

Sexual conflicts are often of the approach-avoidance type. You may be very attracted to the idea of having sex with the person you're dating but want to avoid the obligations and commitment that might entail. Conflicts involving interpersonal commitment also involve approach-avoidance conflicts. You may be attracted to the security and permanence marriage seems to offer but also feel that marriage would put very frustrating limits on your freedom to travel, meet other people, and do things on your own.

The psychologist Neil Miller (1944) developed a theory about the way people behave when they are in approach-avoidance conflicts. Although it is difficult to know from his model how such a conflict will finally be resolved, he does explain some of the consequences of being in an approach-avoidance situation. Miller says that both the tendency to approach a desired object and the tendency to avoid a feared or disliked one increase the closer you get to the object. For example, a young person who likes root beer (or an older one who likes ordinary beer) will be more and more drawn to drinking it the closer he or she gets to it. Similarly, a person who is afraid of snakes will feel more and more like running away from a boa constrictor the closer it is. If we consider a situation in which a person is both drawn to and afraid of an object, we find

that both tendencies, approach and avoidance, get stronger as the situation gets closer. The closer the person is to the object, the stronger the conflict about it is. For example, Miller's theory predicts that a person who is just about to knock on an employer's door to apply for a job will be more excited about the interview *and* more apprehensive about it than another applicant just getting out of the car in the parking lot. The person inside is in a greater bind and is experiencing a sharper conflict than the person in the parking lot. Similarly, a person just about to call up and ask for a date ought to be in more conflict than one further away from the phone.

When we speak of distance from the object of conflict, we can mean distance in time as well as in space. A person who has a job interview today should feel more intense approach drives and avoidance drives than one who has the interview next week. Whether we mean closeness in terms of physical proximity or in terms of time, Miller states that those who are close to an object of conflict will feel stronger approach and avoidance tendencies than those who are far away.

The most important part of Miller's theory concerns the relative strengths of the approach and avoidance tendencies. While both get stronger as the person nears the object of conflict, the avoidance tendency gets stronger *faster* than the approach tendency (see Figure 5.1).

Consider the following: A man is about to register for a course he would really like to take. He is pretty sure he'll get a poor grade in it, however. He wants the course but is also afraid of it. Let's suppose that the place where the student must register for the course is half a mile across campus from his dormitory. He leaves his room, headed toward the registration building, feeling ready to take the course. His approach tendency—that is, his desire to learn about the topic—is stronger than his fear of a low grade. As he gets nearer the registration building, both his excitement about the course and his fear of the low grade get stronger. The conflict becomes more intense. He may be so absorbed that he isn't careful where he walks.

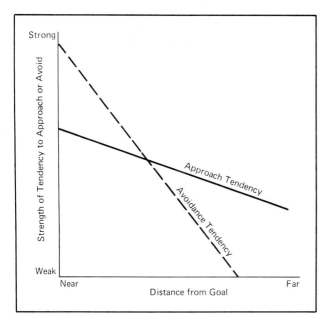

FIGURE 5.1 APPROACH-AVOIDANCE TENDENCY
As people get near goals they are both drawn to and fear, the strength of both approach and avoidance tendencies increases. However, the avoidance tendency gets stronger more quickly. As a result, people may approach such goals up to a point, then back away.

Source: Adapted from Miller (1944).

Suddenly, he's reached the registration building, and because his avoidance tendency has gotten stronger faster than his approach tendency, his fear is now stronger than his desire for learning. He stops, turns around, and heads back to the dorm. But that isn't the whole story. When he gets about a hundred yards from the building, the approach and avoidance tendencies are equal, and he sits down on a bench and tries desperately to decide what to do. He feels awfully foolish, especially since the registration deadline is approaching. This temporal "nearness" to the point of decision also increases his conflict.

Unfortunately, Miller doesn't tell us how people resolve conflicts. The man in a stew over a course must resolve his conflict either by suppressing his fear and deciding that the course would be valuable or by giving in to his fear and deciding that taking the course would be foolish. When either the approach or the avoidance tendency finally becomes stronger, the conflict is resolved in favor of the stronger tendency.

One possible response in some cases is oscillation (also known as indecisiveness and wishy-washyness), going back and forth, approaching until the avoidance tendency is stronger again. Children at the seashore who

are fascinated by the huge waves but also afraid of them will run closer and closer until very close and then, more scared than intrigued, run back. They can run back and forth for a long time, scaring their parents as well as themselves.

DOUBLE APPROACH-AVOIDANCE CONFLICT. A final kind of conflict is the most complex, but probably also the most common in the modern world. This is the double approach-avoidance conflict, in which a person must choose between two objects or courses of action, both with positive and negative attributes. There are approach and avoidance tendencies for both alternatives. This type of conflict multiplies by two all that is involved in the approach-avoidance conflicts discussed above.

Double approach-avoidance conflict can be illustrated by extending the example of the uncertain student we mentioned before. Imagine that instead of deciding about just one course, he is choosing between two. One offers the advantage of being easy and the disadvantage of being worth very little. The other offers the advantage of being highly educational and the disadvantage of requiring a great deal of study. A second example might be a person trying to decide whether to develop a relationship with someone he or she is deeply fond of but who comes from a different social background or with another person for whom he or she really feels less affection but whose background would meet with family approval.

Elvis Presley's early decisions about whether to take uppers to keep him going when he was tired were double approach-avoidance decisions. Taking the pills would enable him to do more and perhaps perform better. On the other hand, he knew his mother wouldn't have approved of him taking pills and that he could develop serious health problems from taking them. Not taking pills would keep him away from a potentially dangerous dependency on drugs and from a behavior that was morally questionable, but it would also deprive him of a needed lift.

Most decisions in human affairs involve double approach-avoidance conflicts. There are almost always good aspects and bad aspects of any course of action. In considering any single alternative one is always held back by the negative aspects of that alternative and the positive aspects of other alternatives. Such conflicts exist about which courses to take in college, where to live, what occupation to enter, with whom to associate, and with whom to establish intimate relations. It can be difficult in many instances to decide which alternative is really in one's best interests, even after you've decided what your best interests are. In order to understand how people make these difficult choices, we will now look closely at the decision-making process.

Making Decisions

Among the difficult decisions Elvis Presley made in his career was to give a live television performance in 1968 after having been out of the public eye, except for the movies, since 1960. Like Elvis's decisions about drugs and Mike Stone, and like any decision any of us makes any day, Elvis's decision about the television appearance can be divided into three parts. There was the period preceding the decision, when Elvis had to consider the possibility that he had lost his support and the public wouldn't

Making choices can be difficult enough to cause stress.
Marc P. Anderson.

like him or even watch him; there was the period of commitment to doing the show, the actual moment of decision; and then there was the period after the decision, when Elvis prepared to go ahead with what turned out to be a highly successful public appearance. Much research has been conducted to investigate what happens during these three periods of decision making. Most debate has centered on the predecisional phase. In fact, three theories have been proposed about what happens then.

THE PREDECISION PERIOD.   One view of what happens prior to a decision is **conflict theory**: When confronted with a double approach-avoidance conflict, people consider the alternatives objectively for a time and then begin a process of bolstering or enhancing the more positive alternative in preparation for the decision (Janis & Mann, 1977). Essentially this means that they begin convincing themselves that the slightly better alternative is really good and that the other alternative is really bad. For example, consider a woman who is going to buy a new car and has narrowed her choices down to a Chevrolet and a Toyota. She feels that the Chevrolet is cheaper and easier to get serviced, but that the Toyota is better made and has a little more "pizzaz." There are positive and negative aspects of both. Let's suppose that the woman is going to make a final decision in three days. Conflict theory suggests that as the time of decision gets closer, the woman will prepare herself for the moment of commitment by tentatively deciding in favor of one alternative, let's say the Chevrolet, and then concentrating more and more on the good points of the Chevrolet and the bad points of the Toyota, until by the time she finally has to choose she is heavily in favor of the Chevrolet. This "predecisional spreading of the alternatives" is what makes the eventual decision possible, or at least easier (Janis & Mann, 1977).

In contrast to conflict theory, **cognitive dissonance theory** simply suggests that people remain objective until after they have made an irrevocable choice between two alternatives; then they "spread" (that is, widen the gap between) the alternatives in order to justify their decision (Festinger, 1957; 1964).

A third theory, psychological **reactance theory,** proposes an entirely different view of what happens during the predecision period: People value their freedoms and whenever a freedom is threatened or taken away, they become more attracted to that freedom and will strive to protect or regain it (Brehm, 1966). For example, new college regulations may prohibit

students from smoking in their dormitory rooms. The result is that they want to smoke more than ever before. As anyone making a difficult decision knows, choosing between alternatives also means the loss of a freedom. That is, you eliminate your own freedom when you make a decision. Before the decision, leaning toward one option threatens your freedom to exercise the other.

Consider the woman thinking about the Chevrolet and the Toyota. She may at one point start leaning slightly toward the Toyota. The consequence of this is that she feels her freedom to buy the Chevrolet threatened. Notice that it is her own emerging decision that is threatening her freedom. When she feels her freedom threatened, she becomes more attracted to that threatened option and thus relatively more in favor of the Chevrolet. This may close the gap between her tentative evaluations of the two cars, it may bring them even, or she may actually switch preferences and begin to favor the Chevrolet over the Toyota. If she starts favoring the Chevrolet, her freedom to buy the Toyota becomes threatened, and the reverse process will take place. Any slight preference for one car over the other poses a threat to the unfavored car as the decision time draws near. Reactance will be strongly felt, and the unfavored car will quickly rise in the prospective buyer's esteem. Thus reactance theory predicts that as the decision draws closer, a person will feel more and more concerned about los-

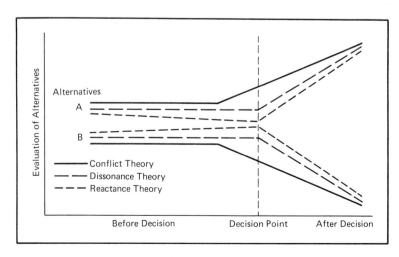

FIGURE 5.2   THEORIES OF PREDECISIONAL EVALUATION OF CHOICE ALTERNATIVES

ing either alternative and more and more in conflict about what choice to make. Studies supporting reactance theory show that the closer the time of the decision is, the more equal in value the alternatives become (Linder & Crane, 1970). This minimizes reactance but makes the decision itself more difficult.

One wonders how a decision is ever made in the face of this process of "keeping your options open." It may be that there is a juggling of favorites until the time of decision actually arrives. At that point one simply chooses whichever alternative happens to be on the upswing at that moment. On the other hand, we can hope that when faced with the final choice people will suspend the distortions of reactance, look squarely and objectively at the options, and make a commitment on the basis of their judgment of the best choice. This is only a hope, however, because research has shown relatively little about how people actually make choices at the point of decision.

THE POSTDECISION PERIOD. In contrast to the debate and uncertainty about the predecision period, we have a relatively clear picture of what happens after a decision is made (Walster, 1964). It appears that there are two parts of this postdecision phase. First, a few minutes after a decision there is a temporary "regret phase" during which people feel very much attracted to the alternative they have just forgone and suspect that they may be committed to a less desirable alternative. This reaction is probably best explained by reactance theory. Your decision has eliminated one of your options, and as a consequence you become more attracted to that option. This desire for an eliminated freedom produces the feeling of regret that follows a decision. Your freedom is gone, you miss it, and you wonder whether you made the right choice. This is an extremely uncomfortable state of affairs. It does not last long, but while it does it is acute.

In the second part of the postdecision phase, people become more and more committed to their choice, more sure they have done the right thing, and more certain that the alternative they chose is better than the one

they gave up. This is explained in terms of cognitive dissonance theory. The bad things about the chosen alternative and the good things about the unchosen alternative are inconsistent with the decision and produce dissonance, an uncomfortable state in which one feels that one has been unwise or, in the case of some decisions, immoral. In order to reduce these unpleasant feelings, people convince themselves that they were right and come to believe strongly in their choice. This kind of dissonance reduction takes place whenever people choose between alternatives. People buying clothes, cars, or houses and people deciding which job to take, which college to attend, or which candidate to vote for show this tendency. In this way any misgivings are finally eliminated.

MAKING GOOD DECISIONS. The research by conflict, dissonance, and reactance researchers outlined above can alert people to some of the motivational pressures that can occur during decision making and often make choices difficult, biased, or both. Being aware of this research is useful, we think, if six specific principles of sound decision making are kept in mind.

First, be as clear as you can about what is in your interests and what your values are. Elvis Presley failed to do this. He started out being guided by his mother's values and expectations. Then he turned over most of the decisions about his career, including the final decision to appear on television in 1968, to his manager, Tom Parker. Elvis never had a clear sense of his own interests. This made it difficult for him to feel at ease with what he was doing.

Second, be as explicit as possible about all the advantages and disadvantages of your alternatives. It may help to write them down. Janis and Mann (1977) have shown that the more thoroughly we have considered these advantages and disadvantages, the better we are able to withstand the stress produced when some of the negative aspects of our final decision begin to affect us.

A third and related point is to think about the long term. Remember, you will have to live with your decision for a long time. Even though it may seem difficult now, your peace of mind will be greatly enhanced if you consider what will be the best in the long run. Elvis never did this very effectively. He considered what would most satisfy his momentary needs, not what was best for him in the long run.

Fourth, be aware of possible conflict reduction or reactance reduction processes that might take place before the decision. In order to reduce the conflict you may go too far in favoring one alternative prematurely, and this can interfere with your objectivity and ability to make the most fully informed decision. On the other hand, worrying too much about keeping your options open can be paralyzing and could lead to a hasty and ill-considered decision at the end.

Fifth, after you have made the decision, be prepared for a feeling of let-down and regret. There may be some yearning for what you have given up and a feeling that you "blew it." Try not to be overwhelmed by these feelings.

Finally, be aware of dissonance reduction processes afterwards. You will want to feel that you did the right thing and so you may distort how good your chosen alternative is and how bad the rejected alternative is. Nothing galvanizes one's feelings like an irrevocable decision. Avoid being too smug and biased as a result of your commitment. At the same time that

you are feeling good about having chosen wisely, try to remain as objective as possible. This will help you make other good choices in the future.

Threats to Physical Well-Being

Many kinds of extreme conditions threaten the well-being, or even the survival, of the human organism. Such threats produce what is called **systemic stress,** because a person's entire system, psychological as well as physical, is in crisis. Systemic stress can be caused by distinct, short-term events, such as a tornado or someone pulling a knife on you and threatening to rape you, or by situations that continue over a long period of time, such as alcoholism or the general abuse suffered by concentration camp victims. Extreme conditions that can lead to systemic stress include severe heat or cold, starvation, excessive physical labor, lack of sleep, serious disease, and severe bodily injury. People in poverty in the United States and around the world suffer chronic threats to their physical well-being: inadequate food, clothing, housing, and health care; often dangerous living environments; and the effects of anxiety about these conditions. Such systemic stress tends to be self-perpetuating, since it drains a person's emotional and spiritual, as well as

Physically exhausting work can generate high degrees of stress.
United Nations/John Robaton.

physical, resources and weakens a person's ability to deal with the conditions that are causing the stress. Systemic stress also threatens the survival of the species as a whole, because negative effects of threats to a person's physical well-being can be passed down, by heredity and by example, to future generations.

War also causes systemic stress. Civilians as well as soldiers experience physical injury, malnutrition, loss of home and livelihood, as well as extreme fear about the possible loss of their own lives and the lives of their loved ones. In the Revolutionary War, General George Washington's troops suffered extreme conditions at Valley Forge in the winter of 1777–1778. Soldiers had to persevere on minimal daily rations, enduring bitter cold for weeks on end. Washington despaired over his army's lack of shoes and bloody footprints in the snow.

People who are able to survive such hardships, whether in the course of "normal" daily life or in war or natural disaster, become what we think of as heroes.

Elvis Presley clearly led a life that threatened, and finally overwhelmed, his physical well-being. Although he had every material advantage, including more than enough to eat and luxurious shelter, the schedule, diet, and drug regimen he forced upon his body constituted an extreme threat to his entire system. How do people cope with these extreme situations? What are the consequences?

The distinguished scientist Hans Selye (1956) has outlined what he calls the **"general adaptation syndrome" (GAS),** which is engaged under stress conditions.

The first stage in the GAS is alarm, which consists first of shock and then of a general mobilization of the body's resources. This alarm phase can be experienced if you are driving and a small child darts into the road directly in front of your car. Even if the child is pulled to safety or you manage to stop the car in time, you can feel the almost immediate mobilization of the body's resources, a readiness to cope with threat and danger. Sometimes drivers find that they must rest for a few minutes after such a scare until they can relax and the body resumes its normal metabolism.

The second stage of the GAS is resistance. At this time the aroused organism does what it can to meet the threat. It may attack or flee or in some other way protect itself. Coping responses are often strongest at this point. The aroused person attempts to do what is necessary to meet the threat, and the general arousal energizes the most effective behavior of which the person is capable. Sometimes people are overwhelmed in the alarm stage and can't function at all, but if there is effective functioning, it occurs in the resistance stage shortly after alarm.

The third stage of the GAS, exhaustion, occurs if, after a period of resistance, threat is not removed. Physical and psychological resources are depleted, and the person's functioning is less effective than normal. It can be extremely difficult for a person to plan or execute adaptive behavior when exhausted. Unless the person has some chance to escape from the threat and to rest, functioning will eventually stop altogether, and death will result. Elvis had the chance to escape from the stress that was destroying him, but he had neither the foresight nor the inner strength to alter his life style.

We've mentioned the fact that a high level of threat can exist for an extended period of time and that the exhaustion stage in such stressful situations is often prolonged. Recent wars have subjected some American soldiers to a unique kind of extended stress that combines extreme conditions of physical deprivation and punishment with unrelenting attacks on the soldiers' values and integrity. One example is the efforts by the Chinese communists in the Korean War to convert American prisoners to their ideologies. A variety of manipulations and propaganda techniques were used, the most effective of which was to try to convince soldiers that their peers believed the propaganda and supported the enemy. As soldiers came into the exhaustion stage of the stress reaction, it became more and more difficult to resist the enemy effectively. The communists seemed to recognize intuitively that it was easier to attack men's minds after they had weakened their bodies.

Ambiguous situations, such as interviews, can be highly stressful.

Rhoda Sidney.

Nevertheless, the attempt at brainwashing was largely a failure. Very few men adopted any part of the communist ideology. The Chinese were successful in getting soldiers to behave collaboratively—men would act as they had to in order to survive—but few changed their minds. Because of the extreme force and coercion used by those who ran the prisoner-of-war camps, it was easy for the GIs to view their collaborative behavior as forced, and they knew it implied nothing about their attitudes. The threats they endured were much more to their well-being than to their integrity.

Of course, as we've already seen, systemic stress doesn't occur only in wartime. Some of the most tragic examples of human responses to extreme conditions have occurred under initially benign circumstances. There are many instances of "panic situations" where an immediate threat to life and well-being occurs. Fires in theaters or crowded dance halls pose such threats. Often the shock of these situations completely overwhelms adaptive behavior, and the result is uncontrolled, irrational mass panic as people struggle wildly in futile attempts to escape and survive. In fires the threat is clear, and there is little ambiguity about what should be done—get to an exit—but there is simply no way to do it.

In other situations in which people are worried about their well-being or survival, there can be a great deal of ambiguity about what should be done, if anything, or even if there really is a threat. Is a burglar really tiptoeing through your living room? Will the flood reach your neighborhood? Is a certain crisis in the Middle East bringing the world to the brink of nuclear war? Such ambiguity itself is stressful. This kind of situation is well-illustrated in Hadley Cantril's (1940) study of the "Invasion from Mars." Luckily, in that case, the invasion took place only on the radio.

On the night before Halloween in 1938, the "Orson Welles Mercury Theatre" on CBS radio in New York presented a dramatization of H. G. Wells's *War of the Worlds*. In that broadcast a supposed program of dance music was repeatedly interrupted by reports of explosions on the planet Mars and meteors landing on Earth, reassurances that there was nothing to fear, and finally the story of a monstrous Martian machine emanating from one of the fallen meteors and destroying a platoon of soldiers at Grovers Mill, New Jersey. Many people who were not aware that what they were hearing was simply a radio play thought there really was an invasion from Mars and panicked. Highways leading away from the Grovers Mill area were congested with traffic. Many other people were uncertain. They didn't want to be captured by the Martians, nor did they want to act foolishly if there really was no crisis. Because there was a threat but the threat was ambiguous, people found themselves in a very stressful situation. They were frightened and in conflict about what to do. Some coped with the stress by trying to escape, others became immobilized, and others acted rationally to find out what was really happening. In his thorough investigation, Cantril found that ambiguous threat can be more stressful than a known emergency.

More recent studies of behavior in crisis situations by Latané and Darley (1970) also show that there can be tremendous stress in ambiguous situations. In one of their studies, subjects were placed in a room which began to fill with smoke. In another study a person in a discussion began to have an epileptic seizure. In both of these situations subjects experienced high physiological arousal and felt severely stressed. They were mobilized to take adaptive action, but the uncertainty of what action to take created even more stress. They didn't want to remain in a burning building or ignore a person in need of help, but they didn't want to panic inappropriately or appear to be fearful, gullible, or inept. They were faced with a serious conflict that had to be resolved in seconds. It was unmistakably stressful.

Threats to Self-Esteem and Integrity

As indicated by the study just discussed, ambiguity is stressful, even when there is no threat to physical well-being, because people don't want to make fools of themselves. They don't want to make choices or take actions that make them feel stupid, weak, or immoral. Such feelings are threats to one's integrity that can create just as much stress and anxiety as do threats to physical well-being.

Elvis Presley faced the most stressful moments of his life just after Priscilla left him to live with Mike Stone. Here his physical well-being was not being threatened. Rather, Elvis was having to face his own failure in marriage, the choices he had made in the past that had undermined his relationship with Priscilla, and the fact that people would know that the wife of the world's greatest entertainer had left him for a struggling karate instructor. He also had to face up to the foolishness and immorality of his ordering Mike Stone's murder and his inability to even think of a more constructive way of responding to the loss of his wife. This threat to his self-esteem created as much stress as his problems with diet and drugs did.

In general, then, stress is produced whenever one's self-esteem is threatened. Threats to self-esteem can be experienced through any of the processes of self-conception we discussed in Chapter 3. For example, other people's negative evaluations can be very threatening and stressful. Certainly minority groups who have been stereotyped negatively and treated unjustly by the majority have found these stereotypes and inequities extremely stressful. Similarly, unfavorable social comparisons, based on looks or money or education, are stressful. An inability to meet the standards of a role model is also stressful. Often, however, as Elvis Presley's case illustrates, it is our own behavior, when we feel it to be inconsistent with our standards of competence or morality, that most threatens our self-esteem and integrity. Such psychological threats, like threats to our physical well-being, lead to efforts to overcome the threats. People may try to attack those who threaten them or escape from threatening situations, or they may attempt to justify their own behavior.

A fascinating example of self-justification designed to reduce psychological threat is found in the study *When Prophecy Fails*. In this book, Festinger, Reicken, and Schachter (1956) discuss what happened to a group of people who predicted the end of the world. They had received secret messages, they believed, from a planet called Clarion, saying that the middle of the United States would be flooded but that they would be rescued just before the disaster by extraterrestrial beings who would take them to safety on Clarion. These people were extremely serious about their beliefs. Realizing that they had no need for earthly possessions or material comforts, they had quit their jobs and given away their belongings. What was interesting was that they had no need to defend themselves to other people. Their belief system was firm, and they took appropriate action based on their beliefs; they were not concerned about the possibility of being mistaken. They felt no need to persuade others that they were correct. The news media had heard about their group and wanted to interview them, but the group shunned all publicity.

When the day of the expected cataclysm came and went and nothing had happened, the group's beliefs were threatened by the failure of their clear prediction. Great stress was experienced by these people who had sacrificed everything for their beliefs. To admit that the beliefs were wrong would have been to admit utter stupidity, perhaps even insanity. In order to protect their integrity, the members of this

Persuading another person that we are correct can reduce threats to our self-esteem.

Christa Armstrong, Photo Researchers, Inc.

group had to maintain their faith even though it had been disconfirmed. As is often the case with such groups, the problem was partially resolved when they received other "messages" from outer space providing a rationalization of the failure of the prophecy. The new explanation was that the faith of the group had actually caused the world to be saved.

As the group members latched onto this explanation, their attitude toward outsiders changed. They welcomed curious bystanders into their homes, contacted the news media to explain what had happened, and took every opportunity to talk to people about their group and recent events. In short, they began proselytizing, trying to persuade others of the validity of their beliefs and hence of their earlier actions. If they could convince others, they would be able to bolster their own shaky confidence and protect their self-esteem. If others accepted their beliefs, they could be more certain that those beliefs were correct and that their actions had not been foolish. The proselytizing represented, then, a mobilization of their resources in an effort to protect their self-esteem and ease the threat to their integrity that the failed prophecy presented.

While this is an extreme example, the general point has been well established in many other studies. When people's integrity is threatened, they try desperately to protect and defend themselves—the psychological self as much as the physical self. Sometimes, however, these efforts to establish or maintain positive self-esteem are overwhelmed. Sometimes people can't overcome the feeling that they are incompetent, that they are failures, that they can't succeed, that they've acted immorally, or that they've wasted their lives. They may accept the negative judgments of others or condemn themselves. When people's resources are not sufficient to meet threats to their self-esteem, they may become intensely anxious or may have feelings of hopelessness, helplessness, and despair. These negative and debilitating feelings can lead to increasingly serious psychological states. (In Chapter 6 we will look at the ways that people try to manage stress and the consequences of failing to do so.)

REVIEW QUESTIONS

1. Individuals respond both physiologically and psychologically to the threats and demands of the environment. The pattern of physiological and psychological reactions is known as _____, while the external threats and demands are called _____.
2. One common stressful reaction that occurs when our actions toward a goal are blocked is _____.
3. Two hypothesized responses to frustration are _____ and _____.
4. The kind of conflict that occurs when our goals contain both positive and negative aspects is called _____-_____ conflict.
5. In an approach-avoidance conflict as one gets closer to the goal the avoidance tendency increases in strength _____ relative to the approach tendency.
6. *Immediately* following a decision people often feel more strongly attracted to the alternative that was not chosen. This "regret phase" is best explained by _____ theory.
7. Hans Selye, in his classic book *The Stress of Life,* explains the individual's response to stress in terms of the General Adaptation Syndrome. The three stages of the G.A.S. are _____, _____, and _____.

RESPONDING TO STRESS

Stress is everywhere in today's world. We all have to face small frustrations in daily living, we must make decisions involving considerable conflict at many points in our lives, and there are many ways that our self-esteem is threatened. Threats to our physical well-being may seem relatively remote to many of us, but violence seems to be increasing in our society, and all of us are affected by it, directly or indirectly. Women's freedom of behavior is curtailed by the threat of rape; children are abducted on their way home from school; and few of us feel safe taking a midnight stroll alone any more. Some people feel the threat of nuclear holocaust hanging over them, and physicians and educators have recently discussed intense "nuclear fears" in children. Many people channel a great deal of their energy and behavior into minimizing these threats and pressures in the modern world, consciously and unconsciously, in thought and in action. Many of these methods are helpful and do not interfere with healthy personal adjustment; but most of them can be abused if stress increases. In this section we will consider some of the most common responses to stress.

Appraising Threats

One of the most important aspects of the way people deal with potentially threatening situations is their perceptions or appraisals of them in the first place (Lazarus, 1982). Some people experience a great deal of stress—and its consequences—because they *perceive* events in their environment to be threatening. Others are relatively relaxed and optimistic about the same events simply because they appraise them to be nonthreatening. For example, some people worried that the falling of the Skylab satellite was a serious threat to their safety because they felt it had a good chance of landing on them. Others blithely reassured themselves that such an event was utterly unlikely. Some people perceive others' achievements and the praise they receive as threats; others do not. Some people perceive a close friend's irritation or anger as a threat to the relationship; others do not. Some people view failures as forecasting doom; others do not. The list is endless. The point is that people vary tremendously in their perceptions or appraisals of what is threatening. Those who do perceive threat will feel stressed. It's worth remembering that you have some choice in how you appraise situations. Are there times when you unnecessarily perceive them to be threatening?

In addition to differing in how threatening they perceive various situations to be, people also differ markedly in their feelings about their capacity to control threatening situations. Some people feel that they are in control of their own destinies. Their general expectancy is that what happens to them and what they achieve in life are due to their own abilities, attitudes, and actions. In contrast, other people see their lives as being beyond their own control and believe that what happens to them is up to luck or fate. These two types of people are said to perceive either an *internal* or *external* "locus of control" (Rotter, 1966; Phares, 1976).

The difference in perceived locus of control is important for personal adjustment to the world. People who believe they can control events in their environment will respond to stress quite differently from those who believe the opposite. The major difference can be summed up in the words of the Avis car-rental commercial, "We try harder." "Internals" believe their efforts make a difference when they are facing a difficult situation, so they try to cope with it. They take whatever action seems appropriate. Externals believe their efforts won't make a difference, so naturally they don't attempt to cope with threatening situations.

Elvis Presley developed a strong internal orientation when his career first soared to success. He saw that he could have a real impact on his audiences, and he tried hard to please them. At this early point in his career Elvis was an extremely dynamic person. This changed in later years, as Elvis's locus of control became more external. Elvis learned that his efforts in fact made little difference. His fans loved him no matter what he did. Most people who feel externally controlled believe there is little they can do to gain success. Elvis discovered the opposite: No matter what he did or didn't do, he was successful. Elvis also learned that he couldn't escape from his success and popularity. He was a prisoner of it. He couldn't leave his estates without a huge entourage to protect him from adoring fans. He also couldn't escape from the boredom his confinement created. And there was nothing he could do to save his marriage and get Priscilla back. His old perception of internal control may have directed him to think about killing Mike Stone, but as the futility of that became apparent to Elvis, he became more and more aware that a good many of his life situations lay beyond his personal control. This increasingly external perspective led to a lack of active engagement with living and Elvis's eventual downfall. Elvis had lost the ability to handle stress by taking action.

Taking Action

When people are faced with a threatening situation or a demanding environment, they may try to take action to cope with the threat or demand. If they do take action, it may be carefully planned and prepared, or it may be taken hastily with little deliberation. Usually the actions that people take fall into one of two broad categories, *fight* or *flight*—that is, acting against the threat to overcome or deflect it, or trying to escape. Sometimes, however, no action can be taken. Then people simply have to await their fate. Let's consider these various forms of response to stress.

PLANNING AND PREPARING. People are usually better able to cope with stress effectively if they've had time to plan and prepare for it (Janis & Mann, 1977). They are least likely to panic if they have taken the time to evaluate the alternatives for dealing with possible threat. The actions that people plan vary tremendously. Elvis Presley was preoccupied with threat and took elaborate measures to protect himself from people who might want to harm him or might accidentally injure him in uncontrolled expressions of affection. He had a number of bodyguards, including Red West, and always carried a small pistol in one of his boots when he performed on stage. Few of us face Elvis's problems of self-protection, but most people have good locks on their doors, and most families have insurance plans to prevent financial disaster should they encounter serious illness or death.

COUNTERACTION. With or without planning, we often try to overcome, defeat, or neutralize the people, objects, or events that threaten us. There are many ways we do this, ranging from overt aggressive attack to calm persuasion. If your roommate is bothering you with loud music, you can try to get him or her to turn it down or turn it down yourself. If an exam is pending, you can "attack" it by studying hard. If people you are working with fail to meet their obligations, you can confront them with your concerns. There are many ways of taking counteraction, some effective and some ineffective, but, in general, directly dealing with the source of the problem and trying to improve the situation is the best way of dealing with stress.

AVOIDANCE. Another way of coping with threatening situations is to try to escape from them. We can see this response in people fleeing from New Jersey during the *War of the Worlds* panic in 1938. Students sometimes avoid threatening experiences such as writing term papers by procrastinating. (Then they may have to avoid further crises by not mentioning their grades to their parents.)

Sometimes people go beyond mere procrastination and avoid challenging situations altogether. Sometimes this way of coping with stress is appropriate in a situation. If you realistically know you have little chance of winning a tennis match or the heart of that dream person sitting across the aisle from you in your psychology class, there's not much point in competing, although you might profit from the experience and the practice in going after what you want. It may be better to avoid or forget such efforts. But we should be careful not to avoid too much. Fear of failure or embarrassment keeps us from doing a great deal that might expand and enrich our lives. This includes listening to new kinds of music, taking difficult courses, trying to get to know people from different backgrounds, and attempting to enjoy new exercises and games.

WAITING AND "CARRYING ON." Sometimes there's nothing we can do about a threat. Nei-

ther fight nor flight will work. During the Three Mile Island nuclear accident in 1979, there was nothing most citizens could do to counteract or escape from possible nuclear disaster. If it was to come, it would come, that's all. In other instances people put a great deal of effort into coping, but then reach a point where no further action is possible. Once you've studied hard for an important exam and taken it, you just have to wait and see if you've done well. During these agonizing periods of waiting for the outcome of events, the adaptiveness of your behavior can still vary tremendously. Some people are able to carry on with normal activities that are productive and enjoyable; others are nearly incapacitated. Being able to carry on under stressful and uncertain conditions is a skill well worth cultivating.

RELATING TO OTHERS. One common helpful response to being in a stressful situation that you can neither fight nor avoid is to affiliate and interact with others. People tend to cluster up with friends and acquaintances when they first arrive at parties, for instance. Doing this allows you to talk to other people and appraise the threat and takes your mind off the fact that you're in danger.

This tendency to seek out others when we're anxious about a threat has been demonstrated in research on anxiety and affiliation (Schachter, 1959). Subjects told to expect painful electric shocks in an experiment became highly anxious and had a great desire to wait with others for the experiment to begin. Subjects who weren't threatened with pain were happy to wait in rooms by themselves. Being with others seemed to soothe the highly anxious subjects and give them a clearer idea of how to respond to the threatening situation.

A surprising but consistent finding from this research was that the tendency to affiliate with others when anxious was strong for subjects who were eldest children or only children. Subjects who had siblings and weren't first-borns didn't show this tendency. It seems that eldest and only children are more accustomed to having anxiety relieved in the presence of others, possibly because parents tend to be highly sensitive and attentive to the fears of their first-born and somewhat more casual with later-born offspring. Thus, as a result of parental treatment, eldest and only children have learned that affiliating with others and talking over their fears can be helpful in reducing stress and anxiety.

Using Drugs

Elvis Presley seldom took action in attempting to cope with stress. To some extent he did try to relate to others, surrounding himself with friends and hangers-on. But these relations were neither open, intimate, nor fulfilling. Consequently, Elvis turned to drugs. This was not a conscious choice, but something Elvis fell into gradually. At first he just used amphetamines to overcome exhaustion and boredom, but then his dependence became more general. It is interesting, however, that he didn't abuse alcohol, the most commonly abused drug in the United States today.

Many people in our society use a wide variety of chemical substances to relieve feelings of anxiety and stress or to gain positive feelings of euphoria or relaxation. Many of these drugs are used to excess or to the point where a dependence on them develops. Such dependence can be purely psychological, where the person experiences a strong need for the drug, or physiological, where the drug must be present in the body for the body to function. Drug dependencies can cause people to become so consumed with using and obtaining the drug that other aspects of their lives are not adequately managed.

ALCOHOL. One of the most habitually used drugs in our society is alcohol. It is a legal and easily obtained drug with tension-reducing properties that make it very tempting for many people. Unfortunately alcohol is often abused, and the social costs due to alcoholism are astounding. Benglesdorf (1970, p. 7) has noted that alcohol abuse "has killed more people, sent more victims to hospitals, generated more police arrests, broken up more marriages and homes, and cost industry more money than has the abuse" of all other drugs combined.

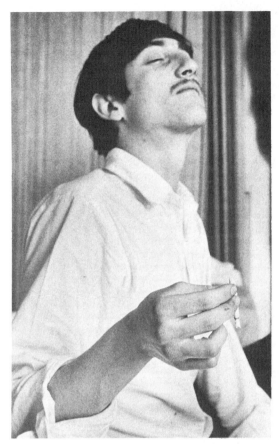

Using drugs is a commonly abused method of reducing stress.

Charles Gatewood.

Alcohol abuse is a serious problem for people when it impairs their performance at school or work, their relationships with others, and their own self-concepts. There are many warning signs of alcoholism, including increased desire for and consumption of beer, wine, and/or hard liquor; needing to drink more to feel the pleasurable effects of the drug; drinking in a fixed pattern; morning drinking; and the need to have a drink before facing a stressful event. Of the nearly 50 percent of Americans who drink at some time, approximately 10 to 15 percent are alcoholics in that their drinking impairs effective functioning.

Interestingly enough, recent studies indicate that occasional drinking, not more than one or two drinks a day, is positively related to health. People who drink moderately have significantly less heart disease than people who are teetotalers. Alcohol in moderate doses may be directly beneficial to the circulatory system, in addition to temporarily reducing tension and social inhibition. The problem is that people with a tendency toward alcoholism may not be aware of it, and one or two drinks a day could become far more.

Using alcohol is clearly a response to anxiety that can be beneficial or harmful depending on degree. There is no question, however, that alcoholism takes hold gradually and is an extraordinarily serious disorder. Using alcohol in excess is dangerous to your health.

MARIJUANA. Other than alcohol, the drug perhaps most commonly used in the United States today, especially by young people, is marijuana. Possession of marijuana is still illegal in most states, although laws pertaining to its use are being relaxed in many areas. Marijuana is a tremendously controversial drug. It doesn't cause physical addiction, and no clear long-term dangers from its use have been documented. On the other hand, it is psychoactive, that is, it affects psychological processes and like any other such drug can produce poor judgment and slowed coordination. Driving, for example, can be impaired by marijuana use (Klonoff, 1974). However, it's difficult to maintain that marijuana is as much of a health problem as alcohol is.

HEROIN. Much of the controversy over marijuana relates to the assertion, which is false, that its use leads to heroin addiction. Heroin is a much more dangerous drug that produces physiological dependence and painful, frightening withdrawal symptoms. Heroin users develop tolerance to the drug and so need stronger and stronger doses to get positive psychological effects or to maintain normal bodily functioning. Withdrawal symptoms are temporary physiological and psychological disturbances that result when a person who is physiologically dependent on a drug is deprived of it. Of course people can be psychologically dependent on a drug and feel an urgent need to take it, even if they are not physiologically dependent on it. With respect to heroin, people who must maintain their addiction often completely disregard other requirements of living and may end up participating in crime to finance their very expensive "habit."

AMPHETAMINES, BARBITURATES, AND TRANQUILIZERS. Other widely abused drugs include amphetamines, barbiturates, and tranquilizers. These are the drugs on which Elvis Presley developed dependency and which contributed in large measure to his early death.

Amphetamines ("uppers") are often used as "pep pills" by college students when studying for tests and are apparently used by entertainers to cope with exhausting schedules and to enhance their performances. Uppers were the first drugs Elvis used. Common varieties of amphetamines include Benzedrine, Methedrine ("speed"), and Dexedrine. These drugs cause no physical dependence, but they can produce uncontrolled and violent behavior if they are used in excess. They produce tolerance and are exceedingly dangerous, sometimes lethal.

Barbiturates ("downers") are freuqently used as sleeping pills. Common varieties include Nembutal, Seconal, and chloral hydrate. These drugs are physically addicting and produce highly dangerous withdrawal symptoms. Stopping these drugs "cold turkey" can be fatal.

Another group of depressants is tranquilizers, or antianxiety drugs, such as Valium, Librium, and Thorazine. In recent years they have been used widely. Current research suggests that while they are not as dangerous as barbiturates, they can produce psychological dependence and withdrawal symptoms.

The actress Marilyn Monroe was a well-known person who had serious difficulties with the barbiturate Nembutal. She developed a tolerance to it, took higher and higher dosages, and showed many of the common symptoms of barbiturate abuse. These included irritability, reduced effectiveness, and depression. The

TABLE 5.1

Commonly Abused Drugs

DRUG	HOW TAKEN	MEDICAL USE	SHORT-TERM EFFECTS	EFFECTS OF PROLONGED USE
Sedatives				
Alcohol	Drinks	Rarely used to reduce tension	Relaxation, impairment of judgment, uninhibited emotions	Damage to liver and brain, hallucinations, other toxic psychotic symptoms
Barbiturate	Pills, injections	Sleeping pills, to reduce pain or tension	Relaxation, anxiety reduction, pain reduction	Addiction, severe withdrawal symptoms, toxic psychosis
Stimulants				
Caffeine	Coffee, Tea, Colas, No-Doz	Rarely for comas	Increased alertness, jitteriness, reduced fatigue	Sleeping problems, restlessness
Nicotine	Tobacco	None	Relaxation for regular users, distraction, satisfaction of physical need	Smoker's cough, cancer, heart and circulatory diseases
Amphetamines	Pills, injections	Treatment of obesity, depression, fatigue	Increased alertness, reduced tiredness, appetite loss, sleeping problems, euphoria	Loss of appetite, weight, irritability, restlessness, toxic psychosis
Cocaine	Snorted, injected	Local anesthesia	Euphoria, alertness, depression on withdrawal	Depression, irritability
Narcotics				
Heroin, opium, codeine, demeral, morphine	Pills, injections, smoking	Treating severe pain, diarrhea, cough	Euphoria, pain relief, relaxation, poor judgment and coordination	Physical addiction, painful withdrawal symptoms, constipation, appetite loss, impotence, sterility
Hallucinogens				
LSD, peyote, psyocybin, mescaline, STP, angel dust (PCP), MDA	Pills, injections, snorted, eaten	None	Increased sensory awareness, hallucinations, anxiety, nausea	Usually none—may intensify psychological problems
Marijuana				
	Usually smoked	Treating high blood pressure, headaches, tension, glaucoma	Relaxation, sometimes euphoria, distorted perception of time, impaired judgment, coordination	Usually none

REVIEW QUESTIONS

8. Much of the variability in the way people respond to stressors can be explained by individual _____ of potentially threatening events.

9. A personality characteristic that may influence the way an individual perceives and responds to threatening situations is the tendency to view life's events as either due to one's efforts and abilities or a matter of chance or fate. Rotter calls this personality characteristic _____ of _____ .

10. People who respond to stressful life events by exerting more effort are likely to have an _____ locus of control.

11. T or F: When given the opportunity, people in stressful situations are more likely to affiliate with others. This tendency does not hold, however, for the oldest child or the only child in a family.

12. An increasingly frequent response to stressful life situations is the use of drugs. Match the drug to its description.

    a. marijuana
    b. alcohol
    c. barbiturates
    d. tranquilizers
    e. heroin
    f. amphetamines

    _____ So called "pep pills"; not physiologically addicting, but can produce violent behaviors in large doses (e.g., Benzedrine, Dexedrine)

    _____ Highly physiologically addicting drugs; increasing tolerance requires larger and larger dosages often resulting in overdoses (e.g., Nembutal, Seconal)

    _____ Depressants that are frequently prescribed for anxiety; these drugs can produce psychological dependence and withdrawal symptoms (e.g., Valium, Librium)

    _____ Most frequently used drug in our society; approximately 10 percent to 15 percent of the users of this drug are physiologically or psychologically addicted

severe depression caused by these and other drugs became her most serious problem in later years. An overdose can be lethal, and one eventually killed her.

The deaths of Elvis Presley, John Belushi, and Marilyn Monroe at early ages illustrate the fact that powerful drugs used in excess are dangerous and that drug dependence is itself a severe stress that should be avoided or counteracted as quickly as possible.

Psychological Defenses

Many people use drugs to reduce the unpleasant symptoms of anxiety and stress. All of us, however, use psychological defense mechanisms for this purpose. These mechanisms represent extremely clever operations of the ego to ward off feelings of fear, guilt, conflict, frustration, and loss of control. Like drugs, defense mechanisms can be abused, but they are absolutely necessary for dealing with the stress of living today. Well-adjusted people use them frequently and regularly, but do not let them dominate their behavior, perceptions, or feelings. Ego-defenses can safely be used to manage stress and anxiety, but you should remain aware of how they work, so that *they* do not manage *you* in maladaptive ways.

The ego-defense mechanisms were first described by Sigmund Freud. His daughter, Anna Freud (1946), has written the most influential account of how they actually work. For convenience, we will organize them into three categories: the behavior-channeling defenses, the primary reality-distorting defenses, and the secondary reality-distorting defenses.

BEHAVIOR-CHANNELING DEFENSES. The three behavior-channeling defense mechanisms are **identification, displacement,** and **sublimation.**

Identification (discussed in Chapter 2) involves emulating or imitating another person—usually a parent, an admired friend, an older person in one's profession, or a leader in a group—and trying to be as much like that person as possible. Identification is important in giving us a clear idea of how to behave in various situations; it thus relieves us of much anxiety, conflict, and confusion. Instead of wallowing in uncertainty, we follow the example of a trusted other. Elvis Presley never had a person with whom he could identify. He adopted many of his mother's values for a time, but never had a satisfactory model for living. His initial independence from traditional ways of doing things in music was a sign of his originality and directly responsible for his success, but a similar independence in style of living left him without long-term goals and direction. Freud regarded identification as one of the healthy defense mechanisms, but there are some pathological instances of it. Inmates in concentration camps have sometimes identified with guards in order to resolve insecurities and conflicts about how to survive. This action is known as "identification with the aggressor" (Bettelheim, 1958).

Displacement is most often used to direct aggression. Consider an employee who is humiliated by her boss in front of other employees or a student who is jilted by his girlfriend. These frustrating circumstances arouse anger and aggressive feelings. But aggressive behavior toward the boss or the girlfriend would be foolhardy: The woman wants to keep her job, and the man wants to keep his relationship. Instead these two injured parties would be likely to redirect, or displace, their anger onto another person or object against whom it's safe to express hostility. The humiliated employee may yell at other drivers on her way home from work, and the jilted student may punch the

wall. Such displacement reduces fear of losing control and fear of punishment or retaliation. Displacement most commonly occurs because of the realization of the dangers of directing anger toward the person who aroused it; but it can also occur when moral restraints prevent the expression of aggression. A father may be furious with his children for breaking a window but feel that it's not right to express his aggressive feelings toward them. He could avoid stressful guilt feelings by displacing his anger. In this case, the family dog may be in for trouble.

The third of this group of ego-defenses is *sublimation,* the major technique a person uses to direct sexual and aggressive urges into socially acceptable behavior. Through sublimation one minimizes anxiety by performing behavior that is socially approved, that will provide some satisfaction of personal needs and impulses, and that is effective in reality. Elvis Presley channeled his energies into performing in order to get women's attention and adulation, as well as to gain financial security. Sublimation is the defense mechanism that usually contributes most positively to an individual's adjustment. It produces effective, socially useful behavior that maintains inner peace and harmony.

These three behavior-channeling defenses are very important means of resolving fears, and they make, in most instances, a positive contribution to personal adjustment. Sublimation nearly always leads to adaptive and productive behavior. Identification can have positive or negative consequences, depending on the person chosen to identify with; if the person is successful and effective by prevailing social standards, then identification with that person will be helpful to one's adjustment to social realities. Displacement is highly tuned to reality and keeps a person out of trouble with those that might harm him or her. However, it may lead to destructive action against others who are powerless and in this way have negative consequences for society as a whole. Overall, however, these defenses usually help us to act effectively. The same cannot be said for the reality distorting defenses.

COPING MECHANISMS VS. DEFENSE MECHANISMS

We all use defense mechanisms to cope with stress. However, we can adjust much more effectively if we try to use the conscious coping mechanisms that are close relatives to the unconscious, more rigid defenses. The lists below show some of the major defense mechanisms and their closely related coping counterparts (after Kroeber, 1963).

Defense Mechanism	Coping Mechanism
Depression—totally blocking out unconscious drives	Suppression—acknowledging drives but holding them in check until it is appropriate to express them
Denial—blocking awareness of dangerous threats	Concentration—keeping attention on tasks despite recognition of dangers
Projection—attributing one's own undesirable characteristics to others	Empathy—feeling how others really feel, and seeing them as they are
Regression—unconsciously returning to infantile forms of behavior	Playfulness—being joyful, childlike, and impractical, while being aware of real problems
Reaction formation—expressing the opposite of one's true unconscious feelings	Substitution—consciously acting in a constructive manner when urges to behave in a negative manner are experienced

PRIMARY REALITY-DISTORTING DEFENSES. One way people minimize anxiety is simply by pushing threatening concerns and the anxiety they cause out of conscious awareness. The most primitive and basic defense mechanisms perform these tasks. **Repression** and **denial** operate on an almost totally unconscious level, seriously distorting both internal and external reality. Repression operates to keep anxiety-producing impulses and guilt feelings out of a person's awareness. Denial operates to ignore or distort reality so that the person is not made anxious by external threats.

Repression usually operates to control sexual impulses and aggression. It does so when we feel guilty about these feelings or worry that we're losing control of our feelings and impulses. When we say that sexual impulses are repressed, we mean that they are never admitted into a person's awareness. Repression keeps them in the unconscious. Similarly, aggressive feelings that people could never admit, such as hostility toward their parents, may be repressed. In addition to repressing basic impulses, people can also repress guilt feelings or feelings of shame. These unpleasant, anxiety-provoking feelings are simply denied awareness. In short, as a result of repression, people are not overwhelmed by powerful and frightening impulses on the one hand or punishing and debilitating guilt feelings on the other. They are left free to cope with the demands of reality.

Coping with reality is not always so appealing either, especially when there are threatening circumstances to be handled. This is when the defense mechanism of denial comes into play. People often simply deny that there is any danger. They ignore warnings and tell themselves that nothing is wrong. One common example of this is parents denying that their children are having learning or emotional difficulties, when it is quite clear that something is wrong and needs correcting. Denying unpleasant facts can mean that harmful behaviors or situations are perpetuated and problems that could be solved are left unattended.

Elvis Presley often used denial, and his misuse of it contributed to his unhappiness and psychological problems. His primary denial was not recognizing that his drug habits were getting out of control and that his life as a whole was coming undone. He also failed to recognize clear signs that Priscilla was unhappy in a marriage where Elvis traveled constantly and that she wouldn't keep up such a life for very long.

SECONDARY REALITY-DISTORTING DEFENSES. Repression and denial push out of consciousness real feelings and real dangers. But the repressed feelings put pressure on the ego-defenses, and sometimes additional techniques come into play to further remove threatening feelings from consciousness. These are the secondary defense mechanisms, so called because they usually do the follow-up work of repression or denial (White, 1964).

Projection is one of the most common defense mechanisms. It involves assigning to others traits, impulses, or attitudes that you feel in yourself but can't acknowledge. Projection presupposes repression, since awareness of the characteristic is first repressed and then projected onto others. A person who feels sexually attracted to someone may project that attraction onto the other person and believe that the other person is seducing him or her. People very often project their own feelings of selfishness or hostility onto others. Thus we see what we think are the worst things about ourselves in other people. The reality-distorting nature of this defense is obvious. A person perceives characteristics in others that simply aren't there. While true feelings and tendencies in the self are not admitted, the anxiety they would cause if they were admitted is avoided.

Another secondary defense mechanism is **reaction formation.** In this case a person who is afraid to admit a certain feeling or attitude about someone else or a particular situation adopts just the opposite attitude as a way of keeping the true attitude from rising to his or her consciousness and avoiding the anxiety that it would cause. For example, maybe someone you see a lot of really bores you, or you feel envious or resentful of that person, and instead of admitting your true feeling you tell yourself what great friends the two of you are. Usually

TABLE 5.2

The Ego-Defense Mechanisms

BEHAVIOR CHANNELING DEFENSES	
Identification:	Trying to be like an admired or powerful other
Displacement:	Aggressing against someone other than the person or thing that has caused frustration
Sublimation:	Channeling sexual or aggressive impulses into socially acceptable behavior
PRIMARY REALITY DISTORTING DEFENSES	
Repression:	Blocking out of consciousness unacceptable or frightening impulses
Denial:	Blocking threatening external objects or events out of consciousness
SECONDARY REALITY DISTORTING DEFENSES	
Projection:	Attributing unacceptable impulses in oneself to other people
Reaction formation:	Expressing feelings or behaving in ways that are opposite to our unconscious impulses
Rationalization:	Offering socially acceptable explanations for behavior that satisfies our impulses
OTHER DEFENSE MECHANISMS	
Intellectualization:	Regarding threatening events or actions in a detached, analytical manner
Regression:	Responding to threat or stress by behaving in an infantile or juvenile manner

the feeling or attitude expressed through reaction formation seems rigid and exaggerated: The person may overdo the act. Thus a person who is romantically and sexually attracted to people of the same sex may become outspokenly antihomosexual. A person who feels drawn toward lurid sexual material may react against those tendencies and become a crusader against pornography.

Rationalization is another extremely common defense mechanism. In this case a person behaves according to his or her impulses but doesn't admit the real reasons. Instead the person justifies or rationalizes the action by offering some socially acceptable reason for doing it. People who are cruel to their children justify their behavior by saying they are only trying to help the child learn right from wrong. People often rationalize selfishness by saying they think needy people should be taught self-reliance. Hungry people may justify overindulging themselves at fast food restaurants by believing the ad that says "You deserve a break today."

OTHER DEFENSE MECHANISMS.   Other defense mechanisms have been discussed by Freud and others from time to time. We believe the ones discussed above are the most important. Others can be mentioned briefly.

Intellectualization occurs when people consider a fear-, guilt-, or grief-producing event or behavior in very cold, detached, and analytical terms, acting as if it didn't really upset them. They distance themselves psychologically from the disturbing emotions. **Regression** occurs when people feel anxious and uncertain and revert to a form of behavior that brought them security in childhood. Becoming very dependent and childlike in the face of danger is a form of regression.

DEFENSE MECHANISMS AND PERSONAL ADJUSTMENT.   In their pure form, defense mechanisms operate unconsciously, but people can also reduce anxiety by using conscious variants of the defenses, which involve much less actual distortion of reality (see Kroeber, 1963). For ex-

ample people can consciously suppress undesirable impulses, rather than unconsciously repress them. Similarly, they can consciously decide to overcompensate for aggressive feelings by being polite and warm without engaging in an unconscious reaction formation. To the extent that defenses involve unconscious denials and falsifications of reality and inner emotions, it seems that they impede adjustment and personal growth. At the same time, they do provide needed relief. On the whole, it seems that the conscious variants of the defenses, often called **coping mechanisms,** offer the best solution. They interfere less with reality and self-knowledge and can be used more flexibly than the rather rigid defense mechanisms. The totally unconscious defenses offer stronger protection against anxiety, but they produce more distortion and more rigidity.

REVIEW QUESTIONS

13. T or F: Psychological defense mechanisms are used regularly by well-adjusted people to counteract stress and anxiety.

14. One of the behavior channeling defense mechanisms whereby individuals redirect the motivating energy associated with sexual and aggressive impulses into more socially acceptable activities is known as _____ .

15. Primary reality distorting defense mechanisms attempt to deal with stress and anxiety by preventing these feelings from entering conscious awareness. Two examples mentioned in this section are _____ and _____ .

16. Denying acceptance of an unacceptable impulse by giving expression to its opposite is called _____ _____ .

17. Conscious strategies, related to defense mechanisms but allowing for less distortion of reality and greater cognitive flexibility, are called _____ _____ .

Conscious and unconscious defenses can have a strong influence on a person's overall pattern of behavior. Some people develop a set of defenses into a "defensive organization" that has a pervasive effect on how they act (White, 1964). Elvis Presley's entourage of bodyguards and yes-men was an external reflection of the psychological defensive organization he developed as a wall between himself and stressful realities. A boy who was taught a a young child that sexual curiosity and sexual play are base and immoral may avoid anything that involves sex, project sexuality onto others, and suppress his own sexual strivings. He may feel very uneasy about any affectionate feelings that seemed tinged with sexual desire and may find security only by rigidly avoiding even the most innocent sexual behavior. A college student who is terrified of academic failure may throw all her energies into achievement, repress any resentments against pressures to excel, and project competitive behavior onto others. She may even rationalize cheating on exams.

In the last two examples the individuals involved develop a pattern of traits that protect them from feelings of anxiety and guilt. Such patterns are self-sustaining precisely because they are effective in reducing these feelings. Is there any reason to regard such defensive organizations as maladaptive? Perhaps not. We all have defensive patterns of behavior to some extent, and most people function perfectly well with their little rigidities, compulsions, fears, drives, and strivings. They are certainly human, they are sometimes endearing, and they give us individuality and identity. On the other hand, too large a part of our energies can be given over to defensive behaviors. To satisfy defensive needs, one person may be consumed with obtaining affection and approval, another may be constantly focused on power issues, and another may always be concerned with rules, regulations, and other safety structures. A major cost of these defensive behaviors can be the inhibition or repression of true feelings and distortion of reality. Fatigue, chronic feelings of dissatisfaction, and insomnia can also result (White, 1964). Still, many people seem locked into these behavior patterns until there is a change for the better initiated by dissatisfaction and desire for a better life, or a change for the worse when the inability to effectively manage increasing anxiety leads to a psychological disorder. In Chapter 6 we will consider the psychological disorders that can result from overloads of stress and anxiety or from other disturbances and problems in living.

SUMMARY

1. Stress is a pattern of psychological and physiological reactions to demands in the environment that threaten our well-being, self-esteem, or integrity and that cause us to devote many of our resources to coping with the danger and defending ourselves.

2. Stress has many sources, including complex interpersonal relations, the pressures involved in making a living, difficult decisions, and many other kinds of demanding realities in our modern world.

3. Frustration stemming from various drives being thwarted produces stress and can cause aggressive or infantile responses in us.

4. Conflict and decision making cause stress when we have to choose between one kind of satisfaction and another. Conflict situations can involve tendencies to approach, to avoid, or both. Most situations involve double approach-avoidance conflicts in which people must choose between two alternatives that each have positive and negative attributes.

5. Decision making usually has three stages: the predecision stage, the actual decision, and the postdecision stage. People seem to strive to keep their options open during the predecision stage by seeing their alternatives as more and more equal as the time of decision draws closer. After the decision is made, there is often a period of regret, when people feel attracted to the alternative they have foregone. This regret is followed by dissonance reduction, when people accentuate the positive and deemphasize the negative aspects of the alternative they have chosen, convincing themselves of its superiority to other alternatives.

6. Other sources of stress include physical danger, ambiguous situations, and fears about being foolish, incompetent, or immoral.

7. Stress reactions include an initial period of alarm and mobilization of resources, resistance to the threat, and, if the threat isn't removed, exhaustion. In some extreme conditions, stress can lead to death.

8. People cope with stress in several ways. Sometimes we take action to overcome the threat or to escape it. This action may be planned or spontaneous. When we have attempted to anticipate difficult or threatening situations, we are usually able to deal with them better. Sometimes we affiliate with others when stress has made us anxious.

9. Another common response to stress is to take drugs. The most often used and abused drug is alcohol, and alcohol abuse involves high social costs. Other drugs such as heroin, marijuana, amphetamines, barbiturates, and tranquillizers can be abused as well.

10. Psychological defense mechanisms are another way people deal with stress. The behavior-channeling defense mechanisms are identification, displacement, and sublimation. The primary reality-distorting defense mechanisms are repression and denial. The secondary reality-distorting defense mechanisms are projection, reaction formation, and rationalization. Intellectualization and regression are other defense mechanisms.

11. People often develop psychological defensive organizations, which are complex sets of behaviors and attitudes used as protection against stressful situations and the anxiety they produce.

KEY TERMS

a. CONFLICT THEORY
b. COPING MECHANISMS
c. DENIAL
d. DISPLACEMENT
e. DISSONANCE THEORY
f. GENERAL ADAPTATION SYNDROME (GAS)
g. IDENTIFICATION
h. INTELLECTUALIZATION
i. PROJECTION
j. RATIONALIZATION
k. REACTANCE
l. REACTION FORMATION
m. REGRESSION
n. REPRESSION
o. SUBLIMATION

1. Conscious and deliberate efforts to manage stressful situations
2. An ego-defense mechanism in which anger felt toward a powerful person is expressed in the form of aggression against a person who cannot retaliate
3. The theory that prior to a decision the choices spread in value so that the person can make a decision between them

4. The theory that people are made uncomfortable by inconsistent cognitions and have a drive to reduce the discomfort by changing a cognition

5. The theory that whenever a freedom is threatened or taken away, people become more attached to that freedom and will strive to protect or regain it

6. In Selye's theory, the body's reaction to threat consisting of (a) an alarm stage marked by a mobilization of the body's resources, (b) a resistance stage marked by the organism's attempts to protect itself, and (c) an exhaustion stage in which the organism can no longer resist the threat

7. An ego-defense mechanism in which unwanted thoughts or impulses are driven from one's consciousness

8. An ego-defense mechanism in which an individual reacts to a stressful situation by reverting to childish or juvenile behavior

9. An ego-defense mechanism in which sexual and aggressive urges are channeled into socially acceptable behavior

10. An ego-defense mechanism by which people convince themselves and others that their behavior was performed for socially desirable reasons

11. An ego-defense mechanism in which anxiety is reduced by repressing one set of feelings and over-emphasizing an opposite set of feelings

12. An ego-defense mechanism in which an individual's unacceptable thoughts or impulses are attributed to others

13. An ego-defense mechanism in which the individual reacts to a stressful situation in a detached and analytical manner

14. An ego-defense mechanism in which an individual refuses to acknowledge an external source of threat

15. An ego-defense mechanism in which anxiety is reduced by identifying with a high status individual or institution

ANSWERS TO REVIEW QUESTIONS

1. Stress; stressors. **2.** Frustration. **3.** Aggression; regression. **4.** Approach-avoidance. **5.** Faster. **6.** Reactance. **7.** Alarm; resistance; exhaustion.

8. Perceptions or appraisals. **9.** Locus; control. **10.** Internal. **11.** False. **12.** f; c; d; b.

13. True. **14.** Sublimation. **15.** Regression; denial. **16.** Reaction formation. **17.** Coping mechanisms.

STRUGGLING FOR CONTROL

Agnes Carpenter discovered her daughter Karen lying unconscious on the floor of a closet in the Carpenter family's Downey, California, home. The rescue team found a weak pulse in Karen's extremely thin body, and one of the paramedics thought she had a good chance to survive. Karen had been struggling with anorexia nervosa for about nine years and had seemingly been making excellent progress. But she suffered a cardiac arrest and was pronounced dead less than an hour after her early morning collapse. Her father and brother, Harold and Richard Carpenter, were in Downey too. The close family group that had been important to Karen her whole life was together when Karen died, in February 1983 at the age of 32.

Karen Carpenter had been the lead singer and star of an enormously successful singing group, "The Carpenters," that she'd formed with her brother Richard. During the early and mid-1970s, the Carpenters sold 80 million records, including 17 million albums, won three Grammy awards and an Academy Award, and were acclaimed by President Richard Nixon as "young America at its very best." In the age of acid rock and rebellious, drug-addicted, and self-indulgent youth, the Carpenters were a clear counterpoint. Although they were highly successful, they were never fully accepted by the critics, most of whom thought the Carpenters' sound too simple, too sentimental, and too "establishment." In 1979 one publication called them "a bubblegum alternative to hard rock" (Simon, 1979). Despite the criticism, Karen and Richard did very well until 1975, when they had to cancel a large European tour because Karen was suffering from exhaustion. By then the demands of Karen's life had taken their toll. She was physically and mentally worn out.

Karen Carpenter was born in New Haven, Connecticut, in 1950. Richard was three years older. Their father was a printer and their mother a housewife. Both Carpenter children, particularly Richard, showed an early interest in music, which their parents strongly encouraged. While still in high school, Richard studied piano at Yale University, and Karen taught herself the drums. Their parents moved to Downey in 1963. In 1966 Karen and Richard were two-thirds of a trio that won a "battle of the bands" competition in Los Angeles County. Later they began singing as a duo and tried to create a career in entertainment. Finally they got lucky. In 1968 Herb Alpert signed Karen and Richard to a recording contract, and they made a hit song, "Close to You." Their second album, named after that hit single, sold 4 million copies. From then on "The Carpenters" were a very popular act, and their songs made the Top 40 hit lists for several years: "We've Only Just Begun," "Rainy Days and Mondays," "For All We Know" (the Academy Award winner), and "Yesterday Once More."

The Carpenters were perfectionists. Richard once remarked that if the critics thought the Carpenters' music was so easy, they should come to the studio and watch Karen and Richard put together their carefully crafted sound. Richard did much of the song writing and arranging, heavily influenced by his favorite "three Bs": the Beatles, the Beach Boys, and Burt Bacharach. He recorded most of the basic musical tracks first, with emphasis on great precision. Then Karen came in and did the lead vocals.

Karen Carpenter was the lead singer in the pop group called "The Carpenters." The group was extremely successful in the early 1970s. Karen died in 1983.

UPI/Bettmann Archive.

Karen is said to have adored Richard and thought of him as a genius. Although he could be "a tyrant" in the studio, Karen herself worked hard to make her vocals perfect. Richard was the controlling figure in "The Carpenters" and the musical mastermind behind their hit records, but the most intense pressure fell upon Karen. She was the lead singer, the one in the spotlight. In a sense the whole act, and the Carpenters' joint career, hinged on Karen's vocals bringing all the pieces together into their beautiful soft-rock sound.

The Carpenters' striving for perfection extended to most aspects of Karen and Richard's lives. One interviewer commented that the Carpenters always tried to give the "right" answers, as if their responses to questions had to be as seamless as their music. Their hard work and striving for perfection paid off. They earned $30,000 for each of their concerts and consistently played to standing-room-only, sold-out audiences. But they paid a price as well. Richard said the problem was that "we were growing professionally during the years most people were concentrating on being a person" (Simon, 1979)*—they never experienced some of the normal development people go through, including rebelling against their parents and establishing their personal identities. As their professional success increased, the pressures on them to present the right sound and the right public image increased also.

Although Karen was a poised and confident singer, people often described her as childlike and sweet, holding her emotions in and taking care of others but not herself. Karen's parents had exercised a great deal of control over her personal and professional development and remained very much involved in her life. Karen didn't move out of her parents' house until she was 26. Both Karen and Richard obeyed their mother when she scolded them for not signing autographs after a concert in Hershey, Pennsylvania. An angry fan wrote and complained, and Agnes Carpenter insisted that Karen and Richard call the fan and apologize. They did.

Karen and Richard's career declined somewhat during the late 1970s. These

*Excerpts from *The Best of the Music Makers* by George T. Simon and Friends. Copyright © 1979 by George T. Simon. Reprinted by permission of Doubleday & Company, Inc.

years coincided with the extreme weight loss and general exhaustion that reflected Karen's struggle with anorexia nervosa.

Karen's concern about her weight began early in her life. She tended to be "pear-shaped" when she was a child and was always worried about being too chubby. In her late teens, Karen managed to slim down. By the time she and Richard had begun making hit records, Karen's slenderness and good looks certainly lived up to popular American standards. But Karen was still constantly obsessed with her weight. In 1975, the year Karen had to cancel a tour because of exhaustion, her weight had slipped from 110—normal for her height of five feet, four inches—to a mere 90 pounds. Karen recovered temporarily from her exhaustion, but in 1982 her weight was down to 82 pounds. Her obvious emaciation was worrying her fans. By then, to purge herself of unwanted calories, Karen had developed a dependence on laxatives she was afraid she'd never break. Only toward the end of her life had she finally admitted that she had a serious eating disorder.

Anorexia took control of Karen's life. Worries about her weight and her career helped contribute to the break-up of her marriage to real-estate developer Tom Burris in 1980. (Interestingly enough, Karen met Tom at a lunch she went to against her own inclinations and at the urging of her mother.)

Sadly, Karen's health and her career seemed to be on the mend when she died. She was in intensive treatment in New York during most of 1982 and had brought her weight back up from 82 pounds to 108, near her normal performing weight. The tour and album she was planning were very exciting for her, and she told a close friend a short two weeks before her death, "I have a lot of living left to do." Ironically, however, an expert on anorexia, Dr. Raymond Vath of Seattle, reports that doctors learned only two months before Karen's death that the greatest strain on the heart of a person with anorexia is when they start to gain back some of their lost weight. Karen felt that she truly was on her way back, but her heart didn't stand up under the strain. Karen's death from cardiac arrest has taken something from us all. As Burt Bacharach said, "She was a magical person with a magical voice."

STRUGGLING FOR CONTROL

Karen Carpenter's tragic story is an example of the way control—in her case, excessive control—deeply affects our lives. Karen was controlled by others in important ways, and one of the few independent controls she achieved, over her weight, had disastrous results. Then she died before her increasing control over her anorexia nervosa had returned her to full health. Perhaps if her heart had not given out she would have been one of those who triumph over anorexia nervosa. There were signs that she was winning her long struggle to survive, but her disorder contributed to her death before the world knew much about what had been happening to her and the gains she had made.

Few of us face the kind of struggle for control that dominated, and ultimately ended, Karen Carpenter's life. In this chapter we will consider several more common examples of control in our lives. Our general concern is with various aspects of personal and interpersonal living that challenge our control over our destinies and with the ways people cope with these challenges. As we shall see, there are many routine problems in everyday living that seem to defy human control. We hope that understanding these challenges will help you see how common they can be, how similar many of them are to each other, and how some of them can be coped with effectively.

Some people believe that their lives are under their own control, while others believe that their fates are controlled much more by other people or chance. This basic belief about the location of control in one's life is an extremely important personality variable that affects the way people handle their life experiences. We will consider it first before looking at a range of challenges people face in the course of living.

PERCEPTIONS OF THE LOCUS OF CONTROL

As we discussed in Chapter 5, people differ markedly in their feelings about their capacity to control life situations. People who feel in control of their own destinies generally believe that their experiences and achievements are due to their own abilities, attitudes, and actions. In contrast, other people see their lives as more or less the toys of external forces—whether other people, "Mother Nature," or "the stars." We noted that these two types of people are said to perceive either an *internal* or an *external* locus of control (Rotter, 1966; Phares, 1976). A psychological test measuring whether individuals perceive an internal or external locus of control has been devised, and some of the items are shown in the accompanying questionnaire. People answering the items in an "external manner" believed their situations to be controlled by forces outside themselves, while those answering in an "internal manner" perceived that they can control what happens to them.

Of course such attitudes have an enormous effect on how people cope with the challenges of living. "Externals" may tend to sigh

and say "why bother trying?" when confronted by difficult circumstances. In the same situation, "internals" are more likely, whatever their fears, to see an opportunity to exercise their abilities to learn and grow.

A good example of the differences between the behavior of people who feel an internal or an external locus of control comes from a study of people in a hospital suffering from tuberculosis. The "internals" tried much harder than the "externals" did to find out about their disease and how they might cope with it. They felt that maybe with some information they could take some action to improve, or control, the state of their health. The "externals" sought out less information and engaged in fewer efforts to do anything about their illness (Seeman & Evans, 1962).

A study with similar results involved college students who had the task of persuading another person to believe something that was counter to the other person's beliefs and values (Davis & Phares, 1967). Before their persuasion attempt, subjects were given as much opportunity as they wanted to obtain any information about the other person. Clearly, this information about the other person would enable them to persuade him or her more effectively. The "internals" sought out more information, by asking more questions, than the "externals" did. They felt that the outcome of their persuasion attempt could be affected by their own efforts. The "externals" didn't.

Karen Carpenter lived a life controlled in personal ways by her parents and in professional ways by her brother. She felt that she could control very little, except her weight. As we shall see later, many anorexics excessively value the control they have over their weight because it is the only area of their lives that they can control.

What implications does research on the locus of control have for you? The most important point is that there is a link between your beliefs about the locus of control and your behavior. If you believe that your experience is beyond your own control, you may expend less effort than you could. You may not try as hard as you are able, because you believe that your

INTERNAL VS. EXTERNAL LOCUS OF CONTROL

For each of the pairs of statements below, choose the one that best describes your feelings, a or b. After you have answered the questions, you can score them as reflecting perceptions of Internal or External locus of control. Score Internal for each of numbers 1, 2, 3, and 6 that you answered a, and for 4 and 5 if you answered them b.

1. _____ a. One of the major reasons why we have wars is because people don't take enough interest in politics.
   _____ b. There will always be wars, no matter how hard people try to prevent them.

2. _____ a. In the case of the well-prepared student there is rarely if ever such a thing as an unfair test.
   _____ b. Many times exam questions tend to be so unrelated to course work that studying is really useless.

3. _____ a. The average citizen can have an influence on government decisions.
   _____ b. This world is run by the few people in power, and there is not much the little guy can do about it.

4. _____ a. Most people don't realize the extent to which their lives are controlled by accidental happenings.
   _____ b. There is no such thing as "luck."

5. _____ a. It is hard to know whether or not a person really likes you.
   _____ b. How many friends you have depends upon how nice a person you are.

6. _____ a. What happens to me is my own doing.
   _____ b. Sometimes I feel that I don't have enough control over the direction my life is taking.

From Rutter, J. B. Generalized expectancies for internal vs. external control of reinforcement. *Psychological Monographs*, 80 (no. 1) (Whole No. 609). Copyright 1966 by The American Psychological Association.

efforts won't make a difference. You may satisfy yourself with poor performances, figuring there's nothing you can do to improve the situation. Certainly some circumstances are more out of your control than others are, but your overall attitude about challenging situations affects every aspect of your life. If in general you tend to be overwhelmed by external forces and to shrug your shoulders, you guarantee a performance much worse than what you are capable of. Be careful not to blame yourself too much for things that go wrong, but believe enough in your own effectiveness and control to make good efforts. You won't do worse with high effort than with low.

SELF-CONTROL IN EVERYDAY LIVING

All of us engage in a variety of everyday activities simply to sustain life. We must eat, drink, sleep, and take care of basic biological needs. It turns out that all of these activities can pose challenges to a successful personal adjustment to the world, and we must be careful to control them. For some people, control over eating, drinking alcoholic beverages, and getting a good night's sleep poses serious challenges. They can't take these activities for granted. Let's consider some of the problems associated with these activities and some of the solutions to them.

OVERWEIGHT AND OBESITY.   There are several different kinds of eating disorders, but the most prevalent one, and perhaps the one that is most difficult to cure, is the one that is obvious to us simply from looking around at people in any large gathering or public place. Overweight, which in its extreme form becomes obesity, is a problem that many of us face. Let us consider the dimensions of the problem, its possible causes, and its possible solutions.

First, how can we define overweight and obesity? Unfortunately there is no consensus on definitions. Insurance companies and physicians have estimated ideal weights for persons of a given sex, age, height, and body type. Obesity is sometimes defined as being over one's ideal weight by 20 percent. Extreme obesity has been defined as 100 pounds over ideal body weight (Coleman, Butcher, & Carson, 1980). However, there is no agreed-upon definition. Our culture seems to define thin as beautiful, and it may be that people are made to feel uncomfortable about their weight when they are really quite healthy. The material we discuss in this chapter applies both to people who are overweight to a moderate extent and would like to be thinner and to those who fit the 20 percent overweight definition of obesity.

How common is overweight or obesity? What proportion of the population faces a problem with weight? A study made in 1977, when the population of the United States was about 215 million, indicated that 40 to 80 percent of the American population was *seriously* overweight—that is, weighed more than medical authorities consider healthy for their age, height, and body type (Jeffrey & Katz, 1977). This percentage range is imprecise, but it signals the pervasiveness of the problem. A 1981 Gallup poll indicated that 36 percent of the population considered themselves to be overweight, while *another* 22 percent were judged overweight according to health charts for their reported heights and weights. These two per-

Being overweight is a common psychological and health problem in our society.

Marc P. Anderson.

centages combine to indicate that 58 percent of the population is, or believes itself to be, overweight. We can't be sure of any particular figure, and of course percentages vary from day to day, but it is clear that overweight is a widespread problem challenging perhaps half of America's population. One other thing that the poll shows is that the struggle to meet this challenge seems neverending and that people are constantly fighting to control their weight. In the Gallup poll, 39 percent of those who thought they were overweight said they were currently dieting, and another 42 percent said they had dieted, but had given up dieting at some time in the past. In other words, more than 80 percent of overweight people are either trying to reduce their weight or have given up trying. These figures suggest that the struggle is a constant one, and the people polled indicated the same thing. They talked about their difficulties resisting food, particularly sweets.

The problem of overweight and obesity is not spread evenly throughout the American population. Adults in lower social classes in the United States are six times more likely to be overweight than are other Americans, while children in lower social classes are *nine times* more likely to be overweight than are other children (Stunkard, D'Aquill, Fox, & Filion, 1972). This suggests that obesity is related to sociocultural factors. For example, there are different social norms in different social classes about what kinds of food to eat, how much to eat, snacking, and when to have meals. These norms can exert an effect on calorie intake. In addition, there are different norms regarding the degree of thinness that is most attractive. People in the upper and middle classes tend to exert more pressure on themselves to be slim.

What can we say about the causes of obesity? The basic problem, of course, is that overweight people take in more calories in eating than they burn off in their daily activities, possibly because they are not very active. But why do they eat too much? One biological approach to this question points out that overweight people have a larger number of fat cells than other people and have had for most of their lives. The number of fat cells is set in early life. Thus a heavy baby may acquire more fat cells as a result of overfeeding in infancy and may for the rest of his or her life have too many fat cells compared to persons of normal weight. In addition, even if this person diets and loses weight, the number of fat cells won't decrease. This has two consequences. One is that the heavy person has more fat cells signaling the brain to eat, especially if the cells have been reduced in size due to dieting. The person is hungry much more of the time than a person of normal weight is, due to the signals from the fat cells. Second, the fat cells will absorb calories from eating. Thus the overweight, or formerly overweight person, with lots of fat cells, will gain weight more easily than a normal weight person from the same amount of food. The person may eat less but gain more than the normal person.

Besides the number of fat cells, another important factor in obesity has been identified by researchers looking at the kind of information that obese and normal people attend to. Stanley Schachter (1971) has shown that obese people pay more attention to external cues, such as the sight and smell and taste of foods, rather than to internal cues, such as messages from the internal organs that the person is full than normal people do. There are a number of interesting studies showing that obese people are more responsive to external cues than normal people, so that their eating is controlled by seeing and smelling food rather than by how much they really need. In one study obese and normal subjects had a chance to eat some crackers either when they were very hungry, because they had not eaten their last regular meal, or when they had just eaten several roast beef sandwiches. The normal people, as you might expect, ate many fewer crackers if they had just eaten some sandwiches than when they were still hungry. Their internal sense of how full they were curbed their appetite. It didn't work that way for the obese subjects. They ate the same whether they had eaten sandwiches or not. They actually ate fewer crackers than the hungry normal weight subjects. The taste and sight of the crackers, rather than feelings of hunger, determined their food consumption (Schachter, 1971). You can imagine obese people being at the mercy of television commercials for food or the sight of a box of cookies or a tasty pot of spaghetti in the kitchen. People without this problem stop eating when they are full. Extremely overweight people continue eating as long as there are appealing external cues for eating.

Research also shows that stress is related to increased eating among obese people. Research with rats suggests that a stressor such as tail pinching can cause rats to eat far more than normal (Rowland & Antelman, 1976). It may be that certain degrees of stress activate motivational systems that control increased or decreased eating (Robbins & Fray, 1980). In one study subjects heard clicks that they thought represented their heart rates. When the clicks sped up, subjects thought that their heart rates were increasing. This stressor caused people of normal weight to eat less and obese people to eat more. In short, when we are stressed, our eating behavior can be affected dramatically. Some people may have a loss of appetite, eat less, and therefore lose weight. Obese people are likely to react to stress by eating more (Slochower, 1976). Those of you who have trouble with eating should be alert to the effects of stress. You will be better able to overcome the increased urge to eat that comes from pressure and stress if you know it's coming.

Research indicates that for reasons such as more fat cells, greater responsiveness to external food cues, and reactions to stress, overweight people eat more than people of normal weight. However, obese people's increased food intake is only one side of the equation. The other side is how many calories they do or do not burn. The problem is that once people become heavy it is increasingly difficult and unpleasant for them to exercise. As a result they become less active. This means that they burn up fewer calories, with the result of more weight gain. It also means that with more empty time on their hands they tend to eat even more, exercise even less, and continue to increase in weight.

What can be done about obesity? Are there any solutions? We can't be very optimistic, although there are some sound approaches to the problem. Our pessimism simply stems from studies showing that people's efforts to substantially and permanently reduce their weight very often fail. The main reason is that eating is an extremely strong drive. Brain researchers are showing that the signals the brain of a hungry person exerts on the person to start eating are extremely strong. The physiological power of the hunger drive defeats many, many people in their efforts to lose weight and keep it off. Less than one-fifth of the people who lose a substantial amount of weight maintain the loss for up to a year (Worchel & Cooper, 1983). The average weight loss for people in Weight Watchers who stay with the program for two years is only 14 pounds, and less than one-third even manage to stay with the program for that length of time. Similarly, a study by Stuart (1967) showed that the average person regains 105 percent of the weight lost in dieting programs. That is, the average person ends up weighing more than when he or she began trying to lose. Although 8 billion dollars are spent every year on dieting pills and dieting books, such expenditures have little to show for them. Diet pills, largely amphetamines, work

temporarily, but the weight loss is not maintained. Nevertheless, most people who are dedicated to losing weight and keeping it off can do so. The key is strong motivation and an effective self-control or self-management program. Let's consider the basic elements of such a behavior management program.

First, we must realize that starvation doesn't work. We must be in the business of weight control over the long term, and that means slow, gradual reduction in intake of calories through eating less and eating differently, and a gradual, carefully monitored increase in the burning of calories in exercise. In order to eat less and exercise more we need to be mindful of the stimuli or cues that lead us to eat and control them; we must be mindful of our actual eating behaviors and alter them in ways that will reduce how much we eat; and we must remember that the consequences of our actions are powerful determinants of our behavior in the future, so that we must reward ourselves for meeting our goals and punish ourselves, in productive ways, for failure. In short, we must control our environment, alter our eating patterns, and administer appropriate rewards and punishments. How, specifically, can we do this?

Let's first consider stimuli in our environment. One thing we can do is to stay away from situations where we can purchase fattening food. Going into a pizza parlor or burger haven can be extremely dangerous. Our homes can be dangerous if they contain tempting, fattening foods. Don't buy them in the grocery store. Avoid advertisements that make your mouth water. In general, try to be around food, especially fattening food and food reminders, as little as possible.

Change the *way* you eat. Obese people tend to eat more quickly than people of normal weight do. Slow down. Wait between bites. Take smaller bites. Chew more thoroughly. Wait several minutes between bites. You can also change what you eat. Munching on carrots and celery does much less damage to your weight control aspirations than eating ice cream, french fries, or pizza.

In addition to staying away from food or

other stimuli that make us eat, we can administer rewards and punishments to ourselves. If you reduce your calorie intake for a day or lose some weight, reward yourself, though not with food. Spend a little extra time watching television or buy a new book. People have suggested you can administer punishment by giving money to a cause you deplore or depriving yourself of using the telephone for an evening. Take away something you like.

In addition to controlling your eating behavior, you should practice similar self-management techniques in increasing your exercise. Get up at an earlier hour, when there is time for exercise and perhaps for not much else. Put on some exercise clothing. That is, surround yourself with stimuli appropriate to exercise. Begin, perhaps under a physician's care, at exercise levels that are appropriate to your physical condition. Reward yourself for meeting your goals. All of these techniques—controlling the stimuli or environment, altering your actions, and administering rewards and punishments—require careful monitoring of your behavior. So keep close track of what you are doing, how you reward yourself, and how you reduce temptation. Set reasonable goals and follow through. And don't give up. Sometimes you will fail but keep it up. It is a long slow process but some people succeed. Try to be one of them.

Anorexia nervosa is an increasingly prevalent disorder among young women. One symptom is distorted body image—thinking you are overweight when you are too thin.

Susan Rosenberg, Photo Researchers, Inc.

ANOREXIA. **Anorexia nervosa** is a serious eating disorder that is becoming more and more common and well-known. The death of Karen Carpenter and the book *Starving for Attention,* by Cherry Boone O'Neill, daughter of singer Pat Boone and sister of Debbie, have helped focus recent attention on this sometimes fatal condition. The major symptoms of anorexia nervosa are a marked loss of body weight and an obsessive fear of being fat. Anorexics lose at least 25 percent of their body weight, but, given their distorted images of their bodies, they feel that they must lose still more. Anorexia occurs primarily among women, usually in adolescence or early adulthood. Women anorexics outnumber men by more than 20 to 1. The death rate among anorexics, due to loss of

weight and related physical disabilities, has been estimated to be as high as 25 percent. Furthermore, anorexia is difficult to overcome. About one-third of those suffering from anorexia remain ill (Bemis, 1978).

The causes of anorexia are still being debated and explored. In many cases cessation of menstruation precedes the noticeable weight loss and the pattern of starvation that many anorexics show. This has led some psychologists to speculate that there is some emotional component, perhaps related to sexual feelings and conflicts, that is at the root of the disorder. Others use the evidence of cessation of menstruation to argue that some kind of glandular or endocrine disorder is the root cause.

Although we can't be sure about these

suggested causes of anorexia nervosa, we do know that cultural factors and personality variables are linked to anorexia. Anorexia has been called the "good girl's disease" and is associated with people who are brought up in families that emphasize tight control over behavior. We've seen what a dutiful daughter Karen Carpenter was and how hard she strived to be sweet, pretty, perfect, and obedient. Anorexics tend to come from the higher social classes, to have dominating mothers and emotionally distant fathers, to be highly intelligent, hard-striving, ambitious achievers (Coleman, Butcher, & Carson, 1980).

Cherry Boone O'Neill argues that the drive for control is one of the key aspects of anorexia. Anorexics often feel that there is very little in their lives that they can control. Naturally, such a feeling is disturbing, especially if you are an active person oriented toward achievement. Once anorexics gain control of their weight and their eating, however—O'Neill reports from her own experience with anorexia—they have an exhilarating feeling that there is something in their lives they can control. Often the reason that anorexics so badly need control over some aspect of their lives is that they feel that their lives, or large portions of them, have been controlled by someone else. Karen Carpenter was always highly controlled by her brother Richard, the mastermind of their joint career, even though she was its most visible star. She gained control over her eating behavior by becoming anorexic, but then lost control of her anorexia itself.

Of course most anorexics by far are female, which is probably not just an amazing coincidence. Do lingering stereotypes about the "proper female role" and "thin is beautiful" help lead certain intelligent, ambitious, and frustrated young women into such a disastrous form of "self-control"? Whether or not these factors directly contribute to a person becoming anorexic, they certainly don't discourage female anorexics' obsession with controlling their weight.

Some anorexics can be helped, through various self-management techniques, to eat and regain weight. Still, the struggle is a long one

TABLE 6.1

Symptoms of Anorexia Nervosa and Bulimia

SYMPTOMS OF ANOREXIA NERVOSA

1. Continual fear of becoming obese, even with great loss of weight
2. Body image distortion; feeling too fat even when extremely thin
3. Weight loss of at least 25 percent of normal weight
4. Refusal to maintain a minimal normal weight for age and height
5. No evident medical explanation for the weight loss

SYMPTOMS OF BULIMIA

1. Repeated instances of binge eating
2. At least three of the following:
   a. eating high calorie food during binges
   b. hidden eating during a binge
   c. stopping binging due to abdominal pain, interruption by another person, sleep, or self-induced vomiting
   d. repeated attempts to lose weight by crash diets, self-induced vomiting, laxatives, or diuretics
   e. frequent variations in weight due to alternating binging and fasting
3. Awareness of abnormal eating pattern and fear of not being able to control it
4. Feelings of depression and worthlessness following binging
5. Binging and purging not due to anorexia or apparent medical explanation

and often fails, as it did in Karen Carpenter's case. Anorexia nervosa is a life-threatening disorder that should be taken very seriously. Anorexics often hide their disorder. If you think someone you know may be anorexic, you should take whatever steps you can to help that person get medical help.

BULIMIA. **Bulimia** is an extreme form of weight control that involves binging on food, followed by self-induced vomiting. Bulimics also attempt to control their weight by using diuretics, drugs that increase urination, and laxatives. Bulimia usually causes no excessive loss of weight and is not life threatening. Nevertheless, it is a troubling and increasingly common eating disorder. Obese people and anorexics often are also bulimics. Karen Carpenter developed an extreme dependence on laxatives. Bulimia, like anorexia, afflicts females more than it does males. It usually begins before or during adolescence.

During the period that a bulimic is binging, the self-induced vomiting can be carried to the point of exhaustion. The person may eat—usually high-calorie "junk food"—vomit, eat, and vomit again in a continuous pattern. Not only can this exhaust the person, but related problems, such as sores on the gums due to the acidity of regurgitated stomach fluid, often result (Thompson, 1984).

People with bulimia are generally aware that their behavior is not normal, but they seldom can control it during the periods of time, lasting from one or two to many days, they are in a binging and purging pattern. Bulimia is usually accompanied or followed by feelings of disgust, self-depreciation, and depression. We do not know how common bulimia is, because it appears to be such a recent phenomenon, and bulimics are secretive about their behavior. We do know that, like anorexia, bulimia is on the increase, and that it can be as difficult to control and cure as the other eating disorders.

Drinking and Alcoholism

We all must eat nutritional food and drink water and other liquids necessary for life. But drinking can get out of control just as eating can. The main problem is associated with a particular kind of drinking, the consumption of alcoholic beverages. As we noted in the previous chapter, drinking alcohol and alcoholism itself are both serious social problems, which seem to be getting more common and more costly. An important difference between eating disorders and drinking disorders is that the abuse of alcohol has serious, even life-threatening consequences for those around the drinker. One serious problem associated with the consumption of alcohol is the danger to others caused by drunk drivers. Many states are cracking down on drunk driving with stiff penalties, es-

pecially for repeat offenders. Government efforts have left many people unsatisfied, however. Organizations such as MADD (Mothers Against Drunk Drivers) are springing up in different parts of the country as citizens themselves try to control a serious social, medical, and psychological problem. As you know, excessive drinking and alcoholism are common problems among many college students, although few students are actually diagnosed as alcoholics. But alcoholism is a serious problem many of you may face in the future, or may be facing right now in your own lives or in the lives of others close to you. Let's consider some of the dimensions and causes of alcohol abuse, as well as some possible solutions to the problem.

As we noted in Chapter 5, alcohol can be a tremendously harmful substance. Alcohol is implicated in 50 percent of all automobile fatalities, 60 percent of all murders, and 80 percent of all deaths in fires. Why, then, do people drink? There are a variety of reasons, but an important one is that people drink because al-

Many people find temporary relief from pressure in alcohol. Alcohol abuse causes vast personal and social destruction.

Arthur Tress, Photo Researchers, Inc.

cohol in small amounts relieves tension, anxiety, and stress, and in general makes people feel good. A very important part of these reactions is that people expect alcohol to have these effects, and their expectations are often self-fulfilling. Peer pressure is important too. Alcohol is consumed in most cultures in the world, and each one prescribes how a person should drink, how much you should drink, and what kinds of effects are likely. You should be aware that other people sometimes exert strong pressure on you to drink, perhaps so that they don't have to "drink alone," and that these pressures have the potential to make you drink more than you know is good for you.

Once people drink, alcohol is taken into the bloodstream and acts directly as a depressant on the central nervous system. It affects higher brain centers and thus impairs judgment and rationality. This makes people feel freer, less inhibited, and more energetic. But the depressant quality of alcohol is made clear when too much is consumed and people "pass out."

A moderate amount of alcohol is actually beneficial (United States Department of Health, Education, and Welfare, 1974). Several studies have shown that people who consume one or two drinks a day have longer life expectancies than those who are teetotalers and never drink. One important danger related to even moderate drinking, however, is the fetal alcohol syndrome: Unborn babies are harmed by alcohol consumed by their mothers. The fetal alcohol syndrome can lead to mental retardation and is the third largest cause of birth defects (United States Department of Health, Education, and Welfare, 1978). It is not clear how much alcohol is dangerous in pregnant women, but pregnant women should be extremely cautious about alcohol consumption.

Drinking does not always lead to problem drinking or alcohol abuse. When it does, signs such as binging, preoccupation with drinking, and craving for alcohol become part of your life. As in the eating disorders, control is a key problem. People with alcohol problems struggle to control their craving and feel that they will lose control over their drinking after just

TABLE 6.2

Indicators of Alcoholism

The first three signs below indicate a behavior pattern that definitely fits the National Council on Alcoholism's definition of an alcoholic. Numbers four through ten are signs that strongly suggest that the person behaving this way is an alcoholic.

1. Drinking despite medical warning to person against it
2. Drinking despite social problems—job, marital, police, driving problems
3. Open, indiscriminate drinking
4. Feelings of loss of control over drinking
5. Morning drinking
6. Changing from one alcoholic beverage to another
7. Loss of interest in activities not involved with drinking
8. Outbursts of rage and anger while drinking
9. Making frequent conversational references to being drunk, or drinking more than other people
10. Drinking to relieve problems such as insomnia, anger, exhaustion, depression, lack of social comfort

one sip. Then it's "no holds barred," and a binge can occur, until the person drinks himself or herself into oblivion. The control struggle is underlined by findings indicating that problem drinkers have a higher perception of external locus of control than other people do. This is especially true among women. The heavy drinker is usually one of those people who feel that life is out of their hands (Rohsenkow & O'Leary, 1978).

What kinds of people are likely to have drinking problems? Alcoholics come from all walks of life, although people from lower social classes suffer from alcoholism more than others. In addition, men are much more likely to be alcoholics than women are. There are also racial differences. Black men drink more than white men, but black women drink less than white women. In fact, black women have lower rates of alcoholism than any other social group (Wechsler, 1980). With respect to age, the data are quite depressing. Young people are drinking more and more. Drinking at the high school level doubled from 1966 to 1975. This increase in alcohol use in part reflects the fact that young people are turning away from drugs such as marijuana that were more prevalent during the 1960s.

What can be done about problem drinking? A variety of psychotherapeutic approaches to problem drinking have had some degree of success. The cure rate is higher among younger people who are better educated and whose problems are not as severe. One notable success story is that of Alcoholics Anonymous (AA), which was founded in 1935 in Akron, Ohio, by two men who had recovered from problem drinking through "fundamental spiritual change." AA emphasizes social support, the importance of higher spiritual authority in causing and curing alcoholism, and the goal of total abstinence. AA reaches only a small percentage of alcoholics, but there is a high success rate for those who stay in AA. AA is one of the most effective self-help and social support groups in our society. We will discuss it further in Chapter 8.

AA is like many other approaches to treating problem drinking in that its goal is total abstinence. However, some people, though still a minority, now advocate a different solution to alcoholism, controlled drinking (Sobell & Sobell, 1978; Miller, 1978). Controlled drinking—that is, drinking in moderation—is a goal that may seem more attractive and attainable to many problem drinkers than total abstinence. Some success has been found in studies that used behavioral self-control methods emphasizing the close monitoring of alcohol intake and intoxication levels and behaviors that are alternatives to drinking. People can learn ways of controlling their drinking, even though we know less about how well-controlled drinking works in the long run. The goal of total abstinence has proved difficult to reach, though, and this new approach, emphasizing coping with the learned behavior disorder of excess drinking, rather than with the disease of alcoholism, is well worth exploring.

If you are one of the 10 to 15 million people in the United States with a drinking problem, you should be aware of the terrible price your problem inflicts on you and others, and that there is a wide variety of therapies and treatments available, with a wide range of goals. The sooner you get into treatment, and the more modern approach you take to treatment, including thinking about followup treatment in the difficult days after initially stopping or reducing drinking, the better your chances of beating this problem will be. Exciting work is going on right now about how to define and understand alcoholism and how to treat it. People struggling to control their drinking should seek more detailed information about this new work.

Insomnia

Just as we all must eat, we all must sleep. Predictably, many people have difficulty controlling or coping with this most common of all activities. How much we sleep varies, but most of us spend more time sleeping than performing any other single activity. Roughly a third of our lives is spent sleeping. For many people sleep does not come easily. Estimates of the number of people who have insomnia—trouble falling asleep or staying asleep—run as high as 30 million (Clark, Gosnell, Shapiro, & Hager, 1981). The disorder is more than twice as common among women than among men. As many as one-seventh of all women over 30 report problems with insomnia.

People who are highly anxious, who have high degrees of muscle tension, and who are depressed or shy have trouble with insomnia. Of course, all of us have periodic difficulties with anxiety or tension or other emotional problems, and during the times we have these difficulties we are likely to have occasional trouble sleeping. Insomnia is often caused by, or made worse by, people's worry that they won't be able to go to sleep. This worry causes further emotional arousal and makes it even harder to go to sleep. Sometimes people try to force themselves to go to sleep. This effort and

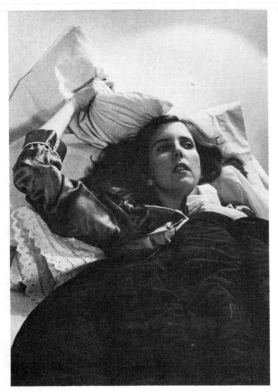

An insomniac can toss and turn for hours waiting for sleep to come.

Susan Rosenberg, Photo Researchers, Inc.

its lack of success create further arousal and more restlessness.

One therapy for insomniacs directs them *not* to sleep, but to stay up late for one purpose or another. People then worry about trying to stay awake, rather than about trying to fall asleep. Often the result is that they do fail to stay up, and they do fall asleep (Ascher & Efran, 1978). A similar therapy based on attribution theory has been used with insomniacs, based on the fact that anxiety and emotional arousal increase when people can't sleep. In this procedure, people suffering from insomnia are given a pill, actually a placebo with no real physiological effect, and are told that the pill will make them feel tense and restless. When these insomniacs are in bed waiting for sleep and feel tense, anxious, and restless, they attribute their arousal to the pill. This breaks the usual cycle where tense, anxious people can't

sleep, and the awareness that they can't sleep makes them more tense and restless and even less likely to sleep. When people attribute their arousal to the pill rather than to insomnia or their life's troubles, they tend to stop worrying about sleep and about their problems. Consequently, they fall asleep (Storms & Nisbett, 1971).

There is an important lesson in these findings: You can't cure insomnia by trying to directly control the tension and arousal associated with insomnia. This will make the problem worse. Somehow you must think of something other than the problem of staying awake, perhaps by concentrating on trying to avoid sleep or by attributing the physiological arousal associated with insomnia to something else.

While we can't willfully suppress the physiological arousal or the worries that keep us awake, there are several things we can do to reduce the tension produced by failing to fall asleep and to increase the chances of a good night's sleep in the future. First, although we can't control the time we fall asleep, we can control the time we get out of bed and start our day each morning. It is important to get up at the same time every day. This will help our bodies get on a regular schedule. Don't try to make up for trouble falling asleep at night by staying in bed later in the morning. This is letting your sleeping problem control you. Gain some control over it by setting the time that you get up. And don't worry about lack of sleep. Most of us need much less sleep than we actually get, and if we are tired, sleep will come.

Second, people can learn various relaxation techniques to help them remain calm when waiting for sleep. One such technique is **autogenic training,** where people give themselves suggestions that their limbs are growing warm and heavy and that their breathing is becoming deep and regular (Nicassio & Bootzin, 1974). One advantage of such relaxation techniques is that they distract your attention from the fact that you are physiologically aroused and not sleeping, and prevent your trying to force relaxation.

Another technique for keeping your mind off your problem is to engage in fantasies. Let

REVIEW QUESTIONS

1. The psychological test devised by Rotter that asks people to what extent they believe that the events and outcomes in their lives are either the result of their own efforts *or* are a result of chance is attempting to measure that person's *perceived* _____ _____ _____ .

2. Sick people with an _____ locus of control are more likely to seek information about their disease and make more efforts to do something about their illness than persons with an _____ locus of control.

3. The most prevalent eating disorder in our society is _____ .

4. T or F: Persons who are overweight are likely to actually have more fat cells than normal persons.

5. Schachter's studies indicate that obese people are more responsive to _____ _____ than normal people.

6. An overweight student eating five pounds of ice cream the night before a major exam illustrates how dramatically _____ can affect eating behavior.

7. T or F: It's not uncommon for a person to weigh more after dieting than before they began.

8. Controlling our weight involves learning to control our _____ , altering our eating patterns, and _____ ourselves appropriately.

9. _____ is an eating disorder whose symptoms include weight loss and an obsessive concern with being fat.

10. The most important aspect of anorexia may be the anorexics' need for _____ which they attempt to exert through their eating patterns.

11. Although there may not be excessive loss or gain of weight in bulimia, weight control is usually attempted through _____ and _____ _____ .

12. T or F: Alcohol is implicated in at least half of all car fatalities, murders, and deaths in fire.

13. T or F: Alcohol is a stimulant which loosens inhibition and increases energy level.

14. Although there have been a variety of approaches to helping alcoholics, in many organizations such as Alcoholics Anonymous the goal of treatment is _____ _____ .

15. Some successful therapies, such as telling the patient to try *not* to sleep or giving them a placebo which is supposed to keep them tense, work by reducing the _____ associated with not being able to sleep.

16. _____ _____ is a relaxation technique in which people give themselves suggestions about their bodies becoming more relaxed, taking their attention away from not sleeping.

your mind wander. Daydreaming, even at night, is good for us (Singer, 1975). Sexual fantasies or fantasies about other enjoyable activities are relaxing and take our minds away from the struggle to sleep. If you find that nothing seems to work, take advantage of the fact that you are aroused and get up and do some reading or productive work. You will either get the work done, or, more probably, find that the work is making you feel awfully sleepy. Then go back to bed. But don't worry about losing sleep. You don't need that much.

Finally, let us issue a caution about sleeping pills. Many people use them, and they can work in the short run. But they present all the problems with drugs that we discussed in the previous chapter, most notably tolerance, so that you need stronger and stronger doses to get to sleep. Also, insomnia tends to increase in severity after using sedatives, even for short periods of time (Schumer, 1983).

SELF-CONTROL IN PERSONAL RELATIONSHIPS

Thus far we've been considering self-control problems that involve an individual's physical well-being and that, aside from alcoholism, mainly have an impact on the person struggling with the problem. Someone like Karen Carpenter, battling anorexia, may go unnoticed for a period of time, and may do everything she can to remain unnoticed. On the other hand, because alcohol abuse leads to actions such as boisterousness and aggression, it affects those around us. In this section we will consider in general terms problems that arise in interpersonal relationships when we can't exert enough control to get what we want and must tolerate some frustration. Frustration makes us angry and arouses aggressive feelings in us, as we saw in Chapter 5. Let's see how we control, or fail to control, frustration and anger in relation with others, and the way anger contributes to important social problems.

Frustration, Anger, and Aggression

All of us experience frustration in our dealings with other people. Our goals may be thwarted, our self-esteem and integrity may be threatened, and our abilities to handle situations may seem overwhelmed. The way we respond to these situations is closely linked to our perceptions of internal or external locus of control. Those who feel that, in general, they can control their own outcomes are more likely to take productive steps to overcome the frustration. Those who feel as if external circumstances control their outcomes are more likely to give up and withdraw or simply to act out their frustration by behaving aggressively. No matter what our perception of the locus of control, all of us can be driven to the point where our anger at frustrating circumstances spills over into aggressive behavior. As we noted in Chapter 5, frustration-aggression theory holds that the greater the frustration is, the more likely it is that aggression will result (Dollard, Doob, Miller, Mowrer, & Sears, 1939). When other people block us from obtaining what we desire, we will be inclined to be aggressive toward them. We know that aggression doesn't always stem from frustration, however. Let's consider some key aspects of frustration-aggression theory, including the important cases where people do not directly attack the people who frustrate them.

One commonly discussed example involves a person who is frustrated by his or her boss. In this case, one might wish to hurt the boss but refrains from doing so for fear of losing one's job. Instead of attacking the boss, one may yell at or deal harshly with a subordinate. The subordinate is often bewildered because

Frustration often leads to aggression. Many aspects of modern living, including commuting in heavy traffic, generate frustration.

Paul Sequeira, Photo Researchers, Inc.

he or she can't imagine what caused this unfair attack. Frustration-aggression theory takes this behavior into account by postulating that while the most preferred target of aggression is the thwarter of someone's desire, people may displace their aggression onto other targets if they fear the consequences of hurting the thwarter. In the example used above, the strongest impulse should be to attack the boss, but if that target is unavailable or the person fears acting in that manner, she or he may displace the aggression onto some other target, such as a subordinate. The subordinate is a "safer" target, since he or she can't fire the aggressive person and probably will be reluctant to reciprocate the aggression.

The **displaced aggression** hypothesis has been used to explain a wide range of behaviors. One explanation of child abuse focuses on a wife who is frustrated by her husband. She is afraid to attack him directly, so she displaces the aggression onto a safer target, the defenseless child. Racial discrimination and prejudice may also represent displaced aggression. According to this explanation, people are frustrated in their daily lives by their bosses, their spouses, and other interpersonal encounters. They don't feel that attacking those targets is safe, so they displace their hostility and violence onto members of minority groups who serve as "safer" targets. Miller and Bugelski (1948) found some support for this line of reasoning. They frustrated workers in the Civilian Conservation Corps (a government agency during the Depression) by not allowing them to see a good movie. Then they measured the attitudes of these workers toward Mexicans and Japanese. The results indicated that the workers expressed more hostility toward the minority groups after they had been frustrated than before the frustrating event, even though the minority group members had nothing to do with the frustration. This discussion suggests that before you behave aggressively toward another individual, you should attempt to understand your underlying motives. Has that person really done something to anger you, or are you upset by the actions of another? Such an appraisal may keep you from hurting an "innocent" individual and may allow you to focus your attention on dealing effectively with the thwarter who is responsible for your anger.

Another aspect of the theory deals with the means of reducing aggression. Dollard, Doob, Miller, Mowrer, and Sears (1939) suggested that frustration builds up in a person, and each frustration adds to the residue and must be released, lest it result in extreme violence. Worchel and Cooper (1979) illustrated this idea by comparing it to the inflation of a balloon: "One breath is not enough to cause the balloon to explode but one breath can cause an explosion if the balloon is already filled to capacity with air" (p. 326). According to frustration-aggression theory, a person must be allowed to vent the tension built up by frustration. One way to accomplish this is to engage in aggression. Participating in aggression should reduce the tension and lower the individual's readiness for future aggression. **Catharsis** is the term used to describe the process whereby an act of aggression reduces the desire for aggression.

The notion of catharsis is important because it suggests that people should be allowed to express aggression in a conflict situation. As we will see later, there is considerable controversy over the validity of the catharsis hypothesis. There has, however, been research demonstrating that, under some conditions, catharsis does occur when aggression is expressed. For example, Hokanson, Burgess, and Cohen (1963) examined subjects' physiological arousal (heart rate and blood pressure) after they were insulted by an experimenter or an experimental confederate. As expected, both their heart rates and blood pressures increased following the insult. Some subjects were given the opportunity to express counteraggression, and physiological measures were again examined. The results indicated that physiological arousal decreased after counteraggression. Clinical psychologists George Bach and Philip Wyden (1968) urge couples who are engaged in conflict to express aggression in a nonhurtful way in order to release hostility and tension. They have developed a sponge-rubber club (bataca club) for couples to use in this cathartic activity; they can beat each other without causing injury. Bach and Wyden report that couples often feel better and less hostile after engaging in this "creative aggression."

This notion of catharsis has important implications. For example, it suggests that having children participate in aggressive games may be a good idea, since the children will be able to "blow off steam." According to the theory, acting aggressively in a game situation will reduce the likelihood that the children will be aggressive toward each other outside the game situation.

More recent reviews of the catharsis literature, however (Konecni & Doob, 1972; Geen & Quanty, 1977), conclude that catharsis occurs only when the aggressor is angry and allowed to be aggressive toward the person or thing he or she is angry at, and that even then the expression of aggression doesn't necessarily decrease the chances of further violence. Furthermore, aggression against a person is likely to result in that person acting aggressively in return (counteraggression). So the expression of aggression is likely to have some undesired consequences and rarely leads to a reduction in conflict.

Say you've been up all night writing a term paper, which is due in 45 minutes, and you still have three pages to type. Unfortunately, your roommate has the long-time irritating habit of using your typing paper and not replacing it, so there's not a sheet to be found. In your frustration and fury you'd like to jump on your sleeping roommate and give him or her a punch in the kisser. But your roommate is a foot taller than you and lifts weights. He or she could knock you flat. And, besides, you have to live with this person every day. So instead you put on your running shoes and race down the block to a friend's apartment to borrow some paper, cursing and yelling and yanking limbs off small trees in your path. According to frustration-aggression theory, this behavior should serve as a catharsis for your anger at your roommate. Later in the day you should be able to have a calm discussion about the typing paper situation, without feeling a need to shake your roommate by the neck until his or her

teeth rattle. Other research, however, now suggests that you'd still feel angry at your roommate and need to vent your aggressive feelings toward him or her in some way. Maybe you kick one of your roommate's stereo speakers. Then your roommate, counteraggressively, throws your digital alarm clock against the wall. And so forth and so on, until one of you moves out or offers to buy the other a pizza.

THE INFLUENCE OF MEDIA VIOLENCE ON AGGRESSION.   There has been a growing concern in the last decade over the possible influence of the media on people's aggressive feelings. The influence of television has received particular attention, since watching television has become almost a national pastime; recent estimates suggest that by the age of ten, a child watches four to six hours of television a day. The concern over the effects of television becomes even greater when we realize the amount of aggression portrayed on the screen. Walters and Malamud (1975) estimate that the average 16-year-old has seen 13,000 murders on television. On the average there is a violent act on the television screen every 16 minutes, and a murder is shown every 31 minutes. In a recent court case, lawyers for 15-year-old Ronald Zamora argued that his "addiction to television crime shows" motivated his shooting of an elderly woman during the robbery of her home.

If we attempt to use theories of aggression to understand the effects of media violence on aggressive behavior, we find two conflicting predictions. The frustration-aggression theory hypothesizes that individuals can experience aggression vicariously by watching or fantasizing aggressive actions. These experiences should result in catharsis and reduction of the aggressive inclination. Social learning theory, on the other hand, predicts that witnessing media violence will encourage aggressive behavior, since the viewer will learn new acts of violence. In addition, the aggressor on television is often rewarded for his or her violence, and the viewer may expect that he or she too will be rewarded for aggression. The example

Hundreds of studies have indicated that watching televised violence, including violent cartoons, leads to imitative aggressive behavior.

Michael Kagan, Monkmeyer.

set by such violent behavior is especially dangerous for children, who often have difficulty separating fiction and reality.

Recent research tends to support the social learning position; watching violence on television often results in increased viewer violence. For example, Parke, Berkowitz, Leyens, West, and Sebastian (1970) divided juvenile delinquents in a minimum-custody institution into two groups. One group watched violent television programs each night for one week, while the other group watched nonviolent programs for that period. The subjects were then observed for three weeks. The results indicated that subjects who watched the violent programs behaved more aggressively than subjects who had been shown the nonviolent programs. The effect was most pronounced during the week that subjects were actually watching the television programs. Findings such as these prompted the United States National Commission on the Causes and Prevention of Violence to conclude, "It is reasonable that a constant diet of violent behavior on television has an adverse effect on human character and attitudes. Violence on television encourages violent forms of behavior, and fosters moral and social values about violence in daily life which are unacceptable in a civilized society" (1969). One of the ways that televised violence does this, of course, is by showing us

that if we are to exert control over our lives, and determine our own outcomes, we can do so by behaving in an aggressive way when we are faced with obstacles. People want to have power and feelings of control, and televised violence teaches them that aggression is a means to achieving that goal.

The wide viewing of violence on television also seems to have an effect on the viewer's reaction to violence in the real world. Thomas, Horton, Lippincott, and Drabman (1977) had young children watch either an aggressive or a nonaggressive television program. After the program, the subjects were shown a scene of "real life" aggression that they believed to be occurring at the time. Physiological measures of their arousal were taken during the program and during the "real life" aggression. The results indicated that the aggressive program did arouse subjects. However, subjects who had watched the aggressive program were less aroused by the "real life" violence than were subjects who had seen the nonaggressive program. These findings suggest that the regular viewing of violence on television may cause individuals to become less disturbed by aggression in their lives and more tolerant of it. This may result in individuals' becoming less sensitive to the plight of victims of aggression and less hesitant to use various forms of aggressive behavior in response to conflict.

Sexual Violence: The Problem of Rape

Much of the aggression that is expressed in our society is expressed by men against women. This may take several forms. Many women are beaten by their husbands. It has been estimated that nearly two million spouses, mostly wives, are physically abused by their mates every year in the United States. This may take the form of punches, kicks, assault with objects, and the threatened or actual use of knives and guns (Gelles & Strauss, 1979). This pattern of behavior sets up self-perpetuating patterns where children who observe the violence, or who perhaps are objects of it themselves, quickly learn to imitate the aggressive behavior and carry it on to the next generation.

Of all the forms of violence between men and women, rape is the one now undergoing the most thorough examination and rapid change in our understanding. It may surprise you to think of rape as a topic under the heading of violence rather than under the heading of sex. But this is a key part of the redefinition. More than being an act of sexuality, rape is an act of violence and aggression, and it is often linked to life-long frustrations, anger, and senses of inadequacy experienced by male rapists.

Our understanding of rape has been greatly advanced by the book *Against Our Will: Men, Women, and Rape* (1975) by Susan Brownmiller. Her analysis of the history of rape has shown that it is an act of aggression and not an act of sexuality, and that many rape laws have been written to protect men's power and to make convictions for rape difficult to obtain. As a result, many laws and courtroom procedures have been changed in recent years. For example, there are more constraints than previously on the extent to which a rape victim's intimate history can be brought into a trial.

What is the frequency of rape, and what kinds of men are involved in it? It's difficult to know the frequency of rape because as few as one in five rapes are actually reported, mostly because of the traumatic and humiliating procedures that rape victims go through in police stations and courts. In 1980, 75,000 rapes were reported. The actual number committed is closer to 400,000. The number of forced sexual contacts short of intercourse is much, much higher.

Studies of rapists reveal that most of them repeat their crimes and that rape is driven by anger and the needs for power and control. More than half of all rapes stem from the need for men to wield power over women—to control, conquer, and subdue women. Most of the rapes motivated by needs for power are called **power-expressive rapes,** where men are actively expressing their felt dominance over women (Groth, Burgess, & Holmstrom, 1977). About half as frequent are **power-reassurance rapes,** where men who feel quite powerless and inadequate are attempting to reassure themselves of their power and adequacy through subjugation of women.

About 40 percent of rape cases are motivated by anger; men retaliate against real or imagined mistreatment at the hands of women (Groth & Birnbaum, 1979). Here anger and rape, and the desire for revenge against women for their supposed transgressions, are dominant. Rapes motivated by anger or the need for retaliation are exceedingly violent.

About 5 percent of rapes involve sadistic anger rather than retaliatory anger. These are committed by pathological sadists who gain sexual pleasure from other people's suffering, often to the point of mutilating or murdering them.

Rapists seek feelings of power and the expression of rage and anger, not sexual pleasure. What can women do to control their own lives and seek protection from rape? The book *Our Bodies, Our Selves* (Boston Women's Health Book Collective, 1979) gives a number of practical suggestions. One is communication. Women who share the same apartment buildings and neighborhoods should organize and work out signals for dealing with danger and other arrangements for getting help. They should make sure their windows and doors are absolutely secure, that more than a key must be used to open them. Entrances and doorways should be well illuminated. Many women list their telephone numbers in directories using only their first initial, so they can't be identified as women. When going to her car, a woman should have her key ready, check the rear seat to make sure no one is concealed there, enter the car quickly, and lock all the doors. And of course most women are very familiar with the need to stay out of dark places at night, especially when they are alone. If you are attacked, be sure to yell. Screaming can often scare away an attacker.

Women are often made more vulnerable to attack by conflicting conditioning they've received. On the one hand, every woman has been told, "Don't talk to strangers, and don't pick up hitchhikers!" On the other hand, women are usually expected to be soft, refined, polite, and thoughtful of others. Traditional stereotypes about women still cause many people, male and female, to view women as "pushovers" and "natural victims." Assuming control of your own life in all sorts of ways, whatever the threatening factors in the environment, can make you less vulnerable to being used and abused. Improving your self-esteem and physical well-being can be a helpful protection against rape or other violence. Contrary to sometimes popular opinion, "real women" don't have to be physically weak. Being in good physical shape, as we've already seen, is crucial to your ability to control and withstand threatening circumstances in our often scary world. Physical fitness increases your sense of personal power and autonomy. It also enables you to run if you have to.

Obviously, attempts to prevent or control rape are not always successful, and the survivor of rape has a new struggle to face in gaining control over her emotional reactions to the violence done to her and getting back to day-to-day living. Rape survivors often experience nightmares and phobias associated with the rape incident; tension, nausea, and sleeplessness; and sexual difficulties such as pain, orgasmic problems, and lack of sexual interest (Becker, Abel, & Skinner, 1979).

A very frequent emotional struggle for raped women is their feeling of guilt, that somehow it's their fault they were raped or that they should have resisted more effectively. Unfortunately, a subtle form of violence against women, still prevalent in our society, maintains that "good women" don't get raped and that women who are raped "asked for it." So rape survivors must deal not only with the effects of the physical violence they've suffered, but also with damaging attitudes about themselves that prejudice against women has conditioned them and others to feel.

The fear of rape and the usual preventative measures against it seriously limit women's freedom of behavior and cause many women to feel somewhat like prisoners in their own lives. Prevention or control of rape, and of other physical abuse of women, requires more than adaptive behavior on women's part; it also requires changes in men's conventional attitudes about women and a reduction of our society's glamorization of violence. Such changes will take time, of course, but concerned women and men have begun to focus attention on these issues. Battered women and women who have been raped are not as isolated as they were in past years. There are now women's shelters and rape crisis centers in many urban areas, and counseling services are also available at many hospitals and mental health agencies. Laws affecting violence against women are slowly improving. The judge who lectures a raped woman on her morality is now likely to shock, rather than to confirm, public opinion.

Prejudice and Violence against Minorities

Many factors are involved in prejudice and discrimination against members of minority groups. One powerful factor is prejudiced attitudes learned from our culture in general or from significant other people in our lives, especially our parents. Aggression is one powerful factor in prejudice, however, and we need to be careful about the possibility of our own frustrations producing scapegoating and aggressive prejudice in us.

As an example of scapegoat theory, let's consider David Smith, an "average" white citizen. David wakes up in the morning and

MEASURING THE PREJUDICED PERSONALITY

One of the classic studies in the history of psychology attempted to identify the kinds of people who are prejudiced (Adorno et al., 1950). Research indicated that people who have "authoritarian personalities" are more likely to be prejudiced, but not necessarily so. The authoritarian person believes in strict authority-subordinate relationships, advocates punishing transgressions, tends not to be introspective, and is generally "tough-minded." The more you or your friends tend to answer the questions from the F-Scale below as true, the higher you score on authoritarianism. This means you have a greater chance of being prejudiced toward minority groups. How many of the questions below did you answer true? Do you consider yourself to be a prejudiced person?

T F 1. Obedience and respect for authority are the most important virtues children should learn.

T F 2. What this country needs most, more than laws and political programs is a few courageous, tireless, devoted leaders in whom the people can put their faith.

T F 3. An insult to our honor should always be punished.

T F 4. Most of our social problems would be solved if we could somehow get rid of the immoral, crooked, and feebleminded people.

T F 5. What youth needs most is strict discipline, rugged determination, and the will to work and fight for family and country.

T F 6. People can be divided into two distinct classes: the weak and the strong.

From Adorno, T. W., Frenkel-Brunswik, E., Levinson, D. J., & Sanford, R. H. *The authoritarian personality*. New York: Harper & Row, 1950. Reproduced by permission.

starts off to work. He seems to go from one traffic jam to another. Each time he runs into a jam, his anger builds up, but he can't do anything about it; he can't run over all the other cars. As a result of the heavy traffic, David is late to work and receives a stern scolding from his boss. Again, anger wells inside him, but again he can't express it; if he were to yell at his boss, he would lose his job. The day wears on, characterized by one small frustration after another. Each one makes David angry, but he doesn't dare explode for fear of being punished or seeming stupid in front of others. When he leaves work, he stops by a bar for a "quick one" to reduce the tension that has built up. Some of his friends in the bar are talking about how blacks are taking more and more jobs that were once held by whites. David joins in and vigorously expresses anger and hatred toward blacks.

In this case, the minority group served as a **scapegoat** against which David could vent the anger that had welled up during the day. He couldn't vent his aggression against his boss, his secretary, or his wife, but he could vent it against blacks. As a group, blacks are a visible minority, and whites may get social support from peers for expressing prejudiced attitudes towards them. Thus the scapegoat theory suggests that prejudice is the result of displaced aggression; it serves as a way to vent repressed anger (Konecni, 1979). The target of prejudice is chosen because it is "safe" to attack (it is a minority), it has visible characteristics, and there is social support for holding a negative attitude about it.

It should be noted that scapegoating fits into our locus of control idea. When people are suffering frustration they often feel better if they can attribute their frustration to factors they cannot control. They hold the scapegoat responsible. Once they have done that they often try to regain a sense of personal control over their lives by taking discriminating action against minority group members. Some leaders like Hitler and some groups like the Ku Klux Klan stir up both the feelings that our negative outcomes are due to minority group members and that we can regain control by acting against them.

There have been several demonstrations that prejudice and discrimination may be caused by frustration. For example, Hovland and Sears (1940) reported a negative correlation between cotton prices in the Depression-era South and the number of lynchings of blacks: The lower the prices for cotton, the more lynchings took place. Hovland and Sears suggested that because many southerners depended on cotton for a living, the low prices created frustration, which, in turn, was directed towards blacks, who were a "safe" scapegoat in the South. In another example, Campbell (1947) reported that the more people were dissatisfied with their jobs, the more anti-Semitic attitudes they expressed.

What can be done about prejudice? We need to build up positive contacts between hostile groups, but research has shown us that contact alone doesn't work. The contact has to be of a special kind. In an interesting study at a summer camp, Sherif and his colleagues (Sherif et al., 1961) created hostility between two groups of campers by having them compete in a series of events. In an effort to see if simple contact would reduce intergroup hostility, Sherif set up a number of situations where members of the two groups interacted without competition. For example, the two groups ate together in the dining hall. The contact, however, did not reduce intergroup hostility. Instead the groups used the periods of contact to hurl verbal abuse at each other, and the conflict was actually heightened during the periods of contact. The contact in the dining hall ended in a food fight between members of the two groups.

Simple contact may perpetuate prejudice in another way. In the old South, there was a great deal of contact between blacks and whites; the whites were in the dominant, supervisory role, and the blacks generally served as laborers and servants. Similarly, contact between males and females in the job setting has been common for years; males generally take the supervisory role, and females hold the clerical and secretarial positions. In both cases, the nature of the contact serves to solidify, rather than to reduce, prejudice. Some research (see Austin & Worchel, 1979) has shown that if contact is to reduce prejudice, people must be brought together on an equal basis.

The Sherif study with summer campers demonstrated another factor that determined the effectiveness of contact in reducing intergroup hostility. During one phase of the study,

---

REVIEW QUESTIONS

17. A man who is frustrated by his boss, but physically abuses his wife instead, could be said to be displaying _____ _____ .

18. _____ is the process whereby an act of aggression reduces the desire for aggression.

19. The frustration-aggression theory predicts that watching violence on TV would _____ aggression; social learning theory predicts it would _____ aggression. Recent research tends to support the _____ theory's predictions.

20. Rape is not an act of sexual pleasure, but rather an act of violence motivated by a need for _____ and expressed as a demonstration of _____ .

21. The scapegoat theory suggests displaced aggression caused by frustration is the underlying cause of _____ and _____ .

22. Sherif's research indicates that prejudice may be reduced by increasing contact in a situation which requires _____ .

the campers were faced with a number of situations that required them to work together for a common goal. In one case, a truck that was bringing them food got stuck. It was impossible for the members of one group to move the truck, but if the two groups worked together, they could get the truck moving. Sherif found that intergroup hostility abated after the two groups cooperated by working for a number of common goals. Further work by Worchel (Worchel et al., 1978) has shown that cooperation reduces intergroup hostility only when the cooperative efforts result in achievement of the common goal. Hostility was not reduced when the groups failed to achieve their common goal through cooperation.

Thus this research suggests that prejudice can be reduced if contact is made between the prejudiced individual and the target of prejudice. However, it is important that the contact occur in a situation that places the individuals in positions of equal status and has them working together and achieving a common goal.

DEATH AND GRIEF

In 1947, Johnny Gunther, the 17-year-old son of the noted writer John Gunther, died after battling a brain cancer for 15 months. He had no chance of defeating death, but his courage led his father to write a moving memoir of Johnny's struggle to maintain his dignity and good cheer and to let death take his body, but not his spirit. The book is aptly entitled *Death Be Not Proud*. Gunther's book is helpful to our understanding of how people can cope effectively with the tremendously deep and searing experience associated with death, both for the dying person and for those the dying person leaves behind. Death, whether our own or that of people we love, doesn't have to be experienced only as an external threat or a "Cruel Fate" over which we have no say. We can choose to experience death as a part of ourselves and the life we love—a valuable, though final, stage in our development as human beings.

Elisabeth Kübler-Ross (1975) has been helpful in furthering our understanding of the process of dying. Our culture generally regards death as a taboo "dirty topic" and tends to react to death with fear and denial. Often terminally ill people aren't even told they're dying. Others around them encourage them to ignore or resist the inevitable, rather than to deal openly with the experience they're having. As a result, many people die without a sense of completion, because they haven't been able to express their feelings or to communicate honestly with their grieving loved ones. Kübler-Ross suggests that dying people can instead come to feel like participants in, rather than victims of, their deaths. She outlines five stages of the dying process that, if allowed to unfold naturally, will result in ultimate acceptance of one's life coming to its close.

Denial is the first stage in dying. The terminally ill person refuses to accept the reality of impending death and interprets his or her illness in a harmless, nonthreatening way. Johnny Gunther denied that he was dying for some time. Even when he had an operation that involved drilling holes in his head and removing part of his scalp in order to try to remove the brain tumor, he made light of it. He made plans to go to college as if he would be able to do it. This is often referred to as the "Not me!" stage of dying.

The "Not me!" of the denial stage is followed by the "Why me?" of the **anger and resentment** stage. People resent the fact that they must die, and their frustration produces great anger and occasionally aggressive behavior. Johnny Gunther's courageous and dignified struggle with death was at times marked by behavior very unlike him. He would make sarcastic remarks to physicians and break out in great anger against his parents. This seemed quite mysterious, as if it were totally unexplainable behavior. Now we know that expression of anger and resentment, even toward those we love and those who are trying to help us, is a normal stage of the dying process and should be allowed, not discouraged.

During the next stage, the **bargaining** stage, people bargain with themselves, with physicians, and with spiritual forces, if they believe in them, to stay alive just for a certain length of time. Dying people strive to live for something in the short term that means something to them, to put death off for at least a time. After they have reached one short-term goal, they may "bargain" for another. A dying man may ask only to be allowed to live until his daughter's wedding. Johnny Gunther wanted very much to live until he graduated from secondary school, and, if he could do that, to live until he could enter Harvard College the next fall. Johnny's struggle to live until graduation was successful. In an experience that moved all who watched it, Johnny marched onto the stage to receive his diploma like all his classmates, although he was severely disabled and could barely walk alone. He died a few weeks after his graduation.

Another interesting example of bargaining involves the second and third presidents of the United States, John Adams and Thomas Jefferson. Adversaries in their political careers, they began writing letters to each other in their old age. They both wanted to live until July 4, 1826, the fiftieth anniversary of the Declaration of Independence, which they had had such important roles in creating. Both were ill and elderly, but both achieved their goal: They died on July 4, 1826.

It is not surprising, then, to learn that most deaths take place within three months after a birthday and that the fewest take place one month before. People who are dying bargain to stay alive until their birthdays.

The bargaining stage is followed by the **depression** stage. Here the dying person experiences the most suffering and grief. People must be allowed to feel and express their depression. It is a mistake to try to cheer people up during this stage of depression, which is a natural part of the dying process. Different people experience it and handle it in different ways. One of the remarkable things about Johnny Gunther's death was that he seldom felt depressed. He hated a diet that he had to endure for some months, but he kept depression to a minimum. Death was not allowed the "pride" of making Johnny feel sorry for himself.

Finally, people move into the **acceptance** stage. This stage may be quite short, but during this stage they achieve the "quiet victory" of accepting the fact that death is coming and standing ready for it. People may want very much to be with their loved ones at this point so that they can share this final moment when inevitability is accepted. Johnny Gunther's parents were with him on the last day of his life, when he died in his sleep.

Death poses severe psychological challenges for those in the process of dying and for those who are left behind to grieve.

David Strickler, Monkmeyer.

Following death, those who are left behind face the difficult job of picking up the pieces and carrying on. This can be exceedingly difficult. Some writers have advocated talking out your grief with others, and even acting it out in appropriate ways, in order to fully explore your feelings (Jackson, 1975). Johnny Gunther's father acted out his grief by channeling his feelings into the task of writing a book in Johnny's memory.

The book *Up From Grief* (Kreis, 1969) makes distinctions about three different stages in the grieving process (see also Kavanaugh, 1974). The first is called the stage of **shock.** Even if death is expected, few people are prepared for the state of shock that follows immediately. This lasts through the funeral and the time of contacting friends and making arrangements. Shock is useful in that it numbs and postpones suffering. Just as shock from physical injury can postpone the onset of pain, shock from psychic trauma can delay suffering. During this phase the bereaved may have difficulty focussing on reality, may feel out of touch with themselves, with their feelings, and with those around them. They may also feel guilt, that they should have done more to prevent the person's death or to help the person during his or her life. But the general feeling is one of detachment from one's own feelings and thoughts. This is a shield from the suffering that comes later.

The second stage of grief is **suffering.** This may begin several weeks after the death or loss. Feelings of pain and grief increase sometimes quite surprisingly, as the shock wears off. This is a long stage in the grieving process, marked by intense loneliness and feelings of lack of purpose, meaning, or significance in living. Most people experience their most intense moments of happiness and significance, their "peak experience," when they form an intimate relationship with someone else. The loss of a partner can take away a person's sense of purpose. A person may feel rudderless and at "loose ends" during this painful period of grieving. This is the difficult time when most actual grieving is done.

The stage of suffering eventually gives way to the stage of **recovery.** This often begins a year after the death. People must begin to

---

TABLE 6.3

Stages of Death and Grieving

STAGES OF THE DYING PROCESS (KÜBLER-ROSS, 1969)

1. Denial: "Not me"
2. Anger: "Why me?"
3. Bargaining: "Let me live a little longer."
4. Depression: Feeling of loss and despair
5. Acceptance: The "quiet victory" of accepting death

STAGES OF GRIEVING (KREIS, 1969)

1. Shock: Living through the loved one's death and funeral
2. Suffering: Nearly year long period of pain, grief, and loneliness
3. Recovery: Reengagement in active living

REVIEW QUESTIONS

23. Elisabeth Kübler-Ross called the first stage faced by a dying person the _____ stage, which is characterized by a refusal to accept the reality of the impending death.
24. The fact that most deaths take place shortly after birthdays and rarely before them illustrates the dying person's attempt to "negotiate" to live for a certain length of time. Kübler-Ross calls this the _____ stage.
25. The final stages a dying person experiences are _____ and finally _____ .
26. The process of grieving also proceeds through stages. The first numbing phase of grieving is the _____ stage, followed by a _____ stage, and ending in the _____ stage during which they begin to reengage in living.

worry about the future and reengage in living. They have choices to make, and they realize that life has to be lived. Sometimes people begin this reengagement process by making impulsive decisions they later regret. For example, a person trying to "get on with it" may throw out pictures of the lost person that are sorely missed later. We should guard against impulsive action at this stage of the grieving process. Also, we should recognize that the line between the suffering stage and the recovery stage can be recrossed, time and time again. You may feel that you have put your grieving behind you and that you are making new plans and carrying on with life—then the pain and suffering, and especially the loneliness, return. You must realize then that more time must pass before you will have put your grief behind you. Eventually, the recovery will take hold, and grief can be overcome.

Grieving, like dying, can seem less like a blow from cruel fate if the grieving person is able to view death as a natural, though deeply saddening, part of life.

SUMMARY

1. People who perceive an external locus of control believe that their life experiences are out of their own hands. They work less hard than people who perceive an internal locus of control and believe that their experiences reflect their own efforts and abilities.

2. Research suggests that more than half of the American population is overweight. There are several theories about the causes of obesity. One is that since early childhood obese people have had more fat cells than people of normal weight. Another theory is that obese people are more responsive to external cues such as the sight and smell of food than to internal cues such as how full they feel.

3. Stress is related to eating in animals and human beings. Stress can cause people of normal weight to eat less, but obese people to eat more.

4. Overeating can be controlled by avoiding stimuli that urge us to eat, changing the behavior patterns we typically use when eating, and rewarding or punishing ourselves for eating appropriately or inappropriately.

5. People suffering from anorexia nervosa lose more than 25 percent of their body weight and risk serious illness or death. The drive for control over one aspect of life and a distorted body image are two key factors in anorexia.

6. Bulimia is an eating disorder where people binge and then purge themselves by self-induced vomiting or laxatives. They do this at times to the point of exhaustion.

7. People drink alcoholic beverages due to the good feelings alcohol produces, or the expectation of good feelings, and because of social norms or expectations that they should drink. Alcohol is a central nervous system depressant that first affects judgment and rationality. People who abuse alcohol may experience a constant craving to drink. Most treatment programs for alcoholics set the goal of total abstinence. Recent studies show that controlled drinking may be a more obtainable and desirable goal for many alcoholics.

8. People with insomnia are often kept awake by worrying about lack of sleep and by futile efforts to force themselves to go to sleep. Treatments for insomnia focus on means of getting people to take their minds off trying to sleep and worrying about failure to sleep. These include training in relaxation, day dreaming, and trying to stay awake. Also, people sleep better if they are given a placebo pill which they believe causes the emotional arousal they feel when they are unable to sleep.

9. Frustration often causes aggression. Sometimes, however, the aggression is displaced onto others. Some theorists believe that expression of anger and aggression has a cathartic or cleansing effect and reduces the desire to aggress. Expression of aggression, however, generally leads to further aggression.

10. Research shows that observing televised violence leads to an increase in aggressive behavior rather than a decrease through vicarious catharsis.

11. Rape is an act of violence rather than an act of sexuality. It is caused by a need for power in men and/or by men's expression of anger and rage against women. Women can reduce the chance of rape by taking various self-protective measures, including banding together, improving their physical fitness and self-esteem, and avoiding dangerous situations.

12. Prejudice can be caused by frustration and using minority group members as scapegoats for our misfortunes. Prejudice and intergroup hostility can be overcome by joint efforts to achieve a goal that can only be accomplished by cooperation.

13. Five different stages of dying have been identified: denial, anger and resentment, bargaining, depression, and acceptance. The grieving process has been divided into the shock, suffering, and recovery stages.

KEY TERMS

a. ACCEPTANCE
b. ANGER AND RESENTMENT
c. ANOREXIA NERVOSA
d. BARGAINING
e. BULIMIA
f. CATHARSIS
g. DENIAL
h. DEPRESSION
i. DISPLACED AGGRESSION
j. POWER-EXPRESSIVE RAPES
k. POWER-REASSURANCE RAPES
l. SHOCK
m. SUFFERING
n. RECOVERY

1. The first stage in the dying process in which people do not accept that death is coming and say "Not me"

2. Rapes in which men who feel insecure about their power and worth attempt to make themselves feel better by overcoming uncertainty about their power

3. An eating disorder characterized by binges of eating followed by purging through self-induced vomiting or laxatives

4. The fourth stage in the dying process in which people feel extremely unhappy

5. The stage in the grieving process in which the person tries to deal with the surprise and finality of another person's death

6. An eating disorder in which the person, usually a woman, loses a great deal of weight, often to the point of endangering her health, but still feels that she must lose more

7. The second stage in the dying process in which people feel unfairly stricken and say "Why me?"

8. The final stage in the dying process in which people feel at peace and able to accept the fact that they are dying

9. An angered individual's attack on a target that was not responsible for the frustration

10. The final stage in the grieving process in which one begins to put suffering behind and tries to continue to live an active life

11. The process whereby an act of aggression reduces the desire for further aggression

12. The stage in the grieving process in which the greatest suffering and loneliness is experienced

13. The third stage in the dying process in which people strive to stay alive for a future event

14. Rapes in which men attempt to assert and show their power and dominance over women

ANSWERS TO REVIEW QUESTIONS

1. Locus of control. **2.** Internal; external. **3.** Obesity. **4.** True. **5.** External cues. **6.** Stress. **7.** True. **8.** Environment; rewarding. **9.** Anorexia. **10.** Control. **11.** Binging; self-induced vomiting. **12.** True. **13.** False. **14.** Total abstinence. **15.** Stress. **16.** Autogenic training.

17. Displaced aggression. **18.** Catharsis. **19.** Reduce; facilitate; social learning. **20.** Power; rage. **21.** Prejudice; discrimination. **22.** Cooperation.

23. Denial. **24.** Bargaining. **25.** Depression; acceptance. **26.** Shock; suffering; recovery.

LOSING CONTROL: PSYCHOLOGICAL DISORDER

Struggling with Stress and Anxiety

Sources of Stress and Anxiety: Past and Present

Anxiety in Childhood / Stresses in the Modern World

Psychological Disorders

Anxiety Disorders / Dissociative Disorders
Psychophysiological Disorders / Affective Disorders: Depression
Schizophrenia / Who Is Psychologically "Sick"?

Summary
Key Terms

"**I** remember waking up from my nap fighting for my life. Something was pressed against my face. It could have been a pillow. I fought with all my strength." Such was the first recollection of the woman who was baptized Norma Jean Baker. The event took place when she was a year and a half old. The person holding the pillow over her face was her grandmother, who was in the grip of a manic-depressive psychosis.

Norma Jean Baker was to become the movie star Marilyn Monroe, and to a large extent her whole life was a fight for psychological, if not physical, survival (Guiles, 1969). It was a fight that she would eventually lose. Marilyn was an extraordinary star, a personality who captured the public imagination like few others in Hollywood history. Yet her life and her image contained profound contradictions. One director commented that she was the meanest woman in the movie industry, but after her death said, "We just happen to miss her like hell! There has never been a woman with such voltage on the screen with the exception of Garbo." Marilyn drew life and energy from the public's adulation but was frustrated that her own employers couldn't appreciate her sensitive and unique gifts as an actor. While she was a vivid "sex symbol," her sensuality was described as that of an angel. As a critic once said, "None but Marilyn Monroe could suggest such a purity of sexual delight" (Mailer, 1975).

Norma Jean spent her early years in foster homes and in an orphanage near Hollywood, where she was born in 1926. Her mother lived longer than Norma Jean, but spent most of her life in a mental hospital. Her father was someone with whom her mother had had a brief affair. Norma Jean never knew him. Her early life was filled with trauma, loneliness, a constant fear of abandonment, and a pervading sense of danger. There was no permanence or trust. There was nobody she was sure really loved her, nobody who would always be there to take care of her.

Possibly the worst years for Norma Jean were the two she spent in the orphanage, from age 9 to 11. There her life was lonely and regimented, and occasionally rebellious behavior got her into trouble. Eventually the Goddards, friends of her mother, took her in, and she stayed with them until she was 16. At that time the Goddards arranged a marriage for Norma Jean to a young man named Jim Dougherty. Her marriage to Dougherty, whom she came to love, was one of the happiest periods of her life.

World War II separated Norma Jean and Jim, and near the end of the war Norma Jean began modeling for a photographer. She was an excellent model whose photographs communicated warmth, vulnerability, and fragility. She knew she had talent and was determined to make an independent life for herself in modeling and eventually, she hoped, in the movies. When she realized that Jim and his family wouldn't approve of her having a career, she unhesitatingly divorced him while he was out of the country in the merchant marines.

Finally an agent arranged for Norma Jean to have a screen test. It was an opportunity she put to good use. On film the new Marilyn Monroe had a uniquely captivating sensuality and sensitivity. Critics also felt that she was a talented actor,

Marilyn Monroe was the best known American sex symbol of the 1950s. People found her to be saucy, but sweet and vulnerable.

Sygma.

but the movie studios simply wanted to exploit her magnetism as a charming, sexy, yet innocent, dumb blonde. Her fans adored her.

By 1953, Marilyn Monroe was one of the biggest names in films, and it was front page news when she married another of America's best-known celebrities, former New York Yankee baseball star Joe DiMaggio. Shortly after their wedding Marilyn and "Joltin' Joe" took a trip to Korea, where Marilyn sang to the American troops who were fighting there. The visit was a sensation, and Marilyn's popularity soared.

Marilyn's marriage to DiMaggio lasted less than a year. The two were simply incompatible as husband and wife. Joe wanted her to quit the movie business, which he considered to be degrading, but Marilyn couldn't stop. She had worked hard for her successful career. By now her identity was totally that of Marilyn Monroe; Norma Jean was long since dead. Still, Marilyn felt tremendously insecure and alone. At this time she began to calm her anxieties by taking tranquilizers.

In 1954 Marilyn left Hollywood to spend a year in New York studying acting in the world's most respected theater circles. As in the past, people who met Marilyn were captivated by her sensitivity and warmth. She made new friends but at the same time abandoned older friends in the West. When she returned to Hollywood in 1955 she began a period during which she made some of her best films, including *Bus Stop* and *Some Like It Hot*.

In 1956, at the same time that Marilyn's acting career peaked, she thought her personal life was also reaching fulfillment. She married the playwright Arthur Miller, author of *Death of a Salesman* and *The Crucible,* a man she had known and admired for years, even before she married Joe DiMaggio. Miller was a sophisticated, intellectual Easterner who she hoped would take her out of the jungle of Hollywood, where resentments and jealousies were making her work difficult. But her marriage to Miller turned sour almost as quickly as her marriage to DiMaggio had although they stayed together for a turbulent four years.

By the time Marilyn had been married to Miller for a year, there was a clear pattern both in Marilyn's personal life and in her professional life. As an actor she was exceedingly difficult to work with. Directors and fellow actors felt sorry for her and wanted to protect her, but it was nearly impossible to work smoothly with her. She was extraordinarily anxious and would consult her acting coach constantly, interrupting filming. She was almost always late, sometimes half a day late, and often she wouldn't come to work at all, leaving actors, directors, and technicians standing around after hours of preparation of their own. Studio executives felt that she was spoiled and neurotic. But, those who worked with her generally felt it was worth it when they saw the magnificence of her performances and the box office successes.

Marilyn's general outlook on life, in her work and in her personal life—was one of mistrust. Her early experience had led her to believe that the world was at best callous and indifferent to her and at worst ominously threatening. She had a tendency to interpret the behavior of others as betrayals. She would then reject them violently. She gravitated to new friends as she needed them and discarded others in just the way she felt people had rejected and exploited her. She was contemptuous and afraid of people she felt weren't on her side. Basically, she was insecure about her existence and her identity because she lacked confidence in her abilities as an actor and her ability to maintain relationships with others. She had a drive to succeed but also felt unworthy because of the ways her fears sometimes made her behave. Marilyn tried to cope with her anxieties and doubts with drugs. These helped somewhat, but they also drove her into deep depressions. She couldn't sleep, and her nights were filled with terror. She seemed to drive away those who most cared about her.

In 1960 Marilyn began a film that was to be her last. It was called *The Misfits* and was written by her husband, Arthur Miller. She became less and less able to cope. Her insecurities were making it impossible for her to work. Finally, she was hospitalized. Then she was able to come back and complete the film. Clark Gable, the male lead, died a few days after the film was finished. This event added to the many things that haunted Marilyn.

After *The Misfits* was completed, Marilyn had little will to continue. She permanently ended her relationship with Miller, but kept up contacts with various doctors and friends, including Joe DiMaggio, who still loved her. She began a new film with Dean Martin but was fired because of her constant tardiness and absences. Her dependence on drugs was increasing. Those who knew her became more and more concerned. Then in the summer of 1962 it appeared as if she were regaining control of her life. She was reinstated on the film with Martin. She was showing her old drive. On August 5, 1962, a Sunday morning, she was found dead in her apartment from an overdose of Nembutal. Her death was ruled a "probable suicide." Many who knew her believed the overdose was an accident. Many felt guilty that they hadn't been able to help Marilyn. Yet she had made it very difficult. She didn't seem to be able to have a complete and lasting relationship with anyone or to be at peace with herself. Marilyn Monroe's life was filled with as much outward success and inward misery as that of anyone in her time.

STRUGGLING WITH STRESS AND ANXIETY

Marilyn Monroe's life was filled with a great deal of stress and with tremendous anxiety, which eventually overwhelmed her and led to her death. Regrettably, stress and anxiety are common in all our lives, though usually not to the extent that they pervaded Marilyn's. In this chapter we will discuss the origins of stress and anxiety and how continued stress or extreme anxiety can lead to psychological disorders and breakdown.

Stress and anxiety are closely related but separable phenomena. A few definitions will help us keep them straight. **Stress,** as we discussed in Chapter 5, exists when we perceive a demand in the environment that threatens our well-being and needs to be met or coped with. **Anxiety** is an emotion we sometimes feel in facing stress. We become anxious when we feel uncertain about how to cope with the stress, when we doubt that we have the capacity to do so, or when we feel certain that the stress will overwhelm us. We also feel anxious in certain situations that remind us of threatening or traumatic experiences we had in the past.

What is the experience of anxiety like? We've all probably experienced intense anxiety at some point in our lives—perhaps as children, when we were lost, or as adults, when we feared that someone close to us may have been harmed—but this happens infrequently. When we do experience intense anxiety, we feel overwhelmed by danger and fear. We feel extreme physiological arousal, such as increased heart rate, perspiration, and trembling. We experience the extremely unpleasant sensation of losing our ''mental balance'' (Mira, 1943). A complete disorganization of behavior can follow. Mira (1943) indicates that actual physiological functioning is as bad as it seems: ''The anarchy present at the conscious level spreads to the internal organs as well.'' While the responses of the sympathetic nervous system are not disorganized, they are intense and make it very difficult for people to remain calm or plan adaptive and effective action.

Natural disasters, such as floods, are one situation that can lead to panic reactions.

Nancy J. Pierce, Photo Researchers, Inc.

Because the experience of extreme anxiety is so unpleasant and debilitating, people generally take whatever measures are necessary to try to control it. For the most part these efforts are successful. Thus the kind of severe upset described above is rare. Still, pressure, tension, and worry are part of modern living. They produce psychological disturbance in the vast majority of us at least part of the time. It is extremely important to understand how people manage stress and anxiety and how stress and anxiety can produce failures to adjust to the pressures of modern living. In this chapter we will consider these questions, and in Chapter 8 we will discuss how to get help. We hope these chapters give you a reasonably complete picture of how intensive struggles can lead to psychological disorders and how people can be helped, and can help themselves, to live more effectively in today's challenging world.

SOURCES OF STRESS AND ANXIETY: PAST AND PRESENT

Many people feel that life today is filled with anxiety. Most of us are able to cope with our anxieties well enough to function adaptively. Others at one time or another have setbacks and suffer periods of psychological disorder. The anxieties most people feel come from two sources. First, people have learned to be anxious about certain objects and situations because of their association with past experiences. Painful failures, humiliations, or threats in the past have led them to fear similar circumstances in the present. Second, people become anxious because of the stresses that exist in the present. These include difficult decisions, impersonal interactions, demanding work, and an uncertain future.

Marilyn Monroe's life is typical in that her anxieties about her career had their roots in past experiences and in present realities. Marilyn was made anxious by a life history that taught her mistrust and fear. Her first memory was of a desperate struggle to hold on against a literally murderous environment. In addition, acting is an extremely demanding and competitive profession. There was always the chance that Marilyn would fail and be discarded by the film industry that had helped create her "sex symbol" image. Let's consider, first, how anxieties develop in childhood and, second, how stresses in modern life can lead to stress, anxiety, and a range of psychological problems.

Anxiety in Childhood

Many personality theorists have argued that the powerlessness of childhood has the potential to make people anxious about living as adults (Harris, 1969). Horney (1945), for example, discusses how children can feel "isolated and helpless in a potentially hostile world." Whether or not people learn to be afraid of the environment or certain aspects of it depends on how they are treated. Variations in how children are treated by their parents have profound effects on how mistrusting they become and how extensive and debilitating their fearfulness is (see Chapter 2). The more children are frustrated in their needs, especially when they have no understanding of the justification for this frustration, and the more they are punished for their behavior and criticized for their impulses and feelings, the more they will come to mistrust and fear themselves and their environment.

When children do have frightening experiences, two things can happen to make their original fears even worse. First, their fear of the threatening object or experience can build up over time, unless the person can be shown immediately that the fear is unwarranted. This phenomenon is called **incubation** and can lead to avoidance of the feared object and an inability to learn that it might not really be dangerous. For example, a child who is frightened by a sailing mishap can become increasingly

Many of the fears we learn in early childhood affect us all our lives.

Rhoda Sidney.

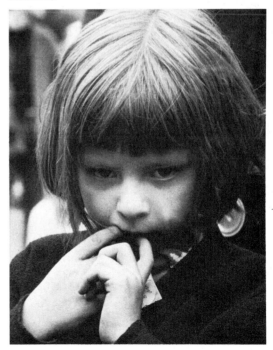

afraid of boats, unless somebody quickly demonstrates that sailing can be safe. Second, a person can come to fear many other objects, people, or impulses that are associated with the original fearful event. These can be either similar to the original source of fear or close in time or distance to the original trauma. This phenomenon is called **generalization** and most often occurs with very little awareness on the person's part. Generalization happened for Marilyn when her first disastrous experiences with those taking care of her led to a generalized fear of people and a feeling that even those who were friendly at present could easily betray her in the future. Marilyn's early years obviously had debilitating effects on her interpersonal relations.

Stresses in the Modern World

In Chapter 5 we noted the variety of factors that produce stress and anxiety in the modern world. Later in this chapter we will consider how life stress can produce psychophysiological disorders. We can underline the problem at this point by considering a recent study of stress reactions that occurred in Othello, Washington, in the seven months following the eruption of the Mount Saint Helen's volcano and the fall of volcanic ash on the town (Adams & Adams, 1984). Investigators considered stress reactions in a period of several months beginning one month after the eruption. The one-month delay was chosen in order to avoid considering only "transient," or temporary, reactions to the natural disaster, since the relatively long-term effects of such a severe stress are of more interest. Results of this study showed increases in physical illness, as indicated by admissions to the emergency room at the local hospitals, and a 19 percent increase in the death rate. Diagnoses of mental illness at the local mental health center increased by over 235 percent! Family problems, such as child abuse, domestic violence, and divorce, also increased, as did alcohol abuse, criminal cases, and other indicators of general psychological maladjustment. In short, in addition to whatever anxieties people may have from their childhood experiences, circumstances in the present will add stress and anxiety to their lives and can lead to sharp increases in health and adjustment problems.

The eruption of Mt. St. Helen's volcano caused stress reactions for more than a year in a nearby town.
UPI/Bettmann Archive.

PSYCHOLOGICAL DISORDERS

As noted before, most of us cope reasonably effectively with stress most of the time and keep anxiety under control. Sometimes, however, our behaviors aren't successful, our defenses break down, and we go through a period of psychological disturbance. In the remainder of this chapter we will consider the major psychological disorders. It is important that you recognize and understand these disturbances. If you do, you will be in a position to be more aware of what you are going through and not going through, more sensitive to those close to you who may be having serious difficulties, and more understanding and sympathetic towards those who are deeply and intensely troubled by psychological problems.

For many years psychologists used a neurotic-versus-psychotic distinction in discussing psychological disturbance. Neuroses were regarded as relatively mild disorders in which people didn't lose contact with reality or the ability to function in society. Psychoses were the more serious disorders that usually entailed loss of functioning and loss of contact with reality, marked by delusions and hallucinations. In a recent reclassification of psychological disorders, the American Psychiatric Association (APA) decided to eliminate the term *neurosis* from its list of disorders, largely because it referred to so many different kinds of problems that it had lost its usefulness. Some disorders are still referred to as **psychoses,** and use of the term neurosis is still permissible, though not preferred. We will classify the disorders considered in this chapter according to the new APA *Diagnostic and Statistical Manual, DSM-III* (APA, 1980). First we will consider several *anxiety disorders, dissociative disorders,* and *psychophysiological disorders.* These are the disorders that are most directly related to anxiety and stress. Then we will consider the most important *affective disorder,* depression, and the related *manic-depressive state.* Finally, we will consider *schizophrenia.* Other disorders will be mentioned when relevant.

MEDICAL STUDENTS' DISEASE: A CAUTION. The term "medical students' disease" originates from the experience of those studying medicine who, on reading about the symptoms of various diseases, find the list of complaints uncomfortably familiar and worry that they have the diseases! This is a common experience among people studying physical illnesses, and it may be even more common among those reading about psychological disorders. Many students read, for example, that obsessive-compulsive disorders are marked by recurring thoughts, often of a socially unacceptable nature, that will not go away. They realize that to some extent they have such thoughts and fear that they are neurotic and perhaps need treatment. The same thing happens when people read that depression is marked by loss of joy, appetite, and interest in outside activities.

Two points need to be mentioned. First, readers should simply be reassured that medical students' disease is common and that there is a strong tendency to think you have more of the symptoms of a disorder than is actually the case. Second, feeling similar to those who are suffering psychological difficulties should alert you to the fact that normal and abnormal behavior have much in common. Those who have breakdowns are human beings with human problems of the kind we all face. Their difficulties may be more extreme, but the chief difference is simply a less adequate ability to cope with common problems.

Anxiety Disorders

The first set of psychological disorders we will consider are called **anxiety disorders.** They appear when intense fears can no longer be contained by the defenses in the normal manner, and one of the following patterns of disordered behavior results.

Anxiety states are characterized by constant feelings of high anxiety and worry interspersed with short periods of intense panic, which include rapid heartbeat and sweating. Feelings of dissatisfaction and tension dominate. Victims may feel somewhat depressed, as well as intensely anxious. Usually the feelings

The term for the fear of snakes is *herpetophobia*. It is a relatively common phobia among men and women.

Susan Rosenberg, Photo Researchers, Inc.

of worry are not attached to any specific event, object, or person. There is simply a feeling of "free-floating anxiety." Marilyn Monroe suffered these kinds of anxiety attacks often, especially at night. A good night's sleep was rare for her, and she used depressant drugs (barbiturates) to try to relieve the anxiety symptoms and get some needed rest.

Anxiety states occur when people are unable to defend themselves against anxiety resulting from an increase in threat in the environment or increased anxiety-causing impulses or feelings. These attacks are usually immobilizing and interfere with coping. One usually improves when the environment becomes less threatening or when one gains more control over oneself, possibly with the help of others.

Phobias are another kind of anxiety disorder. A phobia is an intense fear of a particular behavior, object, or place (see Chapter 5). Some kinds of phobias are common and well known. Perhaps the most famous is claustrophobia, the fear of enclosed places. Another common variety is acrophobia, the fear of high places. Some people suffer from agoraphobia, a fear of open places, and are afraid to go out of their houses or apartments. Still others have phobias about flying or being unaccompanied at social gatherings. Individuals with phobias experience intense fear of these things without really knowing why they are afraid.

Phobias help people minimize anxiety by causing them to avoid threatening circumstances. Their overall ability to function may be protected if they can focus their intense fears on just a few situations and avoid them. Such people are unable to deny all danger in the environment, but they limit their fears to a few avoidable objects. Most people with phobias are able to adapt quite well, unless their intense fears begin to spread and they become terrified of more and more things. Then there may be an inability to behave effectively.

Phobias have received a great deal of attention recently—so much so, in fact, that *Newsweek* magazine proclaimed them the disorder of the 1980s (*Newsweek*, 1984). An estimated one out of nine adults in the United States suffers from some kind of phobia. This makes phobias the second leading psychological and adjustment problem, after alcohol abuse. Phobias are usually experienced at first by young adults, mostly in their late teens and early twenties, and for many people phobias continue for many years after first experienced. Phobias strike women four times as often as they do men. Although phobias are becoming an increasing problem in modern society, they have been around for centuries. The ancient Greek physician Hippocrates, the "father of medicine," reported the case of an individual who experienced intense fear of the sound of flutes at banquets. So this modern disorder has ancient roots.

There are several different general clas-

TABLE 7.1

Phobias

There are long lists of phobias in medical texts, some quite common but some quite rare and obscure. The lists indicate the large and varied number of things people have been afraid of over the years. Below is a partial list of the many phobias that have been named (*Newsweek*, 1984):

Acrophobia: fear of heights
Aerophobia: fear of flying
Agoraphobia: fear of open spaces
Ailurophobia: fear of cats
Amaxophobia: fear of cars and driving
Anthrophobia: fear of human beings
Aquaphobia: fear of water
Arachnophobia: fear of spiders
Astraphobia: fear of lightning
Brontophobia: fear of thunder
Claustrophobia: fear of enclosed spaces
Cynophobia: fear of dogs
Dementophobia: fear of insanity
Gephyrophobia: fear of bridges
Herpetophobia: fear of reptiles
Mikrophobia: fear of germs
Murophobia: fear of mice
Numerophobia: fear of numbers
Nyctophobia: fear of darkness
Ochlophobia: fear of crowds
Ophidiophobia: fear of snakes
Ornithophobia: fear of birds
Phonophobia: fear of speaking aloud
Pyrophobia: fear of fire
Thanatophobia: fear of death
Trichophobia: fear of hair
Xenophobia: fear of strangers

sifications of the various phobias (see Table 7.1 for a list of different phobias). The "simple phobias" include fears of specific objects or events, such as heights, animals, and driving across bridges. The so-called "social phobias" include fears of passing out at parties or eating in public. It has been said that social phobics wear the most attractive and dignified underwear because they're afraid they might have to be taken to a hospital.

Special mention should be made of agoraphobia, the fear of open places. It's unique because it consists not only of a fear of open places, but also of a fear of fear and panic itself. Agoraphobics never know if they can go outside and cope or not, because they never know when they'll suffer a panic attack. They fear the symptoms of high fear or panic we noted before: breaking out in a sweat, a racing heart beat, a shortness of breath, and a feeling of loss of motor control. Agoraphobics' fear of fear leads them to stay inside and avoid any situation where they may be overcome with fear. An estimated 1 out of 20 adults suffers from agoraphobia, and the cause of this disorder is currently unknown.

Although phobias are of increasing concern in our society, the good news is that phobias are one of the most easily treated of all psychological disorders. We'll see how in Chapter 8.

Obsessional disorders involving obsessive or compulsive traits are among the most troublesome anxiety disorders. An **obsession** is an idea or feeling that won't go away. It may well frighten a person or make him or her feel guilty, and there seems to be no way to be rid of it. A **compulsion** is an urge to act that won't go away. After the person performs the act, he or she feels compelled to do it over and over again. Because many people have obsessive thoughts and urges, the obsessional disorders are in some ways the most similar to normal behavior patterns. The difference is only a matter of degree and a question of being able to exert some control over the obsession.

Obsessional thoughts are usually of two types. First there are thoughts of an aggressive or sexual nature. An example might be an urge to throw scalding coffee at someone else whenever one pours a cup. Many people have crude sexual thoughts. These thoughts are common to normal people but can be controlled fairly easily. In the obsessive person they don't go away.

In contrast to these thoughts about impulsive actions are obsessions and compulsions having to do with cleanliness, orderliness, safety, and duty, with accompanying guilt feelings for not repeating these socially approved actions frequently enough. A person may worry obsessively all the way to work that she left her door unlocked at home, knowing full well that she locked it. Before leaving for work she may have felt compelled to check the lock several times. She feels inadequate because of a fear of having been careless and because she can't control that fear. Compulsions to lock, check, clean, help, apologize, and so forth seem to represent an extremely rigid way of compensating for antisocial impulses. They have their roots in feelings of guilt, but do not totally relieve those feelings.

In discussing anxiety disorders we would like to mention briefly the closely related problem of **hypochondriasis.** This is not an anxiety disorder, strictly speaking. Instead it involves the focusing of anxiety on constant worries about physical ailments. Every time the person has an ache, he or she worries that it's cancer. A slight pain in the chest is feared to be a heart attack. The worry about physical symptoms is unending. The familiar term "hypochondriac" is applied to people who are always worried about being ill or becoming ill. Closely related to hypochondria is the disorder known as **neurasthenia,** characterized by chronic tiredness, fatigue, or exhaustion.

In concluding this section we should remember that anxiety disorders represent extreme reactions to stress and anxiety in which normal defensive personality trends, which might seem merely "neurotic," are disturbed and followed by more serious disorders. Still, in most anxiety disorders the person functions adequately on a day-to-day basis. The disorder may impair optimal adjustment, but there is no complete breakdown of functioning or loss of contact with reality. Marilyn Monroe's anxiety state made acting difficult and unpleasant, but not impossible.

Dissociative Disorders

Among the most intriguing of the psychological disorders are those involving **dissociated states.** A relatively mild dissociated state is psychologically caused forgetting, or **amnesia.** An amnesiac usually forgets temporarily who and where he or she is. This loss of memory is caused by some kind of intense anxiety. Cases of amnesia often follow traumatic experiences. Soldiers in combat may feel overwhelmed by fear or by guilt for not acting bravely. Their loss of memory of who they are or what they are supposed to be doing represents an extremely rigid form of denying danger or repressing guilt. In civilian cases amnesia is also associated with extreme threat or conflict. Loss of identity is a mechanism for temporarily escaping the whole problem.

More extreme dissociated states can involve "split personalities," or multiple personalities. One of the most famous of these was dramatized in the film *The Three Faces of Eve* (see Chapter 8). These cases are extremely rare, but there are several well-documented instances. Amnesia involves temporary forgetting of identity, during which time the person is simply "lost." In cases of multiple personalities, one or more new personalities develop during the time the primary identity is dissociated. Usually the later personalities express parts of the person that are incompatible with the normal identity. They are repressed, split off from the primary identity, but somehow gain the power to assert themselves as separate dissociated personalities. A famous case of multiple personalities reported by Morton Prince (1905) was Miss Beauchamp who, like "Eve," had three personalities: a prime and restrained personality, an independent and ambitious personality, and a playful and fun-loving personality. These multiple personality disorders are as intriguing as they are uncommon.

In some ways the classic dissociative disorder is **hysteria.** Freud first became interested in psychodynamic studies in attempting to treat hysteria. He published *Studies in Hysteria* in 1895 with Joseph Breuer. Hysteria involves loss of a physical function when there is no physical reason for it. Most often hysteria involves paralysis of an arm or leg or a side of the body. There may also be **mutism,** an inability to speak, or **tics,** spasmodic jerking. Hysteria seems to be produced by defensive inhibition of a body function that has come to be associated with great stress or anxiety. In one of Freud's cases, a woman developed an arm pa-

MEASURING HYSTERIA

People with an hysterical personality tend to react to stress with physical symptoms, to lack insight into their psychological problems, and to deny their deep feelings. People who answer true to items like the even-numbered questions and false to items like the odd-numbered questions below get higher scores on the MMPI (Hathaway & McKinley, 1943), a test designed to measure hysteria and other psychological symptoms.

1. I'm not bothered by the sight of blood.
2. I frequently feel utterly exhausted.
3. People don't tell the truth unless they have to.
4. I frequently have a very pressing headache.
5. I don't have any aches or pains.
6. One of my biggest problems is concentration.
7. I am often suspicious when I see people being friendly.
8. I often have an upset stomach.
9. I like suspense on TV shows.
10. Sometimes I just want to act outrageous or dangerously.

REVIEW QUESTIONS

1. Uncertainty and/or the inability to cope with stress creates feelings of _____ that, if intense enough, can lead to the development of _____ _____ .
2. _____ _____ are psychological disorders that appear when normal coping mechanisms no longer work.
3. Unlike generalized anxiety states, _____ involve an intense fear of a specific object, behavior, or place.
4. Match the following anxiety disorders with the appropriate description.
   _____ acrophobia   a. fear of enclosed places
   _____ anxiety states   b. fear of open places; people with this phobia seldom leave
   _____ claustrophobia   their house
   _____ agoraphobia   c. generalized feelings of anxiety and worry
                              d. fear of high places
5. T or F: Social phobias are experienced by men more often than women, though women experience anxiety states more often.
6. _____ are reoccurring thoughts that won't go away; _____ are urges to perform certain actions or rituals repetitively.
7. Jane runs to the doctor fearing she is very ill every time she feels a slight pain. She may be said to have _____ .
8. Amnesia, multiple personality disorder, and hysteria are examples of _____ _____ .

ralysis that seemed to be related to a repressed urge to stroke her father in what may have seemed too intimate a fashion. As this case suggests, hysteria seems to result from extreme repression. There is actual physical inhibition, as well as psychological blocking of wishes. Hysteria used to be much more common, especially among women, whose physical freedom and spontaneous desires were curtailed by conventional sex-role conditioning. It is much less prevalent in today's less-repressed society.

Psychophysiological Disorders

Along with anxiety disorders, **psychophysiological,** or psychosomatic, **disorders** are the most common disturbances produced by stress and anxiety. It is often useful to think of anxiety disorders and psychophysiological disorders as two sides of the same coin. Some people respond to intense stress and anxiety with disorders in which their problems are expressed psychologically. Others respond with bodily breakdowns in which their problems are expressed physically.

The most useful analysis of the relation between stress and psychosomatic disorder is Selye's (1956) account of the General Adaptation Syndrome (GAS) (see Chapter 6). Selye suggests that when a person perceives a demand or threat in the environment, there is an emotional reaction of alarm. This initial stress response includes a physiological component that readies the organism for effective behavior to counter the threat, usually some form of "fight or flight." Marilyn Monroe usually felt tendencies in both directions when she believed people in Hollywood were hostile to her. She wanted to strike out at them, and she also had the urge to take flight—literally, to New York, where people might be more congenial. Her constant lateness and procrastination had elements of both fight and flight in them. She inconvenienced, and in that way punished, the movie executives, and she avoided, at least temporarily, the threatening demands of working.

Although we are readied by the GAS for fight or flight, in many instances we take no action, we don't express our fears and anger, or the action we do take doesn't remove the threat. If this is the case, the physiological reaction will continue until we stop thinking about the threat or until it is removed. Over a long period of time, this continuing stress can produce physical illnesses considered to be psychophysiological. They are called psychosomatic, or psychophysiological, because they have their origin in the perception of threat and the emotional reaction to it.

Let's take for example a student who is worried about her future business career. She knows she must do well in college the whole time she is there if she wants to get into business school. The demands placed on her by the requirements of business school produce stress. She has to cope. She does so by studying hard and doing well. But her coping behavior doesn't remove the demand and the threat of failure. She may get an A this week, but she needs another one next week as well. The pressure is constant. If the pressure produces long-term emotional and physiological responses, damage to the internal organs can occur. In sum, continued, emotionally produced physiological responding is what causes psychosomatic illness. Many parts of the body can be damaged, including the digestive system, the circulatory system, and the respiratory system.

STUDIES OF LIFE STRESSES AND ILLNESS. The general idea that life stress can cause physical illness is demonstrated dramatically in Holmes and Rahe's (1967) studies of coping with stressful changes in the environment. Holmes and Rahe attempted to measure the amount of change and readjustment required by more than 40 different life events and to correlate the amount of readjustment required with illness. Not all the events on their scale are threatening, but they all can be regarded as stressful in that they do require adaptive action. The event receiving the highest rating, 100, was the death of a spouse. Other examples were marital separation, 73; marriage, 50; gaining a new family

TABLE 7.2

Social Readjustment Rating Scale

RANK	LIFE EVENT	MEAN VALUE
1	Death of spouse	100
2	Divorce	73
3	Marital separation	65
4	Jail term	63
5	Death of close family member	63
6	Personal injury or illness	53
7	Marriage	50
8	Fired at work	47
9	Marital reconciliation	45
10	Retirement	45
11	Change in health of family member	44
12	Pregnancy	40
13	Sex difficulties	39
14	Gain of new family member	39
15	Business readjustment	39
16	Change in financial state	38
17	Death of close friend	37
18	Change to different line of work	36
19	Change in number of arguments with spouse	35
20	Mortgage or loan for major purchase (home, etc.)	31
21	Foreclosure of mortgage or loan	30
22	Change in responsibilities at work	29
23	Son or daughter leaving home	29
24	Trouble with in-laws	29
25	Outstanding personal achievement	28
26	Wife beginning or stopping work	26
27	Beginning or ending school	26
28	Change in living conditions	25
29	Revision of personal habits	24
30	Trouble with boss	23
31	Change in work hours or conditions	20
32	Change in residence	20
33	Change in schools	20
34	Change in recreation	19
35	Change in church activities	19
36	Change in social activities	18

TABLE 7.2 cont.

Social Readjustment Rating Scale

RANK	LIFE EVENT	MEAN VALUE
37	Mortgage or loan for lesser purchase (car, TV, etc.)	17
38	Change in sleeping habits	16
39	Change in number of family get-togethers	15
40	Change in eating habits	15
41	Vacation	13
42	Christmas	12
43	Minor violations of the law	11

NOTE: The amount of life stress a person has experienced in a given period of time, say one year, is measured by the total number of life change units (LCUs). These units result from the addition of the values (shown in the right column) associated with events that the person has experienced during the target time period.
SOURCE: Reprinted with permission from *Journal of Psychometric Research*, 11, T. H. Holmes & R. H. Rahe, The social readjustment scale, copyright 1967, Pergamon Press, Ltd.

member, 39; outstanding personal achievement, 28; and trouble with one's boss, 23 (see Table 7.2) People whose lives had required a high amount of readjustment in recent months were more likely to suffer an illness than those facing little stress. Subsequent studies have shown that those who faced many life stresses in the past six months were more likely to have fatal heart attacks (Rahe & Lind, 1972; Thiel, Parker, & Bruce, 1973).

In the years since the development of the Holmes and Rahe scale new research has been done to improve the measurement of life event stress and the relationship between this source of stress and other stressors that can affect physical and psychological health (Scroeder & Costa, 1984). One study underlines the fact that day-in-and-day-out stress may have a more powerful impact on health than do the kinds of unusual and short-lived stressors we see in the life events scale (Billings & Moos, 1984). This study showed that both kinds of stressors, acute life events and chronic, everyday strains, are related to depression, but that chronic strains are usually more strongly related to the severity of the disorder. These findings suggest that we

Minor daily stresses can have a significant impact on mood. They can have more impact than major life events.

Lopez & Medina, Photo Researchers, Inc.

need to be alert not only to unusually demanding events, such as taking out a mortgage, but to such common events as work pressures, family strains, and illness. Both kinds of events can lead to psychological difficulties.

Another source of health difficulties is minor daily stresses, such as particular things that can go wrong in your household or customary routine: missing the bus, having an appliance break down, or spilling milk all over the tablecloth. A study of women in the Boston area who used the services of neighborhood health clinics showed that minor daily stressors had a greater direct impact on people's moods than did major life events or even chronic stressors (Eckenrode, 1984).

So we need to be aware of the fact that health and personal adjustment are affected by three kinds of external stressors: major life events, the chronic, day-in-and-day-out pressures of daily living, and minor daily irritations that come and go. All of these stressors challenge us and demand coping. They can produce psychophysiological disorders of many kinds.

ULCERS. Although psychosomatic research has expanded greatly in the past decade, the "classic" psychosomatic disorder is still the ulcer. More writing and research has been done on this problem than any other, and ulcers pro-

vide a useful illustration of how emotional arousal that is not released in effective action can produce physical illness. Emotional tension or worry can stimulate the flow of the stomach acid that is used in normal digestion. If this acid isn't absorbed by food, it can irritate the lining of the stomach and the small intestine, eventually causing an open, craterlike sore. Ulcers can range in size from a pinhead to a coin.

The most dramatic demonstration of the relationship between emotional upset and ulcers was reported in a study by Wolf and Wolff (1947). A man had had a small plastic window put into his stomach as the result of a severe childhood burn. This window permitted doctors to observe stomach secretions and their action on the stomach lining. They found that the acid caused a painful ulcer that went away when the wound was shielded from excess acid. Most important, they found that the flow of acid was markedly increased when the man was feeling anger and resentment due to stress. This study clearly shows the relationship between emotional arousal and ulcer-causing physiological responses. Other studies have shown that ulcers can result either from suppressed aggressive tendencies or from needs for love and tender care that are subordinated to the competitive drives needed for occupational success. Men have more than twice as many ulcers as women do (Calhoun, 1977), although this may be changing. This is probably because men are much more likely to suppress their needs to be taken care of and more apt to experience feelings of hostility and resentment in the competitive business world.

This research and other studies suggest that positions of responsibility in which action and decision making are required can produce emotional upset and ulcers. On the other hand, research by Seligman (1974) suggests that people become severely troubled if they have no control over their lives. Both too much and too little responsibility can be stressful for people. It is adaptive to be able to judge how much responsibility one can manage without feeling overwhelmed, and to take on tasks and challenges that make our lives full but not overloaded.

PERSONALITY AND PSYCHOSOMATIC BREAKDOWN.
Although we know that emotional responses produced by tension and threat can cause physical illness, it is not at all clear why some people get ulcers and other people suffer from hypertension, migraine headaches, or asthma. Selye (1956) suggested that stress produces a "general" physiological arousal and that the weakest part of the body breaks down first. Others (Alexander, 1950) have suggested that specific kinds of emotional reactions, such as anger or dependency yearnings, produce specific bodily reactions and illnesses. This is an unresolved issue.

In spite of the uncertainty involved in knowing exactly how specific stresses in specific people cause specific illnesses, advances are being made in studies of the role of personality factors in determining what kind of psychosomatic difficulties, if any, a person is likely to have. Some people aren't upset by situations that make most people very anxious; they suffer less stress and are less subject to breakdown. Others are able to turn their attention away from worry or to express their agitation in constructive activity, such as exercise or art. One of Marilyn Monroe's difficulties was that she couldn't stop worrying that she was inadequate and that she would fail. At certain points in her life she would overeat and gain weight as a result of worry. Others in the same situation respond differently.

One important line of research has identified some of the factors that make people resistant to stress, giving them a stress-hardy personality. Three important characteristics are challenge, commitment, and control (Borysenko, 1984).

We can understand challenge by remembering that the Chinese word for "crisis" is composed of the word for "danger" and the word for "opportunity." We can look at stress in this way too. Some people look at stress as an opportunity or a challenge, a chance to work hard to succeed and overcome an obstacle. Others look at stress as dangerous and overly taxing. Being able to confront stress as a challenge is one characteristic that makes an individual stress-hardy.

The stress-hardy person sees the demands of the environment as opportunities for making a commitment. He or she sees a task as worth the effort and as something that is important to achieve. Feeling challenged and feeling committed to succeed in the challenge are adaptive responses to stressful situations. Toward the end of her life, Marilyn Monroe could look on *The Misfits* as a challenge worth her commitment. She felt she could handle her role in that movie and that handling it, and herself, was necessary to getting back on the road to productivity and happiness. Unfortunately, her commitment didn't last.

Control is also crucial to the stress-hardy personality. As we noted in Chapter 5, people must feel that they have some degree of control over their lives if they are going to accept challenges and make the commitment to overcoming obstacles. Too much responsibility can overload the circuits and lead to psychophysiological breakdown, but perceiving that one's experiences and achievements are under one's control is important in enabling a person to cope with the demands of a complex world.

One extremely promising line of research on personality differences in response to stress has shown that certain kinds of people, known as Type As, are more likely to have heart trouble than are others, called Type Bs (Glass, 1976). Type A people are hard-driving, success-oriented, and very concerned with time and getting things done on a rigid schedule. They tend to make inflexible work plans and ignore fatigue. They are competitive, impatient, and hostile when criticized. The underlying disposition of the Type As seems to be an unrealistic need for control and predictability. They act in a frenzied but often ineffective manner. Type Bs are more realistic about what they can and can't do, organize other people better, and work better in groups. Because of these skills they often achieve more as managers and leaders. The hard-driving Type A pattern is self-defeating, in terms of both getting things done and staying healthy.

Many other physical symptoms have been associated with stress, emotional upset, and life pressures. These include hypertension (high blood pressure), some forms of asthma, migraine headaches, various skin disorders such as eczema, and colitis (chronic diarrhea). Research on possible psychological factors involved in disease is growing. One of the most interesting is the study of possible emotional factors involved in cancer. Reports by Schmeck (1974) and Marcus (1976) suggest that people who get cancer are emotionally restrained or suppressed even though their lives contain a good deal of stress. They tend to abide faithfully by conventional social restriction. While the link between cancer and emotional constriction has not been proven, it is consistent with other research showing the dangers to health that psychological tension can pose.

REVIEW QUESTIONS

9. The body's physiological response to stress has been implicated in a number of disorders such as migraines, hypertension, and ulcers. These are called _____ disorders.

10. T or F: Both pleasant and unpleasant major life events can negatively affect health and personal adjustment.

11. Suppressed aggressive tendencies as well as unfulfilled needs for love and tender care have been implicated in the development of _____ .

12. Psychologists have identified three attributes that distinguish stress-resistant people from people who seem to be susceptible to stressors. For stress-resistant individuals stress is more likely to be seen as a _____ and an opportunity for _____ . Additionally people who are more resistant to stressors believe themselves to have _____ over the events in their lives.

13. T or F: "Type A" people tend to have an unrealistic need for control and predictability—a pattern that may be associated with their higher incidence of heart trouble.

Thus we can see how stress produces emotional arousal, which includes a physiological component. The physiological response will continue if action is not taken that improves the threatening situation and can eventually cause real damage to organs of the body.

Affective Disorders: Depression

Anxiety, dissociative, and psychophysiological disorders are all usually attributable to specific anxieties and stresses. The affective disorder depression presents a much more mysterious and confusing problem. It is probably the most common of all psychological disturbances, but it is so varied in its seriousness and causes that it is somewhat more difficult to understand than other disorders.

At its core, depression is characterized by sadness and lack of energy. We all have periods of mild depression that shouldn't really be regarded as disordered and certainly aren't psychotic. But millions of people from all walks of life have more severe bouts with depression. Abraham Lincoln was haunted throughout his life by severe depressive episodes, what were then called the "hypos." Other famous figures, such as "Buzz" Aldrin, the second man on the moon, have had shorter phases of depression. And, of course, Marilyn Monroe suffered from severe drug-caused depression in her later years, and, although we can't be sure, she may have committed suicide during a period of depression.

Depression ranges from very mild bouts of feeling "down," to severe sadness, to profound, "psychotic" depression. In its psychotic form, depression often alternates with periods of wild elation and high energy called **mania.** This cyclical pattern of depression and mania forms the manic-depressive psychosis. In addition to involving sadness and lack of energy, depression is characterized by loss of all positive feeling, including joy and humor, loss of appetite, loss of sexual interest, inability to sleep well, and feelings of worthlessness, helplessness, and despair. The depressed person is unable to concentrate on tasks or to function

Depression is a common but severe psychological disorder. New research on biochemical aspects of depression holds out a promise for cure.

Arthur Tress, Photo Researchers, Inc.

effectively. In its extreme psychotic form, depression may also include delusions, such as the belief that one is being punished in hell for one's wrongdoings.

Depression seems to have its roots in low self-esteem. People with negative feelings about themselves and the world often have intense guilt reactions and feelings of self-blame when they encounter failure or disturbing losses. They feel self-hatred, worthlessness, helplessness, and an inability to take any effective action to improve their situation; at the same time they tend to believe that they are responsible for the state they're in and somehow should have been able to do more to prevent it. The result of all these feelings is a lack of interest in doing anything, and eventually depression sets in. Studies of a phenomenon known as "learned helplessness" are relevant here (Seligman, 1974). They indicate that people can become depressed when they have continued negative experiences over which they have no control. They "learn" that there is nothing they can do to control their fate, and they become inactive and depressed. This feeling of being wounded

and having no recourse seems to be at the root of depression.

Evidence suggests physiological causes of depression as well. People with certain chemical imbalances, which may be genetically transmitted, that is, inherited from their parents, are most likely to have the severe forms of depression. It's very possible that Marilyn Monroe's psychological imbalance was in part inherited. Little is known about her father, but her mother was psychotic, as were both her mother's parents. All three spent many years in mental hospitals. In addition, the manic periods of the manic-depressive disorder may be related to physiological cycles, although some psychologists believe that manic periods are caused by denial of the significance of a depression-producing loss and subsequent reaction formation, which in turn produces feelings of euphoria and boundless energy.

DEPRESSION AND SUICIDE. Marilyn Monroe's life is an example of the strong link between depression and suicide. Recent studies indicate

MEASURING DEPRESSION

There are several measures of depression. One personality inventory has items like the ones below. People who answer false to items like the odd-numbered questions and true to items like the even-numbered questions are more similar to depressed people than those who answer the opposite way. When people answer similarly to people who feel depressed, it may indicate that they are feeling low or depressed themselves.

1. I am as sharp as I ever was before.
2. I have a lot of trouble sleeping.
3. I generally believe that my life has been worth living.
4. I often feel that I lack zest and energy.
5. I am involved in many different kinds of enjoyable leisure activities.
6. Other people seem happier than I am.
7. I'm not any more jittery than the next person.
8. I seem to cry a lot.
9. I often feel energetic and excited.
10. I have a deep lack of confidence.

that up to 94 percent of the people who commit suicide have had depressive episodes. As many as 80 percent are depressed prior to committing suicide. In Marilyn's case the overall deterioration in her life, plus excessive use of barbiturates, contributed to depression and eventually to a "probable suicide." The specific feeling associated with suicide is hopelessness, usually precipitated by some crisis in the person's life. These crises could involve difficulties in interpersonal relationships, especially marriage, failure at work, or an inability to achieve something of meaning or significance.

It's difficult to assess the prevalence of suicide and suicide attempts in the United States, because many attempts go unrecorded and many deaths are attributed to other, less stigmatized causes. It seems that about 200,000 to 250,000 attempts are made a year and that at least 25,000 of these actually end in death. Some estimates go as high as 60,000. Somewhere between 1 and 3 percent of people in

the United States have attempted suicide at least once in their lives. College students are twice as likely to commit suicide as are other people of the same age.

One of the most dramatic problems to arise in recent years is the increase in suicides by teenagers and young adults. In the last two decades the suicide rate among people 15 to 24 years old has increased 300 percent (Williams, 1984). In 1981 there were 13 suicides per 100,000 people in this age group. One alarming phenomenon is the tendency for there to be a rash of suicides in a single community or geographical area. In 1983 a series of suicides occurred among young people in Plano, Texas, and in 1984 a similar string of suicides occurred in the New York City area. In many cases the suicides have occurred in prosperous neighborhoods among young people who seem to be accomplished and well adjusted and to have everything to live for. One question that comes up in these cases is whether there is a modeling or imitation effect. Do young people who hear of someone near them committing suicide begin thinking of it themselves? One 13-year-old boy who hung himself from a tree in New York apparently identified with and imitated the suicide of a character in the movie *An Officer and a Gentleman.*

The causes of adolescent and young adult suicide are difficult to establish, but several factors have recently been implicated. One contributor is family breakdown. This can be traced to a divorce, a death in the family, or even to parents becoming so intensely involved in their careers that they lose touch with their children. Youngsters then feel that nobody cares (Brody, 1984). Disruption of social relationships with peers caused by a family moving also increases the risk of suicide.

Ironically, both too little and too much parental involvement and pressure can increase young people's risk of suicide. If teenagers are raised in an atmosphere that's too permissive, where anything goes and there's no structure or discipline, problems can arise. Young people in this kind of unstructured atmosphere are more likely to get involved with alcohol or other drugs, for example. Drug abuse doesn't directly cause suicide, but it does contribute to the lowering of self-esteem that's a factor leading to suicide. Rules and standards are needed to give young lives structure. At the same time, too much parental pressure to succeed and be "the best" can increase the risk of suicide. Young people may feel worthless if they disappoint parental aspirations, even if they perform at a high level.

It is estimated that approximately 80 percent of the young people who commit suicide give a sign of their intentions beforehand. If parents, friends, or teachers can recognize such signs, many of these troubling deaths could be prevented. Sometimes the signs are verbal, such as a teenager saying "I wish I'd never been born." People may also give behavioral signals of their suicidal tendencies. Behaviors to be concerned about are withdrawal of effort from school work or from outside interests, getting into trouble with authorities or taking uncharacteristic risks, and changes in eating or sleeping patterns. Often the loss of a significant

relationship, with a boyfriend or girlfriend or with a close friend of the same sex, can lead to suicide attempts. Parents should be alert to these signs, and peers should report them to parents or other professional helpers. Professional intervention is needed quickly when these signs are present. It may be that suicide is the farthest thing from the young person's mind, but responding when there is trouble is never wasted effort.

While it's true that many people who attempt suicide fail and most are not committed to killing themselves, a suicide attempt should be taken seriously. Twelve percent of those who make an unsuccessful attempt do in fact kill themselves within the next two years. When a person threatens suicide, it's wise to remember that he or she is probably very ambivalent about ending his or her life. Suicide counselors try to remind people contemplating suicide that there is much in living that they value, that the crisis will pass, and that suicide is irrevocable. People who are deeply troubled and thinking about suicide can telephone for help in most communities. Suicide prevention centers and telephone help lines are now common in most areas of the country.

Schizophrenia

Of all the disorders that can be produced by the stresses of living, none is more serious and less understood than *schizophrenia,* a psychosis characterized chiefly by extreme breakdown in the normal processes of thought. The break with reality may for a time be total. Schizophrenia also involves impairments in language, feeling, perception, and behavior. At the core of the disorder, however, is the disordered thought process. Anxiety disorders and depression are debilitating disturbances, but schizophrenia is in a class by itself in terms of its extreme impact. In this section we will consider the basic nature of schizophrenia, when and how it occurs, the different forms it takes, and its causes.

THOUGHT DISORDER IN SCHIZOPHRENIA. As noted above, a breakdown in thinking is the fundamental feature of schizophrenia. At its most basic level, this breakdown can be seen in the association patterns of schizophrenics. When they are asked to say the first word that comes to their minds when a word is read to them, they are apt to give highly unusual responses, responses that are understandable in a way, but clearly seem "weird." Often the association the schizophrenic makes is to the sound of the word. For example, the person might associate *table* to the word *stable*. Sometimes the association is a very remote one. Often the word a schizophrenic supplies is obscene.

In their everyday lives, schizophrenics express their distorted associations and thought processes in *delusions* and *hallucinations*. **Delusions** are false and irrational beliefs that are clearly in contradiction to reality. They usually take the form of delusions of grandeur, where the individual feels he or she is a very important or famous person, such as Jesus, Cleopatra, or Napolean Bonaparte. Schizophrenics also can have delusions of persecution, where they feel that others are secretly plotting to harm or destroy them. **Hallucinations** are disordered perceptions, such as smelling strange odors, hearing voices, and seeing objects floating in space. Sometimes when a schizophrenic talks, the words seem totally incoherent and have no meaning. They are completely confused, resembling a word salad.

In the early stages of thought disintegration, people who are becoming schizophrenic are often aware of the increasing unreality of their thoughts. They feel that they can't exert control over these thoughts, even though the thoughts are "crazy." They may also simultaneously wish to control the unusual thoughts and to give them expression. They're afraid of completely losing control. This lack of control extends into schizophrenics' emotions and behavior. Their feelings and actions can be wild. The breakdown in thought extends to a breakdown of the organization of the personality, an inability to cope with reality, and even an inability to control one's own behavior.

SCHIZOPHRENIC BREAKDOWN. Schizophrenia usually takes hold in late adolescence or early adulthood, as people struggle with difficult life decisions and tasks. Stresses involved in intimate relations, raising a family, or succeeding at work can lead to a schizophrenic episode, the more so as these stresses threaten a person's self-esteem or sense of adequacy. Approximately 1 percent of the population worldwide becomes schizophrenic for some period of time. About 20 percent of those who are admitted to mental hospitals are diagnosed as schizophrenic. Because of the exceedingly long hospitalization the disorder may require, about 50 percent of those who are in mental hospitals at any one time are schizophrenic.

The actual onset of schizophrenia follows one of two patterns. There is the process-type onset, where there is a long, progressive deterioration of functioning that finally results in breakdown. No single event causes this gradual decline. In contrast to this pattern is the reactive-type onset, which is quite sudden, following a highly stressful event that is usually damaging to the person's self-esteem. In general, reactive types recover more quickly, just as they become disordered more quickly.

VARIETIES OF SCHIZOPHRENIA. Whether the schizophrenic is a process or reactive type, his or her disorder often takes one of four classic forms. There is some relationship between the type of onset (process or reactive) and the form of schizophrenia a person develops, but it doesn't always hold. The major varieties of schizophrenia are *simple, disorganized, catatonic,* and *paranoid*—the first two tending to be process types and the latter two, reactive types. Other schizophrenics are sometimes simply categorized as undifferentiated or residual types.

Simple schizophrenia usually develops gradually and is marked by withdrawal, disinterest, and apathy. The person does less and less, and there is a deterioration in the quality of his or her thoughts, feelings, and relationships with others. The person puts little effort

TABLE 7.3

Aspects of Schizophrenia

TYPES OF ONSET OF SCHIZOPHRENIA

Process-type onset: gradual, long progressive deterioration in functioning that finally results in breakdown

Reactive-type onset: sudden onset of schizophrenia following a highly stressful event that is generally damaging to a person's self-esteem

VARIETIES OF SCHIZOPHRENIA

Simple (usually process-type onset): characterized by withdrawal, disinterest, and apathy; person needs nearly constant care

Disorganized (usually process-type onset): more extreme than simple type, characterized by extensive personality disintegration and regressed, childlike behavior; maximally impaired thought and action

Catatonic (usually reactive-type onset): marked by alternating periods of total withdrawal and inactivity with periods of great excitement, lack of control, and potentially dangerous behavior

Paranoid (usually reactive-type onset): marked by delusions of persecution or grandeur, hallucinations and disorganized thinking, with central belief that others are conspiring to cause their difficulties

---

or caring into living and gradually loses the ability to mobilize himself or herself to behave effectively. Then, unless someone at home is available for nearly constant care, hospitalization results.

Disorganized schizophrenia is a more extreme form of the condition. Much more extensive personality disintegration occurs, and behavior is even more regressed and childlike. The person acts very silly, with inappropriate laughing and giggling, often using obscene language and acting in bizarre ways. Thinking and behavior seem most impaired in this form.

In catatonic schizophrenia there is usually an alternation of periods of total withdrawal, inactivity, and unresponsiveness with periods of great excitement and activity, usually marked by wildly uncontrolled and dangerous behavior. During the withdrawal phase the person is in a schizophrenic *stupor*. There is no activity at all, and the person is completely oblivious to his or her surroundings. He or she usually maintains a rigid position and stares off into space.

In the case of paranoid schizophrenia the major symptoms are delusions, usually of persecution and grandeur, accompanied by hallucinations and other disorganized thinking. It seems as if paranoid schizophrenics are blaming their difficulties on others by using extreme and irrational projections. They often act violently against those they think are conspiring against them. Paranoid schizophrenia should be distinguished from another rare psychosis, **paranoia,** in which the person has similar delusions of persecution and conspiracy, but no hallucinations and no overall breakdown in thought.

THE CAUSES OF SCHIZOPHRENIA. There is no clear explanation for what causes schizophrenia. In recent years, however, an account has begun to take shape. Early theories of schizophrenia emphasized environmental factors, usually parental treatment, that stressed the child and led him or her to develop disordered modes of coping that eventually resulted in schizophrenia. For a time, in a more sexist era, the concept of the "schizophrenogenic mother" was popular, blaming schizophrenia on mothers who drove their children crazy, usually by speaking to them in a "double binding," contradictory fashion whereby their behavior was criticized no matter how they responded (see Chapter 9). Other theories also emphasized the stresses in the early years that led to schizophrenic breakdown.

In recent years, more and more attention has focused on the physiological determinants of thought disorder and on evidence suggesting that a genetically controlled chemical factor is involved in schizophrenia (Crider, 1979). The evidence suggests that people inherit from their parents a predisposition for schizophrenic breakdown. This is first manifest in a low weight

---

REVIEW QUESTIONS

14. _____ is an affective disorder characterized by sadness, lack of energy, and sleep and appetite disturbances.

15. Which of the following is implicated in suicide?
    a. depression
    b. family breakdown
    c. suicide threats
    d. low self-esteem
    e. all of the above

16. Delusions of grandeur or of persecution, hallucinations, and disordered patterns of thought are all symptoms of _____ .

17. A major distinction can be made between schizophrenic reactions by looking at the onset of the disorder. The type of schizophrenic reaction characterized by a slow progressive deterioration of function is known as _____ schizophrenia whereas the relatively sudden schizophrenic reaction, usually following some highly stressful event is termed _____ schizophrenia.

18. Match the type of schizophrenia with the appropriate symptoms.
    _____ simple
    _____ disorganized
    _____ catatonic
    _____ paranoid

    a. extensive personality disintegration, regressed inappropriate behavior
    b. gradual deterioration, withdrawal, disinterest, apathy
    c. periods of stupor, alternated with hyperactive periods
    d. delusions of persecution and grandeur

19. T or F: Research has demonstrated that a genetic predisposition is the primary causal factor in schizophrenia.

---

at birth and other signs of weakness and low ability to withstand stress. Often these people are less able to cope effectively than are other children of the same age, and at each stage of development they fall further behind and become less able to cope. Not all people who inherit a predisposition will become schizophrenic. They may be able to withstand the normal stresses of living. Perhaps they can be strengthened in some way. But, overall, they have more of a chance of becoming schizophrenic than others do.

It should be made clear that, while genetic factors may be important, stress also plays a central role in schizophrenia, especially in the reactive types. But it is difficult to say that any *particular* stressor, such as parental double binding, is the key. It seems, as we have emphasized so far, that stress of many varieties can lead to disorders of many kinds in many people. Schizophrenia is likely to be the form that breakdown takes in people with an inherited predisposition. If stress gradually or suddenly overwhelms them, schizophrenia is likely to result.

Who Is Psychologically "Sick"?

Is it appropriate to call psychologically disturbed people "sick"? How exactly can we define "psychological health"? Was it sick for Marilyn Monroe to resent the studio executives' exploitation of her and to be suspicious and uncooperative with them? Her attitudes did cause her difficulty, but they may have been valid, and it seems unfair to call them "sick." Did her difficulties represent her own inadequacies, or did they stem from unhealthy aspects of her environment that needed treatment as much as she did?

On the one hand it seems to make sense to regard those who are functioning effectively as "healthy" and those who are functioning ineffectively as "sick." Yet several psychiatrists and social critics have challenged this view. They have pointed out that there are many things wrong with our society and that those who easily fit in, who conform, are often less psychologically healthy than those who refuse to conform, but want instead to live their lives in their own ways. The problem, according to such critics as R. D. Laing (1967), Erving Goffman (1963), and Thomas Szasz (1974), is that those who act differently and deviate from the normal arrangements make trouble. They are less predictable because they don't follow "rituals of interaction," and they raise questions about the validity of normal ways of behaving. They challenge the common rules of "deference and demeanor" (Goffman, 1967).

The response to such deviants, according to these critics, is to label them "sick," and often to confine them in mental hospitals. When psychiatrists do this, it reassures people in society that their behavior is normal and that deviants are sick. But is this true? Laing, Goffman, and Szasz argue that it isn't necessarily sick to fail to adjust to modern society. Goffman (1963) argues that traditional social arrangements are terribly stifling and require a great deal of conformity and that it isn't abnormal, in the sense of sick, to resent them and fail to live up to them. Szasz (1974) says that mental illness is a "myth" we invent to justify removing deviants from society. Laing (1967) goes further and claims that modern society is insane. In fact, he says, "the behavior and experience that are labeled schizophrenic are a special sort of strategy that a person invents in order to live in an unlivable world" (Laing, 1967, p. 187). Laing has even suggested that schizophrenia is "hypersanity" and represents an attempt to escape the madness of the world and find true freedom and significance without being bound by conventional definitions or customs.

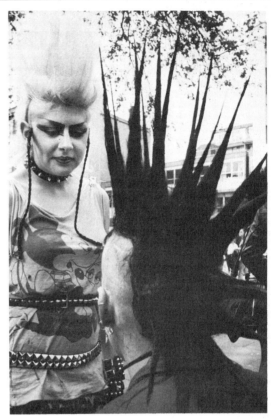

People who are deviant are sometimes labeled as psychologically disordered. Many critics of conventional values oppose this labeling as unfair and unjustified.

Bernard Pierre Wolff, Photo Researchers, Inc.

How should we react to these positions? It seems that the utility of these perspectives is to remind us how cruelly and inhumanly troubled people are often treated. Too often they are thought of as less than human because of their difficulties in managing and behaving effectively. There are extreme stresses in modern society, and those who can't cope with them should still be treated as fully human and helped, with as much respect for their psychological integrity as possible. We don't share Laing's view that it is insane to adjust because the world is insane. But we do believe in not labeling troubled people in ways that make them seem to be lesser human beings. As noted before, the differences between those who cope effectively and those who don't are often rather small.

SUMMARY

1. Anxiety is a major problem in the modern world. It stems from two sources: fears that have been learned in the past and then incubated and generalized to other similar objects and situations in the present; and stresses and pressures in the present.

2. Several kinds of psychological disorder can result from stress and anxiety. Anxiety disorders take the form of anxiety states, phobias, obsessional disorders, and hypochondriasis. Phobias, increasingly prevalent today, are disorders involving intense fears, such as agoraphobia, the fear of open places and of that panic reaction itself. Dissociative disorders include dissociated states (such as amnesia), multiple personalities, and hysteria. Psychophysiological disorders, including ulcers and heart attacks, are caused by excessive stress from life events, chronic everyday pressures, and minor daily irritations.

3. Stress-hardy people regard stress as a challenge, commit themselves to overcome the challenge, and feel control over their lives.

4. Hard-driving, success-oriented, and time-pressured people are called "Type A personalities" and are more likely to have heart attacks than are the more easy-going and realistic "Type B personalities."

5. Depression is a common affective disorder caused by feelings of helplessness and worthlessness. Depression takes many forms, from mild "blues" to deep psychotic depression including delusions.

6. Suicide is closely linked to depression and is on the rise among young people ages 15 to 24. Teenage suicide is linked to family breakdown, disruption in peer relationships, lack of structure in daily living, and excessive pressure to succeed.

7. Some people become so overwhelmed by the stresses of living in adolescence or early adulthood that they become schizophrenic. For some the onset of this severe disorder is gradual (process type); for others it results from a sudden increase in stress (reactive type). The causes of schizophrenia are far from certain. Recent evidence strongly suggests a genetic component.

KEY TERMS

a. AMNESIA	g. INCUBATION
b. COMPULSION	h. MUTISM
c. DELUSION	i. NEURASTHENIA
d. GENERALIZATION	j. OBSESSION
e. HALLUCINATION	k. TICS
f. HYPOCHONDRIASIS	

1. A perception or mental image occurring without any external stimulus to cause it

2. Complete or partial loss of memory

3. A period of time in which a phobic reaction intensifies as a person avoids the original stimulus

4. Recurring thought or image experienced as uncontrollable intrusions into consciousness

5. A process by which a person comes to fear other stimuli that are associated with an original fearful event

6. Constant worrying about physical symptoms caused by anxiety
7. Chronic tiredness, exhaustion, or fatigue
8. Recurring, ritualistic behavior pattern experienced as irresistible
9. An inability to speak associated with hysteria
10. Spasmodic jerking or involuntary twitches associated with hysteria
11. A false belief held by a person without any objective evidence

ANSWERS TO REVIEW QUESTIONS

1. Anxiety; psychological disorders. **2.** Anxiety disorders. **3.** Anxiety states; phobias. **4.** d; c; a; b. **5.** False. **6.** Obsessions; compulsions. **7.** Hypochondriasis. **8.** Dissociative disorders.

9. Psychophysiological (or psychosomatic). **10.** True. **11.** Ulcers. **12.** Challenge; commitment; control. **13.** True.

14. Depression. **15.** e. **16.** Schizophrenia. **17.** Process-type; relative type. **18.** b; a; c; d. **19.** False.

GETTING HELP AND HELPING YOURSELF

T he patient, Eve White, was under hypnosis and discussing a very early and traumatic recollection when she gradually went into a trancelike state.

After a few minutes she seemed to wake up. She looked around the room with a bewildered expression and asked the therapist, with whom she had been working for months, "Who are you?" It was immediately apparent to the therapist that Eve White was exhibiting a completely different personality. The new one called herself Jane. Although this event was extremely surprising, there was some precedent for it. Jane was the third personality shown by this patient. Much earlier in treatment Eve White had come out of a similar moment of stress with an uncharacteristically bright and sassy "Hi there, Doc," manifesting the second personality, Eve Black.

Eve White, Eve Black, and Jane are pseudonyms that were used to protect the identity of the woman whose multiple personality was dramatized in the movie *The Three Faces of Eve*. This movie and a book of the same title by her therapists, Corbett Thigpen and Hervey Cleckley (1954; 1957) told only part of the story, however. Nearly a quarter of a century later, the woman, whose real name is Chris Costner Sizemore, told her own story in the remarkable book *I'm Eve* (Sizemore & Pittillo, 1977).

At the beginning the patient called Eve White appeared at a clinic in Augusta, Georgia. She was 25 years old, separated from her husband and their four-year-old daughter, and complaining of severe headaches and occasional blackouts. Initial interviews revealed nothing unusual except that the patient was unable to recall a recent trip she had made. But hypnosis quickly cleared up her amnesia. Then in one session Eve reported that she was hearing "voices" and was afraid that she was "insane." The therapist was startled by this revelation, and while he considered what to say, Eve White seemed to suffer a splitting headache. She emerged from this attack manifesting the personality of Eve Black for the first time in therapy.

Eve White and Eve Black couldn't have been more different. Eve White was quiet, reserved, kind, considerate, and very proper. She was extremely responsible in her attitude toward her young daughter, who was then living with Eve's parents. She had compassion and spirituality. Eve Black was saucy and childlike. She was mischievous, sensual, and somewhat irresponsible. She had many of the characteristics of a "swinger" and enjoyed meeting men and drinking in bars. She was aware of Eve White, who wasn't aware of her. Eve Black enjoyed playing tricks on Eve White, such as leaving her to face the consequences of Eve Black's pranks and excesses. She thought Eve White's great concern for her daughter was "pretty corny."

Once Eve Black had "come out," Thigpen and Cleckley planned a treatment that would make extensive use of hypnosis and depth interviews to explore the pasts of both personalities. They wanted to understand how Eve Black's character had split off from Eve White's, and they hoped to effect some kind of integration of the two personalities. Short of that, they aimed at relieving Eve White of her troublesome headaches and blackouts and at getting Eve Black to be more cooperative and less troublesome for her counterpart.

In a scene from the movie *The Three Faces of Eve*, a therapist attempts to help Eve deal with her multiple personalities.

The Museum of Modern Art/Film Stills Archive.

Thigpen and Cleckley were medically trained psychiatrists. They consulted a clinical psychologist trained in techniques of assessment, who tested both Eves in order to explore their intellectual capacities and personality structures. Both personalities proved to be intellectually competent, Eve White more so than Eve Black. The two personalities represented to some extent the same person at two different stages of life. The latter conclusion was based on two psychological tests, one in which a subject is asked to draw human figures and another, the famous Rorschach inkblot test, in which a subject is asked to report what she sees in ambiguous ink figures. These devices are both called "projective" tests, and the assumption is that in her drawings and discussions of the ambiguous inkblots the patient will reveal her fears, wishes, conflicts, and feelings. The tests indicated that Eve White had unconscious conflicts and anxieties about being a wife and mother that had led to her regression into the less mature and responsible Eve Black personality. Eve Black's taunting of Eve White came from Eve White's anger at herself for her present life difficulties.

After eight months in treatment, the two Eves seemed to be making good progress. Eve White got a job that was steady and began making some financial gains. She was having no headaches or blackouts. Her life seemed more stable and generally well-adjusted. Most important, perhaps, Eve Black was causing her less difficulty. She was "bored" with Eve White's hard work and long hours. She did "come out" at night for some fun occasionally, but she was less likely, for example, to get drunk and leave Eve White with a painful and inexplicable hangover. This good behavior on Eve Black's part was accomplished in therapy essentially through negotiation. Through the therapeutic process, Eve White was made aware of Eve Black's existence and could exert some, though not total, control over her "coming out." Eve Black was rewarded with more time out for good behavior. But because she was bored unless she could be wild and prankish, she began to recede more and more.

At this point in Eve's treatment things took a marked turn for the worse. Eve White began having more severe headaches and blackouts, and for the first time Eve

Black was suffering these symptoms too. Several times Eve was found lying unconscious in her room. Thigpen and Cleckley were again afraid that their patient might be approaching psychosis. These setbacks may have been related to efforts by the therapists to unite Eve's two personalities. They attempted to call out both personalities at once. Eve White reacted with severe headaches and Eve Black with "such a funny, queer mixed-up feeling that I ain't gonna put up with it no more." It was not long after this time that Jane first "came out."

Thigpen and Cleckley were very impressed with this new personality and seemed to view positively the trend toward Jane's becoming more and more dominant. They felt her strengths were greater than the combined strengths of the other two. A psychological assessment procedure measuring brain waves (the electroencephalogram, or EEG) indicated that Jane was the least tense of the three personalities. The therapists felt she had great strength and initiative and seemed less constrained by the past. She appeared to have the capacity and energy to build a new and productive life.

When Eve left treatment in Georgia after 14 months, it seemed as if she had been cured. Although she had some misgivings about her health, she decided to remarry, her first marriage having ended in divorce. She married Don Sizemore in December of 1953. At this time only the Jane personality was still present. Don knew about Eve's history but shared her psychiatrists' optimism that she was well. Then shortly after the wedding another personality appeared. This was the so-called "Blind Lady," who couldn't see. Many other personalities followed, usually in groups of three, often with at least one personality change a day, with each personality unaware of the others and mystified at the situations one of the others had left her in. Some of Eve's personalities could drive or sew and some couldn't. At times one personality would hopelessly try to pass an examination on material studied by another personality. Among these personalities were the Purple Lady, who loved everything purple, and the Banana Split Girl, who was obsessed by the fattening dessert.

By this time Jane had "died," and there was little stability in Eve's life. Her husband remained supportive, however, and she decided to see psychiatrists in Virginia where she was then living. One of the therapists suggested that she reveal to her friends and to the world who she was and what she had been going through. She started work, with her cousin, Ellen Pitillo, on her book, *I'm Eve*. Her new therapists helped her realize that all her personalities were really the same person. This and her decision to tell others about her experiences helped to give her a more enduring identity. This has been very important. She says, "You don't know how wonderful it is to go to bed at night and know that it will be you that wakes up the next day" (*New York Post*, September 15, 1975). For the past several years Eve has been herself, she says. "I am not well, but I am stable" (Associated Press, December 17, 1978).

HELP IN TODAY'S WORLD

The fascinating case of Eve offers some revealing glimpses into the process of therapy. We will find it useful in discussing the therapeutic process and other methods used to help people who are having difficulty adjusting to life. Having some knowledge and appreciation of the process of therapy is important for two reasons. First, therapy is such a commonly known and widely discussed part of society today that it is important to be well informed about it. Although many people espouse opinions about psychological treatment, fewer have actually experienced it. Probably about 15 percent of people in the United States seek psychological help of some kind during their lives, though estimates of the number who may *need* help from time to time run to as high as 80 percent. In any case, opinions about therapy are often extreme and controversial. This makes it doubly important to have knowledge of the basic processes and basic varieties of treatment.

Second, and of more immediate relevance, the chances are that you or someone close to you will one day consider getting some counseling or therapy. You may then want to think about whether any form of help should be sought at all, and, if so, what kind. Knowing the range of therapies available and what each can accomplish will help you make this decision.

In addition to providing information about various kinds of therapy and treatment, we think it is crucial to deal with two related questions. One is whether therapy in general is effective, and the second is what kinds of therapists are most helpful. Research suggests that the personality of the therapist and the relationship that she or he establishes, or fails to establish, with the patient or client is the critical determinant of the outcome of therapy. These human factors are much more important than the therapist's theoretical beliefs or techniques, although we will see that certain practices make the most sense for particular problems.

People with difficulties can also do a great deal to help themselves. People's attitudes toward themselves, their ability to understand, accept, and nurture themselves, as well as to make positive decisions about their lives, are crucial determinants of personal adjustment and of satisfying relations with others. Helping yourself is also related to helping others. Self-knowledge and self-acceptance usually increase your understanding and acceptance of other people. Active empathy for other human beings is a quality well worth developing, and there is a great deal that each of us can do to affect others positively and help them with their difficulties. More than anything else, helping others requires caring and genuine desire to be helpful, as well as a fundamental awareness of what an untrained person, as a friend, can and can't do. We believe that concern about others, and mutual caring and support, are of great importance and enhance our collective well-being in a complex and stressful world.

PSYCHODYNAMIC THERAPIES

Several therapies are based on the exploration with a therapist of a single patient or client's personality structure. These psychodynamic therapies differ tremendously among themselves, but they can all be contrasted with behavior therapies, in which there is much more emphasis on changing specific maladaptive behaviors than on exploring the forces and patterns in the client's psychological makeup that perhaps cause maladaptive behaviors. They also differ from group therapies, where more than one client works with a therapist at a time.

One assumption all the psychodynamic therapies share is that an improvement in behavior and personal adjustment will occur if a person's underlying personality structure can be changed for the better. They also share the closely related assumption that your personality structure can be changed through greater insight into the origins of your difficulties, the reasons for your actions, and the rich potentials for healthy self-enhancing behavior. And they have in common the belief that unconscious motives and distortions of reality can be eliminated or controlled once they are fully exposed to view. The principal goal is to make more and more in the person conscious, known, and understood—to leave less and less unconscious. Freud's famous statement of this goal is "Where there is id, there shall ego be."

Thigpen and Cleckley's treatment of Eve White essentially followed a psychodynamic approach. The two psychiatrists were concerned with finding out about Eve's past fears, wishes, and behaviors and how unconscious forces might have led to the splitting off of a separate personality. They assumed that once these matters were understood and the patient could deal with her fears and accept her wishes, wholeness in her personality could be restored.

As mentioned above, many therapies can be called "psychodynamic." Here we consider several therapies that illustrate the variety of ways that self-knowledge and growth are attempted through psychodynamic methods.

Sigmund Freud's theories of personality and psychotherapy have had a great impact on our society and our culture.

Bildarchiv d. Ost. Nationalbibilothsk.

Freudian Psychoanalysis

Once again, we start with Sigmund Freud. It was Freud (1940) who pioneered psychological treatment, and many psychotherapies represent some kind of modification of his methods. Freudian therapy is the longest, most complex, and most extensive of all therapies. The emphasis is on discovering unconscious wishes, fears, and defenses that originated in childhood but that affect the personality in the present. Psychoanalysis attempts to explore all the significant emotional experiences that occurred in a person's early life and to connect the effects of these experiences with present functioning.

In Freudian therapy a client may meet with his or her therapist several times a week for many months or even several years. Therapy consists of continual exploration of the unconscious in the hope that knowing and accepting what is hidden will give a person more control and happiness. In order to explore the unconscious, the Freudian analyst uses several techniques. The most important are free association, hypnosis, and dream analysis.

FREE ASSOCIATION. The primary tool for uncovering unconscious material is **free association.** The client is asked to sit or lie in a comfortable position, often with eyes closed, almost always with the therapist out of view, and to say whatever comes into his or her mind. The client simply talks and is required to hold nothing back, no matter how silly, cruel, obscene, or ridiculous it may seem. Try doing this out loud for a minute and see how difficult it can be! It is assumed that in the relaxed, unguarded process of free association, ideas that are usually kept hidden from awareness will emerge into consciousness. The ego eases its censoring of unconscious material once the person is involved in free association.

HYPNOSIS. Many Freudian therapists use hypnosis. In an induced psychological state of deep relaxation the client is encouraged to let down his or her guard and trust the hypnotist. In this relaxed state the client is suggestible and will do what the hypnotist asks, as long as it doesn't violate strong values or fears. People will do things under hypnosis that are unusual, but never things that are flagrantly immoral or dangerous. One of the things a client will do is think over past events with less inhibition than normal and report things that are usually hidden, even from his or her own awareness. Thus hypnosis provides access to unconscious memories and feelings. Thigpen and Cleckley used hypnosis extensively with Eve White to help her recall past experiences and also, at first, to let Eve Black come out. Later in treatment, either Eve White or Eve Black could come out on request. Interestingly Eve Black was never successfully hypnotized, probably because she was the most tense of Chris Sizemore's original three personalities. It was because of the difficulties in using hypnosis with some patients that Freud began to favor free association.

DREAM ANALYSIS. The censoring functions of the ego are disarmed to a great extent in free association and hypnosis. As a result, much unconscious material can be brought into awareness and reported through these methods. Another time the ego's censoring functions are relaxed is during sleep. Then unconscious wishes and fears make themselves known in dreams. For this reason dreams have been referred to as the "royal road to the unconscious." However, Freudian theory holds that the ego doesn't completely lift censorship during dreaming, and the unconscious material in dreams is rarely expressed in direct form. For example, one woman in analysis had a dream about opening a boutique to which her sister came and bought a dress on sale. This dream indirectly expressed the woman's guilt for not having been generous with her sister in the past and a wish to make up for her behavior by giving her sister presents.

PROBLEMS IN INTERPRETING ASSOCIATIONS AND DREAMS. Obtaining associations and dreams is only part of the long process of psychoanalysis. The most difficult part lies ahead. The therapist must offer interpretations that help the client understand his or her unconscious wishes, fears, and conflicts. This requires first that the therapist be accurate in his or her interpretations. Second, great skill and competence is needed in giving the interpretations to the client. Many clients show **resistance** in dealing with sensitive matters during free association and show resistance to interpretations that touch on strong unconscious feelings. Eve White might have shown a lot of resistance to the idea that Eve Black represented wishes that weren't allowed expression in Eve White's personality. The psychoanalyst must be extremely sensitive in knowing how and when to analyze and overcome resistance so the client can genuinely and fully see what is in his or her own unconscious.

A second problem in interpreting unconscious feelings is the phenomenon of **transference.** Transference occurs when the client projects the attitudes of significant people in his or her life, especially parents, onto the therapist and then begins acting toward the therapist as he or she acted, or unconsciously *wished* to act, toward these significant others. Transference occurs because of the deep emotional relationship that develops between client and therapist and needs to be carefully understood by the client before therapy can succeed. Transference is useful because it often reveals repressed feelings about other people, as when a person's anger in therapy is seen as coming from unconscious hostility felt toward a parent. Again, a delicate interpretation of the transference process is needed.

Client-Centered Therapy

One of the most widely used and well-respected alternatives to the long and often stormy process of psychoanalysis is client-centered therapy. It has been developed and modified by Carl Rogers (1951; 1961) over three decades. Like psychoanalysis and other dynamic or insight therapies, Rogers's approach emphasizes getting in touch with your feelings and discovering your true and unconscious self.

In client-centered, or "nondirective," therapy, the client rather than the therapist is the one who is active. He or she does most of the talking. Rogers believes that the client must

In client-centered therapy, the therapist provides a safe setting for the client to explore his or her psychological problems.

Ken Karp.

take the lead and that therapy will only be successful to the extent that the client is talking about what is really on his or her mind. The therapist's role is to provide a safe, nonthreatening atmosphere in which the client can explore his or her true feelings. This atmosphere exists when the therapist shows complete acceptance of the client as a person. This complete acceptance is called **"unconditional positive regard."** In addition, the therapist must help the client clarify feelings and insights that are difficult for the client to understand or express. Often nondirective therapists do little other than articulate what clients are groping to say so that clients can more vividly and directly experience their own feelings and learn to accept and reflect on their own inner worlds. Client-centered therapy assumes that listening intently and helping the client reflect upon his or her feelings will enable the client to gain insights independently, which will be all the more powerful for having come from within.

If Eve White had entered client-centered therapy and Eve Black had appeared, any decision about attempting a unification or melding of the two personalities would have depended on what the two Eves themselves wanted. A therapist following the Rogerian school of thought would hold that an attempt to integrate the two personalities would work only if that is what each one wanted. On the other hand, Freudians might argue that the therapist must push the client toward dealing with problems that he or she doesn't want to face. This is sometimes one of the key differences between Freudian and Rogerian therapy.

Humanistic-Existential Approaches

Other approaches to therapy share the Rogerian emphasis on creating an environment in which a person can discover himself or herself. They put even more emphasis on developing all a person has the potential to become and finding meaning and significance in present life.

One such therapy was developed by Viktor Frankl (1963) and is called **logotherapy,** after *logos,* the Greek word for "meaning." The essential tenet of logotherapy is that human beings' basic need is to find meaning and that unhappy and maladjusted people need help in finding something to give their lives meaning and significance. Frankl explores the client's life with him or her and helps the client discover aspects of living that are important and can give him or her purpose. The therapist helps the client find a goal; in pursuing the goal, the client can develop his or her potential.

Other related therapies are existential (see May, 1958), gestalt (Perls, 1970), and reality therapies (Glasser, 1965). All of these therapies emphasize that people must be responsible for their lives in the present and make the choices that will define and enact their values and actualize their potentials.

Rational-Emotive Therapy

One of the more interesting therapies to be developed during the past several decades is **rational-emotive therapy.** Its major proponent and founder is Albert Ellis (1962). We will examine rational-emotive therapy in some detail because of its uniqueness and the fact that it raises many key issues about what a therapy and a therapist should do, especially when Ellis's approach is contrasted with other treatments.

The major assumption underlying rational-emotive therapy is that people have beliefs, usually learned from their parents and reinforced by society, that cause them great misery and lead to self-defeating behavior. The rational-emotive therapist tries to show the person in therapy that these beliefs are irrational and debilitating and tries to get the person to change them. Among the beliefs that bedevil people are the ideas that one "must" meet up to others' expectations and that one "must" be competent and skillful to have worth. In changing these beliefs the therapist plays as active a role as Freudian therapists do, perhaps even more so. Yet the emphasis, as in gestalt and reality therapies, is on the present and on how one can change it for the better. In this case the change for the better is accomplished by realizing and changing the debilitating beliefs. If Ellis were treating Eve, he might challenge the belief that she had to have a single unified personality, in order to free her from any compulsion to be like everyone else and at the same time help her to be more stable and consistent in a relaxed, noncompulsive way. Let's consider an example of rational-emotive therapy to see how it actually tries to work. The following exchange is excerpted from Hersher (1970).

> *Ellis:* Well, I understand . . . that you have the problem of feeling intellectually inferior, is that correct?
> *Patient:* Yes, I've always felt that that's been very important to me, and I've felt that

---

TABLE 8.1

Varieties of Psychodynamic Therapies

Psychodynamic therapies emphasize changing a person's personality structure by insight into the origins of our difficulties, the reasons we behave as we do, and the potential we have to behave in more effective ways. These therapies include the following:

A. Freudian psychoanalysis: Exploring unconscious wishes, fears, conflicts, and defenses using free association, hypnosis, dream analysis, and interpretation

B. Rogerian client-centered therapy: Getting in touch with our feelings and discovering our true and unconscious self in a safe, exploratory atmosphere of unconditional positive regard

C. Humanistic-existential therapy: Finding meaning and significance in our lives by finding goals and developing potentials

D. Ellis's rational-emotive therapy: Learning that our beliefs that we have to live up to other people's expectations are debilitating and irrational

---

I. . . . I always doubt that I have what it takes intellectually, yes.

Ellis: Well, let's suppose you haven't. Let's just suppose for the sake of discussion that you really are inferior to some degree, and you're not up to your fellow—your old peers from childhood or your present peers. Now what's so catastrophic about that, if it were true?

Patient: Well, this is a fear, I'm not . . . if they found out, then . . . if I can't keep my job teaching then I . . . .

Ellis: You've done pretty well in keeping your job. You're not that concerned about your job. . . . You're saying you don't respect yourself, if you act ineffectively as a teacher. Right?

Patient: Yes, I wouldn't respect myself.

Ellis: Why not?

Patient: Well, it wouldn't be right to say that I'm teaching when . . . if I haven't got the qualifications, if I'm not capable to do the job.

Ellis: Let's assume you're a lousy teacher. Now why are you tying up your performance? Lousy teacher, we're assuming now. You are a lousy teacher and may always be a lousy teacher. Why are you tying that aspect of you up with your total self? I am a slob because my teaching is slobbish. Now do you see any inconsistency with that conclusion?

Patient: Yeah, but it still feels that it would be a terrible thing that if I should be a teacher and not really have the stuff to do it.

Ellis: Why? Why is it terrible? It's unfortunate. Why is it terrible? Who said so? Where is the evidence?

Patient: Well, everybody says so. I feel that way about the other teachers too. If they don't . . . .

Ellis: You're a moralist. You blame human beings for being [imperfect].

Patient: You mean I'm expecting too much of them? . . . I got to believe it's okay to be mediocre?

Ellis: That it's a pain in the ass to be mediocre. But I in total am not a louse for having a mediocre performance. Not good, so your performance would be deplorable, sad, frustrating if you were mediocre. But you are not your performance.

Patient: But people judge me on . . . .

Ellis: That's right. They're just as nutty as you are, and they think if this guy is no good in teaching . . . then he is no good as a whole. Are they correct in that kind of thinking? Is this a good generalization, from the evidence?

Patient: I never thought of it.

Ellis: That's right. That's what I'm trying to get you to think of.

Patient: You mean if they don't like me I should say that's tough, that it doesn't matter?

Ellis: That's exactly right. Not that "It doesn't matter at all because I would like them to like me," but "I don't *need* them to like me." What I want you to do, in conclusion, is every time you get upset from here on—but especially this feeling of worthlessness, or crumminess which you get—assume ex-

perimentally that it doesn't come from that fact that you screwed up in some way, but from what you told yourself, your negative evaluation of your total self for this performance, and question and challenge that, just

REVIEW QUESTIONS

1. Which of the following is *not* an assumption of all psychodynamic therapies?
   a. A change in the underlying personality structure can result in a behavioral change.
   b. An examination of the client's past can provide important clues as to his or her current psychological difficulties.
   c. Maladaptive behavior is maintained almost exclusively by external reinforcers.
   d. Unconscious forces are powerful determinants of maladaptive behavior.
2. The use of techniques such as free association and dream analysis to uncover unconscious motives is most likely to be found in the therapeutic approach known as _____.
3. The therapy in which the therapist's role is to provide the client with a safe, nonthreatening atmosphere of "unconditional positive regard" is _____-_____ therapy.
4. T or F: Insight is unimportant in client-centered therapy.
5. The therapeutic approach that emphasizes human potential and finding the meaning in one's life is the _____-_____ approach.
6. The therapy that attempts to change behaviors by forcing the client to confront irrational and destructive beliefs and attitudes that they hold toward themselves is called _____-_____ therapy.

like you question and challenge any other hypothesis. Now, just try that, be open-minded, you've got nothing to lose. You feel like a worm now, you've got nothing to lose by it. And let's see. You come back next time and tell me what happened.

These excerpts give some flavor of what Ellis tries to do in therapy. Elsewhere in this interview he tried to make the point that the client's performance is probably negatively affected by constantly evaluating himself, and that if he stopped berating himself he would enjoy teaching more and do better. Ellis makes the point that students need to be taught and that the patient should work on ways of doing the best he can and improving, without worrying about what others think or becoming undone by his own evaluative concerns. We will return to Albert Ellis and rational-emotive therapy when we consider the question of what makes an effective therapist.

BEHAVIOR THERAPIES

Several therapeutic techniques derive from principles of reinforcement and learning. These **behavior therapy** approaches differ from psychodynamic, or insight, therapies in two important respects. First, they assume that a person's maladaptive behaviors and feelings have been learned and are maintained by external reinforcers. In order for these behaviors to be changed, new and more adaptive responses have to be learned and reinforced. This enables people to respond differently and more adaptively in previously debilitating circumstances. A second difference between insight therapies and behavior therapies is that behavior therapies work directly with the symptomatic behavior itself rather than with the underlying personality structure. They don't concern themselves with self-actualization directly, but may work toward it indirectly by teaching adaptive behavior. Before considering specific therapeutic techniques, we'll review the principles of conditioning on which they are based.

Principles of Conditioning

CLASSICAL CONDITIONING. **Classical,** or respondent, **conditioning** was first discovered by the great physiologist Ivan Pavlov in Russia in the early part of this century. Pavlov received a Nobel Prize for his work in 1904. In classical conditioning an animal or person is conditioned to make a response to a stimulus that previously didn't evoke that response (see Chapter 4). This is accomplished by consistent pairing of the new stimulus (conditioned stimulus) with another stimulus (unconditioned stimulus) that naturally elicits the response. Pavlov's classic demonstration of this phenomenon showed that a dog would salivate to a bell if that bell had been rung consistently just before giving the dog meat powder, which naturally elicits salivation. A common example in human affairs occurs with thunder and lightning. Lightning usually precedes thunder. The sound of thunder is enough to elicit a startle reaction from most people. A flash of lightning by itself isn't. However, since thunder so often follows lightning in just a few seconds—since nature has paired the two—lightning gains the power to elicit the startle reaction because of its association with thunder. This kind of association or pairing is important in leading to positive or negative attitudes and emotions about many objects, events, and people in everyday life. Especially common, as pointed out in Chapters 4 and 7, is learning to fear perfectly innocent objects because of their pairing or association with other, more sinister objects. Behavior therapies, as we shall see, are often directed at reducing fears of these benign objects.

OPERANT CONDITIONING. **Operant conditioning** is closely associated with the name of B. F. Skinner. Skinner (1953) has researched this phenomenon extensively and written volumes about its implications. The idea of operant conditioning is extremely simple. The basic premise is that behavior is under the control of its consequences and that if positive consequences follow a behavior, the tendency to

B. F. Skinner's research with animals such as pigeons teaches us a great deal about operant conditioning and learning.

Monkmeyer.

perform the behavior is increased. Such a positive consequence is called a **reinforcer;** it strengthens the behavior. A rat in a box that is given a food pellet after it pushes a bar will begin to push the bar more and more. This behavior, under the control of the reinforcer, food, is called an **operant.** It is a behavior that has been learned or conditioned on the basis of reinforcement. Similarly a child who cleans up his or her room in anticipation of a parent's smile or 25 cents is emitting an operant. He or she has been conditioned to clean up the room. Unfortunately there are many behaviors that are highly maladaptive that are nevertheless repeated because of some kind of reinforcer. A therapist using operant conditioning principles in therapy would attempt to remove or change the reinforcers that strengthen the client's maladaptive behaviors or provide reinforcement for adaptive behaviors, especially those that can replace maladaptive ones. We will see how this can work in the sections that follow.

EXTINCTION. An important learning phenomenon involved with both classical and operant conditioning should be mentioned here because of its importance in behavior therapy. This is the phenomenon of **extinction.** A con-

ditioned response will gradually be extinguished, that is, cease to occur, if it isn't paired with its unconditioned stimulus or reinforcer. In classical conditioning, the dog will stop salivating at the sound of the bell if the meat powder is never again given after the bell. A rat will cease to press a bar if it never again receives a pellet after doing so. When these conditioned responses stop being emitted, extinction is said to have occurred.

Techniques of Behavior Therapy

The principles of conditioning outlined above have wide application to the challenge of changing or modifying maladaptive behavior. We'll consider several specific techniques. Each of them is based on some combination of classical or operant conditioning.

SYSTEMATIC DESENSITIZATION AND IMPLOSIVE THERAPY. Perhaps the most widely used form of behavior therapy is a technique developed by Wolpe (1958) called **systematic desensitization.** It is most applicable to curing phobias and other severe forms of anxiety. The first step in systematic desensitization is to teach the client a new response, **relaxation,** that is incompatible with feeling frightened. Relaxation is essentially taught through operant conditioning. The therapist gives careful instruction in exactly how to relax. The client is told precisely how to behave and what to think about. When the client behaves in a way that approximates what the therapist wants, he or she is praised. When the person learns to perform the approximation easily, the therapist demands another approximation that is even closer to the precise relaxation response desired. Then the client is only reinforced for this improved approximation. As the client gets more adept at relaxing, the therapist demands and then reinforces progressively improved approximations. This procedure is a form of operant conditioning called *shaping.*

The next step in systematic desensitization is for the client to construct a list of about

Teaching clients to relax is a key step in systematic desensitization.
Van Bucher, Photo Researchers, Inc.

eight or ten situations beginning with situations that are hardly frightening at all and ending with the scariest circumstance imaginable. A person who was terrified of the dark might start the list with a late afternoon scene or a sunset and end it with a dark moonless midnight. This list is called a **hierarchy.** The client is told to relax and to imagine the least frightening situation in the hierarchy. This continues until a scene is imagined that begins to make the client feel anxious. Then a therapist instructs and encourages the client to relax, perhaps goes back one step on the hierarchy, and try again until the anxiety-provoking situation can finally be imagined fully with complete relaxation.

Through this procedure a person is taught a new response, relaxing, that is associated with formerly frightening circumstances, and eventually this new response replaces anxiety as a response to the situation involved. This technique is widely used and is highly successful. It takes only a small fraction of the time of psychoanalysis and usually does a better job of relieving symptoms. The cause of the anxiety is not explored, but the anxiety itself is cured. As noted before, this form of therapy is highly successful with phobics. An organization called TERRAP, run by Arthur Hardy, a California psychiatrist, reports that this kind of behavioral therapy is effective with agoraphobics, those who fear open spaces and their own unpredictable panic attacks. Hardy's program treats more than 10,000 agoraphobics a year all over the country and has an 85 percent cure rate (Adler, 1984).

A similar technique that is also used to deal with anxiety is called **implosive therapy** (Stampfl, 1961). In this case instead of working through a hierarchy the client is asked to think as vividly as possible of the most frightening situation imaginable and to feel fully and deeply the dread of this situation. A man who is afraid

TABLE 8.2

Important Terms in Behavior Therapies

Classical conditioning: Learning through the consistent pairing of a neutral stimulus with a stimulus that elicits a response until the neutral stimulus also elicits the response

Operant conditioning: Learning in which a response or change in behavior is strengthened with a reinforcer

Systematic desensitization: A behavior therapy in which the client is taught to relax, is presented with a hierarchy of anxiety-arousing situations, and learns to relax even when contemplating the most threatening situation

Implosive therapy: A behavior therapy in which the client is asked to imagine as vividly as possible the most frightening situation possible; gradually, the anxiety response to these situations extinguishes

Assertiveness training: A behavior modification technique in which a person is trained to act appropriately assertive in interpersonal situations

Token economy: A form of behavior therapy in which desired behavior is rewarded with tokens which can be used to purchase reinforcers of snakes might be asked to imagine going to the zoo and letting a python wrap itself around his neck and arms. A woman who is afraid of speaking in public would be asked to imagine herself speaking to a large public gathering. The idea is that if the client continues to do this, he or she will see that no negative or harmful consequences follow the frightening stimulus. In the safety of the therapist's office, the threat doesn't actually lead to harm. The client can even practice thinking about the frightening situations on his or her own for "homework." Because the imagined situation doesn't lead to danger, the anxiety response is eventually extinguished. The client can learn to imagine a situation and then to actually experience it without becoming anxious. The "implosion" of anxiety that occurs when frightening situations are first imagined in detail gradually gets weaker and disappears after repeated trials.

TEACHING NEW BEHAVIORS. Other forms of behavior therapy involve getting the client to learn to perform effective behaviors in situations that ordinarily cause debilitating anxiety. First the client learns to relax in the frightening situation; then he or she is taught to perform new behaviors that further eliminate anxiety because they are incompatible with it. Role playing is generally used to teach the new behaviors. The therapist acts out the effective behavior in an imaginary situation to give the client a model to imitate, and then the client has to role-play the effective behavior himself or herself. The therapist uses approval to shape and reinforce the client's role playing until the client is able to perform the desired behavior effectively. Finally the client attempts the new adaptive behavior in a real situation.

One form of this technique being widely used today is **assertiveness training.** People who are afraid to express their opinions or to protest being manipulated or people who lack the knowledge or ability to assert themselves appropriately can be helped through assertiveness training. Although this form of therapy can be used with anyone having difficulties with assertiveness, it has been used particularly by women as a means of overcoming traditional

conditioning that encourages women to be meek and submissive. Many women feel that only by learning to be as assertive as men generally are can they make the most of their potential in a male-dominated world. Skilled trainers work with clients through exhaustive role playing, demonstrating how to be assertive and shaping the client's behavior until the client can behave flexibly and effectively. It is important that assertiveness be learned but that it not boil over into unnecessary and ineffective aggression.

It is highly likely that a behaviorally minded therapist who was informed of the psychologist's analysis of Eve White and Eve Black discussed earlier would have used assertiveness training. One of Eve White's major problems was her inability to be appropriately assertive in her first marriage. She got herself into an unsatisfying marital situation and couldn't find a way out. All her anger was held in and unconsciously directed at herself. She then regressed into the immature Eve Black personality in which she was free from marital constraints (she even used her maiden name) and free to express her hostility toward Eve White for the situation the latter had created for herself. If Eve White had learned to be assertive and to work on her marital problems more effectively, the need for the extreme Eve Black "solution" might never have been so strong. Eve White might have acquired some of the desirable characteristics of Jane and reduced the necessity for an Eve Black, without having gone through the self-alienation represented in her succession of multiple personalities.

BEHAVIOR MODIFICATION THROUGH OPERANT CONDITIONING. Several forms of behavior therapy work on the elegantly simple principle of reinforcing desirable, adaptive behavior and ceasing to reinforce maladaptive behavior. Many involve what is known as a **token economy.** This form of therapy is often used in institutional settings such as mental institutions and prisons. When inmates perform desired behavior, they are rewarded with a "token," which can be used to "purchase" desired reinforcers such as watching television, exercising, or having free time. Operant behavior modification can also be self-administered. People can make careful plans of adaptive behavior and reward themselves if they carry out the behavior according to plan and schedule. Students trying to write a paper or finish a long project can reward themselves by watching TV, having a snack, or other appropriate indulgences if they complete a unit of adaptive behavior as planned. A successful program of self-administered behavior modification requires realistic goals that aren't too hard or too easy.

With realistic goals, this can be a remarkably effective "self-help" technique.

Endless varieties of operant behavior modification are used in therapy. One form was used by Thigpen and Cleckley with Eve Black, although they didn't call their treatment "behavior modification." Once Eve White was able to get some control over Eve Black's coming out, Eve Black could be rewarded, with the opportunity to "come out" if she behaved in ways that would not irritate or debilitate Eve White. For a time this unwitting form of behavior modification was successful.

REVIEW QUESTIONS

7. Which of the following assumptions is(are) true regarding behavior therapies?
   a. Maladaptive behaviors are learned and maintained by external reinforcers.
   b. Past events in one's life are not as important as current circumstances.
   c. The visible symptoms are more important than the underlying personality.
   d. All the above are true.

8. A loud noise will elicit a startle response in most people. By repeatedly sounding the loud noise in the presence of a neutral stimulus, such as a stuffed toy, the startle response will eventually be elicited when the stuffed toy is presented by itself. This is an example of
   _____ _____ .

9. If by rewarding a behavior you increase the likelihood that the behavior will be repeated, you are demonstrating the principle of _____ _____ .

10. An important goal of behavior therapy is the removal of maladaptive behavior. The gradual disappearance of a conditioned behavior when reinforcement is withheld is known as
    _____ .

11. Match the following behavior therapy techniques with their description.
    _____ systematic desensitization
    _____ shaping
    _____ implosive therapy
    _____ token economy
    _____ assertiveness training

    a. reinforcing successive approximations to the target behavior
    b. a procedure used for people who are submissive and easily manipulated; often involving the use of role-playing
    c. practicing relaxation techniques as one imagines anxiety provoking situations arranged in hierarchical progression from least frightening to most frightening
    d. reinforcing positive behaviors by presenting rewards that can be later exchanged for special privileges
    e. desensitizing oneself to an anxiety-provoking situation by imagining the most frightening scenario

DOES PSYCHOTHERAPY WORK?

Do the forms of therapy we've discussed really work? There have been many studies of this question, particularly with regard to psychodynamic therapies, and they have led to some confusion. The reason for the confusion is that the question is terribly difficult to answer. How does one judge whether therapy has worked? How can we know whether the patient would have gotten better (or worse) without therapy? We will approach this issue in terms of *when therapy is likely to work.*

EYSENCK'S CHALLENGE TO INSIGHT THERAPIES. Psychotherapy, especially Freudian psychoanalysis, has been controversial as long as it has been in existence. But the first really substantive challenge didn't come until 1952, when Hans Eysenck, a British behavioral psychologist, published his first article attacking traditional psychotherapy. In this article and several others, Eysenck (1961; 1964) consistently argued that insight therapies do little good. In 1964 he cited the finding that 44 percent of people in psychoanalysis were helped by their treatment, 64 percent of people in other forms of insight therapies were aided, and 72 percent of those who were *untreated* improved. From these data he argued that psychotherapy is no better, or perhaps even worse, than no treatment at all.

Eysenck's conclusions have been challenged repeatedly. One major problem is that it's very difficult to define "cure." Could Eve White have been considered "cured" when her headaches went away? Was she "cured" when she left Thigpen and Cleckley with Jane in control? Were her later breakdowns indicative of the failure of therapy, or were they new problems? In many cases it's difficult to say definitively whether therapy has been beneficial or not. Another problem with Eysenck's study is that those who received treatment and those who didn't might not have been similar to begin with (see Pizer & Travers, 1975).

The controversy has raged. For example,

Eysenck has been attacked for being less than objective because of his involvement with behavior therapy (Lazarus, 1976). Still, the effectiveness of psychodynamic treatment has not been demonstrated statistically (Luborsky & Spence, 1971). The debate continues.

LATER RESEARCH ON PSYCHOTHERAPY'S EFFECTIVENESS. Many studies have followed Eysenck's findings and shown on the average a 60 percent cure rate for a variety of forms of psychotherapy. This is the same as the general rate of improvement for people who have had no treatment—which doesn't mean that, for a given individual, therapy is no better than no therapy (Pizer & Travers, 1975). It simply reflects the fact that many, many variables determine whether treatment works. One variable is the nature of the disorder. Schizophrenia can be much more difficult to treat with psychotherapy than anxiety disorders are (see Chapter 7). People who are totally withdrawn or who have lost contact with reality are difficult to reach with either insight or behavioral approaches. Another important factor is the person seeking treatment. It has been shown that people with high intelligence and good verbal skills are the most likely to benefit from insight therapy, where great understanding and the ability to express confused feelings is crucial. People who lack verbal facility may not be able to gain real insight into their problems or explore their potential in therapeutic interaction. Another factor is the aims of the patient and whether these fit with those of the treatment. If the patient wants to find meaning in his or her life and is concerned with self-discovery, a behaviorally oriented therapist might not be very helpful. On the other hand, behavior therapy works very well for reducing anxiety (Wolpe, 1974). Thus there are many factors that influence whether a particular therapy will be beneficial for a particular person.

Where does this leave the person trying to decide whether to seek psychological help? Our feeling is that if people feel a need for help they should seek it out, remembering one key conclusion from the literature on the effectiveness of therapy: Many studies have shown that the most important determinant of success in therapy is the therapist himself or herself. More than any other factor, this can determine whether therapy is successful. Bergin (1966) states that research shows that some therapists make people better and others make people worse. It's critical to get good advice on a good therapist from one or more responsible people who are in a position to know. Advisers, clergymen, and physicians can often give good suggestions. Peers sometimes can too. Choosing the right therapist is the most important decision you make in seeking help.

The Characteristics of an Effective Helper

Carl Rogers (1961; 1967) has not only made a great contribution by developing his own psychotherapy, he has also been a consistent advocate of doing research to test the effectiveness of psychological treatment. His work agrees with the general conclusion that one kind of therapy is not more effective overall than others and that the characteristics of the therapist are most important. Rogers and others have found three major personal characteristics to be important in a successful counselor or therapist.

CONGRUENCE. The first important characteristic of a therapist is his or her **congruence,** or genuineness, in dealing with the client. This means being absolutely honest. The key here is that what the therapist says must match his or her inner feelings. If the therapist feels anger, she must make that plain. If he is skeptical, he must show that. Whatever the therapist's feelings and attitudes, they must be shown plainly to the client. In Rogers's words, the therapist must be "dependably real." This is important in establishing dependability and trustworthiness, two absolutely crucial elements in the therapeutic relationship. In addition, Rogers points out, it isn't sufficient merely to *be* congruent and real; the therapist must also be ex-

pressive enough and communicative enough to make his or her congruence felt in the treatment.

UNCONDITIONAL POSITIVE REGARD. A second critical characteristic of the successful helper is what Rogers calls **unconditional positive regard.** As noted before, this term refers to warm caring for the client as a human being, with no strings attached. The therapist must be willing to accept all that the client is as a human being, good and bad, desirable and undesirable. Positive regard, warm acceptance, and caring must be present no matter how much the therapist may not like specific behaviors or attitudes. Again, the unconditional nature of this attitude helps establish trust.

EMPATHIC UNDERSTANDING. The effective therapist must be able to see the world from the client's point of view, to understand what the client understands, see what the client sees, and feel what the client feels. The therapist must be able to keep these feelings and perceptions separate from his or her own, but must have an **empathic understanding** of the client's inner world, even to the point of being able to make clear to the client things the client presently "sees dimly." Again, expressiveness is important. The therapist must be able to communicate that he or she does understand and can feel what is going on inside the client.

BEING CONGRUENT, CARING, AND EMPATHIC. Research has shown that the three characteristics of congruence, unconditional positive regard, and empathic understanding are absolutely necessary in therapy. This doesn't mean that all therapists should act the same. There are many ways to express these characteristics. For some patients, a particular therapist's expression of these traits may be appreciated and accepted. Other patients may not view the therapist as caring or understanding. Let's consider the session between Albert Ellis and a client that we presented earlier. Does Ellis manifest the critical traits?

Most people would say that Ellis does demonstrate congruence. He says exactly what is on his mind, in a no-holds-barred, rapid-fire style. He calls the patient's ideas "nutty." He curses to show his disgust at illogical perceptions. Congruence is evident. It also seems clear that Ellis is empathically understanding. After a long intake interview in which the client mentioned a variety of problems, Ellis zeroes in with his first question about what he believes—accurately, as it turns out—to be the core of the client's problem: feelings of inferiority, especially intellectual inferiority. It seems obvious from the client's response that Ellis has correctly raised the major problem.

Now, what about unconditional positive regard? Surely it is essential. Without it congruence and empathy are worthless in building a successful relationship in therapy. All three must be present. Many people feel that Ellis definitely doesn't show unconditional positive regard, that he is too critical and sarcastic, and that he demeans the client. Others feel that while he doesn't show a superficial or conventional positive regard, he shows that he does care for the client as a person by demonstrating his belief that the client is a good man, worthy of being helped. Ironically, what he criticizes is the client's conclusion that he's no good. Ellis's message is, Even if you're a bad teacher, you are still a good person, *and* we can improve your teaching. Ellis obviously feels personally involved wtih the problem; he cares.

The crucial question is not whether we as observers sense that Ellis shows unconditional positive regard, but whether the client feels that Ellis cares, that Ellis accepts him as he is, and that Ellis will unconditionally give his help. But Ellis's style does make it clear that there are many ways to demonstrate or express acceptance and genuine caring about a client. Different kinds of expression probably work for different clients. The key point to remember is that all three characteristics of the effective therapist must be perceived by the client if there is to be a relationship in which the client can explore his or her problems and potentials and work toward a better adjustment.

THE GROUP EXPERIENCE

Thus far we have been considering forms of therapy in which a single client works with a therapist. However, there is a marked trend in the United States today toward seeking help and self-improvement in groups. Sometimes people seek help for specific problems in group psychotherapy. Other times they join sensitivity or encounter groups to find the opportunity to fully explore their potentials, to discover deeper facets of their feelings and beliefs, and to improve their individual and interpersonal functioning.

There are many reasons for the phenomenal rise of group therapy and encounter. One reason is that more and more people are trying to improve their lives by dealing actively with their psychological shortcomings. More people can get help in a shorter time in groups than in individual therapy. Thus group therapy is more efficient. Another reason for the rise of groups is that they emphasize interpersonal relations, the aspect of living that many people feel is most important and most worth improving. In general, people want to explore their potentials fully and become more aware of how others see them, how they can grow, and how they can help others. They also want to be more effective in dealing with others in personal relations and at work. Group experiences seem to offer the opportunity to pursue this kind of development.

We will first look at several forms of group psychotherapy, then consider the encounter group. Encounter is the kind of experience college students seem most interested in. We'll consider its risks and benefits.

Forms of Group Psychotherapy

GESTALT THERAPY. One of the most important forms of group psychotherapy today is Fritz Perls's (1951; 1967; 1969) **gestalt therapy.** The word *gestalt* means whole or complete. Gestalt therapy grew out of Freudian principles but took on a highly distinctive humanistic flavor. It emphasizes personal integration and taking responsibility for one's own life. It recognizes that the past is important in influencing what we are like today but emphasizes that people must live in the here and now. In order to become whole, we must thoroughly experience and accept all that is inside us in as vivid and active a way as possible. We must "take care of unfinished business"—such as conflicts and compulsions from the past—by living responsibly in the present. Instead of blaming others, we must make an active commitment to becoming more honest, aware, and decisive on our own.

Gestalt therapy groups are designed to help people meet these goals. Various exercises and role-playing techniques are used. People may act out the "top dog" role, playing the moralistic part of the personality, or they may play the "underdog," the aspect of the self that has low self-esteem. There is also the "hot seat" technique, whereby the group members focus on an individual and give that person honest feedback about how they view him or her. This helps people see parts of themselves they might have been unaware of. Often people reenact past conflicts to make themselves more aware of their inner feelings. But the objective is always to "take care" of this "unfinished business" and then put it aside. The emphasis in gestalt therapy is on the present and future, on living fully and taking responsibility for one's own growth and development.

TRANSACTIONAL ANALYSIS. Another widely used form of group therapy is based on Eric Berne's and T. A. Harris's (1969) theories of **transactional analysis.** Berne (1963) distinguished three "ego-states" of the personality, the Parent, the Adult, and the Child, which correspond roughly to Freud's superego, ego, and id. The Parent is the person's voice of unquestioned authority; it is often judgmental and harsh. The Adult is the objective and rational voice of the personality. The Child is the impulsive, feeling side of the person that often voices negative feelings about the self and hostility toward the Parent in other people. In the case of Eve, Eve Black seems to represent the Child ego-state; Eve White, the Parent; and Jane, the Adult. In analyzing transactions Berne believed that people play "games" by pretending to interact and converse in a factual and objective way, with their Adults in control, but actually "come on" with their Child or Parent.

A common "game" is Why Don't You, Yes But (WDYYB), in which one person, It, asks for help with a problem, and others make suggestions, saying "Why don't you. . . ," whereupon It rejects the suggestions with "Yes, but. . . ." In this game It pretends to be an Adult, objectively seeking advice, but actually It's Child elicits Parent reactions from others and then confounds or defeats the Parents. This game, like many, is self-defeating in that It simply turns others away and proves that his or her problems are insoluble. It comes to believe this by successfully playing the game. The purpose

FIGURE 8.1   TRANSACTIONAL PARADIGM FOR "WHY DON'T YOU, YES BUT"
In Berne's (1963) theory of transactional analysis, people play games when on the surface they communicate from Adult ego-state to Adult ego-state but underneath they actually communicate from Parent ego-state of one person to Child ego-state of the other. There are games involving other kinds of communications between ego-states, but this is the most common. It can be diagrammed as follows:

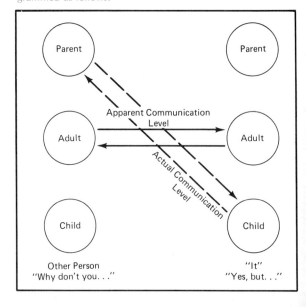

of therapy is to explore the games that people play in groups and how group members' three ego-states are really communicating, both on the surface (usually Adult to Adult) and below the surface (usually Child to Parent). This helps make people more aware of the ways they sometimes deceive, confuse, or manipulate others.

FAMILY THERAPY.   One form of therapy undertaken in groups is **family therapy.** Here the therapist may work with a couple, two parents and a child, or perhaps a whole family. This is a fast-growing approach to helping people with their adjustment problems. Many psychologists believe that for anyone who lives in a family the only rational approach to problems is family therapy. This belief stems from general systems theory, which holds that in any group, or "interactional system," the behavior of all the members is interdependent, and they all adjust to each other and to some extent dictate each other's actions (see Watzlawick, Beavin, & Jackson, 1967). Each member of the group reinforces certain behavior patterns in the others. If this is true, in order to understand a person fully one must understand the others he or she interacts closely with and see firsthand how they relate to each other. This can be done by working with the whole family. Also, it makes little sense to attempt to help one person if the group or family that the person lives with keeps reinforcing—even if subtly—the maladaptive behavior that is troubling the person. For these reasons family therapy makes a good deal of sense. The total picture of forces affecting the troubled person can be gained, and ways of encouraging more adaptive behavior among all concerned can be explored. It might have been very beneficial if Eve had had family therapy when she first sought help. Her conflicts about her marriage and her child could have been more fully explored, and her basic problems might have found more lasting solutions.

Encounter Groups

Most **encounter groups**, though conducted by psychologists, aren't for the specific purpose of psychotherapy. Many people without troubling

psychological difficulties participate in groups in order to explore, and improve, their patterns of relating to other people. The encounter group or sensitivity-training group was originally devised by Kurt Lewin and his associates in the late 1940s at the National Training Laboratory at Bethel, Maine. Their purpose was to work with business people and managers of organizations to help them interact more effectively with their colleagues. Since then, encounter has been affected greatly by the "human potential movement," which has adapted the original formula for sensitivity training to promote personal growth in groups.

THE GOALS OF ENCOUNTER.   The goal of group encounter can best be summarized as "personal growth." People join groups in order to develop their potential more fully. Usually this growth takes the specific form of improving relations with others. Aronson (1976) has outlined some of the specific kinds of improvement people seek: developing more awareness of others and of what they have to offer; being more honest, "congruent," or "authentic" in relations with other people; being more cooperative and egalitarian in relations with others, with less concern about status differences; and being better able to resolve conflicts.

Many of these goals are related to each other. Probably the most central is the attempt to become more authentic. This means that instead of conforming to the superficial "interaction rituals" that we use to make interaction go smoothly (see Chapter 7), people want to be able to say what is really on their minds, even if this means dealing with others uncomfortably on occasion. They believe that it will be better in the long run if there is more authenticity and less ritual in personal interactions. This is a highly debatable point of view, one well worth some discussion, because some people feel more honesty would mean more painful criticism and unhappiness. Regardless of what is best for society in the long run, it's clear that authenticity is needed in encounter groups if they are to achieve the goals of teaching people to improve interpersonal relations and develop their potentials. Let's see how people actually behave in groups and then consider what the results are.

THE ENCOUNTER EXPERIENCE. Carl Rogers (1970) has given the most useful account of the basic encounter group process. Encounter groups are guided by a leader who should be knowledgeable and experienced about human behavior in general and group processes in particular. Usually the leader begins with some introductory comments that establish the basic rules and then turns the group over to the participants. There may be long periods of silence. Usually there is an initial "milling around" stage. Gradually the participants will overcome their discomfort and begin to express what is on their minds, often anger at the leader for not providing more structure. After a while people become more able to talk about personally meaningful concerns and their feelings about what is happening in the group and the people in it. At this point trust begins to grow, as people learn that it is acceptable to say what they feel. People begin to express concern for the pain and problems of others and to help one another. This is done by sharing experiences and giving honest feedback to other people about their behavior. Once trust is established, and people learn to be free in the group, to do their "own thing" within limits set by the leader, people can drop facades, be helpful, and give feedback. The feelings that are expressed become more and more positive as the participants get closer, learn from each other, begin to find out more about themselves, and help others to do so too.

Encounter groups vary greatly. Some last for only a few hours, and some may last for months, meeting for a few hours every week. More and more people are participating in marathon sessions, an encounter that runs for an entire weekend. The intensity of the marathon helps people move into the most productive phases of encounter relatively quickly. There are also great differences in the basic rules and styles of encounter groups. Sensitivity training groups are often the most "conservative," and they emphasize talking things through and exploring the group process intellectually, in addition to more personal considerations. The human potential groups are somewhat less restricted, with more emphasis on touching and bodily expression. Will Schutz is one of the advocates of the more open encounter style. His principles are honesty, awareness, free choice, responsibility for one's behavior, and naturalness. He believes in the unity of mind and body and in expressing things physically—for example, "Take off your clothes if it feels right" (Schutz, 1973).

FEEDBACK IN GROUPS. No matter what schedule or style a group is following, the key element is **feedback.** People must express their reactions to other people and their feelings in general as honestly and openly as possible. This is the crucial tool to develop awareness and growth. Feedback is often negative, and it is the responsibility of the leader to make sure that the feedback in the group is constructive and facilitative of growth, rather than diminishing and destructive. Aronson (1976) has outlined how this can be accomplished. Group members must learn the crucial distinction between expressing feelings and making evaluations of others. If another person in the group makes you feel angry, it is much more constructive to say, "When you say that, I feel very upset and angry" than to say, "You are a stupid and immoral fool for saying that." Feelings that are expressed can be better explored without meaningless categorizing and name calling. Expressing real and complex inner states, rather than attaching labels, is consistent with the encounter emphasis on the "here and now" and leads toward personal growth.

EVALUATION OF ENCOUNTER. As with therapy, we can ask whether encounter groups are effective, but here too the question is very difficult to answer. Rogers (1970) observes that most people report very positive experiences in groups and indicate that the experience has been helpful to them in their daily lives. Most research has shown that for the most part the outcome, in terms of how people feel about their encounter experience, is positive. A study of Lieberman, Yalom, and Miles (1973) showed that 61 percent of the participants in groups they studied felt that they had undergone positive change. This result is encouraging. At the same time, however, about 10 percent of the participants were regarded as "casualties," people who were harmed by the intensity and/or negative feedback of the group. These people showed enduring psychological harm six to eight months after the encounter was over. Thus some individuals are helped by group encounter, but others are definitely hurt, even though they may be few.

These results, especially the figure of 61 percent, are much like the results from studies of the effectiveness of psychotherapy. Not surprisingly, one of the key determinants of positive or negative outcomes in the group is the leader, as is the case in psychotherapy. Before joining any group, one should be sure that the leader is well qualified and known to be effective. Lieberman et al. (1973) have distinguished two different types of group leader and found that one has more casualties than the other. The first is called the "energizer." Energizers are more charismatic and dynamic and stimulate the group more. Their casualty rate is higher,

REVIEW QUESTIONS

12. Which of the following statements regarding the effectiveness of psychotherapy is true?
    a. No relationship has been found between verbal skills and success in psychodynamic therapies.
    b. For any particular individual, therapy has only a 50-50 chance of being successful.
    c. People with phobias and other anxiety disorders are more likely to be helped by insight-oriented therapies.
    d. It is probably the case that the most important determinant of success is the therapist himself or herself.
13. The three personal characteristics found to be most important in a successful therapist are _____, _____, and _____.
14. Match the following group psychotherapies with their descriptions.
    _____ gestalt therapy
    _____ family therapy
    _____ transactional analysis
    _____ encounter groups

    a. emphasizes the interactional system; the individual must be understood in the context of how he or she relates to the other members.
    b. focuses on the Parent, Adult, and Child communication games people play
    c. emphasizes personal integration and taking responsibility for one's own life in the here and now
    d. not specifically for the purpose of psychotherapy; goal is often "personal growth"
15. T or F: One of the differences between sensitivity groups and encounter groups is that the latter are generally more conservative in their approach to personal growth.
16. If group therapy is to be meaningful it is essential that group members provide _____ to each other.
17. T or F: At best, group therapy can be a positive experience; at worst it has no effect at all on the participant.

probably because of the intense energy in their groups, which sometimes takes the form of aggression or attack. The other kind of leader is the "provider." Providers show substantial caring for individual group members and help clarify what is happening in the group. They are called "big daddies" by Lieberman et al. These leaders have fewer casualties. They seem to have some of the key characteristics of effective therapists.

HELPING YOURSELF

Sometimes people are troubled enough to need help from a qualified professional. Sometimes they have such a strong need for self-exploration, development, and actualization that they seek out groups to find intense growth-enhancing relations. This is fine, as long as the therapist or group leader is known to be well qualified and responsible. But no one should overlook his or her own inner resources. There is a great deal we can do to help ourselves. In this section we'll consider several aspects of self-help.

The Importance of Self-Acceptance

There are many ways to define a psychologically healthy personality. One of the most influential definitions, that by Maire Jahoda (1958), lists several characteristics of psychological health, such as accurate perception and autonomy; but nearly every definition, including hers, emphasizes the importance of self-acceptance. We think self-acceptance is of critical importance. Eve's eventual improvement in recent therapy was related to her acceptance of the fact that all her personalities were a part of her and represented aspects of herself that she had to accept.

Self-acceptance has several elements. Let's begin with one of the classic statements in psychology, William James's (1890) simple definition of "self-esteem." James defined self-esteem as one's achievements divided by one's pretensions or aspirations. The more you achieve relative to what you desired or aspired to achieve, the better you feel about yourself. This definition signals the importance of our expectations or aspirations in our evaluation of ourselves. Other ideas in psychology sound a similar note. Carl Rogers (1951) defines mental health in terms of the relation between ideal self-image and actual self-image. The closer you are to what you want to be, the more self-esteem and psychological health you have. In general, if we do better than we expect, we're happy; if we do worse, we can be miserable. How can these definitions be used to improve self-acceptance?

If self-esteem, as James suggested, is a function of both achievement and expectations, we could, theoretically, increase our satisfaction either by achieving more or by expecting less. Achieving more is usually considered first. Our culture encourages us to achieve and in fact teaches us to evaluate ourselves according to our achievements. But improving our abilities and achieving more can be difficult. What about the alternative, lowering our expectations? Even if we wanted to lower them, there would be some difficulties there too. As noted above, much of what we aspire to is culturally determined. Nevertheless, it's crucial to realize that we have much more control over our expectations than we do over our achievements, and if we are willing to be satisfied with less—to accept ourselves and be happy with less—we can increase our self-esteem and happiness. The philosopher Thomas Carlisle made the point this way: Happiness "can be increased in value not so much by increasing your numerator as by lessening your denominator."

Lowering your aspirations and expectations doesn't mean that you should work less hard or take fewer risks in trying to succeed. We believe that people should develop their potentials as much as possible and do all that they can. We are talking about your attitude toward yourself *after* you have done all you can. It undermines your self-concept to be punitive toward yourself after you've tried your best. One should be willing to lower one's expectations and accept what one has done. Continue to work hard and push yourself, but learn to live with whatever the outcomes are. One motto puts this well: Expect the worst, hope for the best, take what comes. Albert Ellis would add: You aren't your performance. Again, the message is, Do all that you can, but don't berate yourself if what you do falls short of your hopes, be prepared for possible failure or disappointment.

Another point to remember is that what we expect or want for ourselves is often determined by what we see others receiving or achieving. This kind of social comparison may be natural, but it is ultimately self-defeating if it becomes a source of low self-esteem or unhappiness. Be willing to see others do well without becoming jealous or down on yourself. This is hard to do, but important. Continue to make the effort to do well yourself, but be prepared to accept the outcome regardless of what happens to you or others.

SELF-ACCEPTANCE AND ACCEPTANCE OF OTHERS. Whether one becomes jealous or envious of others is ultimately related to one's own level of self-acceptance. The person who can accept herself or himself is more able to accept others, and the person who can accept herself or himself and others is well on the way to psychological well-being. This point is central to Thomas Harris's (1969) book on transactional analysis, *I'm OK, You're OK.* In it Harris outlines the four "life positions" that orient people's lives. He believes that during the first six months of life, children begin to try to gain clarity about their experience by drawing tentative conclusions about themselves and the world. Most children draw the conclusion "I'm not OK, You're OK." They decide "I'm not OK," according to Harris, because of the powerlessness and frustration of early childhood. They decide that others "are OK" because, even though those people don't supply instantaneous gratification to the child, in most cases they do provide basic care and nourishment. Harris goes on to say that most people adopt this life position and never change it. It doesn't make them feel very good, but it does bring

TABLE 8.3

I'm OK–You're OK and Life Positions

T. A. Harris (1969) outlined the four life positions that people adopt. These life positions define self-worth and the worth of others, and they are used to understand experience and to direct behavior.

1. I'M NOT OK—YOU'RE OK: This is the life position in which all people begin. At about six months they conclude I'm Not OK—You're OK on the basis of the powerlessness of childhood and the power of adults. If people remain in this position they constantly seek approval from others but never feel worthy.

2. I'M NOT OK—YOU'RE NOT OK: At about age two, some children with negligent and distant parents move to this life position where they feel that they and others, and life generally, is worthless. They withdraw completely from interacting and living.

3. I'M OK—YOU'RE NOT OK: At about age two, some children with brutal parents feel that they are fine if left alone and decide I'm OK—You're Not OK. They behave in aggressive, antisocial ways which they justify by saying other people deserve no better than antisocial treatment.

4. I'M OK—YOU'RE OK: Some people as adults make a conscious decision, and act on it, to accept themselves and others. They commit themselves to this decision and by acting in accord with it, they begin to think much more positively about themselves, other people, and living in general.

some predictability and stability to their experience. They go through their lives seeking approval from others they regard as OK and generally lead productive if somewhat miserable lives. Certainly Eve White falls into this category.

Harris thinks that at around the age of two some people adopt life positions that are even worse. Children who have parents who ignore them and show no caring may conclude "I'm Not OK, You're Not OK" and withdraw totally from living, even to the point of committing suicide as adults. Children who are brutalized by their parents may realize that they're happier and safer when they're alone and may conclude "I'm OK, You're Not OK." These people may become very aggressive as adults, turning against society, even to the point of killing other people and feeling justified because of their alleged brutality.

The one desirable position, according to Harris, is the "I'm OK, You're OK" position, in which both self and others are actively accepted. Harris believes this position can only be achieved in adulthood, perhaps through therapy, when one makes a conscious decision to accept oneself and others and then makes a commitment to live by that assumption and to act on it continually. The other life positions are adopted on the basis of the feelings of an earlier age. The "I'm OK, You're OK" position is adopted on the basis of adult thought and decision, but it's a decision that must be followed with action, a commitment that needs to be lived up to. Harris believes that once people decide to commit themselves to this life position, they can function more fully and effectively. Jealousy, hostility, and self-doubt can be put aside, energies can be channeled effectively, and potentials can be developed. Following through on an "I'm OK, You're OK" decision is difficult. It may need to be supported by therapy, as Harris suggests. We feel that it can be a crucial step to better adjustment that you should think about taking on your own and working hard to live up to.

If you do decide to try to follow through on an "I'm OK, You're OK" decision, remember that it will involve acting and thinking in new ways. This means doing some things that you aren't doing now and stopping other things you presently are doing. For example, you may need to remind yourself to act considerately toward others whom you haven't treated with kindness before. This could be as simple as saying "Hello" or taking the time to listen carefully. In another case, if you're consuming time and energy by worrying and berating yourself, you need to learn to tell yourself to stop and help yourself follow that command by engaging in some other activity, perhaps volunteer work or running, that is incompatible with unpleasant and disturbing thoughts. Getting yourself to think and act differently about yourself

and others involves work and practice. But you will find it's worth the effort.

Finally, we should note that a positive attitude toward yourself, others, and the world around you has a significant impact on your physical health as well as your psychological well-being. We've seen that when a person perceives threat the body reacts, and the continual reactivity of the body can upset its immune system and lead to physical breakdown. A positive mental attitude means that less threat is perceived. Recent studies indicate that a positive attitude lessens the risk of ulcers, hypertension, and heart disease (UPI, 1984).

Planning Effective Action

Accepting yourself and others, and maintaining a positive attitude in general, are critical first steps in psychological well-being, but acting effectively in the environment is also crucial. We need not punish ourselves for our failures, but we must consider how to act so as to maximize our potentials. One helpful approach to effective behavior is contained in the book *Decision Making* by Irving Janis and Leon Mann (1977). Janis and Mann underline the fact that decision making is painful, and that people often plan and act without carefully weighing all the alternatives because making choices in important situations produces so much conflict. People avoid such stress and conflict by procrastinating and denying that there is anything wrong with their current behaviors.

The most useful part of Janis and Mann's analysis points to the conditions under which people will plan thoroughly and successfully: When people retain hope of finding a better course of action *and* believe they have time to search for and find it, they make the best decisions. Retaining hope may simply be a matter of commitment, similar to deciding "I'm OK, You're OK." Trying to be open to possibilities also helps keep up your confidence in doing better. Careful scheduling and anticipation of your future needs ensures that you have time to search for the best alternatives. It should be remembered that procrastinating almost always puts you in a situation in which alternatives can't be carefully and rationally weighed and leads to snap decisions that are often regretted later. Give yourself enough time to search for and appraise alternatives.

A thorough search for alternatives and careful consideration of the advantages and disadvantages of each is important both in selecting the right course of action and in adapting to the consequences of your decision. Problems and setbacks are always associated with any major life decision, be it going to school, getting married, or taking a job, and the more you have thought through the alternatives beforehand, the better able you are to withstand these stresses and persevere, to "take what comes." This is helpful in living up to your commitments and realizing when it is and when it is not time to consider making appropriate revisions in your plans.

Janis and Mann's decision-making analysis makes many points, but the most important underlines the benefits of maintaining some degree of optimism and allowing yourself the time to deliberate your future actions rationally and thoroughly.

Exercise is an important element in helping yourself by staying physically fit and psychologically well-adjusted.
Hugh Rogers, Monkmeyer.

Physical Well-Being

One of the most beneficial ideas to emerge from the human potential approach to psychological health is that body and mind are related and that physical well-being can directly affect psychological well-being. This isn't a new idea, of course, but it's one that has until recently been forgotten in our culture. Now, more and more people are finding that tennis, yoga, jogging, swimming, isometrics, or some other form of exercise are very helpful to mental health. Physical exercise isn't necessarily *the* answer, but studies show that it makes a significant contribution. One investigation of middle-aged business and professional men who were put on a four-month exercise program showed that the exercise produced marked improvements in openness, social motivation, stability, and self-assuredness. Subjects also became more imaginative and venturesome and less neurotic (Ismail & Trachtman, 1973). Recent studies at the University of Rochester (Treadway, 1984)

show that physical conditioning can have beneficial effects on depressed people. Psychologist Elizabeth Doyne has shown that both aerobic exercise (running) and nonaerobic exercise (weightlifting) in moderate amounts make stress reactions less severe. Additionally, women participating in this program achieved a greater sense of general competence and self-confidence.

These findings shouldn't surprise us. Just as a positive mental outlook contributes to physical health, exercise leads to increased physical health that can positively affect psychological well-being. Good health can increase day-to-day efficiency. Exercise can add richness and variety to life and provide an enjoyable activity that's a welcome distraction from daily stresses. Regular exercise can also contribute to a sense of achievement.

LEARNING TO RELAX. Another benefit of exercise is thought to be that it contributes to being and feeling relaxed. This may be true, and if so it is important. Relaxation is obviously desirable in its own right, and we have seen the effects it can have in helping to reduce anxiety in the systematic desensitization procedure. Relaxing is something people can easily practice by themselves.

Here are brief instructions for a relaxation procedure that can be practiced in less than half an hour a day (Calhoun & Accocella, 1978). The basic principle of this procedure is to tense a muscle for five to ten seconds, then relax it. Pay close attention to how it feels as the muscle that has been tensed gradually becomes more and more relaxed. Start with your hand, making a tight fist, and then relaxing it. Do this two or three times until you are certain that your hand and forearm are totally relaxed. Then you can proceed to your upper arm (bend your elbow and tense your biceps), your other hand and arm, your forehead (try frowning hard and then relaxing), your face (squint), and then your trunk and legs, until all the muscle groups in your body have been tensed and relaxed. You will soon learn what it feels like to be completely relaxed.

You can also relax yourself psychologically. In this relaxed state you can begin to meditate. Focus on your breathing or some other simple, nonthreatening scene or repetitive action, such as a beach or walking in the woods. On each breath imagine the relaxing scene. Let in anxiety-arousing thoughts briefly, then usher them out with the next breath. Both mind and body should be passive and relaxed (Benson, 1975). It's important to do this when you have enough time and are in an undisturbed, quiet, and comfortable place.

Try to build relaxation and meditation time into your schedule for several days, and see if it makes you feel better. Finding some form of exercise or physical relaxation that works for you can be highly beneficial to your general well-being. Exercise and relaxation can help you feel at home with your body and with your psychological self. In addition, both exercise and relaxation give you an added sense of control over your life.

THE ROLE OF MEDICATION

In addition to psychotherapy and self-help, you should be aware of an important form of help you can get from a physician or psychiatrist—medication. As biopsychologists and neuropsychologists penetrate further into the secrets of the brain and nervous system, they have discovered more and more about the neurological correlates of various psychological states, including various disorders. This means that they know with great precision what is happening in the brain and nervous system when people are feeling depressed, panicked, or in danger of losing their minds. Thus they are able to prescribe drugs that will stop the action in the nervous system, with the result, very often, that people no longer experience psychological symptoms. For example, there are now drugs available that are effective in treating the spontaneous panic attacks of agoraphobics, although it has been more difficult to find drugs that stop the specific fears associated with other phobias, such as the fear of flying.

Some people believe that the powerful effects of drugs in reducing psychological symptoms mean that disorders such as depression are "all chemical" or "all physical." This isn't true. The fact is that mind and body are interrelated. When a person has a psychological experience, there is also a physical event in the nervous system corresponding to it. This is true of disordered psychological states just as it is true of normal states. But it may be that external events or psychological processes, such as feelings, rather than the neurological events, led to the disordered psychological states. All we know is that psychological state and neurological state occur together. We can't say which is the first cause. But we can still act directly on the nervous system using drugs, and changes in the nervous system can have positive effects on psychological symptoms. Similarly, we expect that processes, such as psychotherapy, that act directly on psychological states can cause changes in the neurological processes that go hand in hand with those psychological states. You don't have to worry in detail about the complex relation between mind and body, but you should be aware that many disorders can be helped through medication. Only a qualified physician or psychiatrist should prescribe such medication to you or others you know.

HELPING OTHERS

The key to helping yourself, we have suggested, is self-acceptance. We also think that you can do a great deal to help others, and again the key appears to be acceptance. Carl Rogers has written extensively on the importance of congruence, unconditional positive regard, and empathic understanding in therapy. In an important paper called ''Characteristics of a Helping Relationship'' Rogers (1961) suggests that these traits are important in *any* relationship in which one person is interested in helping another. It applies to teacher-student relationships, parent-child relationships, and friendships between peers as much as it does to therapy. Any person who is able to offer caring acceptance, an ability to see another's problems clearly, and an ability to be entirely candid and honest can be very helpful. We

Helping other people is a source of satisfaction to ourselves and makes a big difference for others.
Rhoda Sidney.

CAN YOU HELP?

Carl Rogers (1961) wrote that his extensive experience as a psychotherapist showed him that people can help each other in many situations, in therapy, in the family, in groups, and simply among friends, if they can answer yes to each of the following questions. Consider one or two people that you would like to help, and ask whether you could say yes to the questions below and help the person.

1. Can I behave in a way which will be perceived by the other as trustworthy, dependable, and consistent in a deep sense?
2. Can I be expressive enough to be perceived clearly?
3. Can I let myself experience positive attitudes toward this person?
4. Can I be strong enough to be separate from the other?
5. Can I be secure enough to let the other have his or her separateness?
6. Can I let myself enter fully into the other's world of feelings and see things as he or she does?
7. Can I be accepting of each facet of this other person?
8. Can I act with sufficient sensitivity that my behavior will not be perceived as a threat?
9. Can I free the other person from the threat of external evaluation?
10. Can I meet the other person as a person who is *becoming*?

Adapted from Carl R. Rogers: *On Becoming a Person,* copyright © 1961 Houghton Mifflin Company. Adapted with permission.

know that social support is a key factor in helping people withstand stress and in making them stress-hardy (Borysenko, 1984).

We aren't suggesting that one person should play "therapist" with another. Being willing to care, listen actively, and say directly and honestly what you feel and perceive doesn't involve being a therapist, but simply being a friend. If we recall Harry Stack Sullivan's observation about intimacy and the chum relation, we can see that its qualities are very much like those we've been discussing. Sullivan (1953) emphasized caring, being as concerned with the other person's problems as with your own. It's clear that the caring he describes is unconditional. Your chum is as important to you as you are. It's also clear that congruence is involved. One talks freely and openly with one's chum, and each gives the other an accurate reflected appraisal and helps the other to correct errors in his or her self-concept. There is also a clear ability to see things from the other's perspective in the chum relationship.

Behaving in this helping way, with no strings attached, is easy if one makes a commitment to it. We think it can be of inestimable value for all concerned. If you can keep in mind the simple things you can do to have a "helping" effect on others around you, we feel you have learned an important lesson. We hope you apply it.

SELF-HELP GROUPS. One setting in which people help each other is in groups. In this instance we aren't talking about therapy or encounter groups run by experts, but about groups run by people who are sharing or have shared a common problem they are working on together in a supportive social atmosphere.

Instead of relying on experts, people use their own experience and the experience of others who have "been there" to gain insight into problems and support in trying to modify their behavior. The most famous such group is Alcoholics Anonymous (AA). AA emphasizes helping people to abstain from drinking, making people feel part of a group that shares a problem, and helping and supporting those who aren't presently able to refrain from drink.

Honestly, understanding, and support seem to be the key factors in the remarkable success of AA. Weight Watchers and Parents Anonymous help people who have difficulties with overeating and mistreatment of children. There are many such mutual support groups in the United States today, and if the group you need doesn't exist, other people who share your concern would probably help you create it.

SUMMARY

1. There are many kinds of help available to people who are troubled. There are also ways that people can help themselves and help others. The varieties of help available can be divided into individual therapy, group therapy, and self-help.

2. Many individual therapies have an "insight," or psychodynamic, orientation. These range from classical Freudian psychoanalysis, emphasizing free association, dreams, and transference, to humanist approaches emphasizing the actualization of a person's inner potential. All these therapies aim to make people more aware of the causes of their psychological problems.

3. Behavior therapies concern themselves with changing maladaptive responses to the world without exploring the causes for those problematic attitudes and behaviors. Clients in behavior therapies go through conditioning procedures that lead to extinguishing maladaptive behaviors or acquiring new and more effective ones.

4. Many people question the effectiveness of therapy. Although the empirical evidence is unimpressive, there is enough evidence to conclude that therapy can be effective in helping people overcome their problems. Therapy is most likely to be effective when there is a good match between what the client is seeking and what the therapist can offer, and when the therapist shows genuineness, unconditional positive regard, and empathic understanding in his or her interactions with a client. The right therapist is the most important factor in effective therapy.

5. Many forms of treatment are undertaken in groups. Several group psychotherapies emphasize helping individuals solve specific problems in a group setting: gestalt therapy, transactional analysis, and family therapy. In addition, several varieties of encounter groups emphasize self-exploration and improvement rather than correcting specific maladaptive behaviors. Although most people find that they benefit greatly from the encounter experience, some are hurt by the intensive, no-holds-barred group interaction. The quality of the group leader is the most important determinant of a person's successful experience in an encounter group.

6. There are many things people can do to help themselves with their psychological problems. Self-acceptance, acceptance of others, careful planning of alternative ways of thinking and acting, nurturing, physical well-being, and learning to relax can greatly improve a person's outlook on life. Medications can sometimes also be helpful.

7. Helping others can also be a way of helping ourselves. Most people's problems include concerns about their personal relationships. The effective therapist, the good group leader, and the helping friend all have many of the same characteristics. The most important is being willing to listen carefully and give others our honest reactions, always in the context of caring and friendship. Genuinely caring about other people seems to be the key to both helping others and being at peace with ourselves.

KEY TERMS

a. CONGRUENCE
b. EMPATHIC UNDERSTANDING
c. EXTINCTION
d. FREE ASSOCIATION
e. OPERANT
f. OPERANT CONDITIONING

g. REINFORCER
h. RESISTANCE
i. SYSTEMATIC DESENSITIZATION
j. TRANSFERENCE
k. UNCONDITIONAL POSITIVE REGARD

1. In Freudian psychoanalysis, the patient's avoidance of thinking about or discussing anxiety-provoking thoughts or feelings
2. A psychoanalytic technique in which the patient verbalizes whatever thoughts or feelings come to mind without any censoring
3. In psychotherapy, complete acceptance of the client by the therapist along with the therapist's warm caring for the client as a human being, with no conditions attached
4. In psychotherapy, the matching of a therapist's inner feelings with what he or she expresses overtly
5. The process by which a conditioned response gradually disappears when the unconditioned stimulus or reinforcer is removed
6. A behavior that has been acquired on the basis of reinforcement
7. In psychoanalytic therapy, the process by which the patient projects the attitudes of significant others onto the therapist and acts toward the therapist as he or she may have acted toward those significant others
8. A behavior therapy developed by Wolpe in which the patient is trained to relax, is presented with a hierarchy of anxiety-arousing situations, and learns to relax even when contemplating the most threatening situation
9. In psychotherapy, the therapist's capacity to view the world from the client's point of view and to understand his or her feelings
10. A form of conditioning in which a response or change in behavior is strengthened with a reinforcer
11. A desired stimulus that strengthens a behavior, a reward

ANSWERS TO REVIEW QUESTIONS

1. c. **2.** Psychoanalysis. **3.** Client-centered. **4.** False. **5.** Humanistic-existential. **6.** Rational-emotive.

7. d. **8.** Classical conditioning. **9.** Operant conditioning. **10.** Extinction. **11.** c; a; e; d; b.

12. d. **13.** Congruence; unconditional positive regard; empathic understanding. **14.** c; a; b; d. **15.** True. **16.** Feedback. **17.** False.

RELATING
TO OTHERS

B arbara Walters faced the interview with considerable anxiety. Her subject, Prince Philip, husband of Queen Elizabeth II of England, had a reputation for being testy, and she was afraid he would be highly irritated at having to grant an early morning interview before he assumed control of his jet plane and flew back to the British Isles. The interview had been arranged only through the personal intervention of the president of the United States, Richard M. Nixon. Barbara had been interviewing President Nixon's daughter Julie in the White House and had mentioned that she had been trying to interview the prince but had been told that he would be available only for a "Meet the Press" interview. The president had felt that Prince Philip would enjoy appearing on the "Today" show with Barbara and apparently had mentioned this to him. So Barbara unexpectedly received a call from the British Embassy saying the prince would be available early the next morning for an interview. Barbara was happy to have the chance to interview the prince, but she wasn't optimistic that it would go well.

At the beginning of the interview Barbara's pessimism seemed justified. Prince Philip criticized the lighting and nearly everything else involved in setting up the interview. He curtly replied "No" when Barbara asked him if there was anything in particular he wanted to talk about at the beginning. When they went on the air, Barbara tried to break the ice by saying how much she had enjoyed being in England when Prince Charles had formally been invested as Prince of Wales. Philip simply said, "Can't we get on with it?"

The prince's response to Barbara's first question continued in this disastrous manner. Barbara mentioned a recent poll indicating that the English people would elect Prince Philip if they were ever to choose a president; she asked the prince if he would have liked to have been a politician. Again he seemed irritated and said that he made it a practice not to answer hypothetical questions. Instead of panicking and losing her composure, Barbara realized that she had better shift gears fast. She remembered that people usually respond best when they can deal with a personal question related to their feelings and specific interests. So she asked Prince Philip if it was difficult for him to deal with the fact that a good deal of what he said was highly controversial. He responded with interest to her question: Yes, it was difficult, but he didn't enjoy simply mouthing platitudes. Barbara went on to ask Prince Philip's feelings about a range of things and obtained a very full interview.

In the many years of her broadcasting career, Barbara Walters has become one of the most prominent women in the television industry. Her skills as a broadcaster and interviewer first became noted in the 1960s, when she was an anchorperson on television's popular "Today" show and conducted interviews with newsmakers from all walks of life. In the 1970s she left the "Today" show to become coanchor of the ABC evening news, for the unheard of sum of one million dollars a year. Since her years on the evening news she has worked with ABC as an incisive interviewer, hosting her own show, "The Barbara Walters Special." She has become well known for her ability to elicit interesting personal revelations from all sorts of prominent

Barbara Walters.
Springer/Bettmann Film Archive.

people. During the 1984 presidential primaries, Barbara conducted one of the most revealing debates ever between Democratic presidential candidates, in what amounted to a joint interview. Each of the candidates spoke in highly personal and revealing ways in answer to Barbara's questions about their backgrounds and their aspirations for America. They showed themselves in much more human and humane light than usual and revealed a genuine sense of respect for each other that is not generally noticeable in America's televised political debates. Over the years, Barbara Walters has developed great skill in encouraging others to communicate with her about themselves, and she has shared a great deal of her wisdom in her best-selling book, *How to Talk with Practically Anybody about Practically Anything* (1970).

Barbara Walters learned a key lesson about talking with other people in an interview with Greek shipping tycoon Aristotle Onassis, who until his death had been married to Jacqueline Kennedy, the widow of United States President John F. Kennedy. Onassis had just been through a lengthy meeting about shipping issues and was trying to relax at the New York restaurant where Barbara joined him for lunch. He was an intimidating and uncooperative subject. Walters had no choice but to plunge in anyway. She asked Onassis how he got involved in shipping and what was his very first job. To her surprise, Onassis opened up. He talked on and on about his boyhood and the way he built his shipping empire. The lesson Barbara derived from this experience was clear: People love to talk about themselves in specific terms, to reminisce, and to discuss whatever is personally important to them. There are many tricks to the interviewing trade, but helping people relax and expressing specific interest in what they have done are crucial.

Drawing people out can require a great deal of sensitivity. Barbara Walters was the only woman in a group of reporters who interviewed former President Dwight D. Eisenhower and his wife, Mamie, on the occasion of the Eisenhowers' fiftieth wedding anniversary. During a break in the proceedings, Walters helped Mamie Eisenhower serve soft drinks and asked her how she managed to arrange her own life so as to have time for herself and her busy husband. Later, Mamie Eisenhower remembered Barbara's having taken a personal interest and granted her an exclusive interview shortly after President Eisenhower died. As they talked about the former president's final days, Barbara sensed that Mamie was feeling a lot of sadness, so she suggested they talk about something else, about the happy times. Mamie Eisenhower replied that those final days actually were the happy times and went on to talk in revealing terms about her husband. Barbara showed that she was sensitive to Mamie Eisenhower's grieving and let her lead the way in talking, or not talking, about her personal feelings.

Barbara Walters advises us to keep in mind that people may want to keep their feelings private, but also to recall Shakespeare's advice, ''Give sorrow words'' and ''The grief that does not speak whispers the o'erfrought heart and bids it break.'' Express an interest in what is personally significant to others, Barbara suggests, but be sensitive about pushing into private territory.

Asking personal questions can also be difficult if you don't know much about the person and so don't know what to inquire about. Barbara Walters once found herself sitting next to a certain Sir George Weidenfeld at lunch. She had no idea who he was and knew absolutely nothing about him. Here some quick wit and creativity were in order. Seeing the ''Sir'' on Weidenfeld's place card, Barbara asked him what he had been knighted for, and Weidenfeld explained that his knighthood was a reward for his work in British publishing. Using the tactic she'd learned with Aristotle Onassis, Barbara asked Weidenfeld how he got into publishing. Weidenfeld explained that he had wanted to publish the interesting views on labor that one of his early professors had espoused. That professor was Harold Wilson, the future prime minister of Great Britain. By trying hard and taking a personal interest in Weidenfeld, Walters learned something that was of interest to her and that permitted the two of them to have an enjoyable meal together.

These are a few of the lessons that Barbara Walters has learned in her many years as an interviewer. She has overcome the considerable shyness she felt in her early years, and, by attending carefully to the lives of others and communicating to them openly, she has truly learned how to talk with practically anybody about practically anything.

RELATING TO OTHERS

Barbara Walters's success in having interesting conversations with all types of people depends on her ability to perceive people accurately and to communicate with them effectively. These skills are important for more than highly paid interviewers. All of us must relate to other people daily, and being able to perceive them accurately and communicate with them effectively is of utmost importance. As John Donne wrote, "No man is an island," and the well-adjusted person needs to understand the key aspects of relating to others. In this chapter we will consider how we perceive, and misperceive, other people and the ways we communicate ourselves to others and they communicate themselves to us, especially through the highly important channel of nonverbal communication. Let's first consider how we perceive other people through the process called **person perception** and the ways our impressions of others affect our interactions with them.

PERCEIVING OTHERS

Our perceptions of others are crucial determinants of personal interaction. We respond to people as we perceive them to be, not as they really are. Whether we think another person is friendly, intelligent, or sincere makes a vast difference in how we treat them. Because our impressions of others are so important in determining how we relate to them, and because we are so deeply interested in other people, it seems very important that we judge them accurately. In many cases, perhaps, we are accurate, but human beings are extraordinarily complex, and there are many ways in which our impressions can be biased. When they are biased, there is trouble in store. Sometimes that trouble is a problem for us. For example, if we believe that a crooked real estate agent is honest, we can easily be swindled. In other cases, our misperceptions can lead to unfair and harmful treatment of others. A juror who doesn't like someone's looks and therefore helps convict that person of a crime of which he or she is actually innocent is committing a serious injustice. Thus anything we can do to minimize bias and inaccuracy in forming impressions is important. It can protect our own well-being, as well as that of others. Getting the facts straight about other people is critical to making the proper decisions about people and treating them fairly in a free and democratic society.

We believe that perceiving others accurately is important for effective behavior. Erroneous impressions can contribute to self-defeating action and poor personal adjustment to the world as it really is. Perceiving the world accurately—including, of course, other people in it—is a mark of the healthy personality. Therefore our aim in this chapter is to outline the basic processes of person perception and to show how our impressions can go awry. We hope the reader will become more aware of the ways in which his or her judgments can be in error and use this awareness to guard against bias.

THE PROCESS OF FORMING IMPRESSIONS. The overall process of perceiving others can be separated into two related phases. First, we make inferences about a person's specific traits. Second, we resolve conflicting data we may have about a person into an organized and coherent impression.

There are many ways we make inferences about people's traits. The key process here is interpreting another person's behavior and drawing conclusions about why he or she acted in a specific manner. On the basis of our interpretations we may be able to attribute one or more traits to the person. This process of *attribution* is often exceedingly difficult. For example, when Barbara Walters interviewed Prince Philip she had to infer why he acted in a remote and nearly hostile manner. Was he simply tired, did he not like Americans, did he have a particular dislike for her, was he angry with the British Embassy for arranging the interview, or was he just a bad-tempered snob? It was hard to know. Making inferences on the basis of behavior can be extraordinarily complex. Of course not all traits are inferred from behavior. Sometimes we make snap judgments about other people on the basis of their appearance or their nonverbal communication. Sometimes simply knowing one trait allows us to infer others.

In addition to attributing traits to people we have to integrate information related to several traits. Often the information is contradictory. Sometimes we may have information that suggests that a person is friendly, but someone else may tell us that the person is unfriendly or cruel. Or we may see a person act in a clumsy fashion in one situation but later perform with skill and grace. How do we resolve these discrepancies?

Because people are complex, we have several ways of organizing all the information we have about them. We inevitably take shortcuts and make summary judgments; but we have to integrate our impressions in some way or else be overwhelmed with information. The ways we do organize our impressions are often sound. But there is room for considerable error because of the complexity of the information and the strength of our own motives. As we shall see, bias is pervasive in people's perceptions of each other and affects both our inferences about others' specific traits and our overall picture of them.

Inferring Traits

ATTRIBUTION PROCESSES. Among the most complex and important of the person perception processes are those involving attributions about the causes of behavior. Making attributions that explain why a person did something is very common. Whenever a person makes a statement about a political issue, succeeds or fails at a task, or treats someone with respect or neglect, we are likely to ask why. What is the reason for the person acting that way? We don't only make attributions about other people's behavior; we do the same for our own behavior as well. We may wonder, Why am I so scared?—or, Why did I do so poorly on that exam?

Answering these questions correctly, that is, making accurate attributions, is extremely important. We base our actions toward others on our interpretations of their behavior, and we make decisions about our own future actions on the basis of self-attributions. For example, if we attribute our failure on a test to low ability in a certain subject, we may not study that subject any more. If the reason for the failure was actually inadequate effort, not studying would be a serious mistake. In this section we will talk about the rational principles of attribution, and in the next section we will show some of the many ways that attributions can be biased. We hope that once you are aware of these attributional errors you will be less likely to make them.

The starting point for discussing attribution is Fritz Heider's (1944) distinction between internal and external causes of behavior. Heider pointed out that when observers watch another person act, they try to judge the extent to which the behavior reflects either underlying personality traits and dispositions or external and situational pressure. In other words, Is some trait of the person causing his or her behavior, or is his or her behavior attributable to external forces in the environment? This is frequently a key question when Barbara Walters interviews a well-known person. Do you really love what you are doing, or do you do it for the money or fame that goes along with it? Although we can use logical processes to attribute people's behavior to internal traits or external influence, oftentimes we don't. Research shows that people are often sloppy and lazy in collecting data needed for accurate impressions and that many motives get in the way of objectivity in even the simplest situations.

BIAS TOWARD INTERNAL ATTRIBUTION. People seem to have a fundamental bias toward making internal rather than external attributions in judging others. Heider (1958) first pointed this out. He said that human beings like to be able to predict their environment so they can be in a position to control it. They especially want to be able to control other people. As a result of this desire to predict situations and to control others, there is a desire to learn as much as possible about other people's traits—and therefore a bias toward making internal attributions. You should be aware of this bias because it's very common. Notice how often you attribute a trait to a person and get the feeling that you know and understand him or her. Have you really been accurate, or might you have made an attribution error?

BIAS TOWARD STABLE ATTRIBUTION. Heider (1958) also suggested that people have a bias toward making attributions to stable characteristics in others, such as long-term attitudes and values, rather than to temporary characteristics, such as excitement or fatigue. You know more about a person if you know about an ever-present trait than if you know about something that can vary, such as a person's mood. This tendency, combined with the more general tendency to make internal attributions, has special relevance when people are trying to understand performances that are related to ability. Heider suggests that we perceive success or failure in various situations—taking a test, running a race, or giving a

speech—as a function of four factors. The first is the ability of the person acting. If a person succeeds, that may indicate high ability. The second possible cause of success or failure is effort. Failure may result from the person not having tried hard enough. Third, the difficulty of the task is a major determinant of how well a person performs. Sometimes a very able person will try hard but still fail if the task is very difficult. Failure to find a cure for cancer is generally not attributed to the incompetence or laziness of researchers because finding a cure for cancer is recognized as a very difficult task. Finally, success or failure can be attributed to good or bad luck.

Heider noted that ability and effort are internal causes and that task difficulty and luck are external factors. He and Weiner et al. (1970) also noted that ability and task difficulty are *stable* attributes of the person and of the environment, respectively, and that effort and luck can *vary*. Therefore we can expect people to have a significant bias toward attributing success or failure to ability, because it is both internal and stable. Thus, for example, when we learn that a child did poorly on a spelling test, we may tend to attribute the child's poor grade—his or her "failure"—to lack of intelligence. This attribution is the one that makes us feel we know most about the child.

Attributions about success and failure are complex and can be biased in many ways other than a tendency to make judgments about ability. We all have a tendency to bolster our self-esteem by attributing our successes to high ability and our failures to temporary bad luck or lack of really trying. At the same time we have a tendency to dismiss other people's successes as being just due to luck or only reflecting the fact that they are serious "grinds." These biases are not always strong, but we should be aware of them as traps that can interfere with looking at ourselves and others objectively.

In sum, Heider proposed that there is bias toward making attributions to internal and stable causes. In the case of success and failure, this means we often have a tendency to overestimate the role of ability and underestimate

---

TABLE 9.1

Biases in Attribution

1. Bias toward internal attribution: The tendency to try to infer personal characteristics rather than external circumstances as the cause of behavior
2. Bias toward stable attribution: The tendency to try to account for behavior in terms of stable, invariable causes rather than temporary factors such as mood or luck
3. Ignoring situational constraints: Also called the fundamental attribution error, the tendency to disregard situational or external factors that are plausible causes of a person's behavior
4. Actor-observer bias: The tendency for people to attribute their own behavior to external, situational factors and other people's behavior to internal, personal characteristics
5. Salience bias: The tendency to attribute behavior to the most obvious or conspicuous possible causes

TABLE 9.2

Possible Attributions for a
Successful or Unsuccessful
Performance

People can attribute success or failure to causes that are either stable or unstable and that are either internal or external. This results in four possible causes. These are used to understand most good and bad performances (Weiner et al., 1971).

	STABLE CAUSE	UNSTABLE CAUSE
INTERNAL CAUSE	Ability	Effort
EXTERNAL CAUSE	Task difficulty	Luck

the roles played by effort, the difficulty of the task, and luck. But when our own self-esteem is involved, our bias is toward attributions that make us feel good. In such cases we will tend to attribute another person's success to external factors, such as luck, or to negative, rather than positive, internal traits.

BIAS TOWARD IGNORING SITUATIONAL CONSTRAINTS. Research has also shown that, in addition to being biased toward internal attributions, perceivers sometimes ignore environmental constraints when judging other people's behavior. We fail to take into account that the person might be overworked or tired, or that it's his or her job to be friendly or, in other cases, unfriendly. In many such cases, the person's behavior occupies so much of our attention that it "engulfs the field," and we fail to pay enough attention to external constraints. Then we infer that the person must have a trait corresponding to the behavior.

One demonstration of this tendency was found in a study by Napolitan and Geothals (1979). Subjects had a discussion with a female "consultant" who was actually a confederate of the experimenter, trained to act either very friendly or distinctly unfriendly. In some cases subjects thought the consultant's behavior was spontaneous, and in other cases they were told that she was practicing a friendly or unfriendly role as part of her training as a consultant. Subjects who encountered forced friendly behav-

ior thought the woman was just as friendly as did subjects who thought her friendliness was freely chosen. Similarly, subjects who knew the woman was forced to be unfriendly thought her to be just as unfriendly as did subjects who thought her unfriendliness was her own. That is, subjects totally ignored the constraints on the woman's behavior and believed her to be as friendly or unfriendly as she behaved on that occasion.

Some subjects interacted with the woman twice. When her behavior was the same as in the first encounter, their attributions didn't change. They had already made very strong attributions on the basis of her initial behavior, whether they thought it to be free or forced. When the confederate's behavior on the second occasion was different from that at the first encounter, subjects were somewhat confused and began to consider the causes of the woman's behavior. For example, if she was spontaneously friendly and then forced to act unfriendly, they tended to believe she was more friendly than unfriendly. Still, they didn't completely discount the unfriendly behavior.

This study provides a dramatic example of people ignoring the causes of behavior and taking behavior too much at face value. It suggests that people are lazy in forming impressions of others and won't think about the reasons for other people's behavior unless they are forced to by inconsistent information. In general, people don't give enough consideration to the external constraints that may be forcing others to act in particular ways.

Barbara Walters has learned this lesson, and it has been a significant factor in her successful interactions with others. People do behave differently in different situations, and their present behavior may have more to do with the situation than with their personality. Try to change the situation for people if you want to get their behavior to change. Barbara Walters did this in interviewing Prince Philip. She created a situation where she was genuinely interested in his reaction to real and meaningful problems. Prince Philip then opened up considerably. You will probably have better luck trying to change the social situation that you create for others than in trying to change their personalities. In general, be aware of the external constraints that are acting on another person, and remember them when judging an unfriendly police officer or a friendly salesperson. To some extent their behavior is forced upon them by their jobs.

ATTRIBUTION TO SELF AND OTHERS. Attribution theory provides an account of the rational principles people use to make accurate judgments. But the research on attribution shows that people don't always apply these principles and consequently often form erroneous impressions. We have already noted people's tendency to be insensitive to external factors that might account for other's behavior. This is understandable in terms of our desire to attribute traits to others so that we feel we know them and can predict them, but it is faulty nevertheless. Jones and Nisbett (1971) underscore this point; they describe the differences between our attributions about our own behavior and that of other people.

Jones and Nisbett suggest that when people are explaining the behavior of another person they tend to see it as a function of the person's internal dispositions and traits, but when they judge their own behavior, they tend to explain it in terms of situational constraints. That is, a person is likely to see his or her own behavior as responsive to external pressures and as appropriate to the situation. An observer is likely to attribute that same behavior to the person's personality traits.

There is much evidence for the difference in the way we make attributions about ourselves and others. One study by Nisbett, Caputo, Legant, and Marecek (1973) showed that when subjects were asked to explain why they chose a particular major or why they were dating a particular person they gave as reasons the interest of the subject matter or the attractiveness of the person. That is, they saw their behavior as natural responses to objects and people in the environment. Subjects were also asked to explain why a friend made these same choices. When explaining the friend's choices, they tended toward explanations of the friend's needs, interests, and traits. That is, their own behavior reflected the intrinsic desirability of the choices. The friend's actions reflected the kind of person she or he was.

These differences in attribution raise the question of who is correct, the person acting or the observer. Most evidence seems to suggest that the actor is correct. We are usually accurate when we explain our own behavior in terms of the situation. We are less apt to be correct when we explain someone else's behavior in terms of traits. People are not as stable as we assume when we make trait attributions. They are adaptive, complex, changing, and inconsistent. People are indeed hard to pigeonhole, and we should resist the tendency to ignore constraints and to infer traits. Greater accuracy and possibly greater appreciation of others will result from being sensitive to the obstacles and constraints in other people's environments and the complexity and richness of their inner lives. Before you make an attribution or judgment about someone else, consider how comfortable you would feel having it applied to you, and ask how fair and accurate it is, given the facts. The golden rule can very usefully be applied in person perception.

People often think that their own behavior reflects external stimuli but that others' behavior reflects internal traits—even if they are doing the same thing, such as cooking.

Teri Leigh Stratford.

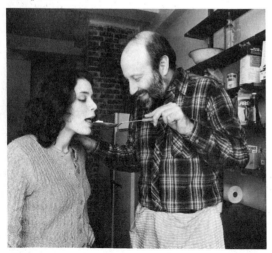

IMPLICIT PERSONALITY THEORIES. Attribution theory shows how we infer single traits on the basis of behavior. Sometimes our inferences aren't really justified by the data—but that doesn't seem to stop us. In fact, research on what are called ''implicit personality theories'' shows that once we infer one trait we are likely to infer more, sometimes many more (Schneider, 1973). An ''implicit personality theory'' is simply a person's ideas about what traits are connected to what other traits. We all have these ideas or theories, and they come into play once we've inferred an initial trait. As the word ''implicit'' implies, we are often unaware of these processes.

As an example of how implicit personality theories work, suppose we've made the inference that someone is intelligent. Suppose also that we know very little else about the person. Our implicit personality theory may tell us that intelligent people are industrious, practical, and arrogant. Or we may believe that intelligent people are creative, friendly, and disorganized. People have different notions about what traits go with what others. Depending on your theory, you may or may not infer any number of other traits about a person from knowing only that he or she is hardworking, liberal, cautious, athletic, or generous. Sometimes we infer traits knowing only that a person belongs to a particular group.

One of the interesting aspects of Barbara Walters's interviews is that they give us an opportunity to go beyond our implicit personality theories. In an interview with Burt Reynolds, Barbara got Burt talking about his very emotional relationship with his father. The feelings Burt expressed showed a side of his personality that didn't fit our usual notion of the tough, independent, ''macho'' actor. Similarly, Barbara's interview with Jesse Jackson during the 1984 presidential primaries enabled Jackson to show a complex set of personal characteristics that couldn't be simply inferred from the fact that he was the first black man to run for president. We are intrigued by the unexpected personal characteristics people reveal, but sometimes in our hurry we fall back on implicit personality theories rather than look slowly and carefully at another person.

Integrating Inconsistent Information

When Barbara Walters began her luncheon interview with Aristotle Onassis many years ago she was distinctly uneasy. She expected him to be uncooperative, intimidating, and uninterested in chit-chat that wasn't related to his business concerns. Onassis had a reputation for being quite brusque. But after Barbara broke the ice with her question about Onassis's first job, she found that he was quite charming.

Consider how you integrate information that is clearly at odds with your first impression of a person. We often have contradictory information about other people, and you need to be aware of the processes you use every day to resolve the inconsistencies and form coherent impressions of others.

One way we achieve coherent assessments of others is by insulating ourselves from information that violates our impressions: We perceive the facts as conforming to our own initial expectations. This tendency is shown clearly in an experiment by Harold Kelley (1950). In this study students in an economics class were told that they would have a guest speaker during the hour and that some information would be given about him beforehand so that people would be able to get to know him quickly and be able to evaluate him at the end of the class. Half the students were given the following description:

> Mr. ____ is a graduate student in the Department of Economics and Social Science. He has had three semesters of teaching experience in psychology. This is his first semester teaching this course. He is 26 years old and married. People who know him consider him to be a rather cold person, industrious, critical, practical, and determined.

Kelly gave the other half of the students in the class the same description except that "very warm" was substituted for "rather cold." After the class period, students evaluated the instructor. Students who had been given the "cold" description rated the instructor as more self-centered, formal, proud, unpopular, humorless, irritable, and ruthless than did people who had been given the "warm" description. Subjects saw exactly what they expected. The single adjective, *warm* or *cold,* created an expectancy that biased subjects' impressions of everything the instructor did during the entire class period. Kelley's study shows how easy it is to distort the facts to fit your biases and to see what you are expecting to see. It also underlies what Solomon Asch (1952) found, that "warm" and "cold" are traits central to our impressions of others.

The Kelley warm/cold study demonstrates how biased our impressions can be, but it doesn't tell the whole story about resolving inconsistent information. Sometimes a perceiver's data about another person are more directly contradictory than was the case in the Kelley study. The major question then is whether the perceiver's final impression of a person will be more influenced by initial impressions or by the latest information. We can imagine Barbara Walters maintaining the impression that Aristotle Onassis was uncooperative and brusque, but we can also imagine her changing her mind and deciding that he was really delightfully friendly. What usually happens in cases like this?

PRIMACY EFFECTS.   Solomon Asch (1952) conducted the first study of the effect of initial impressions on final impressions. Asch gave subjects the following adjectives as descriptions of a hypothetical person: *intelligent, industrious, impulsive, critical, stubborn, envious.* He found that when the adjectives were given in that order, with the more positive traits first, the subjects' impressions were more positive than when the list was presented in reverse. That is, different impressions resulted from giving the same traits in different orders; the results seemed to suggest that the adjectives first

Our first impressions of other people last a long time. They are strongly affected by how attractive the other people are.
Rhoda Sidney.

in the list had the strongest impact on the final impression. This finding is called a **primacy effect.** It means that people are most heavily influenced by initial impressions. (If subjects had been more influenced by information received at the end of the list, the most recent information, their reaction would've been termed a **recency effect.**)

A primary effect was also shown in a famous experiment by Luchins (1957). In this study subjects read two paragraphs describing a boy named Jim. One described Jim as introverted. It read as follows:

After school Jim left the classroom alone. Leaving the school he started on his long walk home. The street was brilliantly filled with sunshine. Jim walked down the street on the shady side. Coming down the street toward him, he saw the pretty girl whom he had met on the previous evening. Jim crossed the street and entered a candy store. The store was crowded with students, and he noticed a few familiar faces. Jim waited quietly until the counterman caught his eye and then gave his order. Taking his drink, he sat down at a side table. When he had finished his drink he went home.

The second paragraph describes Jim as extroverted:

Jim left the house to get some stationery. He walked out into the sun-filled street with two of his friends, basking in the sun as he walked. Jim talked with an acquaintance while he waited for the clerk to catch his eye. On his way out, he stopped to chat with a friend who was just coming into the store. Leaving the store, he walked toward school. On his way out he met the girl to whom he had been introduced the night before. They talked for a short while, and then Jim left for school.

Luchins's results showed that of subjects who read only the first paragraph, 25 percent believed that Jim was friendly. Of those who read only the second paragraph, 90 percent believed that Jim was friendly. For subjects who read both paragraphs at one time, 54 percent rated Jim as friendly if they read the "introverted" paragraph first, and 71 percent rated him as friendly if they read the "extroverted" paragraph first. These results show that subjects with the same information will have different impressions, depending on which part of the information they receive first. Subjects form quick impressions of what a person is like on the basis of the first information they get and then explain away contradictory behavior as the result of external or temporary factors. For example, most of the subjects who read the introverted paragraph first believed that Jim was shy and unfriendly and that his later friendliness was due to being in an unusually good mood or to others being unusually considerate of him.

What happens when people are judging another person in a live, face-to-face interaction and are making ability attributions on the basis of performance?

In an experiment by Jones, Rock, Shaver, Goethals, and Ward (1968), subjects and a female confederate tried to solve 30 very difficult problems drawn from intelligence tests allegedly "designed to discriminate at the very highest levels of ability." The test contained items of this type: "Quality is to benevolence as judgment is to what? Praise, endearment, criticism, or malevolence?" "Tim, tan; rib, rid; rat, raw; hip, . . . hid, hit, his, or him?" (The first item is actually insoluble and has no correct answer. The second has a correct answer and is left as an exercise for the reader.*)

The confederate met with one subject at a time. All subjects were given false feedback indicating that they had gotten 10 problems correct in random order. The confederate always got 15 problems correct, but she did so in different orders. With some subjects the confederate got seven of the first eight problems correct but then started to do less and less well toward the end. With other subjects she started off poorly but got better and finished with seven of the last eight correct. The question was whether subjects would perceive the confederate as more intelligent when she had started off well or when she had a strong finish. The Luchins study had suggested the former. But Jones and his colleagues predicted a recency effect, essentially a "What's she done lately?" phenomenon, whereby subjects would think that the person who had done well at the end had demonstrated the most definitive mastery of the test.

The results, however, showed a strong primacy effect. Subjects thought the woman was much smarter when she had done well at the beginning. The explanation seemed to be identical with that mentioned for the Luchins experiment. Subjects jumped quickly to a conclusion about the confederate's intelligence on the basis of the first few trials. Then they explained away later discrepant performances in terms of external or unstable factors. For example, subjects who saw the woman do well at the beginning believed that her early performance proved she was brilliant and that she must have gotten bored or careless at the end.

*The correct answer is hit. In the first pair of words the last two letters are one letter apart; in the second pair two letters apart, and so forth.

Those who saw her do well at the end concluded that the later problems were a bit easier for her and that she was trying extra hard.

In both studies, then, we see that people are willing to make quick judgments about others, but less willing to change those impressions in the face of contradictory information. They rather glibly attribute any later discrepant behavior to external causes and maintain their original perceptions. Kelley's warm/cold study showed that we often interpret other people's behavior in ways that fit our expectations. These studies show that this happens even when a person's behavior is inconsistent with our expectations. In other words, it's difficult to get people to change their minds about someone after they've formed an initial impression.

RECENCY AND OVERCOMPENSATION EFFECTS.
Although studies showing primacy effects are legion, there are certainly circumstances in which recency effects appear. For example, if subjects in the trait-adjective studies are asked to delay making any judgment until the end, primacy effects disappear and recency effects sometimes occur. Still, primacy effects prevail, indicating that people have interpreted later information to fit their initial expectancies. There is one important kind of exception, however, which actually results in another kind of bias. This is the **overcompensation effect** shown in studies by Elaine Walster and her colleagues (Walster & Prestholdt, 1966; Walster, Walster, Abrahams, & Brown, 1966).

In these studies subjects are given information that leads them to form a first impression of someone else. Usually the impression is that the person is very kind or cruel. Then subjects are given later information that explains away the initial behavior and indicates unequivocally that the person actually has the opposite disposition. Under these circumstances, subjects do change their minds. There is no primacy effect. Instead, people overcompensate for their original erroneous assumptions. For example, if the later information

shows the person to be kind, subjects who had received the initial, misleading information think that the person is more kind, generous, and altruistic than do subjects who had never formed the erroneous impression in the first place. That is, subjects first led to think that the person was cruel and then shown that he or she is kind rate him or her more favorably than do those who were only shown that he or she is kind. It's as if subjects overreact to their mistakes and compensate for them by going too far in the opposite direction, once they realize that they were wrong.

There are probably many examples of overcompensation effects in everyday life, especially in college situations in which people meet in an environment that is new for everybody, with lots of room for erroneous first impressions. For instance, suppose that on your first day of school you meet someone who seems dazed by the whole experience and panicked by her classes. You might conclude that she is unintelligent and will probably flunk out of school. If it should turn out that she gets very high grades, you might overcompensate and think that she is extremely brilliant. You might attribute more intelligence to her than to someone who did equally well but whom you didn't misjudge in the first place. Or, early in the fall you might get to know someone who wears a Dallas Cowboys jersey, can explain complex team plays, and has an ideal physique for football. You might think that this person will probably play quarterback for the freshman team. When it turns out that this person is unable to handle a snap from center or throw with any accuracy, you might judge him to be clumsier than if you had not been misled in the first place.

In case you're wondering, it turns out that Barbara Walters showed overcompensation in her final impression of Aristotle Onassis. After her interview with him she decided he was extremely warm and friendly. She even went so far as to buy her first bikini, in anticipation of spending time with Onassis on his luxury yacht, *Christina*. Barbara wrote that "the now too tight bikini remains my only memento of a dazzling

REVIEW QUESTIONS

1. T or F: Perhaps the most important requirement of effective social interaction is that we accurately perceive the actions and intentions of others.

2. Because people's actions are often ambiguous and their intentions often vague, a key aspect of perceiving others is to interpret their actions and draw conclusions about their intentions. This is known as the process of _____ .

3. Judging that a person's behavior is caused by an underlying disposition or personality trait is called a(n) _____ attribution, while a judgment that the behavior is caused by situational or environmental influences is called a(n) _____ attribution.

4. Our need to predict and control the actions of others creates in us a fundamental bias toward making _____ attributions.

5. Which of the following is(are) a factor(s) to be considered when we make attributions about why people succeed or fail in a particular situation?
   a. ability
   b. luck
   c. effort
   d. task difficulty
   e. all the above

6. When we attribute a certain trait to a person, this trait may imply for us the presence of certain other traits. Our idea about what traits are connected to what other traits is called our _____ _____ .

7. In a study, Harold Kelley (1950) substituted the trait terms "warm" or "cold" into his description of a person who was to speak to his class. His finding that these "central traits" could differentially influence the subsequent impression that the class formed of this speaker is an example of how we perceive behavior to fit our _____ .

8. The order in which we receive information about a person is very important to the overall impression that we form. When the initial information received has the strongest influence on the final impression, this is a demonstration of a _____ effect.

9. Changing an erroneous first impression in the face of overwhelmingly contradictory evidence often results in a new impression that is too strong in the opposite direction. This is known as _____ .

lunch." Such is the power of overcompensation.

In short, people's original impressions seem to set traps for them. Research shows that the more people are able to resist premature judgments, and the more they are able to tolerate the ambiguity of not drawing definitive conclusions, the more accurate their impressions of others will be in the long run. But this kind of self-restraint is difficult. Our natural tendency is to make immediate confident pronouncements about others—which is unfair to both the perceiver and the perceived.

Motivated Biases and Their Consequences

What we have discussed thus far shows that person perception is often far from accurate and objective. Still, we haven't discussed the ways specific needs and motives can bias impressions and how we often see exactly what we want to see. We have only discussed the general desire to attribute traits to people in order to gain a feeling of being able to predict them. In addition, we have noted the fact that self-esteem needs can cause us to make negative attributions about others so that we can look better by comparison. This is the practice that Harry Stack Sullivan (1953) referred to as "disparagement" (see Chapter 2). At this point we will consider some specific motives and the errors they produce in impression formation.

First it is worth emphasizing this major point: To a large extent people perceive what they want to perceive. This is nicely illustrated in a classic study by Hastorf and Cantril (1954) entitled "They Saw a Game." The game referred to was a 1951 football contest between Dartmouth and Princeton. The teams were traditional rivals who that year were both vying for the Ivy League championship. It turned out to be an extremely rough game in which several players, including Princeton's Heisman trophy winner, Dick Kazmaier, were seriously injured. For several weeks the newspapers on both campuses blamed the other school for the "dirty" play. Hastorf and Cantril showed a film of the game to students at both colleges and asked them to note how many infractions each team made and to indicate who started the rough play. Not surprisingly, Princeton students perceived lots of Dartmouth violations, and Dartmouth students did the opposite. Both groups of students felt sure that the film indicated that the other side was to blame. That was what they wanted to see. (By the way, Princeton won.)

PERCEPTIONS OF RESPONSIBILITY. Motives affect impressions in many ways. One motive that has subtle but devastating effects has been discussed by Melvin Lerner (1970), who originated the "just world" hypothesis. According to Lerner, people have a need to perceive the world as fair and just and to believe that good things happen to good people and bad things happen to bad people. One result of this is that when misfortune occurs, observers have a tendency to believe that the person stricken must be bad and must have in some way deserved that fate. This is probably an unconscious tendency, which we can see operating in typical knee-jerk assumptions such as "Poor people are just lazy and stupid" or "Fat people are just weak-willed and gluttonous." Ryan (1971) discussed the same phenomenon as a tendency

he calls "blaming the victim." Several studies have demonstrated this tendency, including several provocative ones (e.g., Jones & Aronson, 1973) showing that rape victims are often assumed to have committed some specific action that makes them responsible for having been raped. It distresses us when people are victimized. Feeling that they are in some way responsible reassures us that the world is really just. We should guard against this especially dangerous bias because, unfortunately, it is quite common.

Closely related to the "blaming the victim" phenomenon is a tendency toward making self-protective, defensive attributions of responsibility for accidents. An early study on this problem by Elaine Walster (1966) showed that when a person had an automobile accident, he or she was blamed more if the consequences were serious than if they were not. Subsequent research by Shaver (1970; 1975) and Shaw and Skolnick (1971) suggests that people want to maintain the perception that serious accidents can't happen to them, but that if such accidents can occur, they don't want to be blamed. These desires lead to several kinds of assignment of responsibility for accidents. We will consider what happens when the accident happens to someone who is very different from you, someone who is fairly similar to you, and someone who is very similar to you.

If a serious accident happens to someone who is very different from you, in a situation in which you would be very unlikely to find yourself, the accident is not threatening because it doesn't seem likely that any such thing could happen to you. For instance, an industrial accident would be unlikely to happen to a business executive. Therefore he or she wouldn't be worried about such an event and would assign responsibility objectively and rationally. However, other blue-collar workers who work in fairly similar situations might be worried about exactly that kind of accident happening to them and would be motivated to protect themselves from the threat of such an accident. One way to do this is to hold the victim responsible, blaming the accident uniquely on him or her rather than his or her circumstances or the situation. If the injured person's fellow workers made an external attribution, that would mean that the situation, one in which they might find themselves, is dangerous. By saying that the accident was caused by the victim's own carelessness, the situation itself seems less threatening. This distorted perception has harmful consequences for everyone involved. It is harmful for the victim, who is unfairly blamed and thus perhaps not justly compensated or helped. It is also harmful for the perceiver because it leads to underestimating the danger, which if realized might be minimized or avoided. But people often prefer to deny danger rather than admit it exists and cope with it realistically.

Another kind of distortion occurs when an accident happens to someone whose life situation is very similar to yours. In this case it might be clear that a similar accident could easily happen to you. It is too difficult to deny the threatening implications of the accident. In this case you might put yourself in the place of the victim and realize that you wouldn't want to be blamed if the same thing did happen to you. Thus you would tend to regard the present victim as not responsible for the accident. This attribution is just as biased as overly attributing fault in order to convince yourself that an accident couldn't happen to you. It seems that only people who feel distant from an accident can look at it objectively.

What are the implications of these studies of motivated biases and the assignment of responsibility? If you are interested in perceiving others accurately, in order to be fair to others and to make your own behavior optimally adaptive to reality, you should beware of motivated biases. If you are judging someone in a situation that is stressful or threatening and you make an attribution that is reassuring and makes you feel good, be careful. Ask yourself if you are really being objective, and answer the question as honestly as possible. If you are sure that you have been objective, fine. It's easy to be smug *and* wrong, however. An extra measure of caution in making judgments of others is worth it in the long run.

EFFECTS OF FALSE IMPRESSIONS. We have pointed out that inaccurate impressions can lead to inappropriate behavior. Erroneous perceptions about someone being likable or unlikable, intelligent or unintelligent, can lead to action that is in the worst interests of both the perceiver and the perceived. One interesting but disturbing consequence of such errors is that they sometimes lead to behavior that makes the error come true. Sometimes inaccurate impressions become what are called **self-fulfilling prophecies.** A self-fulfilling prophecy has been defined by Robert Merton (1957) as a prediction that is false but that produces behavior that makes it come true. A hypothetical example is the incorrect prophecy in a small city that the bank is about to fail. The bank is sound, but panic causes all the depositors to withdraw their money, which does make the bank go broke. A real example in times of high inflation is that people are worried that inflation will continue and that it will be impossible for them to buy a house if it does. Consequently many people buy a house immediately, which causes inflation to continue or get worse.

Self-fulfilling prophecies are also common in interpersonal behavior. For example, if people form an initially negative impression of someone, they may avoid interaction with that person, which makes it impossible for the perception to be corrected by new information. Newcomb (1961) has referred to this as the "autistic hostility" phenomenon. The opposite can work as well. If you decide that another person is friendly and likable, you will treat her or him in a way that is most likely to lead that person to behave in a friendly way.

One startling demonstration of the self-fulfilling prophecy was reported in a study by Rosenthal and Jacobson entitled "Pygmalion in the Classroom" (1968). Rosenthal and Jacobson wanted to know whether the self-fulfilling prophecy might operate among teachers of elementary school children in ways that would have grave consequences for the pupils. Suppose a teacher expected that a student would do poorly and that another would do well. Could this affect the teacher's behavior in some way that might ultimately confirm the expectations? Perhaps teachers would give more help and more sustained attention to students they thought to be talented and ignore students they considered less capable? To examine this possibility the researchers tested children at an elementary school and told their teachers that some of these children, who were actually selected randomly, were "late bloomers." The researchers said that the tests had shown that these children had a great deal of intellectual potential, which would start developing in the near future. At the end of the year all the children were retested. The ones who had been designated late bloomers actually showed greater increases in intelligence scores than other children. Rosenthal and Jacobson suggested that these effects were achieved because teachers who thought that specific children had exceptional potential gave them extra encouragement, dismissed their short-

comings as temporary, and fostered a good climate for their intellectual development (Rosenthal, 1973).

Although the Pygmalion study didn't look at the effects of negative expectations, it's not unreasonable to believe that teachers who expect pupils to do poorly might be less helpful and supportive to such students. In some cases the negative expectations might be based on ethnic stereotypes. A prejudiced white teacher, for example, might expect a black child not to be intelligent. The teacher's behavior might then actually retard the pupil's development.

In general it is important to be aware that our perceptions and the behavior they lead to have a profound effect on the way others act toward us. To a significant degree, "What you see is what you get." No matter what their internal predispositions, the more favorably we treat others, the more favorably they are likely to treat us in return. While we don't want to make ourselves vulnerable to people who would exploit us, it seems to make sense to foster good will and caring in relationships as much as possible, regardless of our initial expectations. It's hard to see why this would not be a good approach to other people.

Accurate Perceptions and Personal Adjustment

We began this chapter by noting a strong relationship between personal adjustment and person perception. Accurate perception contributes immeasurably to adaptive action in the world as it is and to good interpersonal relationships. In our review of impression formation processes, we have seen that error is more common than accuracy. Forming correct impressions is difficult because people are complex and in many ways fundamentally inconsistent. This, of course, is part of being human, and is what makes humanity rich and fascinating.

While being accurate in our perceptions can be difficult, there are a few things that can help. First, we should try to be as sensitive as possible to the external forces that contribute

---

TABLE 9.3

Common Biases in Impression Formation

1. Primacy effect: The general tendency to base our impressions on the earliest information we have about a person and to explain away inconsistent information as reflecting external or temporary causes

2. Overcompensation effect: The tendency to overcorrect for an original incorrect perception in order to see a person as more in line with later information than the mistaken first impression. For example, seeing a person as smarter than we would have if we hadn't seen him or her as unintelligent at first

3. Just world hypothesis: Our tendency to see the world as a fair and just place and to therefore "blame the victim" when bad things happen, thinking that they must deserve their bad fortune

4. Self-fulfilling prophecy: Making predictions about other people and then behaving so as to make our predictions come true, for example, predicting that someone is unfriendly and then not talking to that person, with the result that the person acts unfriendly

to other people's behavior. A reasonable goal is to try to be as sensitive to the constraints on other people's behavior as we are to the constraints on our own. Second, we should avoid jumping to conclusions, on the basis of behavior, hearsay, or stereotypes. A lot of evidence shows that the simple effort of waiting for a little more information is rewarded with increased accuracy. Sometimes a quick decision is required because of the need for action, but most often there is no penalty attached to patience and caution. Third, remember that a great deal of what a person does—and, in the final analysis, is—depends on how we treat her or him. Little is lost and much is gained by hoping for the best in others and doing all we can to cultivate the best. Without being naïve, we can do much to call forth the better impulses in others. So why not?

REVIEW QUESTIONS

10. In which of the following situations would you most likely have a motivated bias toward making an *external* attribution of responsibility?
   a. Your daughter's friend is raped.
   b. A neighbor is involved in a serious automobile accident.
   c. A long-time friend and co-worker who operates the same machine as you severs a finger in an industrial accident.
   d. An aquaintance at the plant where you work breaks his leg in an industrial accident.

11. One of the consequences of forming an inaccurate impression of someone is that it can produce behavior that makes it come true. This is called a _____ - _____ _____.

12. T or F: Although the process of forming correct impressions of people is complex, the fact is that most of our perceptions are accurate, not erroneous.

13. Which of the following is *not* recommended as a way of countering erroneous perceptions?
   a. Be aware of external constraints on behavior.
   b. Avoid stereotypes.
   c. Look for the best in others as a way of cultivating the best response.
   d. Learn to trust your initial impression; it is often the most accurate.

COMMUNICATING WITH OTHERS

In her discussion of interpersonal relations Barbara Walters makes it plain that a good interaction involves *two* interesting people, not just one person drawing the other person out. There is a lot that each of us can bring to any interaction with others, even with those who may be better known or more prominent than ourselves. Almost everyone we interact with wants to relate to us as human beings too. We should, Barbara emphasizes, be willing to be open about ourselves—our feelings, fond memories, and special interests. This can be difficult to do, especially if we tend to be shy or doubt that others will be interested in us and what we have done or want to do. Barbara says it is important to remember the advice of the wife of a former United States senator, who overcame her feelings of inadequacy by telling herself, "I am the way I am; I look the way I look; I am my age." Remember that you can't expect others to accept you if you don't accept yourself. Barbara also emphasizes the importance of "radiating friendliness."

Having self-confidence in our everyday interactions with others can be challenging enough at times, so more formal interactions, such as job interviews, can seem especially formidable. How can we go about making the most favorable impression on someone important to us for one reason or another? Barbara Walters emphasizes three rules you probably heard in a different context when you were a child: "Stop, look, and listen."

"Stop" means take the time to prepare for an interaction and anticipate any possible problems. In formal interactions this can entail doing homework—finding out about the person and about what will be successful topics of conversation. If you're being interviewed for a job, for instance, you should be able to communicate your own needs and interests and be prepared to ask relevant questions. Homework is a key solution to the destructive anxiety that can ruin any social interaction.

"Look" means giving the other person your total attention when you're talking to them. Barbara said that her husband once criticized her for not looking at the camera enough when she was doing a television interview. Barbara responded that she's much less concerned about making eye contact with the camera than she is about signaling to the person she's talking to that he or she has her undivided attention.

"Listen" simply means taking the time to show people that you care about them and are sensitive to what they are saying. Equally important may be to listen well enough to hear what the person is *not* saying as well as what they are saying. In an interview with dancer Fred Astaire, Barbara noticed that Astaire didn't seem to talk about himself very much. She told him that he didn't seem to have the giant ego that some show business people do. That observation led Astaire to admit his desire for privacy and the wish to keep some things about himself for himself and his family alone. It was an extremely touching and revealing interview, although Astaire revealed only that he liked not to reveal very much.

Barbara Walters's message is that we can interact successfully with almost anyone if we take interest both in ourselves and in the other person. Self-acceptance and openness to others are important themes throughout this book, and Barbara Walters has shown how important they are in talking with practically anybody.

Knowing that successful interaction depends on what we bring to the relationship as well as what we perceive in the other person, let's take a closer look at the ways people communicate. Communication can be divided into two important categories. First, there are communications about external matters, such as tasks that people are working on, problems they are solving, or perhaps politics or the weather. Second, there are communications about internal matters, our feelings and the way we view relationships. This latter kind of communication primarily concerns us here, and it is expressed mainly through nonverbal channels. When we communicate about external tasks or problems we generally communicate verbally, but when we communicate about feelings and relationships, what we say nonverbally is much more important than words. Barbara Walters illustrates this when she talks about looking and listening. The act of looking intently at others while they speak communicates our interest in them and what they are telling us more effectively than any words about how fascinated we are. Our nonverbal behavior clearly communicates important messages about our emotional state and our feelings about the particular interaction or relationship we have with another person. Let's look at some of the features of nonverbal communication and exactly how we communicate through this unspoken channel.

Nonverbal Communication

When we consider nonverbal communication we usually think of body language, communication through posture, gesture, and facial expression. Popular books on body language have been sold in the millions, often to young people who are offered the promise that they will be able to use their knowledge of body language to determine whether others are sexually aroused by them. Not surprisingly, this sales angle is highly successful. More modest claims suggest that you can determine people's attitudes toward you, their degree of dominance, intelligence, and so forth from their posture, stance, and facial expression. These assertions are generally exaggerated, but there is a grain of truth to them. Studies have shown that "open" body postures—for example, uncrossed legs, leaning forward, and general re-

We can convey a good deal about what we think and feel through gestures and other nonverbal behaviors.

Sam C. Pierson, Jr., Photo Researchers, Inc.

laxation—indicate liking and attraction. Head nodding, orienting the body directly forward, gesturing, and frequent body movements are also common when people are trying to make friends or get others to be interested in them (Kleinke, 1975). Thus knowing about nonverbal language can sensitize us to feelings that others have about us but are not directly stating. This knowledge can certainly be useful in getting close to, or away from, others.

Although body language is important, there is more to the domain of nonverbal communication. Our behavior communicates in many other ways without using spoken or written words. For example, how we use time, our own and other people's, often communicates a great deal. Keeping people waiting could indicate that we don't like them or that we regard them as having less status than we do and that therefore our time is more important than theirs. Thus even the nonverbal behavior of being late carries a message.

The complete list of nonverbal behaviors that can be regarded as communication includes how we use time, how we position ourselves and others, what body posture we adopt, how we dress and groom, how and where we touch other people, how much eye contact we maintain, and how much attention we pay to someone else. All these behaviors communicate nonverbally. In addition, a complete list must take into account behaviors that are partly

verbal but yet do not communicate direct linguistic messages. For example, tone of voice and pace of speech are aspects of language that do not directly "say" anything, but do qualify and add meaning to words actually spoken.

THE NATURE OF NONVERBAL COMMUNICATION. Virtually everything we do conveys some message about our view of another person. In fact, in many instances our nonverbal behavior communicates a great deal more than what we say. Given that there are so many different kinds of nonverbal communication, is there anything we can say about the nature of nonverbal communication in general? There are several overall points of importance.

NONVERBAL COMMUNICATION: THE LANGUAGE OF RELATIONSHIPS. We have already noted that nonverbal communication is the "language" that people use to communicate about their relationships. This has been noted by many researchers (e.g., Ekman, Friesen, & Ellsworth, 1972), and there are two reasons for it. The first is that we really have a very poor vocabulary for talking about relationships. Many of the words are stilted and awkward and don't express our feelings about others with any precision. Much more information about how we view our relationships with others is conveyed by how we actually

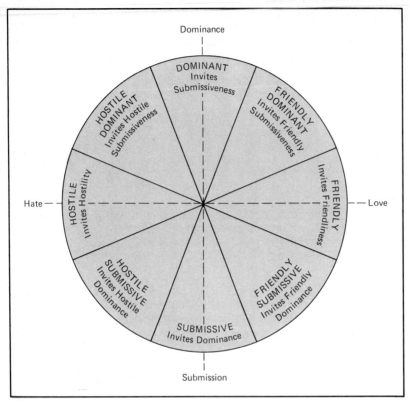

FIGURE 9.1 VARIETIES OF INTERPERSONAL BEHAVIOR
When we communicate nonverbally we generally express our view of the relationship by behaving in ways that are to some degree friendly versus hostile and to some degree dominant versus submissive. These behaviors communicate whether we see the relationship as warm or cold and whether we see it as one of equal status or one where we or the other is in charge. These behaviors also invite a complementary behavior from the other person. Leary (1957) has represented the varieties of interpersonal behavior in the format of the circle above.

treat them and act around them than by what we say. A second reason for using nonverbal communication for relationships is that talking about relationships can feel awkward and embarrassing. People are shy about making declarations of love, and there are social restraints against expressing hostility and anger. Because of these social inhibitions and restraints, people usually find it easier to communicate their feelings about others through their actions. Barbara Walters demonstrated this when after a very warm interview with president of the United States, Lyndon Johnson, she asked if she could kiss him on the cheek. A kiss on the cheek communicated her admiration much more efficiently and convincingly than anything she could have said.

NONVERBAL COMMUNICATION: THE LANGUAGE OF EMOTIONS. In addition to expressing our views about relationships and our feelings about other people, per se, nonverbal behaviors have also been shown to be a channel for expressing a wide range of emotions (Ekman & Friesen, 1968). Facial expressions, especially, convey a whole range of emotions, including fear, surprise, anger, disgust, and sadness. In addition, one's overall feelings of self-worth are expressed through nonverbal behaviors. Whether we like it or not, our emotions and self-evaluations are easily read from our nonverbal behaviors.

CONTROLLING NONVERBAL EXPRESSION. Nonverbal communication naturally expresses very important feelings, attitudes, and emotions. In many cases we might rather not communicate these sentiments. But it's pretty hard to hide our feelings.

Social psychologist Roger Brown (1965) comments that the person who thinks he or she is the only one who knows his or her "smile is forced should see the face the rest of us see." Sigmund Freud (1905) noted that if a man's "lips are silent, he chatters with his fingertips; betrayal oozes out of him at every pore."

Nonverbal communications are partly innate and partly learned. We are probably born with tendencies to wrinkle up our faces when we smell something bad, to yawn and slouch in our chairs when we are bored, and to draw close to people we love or admire. Charles Darwin (1872), who originated the theory of evolution, believed that facial expressions in humans and animals are inherited, having evolved as an effective way to regulate interaction. But there is a learned element of nonverbal communication as well. Much of what we are taught about nonverbal communication has to do with controlling it so as not to reveal

our feelings and attitudes. Often we are taught that it is desirable to suppress our emotions and particularly to control the expression of our feelings. The reason for this is probably that conveying emotions and feelings, especially about the people we are interacting with, can be a nuisance. Feelings are often intrusive and can make it difficult to conduct "business" quickly and efficiently. We learn that other people, especially our superiors, should not have to be bothered with, or embarrassed by, our emotions. Thus we are taught to control all nonverbal communications except those that might express deference. For example, as children we are told, "Don't point! Sit up straight! Don't put your feet up! Don't stare! Let's see a smile!" These nonverbal behaviors are the very ones that lower-status people use to show deference to higher-status people (Henley, 1977).

It is interesting that so much of our childhood training centers around controlling emotions and their expression and showing deference to those of higher status. Of course, not all these efforts at control are successful. Our nonverbal expressions often leak out and

THE ORIENTATION TOWARD MANIPULATION IN INTERPERSONAL RELATIONS

People identified as Machiavellians in research by Christie and Geis (1970) tend to be manipulative in their orientation to other people. They are somewhat cool and detached and keep an emotional distance from others. They are more interested in getting what they want from others than in having a close personal relationship. High Machiavellian scorers answer true to statements 1, 3, 4, and 5 below and false to 2 and 6. How do your answers compare?

T F 1. The best way to handle people is to tell them what they want to hear.
T F 2. One should take action only when sure it is morally right.
T F 3. Anyone who completely trusts anyone else is asking for trouble.
T F 4. The biggest difference between most criminals and other people is that the criminals are stupid enough to get caught.
T F 5. It is hard to get ahead without cutting corners here and there.
T F 6. When you ask someone to do something for you, it is best to give the real reasons for wanting it rather than giving reasons which carry more weight.

Christie, R., & Geis, F. L. (Eds.) (1970) *Studies in Machiavellianism.* New York: Academic Press. Copyright © 1970 by Academic Press, Inc.

tell a great deal about inner feelings we would rather hide. A study by Haggard and Isaacs (1966) shows that emotions and feelings we try to control are expressed in what are called **micromomentary expressions** (MMEs). These are facial expressions that are so small and so short that the eye can barely see them. They last only about a fifth of a second and in fact were only discovered in slow-motion films.

In many cases MMEs are incongruent with both the verbal expression of feeling and the facial expressions just before and after them. You might be telling a date that you really had fun at a party and be maintaining a pleasant facial expression—except for MMEs that express anger (Swensen, 1973). MMEs serve as a safety valve. They allow some expression for feelings and emotions that a person wants to control but that demand outlet. In other words, even when we try hard to control our feelings and the expression of emotions, our bodies will betray us and unknowingly express our true feelings in very subtle ways. In some situations these maverick expressions are perceived and in some they aren't. Sometimes they can affect the interactional behavior of both the person sending the messages and the one receiving them, without either person being aware that this is happening.

THE BODY AND ITS MESSAGES. We have seen that nonverbal communication clearly and convincingly communicates our feelings about relationships with others and also reveals our emotions and self-evaluations. Nonverbal forms of self-expression are taken as highly credible signs of our feelings and attitudes toward others because we know how difficult they can be to control.

For this reason Barbara Walters encourages us to radiate friendliness and to do so by actually feeling friendly. She also knows that, since people can't control nonverbal communication as well as what they say, she can learn from nonverbal communications how others feel about her. But Barbara Walters is limited in interpreting the nonverbal messages of people she interviews from all over the world because there are distinct cultural differences in nonverbal expression. The meaning of a particular gesture, smile, or tone of voice varies from culture to culture. People in different lands have different nonverbal styles. Aristotle Onassis wasn't as brusque as Barbara Walters thought he was at first. To some extent, she was misled by his characteristically Greek manner of nonverbal expression. One interesting illustration of cultural differences in nonverbal styles is shown in a study of a former mayor of New York City, Fiorello La Guardia. It is possible to tell from silent films whether the mayor was delivering a speech in English, Italian, or Yiddish (Birdwhistell, 1952): Each spoken language has its own distinct body language and gestures.

There are further complications in reading the significance of nonverbal behaviors. Their meanings vary from situation to situation. A stare means one thing from a superior to a subordinate. It means something entirely different between intimate lovers. Despite the difficulties posed by cultural and situational differences in nonverbal behavior, however, there is enough uniformity in gesture and expression, at least among North Americans, to allow us to infer the meaning of specific nonverbal communications in most cases. In this section we will consider the meanings of various aspects of facial expression and body language in our culture.

THE HEAD AND FACE. Movement of the head as a whole, or nodding, can be very expressive. Birdwhistell (1952) suggests that different numbers of nods have different meanings, and each nod has a distinct impact on conversation. One nod simply indicates that the listener is paying attention. Two or three nods can slightly disrupt or stop the flow of conversation. A series of rhythmic nods may indicate that your listener has lost interest and is not paying attention. Barbara Walters is implicitly aware of the effects of nods on conversation, and she clearly uses them to encourage a person to keep talking, or to signal that it is time for him or her to stop and move on to a new topic.

The face has received more attention than movements of the head as a whole. This is

Facial expressions vividly convey emotions.
Mimi Forsyth, Monkmeyer.

probably because of the large number of emotions that are communicated by facial expressions. Research by Ekman and Friesen (1975) shows that emotions such as surprise, fear, disgust, anger, happiness, and sadness are clearly manifested in facial expressions. In addition, various subcategories of these emotions, such as different intensities of happiness or fear and blends such as the happy-surprise combination, are also clearly shown in the face.

While we are very often accurate in judging other people's emotions from their facial expressions, we can also be deceived. People sometimes try to mislead us about their thoughts and feelings. This may occur because they have been brought up to control their emotional expressions or because of the requirements of a particular role or situation. Actors and lawyers must control the feelings they display in order to be successful in their careers. Situations such as funerals and blind dates may call for the control of emotional expression. Certainly when people are negotiating or playing cards they may try to keep a "poker face."

How do people try to deceive others

about their true feelings? Ekman and Friesen suggest three tactics. First, people often try to **simulate** emotions that they don't feel, such as surprise at a "surprise party" they already know about or happiness at seeing an old acquaintance they would just as soon have forgotten. Second, people often try to **neutralize** emotions they do feel. This means attempting to show no emotion at all. You might try to neutralize the happiness of seeing your secret lover if your spouse is with you. Finally, people also attempt to **mask** their feelings by covering them with the appearance of another emotion. A parent who is really amused by the prank of a child may feign anger in order to prevent the prank's reoccurrence.

People can be trained to manage their expressions through specific techniques of controlling the mouth and lips or brows and forehead. At the same time, others can learn to pierce these attempted deceptions. By looking very carefully at certain parts of the face and the timing of expressions and by watching for short microexpressions (like the MMEs just discussed), we can detect deceptions. For example, people usually exert more control over the lower face, including the mouth and lips. As a result the eyes will "leak" the true emotions.

GAZE AND EYE CONTACT.   The idea that our eyes will reveal our true feelings is widely believed. People use the expression "I could see it in her eyes," as if the eyes unmistakably reveal what a person is thinking. In his moving testimony during the Senate Watergate hearings that eventually led to President Richard Nixon's resignation from office, Herbert Kalmbach told how he asked his close friend John Ehrlichman to look him in the eye and tell him directly that he wanted illegal fund-raising activities to be covered up. Kalmbach believed he could only act if Ehrlichman's eyes showed he was telling the truth. Because the eyes can be so important in revealing what people think and feel, they have been studied intensely.

One of the most researched aspects of the eyes is whether or not people gaze at each other and how they use eye contact. Research shows that people look at others who are speaking to show that they are paying attention. By watching other people we indicate our respect for them, our feeling that what they do or say is important. At the same time, norms dictate that higher-status people are not to be stared at. They are given the privilege of ignoring lower-status persons if they choose or staring at them if they are trying to assert their dominance. The lower-status or submissive person is expected to avert his or her glance if stared at directly, but to otherwise watch and pay careful attention.

An intriguing study by Ellsworth and Carlsmith (1968) shows that lots of eye contact makes an interaction more intense and heightens whatever feeling or emotion is being communicated. If one person is verbally communicating very pleasant information to the other person, a high degree of eye contact makes the situation even more enjoyable. It can communicate greater liking and elicit greater liking in return. On the other hand, when unpleasant or threatening things are being said the speaker

who maintains eye contact makes the situation more severe. Usually people look at each other less if the interaction is unpleasant, so it doesn't take much eye contact to intensify the emotions in a stressful interaction.

Research by Argyle and Dean (1965) is consistent with the idea that eye contact intensifies whatever emotion is being felt in an interaction. These researchers showed that when two people interact at very small distances, as little as two feet, the amount of eye contact decreases markedly. People look away when interacting at such a small distance. Argyle and Dean developed the theory that an interaction can be too intense or too "hot." This can happen if the interaction distance is too close, if there is too much direct eye contact, or if the topic of conversation becomes too personal or intimate. If the interaction becomes too intense along one dimension—for example, if people are forced to sit very close together or if they get into a heated or emotional discussion—the interaction will be "cooled off" by the avoidance of direct eye contact. Argyle and Dean suggest that there is an ideal degree of intensity in an interaction, depending on the relationship of the people involved and the situation, and if the interaction gets too intense along one dimension, such as topic of discussion or interaction distance, it will be cooled off along one of the others. Thus people might want to sit further apart to discuss a very emotional matter.

BODY POSTURE AND POSITION. Argyle and Dean's work on eye contact and interaction distance alerts us to the fact that the body itself, in addition to the face and eyes, communicates a great deal. Ekman and Friesen (1975) suggest that body posture is critical in communicating or expressing how relaxed or tense we are in interacting with someone and also how we define our relationship with that person. When people are relaxed they are likely to have a less formal posture, less likely to have both arms or both legs in the same position, more likely to have their arms and legs open, and more likely to be leaning. Lack of relaxation can often be reflected in frequent

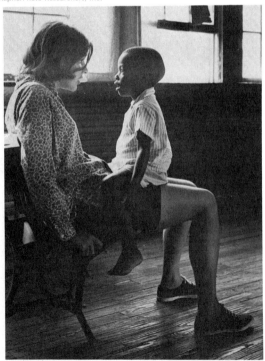

Eye contact intensifies either positive or negative feelings in interpersonal interaction.

Rapho/Photo Researchers, Inc.

shifts of posture as the person tries to find a comfortable position for interacting. People are often most relaxed with people of lower status and, surprisingly, with those they don't like (Swensen, 1973). Being relaxed, rather than sitting up straight and paying careful attention, may communicate that another person is of little significance to you. Generally, leaning toward another person indicates liking for them.

Another important aspect of nonverbal communication is positioning. Studies of positioning make up the area of social psychology called **proxemics.** These studies of how closely people interact often deal with the concept of **personal space.** Personal space is closely related to the idea of territory that figures prominently in studies of animal behavior. A territory is an area that an animal will defend and try to keep free of intruders (see Chapter 15). An individual's personal space is like a portable territory. It is an area around the body that the person wants others to keep away from. People show tension when their personal space is "invaded" by others. The personal space tends to be oval shaped, such that others can get reasonably close from behind and an intermediate distance from the sides, but must maintain the greatest distance directly in front.

The actual size of people's spaces depends on their relation to those they're interacting with. In general, people of high status are given a great deal of space. Others keep a respectful distance from them. People of low status are given little personal space, although some may not want to get too close to them. Studies have also shown that people express liking by moving close to each other, and of course, the interaction distance between highly intimate people can be zero.

Other studies of positioning show that people like different kinds of arrangements from different kinds of activities and for different kinds of relationships (Sommer, 1967). When people want to have a friendly conversation, they usually sit about 5 feet apart and at an angle so that eye contact is both easy to make and easy to break (Rosenfeld, 1965). A situation in which eye contact can be comfortably established but is not demanded is

The area around us that we want others to stay out of is a "portable" territory called our personal space.
Balkin, Monkmeyer.

ideal. When people are in a more competitive situation or with someone that they don't like, they sit at a more direct angle, one that demands eye contact. This has a confronting, challenging aspect to it. Another alternative is to sit farther apart, in an effort to try to avoid the other person as much as possible.

The dynamics of proxemics and personal space are involved in Barbara Walters's interviews in ways you may have noticed in watching television. People conversing before a camera often have to sit closer together than they normally would in order to be clearly visible to viewers on the small television screen. The fact that Barbara Walters and her interviewees may be sitting closer together than the person being interviewed is used to may make the person somewhat uncomfortable and give the interviewer more control over the situation than the interviewee expects.

TOUCHING. Studies of touching show again that nonverbal behavior varies with the nature of the relationship. Touching is sometimes a sign of affection and liking. We are more apt to touch people we like than people we want to avoid. Touching is also linked to status. Those of higher status often exercise the privilege of touching others. The boss lays a hand on the shoulder of an employee. Adults pat little kids on the head. Some men guide women by the elbow. This can be a gesture of solidarity, but it usually communicates one person's assumed right to direct the other person's behavior.

Just what a given degree of touching means is hard to determine, for, as with other nonverbal behaviors, touching varies with culture. This is dramatically shown in a study by Jourard (1966), who counted the frequency per hour of touching by couples in cafes in different countries. His results: San Juan, Puerto Rico, 180; Paris, 110; Gainesville, Florida, 2; London, 0. (In relation to the London figure, it's interesting to note that the first international hit record of the Beatles was called "I Want to Hold your Hand.")

PARALANGUAGE. Nonverbal aspects of speech—such as speed, voice inflection, tone of voice, loudness, and pitch—also communicate feelings. Studies show that active emotions such as anger are communicated by fast, loud, and high-pitched speech. Passive emotions such as sadness are expressed through slow speech and lower volume and pitch (Williams & Sundene, 1965; Swensen, 1973). Other emotions—happiness, grief, and fear—also have their own distinct **paralanguage.** Interviewers like Barbara Walters well understand the impact of paralanguage on the communication of emotions.

An interesting study by Davitz (1964) suggests that people differ greatly in their ability to recognize emotions from speech patterns. Some people seem to have a talent for identifying feelings in other people, a talent others seem to lack. Davitz suggests that this important ability in interpersonal relations can be improved through training and practice.

SEX DIFFERENCES IN NONVERBAL COMMUNICATION. Many of the studies of nonverbal communication show consistent differences between men's and women's nonverbal behavior. Women have been found to show more emotion in their nonverbal expressions than men. When women are with men they smile more than the men do, they have a more tense and controlled posture, and they stay farther away. Women tend to watch men more carefully when men are speaking than vice versa, but are more inclined to avert their eyes rather than stare when they are looked at. Men are more likely to touch women than women are to touch men.

What do these differences have to do with the relations between men and women? It could have something to do with the closeness of their relationships, but neither sex consistently uses nonverbal behaviors that are associated with closeness or distance. Women's not touching and averting eyes suggest low solidarity, but their smiling and showing emotions suggest affection. Men's touching suggests closeness, but their not smiling suggests distance.

On the other hand, the sex differences in nonverbal communication do seem consistently related to status. In an interaction of two people of unequal status, the subordinate is supposed to be more controlled in posture, to keep a distance, to not touch, and to pay close attention, but not stare back. The superior has the privilege of being relaxed in posture (feet up on a desk), to come close and touch (arm around the shoulder), and to stare. The superior is supposed to hide emotions, but the subordinate is not. The behaviors prescribed for the subordinate are those most typically used by women, and the behaviors prescribed for superiors are those most typically used by men.

Henley (1977) argues that nonverbal behavior has political implications and that women are kept in their place by being trained to behave like subordinates. Every time women play the subordinate role, they reinforce the existing political system that assigns privilege to men and lesser status to women. Henley's persuasive analysis lists staring, touching, interrupting, crowding another's space, frowning, looking stern, and pointing as gestures of dominance among humans. Gestures of submission are lowering the eyes, averting one's gaze, blinking, cuddling to the touch, stopping talk, yielding ground or moving away, smiling, and moving in a pointed direction. Henley asserts that men are taught to perform the gestures of dominance and women are taught to perform the gestures of submission. Henley's work is important in alerting us to the ways nonverbal communication defines relationships along the dominance-submission dimension. Most other research has focused on how nonverbal communication expresses affection or hostility. Henley's work also stresses the importance of nonverbal behaviors in maintaining traditional sex roles by providing sex-typed behavior norms for men and women.

CONCLUSIONS ABOUT NONVERBAL COMMUNICATION. We have seen that nonverbal communication is the language of relationships and emotions. What people "say" nonverbally is taken to be the most reliable indicator of what they are thinking and feeling about themselves, about others, and about the situations they face. The reason that various nonverbal communications are taken so seriously is that we know how difficult it can be to control or fake them. Although nonverbal behavior is difficult to contain and manage, in many instances people do try to gain control over it. They may not want their feelings to intrude into their business transactions with other people, they may not want to express feelings that they feel might be inappropriate, or they may feel that they are vulnerable if others know what they really believe or want.

At the same time that some people are trying to manage their nonverbal expression, others are trying to "pierce" those controlled self-presentations and read, from what they regard as the less controllable nonverbal cues, what those people are actually feeling. The result of these efforts can be a spiraling cycle of strong efforts to hide the truth and equally strong efforts to discover it. Consequently, interaction can become very stressful and unsatisfying. Fortunately, when people trust each other and feel ready to be open, this kind of hide-and-seek isn't necessary, and interpersonal relations become more spontaneous and relaxed.

One thing the research makes clear is that, because nonverbal communications are assumed to be highly reliable, people must match their verbal statements with correspond-

REVIEW QUESTIONS

14. We often control overt displays of emotions and feelings that we feel are socially inappropriate. On these occasions our body provides a mechanism for the release of these emotions through minute, fleeting facial expressions, which are often imperceptible to the observer. These facial expressions are called _____ _____ .

15. T or F: When expressing our true feelings, nonverbal forms of self-expression are not as reliable or credible as our verbal communications.

16. One way to nonverbally regulate the intensity of an interaction is to either maintain or avoid _____ _____ .

17. Social psychologists call the study of body positioning _____ .

18. T or F: We are often more relaxed with people we don't like than with people we like.

19. Which of the following statements is(are) true regarding sex differences in nonverbal communication?
    a. Women are more likely to touch men than men are to touch women.
    b. Men show more emotion in their nonverbal expressions than women.
    c. When women are with men they have a more tense and controlled posture than the men do.
    d. All the above are true statements.

20. Often we are presented with a communication that simultaneously conveys two messages that are inconsistent and contradictory. This kind of ambiguous communication is known as a _____ _____ .

21. A person whose dependent position in a relationship heightens the confusion and anxiety created by paradoxical communications is said to be in a _____ _____ .

ing nonverbal expressions if they are to be believed and trusted. If there is a good match, communication and interaction can proceed easily and be rewarding. If there is not a good match, confusion and difficulty may arise in people's interactions, which in some cases can cause serious problems.

Problems in Communication

The key problem in communication is ambiguity. We often wonder what other people are really saying to us. Can we believe what they are telling us? Are we getting the truth or some kind of double-talk? Why does what someone says seem "fishy"? Why does it seem confusing? All these questions reflect ambiguity about what other people are trying to convey about their thoughts or feelings.

These kinds of ambiguities are common and cause problems in many different kinds of interaction. They can cause problems for people in a very casual first meeting and problems for people long involved in a very deep relationship. One example is ambiguity about what people mean when they flirt or make sexual comments. Barbara Walters says that, compared to Europeans, Americans are clumsy and inhibited in expressing their romantic and sexual attraction to a person in a nonthreatening and nonseductive way. One time she was interviewing the European actor Oskar Werner, whom she'd heard was difficult, and she asked him about it. He smoothly remarked, "How would you know? We've never had an affair." She was flattered and floored. This "sexual recognition" is something Americans tend to do poorly, so our romantic interest in other people is often awkwardly expressed.

Awkwardness in flirtation and in expressing sexual recognition is just one source of ambiguity and problems in communication. Let's consider two other important communication irregularities and the consequences of the ambiguities they create.

GAME PLAYING.   In Chapter 8 we discussed transactional analysis and Eric Berne's *Games*

People Play. Game playing involves ambiguous communications, usually where the game player deliberately misleads or confuses another person for some psychological gain. Games may give temporary satisfaction, but in the long run they are extremely destructive to interpersonal relations.

Games use a form of communication Berne called "ulterior transaction," whereby a person says something that communicates one thing on the overt, social level but something entirely different on the covert, psychological level. The responder may be trapped by the double message, confused about how to react, or may continue the game by responding with his or her own double message. One common game is called See What You Made Me Do (SWYMD). A specific example involves a woman who asks her husband if he has time to help weed the garden. He says he is willing to help, even though he really doesn't want to. When he inevitably steps on a tomato plant or trips over the hose he reveals his anger at his wife by saying, "See what you made me do!" The fight that follows is attributable to the husband's not giving an honest answer in the first place. A clearer communication of his attitude would have avoided this situation.

Another game Berne discusses is called Rapo. This is a sexual game that can be played by either men or women. When a woman plays it, it usually takes the form of a nonverbal indication on her part that she is interested in a physical relationship with a man. When he is encouraged enough to make an explicit suggestion of intimate contact such as "My place or yours?" the woman reacts indignantly and asks how he could possibly have thought she was interested in such an affair. The man is confused and embarrassed, having taken the bait and been trapped by the woman's ambiguous communication. When a man plays Rapo, the game involves him gaining the woman's trust by denying any interest in sexual relations. She then relaxes with him and lets her guard down. This makes her more vulnerable to him, and he attempts to take advantage of her sexually. In this case the woman is trapped by the man's ambiguous communication.

A final example is the game of Sweetheart, where a person in a relationship makes a criticism of the other person, but concludes with the endearing term "sweetheart." For instance, "Don't you think you should have let me know, sweetheart?" The use of the word *sweetheart* blunts the criticism so that it's difficult for the partner to be angry about it. The game player may criticize the other person severely, but in effect deny that he or she is being critical by using the term of affection.

When people play games, the chances are that the end result will be bitterness and hostility. A game player may be able to enjoy a moment of feeling one-up, having outwitted the other, but the confusing communications are likely to produce ill will. People can avoid initiating games by being as honest as they can in their communications with other people and by helping to clarify ambiguous communications. When other people seem to be playing games, the best tactic is to be as candid as possible about how the other person's remarks seem to be ambiguous or even dishonest.

PARADOXICAL COMMUNICATION AND THE DOUBLE BIND.

Games can be harmful to interpersonal relations. Even more destructive, however, can be the ambiguous communication known as **paradoxical communication** (Watzlawick, Beavin, & Jackson, 1967). A paradoxical communication can be defined formally as a message that contradicts itself. It conveys at the same time two things that are inconsistent and contradictory. In most cases there is a discrepancy between what is stated verbally and what is expressed nonverbally. Say a parent takes a young child to nursery school for the first day and tells the child not to be afraid, that school will be fun and safe. In reality the parent is very anxious about whether the child will be adequately cared for, and this anxiety shows in the parent's nonverbal behavior. Consequently the child is confused about whether nursery school is really a good place to be left.

The most common and troublesome paradoxical communications are those that put people in a position in which there is no appropriate way to act. Sometimes a person is asked to do two things that contradict each other. For example, consider two high school students who are dating steadily. The girl asks the boy if he minds if she dates other boys and he replies "It's fine with me if you date other guys," but says it in a downcast manner that communicates nonverbally that he would prefer that she didn't. Another example is a couple of kids taken to a dull concert by their parents

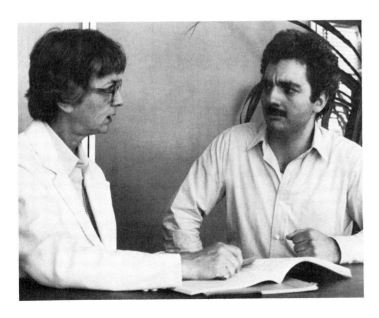

Paradoxical communication can put us in a situation in which we are confused about how to act.
Irene Springer.

and then asked whether they liked it. Their folks say, "Tell us what you really thought of it," while nonverbally indicating that they want the answer to be a rave.

The common factor in all three examples is that one person's communications inevitably put the other in the wrong. This is known as an untenable position, and the result is that you're "damned if you do and damned if you don't." There is confusion about how to act, and, no matter what choice you make, the other person is likely to be critical. Two important questions can be raised about these kinds of paradoxical communications. First, is there any good way to respond to them? Second, what are the consequences of interactions that contain a large degree of paradoxical communication?

RESPONDING TO PARADOXICAL COMMUNICATION.   There are several ways to try to cope with the confusion caused by paradoxical communication. But there's no guarantee that these approaches will be successful.

One approach is to try to figure out what the other person really wants. In most cases this will probably be what the person communicates on the nonverbal level, rather than what he or she states directly. Ascertaining this may be impossible, however, because the person may not know what he or she wants. The reason that people give paradoxical "double messages" is that they are confused, in conflict, and ambivalent about their needs and desires. For example, the young man who says it's fine for his girlfriend to date others, but acts hurt, is probably not sure how he really feels. On one hand, he realizes that his girlfriend can do what she pleases. He knows he can't force her to care for him or to lose interest in being with others. Rationally he knows he must agree to her dating other people. On the other hand, he is afraid of losing her and wants to do whatever he can to keep her. He can't wholeheartedly tell her to go ahead and see other people. His confusion and ambivalence are reflected in his paradoxical communication. In short, it may be hard to respond to the real message because the communicator may be confused.

Another way of handling double messages is to **metacommunicate,** that is, to communicate about the communication. This means calling the paradoxical communication exactly what it is. You don't try to respond to the paradox; you just say, "You're giving me a double message. You're going to be mad at me no matter what I do. I can't respond. Tell me what you really want." Or you may say, "You're twisting everything I do so that nothing I do is right."

Metacommunicating can be very difficult. It takes a good deal of sophistication about what is happening, a better-than-average ability to articulate the problem clearly, and a lot of nerve. It actually disconfirms the other person's communication, saying it doesn't exist, which happens to be true. It can be very difficult for a person in a dependent relationship, like a child, to metacommunicate with someone with a great deal of power, like a parent. Such a person is in serious trouble.

THE DOUBLE BIND.   A person who is in a dependent position in a relationship and is receiving paradoxical communications about which he or she can't metacommunicate, because either of lack of awareness of the problem or fear of the consequences, is said to be in a **double bind** (Watzlawick et al., 1967). Many psychologists have studied the consequences of being in a double bind and have suggested that it can cause serious psychological disorder. Several theorists have argued that double binding by parents can cause schizophrenia in children (Bateson, Jackson, Haley, & Weakland, 1956). They cite evidence indicating that double binds produce so much confusion and uncertainty that people caught in them begin to respond with their own confusing and ambiguous communications and thus manifest the thought disorders that are seen in schizophrenics. Although the double-bind hypothesis of schizophrenia is not given much weight today (Crider, 1979), studies have shown that paradoxical communications can cause serious disturbances in children and adolescents. More generally it's clear that paradoxical communications or other ambiguous messages greatly detract from the quality of a relationship. This underlines the importance of being aware of one's feelings and communicating them clearly.

AVOIDING AMBIGUOUS COMMUNICATION. We have seen that ambiguous communications can cause problems in human relationships that range from annoying to severe. How can we avoid ambiguity in our interactions with others? How can we be clear and straightforward? The key may be in recalling that ambiguous communications stem from ambivalent feelings. This means that we should be aware that when we are in conflict about something, there is a greater than normal chance that our communications will be ambiguous and cause con-

fusion for others. We should be aware of this increased probability and guard against it. Most important, ambiguous communication can be reduced by minimizing ambivalent feelings. While we can never completely eliminate conflict, the more insightful we can be about our real needs and feelings and the more decisive we can be about what we want, the easier it will be to communicate clearly to others. Thus self-knowledge, a willingness to make clear choices, and trust and confidence in our decisions will aid clear communication and honest interaction. Communication is too important a part of relationships to let it become sloppy due to ambivalence. Being clear and honest with ourselves allows us to be clear and honest with others.

SUMMARY

1. The process of perceiving others can be separated into two phases: making inferences about a person's specific traits and resolving various and often conflicting data about a person into a coherent overall impression.

2. People infer others' traits by observing behavior and deciding whether it is indicative of an underlying personal characteristic or is a reflection of environmental contingencies. People also infer some traits using implicit personality theories and stereotypes. Many biases are involved in trait attribution, including strong tendencies to attribute behavior to internal and stable traits and to pay too little attention to situational forces that affect people's actions.

3. Combining trait information into an overall impression is a complex process. Often the overall impression is highly influenced by what the observer sees as a person's central traits, such as whether the person is emotionally warm or cold.

4. When later information about a person is inconsistent with a perceiver's initial impressions, there are three possible results. Sometimes there is a primacy effect, where people force later information to fit their original impression, even, if necessary, seeing the later behavior as reflecting merely temporary moods or situational pressures. Sometimes people are strongly affected by the later information and show recency effects, where their impression of a person is more heavily affected by the later information than by the earlier. There are also overcompensation effects, where people overcorrect for initial mistaken impressions.

5. Our impressions of people are biased in many ways. We see what we expect to see and what we want to see. Often our false impressions have significant impact on the people we are perceiving. Behavior toward them that is based on our false impressions may cause them to behave in ways that are consistent with our impressions.

6. Nonverbal behavior—including facial expressions, body gestures and positioning,

and paralanguage—communicates internal feelings and emotions. Nonverbal communication is harder to control than verbal statements are and is therefore a more reliable indicator of what people deeply feel and believe. If what people say is not supported by appropriate nonverbal expression, it will have little credibility.

7. Problems can arise in communication when there is ambiguity about what people really mean. This ambiguity is generally caused by paradoxical communication, discrepancy between what is communicated verbally and what is communicated nonverbally. Sometimes people deliberately create ambiguity in order to play games. These games may give them momentary feelings of being clever and one-up in a situation, but they are confusing and embarrassing to their targets and lower the quality of relationships. In other cases people may give paradoxical communications because of their own ambivalent feelings. The recipients of paradoxical communications often find themselves in untenable positions where no matter how they act they will be violating part of the other person's communication. Metacommunicating can be an effective way of responding to a paradoxical communication, but it is difficult, especially for those in a dependent position in a relationship. People in such a position often find themselves in double binds that can cause great confusion and conflict and ultimately lead to psychological disturbance. Ambiguous communication can be avoided by being sure of your own needs and feelings.

KEY TERMS

a. DOUBLE BIND
b. MASK
c. METACOMMUNICATION
d. NEUTRALIZE
e. OVERCOMPENSATION EFFECT
f. PARADOXICAL COMMUNICATION

g. PARALANGUAGE
h. PERSONAL SPACE
i. PRIMACY EFFECT
j. RECENCY EFFECT
k. SELF-FULFILLING PROPHECY
l. SIMULATE

1. The attempt to display emotions that seem appropriate to the situation but are not genuinely felt
2. The heavy influence of the most recent information about another person in the creation of one's impression of that person
3. An impression of another that is most heavily influenced by the earliest information received about the person
4. A prophecy or prediction that may not be inevitable but that leads to behavior which makes it come true
5. The space individuals keep when interacting with others, felt as owned by the individual and met with retreat or hostility when invaded
6. A message that contradicts itself
7. Aspects of speaking, such as pace of speech and tone of voice, which qualify the meaning of what is stated
8. A tendency to overcorrect for an initial incorrect impression and overemphasize the most recent information
9. A communication about another communication
10. The attempt by an individual to hide one emotion by displaying another

11. To attempt to conceal an emotion from another
12. A situation characterized by paradoxical communication, dependence on the communicator, and inability to metacommunicate

ANSWERS TO REVIEW QUESTIONS

1. True. **2.** Attribution. **3.** Internal; external. **4.** Internal. **5.** e. **6.** Implicit personality theory. **7.** Expectations. **8.** Primacy. **9.** Overcompensation.

10. d. **11.** Self-fulfilling prophecy. **12.** False. **13.** d.

14. Micromomentary expressions. **15.** False. **16.** Eye contact. **17.** Proxemics. **18.** True. **19.** c. **20.** Paradoxical communication. **21.** Double bind.

10

AFFILIATION AND ATTRACTION

J
ohn R. Cash was born on February 26, 1932, in Cleveland County, Arkansas. His family was poor, and the Depression added to their worries. John's father eked out a living by cutting pulpwood and working in sawmills or on the railroad. In 1935, the Cash family moved to Dyess, Arkansas, where they began farming in the black river delta land. Johnny Cash (1975) reports two vivid memories of his early childhood. The first was the deep religious convictions of his family. His grandfather had been a minister, and, at the age of thirteen, Jack Cash, Johnny's older and favorite brother, announced that "he had been called to preach" the gospel. While Johnny was not as religious as his brother, he was awed by the "power of religion."

Johnny's other vivid memory is his craving for country music. He recalls pressing his ear against the family's battery-powered radio late at night to listen to music. He would turn down the volume so that his parents wouldn't know he was still up listening to it. He also remembers rushing to the radio during his noon break from the cotton fields to listen to "High Noon Roundup," featuring Smilin' Eddie Hill and the Louvin Brothers.

In 1950, when he was 18, Johnny entered the air force and was stationed in Germany. His fascination with music continued, and he bought a guitar and began to sing at local shows. In 1954, he returned to the United States and married Vivian Liberto. He had known Vivian for some years, and they had corresponded while he was in the service. There were many differences between Johnny and Vivian. For one thing, Vivian was a devout Catholic from a strict Catholic background, while Johnny's family was fundamentalist Protestant. The early years of their marriage were frustrating for Johnny. He had decided that he wanted a music-related job. But he couldn't even get a job as a disc jockey, much less as a singer. So he began selling household appliances door-to-door.

After a year as a salesman, Johnny met two mechanics who were also musicians, Marshall Grant, a bass player, and Luther Perkins, who picked electric guitar. They began to write and play songs and recorded "Hey Porter" and "Folsom Prison Blues." The songs were hits, and Johnny began appearing with such artists as Elvis Presley, Sonny James, Carl Perkins, and Jerry Lee Lewis.

But as Johnny's fame grew, his home life began to crumble. Vivian had little interest in country music; she was more concerned with having a home and raising their three daughters. Johnny and Vivian saw less and less of each other. After a brief visit home, Johnny would get up early in the morning and leave for Shreveport and Gladewater and all the other towns where he was doing one-night shows. "Even then," he says, "I think Vivian realized a lot better than I did that my trips away from home, the tours, my complete involvement in the music business would be the beginning of the end of our marriage."* A few years later, Johnny and Vivian were divorced.

*Johnny Cash, *Man in Black*, p. 84. Copyright © 1975 by Johnny Cash. Used by permission of Zondervan Publishing House.

In addition to these troubles, Johnny was beginning to face another problem. All the traveling from one concert to another began to wear on him; he had difficulty staying awake. On one trip, a friend gave him some "little white pills" to help him stay alert. These amphetamines seemed to do the trick; Johnny reports that the pills helped him discover "newly expanded limits to my stamina and performing ability." By 1959 Johnny was addicted to amphetamines, sometimes taking as many as 25 pills a day. Then, in order to counteract the effects of these stimulants, Cash had to take tranquilizers to "calm down."

Johnny's life became a living hell. He began missing engagements or showing up to concerts so high that he couldn't sing. The pills affected his voice and he fought a case of constant laryngitis. He was kicked off the Grand Ole Opry for failing to make scheduled appearances. Over a seven-year period, he was arrested seven times on drug charges and had numerous automobile accidents during this time. Many of his friends, including his relatives, felt he was trying to kill himself.

Johnny was a handsome and charismatic young star. Women were very attracted to him. Even the effects of his drug addiction seemed to add to his appeal. He was surrounded by people who would've loved to get close to him, yet he felt lost and lonely, unable to confide in anyone or to ask for help.

Then in the early 1960s, the Carter Family, a well-known country music group, began touring with Johnny. The Carters saw the state he was in and they "sorta adopted him." June Carter had the greatest concern for Johnny and was determined to help him break his drug habit. June was brought up in a deeply religious home. She had been singing country songs for years and was a star on the Grand Ole Opry. She had two daughters from a previous marriage to country singer Carl Smith.

June was drawn to Johnny. She saw the sadness in his eyes and she "felt his pain." She was struck by his physical appearance, the 6-foot-2-inch frame that was constantly draped in black. She reports feeling gentleness and kindness in Cash, when he wasn't controlled by his drugs. She begged him to give up the drugs. She even attempted to intercept the doctors and friends who brought him the pills. She tried to get Johnny to see a psychiatrist about his drug problem. Johnny rebuffed her efforts and tried to avoid her, but she doggedly persisted in her crusade to help Johnny straighten out his life.

In 1967 Johnny almost died from a drug overdose. He had reached the low point in his life. He wanted to run away but he also knew that "this isn't the answer, getting away by myself when I can't *stand* myself."* At this point, he decided to try to kick his drug addiction. The Carter family moved in with him so they could watch him and help him. June went through Johnny's home searching for pills he had hidden and threw them out. For four weeks, June and others stayed with Johnny as he fought to kick his addiction. June talked with Johnny and comforted him as he went through the agony of withdrawal.

Johnny finally began to confide in June, to talk about his fears and his self-hate.

*Johnny Cash, *Man in Black*, p. 121. Copyright © 1975 by Johnny Cash. Used by permission of Zondervan Publishing House.

June listened patiently and pointed out that Johnny could "turn his life around" if he could break his addiction. Through these intimate discussions, Johnny came to trust and respect June. By November 1967, Johnny had conquered his drug addiction.

He had also fallen in love with June, the woman who had helped him through his agonizing bout with drugs. They were married in March of 1968.

Johnny was determined not to let his love for June fade as his love for Vivian had. Johnny and June toured together. They sang together. In 1969 they went to Vietnam to give benefit shows to the United States troops fighting there. When Johnny Cash signed to do a television series, his costar was June Carter Cash.

The love between Johnny and June grew as they helped foster each other's interests. Johnny became deeply religious, and he

Johnny and June had lived similar lives and had a deep appreciation of each other's needs and desires. Their attraction for each other increased as they shared more experiences.

Springer/Bettmann Film Archive.

and June spent hours discussing the Bible. They toured the Holy Land a number of times, and in 1973 they made a religious film in Israel.

The emphasis on togetherness continued even after their son, John Carter Cash, was born. As soon as John Carter was old enough to travel, the Cashes hired a nurse and John Carter went on their tours. He even appeared in many of their shows.

Both Johnny and June had gone through a great deal of sorrow and pain in their lives; they both had had their ups and downs. Now they were clearly at the top. They both had successful careers and were well respected throughout the world; they had even sung at the White House for two presidents. And these days, in the world of show business, it is still generally acknowledged that Johnny and June "have something special."

THE NEED FOR OTHERS

When we examine the story of Johnny Cash's life, one point stands out: From the time he began to sing hit tunes, Johnny's life was filled with people. Wherever he went, he went with other people. At the height of his career, he turned to other people to share his glory. At the depths of his depression and drug problem, he turned to other people for help. While Cash may have been somewhat unusual in the number of people with whom he dealt, he was not unusual in the fact that he spent much of his time with others. In an interesting survey of college students' lives, Deaux (1978) found that students spent more than 75 percent of their waking hours with other people, and some students spent over 90 percent of their waking time with other people. This suggests that we are social animals who need others.

ISOLATION

One way to see how much we need other people is to look at the effects that being isolated from others has on human behavior. Some of the most interesting accounts of the effects of isolation can be seen in the diaries of solitary sailors and explorers. For example, Admiral Richard Byrd, who explored the North Pole and spent many weeks alone, gives a vivid account of the effects of isolation. His first feelings were fear and loneliness. After a time he began to have hallucinations about seeing people. He hungered for someone to talk to, so he talked to himself, to animals, and to inanimate objects.

Closer examination shows that isolation does not affect everyone the same way. Some people become very uncomfortable after only a short time alone, while others may spend days alone without being severely affected. In all cases, though, it seems that long periods of social isolation are unpleasant. Most people want to be with other people very much.

Loneliness and Privacy

When we think about being away from other people, loneliness and privacy are two very different terms that come to mind.

Loneliness results when people either erect mental barriers to wall themselves off from others or are afraid or unable to break down existing barriers (Worchel & Cooper, 1979). People who are lonely report feeling depressed, helpless, and bored. Being lonely also leads people to tear themselves down and feel useless.

Interestingly enough, being alone is only one of the conditions that leads us to feel lonely. The most important factor in loneliness is having no close companion or friend in whom we can confide (Derlega & Margulis, 1982). Some of the most lonely times are when we are around a number of people but do not feel close to any of them. Johnny Cash echoed this point: He reported being most lonely and depressed when he had crowds of people constantly around him but wasn't close enough to any of these people to talk to them about his problems and fears.

People's reactions to loneliness vary a great deal (Peplau & Perlman, 1982). Some people blame themselves for their condition; they cry, sleep, watch television, drink, or take drugs. This pattern of behavior only prolongs their loneliness. In these cases, they remove themselves from the company of others, and their barriers against allowing others to become close increase. Activity is a more productive approach to loneliness (Shaver, 1982). People may exercise or work on hobbies. They may go on shopping sprees where they interact with people, even if those people are strangers, and buy themselves objects that make them feel better. Or they may attempt to make social contact, calling old friends or going to places where they will meet new friends. Activity, sense of purpose, and social contact help people overcome loneliness. But even active lonely people have to make an effort not to become desperate or panicked by their loneliness. No matter what you do, the feeling may not disappear immediately. It often takes time to remove the barriers we erected to keep others at a distance. What is important is that we realize this and not wall ourselves into solitude behind these barriers.

While isolation from others may lead to the negative state of loneliness, social isolation is also an important part of a very necessary and positive state in our lives, **privacy.** Privacy may be viewed as the person's freedom to *choose* what he or she will communicate to whom and under what circumstances. In other words, privacy can be viewed as chosen isolation, while loneliness often results from isolation over which we have little choice. All of us retreat from interaction with others; we may do this by finding a place away from other people, or we may simply retreat into our own thoughts even when there are many people around us.

Johnny Cash was well aware of the importance of privacy. One of his greatest complaints was that fame made it difficult for him to have privacy. People were always following him, watching him, and wanting his attention. He had no opportunity to collect his thoughts or rest. The craving for privacy was one of the reasons he turned to drugs; the drugs allowed him to shut other people out of his thoughts. June helped Johnny get the privacy he so desperately needed. She helped him learn to turn down engagement requests and seek privacy in his home away from the demand of others, instead of using drugs.

As Johnny learned, privacy plays many roles in our lives. It allows us the opportunity for emotional release from the tensions of every life. It gives us a chance to reflect on ourselves and our lives and to plan our activities. It also gives us a chance to control our own environment and to determine what feelings we will express and to whom.

We have all developed ways to gain privacy. Some, like Johnny Cash, have homes surrounded by high fences where they can go to be alone. Others may simply retreat into their rooms and lock their doors to find solitude.

An important difference between loneliness and privacy involves the degree of choice in isolation.

Ed Lettau, Photo Researchers, Inc.

Even in our day-to-day interactions, most of us have developed effective nonverbal cues, such as a glare or "blank stare," to signal others that we do not wish to have social contact (Altman, 1975).

As we can see, everyone experiences social isolation. Whether this isolation leads to loneliness and depression or is welcomed as a time for privacy is largely a function of control. Controlled or chosen isolation is a necessary part of our adjustment to our world. While we all experience forced isolation and loneliness at times, our responses to these states will determine whether they are only passing conditions or become an anchor that drags us down and erects further barriers that wall us off from social contact.

MOVING TOWARD OTHERS: AFFILIATION

Our discussion of the effects of isolation shows that people can't exist for long periods of time "by themselves" without suffering sometimes severe psychological effects. We are naturally drawn to other people; in fact, psychologists have suggested that **affiliation,** being with other people, is a basic human need. Interestingly, while we all spend time with other people, our patterns of affiliation are influenced by a number of factors. Research suggests that women are more likely to appear in public places with another person than men are (Deaux, 1976). Men tend to spend less time engaged in conversation with others than women do.

In order to see another condition that influences our desire to be with others, we can look at the Cash-Carter relationship. Johnny Cash knew June Carter for years before he began to seek out her company. What were the circumstances that led to his affiliation with June when he did, rather than at some earlier period?

During the time when his relationship with June really began to grow, Johnny's life was dominated by feelings of fear. He was afraid he was losing popularity with his fans; he missed show dates and at times was so drugged he couldn't sing because of hoarseness. He had fears about the effects of the drugs he was taking; he had little control over his actions and his close brushes with death because of overdoses or automobile accidents scared him tremendously. Could this fear have affected his desire to seek out June?

An experiment by Stanley Schachter (1959) suggests that it could. In Schachter's study, female subjects were met at a laboratory by a Dr. Zilstein. To create a high-fear condition in the subjects, Dr. Zilstein was dressed in a white laboratory coat with a stethoscope hanging from his pocket, and the laboratory room was filled with electronic apparatus. In a very serious manner, Dr. Zilstein told subjects that they would be given painful electric shocks: "Again, I do want to be honest with

you and tell you that these shocks will be quite painful, but of course, they will do no permanent damage." With other subjects a low-fear condition was created: Dr. Zilstein was dressed in street clothes, smiled at the subjects, and told them that, while they would receive a shock during the study, "I assure you that what you will feel will not in any way be painful." Following these instructions, subjects were told that it would be a few minutes before the experiment was ready to begin. Subjects were told that there were a number of rooms where they could wait for the experiment, and that some of these rooms were empty while others had students waiting for other studies. Dr. Zilstein then asked the subjects in which type of room they preferred to wait. Subjects in the high-fear condition showed a definite preference to be with other people, while there was no such preference on the part of subjects in the low-fear condition. The fear-affiliation relationship was most strong for subjects who reported being firstborn or only children.

The Schachter experiment clearly demonstrated that fear often leads to the desire to affiliate. Other experiments (e.g., Morris et al., 1976) have found that people not only prefer to be with others when fearful, but also stand closer to others and talk more when they are afraid. (Interestingly enough, while fear leads to affiliation, embarrassment does not.)

Obviously, we seek out other people because we need them, in various ways. Our different needs are reflected in the different types of affiliations we make. Given this, we may ask what needs other people can fulfill.

The first and most obvious answer is that we often need other people to *perform certain activities.* You couldn't play tennis alone, for example. However, this cannot be the only reason we seek out others. Johnny Cash didn't necessarily need June Carter in order to sing his songs.

A second reason for wanting to be with others is that they often *reward* us. Other people may compliment us or give us material rewards. We get status from the way other people evaluate and treat us.

A related, and very important, reason for affiliating with others is that we often need them to *help us evaluate ourselves,* our activities and attitudes. Could Johnny Cash tell how "good" his songs are without seeing how others react to them? In order for you to evaluate how good a tennis player you are, you must find out what other players you can beat at the game. If we want to know what is right or wrong, we must turn to others and use what they believe as a yardstick for evaluating our own attitudes. For example, most of us have never lived in a communist country, but many of us believe that living under a communist government would be bad. How did we arrive at this attitude without having experienced communism firsthand? Clearly, we base our attitudes on what others believe. The importance of others for *social comparison* was discussed in Chapter 3; it is sufficient for our present purposes to point out that we do seek out other people for self-evaluation.

And of course, as we've already discussed, we need and want to be with other people because they comfort us and reduce our fear and anxiety. When he turned to June Carter, Johnny Cash was living a dreadful life and was afraid he was going to die. June comforted him and helped reduce his fear. As children we learn that our parents will protect us in scary situations. You may remember the comfort you got from your parents when you were a child and woke up from a bad dream or were scared by thunder and lightning. Our desire for this kind of comfort leads us to affiliate with others throughout our lives.

So there are many ways and reasons we affiliate with other people. Despite this general desire to be with others, however, we don't simply turn to anyone. There are certain people we want to be with and are attracted to. There are others we find ourselves repelled by. Again, looking at Johnny Cash, we can ask why he was attracted to June Carter when his life was filled with many other people who would have been happy to be with him. To answer this question, we now turn our attention to the factors that determine who we're attracted to.

REVIEW QUESTIONS

1. Isolation from others may lead to the negative state of _____ in which people often report feeling depressed, helpless, and bored.
2. Although isolation over which we have no choice may lead to loneliness, isolation which we choose is _____.
3. The desire to be with other people is called the need for _____.
4. T or F: Persons who are fearful are more likely to want to be with others than persons who are not.
5. In addition to needing others to perform activities with, we want to be with others because they often _____ us and help us _____ _____.

More specifically, we can ask, Why do we choose certain people as friends and reject others?

CHOOSING FRIENDS: THE FORMULA FOR ATTRACTION

Psychologists have identified a number of regularities in the way people choose their friends. They have isolated variables that allow us to predict the type of person who is likely to attract friends and the type of person who is not. Psychologists have even begun to identify those variables that may determine who you'll fall in love with (see Chapter 11).

It is important to be aware of these variables as we adjust to today's world. One of the major causes of depression is that people do not feel that they have friends they can count on. Years ago people tended to live either with or within easy traveling distance of their family. When children grew up and married, they often continued living with their closest kin in an extended family arrangement. If they didn't live in the same home, they would at least continue

The average American moves 14 times during his or her lifetime. This makes it difficult for some to establish lasting friendships.

Laimute E. Druskis.

to live in the same town or city. Family gatherings were frequent, and if someone needed help or simply wanted to talk about a problem, he or she could seek out a parent, an aunt or uncle, a cousin, or some other relative.

The situation today is very different. The extended family is the exception rather than the rule. After children grow up, not only is it unlikely that they will continue to live in their parents' home, but it is even unlikely that they will continue to live in the same community. Packard (1972) points out that each year 40 million Americans change residence and that the average American moves 14 times during his or her lifetime. As a result of this mobility, individuals must constantly make new friends and rely on those friends for support, help, and companionship. Finding people we can relate to, and acting on our attraction to them, thus becomes a pretty crucial issue.

THE SIGNS OF ATTRACTION

It is often said that we live in an emotionally closed society. A common complaint of many people is that they have great difficulty telling

---

HOW MUCH DO YOU LIKE OTHERS?

A researcher (Rubin, 1970) has developed a questionnaire to measure liking and loving. Liking is generally viewed as a tendency to evaluate another person in a positive way. Below are a number of dimensions that have been found to measure liking. Think of some people you know and rate them on these dimensions using a scale of 1 (lowest rating or statement does not describe person) to 10 (highest rating or statement fits person well). When you add your ratings, you should find that your highest ratings were given to those people you liked the most.

1. Shows good judgment   _____
2. Others react favorable to him or her   _____
3. Unusually well adjusted   _____
4. Exceptionally mature   _____
5. Is sort of person I would like to be   _____
6. Easily gains admiration   _____
7. Could easily handle a responsible job   _____

others how they feel. This is especially true when these feelings involve strong attraction. Many times we may feel strongly attracted to others but tell ourselves, ''I don't know them well enough to tell them I'm attracted to them.'' Often school-aged children resort to writing anonymous notes to express their liking for another child.

This fear of openly expressing attraction has a reciprocal consequence: We have difficulty knowing when others are attracted to us. Frequently we play the role of detective in trying to determine if someone is attracted to us. We review the history of our relationship, asking, ''Did the other person smile at me? Seek me out to have a conversation with? Look at me longer than at other people?'' You may wish to look at your own relationships. How did you communicate your attraction to your friends, and how did you decide that they really liked you?

The lack of openness in the expression of attraction is clearly unfortunate. The feeling that we must inhibit the expression of attraction or that others are inhibiting this expression places roadblocks in the way of our interpersonal interactions. Individuals often resort to ''playing games'' to avoid directly expressing their attraction, and these ''games'' may be misinterpreted by the other party. Johnny Cash reports trying to hide his attraction to June Carter because he felt he was unworthy of her. He would tell her to ''leave him alone,'' even though he desperately wanted her to comfort him. The result of Johnny's rebuffs was to impede their relationship and keep Johnny from getting the help and comfort he desired from June.

We may ask why we are so unwilling to tell someone ''I like you'' or ''I am attracted to you.'' In most cases our fear of being rejected or rebuffed inhibits us. We fear being hurt if the other person fails to reciprocate our attraction. So we end up playing the ''waiting game,'' waiting for the ''right time'' to tell people that we like them. The risk here is that the ''right time'' may not come, and we may lose the opportunity to enrich our relationships with people we like. We should strive for open interpersonal communication; we should not feel

paralyzed by fear of rejection when we want to express our attraction. Certainly it would be unwise to ignore the possibility that our attraction may not be reciprocated, but this risk must be weighed against the possibility that our unwillingness to openly express our feelings may seriously reduce the chances of forming a satisfying relationship.

While we may have the goal of open communication, we are often very reluctant to express our liking of others verbally. Yet, despite this reluctance, individuals often sense when someone likes them. In spite of Johnny Cash's verbal rejections of June Carter, she stuck by him. She sensed that Johnny both needed her and was attracted to her. How could June get this feeling when Johnny was giving her the verbal message ''Leave me alone''?

The answer is that humans express attraction in a number of ways; the verbal message is only one type of expression. We also use many forms of **nonverbal communication** to signal our affection. A line from one of Johnny Cash's songs points to one type of nonverbal expression: ''You've got that loving look in your eyes tonight.'' In fact, our eyes may well give our feelings away.

The jade dealers of ancient China were well aware of the importance of communication with the eyes (as we mentioned in Chapter 4). If the seller knew that a buyer was attracted to a particular piece of jade, the seller could hold out for a high price for the piece. The buyer would try to conceal attraction to the jade in hopes of getting it at a lower price: ''I really don't like that piece, but if you really must sell it, I'll reluctantly give you half the price you are asking.'' The jade dealers often ignored these verbal messages and watched the eyes of the buyer. They believed that the pupils of the buyer's eyes would dilate when the buyer was attracted to a particular piece of jade. When the buyer's pupils dilated, the seller held out for the high price for the jade and resisted the buyer's early offers. Hess and Polt (1960) carefully studied subjects' eyes and found that pupils did dilate when the subjects were looking at an object they liked. Unfortunately for buyers of jade and curious lovers, later research has shown that many different emotions, such as fear, also cause pupil dilation!

Before you strain your own eyes attempting to gauge the size of that special person's pupils, consider another more easily measured sign of attraction. Research has found that we look more at people we like than at people we dislike (Exline & Winters, 1965). Going one step further, it has also been found that when someone gives a compliment, we are more likely to be attracted to that person if they hold *eye contact* with us than if they don't. Thus eye contact not only signals our attraction to someone, but also paves the way for their attraction to us.

Another nonverbal channel that communicates attraction is *touching*. We are more apt to touch people we like than people we want to avoid. Although touching is such an important means of expressing attraction, our own culture has many taboos against touching. (See the study by Jourard [1966] noted in Chapter 9.) In addition to differences among cultures, there are interesting differences between the sexes where touching and perceptions of touching are concerned. Females are more

Touching is a sign of attraction; we touch people we like more than people we don't like.

Stan Wakefield.

likely to touch other females than males are likely to touch other males. Women make a distinction between touching that signals warmth or friendship and touching that indicate sexual desire; males do not seem to make these distinctions (Nguyen et al., 1975). Research has also found that females respond more positively to a brief touch than do males. All this suggests that there is a "language of touching," but this language is often choked off by our own culture.

Taking a step back from touching, we find that **interpersonal distance** is another nonverbal channel used to communicate attraction. We will discuss the concept of personal space in greater detail in Chapter 15, but, for our present purposes, it is sufficient to point out that we tend to interact at closer distances with people we like than with people we dislike.

One interesting aspect of nonverbal communication is that people often are not aware that they are communicating through nonverbal channels; hence their communication is mostly unconscious, and as a result a person is less likely to lie nonverbally than verbally. In fact, Mehrabian (1971) found that nonverbal behaviors may actually "give away" a person who is lying. Mehrabian noticed that when people were lying, they exhibited less frequent body movement, placed more distance between themselves and the listener, smiled more, and tended to lean backwards.

Given this information, we may get some clue as to how June Carter "knew" Johnny Cash was attracted to her even though he gave her verbal messages to the contrary. It is possible that Johnny revealed attraction through nonverbal channels. He may have held eye contact with her when they talked or stood close to her when they interacted. June may even have been able to use Johnny's nonverbal behavior to determine that he was not telling the truth when he told her to leave him alone. This discussion should encourage you to pay closer attention to your own nonverbal behavior and that of others. An interesting exercise involves observing the nonverbal behavior of couples and trying to determine how attracted they are to each other.

WHY ARE WE ATTRACTED TO CERTAIN PEOPLE

While it is important to understand how attraction is communicated, it is equally important to understand the variables that help determine who we'll be attracted to. People often take interpersonal attraction for granted; they rarely think about why they are attracted to one person and not to another. In order to demonstrate this you might try approaching a friend and asking "Why do you like me?" Chances are the friend will be surprised by the question and will probably hem and haw, trying to find an answer. It is unlikely that your friend will have given much thought to the specific reasons for his or her attraction.

The reasons for interpersonal attraction may be very valuable for most people to know. Often people complain that they have difficulty making new friends. They attempt to get others to like them but feel thwarted in this effort. Or they wonder why one particular individual is attracted to them even when they think they have done little to invite this attention. People are also concerned when they lose friends. This is particularly true for couples who have dated for some time and then move apart, vowing to write each other faithfully. Generally, the writing becomes more and more infrequent, and the relationship deteriorates.

We may ask related questions about Johnny Cash. Why did his first marriage end in divorce? Of all the people he met in his busy life, why was he attracted to June Carter? Why is he still very much attracted to June? To answer these questions, let's turn to some of the variables that have been identified as the barometers of attraction.

Physical Proximity

There are a number of differences between Johnny's relationship with his first wife, Vivian, and his relationship with June. Johnny's major problems in his first marriage occurred while he was becoming a star and spending much of his time on the road. Some of these trips were long, and Vivian and Johnny often went for weeks without seeing each other. Johnny was away from home more than he was home. Though they would write and talk to each other on the telephone, he realized that these absences were eroding his affection for Vivian and hers for him. The situation was very different with June. June toured with Johnny. When Johnny was lonely, he would spend days with the Carter family. When Johnny decided to break his drug habit, June attempted to stay near him constantly. Johnny reports that she would often try to be there to intercept and discourage individuals who tried to sell him pills. During the four weeks that Johnny was locked in his home to break his addiction, June and the Carter family were ever-present. Even after Johnny and June were married, they still traveled together. They did shows together, made movies together, and vacationed together.

Could a seemingly simple variable such as physical **proximity** affect interpersonal attraction? Research over the last 35 years suggests that it can have strong effects; in fact, in many cases proximity is a prerequisite to attraction. Festinger, Schachter, and Back (1950) studied friendship patterns that emerged in a married-student apartment complex. Couples were randomly assigned to apartments, and few knew each other before moving into the complex. After some time, the residents were asked whom they saw socially. The closer together people lived, the more likely they were to see each other on a social basis. Couples who lived on the same floor were more likely to be friends than were couples living on different floors.

In another interesting study, Segal (1974) investigated friendship patterns among Maryland state police trainees. She found that the closer together the first letters of the trainees' surnames were, the more likely it was they would be friends. It turned out that the trainees were assigned to seats in the classroom by alphabetical order. Hence, the closer together the first letters of their last names were, the closer they sat together in class. In a study of heterosexual attraction, Clark (1952) found that over half the people who married in Columbus,

Ohio, lived within 16 blocks of one another at the time of their first date.

This evidence clearly suggests that physical proximity can lead to interpersonal attraction. We like the people who are physically close to us. Furthermore, unless some prior dislike is present, we may be able to get others to like us by simply being physically close to them. The Johnny Cash story illustrates this point. His attraction to his first wife, Vivian, waned when he was away from her for long periods of time, and he became more attracted to June Carter the more time they spent together.

Why should proximity lead to liking? There are a number of possible reasons. First, it has been shown repeatedly that we like things (and people) with which we are familiar, and we dislike those things that are strange to us. A young child will generally smile with happiness upon seeing a familiar face, but the same young child may burst into tears when a stranger approaches. Zajonc (1968) has shown that familiarity leads to attraction even with adults. He showed subjects a series of photographs; some of the photographs were shown often in the series, while others were shown less frequently. People whose pictures had been seen often were rated as more likable than people whose pictures had been seen infrequently. These results support the idea that "to know him is to love him." Recently, researchers (Moreland & Zajonc, 1982) found that people assume that others familiar to them are also similar to them; as we will soon see, similarity leads to attraction.

Still another possible explanation for the relationship between proximity and attraction is that people who are around us are often in the position of giving us rewards (Hendrick & Hendrick, 1983). For example, simply because June was with Johnny during his performances, she was able to give him reinforcement and encouragement about his work. Likewise, Johnny was also in the position of rewarding June for her performances. As we will see in the next section, we like people who reward us and are generally repelled by those who punish us.

Before you jump to the conclusion that making yourself attractive simply means that

Proximity often leads to attraction. People who are around us often are in a position to supply rewards.

Mark Mangold, U.S. Census Bureau.

you should make yourself constantly present, there are a few other eye-opening statistics. Berscheid and Walster (1978) cite an FBI report that one third of all murders and most aggravated assaults occur within the family unit or between neighbors. Another report shows that robberies often occur between family members or within neighborhoods.

These and similar statistics suggest that proximity does not always lead to attraction. Johnny Cash had close contact with a number of people who didn't attract him, or ease his loneliness, like June Carter did. It may well be that being close to another person simply intensifies the relationship. That is, if two people have a basis for attraction, spending lots of time together will increase the chances of attraction. If two people are likely to frustrate or repel one another, however, closeness will increase the chances of that happening.

Regardless of the exact effects of proximity, one point should be clear: Proximity is an important ingredient for fostering attraction. The research on attraction does not support the popular saying "Absence makes the heart grow fonder." While short periods of absence may lead to increased attraction, long absences reduce interpersonal attraction ("Out of sight, out of mind"). This is an important point to remember, because some people feel guilty or shallow when they find their attraction for another dwindling after long absences. This process is part of human nature and is neither shallow nor unusual.

Rewards

Most of use would like to view our personal relationships as being based on some spark that does not apply to our other day-to-day interactions. We may choose a grocery store because it has the freshest meats and vegetables and we get "the most for our money" by shopping there. But we like to think something more is involved in the way we choose our friends. A number of psychologists (Kelley & Thibaut, 1978; Lott & Lott, 1974) have argued against such an idealistic view of friendship. They say we can better understand our social relationships if we view them on a cost-and-rewards basis. They propose a **social exchange theory** to help predict who we'll be attracted to.

Simply put, social exchange theory suggests that in every relationship there are costs and rewards. For example, our interactions with others "cost" us time and effort: We may have to expend money or other material goods in the relationship, and being in one interaction costs us the freedom to engage in another interaction at that time. On the other hand, we get certain "rewards" for our interactions— love, status, money, services, material goods, or information. Our outcome from an interaction is the difference between the rewards and the costs. If the costs are greater than the rewards, our outcome is negative. If the rewards are greater than the costs, our outcome is positive. One of the basic positions of social exchange theory is that we are attracted to relationships that earn us the greatest positive outcome.

This may seem like a crass way to view social relationships, but it does point out that we want to be with people who will reward us. For example, it has been suggested (Levinger, 1983) that many people consider the gains and losses in deciding who to marry. While social exchange theory may seem to equate the way we choose friends with the way we choose grocery stores, there is an important difference to remember. As can be seen from the above discussion, the economics of interpersonal relationships is not measured in terms of dollars and cents. Rewards in relationships can come in many forms, and what is valuable to a person at one time may not be so valuable at another time.

Aronson and Linder (1965) demonstrated this latter point in a clever experiment. They had a subject hold a conversation with another person. The subject didn't know that this person was a confederate working for the experimenter. Later the subject was given the opportunity to "overhear" the confederate talking to the experimenter on a number of separate occasions. The topic of their conversations was the confederate's evaluation of the subject. Unknown to the subject, the conversations were preplanned, and the sequence of positive reward in them was varied. Some subjects, in the positive-positive condition, heard the confederate begin by making positive statements about the subject and continue making these positive statements throughout the series of conversations. In the negative-negative condition, the confederate began making derogatory statements about the subject and continued making these statements throughout. In the negative-positive condition, the confederate began making negative statements about the subject, but the remarks became increasingly positive as the conversation continued. In the positive-negative condition, the subject heard the confederate make positive statements about her, but the statements subsequently became increasingly negative. After the subject had "overheard" the conversation, the experimenter asked her to rate how much she was attracted to the other person.

In what condition do you think the subject's attraction to the other person was highest? The subject was most attracted to the confederate when she began with negative comments but switched to positive ones. Interestingly, the number of positive statements (reward) was smaller in this condition than in the positive-positive condition. Also, it can be seen that the confederate was considered least attractive when she began with positive statements but later switched to negative ones. Aronson and Linder call this process the *gain-loss phenomenon of attraction*. Supposedly, a need for positive reward was created when the confederate began with negative statements. When she then switched to positive statements, she was fulfilling the subject's need. In the positive-positive condition, the subject did not have such a strong need for positive reward.

The results of the Aronson and Linder study make the point that the value of a reward in a relationship is determined by many things, among them, the needs of the person being rewarded, any previous interaction between the two people, and other possible relationships the person could choose to be in. This study also shows that we will not necessarily win friends by indiscriminantly giving others rewards. It is important that we be sensitive to the situation and the needs of others in deciding what value others will place on our actions.

Before leaving the topic of rewards, we want to offer encouragement to the individual who may feel that he or she has nothing particularly rewarding to offer that "special person." Is such an individual doomed to a life of unpopularity? According to Lott and Lott (1974) there is hope for such a person because we are attracted not only to people who directly reward us, but also to those who are associated with rewards. For example, Griffitt and Guay (1969) administered either a reward or a punishment to a subject when a bystander was present. Even though the bystander had nothing to do with the reward or the punishment, subjects tended to like him when they had been rewarded and dislike him when they had been punished. Thus simply being present when others are rewarded may increase our attractiveness to them. Again, we can see the applicability of this principle in the Johnny Cash story. Because June Carter was touring with the group, she was present when Johnny received the wild ovations from crowds after a concert and when he read the enthusiastic reviews in the newspapers. It is possible that her mere presence when Johnny was rewarded increased Cash's attraction to her. Thus, if you're down to your last dime (or word of praise), you still may be able to make yourself attractive to people simply by being present when good things happen to them.

Similarity

One of the most striking aspects of Johnny Cash and June Carter's relationship is the similarity of the two. Both came from very religious families. Both loved and wrote country music and had aspirations in the country music field. When they met, Johnny and June had lived similar lives, spending a great deal of time, for many years, traveling and performing. They had many friends in common and had traveled many of the same tours.

The situation with Johnny and his first wife was very different. Vivian was a devout Catholic, while Johnny's roots were in a fundamentalist Protestant background. Vivian was not particularly fond of country music and was not a performer. Her desires were very different from Johnny's; she wanted to settle in one place and raise a family, while he was strongly committed to his music and his dream of fame.

Recent research on attraction would allow us to predict that Johnny and June would be attracted to each other, while a relationship between Johnny and Vivian would be more unlikely. In short, research has shown that *similarity leads to attraction*. This rule seems to hold almost regardless of the dimension on which the similarity occurs. While the **similarity-attraction** effect seems to be strongest with regard to attitudes, research has also shown that we are attracted to people who come from backgrounds similar to our own, who are in a similar economic bracket, who have similar abilities, and who even have similar physical characteristics (for example, short people are often attracted to short people).

Similarity is clearly not the only dimension that leads to interpersonal attraction, and there are qualifying aspects to the relationship between similarity and attraction. For example, the importance of the dimension on which the

Similarity generally leads to attraction. We also assume that similar others will like us.

Matusow. Monkmeyer.

similarity occurs influences attraction. We are more attracted to others who are similar to us on important dimensions than to those who are similar on less important dimensions. For example, if you have very strong interests in politics, you will be more attracted to someone who holds similar political attitudes than to someone who holds similar attitudes about a less important topic (for example, about whether a Ford or a Plymouth is a better automobile).

The dimension that is important may vary from one individual to another, however. For example, Touhey (1972) asked subjects for their attitudes about religion and sex. Then under the guise of a computer dating format, he matched some couples by religious attitudes and others by sexual attitudes. He also mismatched other couples on these dimensions. After the couples had been on their dates, he measured interpersonal attraction. While he found greater interpersonal attraction in matched than in mismatched couples, he found that males were more attracted to females who had similar attitudes about sex than to females who had similar attitudes about religion. On the other hand, females were more attracted to males who had similar attitudes about religion than to those who had similar attitudes about sex. It seems that in this case sexual attitudes were

more important for males, while attitudes about religion were more important for females. Thus one way to enhance our attractiveness to another person is to accentuate our similarity to the other, especially on important dimensions.

Knowing the similarity-attraction relationship exists is only half the battle; it is also important to understand why it exists. Why should you be attracted to someone who holds attitudes similar to yours or who drives an automobile similar to yours? There seem to be a number of reasons for this relationship. First, we often assume that others who are similar to us will like us. Since we enjoy being liked, we are attracted to those we expect to like us. Another reason is that similar others often validate our opinions or actions, and this validation may be very rewarding. Johnny Cash was determined to "make it big" in the country music world. He went through many hardships to break into that world, and he was often criticized by others, including his family, for his desire. He probably questioned the wisdom of his desire sometimes too. However, when he was around others who had the same goals and who had made similar sacrifices, like June Carter, he could receive assurances that his own actions were not so crazy or unusual. These similar others encouraged Johnny and supported his actions. This support was very gratifying, and hence he was attracted to those he felt would offer him support. A third reason for similarity-attraction is that we expect to enjoy the company of others who have similar interests and abilities. In Johnny Cash's case, he knew he could sing songs and discuss country music with other country singers. He enjoyed doing this and therefore sought out the company of those other singers. He would have had less to discuss with a person whose main interest was nuclear physics or world banking practices.

While similarity often leads to attraction, we also find cases in which individuals are attracted to others who are different from them. We have all probably seen instances in which an older person marries a younger person or a relatively meek individual has an overbearing spouse. We probably all have friends who have backgrounds or interests different from our own. In many cases, these examples of **complementarity** exist when individuals are able to satisfy each other's needs. For example, an older man may be attracted to a younger woman because she satisfies his need to view himself as still possessing youth and being attractive to younger people. On the other hand, the older man may fulfill the security or stability needs of his younger friend. Thus, while the similarity-attraction relationship will be found in most cases, the complementarity-attraction phenomenon may be found when individuals' personal needs are better satisfied by the coupling of opposites.

When Doing for Others Leads to Attraction

It is very easy to see why we like people who reward us and do favors for us. Thus it is easy to see why Johnny Cash was attracted to June Carter. She cared for him and helped nurse him through his drug addiction. While this is understandable, June's attraction to Johnny is not so easy to comprehend. Johnny was often unkind to June, and he made it hard for her to be nice to him. June was generally on the giving end and rarely on the receiving end when it came to favors or rewards. June had to fight Johnny's moods, his drugs, and his arroagance in her effort to be kind to him. However, the more she did for him, the more she came to like him.

At first glance we might be tempted to question June's sanity. Was she a masochist or someone who enjoyed wrangling with "hard luck cases"? Was her attraction for Johnny unusual, following no predictable pattern? Not at all.

Cognitive dissonance theory hypothesizes that individuals attempt to keep their attitudes consistent with their behavior. It's consistent for an individual to like someone he or she has done a favor. A dissonant relationship between attitudes and behavior would result if the individual were to say, "I did a favor for someone I dislike." Thus, dissonance theory suggests that we like people *because* we do favors for them. The theory also hypothesizes that the bigger the favor is, the more we should

---

REVIEW QUESTIONS

6. In signaling our attraction for others, we may look at them more and touch them more. These channels of communication are called _____.

7. T or F: Nonverbal communication is primarily conscious.

8. Liking those who are familiar to us and who are in the position to reward us may be reasons why _____often leads to attraction.

9. The theory which views social relationships in terms of the costs and rewards is called _____.

10. Aronson and Linder found in their experiment that subjects were most attracted to the confederate when he/she heard the confederate begin with negative statements about the subject but end with positive statements. The subject was least attracted to the confederate when the reverse occurred. Aronson and Linder called this process the _____ _____of attraction.

grow to like the other person. The reason for this tendency is what is called "effort justification": It is more dissonant to dislike someone we've done a large favor than to dislike someone we've done a small favor. Thus we like those things (and people) for whom we have suffered.

Jecker and Landy (1969) demonstrated this relationship between favors and liking in interpersonal attraction. They had subjects perform a concept-formation task. The experimenter behaved in a rude, unfriendly manner toward the subjects. In the course of the experiment, the subjects won either sixty cents or three dollars. After the experiment was over, the experimenter told subjects he was "running out of money" and requested that they give him back the money. Most subjects did return the money they had legitimately won. Later the subjects were asked to rate how much they liked the experimenter. The subjects who had returned three dollars liked the experimenter more than those who had returned only sixty cents. The former group had done a larger favor for the experimenter than the latter group had.

Thus, while we like people who do favors for us, we also like people because we do favors for them. In June Carter's case it is possible that she actually came to like Johnny Cash more because she did favors for him. Many of these favors were difficult and were carried out in unrewarding situations. June's attraction for Johnny may not have been "craziness," but it may have been the result of dissonance reduction.

Physical Attractiveness

One of the lessons that most of us were taught by our grandmothers (or some other wise matriarch) is that "you can't judge a book by its cover." Most of us were probably also cautioned that "beauty's only skin deep." The major thrust of this advice is that we shouldn't let an individual's looks determine our attraction for that person. Most of us would probably agree that physical attractiveness *should not* be a major factor in interpersonal attraction. In

light of this, it is staggering that Americans spend over $3 billion a year on "beauty aids." In fact, some people spend more on such beauty aids than they do on food! A walk through the local drugstore reveals such marvels as false eyelashes, hair dyes, wigs, hair sprays, perfumes, after-shave lotions, deodorants, vitamins to inhibit acne, special soaps to wash away pimples and give "soft skin," lipstick, rouge, and almost every conceivable color of "paint" to be put on the face or the eyelids. In the grocery store we are offered diet foods to slim our bodies or other foods to "put on weight in the right places." If we are wealthy enough, we can have our doctors "lift our faces," remove excess fat from our midsections, or add silicone to increase the size of our busts. Our television advertisements are permeated with the idea that "beauty is good" and we must "stamp out ugliness." In essence, despite cautions from the wise, Americans are preoccupied with beauty.

Can beauty buy attraction? Can skinny Bob get more friends by building his muscles and wearing tailored clothes? Can shy Sue gain popularity by dying her hair blond, painting her face, and wearing contact lenses instead of glasses? Surprisingly enough, the answer to these questions seems to be yes: Physical beauty does lead to interpersonal attraction.

Physical attractiveness has a number of effects on our social interactions and perceptions. Over all, we are attracted to physically attractive people, but the effects of this concern with appearances are much greater than simply making us want to be with those who are beautiful or handsome. Research shows that physically attractive people are rated as being more sensitive, kind, exciting, sociable, and poised than unattractive people. The view that "good-looking is good" has a number of effects on behavior. For example, research suggests that for many crimes an attractive defendant will be given a less severe sentence than an unattractive defendant will be given (Landy & Aronson, 1969). Even children rate the misdeeds of attractive people as being less "bad" than the same misdeeds committed by an unattractive person. The work of an attractive person is rated as being better than the same work performed by an unattractive person (Landy & Sigall, 1974). Given a choice between two equally qualified applicants, interviewers are more likely to choose the attractive person than the unattractive person for the job (Dipboye et al., 1977).

Physical attractiveness has an interesting effect on *heterosexual behavior*. Research has shown that people *desire* to date the most attractive person possible; but when given the opportunity to actually *choose* a date, people tend to choose someone of attractiveness nearly equal to their own (Berscheid et al., 1971). It seems that while people desire a very attractive partner, they temper their actual choices with realism. They're afraid of being rejected by people who are much more good-looking than they are and therefore choose a person whose looks are about on par with their own and thus who is less likely to reject them.

This overwhelming emphasis on attractiveness gives us reason to pause. Why should physical appearance be the key that opens so many doors? There seem to be a number of reasons for our preoccupation with physical appearance. First, research suggests that attractiveness "rubs off" on others. For example, it has been found that people are rated by observers as being more attractive when they are seen with an attractive partner than when they are seen with an unattractive partner (Kernis & Wheeler, 1981). In other words, attractiveness seems to have a "halo effect"; our own status is enhanced if we are seen associating with attractive people.

People also tend to see themselves as being more similar to attractive people than to unattractive people. In one study (Marks et al., 1981), subjects were shown a number of pictures and asked to rate how similar they were to the people in the pictures. There was a tendency for the subjects to report themselves as being similar to the more attractive people. As we discussed earlier, there is a strong relationship between similarity and attraction.

Finally, attractive people may well be more socially skilled and have more pleasing personalities. In other words, there may be

some truth to the relationship between physical attractiveness and "goodness." This relationship may be easier to understand if we think of the lives of an attractive child and an unattractive child. The attractive child is likely to be the center of attention (Hatfield & Sprecher, 1983). His or her parents are likely to buy that child nice clothing and place him or her in social situations. Through being "shown off" the child will have numerous opportunities to interact with others, develop social skills, and develop a positive self-image. On the other hand, the parents of the unattractive child may not give that child the same opportunities. He or she will not be pushed to center stage and "shown off" to the same extent as the attractive child is. So this child's self-concept and social skills will not develop in the same way as those of the attractive child.

Johnny Cash's song "A Boy Named Sue" illustrates this point. A boy's father named him Sue, then left the family. The boy was teased about his name and, without a father to stand up for him, became a tough fighter to protect himself from such kidding. He's always hated his father for naming him Sue. The boy goes looking for his father, intending to kill him. But when he finds his father, his father points out that it was the unusual name that shaped the boy's personality and prepared him for an independent life. In a similar way, our physical appearance may influence our self-concept and personality.

The data on physical attractiveness suggest at least two important points. First, if you are looking for a formula to increase your attractiveness to others, one factor to consider is your physical appearance. Unfortunately, people do judge the book by its cover, and the way you look will influence how much people like you. There is some agreement on what characteristics are physically attractive. Tall men seem to be viewed as more attractive than short men. In general men prefer women with medium-sized legs and breasts (Wiggins et al., 1978). Smiling, eye contact, and straight posture are considered physically attractive in both men and women. Beyond these general characteristics, however, there is no complete agreement about what is physically attractive. So we can't make a list of steps you should take to become certifiably "beautiful" or "handsome."

The second point is that we should be careful not to be "blinded by what we see." Research clearly shows that our judgments about individuals and their actions are affected by their physical attractiveness even when this is an irrelevant factor (Efran, 1974). Unfair and unwise judgments often result. Hence we must be careful to determine that we are using relevant variables to judge people and to guide our attraction to them.

Self-Esteem

We have examined a number of variables that influence who will be attractive to us. For the most part these variables could be divided into situations (proximity) and actions/characteristics of the other person (reward, similarity, favors, and physical attractiveness). But just as beauty is often in the eye of the beholder, so too are the seeds of attraction. That is, our own characteristics influence who will be attractive to us and when we are most likely to be attracted to other people.

At the time Johnny Cash and June Carter began their relationship, both had recently experienced some hard times. Johnny was heavily into the use of drugs, he was the target of criticism because of his numerous missed engagements, he had been expelled from the Grand Ole Opry, and he was in the process of being divorced by his wife. He had many doubts about his worth as a person, and it would be an understatement to say that his self-esteem was very low. June too had recently gone through a divorce, and she was struggling to make her own name in music. Much of her musical acclaim had come from being part of the Carter Family singing group headed by Mother Maybelle. At times June questioned whether she would be a popular singer on her own.

There is wide recognition, both in scientific psychology and in "folk" psychology, that our **self-esteem** affects our attraction to others: We are more apt to be attracted to others when our self-esteem is low than when it is high. Many a parent has cautioned a child against rushing into a new relationship immediately after ending an old one. The concern is that being "on the rebound" is likely to lead to taking the first person who comes along, rather than to being patient and exercising good judgment in choosing an object for one's affections.

This fear is well founded. Walster (1965) found that women whose self-esteem had been lowered were more attracted to a male experimental confederate than were females whose self-esteem was high. In another study, Walster et al. (1972), found that individuals who had high self-esteem were more demanding and expected more from their dates than was true of individuals who had lower self-esteem. It seems that people with lower self-esteem have a greater need to be accepted by others. Hence people with low self-esteem are likely to seek

People with high self-esteem tend to be more demanding and expect more from others around them than do people with low self-esteem.

M. E. Warren, Photo Researchers, Inc.

out others who will reward them and to be very accepting of anyone who does offer rewards and acceptance. As we pointed out earlier, our needs define what we will view as a reward. Thus a friendly smile or word will be more likely to be seen as rewarding by a person with low self-esteem who has great need for acceptance than by a person with high self-esteem who does not have this strong need.

In spite of the fact that the person with high self-esteem has a less strong need for rewards from others, such an individual often faces a difficult problem. A person with high self-esteem is often one who has some degree of high status in the social world. When others give him or her praise, is the praise genuine, or is the praiser simply trying to get something in return? Because the person with high self-esteem and high social status does have something that others want, it is very likely that the praise is simply an attempt at **ingratiation** (Jones, 1964), not an expression of the other's true beliefs. Individuals with low social status do not face this dilemma; they have little that others want, so there is no need to be concerned about attempts at ingratiation. Thus people with low self-esteem are more likely to accept another's praise as genuine than are people with high self-esteem.

The Johnny Cash—June Carter relationship was probably more authentic by the temporary states of low self-esteem that both of them were experiencing. They both had strong needs to be accepted, and these needs made them both more vigilant toward and more vulnerable to each other's reinforcement.

This discussion should alert us to the need to work for a better understanding in our own lives of our reasons for being attracted to others. Are we simply attracted to someone because of our own temporary need to bolster our self-esteem? Are we so suspicious of ingratiation that we automatically reject praise and thereby erect walls that inhibit our relationships? It is important for us to understand how our self-esteem can affect our relationships, and it is also important that we not let our own self-esteem be the only factor guiding these relationships.

CATCHING THEIR EYE: THEN WHAT?

Groucho Marx used to joke, "Any club that would have me is not worth belonging to." Some people seem to adopt this point of view in their personal relationships: "Anyone who's attracted to me, I'm not attracted to." Advice based on this kind of attitude was given to most of us by our parents or other coaches when we began to seek out social relationships. In most cases, we were cautioned, "Don't appear too eager," or "Play hard-to-get."

Whether by design or by circumstance, Johnny Cash played "hard-to-get" when he first met June. He avoided her and at times even hid from her. Yet she ended up "getting" him. Does this mean the hard-to-get approach is a smart way of inviting attraction?

As it turns out, the answer to this question is not a clear yes or a clear no. Walster et al. (1973) designed a number of studies where a woman acted either "hard" or "easy" to get. The situations ranged from dates to interactions between a prostitute and her client. The con-

---

REVIEW QUESTIONS

11. The theory which predicts we will be attracted to those for whom we do large favors is called _____.
12. One reason why physical attractiveness leads to interpersonal attraction is that people see themselves as being more _____ to attractive people than to unattractive people.
13. Attraction to others due to strong needs for rewards is more likely to be found in those with low _____.
14. A person with high self-esteem may be likely to suspect someone who praises him or her of _____.
15. T or F: Walster and her colleagues found that males were most attracted to women who were hard-to-get for others but easy-to-get for themselves.

clusion was that playing hard-to-get did not increase attractiveness. However, men were most attracted to women who were hard-to-get for others but easy-to-get for themselves. A woman who always played hard-to-get was rejected as being unattainable, and a woman who was always easy-to-get was viewed as undiscriminating. But a woman who rejected everybody else was seen by the man she accepted as being choosy and showing good taste. It seems that we are attracted to people who treat us as if we are "special." These data may explain why exclusive relationships are so important to many of us. In an exclusive relationship, someone is telling us that we are special by rejecting all others.

INTERPERSONAL ATTRACTION: SOME CONCLUSIONS

We can learn a number of lessons from this discussion of attraction. The first is that we are attracted to others for a variety of reasons and that they are attracted to us for an equally wide variety of reasons. Often we may get confused by our liking for a person. We may say to ourselves, "I can't understand why I like that person. We're so different." However, we have seen that similarity is only one of many reasons why we like people. An understanding of the reasons for attraction may make us more ac-

cepting of our attraction to others and their attraction to us.

Another point to remember is that there are some aspects of ourselves or some types of behavior that we can emphasize to increase our desirability for others. For example, we should be aware of the needs of others and know that they will want more reinforcement at some times than at others. This is not to say that we should invent or manufacture kindness when we don't feel it. Genuineness and openness in interpersonal relations should be a constant goal. However, it is important to be sensitive to the needs of the other person in a relationship while working to achieve this genuineness.

Finally, this discussion may shed some light on the reasons why we aren't attracted to others or they aren't attracted to us. At times we may be in a position where we feel we are doing everything possible to attract another person, but it isn't "working." We may interpret this rejection as a reflection on our own worth and abilities, which may have serious negative consequences for our self-esteem. We should know, however, that the interpersonal attraction process is many-faceted and determined by the characteristics of both individuals in the interaction, by the nature of the present situation, and by the past histories and needs of the two participants. So to assume the blame for the failure of a relationship is unwise and clearly not in line with what we have learned about interpersonal attraction.

SUMMARY

1. People are social animals who need to be with other people. Most of us spend the majority of our waking hours with other people. Most people find long periods of social isolation to be unpleasant and depressing.

2. Loneliness results when people erect mental barriers to wall themselves off from others or when they are afraid or unable to break down existing barriers. The most important factor in loneliness is having no close companion in whom to confide.

3. Privacy involves a person's freedom to choose what to communicate to whom and under what circumstances. Privacy allows us the opportunity for emotional release; it also gives us the opportunity to control our environment and to reflect upon ourselves.

4. Affiliation, or connection with other people, is a basic human need. The ways we affiliate with others are influenced by sex roles, emotional states, and our need for other people to help us perform certain activities, reward us, evaluate us, and comfort us.

5. We express attraction to others through verbal and nonverbal channels. Nonverbal communication includes facial expression, eye contact, touching, and maintaining interpersonal distance.

6. We are attracted to certain people for a number of reasons.

7. Physical proximity increases a person's attractiveness to us. We tend to like people we are physically close to and spend a lot of time with.

8. We are attracted to relationships we expect to have the greatest positive outcome. Social exchange theory views relationships in economic terms, people weigh the possible costs and rewards of a relationship to determine the likely outcome.

9. Similarity can lead to attraction between people. Research shows that we tend to be attracted to people who are similar to us in attitudes, background, physical characteristics, economic condition, and experience. Sometimes we're attracted to people who are different from us because they complement us and satisfy our needs.

10. We are often attracted to people for whom we do favors and expend effort. Cognitive dissonance theory explains this in terms of people wanting to keep their feelings consistent with their behavior.

11. We tend to be attracted to good-looking people and to equate physical attractiveness with sensitivity, kindness, being exciting, and being sociable.

12. We are more likely to be attracted to others when our self-esteem is low than when our self-esteem is high. At such times we tend to be attracted to people with high self-esteem. People with high-esteem, and therefore high social status, often face the dilemma of deciding whether others' interest and kindness is genuine or aimed at ingratiating the high-status person.

13. We are often attracted to people who seem hard-to-get for others but easy-to-get for ourselves.

KEY TERMS

a. AFFILIATION
b. COGNITIVE DISSONANCE
c. COMPLEMENTARITY
d. INGRATIATION
e. INTERPERSONAL DISTANCE
f. LONELINESS

g. NONVERBAL COMMUNICATION
h. PRIVACY
i. PROXIMITY
j. SELF-ESTEEM
k. SIMILARITY-ATTRACTION
l. SOCIAL EXCHANGE THEORY

1. One person's geographical closeness to another person; an important factor in influencing interpersonal attraction
2. The distance people keep between themselves and others when interacting
3. The theory that views social relationships in economic terms such as inputs, costs, and outcomes
4. Being close or interacting with other people
5. Attempts by an individual to enchance his or her image in the eyes of another by expressing attitudes that he or she thinks the other person wants to hear

6. Finding that people are attractive to others who have attitudes, appearance, background, or desires in common

7. Sending messages through body language rather than speech

8. The degree to which one likes and respects oneself

9. A state of mental stress and anxiety that results when people either erect mental barriers to wall themselves off from others or are afraid to break down existing barriers

10. (a) A relationship among cognitions such that one cognition follows from the opposite of another; or (b) a feeling of discomfort resulting from inconsistent thoughts

11. Chosen social isolation

12. Having opposite but congruent needs

ANSWERS TO REVIEW QUESTIONS

1. Loneliness. 2. Privacy. 3. Affiliation. 4. True. 5. Reward; evaluate ourselves.

6. Nonverbal channels. 7. False. 8. Proximity. 9. Social exchange theory. 10. Gain-loss phenomenon.

11. Cognitive-dissonance theory. 12. Similar. 13. Self-esteem. 14. Ingratiation. 15. False.

11 LOVE AND INTIMACY

I n March 1981, at the beginning of a traditional ceremony honoring subjects of the British Commonwealth, the lord chamberlain to Queen Elizabeth II quieted the throng of observers at Buckingham Palace. He smiled and said, "The Queen has asked me to let you know that an announcement is being made this morning." After a pause he went on, "It is with the greatest pleasure that the Queen and Duke of Edinburgh announce the betrothal of their beloved son, the Prince of Wales, to the Lady Diana Spencer." There was applause, the popping of champagne corks, music by the Coldstream Guards, and the firing of congratulatory salvos from the HMS Bronington in Portsmouth Harbor. Charles, Prince of Wales and heir to the throne of England, had at age 32 finally chosen his bride, the 19-year-old Lady Diana Spencer. She was the first Englishwoman to be engaged to a Prince of Wales in more than 300 years. The entire country celebrated the announcement.

Although the next day's headlines reflected the country's jubilation over the engagement, the English press may have felt a little rueful as well. For years popular newspapers had been boosting their circulations with the latest in an endless series of "revelations" about who Prince Charles would marry. Nearly every time Charles was seen with a woman in public the papers raged with speculation that she was "the one!" There had been considerable speculation about Diana herself of course, and Charles's parents had rather forcefully encouraged him to make his decision. His mother, Queen Elizabeth II, reportedly told him, "The idea of this romance going on for another year is intolerable to everyone concerned," and his father, Prince Philip, reportedly said, "You better get on with it or there won't be anyone left" (Wallis, 1981; Deming, 1981).

Indeed, many young women had come into Charles's limelight during the preceding ten years, and all of them were done in by press speculation, family objections, or Charles's own reluctance. Princess Marie Astrid of Luxembourg seemed to be the official favorite for some time, but she was a Catholic, and the law would have had to be changed for Charles, as future king and therefore future head of the Church of England, to marry Astrid. Another woman who had seemed to be seriously in the running for the title of Princess of Wales was Davina Sheffield. But she and Prince Charles were highly embarrassed when Davina's ex-boyfriend revealed intimate secrets of Davina's and his lives together, including the fact of their sexual relationship. Other women figured prominently in newspaper speculations from time to time, but for one reason or another they all fell by the wayside.

Why, then, did Charles finally settle on Diana? Was it love, or was it simply that Diana met the stringent standards his family, position, and background set for her? Diana herself answered a reporter's question about whether they were in love by saying, "Of course." Charles clouded the matter by adding, "Whatever 'in love' means." The couple certainly appeared to be in love when they met the press and were photographed during their engagement, and Lady Diana Spencer clearly satisfied all the principal requirements for a Princess of Wales. She was a member of the nobility herself, and her family had an impressive history. Diana was a descendant of the seventeenth-century Stuart king, Charles II, one of the few English monarchs who wasn't an ancestor of the future King Charles III. The Spencers had been close to the royal family for many years, the Queen herself being godmother to Diana's younger brother.

In addition, Diana's personality and appearance completely captivated the English public, and they apparently engaged Charles in the same way. He remembers meeting her when she was 16, while on a hunt with Diana's sister, Sarah, one of Charles's earlier interests. Charles was struck by "what a very amusing and jolly—and attractive—16-year-old she was." Her father, Earl Spencer, recalls with a grin that Diana at birth was a "superb physical specimen." Thus Diana would be a perfect Princess of Wales in terms of family background, attractiveness, personality, and health. And her interests in athletics, children, and the outdoors fit Charles's inclinations beautifully.

Two other aspects of Diana's behavior were crucial to her acceptance by Charles's family. First, unlike Davina Sheffield, Diana was "a girl without a past." One commentator who noted the importance of this fact added that "there aren't that many 19-year-old virgins available" (Deming, 1981). In addition to showing that her past behavior measured up to royal standards, Diana had to prove herself in the present after the press began to suspect romance between Charles and herself. Diana was constantly pursued and harassed by reporters and photographers, and this trial-by-fire proved her mettle. She responded to the press with cleverness and good humor, she showed she could parry with reporters, and she demonstrated that she could stand up to the glare of publicity that would follow her all her days as Princess of Wales. The press got the better of Diana only once, when photographers maneuvered her into a pose where the sun shone through her diaphanous skirt, revealing her legs and hips in sharp outline. Even this embarrassing incident blew over easily, and Diana later asserted her own taste and poise, despite some raised eyebrows, when she wore to an official function a dress more stylish and revealing than Charles's mother would have chosen.

Once Diana had proved herself, the engagement was announced, and all England impatiently waited four months for the royal wedding, which was certainly "the event of the year." Diana, in a very romantic wedding gown, rode in a glass coach to St. Paul's Cathedral, where the ceremony was held in front of 21 television cameras and an audience all over the world estimated at 750 million. In the United States, people on the East Coast woke up at five in the morning to watch Diana's ride to the cathedral and the wedding itself. West Coast viewers had to get up three hours earlier to watch the festivities, and many did. Security was tight all along the procession routes, but the large and elated London crowds, including thousands of summer tourists, were on their best behavior. The strain of the occasion showed only when both Diana and Charles made verbal slips in speaking their wedding vows. The wedding was a splendid celebration for all of England.

Some people wondered how genuinely in love Charles and Diana could be, given the impossibility of their having a long courtship and the strain of being constantly in the public eye. One writer noted that Charles and Diana seemed to have spent very little time together and suggested that when Charles left on a five-week trip to Australia during their engagement, absence made the heart grow fonder. This observer felt that the marriage would become, though it might not have been from the start, ''a genuine love match'' (Cocks, 1981).

Charles and Diana appeared to be in love at their wedding, on their honeymoon stop at Gibraltar, and when they

Many people in North America got up before sunrise to watch the wedding of Prince Charles and Lady Diana on television.
UPI/Bettmann Archive.

returned to Balmoral, the royal estate in Scotland where they spent many of their first married days. Interviewed shortly after their honeymoon at Balmoral, Diana indicated that she ''highly recommended'' married life. Shortly thereafter, Buckingham Palace announced that the Princess of Wales was expecting a baby, and Prince William was born in 1982. He is, after his father, second in line to the British throne, and many of us may someday see William crowned king of England. A second child was expected at the time this book went to press.

All in all, Charles and Diana's relationship seems to be a great success. In a time of some controversy about the British monarchy, Diana has captured the hearts of the British people and enhanced the image of British royalty to a considerable degree. She has carried off the difficult role of Princess of Wales with great aplomb. Charles seems happier and more relaxed than he was before marriage. Queen Elizabeth was reported to have told close friends at the time of the engagement: ''Diana is a delightful girl. Charles could not find a more perfect partner.'' He seemed to agree completely, and so have millions of people around the world.

WHAT IS LOVE?

In lots of ways Prince Charles and Princess Diana's relationship seems like a fairy tale. Their storybook courtship and wedding, complete with a glass coach and a postnuptial kiss on the balcony of Buckingham Palace, satisfied many people's romantic ideals about love. But few real love affairs, even among royalty, end with ". . . and they lived happily ever after." Love and intimacy provide moments of great pleasure and great pain, and involve work as well as hearts and flowers. In this chapter we will examine love and intimate relationships, considering their satisfactions and their problems, and try to point out some of the more important aspects of a loving bond between two people.

First of all, what *is* **love,** and how is it different from liking? Zick Rubin (1973) has shown that liking is based in large part on feelings of respect, high regard, and similarity between yourself and the person you like. Loving may include these feelings of respect and perceived similarity, but it's also defined by more emotional reactions. As relationships develop we often wonder, "Do I love this person or just 'like them very much'?" Often couples will engage in lengthy discussions, attempting to decide whether they love each other or are simply very attracted to each other. Often a crisis is reached when one partner says that he or she is truly in love with the other, whereupon the question "How do you know you love me?" arises. This question may bring the partners to the realization that they don't really know what love is, or at least that they can't put it into words.

People shouldn't feel alone when they wonder whether or not they know what love is. A number of psychologists have attempted to define "love." Horton (1973) pointed out that the 1967 edition of the *Random House Dictionary* gave 24 definitions of "love" and only five definitions of "hate."

Rubin (1973) felt that love is made up of three components. The first is **caring,** the feeling that the other person's satisfactions and wellbeing are as important as your own. The second component is **attachment,** or the need to be with the other person and to be approved of by that person. The final component, **intimacy,** involves close and confidential communication.

In an effort to identify love more clearly, Rubin developed two scales, one to measure love and the other to measure liking. To determine if his scale did discriminate between these two concepts, Rubin asked each person in a dating couple to fill out the two scales in reference to his or her partner. He then asked the subjects to complete the same two scales with reference to a same-sexed friend. The results indicated that while friends and lovers were both well liked, only lovers scored high on the love scale.

Further work on love has focused on passionate or romantic love in particular. Passionate, romantic love is defined as a state of intense absorption in another person, longing for the partner, physiological arousal and feelings of ecstasy at having attained the other person's love, and a sense of complete fulfillment

Passionate love can be painful at times, but its joys are expected and sought out just the same.

Jan Lukas, Rapho/Photo Researchers, Inc.

as a result of having the relationship. This is the kind of feeling that Lady Diana seemed to reveal when she looked at Prince Charles and talked about him after their engagement. Charles was always somewhat more reserved in expressing his feelings about Diana, even when asked directly if he was in love with her.

There are three conditions that, taken together, give rise to feelings of passionate, romantic love (Walster & Walster, 1978). First, there must be a culturally based expectation of falling in love. Certainly in our lifetime the romantic ideal is alive and well, and we expect to fall in love in a romantic way. The royal wedding of Charles and Diana satisfied people's expectations about romantic love. Their relationship seemed to be a perfect example of such love, largely because Diana seemed so romantically in love and her charm led lots of the public to share her romantic feelings.

The second condition for falling in love is that the right person must come along to fulfill our expectation of the romantic ideal. Before Charles met Diana, the public wondered what kind of woman the "right person" would be for Charles, and whether she would meet their own standards of the romantic ideal as well as his. Obviously, she did. Having the expectation of falling in love and finding the right person leads many people to experience the feeling of "love at first sight." As soon as we meet someone who fits our ideal image we experience love. Half of all adult men and women report that they have experienced love at first sight (Berscheid & Walster, 1974). Charles and Diana have kept alive the expectation of love at first sight by talking romantically about their first impressions of each other. Diana said Charles was "pretty amazing." He said she was very attractive, amusing, jolly, and full of life. In one of their big hit songs, the English singing group, the Beatles, asked "Do you believe in a love at first sight?" Charles and Diana's royal love story helps people answer yes.

The third and final condition for feeling passionate, romantic love is physiological arousal that is *interpreted* as love. We saw in Chapter 4 how physiological arousal can be experienced as one of several emotions, depend-

Because of the expectation of experiencing romantic love, many people report that they fell in love at first sight.

Monique Manceau, Photo Researchers, Inc.

ing on the cues in the environment. Several studies show that arousal from other sources can be labeled as love and lead people to experience passionate feelings for potential romantic partners they encounter. In one study (Dutton & Aron, 1974) male subjects were interviewed after walking across a rickety, scary bridge or over a very solid one. The interviewer was an attractive female. The male subjects showed more romantic interest in her if they were physiologically aroused from crossing the dangerous bridge.

Romantic passion is strong and intense. It preoccupies us during the time we experience it. We have constant fantasies about our loved one. But this powerful emotion diminishes in intensity quickly and must develop into companionate, or mature, love if a relationship is to last. Companionate love is sometimes referred to as the warm afterglow of romantic passion; it's the affection we feel for those with whom our lives are intertwined. The lover may seem more like a friend, and the attachment is peaceful and tender. Let's consider some important aspects of love and then some of the stages of intimate relationships that may lead to mature, companionate love.

Love and Sex

The relationship between love and sex usually becomes an issue when people try to define love (see Chapter 12). Often love and sex are incorrectly talked about as if they're the same thing. Indeed, the phrase "making love" is often used to denote sexual intercourse, as Bob Dylan observed in his song, "Love Is Just a Four-Letter Word."

Sexual attraction and sexual relations do play an important part in love. As Rubin (1973) points out, intimacy is a component of love, and sexual intercourse is a medium of intimacy. According to Hull (1943), reproductive and sexual drives are basic to humans; so partners may fulfill each other's needs through the act of sexual intercourse. Thus tenderness and intimacy can be expressed through sexual behavior, and interpersonal needs can be filled through sexual union.

Clearly sexual behavior can be viewed as one component of love. But it's important not to identify sexual behavior as being love, or even an expression of love. Love isn't a necessary prerequisite for sex. People may have sex because it's a physical pleasure, or to express simple affection or momentary elation. And there are also less positive reasons for people's sexual behavior. As pointed out in Chapter 12, some use sexual behavior to express dominance or to assuage feelings of inadequacy. Others engage in sexual behavior because they feel that they must do so in order to be accepted by others or because they feel peer pressure because "everyone else is doing it."

Sexual intercourse is an act of interpersonal union. The meaning of the act is based on the context in which it's performed. If two people have sex to fulfill the needs of *both* of them in a caring and tender atmosphere, and if both partners have freely chosen to be sexual with each other, sex can increase interpersonal intimacy and foster love. Like other aspects of an intimate relationship, a good sexual connection requires practice and caring. The caring component of sexual behavior involves a consideration of the other's needs and the genuine desire to satisfy the other person's needs in addition to your own. If the partners aren't aware of each other's needs, or don't care about them, and engage in sexual behavior for self-gratification only, sexual behavior can inhibit a love relationship.

Learning to Love

It may come as a surprise to some, but research suggests that love isn't an emotion that comes naturally to everyone. Unfortunately, some people don't have the ability to experience love. Harry Harlow identified five stages of loving relationships (1971). The first is maternal love, the love of a mother for her child. Infant love, the love of the infant for its mother, is the second stage. Next is peer love, which is the love of a child or preadolescent for another child or preadolescent. The fourth stage is age-mate passion, which is sexual love, and the final stage is parental love, or the love of an adult male for his family. According to Harlow, our experiences at each stage prepare us for the next stage. For example, "age-mate experience is fundamental to the development of normal and natural heterosexual love" (1971, p. 4). If we are deprived of love at an early stage, we will have difficulty experiencing love at the later stages.

In a dramatic series of experiments with monkeys, Harlow demonstrated how crucial the early experience of love is to the ability to feel and express love later in life. Harlow removed some infant monkeys from their mothers shortly after birth. They were raised in isolation without maternal love, though they

Harlow's famous studies with monkeys showed that they craved intimate, loving contact as well as safety and nourishment.

University of Wisconsin Primate Laboratory.

were adequately cared for and fed by their human handler. Three months, six months, and two years later, these monkeys were introduced to other monkeys of their age, and the interactions were observed. Harlow found that the isolated monkeys couldn't form friendships or play with their age-mates. The longer the period of isolation had been, the more impoverished were the monkey's relationships. The isolated monkeys were also unable to engage in sexual behavior and weren't receptive to the sexual advances of other monkeys. In some cases, Harlow impregnated female isolated monkeys in an effort to study whether they could develop a loving relationship with their offspring. The results were most startling: These mothers not only failed to feed and care for their infants; they treated them brutally. The infants would have been killed had the experimenters not removed them from the care of their own mothers. Thus the failure of these isolated monkeys to experience love at the early stages of their development prevented them from being able to express peer love, age-mate passion, or maternal love at later stages in their lives.

Erich Fromm (1956) also points out that early experiences are important for the development of love. Fromm states that we must learn to love ourselves before we can love others. In loving ourselves we learn to foster our own growth and happiness, and we can then transfer this learning into the loving of others. According to Fromm, without learning these lessons, we can't truly know how to care about the happiness of others.

The important lesson to be learned from these theories is that our ability to love others is strongly affected by our own early experiences. Someone who is raised in an emotionally impoverished environment in which love is absent will have difficulty loving others later in life. We must learn how to love by experiencing love from others and practicing love on ourselves. People who have not had these opportunities may require therapy to help them "learn to love."

A true loving relationship takes time to develop. Each partner must learn about the other. Each must understand the needs of the other and learn how he or she can fulfill those needs. In order to do this, two people must work to develop open and honest communication with each other. The love relationship will continue to grow as long as the partners trust each other enough to disclose their emotions, hopes, aspirations, inadequacies, and feelings about each other (see Chapter 9). To the extent that this honest communication can be achieved, each person in the relationship will be able to experience personal growth. To reach these goals takes time.

A love relationship is complex and often delicate. In addition to learning to understand each other, the partners must learn to accept each other as individuals who are likely to have different needs and desires. Berscheid and Walster (1978) point up one of the dilemmas that often make love relationships fragile and lead to misunderstanding between partners: the conflict between feelings of dependency on the relationship and desire for independence. As the love relationship grows, each partner becomes more giving and, at the same time, receives more and more need fulfillment. On the one hand, it's great to have your needs satisfied by someone you love. On the other hand, this satisfaction itself often causes people to feel increasingly dependent on the relationship. Feeling dependent can be frightening, since it may seem to threaten the independence people also desire. The result of this conflict is that people may be afraid of falling in love or may begin to feel strong ambivalence about their intimate relationship.

These feelings are common in most love relationships, and it's important to discuss them. Too many times one of the partners may sense this ambivalence on the part of the other and interpret it as a sign of rejection. This then leads that person to withdraw from the relationship, and the love and trust is quickly destroyed. In order to avoid this problem, individuals in a relationship must respect, and even encourage, each other's independence. There must be room for individual growth within the relationship and a willingness to openly explore each other's feelings of ambivalence without immediately assuming that they are signs of rejection.

So love is an emotion that grows slowly into its mature forms and that requires practice and constant nurture. With proper attention, it can lead to tremendous happiness and satisfaction for the partners and result in a relationship that blends dependence and independence in a way that encourages both individual growth and growth of the relationship itself. The development of a loving relationship depends on the willingness of the partners to be truly accepting of each other and to discuss their feelings honestly.

Pitfalls in Love

We have pointed out that love is a fragile, complex emotion. Clearly Prince Charles and other members of the royal family in England were aware of this during the prolonged time Charles waited for just the right woman to come along. Charles had romances with various women, but they didn't last. The family was familiar with divorce, since the queen's sister, Princess Margaret, had been divorced herself. Perhaps Charles's awareness of the complexity and fragility of love led him to say "Whatever 'in love' means" when he was asked whether he was in love with Diana. He must have recognized that a number of common problems make it difficult to form and sustain a truly loving connection with another person.

People's problems in love often stem from a lack of self-understanding and self-acceptance, from communication that's less than honest, and from unrealistic expectations about what love "is supposed to be like." Some of these problems involve the way people behave at the beginning of a relationship. Taylor (1969) identified two self-defeating behaviors that often kill love before it begins.

First, some people go to great lengths to present their best front to prospective lovers. They attempt to appear always happy and kind and to inhibit feelings of anger or criticism, even though they feel them strongly. They go out of their way to do favors for others even though they may not genuinely feel like doing those favors. Once another person is "hooked" and falls in love, the pretender stops acting and expresses unhappy and unkind feelings such as anger and disappointment. The partner is taken by surprise and may openly express the impression that "you've changed since we met." The partner may feel deceived, and rightly so. The change may not necessarily be intentional, and deceit may not have been planned. Insecurity may have led the person to believe that no one could fall in love with him or her if they saw what he or she was really like. But a facade can be maintained only so long, and hidden emotions, such as anger, must begin to show. Also, the partner is likely to be upset by the other's unwillingness to be open at the beginning of the relationship, and this will dampen the feelings of love and trust.

A second self-defeating behavior involves taking the opposite role: People may present the worst sides of themselves to challenge others to love them at their worst. The feeling may be "If they can love me when they see my worst side only, then we should have an easy time later when I show my better qualities." Again, this tactic may be unintentional and may be motivated by the fear that no one could love them for what they're really like. So some people present the severest test to love at the beginning. The problem is that this behavior is likely to ensure that no one will love them. Certainly it is unfair to ask someone to fall in love with only our worst qualities. Upon seeing that others don't fall in love with them, these people confirm their worst fears: No one can fall in love with them. Essentially, they create a self-fulfilling prophecy. But, they fail to realize that they haven't really given others the opportunity to fall in love with their true selves; they have only shown that a conglomerate of their worst qualities is not love-inducing.

Both of these behaviors are dishonest and work against self-disclosure, which is one of the major prerequisites for fostering love. Clearly it's important to "be ourselves" in relationships. Only by acting honestly will we find love relationships that are enduring. It's important to realize that even if we behave in an open way, not everyone will "fall in love" with us. We won't satisfy the needs of everyone by being ourselves, but we will be more likely to discover those people whose needs we can satisfy and who can satisfy ours.

Another hazard to love relationships occurs when people fail to truly know themselves and don't clearly perceive the other person. We have pointed out that one of the major factors that lead people to fall in love is the desire to have their needs fulfilled and to help satisfy the needs of the other person. So it's important for people to know what their own needs are and to understand the needs of the other person. This is often a tall order, since we rarely take the time to look carefully at ourselves and determine what our own needs may be. And, as we pointed out in Chapter 10, it's often difficult to make accurate attributions about the needs or traits of others. But when we make an effort to identify our own needs and those of our partners, we often save ourselves a great deal of heartache in the long run.

Sometimes people enter relationships with needs their partners shouldn't really be expected to satisfy. If your self-esteem is low, for example, a love affair is likely to be only temporarily reassuring. We can kid ourselves about our motivations or use our relationships to solve problems in other areas of our lives. We've all heard of young people getting married as a way of running away from home. In Chapter 4 we discussed how parental interference may lead people to believe that they are in love. The interference causes physiological arousal, which is then attributed to love for the person the parents don't approve of. In such

---

HOW ROMANTIC ARE YOU?

Charles Hobart (1958) developed a questionnaire to measure how romantic people were during courtship. One of his interesting findings was that men had higher romanticism scores than women. You can get your own romanticism score by indicating whether you agree or disagree with each of the following statements. Agree answers to numbers 3, 5, 6, 7, 8, and 11 and disagree answers to 1, 2, 4, 9, 10, and 12 indicate romanticism. How do you score?

T F   1. Lovers ought to expect a certain amount of disillusionment after marriage.
T F   2. True love should be suppressed in cases where its existence conflicts with the prevailing standards of morality.
T F   3. To be truly in love is to be in love forever.
T F   4. The sweetly feminine "clinging vine" girl cannot compare with the capable and sympathetic girl as a sweetheart.
T F   5. As long as they at least love each other, two people should have no trouble getting along together in marriage.
T F   6. A girl should expect her sweetheart to be chivalrous on all occasions.
T F   7. A person should marry whomever he or she loves regardless of social position.
T F   8. Lovers should freely confess everything of personal significance to each other.
T F   9. Economic security should be carefully considered before selecting a marriage partner.
T F 10. Most of us could sincerely love any one of several people equally well.
T F 11. A lover without jealousy is hardly to be desired.
T F 12. One should not marry against the serious advice of one's parents.

Reprinted from *Social Forces* (Vol. 36, May 1958). "The Incidence of Romanticism during Courtship" by Charles W. Hobart. Copyright © The University of North Carolina Press.

cases, people may also intensify love relationships as a means of "getting back" at their parents for interfering or as a means of asserting and satisfying their need for independence. A similar problem results when people misidentify sex as love. Sexual behavior is arousing, and too often we misattribute this arousal to love. Sometimes we try to see more in a sexual relationship than is really there. Often if a person seriously attempted to identify his or her motivations for "falling in love," he or she would see that the feelings were based on rather temporary needs or unrealistic expectations and that the relationship would be unlikely to grow.

Berscheid and Walster (1978) identify yet another problem that many lovers face. We are raised in a society that glorifies romantic love. According to the majority of our television programs and even advertisements, true love means that lovers should become wildly excited and sexually aroused each time they see or think about each other. According to such programs, lovers should spend 90 percent of their waking hours thinking about each other, and the night should be devoted to passionate lovemaking. Many of us are captured by these stimuli and the lessons about love they promote. As a result we tend to idealize our lovers and our relationships. The intense passion in the early stages of romance certainly encourages such idealization. But Berscheid and Walster point out that the intense passion is a fleeting phenomenon that ebbs over time. To the extent that a person has idealized his or her lover and equates love with passion, disappointment will set in as passion diminishes. Hence, Berscheid and Walster caution against basing one's love on fantasy and idealization. Clearly, love is more than passion, and while the passion may diminish over time, love can grow. But it can only grow if we are able to recognize the difference between love and passion and deal with the ebb and flow of passion as only a part of the loving relationship.

Forming and Maintaining a Relationship

Charles and Diana had to begin and develop their relationship under circumstances very different from those most of us face. They had relatively little time to spend together before their wedding, and in talking about his difficult love life Charles told one reporter, "You can live with a girl before you marry her, but I can't. I've got to get it right from the word go."

How do people decide who they want to form a relationship with from all those who are initially available? And after a relationship begins, how does it blossom into an intimate relationship? How are intimate relationships maintained? Once people are married, how likely is it that they will stay married, and what are some of the things that pull marriages and other intimate relationships apart? In the rest of this chapter we will look at the major aspects of building an intimate relationship. The value of understanding intimate relationships is probably obvious. Since they are such an im-

---

REVIEW QUESTIONS

1. Although both love and liking may involve feelings of respect and perceptions of similarity, love is distinguished from liking by its strong _____ reaction.
2. Rubin believes that love consists of three components: caring, _____, and _____.
3. Several conditions together give rise to feelings of passionate love: the expectation of falling in love, meeting someone who fulfills our expectation of the romantic ideal, and _____ _____ that is interpreted as love.
4. Mature or _____ love is the warm afterglow of passionate love, the affection we feel for those with whom our lives are intertwined.
5. T or F: Harlow found that even isolated monkeys who did not experience nurturing were instinctually able to express agemate passion and maternal love later in life.

portant part of living and psychological adjustment, it is crucial that we explore them as fully as possible. Establishing intimate relationships is one of the most important steps in achieving happiness and successful personal adjustment. We hope the information in this chapter will be useful to you in understanding how relationships work and how they can be improved.

In discussing the development of relationships we will use some of the ideas of Thibaut and Kelley (1959), who outlined the stages of relationship development and some of the events that occur in each stage. There are four such stages: sampling, bargaining, commitment, and institutionalization.

Sampling refers to the process of looking over the possibilities and then deciding on a person with whom to attempt to form a relationship. It involves a quick "forecasting" of how satisfying a relationship with various people might be. It is based on a small amount of information, usually just watching or looking at other people, or possibly conversing with them at a superficial level.

The second stage of a relationship is called **bargaining.** This is the stage in which the relationship is actually built. During this phase people try to "negotiate" or work out mutually satisfying ways of interacting, although no formal bargaining actually takes place. This is the stage where two people get to know each other well and try to pattern a successful way of being together.

If the bargaining or building process is successful, two people might decide to make a **commitment** to each other. This may mean being best friends who can count on one another to spend time together and engage in mutually satisfying activities, or it may mean living together as exclusive partners in a complete adult relationship. A relationship in the commitment phase is clearly an intimate one.

The final stage of relationship development, **institutionalization,** is simply an extension of the commitment stage. In this final stage there is some formalization of the commitment. This may involve marriage, as in the case of Charles and Diana, or some other ritual or ceremony that more or less formally recognizes

the relationship as highly intimate and committed. One example of institutionalization is young boys and girls becoming "blood brothers" and "blood sisters" by pricking their fingers and letting their blood run together. We will consider each of these stages, with special emphasis on the process of initiating and building a relationship.

INITIATING A RELATIONSHIP: SAMPLING

Sampling, the initiating stage of a relationship, usually occurs when one person enters a crowded room, perhaps at a party, and looks at the other people in the room and decides who to approach and talk to or, after some initial conversation, who to try to contact later. Sampling can occur at parties, dances, and singles bars, as well as in offices, buses, and classrooms. We are all aware of this and govern our behavior accordingly. We try to present ourselves in a positive light and make a good first impression on other people. Thus sampling generally takes place in the context of self-presentation. We have learned a great deal about how self-presentation works from the sociologist Erving Goffman (1959).

Goffman suggests that we all try to control other people's impressions of us so that we can influence how they treat us to some extent. We usually do this by trying to present ourselves in a positive way. Specifically, Goffman says that in a first-impression situation, people often give what are called **idealized performances,** acting as if they support and conform to ideal standards of good conduct more than they actually do. For example, you might dress up for an interview with an industrial recruiter and say things to try to make the recruiter think that your life style and attitudes are more in accord with corporate philosophy than is really the case. Also, we often display magazines and books in our living rooms that may suggest better taste than we really have.

We are probably more aware of others

Parties, dances, and bars are places where men and women engage in the sampling stage of forming relationships.

Bill Bachman, Photo Researchers, Inc.

presenting themselves in an idealized way than we are of doing it ourselves. But there is an overwhelming tendency in human interaction not to challenge or contradict other people's idealized performances. Goffman says we act so that open contradiction seldom occurs. Instead we act as if we accept other people's presented or "projected" selves. If they claim they run six miles every morning, we commend them even if we doubt that it's true. This doesn't mean that we really agree with the image another person tries to project. We simply appear to accept and believe in someone's idealized performance. We suppress our true feelings and go along with the other person's act. In this way a working agreement is achieved, and people can conduct their business easily. Goffman claims that societies everywhere regulate people to behave in this way so that interaction can proceed smoothly, without fear of embarrassment or challenge.

Although we seldom openly challenge other people's idealized performances, we do make private judgments about how honest and straightforward they seem to be and to what extent they are inflating themselves and pretending to be something they aren't. We admire the person who seems to behave according to honest feelings and shows others exactly who he or she is.

Problems in the Sampling Stage

We face several problems during the sampling phase of interaction and in moving past it into more meaningful relationships. We've already discussed how "putting up a good front" can squelch possibilities for genuine intimacy. Ritualized self-presentation patterns make interaction very superficial. When two people pass each other and say "Hi. How are you?" and "Fine thanks. How are you?" they learn very little about each other. We often present only the part of ourselves that is "appropriate" to the situation and reveal very little of a personal nature. Under these circumstances, it can be very difficult to forecast accurately how much value any future interaction might have. We're forced to choose potential candidates for future relationships largely on the basis of appearance and first impressions. Furthermore, it can be very difficult to move a relationship beyond this superficial chat. If people are to develop relationships beyond formalities, they must open up a little more. This involves taking risks, but such risks are necessary if relationships are to grow.

Ritualized self-presentation was a special problem for Prince Charles. Especially during the several years before he married Lady Diana he realized that nearly every young woman he met might be trying to interest him in her and that she might be "on her good behavior." This made it hard for him to see past her "front" and decide whether she was the kind of woman with whom he might want to have an intimate relationship. In the case of Diana, Charles was able to see her from afar before she was concerned with attracting him. When she was younger she actually played with Charles's little brothers, and he observed how full of life she was. He also had a chance to observe the "real Diana" when he was dating her older sister, Sarah. In neither case did he have to worry about ideal performances. He could catch a glimpse of Diana as she really was. He didn't have this opportunity with all women, most of whom he saw only in a context where the possibility of an intimate relationship, and marriage, controlled their behavior.

Another serious problem in this early stage of relationship development can be *shyness*. Studies by Zimbardo (1977) and his colleagues show that shyness is a very common obstacle to forming relationships. Forty percent of the populations that Zimbardo studied in large surveys considered themselves to be shy, and more than 80 percent said that they had been shy at one time. Shyness, or "people phobia," as Zimbardo refers to it, manifests itself in physiological reactions (increased heart pounding and blushing), various thoughts and feelings (self-consciousness and concern about others' impressions), and overt behaviors such as being silent and avoiding eye contact. Shyness is so unpleasant that it can prevent people from interacting with others and cause them to suffer some serious losses as the result of diminished interpersonal contact.

We all find great rewards in being with other people. People who are shy are less likely to develop relationships and more likely to miss out on these rewards and satisfactions. They are also less likely than others to have close friends to draw on for social support in times of stress or crisis. Shy people may also have more difficulty in accurately appraising themselves, especially in appraising the seriousness of their shyness-related problems, because they have

Shyness can be a difficult problem to overcome in the early stages of a relationship.

Ed Lettau, Photo Researchers, Inc.

few people with whom they can compare themselves. In short, their relationships and interactions with others are limited, and so they lack the rewards, support, and comparison information that normally come from others.

What are the consequences of losing contact with others in these ways? Not surprisingly, there are indications that the personal adjustment of shy people suffers. They are more socially anxious, show more signs of being neurotic, show memory lapses in stressful situations, and are more easily influenced by others. They even have difficulties in their sexual adjustment. Zimbardo reports that shy people have fewer sexual contacts than nonshy people do and that they enjoy less those sexual contacts they do have. Shy people also show more

MEASURES RELATED SHYNESS

Psychologist Arnold Buss (1980) developed questionnaires that measured public self-consciousness and social anxiety. People who agree with the public self-consciousness statements tend to be concerned about their appearance and the impression they make on other people. These people also tend to have higher scores on social anxiety, a more direct measure of how shy, how easily embarrassed, and how anxious with other people someone is. You can get some idea of your own public self-consciousness and social anxiety by seeing how many of the statements in each group below you agree with.

Public self-consciousness:
1. I'm concerned about what other people think of me.
2. I usually worry about making a good impression.
3. I'm concerned about the way I present myself.
4. I'm self-conscious about the way I look.
5. I'm usually aware of my appearance.
6. One of the last things I do before leaving my house is look in the mirror.
7. I'm concerned about my style of doing things.

Social anxiety:
1. It takes me time to get over my shyness in new situations.
2. I get embarrassed easily.
3. Large groups make me nervous.
4. I find it hard to talk to strangers.
5. I feel anxious when I speak in front of a group.
6. I have trouble working when someone is watching me.

From *Self-Consciousness and Social Anxiety* by A. H. Buss. Copyright © 1980 by W. H. Freeman and Company.

dissatisfaction with their jobs and tend to feel "passed over."

Although shyness can be a serious problem in starting relationships and in interaction generally, it is a difficulty that can be overcome. Zimbardo reports that in his shyness clinic people are helped by various treatments. Some are helped to practice social skills such as smiling or making eye contact, some are helped to control anxiety through the use of relaxation techniques, and some are helped to improve their self-concepts through self-acceptance. You should consider exactly what forms your own shyness takes and how it might be alleviated.

BUILDING A RELATIONSHIP: BARGAINING

After you've made an initial judgment on the basis of sampling about who it might be worthwhile to get to know better, the relationship can begin in earnest. The postsampling phase may start with a telephone call asking for a date, a suggestion that you and the other person might enjoy playing tennis or skiing together, or simply the initiation of a more than casual conversation on the dance floor. It will usually be clear to both people that the relationship is entering a new stage.

Once the conversation, date, game, or stroll has started, and it's clear that both of you are interested in exploring the possibility of some kind of mutually satisfying relationship, bargaining can truly begin. This is the stage where people begin to "negotiate" with each other about what kind of relationship they might have. Each of you will have interests to promote, things you want from the relationship and that you will try to get, with the hope that some sort of accommodation can be reached that is satisfactory to both. Usually you will want the other person to behave in certain ways, and he or she will also have preferences about how you act. These preferred behaviors may involve working on certain tasks, adopting particular beliefs, solving difficult problems, or being attentive to important needs, including needs for companionship, protection, warmth, feeding, sex, and self-actualization. Prince Charles no doubt wanted Lady Diana to be loyal, understanding of the demands of royalty, and able to bear children. Diana had to be examined by royal physicians to assure all concerned that she would be able to be a royal mother. From Charles, Diana too would've wanted loyalty, as well as help in making the transition into royalty. She admitted that the jump would be "quite daunting," but she said with Charles beside her she couldn't go wrong.

We can see, in short, that each person in a relationship has things he or she wants from the other. The question then is how much each person will want to behave in the way the other prefers. Both people will probably be willing to do some things and unwilling to do others. The issue is whether a mutually satisfactory pattern of interaction, a successful accommodation, can be reached. Can the two of you work it out?

Self-Disclosure

One of the most important aspects of trying to work out a successful accommodation and building a rewarding relationship is self-disclosure. This means talking to the other person about your thoughts and feelings, your aspira-

Self-disclosure is a key aspect of getting to know someone well.

Chester Higgins, Jr., Photo Researchers, Inc.

tions and dreams, your fears and doubts. It may even involve talking about things you're ashamed of. Only through honest self-disclosure can people really learn about each other's needs and wishes for being together and begin to build a truly intimate relationship. Through this process people discover who their partners really are and come to love and respect them for who they are. Self-disclosure is a critical part of relationship building. It is closely related to the quality of relationships and to an individual's degree of personal adjustment.

SELF-DISCLOSURE AND PERSONAL ADJUSTMENT. One of the most important findings about self-disclosure is that it has a great impact on the self-disclosing person. Specifically, Jourard (1971) has suggested that the ability to talk about oneself to another person is a sign of psychological health and good adjustment. He believes that openness to other people is necessary for self-actualization and growth. Hiding oneself from others stunts our growth in a number of ways.

One result of keeping information about ourselves from others is that we never get feedback from them. We don't learn what others think of our thoughts, feelings, and actions.

Also, as we will see later, people who don't disclose information about themselves to others, who are unwilling to talk about their own personal matters, aren't likely to be taken into the confidence of others. They will be cut off from intimate interpersonal contact. Thus they aren't likely to learn what others are really like and what they care deeply about. Most important, Journard suggests that not talking about ourselves to others leads us to become less and less in touch with ourselves. A lack of awareness of our own inner lives sets in, and our self-concepts weaken and get lost (Chaikin & Derlega, 1976).

Another problem is that an unwillingness to talk about oneself, and to talk honestly, means that one is, in effect, hiding important parts of oneself from others. This means that what one does present to others is partially a facade. Presenting a facade makes interaction stressful. Other people become a source of threat. Being with others is painful if we are unwilling to talk personally with them. Many psychologists advocate the necessity of self-disclosure and strongly urge people to become more "transparent" to others (e.g., Mowrer, 1971). In general, they believe that self-disclosure and feedback increase the public area of a person's life and that this contributes to effective personal adjustment (see Figure 11.1).

Being able to share deep personal feelings in an intimate relationship is undoubtedly important. Still, just how open and self-disclosing we should be in a particular situation needs to be judged carefully. There are very strong social norms about how much self-disclosure is appropriate. People who violate this norm are thought to be "weird" and are not liked. Those who disclose too much too soon, the "plungers," make others feel very uncomfortable and are strongly avoided (Luft, 1969). Psychologically healthy people follow the norms, revealing a great deal to a few significant others with whom they are intimate, or who are helping or counseling them, and a medium amount to others in general (Cozby, 1973). They are sensitive to a given situation and can accommodate themselves to the needs of others. They are open, but they don't rush things. They don't

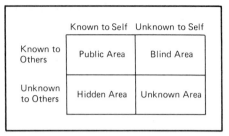

FIGURE 11.1   SELF-DISCLOSURE AND FEEDBACK
As people disclose what they know about themselves to others the Public Area of the personality gets larger and the Hidden Area gets smaller. In addition, self-disclosure often leads to feedback from others that further extends the Public Area by decreasing the Blind Area.

SOURCE: Adapted from *Of human interaction* by Joseph Luft by permission of Mayfield Publishing Company. Copyright © 1969 by the National Press.

seem to be desperate for contact, approval, or information about others. They don't ask more of others in terms of disclosure than others are willing to give, and they don't tell others more about themselves than others would want to hear.

DETERMINANTS OF SELF-DISCLOSURE.   Many studies have indicated that self-disclosure is reciprocal (Jourard & Friedman, 1970; Rubin, 1973; Cozby, 1972). That is, the more one person discloses about herself or himself to another, the more the second person will disclose in return. This finding has been demonstrated repeatedly (see Chaikin & Derlega, 1976), and it is clear that the best predictor of how self-disclosing one person is being with another is how self-disclosing the other has just been. It has even been shown that when others reveal too much, we don't like them as well as we do when they reveal the normative amount, but we still disclose more to them, closely following the reciprocity principle.

Reciprocity is a powerful determinant of self-disclosure, but it is by no means the only one. As we indicated before, people try hard to disclose the normative, or "appropriate," amount of information about themselves, depending on the situation. If someone else's self-disclosure seems too personal, we will probably compromise between the wish to reciprocate and the wish to act appropriately. The more others disclose to us, the more we will disclose to them in return, but this doesn't mean that we will exactly match their level of self-disclosure. The appropriateness norm can exert a restraining force. Thus we might disclose a great deal to people who tell us about their love affairs, but perhaps not reveal the details of our own intimate relationships.

Another restraining force on self-disclosure is fear of the possible negative consequences of revealing too much. We may feel that we will be ridiculed or rejected for some of our thoughts and feelings, or that information we have shared may not be held in confidence or may be used against us in some way. Trust is therefore a key factor in determining how much we will disclose about ourselves to others. If we can count on people not to exploit our confidences, we're likely to tell them a good deal, especially if they've indicated that they trust us by making their own self-disclosures. How much we trust another person is affected by two things, how trustworthy they seem compared to other people and how much *basic trust,* in the Eriksonian sense, we have in our own psychological outlook (see Chapter 2). In short, self-disclosure is affected by how much others disclose, norms of appropriateness, and our degree of trust in another person.

SELF-DISCLOSURE AND THE QUALITY OF RELATIONSHIPS. Self-disclosure has a great impact on relationships and in turn is very much affected by the quality of a relationship. For example, Altman and Haythorn (1965) suggest that as relationships become more intimate there is an increase in both the number of topics that are mutually disclosed and the depth with which any one of them is discussed. Thus both the breadth and depth of self-disclosure are greater in intimate relationships.

While studies indicate that self-disclosure is greatest in highly intimate relationships, research also indicates that strangers often disclose a great deal to each other. Georg Simmel wrote: "The stranger often receives the most surprising openness—confidences which sometimes have the character of a confessional and which would be carefully withheld from a more closely related person" (1950, p. 404). Toffler (1970) quotes a college student who remarked about her behavior in Fort Lauderdale during spring vacation, "You're not worried about what you do or say here because, frankly, you'll never see these people again" (p. 96). These observations suggest that we'll open up to strangers about highly personal matters because we don't need to trust them. We simply have to be sure we'll never see them again. This underscores the fact that, in ordinary relationships, fear of being vulnerable to manipulation as a result of having revealed too much is a powerful inhibitor of self-disclosure.

While most research and theory have focused on intimacy as a factor related to self-disclosure, it has also been shown that status is an important determinant of who discloses what to whom. Erving Goffman (1967) provides an illustration: "In American business organizations the boss may thoughtfully ask the elevator man how his children are, but this entrance into another's life may be blocked to the elevator man, who can appreciate the concern but not return it." That is, those who have high status are allowed to intrude into the lives of those of lower status and ask for self-disclosures. Those with low status would be regarded as impertinent if they asked similar questions. By obtaining information about others, high-status people put themselves in a powerful position; by not reciprocating, they indicate that they don't consider themselves to be at the same level as others. Thus they reinforce the difference in status and power.

SEX DIFFERENCES IN SELF-DISCLOSURE. Studies of intimate self-disclosure have consistently shown that women disclose more than men do (see Cozby, 1973). Men disclose very little in general, and individual males who reveal deep personal feelings are often regarded as weak and inadequate. Jourard believes that men pay dearly for adhering to norms dictating low self-disclosure; he contends that keeping their feelings inside imposes "an added burden of stress" on men. Men do sometimes disclose their innermost feelings, usually to a woman, most often a girlfriend or wife. Writing from a feminist perspective, Henley (1977) notes that this pattern is bad for men, because it reinforces the severe limits on appropriate channels for male self-disclosure and emotional release, and that it is also bad for women, because it keeps them in the subordinate position of having to serve as "emotional service stations" for use at male convenience. Whether you are a man or a woman, you might consider how your self-disclosure patterns are limited by cultural norms.

CONCLUSIONS ABOUT SELF-DISCLOSURE. Research on self-disclosure shows that many people find the intimate exchange of personal information very rewarding. They are willing to take the risks that are often involved. We seem more attracted by the high rewards that can come from self-disclosure than we are repelled by the vulnerability it creates. The reason for this is that self-disclosure involves the highly satisfying experience of self-expression and acceptance by others. When we reveal ourselves to others, there is a good chance that we can show them what we are really like, what really concerns us and makes us feel good or bad, and that they will appreciate and accept who we are. There is no more rewarding experience than having other people interested in listening to us, in sharing and validating our concerns, and in showing their affection and trust by disclosing themselves in return. This kind of sharing of personal feelings and concerns, and the affection and trust that go along with it, is the core of intimacy. It is tremendously self-validating. It feels exhilarating. It can contribute greatly to personal adjustment. It is this kind of communication and interaction that people strive for in intimate relationships.

EVALUATING A RELATIONSHIP

Disclosing oneself to another person is one of the most important aspects of intimacy. When one's self is understood and accepted in an intimate relationship there can be no greater re-ward for the effort required to build and maintain an honest, trusting bond with another person. Still, there is more to relationships than self-disclosure. People do many other things together: They run, play tennis, watch television, play backgammon or bridge, go dancing, discuss books and movies, debate politics or religion. This sharing of activities is clearly the case for Prince Charles and Princess Diana. Of course they share the royal pomp and circumstance, their job, yet they also have similar interests when they relax. Diana, like other members of the royal family, loves the outdoor country life. At Balmoral, the family's country estate in Scotland, the royal couple relax by fishing, shooting, and taking walks with their dogs. Their intimate relationship began when they were fishing together in the River Dee, and one columnist wrote that Diana's "idea of heaven is to spend an afternoon fly-fishing, waist-high in freezing water" (Kennedy, 1981). Charles has a similar idea. These shared interests are very important in a relationship because they have a large impact on two people's total evaluation of their relationship. People who are relating directly to each other, through self-disclosure and sex, *and* two people who together are enjoying things outside themselves, such as children, hiking, or the movies, have a great deal going for their relationship. Enjoying the other person, enjoying that person's enjoyment of you, and enjoying external things together are all important.

Given the pleasure they find in various mutual activities, how do people decide how satisfied they are with their overall relationship? What keeps people in a relationship with each other?

Satisfaction and Dependence in Relationships

Very few relationships are completely satisfying in every way to both people involved. The two of you may have great affection for each other and lots of things in common while still disagreeing about certain tastes, interests, and patterns of relating. No one relationship can satisfy all a person's needs for human interaction. An overall sense of satisfaction seems to be one thing that keeps couples together. Sometimes, however, people choose to stay in relationships that are basically unsatisfying to them or break up with lovers they get along with very well. Thibaut and Kelley (1959) outlined some principles that help explain how we evaluate our intimate relationships and why we choose to sustain or end them.

SATISFACTION.   Satisfaction in a relationship, according to Thibaut and Kelley, depends first on what is called the **outcome level** (OL). The outcome level is defined as the average level of pleasure or gratification a person gets from interactions in the relationship. Each time you interact with another person there will be some rewarding or pleasant aspects of the interaction, such as recognition of interesting conversation, and some costly, painful, or unpleasant features, such as disappointment, embarrassment, or effort. Thus each interaction will have a net positive or negative degree of satisfaction. The average amount of satisfaction, positive or negative, that you receive from all the interactions in the relationship determines the outcome level.

The outcome level is crucial in determining how happy you are in your relationships, but it doesn't tell the whole story. The other critical factor is what Thibaut and Kelley called the **comparison level** (CL). The comparison level is the baseline, or neutral point, to which you compare outcomes to determine your satisfaction. It is based in part on outcomes you have experienced in the past and in part on outcomes you observe other people receiving. When your outcomes in a relationship are above your CL, you will feel satisfied; when they are below your CL, you will feel dissatisfied. For example, if the outcomes in your relationship with a person you've been dating casually for the past two weeks are greater than the outcomes you have had in similar relationships in the past and the outcomes levels other people around you seem to be having with their dates, you will feel relatively satisfied with your new relationship.

DEPENDENCE.   If you're satisfied spending time with the person you've been dating—that is, if your OL is above your CL—chances are that you will remain in that relationship. But your degree of satisfaction isn't the only determinant of whether you continue a relationship or not. Sometimes people remain in relationships where they are unhappy and leave relationships they enjoy a great deal. Their degree of dependence on the relationship helps explain why this happens. Dependence is determined by the difference between your outcome level and what Thibaut and Kelley called the **comparison level for alternatives,** the *CLalt*. The comparison level for alternatives is simply the level of outcomes that one could get in the next best available relationship. It is assumed that the CLalt is the lowest level of outcomes a person will accept in a relationship. If your outcomes in a relationship are lower than your CLalt, you will move to the next best available relationship.

If a person has an outcome level in a relationship that is much higher than his or her CLalt, he or she is very dependent on that relationship; if the relationship were to dissolve, the person would have to move to an alternative in which the outcomes would be much lower. You are in a much better position if you have a high CLalt, one nearly as high as your outcome level. Then you aren't dependent on your current relationship. If that relationship should end, you would still have another appealing option, one that is almost as satisfying. Because you aren't dependent on the relationship, it's hard for your partner to exert much control over your behavior. You are much more susceptible to control by the other person's rewards and punishments when your CLalt is low.

Talking about dependency and control in a relationship seems somewhat crass, but it's an important, if unspoken, aspect of relationships that should be recognized for your own benefit.

KINDS OF RELATIONSHIPS.   In light of what we have said about outcome levels, comparison levels, and comparison levels for alternatives,

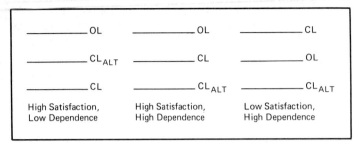

FIGURE 11.2   THREE KINDS OF RELATIONSHIPS
This figure shows three kinds of relationships as determined by the relation of the comparison level (CL) to the outcome level (OL) and the comparison level for alternatives (CLalt).
SOURCE: Adapted from Thibaut and Kelley (1959).

we can distinguish three kinds of relationships with varying degrees of satisfaction and dependence. First, we can assume that in all relationships that last awhile the OL will be above the CLalt, otherwise the person would have already left for the alternative relationship. Given this assumption, one kind of relationship would be one in which both the outcome level (OL) and the comparison level for alternatives (CLalt) are above the comparison level (CL). Here people are in a good position because they are satisfied but not dependent. They have an alternative relationship where outcomes are still above the CL (see Figure 11.2). A somewhat less desirable kind of relationship is one where your CL is below your OL but above your CLalt. In that case, you have satisfactory outcomes, but no alternative relationship with acceptable outcomes. Finally, people may have the misfortune to be in relationships where their OL is below their CL, but where they can't change because their CLalt is even lower. This is called a "nonvoluntary relationship." An example might be a person in an unhappy marriage with no alternative available. A worker who is getting paid very little but can't do even that well anywhere else is dependent on his or her employer and in a nonvoluntary relationship with it.

Equity in Relationships

Another very important aspect of a relationship is how fairly two people treat each other and how much happiness each partner gets out of

their interactions relative to what he or she puts into it. Psychologists have done much research on the question of fairness in relationships and have developed what is known as "equity theory." There are several different versions of equity theory, but they agree on one basic point: We've learned that behaving equitably is desirable, that people will attempt to be fair, according to their own standards, in their dealings with others, and that they will be distressed when they perceive their relationships to be unfair. Psychologists assume that people will feel distressed whether the fairness is to their advantage or disadvantage (Walster, Walster, & Berscheid, 1978).

PERCEIVING EQUITY. What determines whether a relationship is perceived as equitable? The answer can be best stated in this formula:

$$\frac{O_A}{I_A} = \frac{O_B}{I_B},$$

where O refers to outcomes, I refers to inputs, and A and B are persons (Walster et al., 1978). If either person perceives that this formula holds, that the ratio of what one of them is getting relative to what he or she is putting in is equal to the other person's outcome-to-input ratio, the relationship will be perceived as equitable. For example, if two people are both working equally hard in a relationship and making equal sacrifices (equal inputs) and each is deriving as much satisfaction from it as the other (equal outcomes), the formula holds and the relationship is equitable. Another possibility is that one person contributes more to the relationship but also gets more benefit from it. The formula would also hold in this case. An instance of this might be seen in the relationship between two roommates. One works hard to arrange their room for a party and the other spends most of the time in the library and makes minimal contributions. If the first partner is given more say about who comes to the party and what records are played, the equity formula holds, and both roommates probably feel that justice has been done.

RESPONSES TO INEQUITY.   When people perceive themselves to be in an inequitable relationship, they will feel distress and take steps to change the situation (Walster et al., 1978). There are two ways to do this. One is simply to alter one's perceptions of one's own or the other person's inputs or outcomes so that *psychological* equity is restored. The other is to really change inputs or outcomes to restore *actual* equity. Walster et al. predict that people will choose the mode of restoring equity that most simply and completely eliminates unfairness. In some cases it might be easy for the people involved to actually change their inputs or outcomes. For example, two people who are living together might make an adjustment in how much work each of them does around the apartment if they recognize an inequity in the division of household tasks. In other cases, however, there may be little anyone can do to restore actual equity. Then the predictable result is distortion of reality through reliance on psychological equity.

Consider the case of a business executive in an industrial setting who feels that it's unfair how little workers are paid, given how much they contribute to the success of the company. At the same time she realizes that there is nothing she can do that will have any real impact on company policy. Equity theory holds that the executive will feel distressed and seek some kind of psychological relief. Usually the relief takes the form of distorting the situation so that it is perceived as fair. In the case of the execu-

tive she may decide that the workers really contribute very little to company success compared to the "brains" at the top, and that their wages are really very high, given their low level of education and sophistication. Ironically, the executive's initial concern about a social injustice causes her to convince herself that there is no injustice after all.

Very often people who are on the advantaged end of an unfair relationship use psychological distortion to convince themselves that equity actually exists. This is relatively easy, and it allows them to maintain their favored position. How does the person who is disadvantaged respond? He or she should be doubly

REVIEW QUESTIONS

6. Thibaut and Kelley identified four stages of relationship development. In the _____ stage, people look over the possibilities for relationships and decide with whom to have a relationship.

7. In initiating a relationship we may try to present ourself in a more positive way than we normally act. Goffman called these initial self-presentations _____ _____ .

8. T or F: Although it may be experienced as an unpleasant emotional response, shyness is not a major obstacle to forming relationships.

9. If a person's outcome level (level of gratification) in a relationship is higher than his/her comparison level of outcomes, then the person is likely to be _____ with the relationship.

10. A person whose inputs into a relationship are equivalent to their outcomes is likely to perceive the relationship as _____ . Someone whose outcomes are greater than their inputs may use _____ to reduce the psychological tension created by the unbalanced relationship.

distressed—first, that an inequity exists, and, second, that he or she is getting the short end of it. Much to the dismay and frustration of social reformers, however, people in this position often use psychological distortion just as much as those whom the inequity favors. If they believe they can do nothing about the inequity, denying reality and viewing what exists as fair and satisfying can be the best way of feeling happy. Of course an unwillingness to perceive unfairness perpetuates the unfairness.

MAKING
A COMMITMENT

Strong relationships are built on mutual acceptance, mutual satisfactory outcomes, and a style of living and working within the relationship that both people feel is fair. Once two people feel they have a strong, satisfying relationship they may decide they want to make a commitment to each other to further strengthen and extend the relationship. What is involved when we take the important step of making a commitment in a relationship? How do we move beyond bargaining, and what makes a commitment work or not work? Prince Charles realized that a commitment was not only an important matter for him, as future king of England, but that it was also an important step for Diana to make as a person. When he proposed to her a month before their engagement was publicly announced, at a private dinner for two in his quarters at Buckingham Palace, he "wanted to give her a chance to think about it—to think if it was all going to be too awful." He realized that there would be difficult parts as well as exhilarating parts for Diana in her role as Princess of Wales and, later, queen. Diana, deeply in love, knew she wanted to make the commitment. "I never had any doubts about it," she said, and Charles remarked, "I feel positively delighted and frankly amazed that Di is prepared to take me on" (Deming, 1981). Few of us have to think about as much as Charles and Diana had to think about when they made their commitment, and

few of us have to make it with an audience of hundreds of millions of people. Still, for all of us, commitment is a serious decision, and we can make mistakes. Let's see how people make commitments, and how their commitments are likely to work out.

Deciding to Make a Commitment

It's not entirely clear how and when commitment begins. At some time and in some way, two people in a relationship decide that their satisfaction or happiness with each other is significantly greater than in their relationships with other people, and they agree to begin a relatively long-lasting, more intimate relationship that to some extent excludes other close relationships. They agree to depend on each other for satisfaction of important needs, including companionship, love, and sex. The commitment may or may not involve a decision to live together. The most important element in their commitment is the decision to become more intimate and to forgo intimate relationships with others.

Commitment is based on the conviction that you'll get more happiness with one special person than you would get with others. Beyond that, commitments can vary tremendously in how lasting partners expect them to be. Most are based on faith that the relationship can be enduring. Some people hold this conviction rather casually, willing to remain committed as long as they feel satisfied with the way things are going, but frankly acknowledging that at any time either partner may become unhappy or bored or may find a better relationship. For others, commitment and faith in the longevity of a relationship include a determination to see that the relationship does last. Charles and Diana have to have this kind of determination, and they have to stand ready to do whatever is necessary to keep their relationship strong and happy; divorce isn't considered permissible for people in their position. For them, and for all of us with such determination, there's a lot of work ahead.

Freedom and Commitment

Making an agreement with another person to enter into a deeper, more exclusive, and lasting relationship is a crucially important life decision that must be made freely and with careful thought. In many cases you may find yourself under various pressures to enter into a commitment that you aren't sure is good for you. Sometimes parents push their children into making commitments, worried that they'll lose a good relationship. Prince Charles's parents obviously put some pressure on him to make up his mind about Lady Diana Spencer. Sometimes friends push you to become more committed so that your relationship will be as exclusive as theirs. Most common perhaps is the situation where one person in a relationship feels committed and wants the other to make an equal commitment. It often happens that one person is sure of the high value of the relationship sooner than the other and wants the other person to feel equally strongly. This can easily lead to pushing the other person. The person who is pushed may react negatively and lose interest or may be pressured into a commitment. Either of these outcomes is regrettable. We can't emphasize enough that a commitment that isn't truly felt is unlikely to last. Any agreement to form an exclusive relationship must be based on a clear individual decision that is made freely.

Although a commitment must be made privately and freely, it's also true that once a commitment is made privately, public behaviors afterward can serve to further strengthen it. After two people have decided to live together, for example, they may have to exert a lot of energy to move, they may have a break off or at least "simmer down" other relationships, and they may even have to change jobs. In other cases a decision to have sexual relations for the first time may follow a decision about commitment. All the behaviors that one engages in after a commitment to another person are justified because of the commitment, and they strengthen the commitment (Linder, Cooper, & Wicklund, 1968). People who have taken action following a commitment will work hard to maintain their relationship.

Just as a commitment is usually weaker and less enduring if it's made under pressure, so a commitment that is made in defiance of pressure from parents or peers can be very strong (Darley & Cooper, 1972). Parental disapproval of a relationship can in time undermine it, but at least initially, the perception that one was willing to defy parental pressure and perhaps forgo parental support for a relationship demonstrates the depth of one's love and can greatly strengthen a commitment. Rubin (1973) has referred to this as the "Romeo and Juliet effect," after the two young lovers in Shakespeare's play whose commitment was deepened by the knowledge that they risked the wrath of their families by being together. In sum, a commitment is likely to be strongest when it is arrived at freely and when it is cemented by taking action as a result of the commitment.

MARRIAGE, ENDURING RELATIONSHIPS, AND DIVORCE

For many people commitment to an exclusive, intimate relationship is closely followed by a decision to formalize and make public their commitment in some way that is sanctioned by the society as a whole. This final stage of relationship development is referred to as "institutionalization" by Thibaut and Kelley (1959). For most relationships between adult men and women in our society, this means marriage. This was obviously the case for Charles and Diana. Given the glare of publicity, Charles could only carry on an enduring relationship with Diana through marriage. Living together was out of the question. The British public would not stand for it, and, besides, they wanted a Princess of Wales and children to continue the royal line. Once Charles and Diana's relationship began to grow intimate, marriage was the logical outcome. Diana said she never had any doubt about it. For many other people, however, whether or not to marry can be an agonizing decision. Even though marriage can be terminated, many people view it as the biggest decision and commitment of their lives. They realize that while courtship was fun and living together worked well perhaps, marriage means entering uncharted waters. It has its own satisfactions and its own stresses. What studies have shown about the joys and sorrows of wedlock is relevant information for anyone contemplating this major step.

Sources of Gratification in Marriage

People get married for many reasons. We live in a culture in which marriage is encouraged and rewarded with social approval and economic advantages. Throughout our lives we develop ideas about what lies ahead in marriage and what its rewards are. As a result of these expectations we generally look forward to getting married, thinking of the pleasures of having a family, being financially secure, and developing a stable home life. What people find rewarding in marriage can be very different from their expectations. A recent study revealed that the most important factors in marital satisfaction for married women are love, respect, and friendship (Tavris & Jayarante, 1976). Sexual compatibility is a distant fourth, and shared interests and having children are much lower than that. People enjoy being together, loving and respecting each other, and being loved and respected in turn. Sex is important, but the more basic psychological factors that have been part of intimacy since chum relationships in the juvenile era, and which are known to enhance sexual pleasure, are at the core of marriage. These are the things that give people meaning and pleasure in living. They hold people together. When it becomes impossible to have respect for one's partner, difficult to be a friend, and hard to love, unhappiness is inevitable. Unfortunately, love, respect, and friendship between two people are fragile and can be lost as a result of other stresses of living. Once they are lost, most people find them impossible to recover. Let's consider how this can happen.

Stresses in Marriage

One of the most positive and exhilarating aspects of living is building an intimate relationship with another person. It's a joy to learn what someone else is all about, to have that person care about you, and to enjoy a relationship of total openness and acceptance that

People in our society and many others institutionalize their commitments to relationships by getting married.

Ken Karp.

Children bring both joy and lots
of stresses to marriage.
Ed Lettau, Photo Researchers, Inc.

includes the powerful attractions of sex. Usually a relationship is built before marriage. After marriage people must stop working on building the relationship to some degree and use it as a foundation from which other aspects of living can be built. These include pursuing careers, raising a family, and finding satisfying ways of enjoying leisure time. Relationship building can still go on, and must go on, but the focus of living turns to other things after the early, exciting formative period. Sometimes a great deal of stress is involved in this shift in energy and attention from building the relationship itself to using the relationship as a foundation for solving other problems and coping with other aspects of life.

As committed couples spend more and more time and energy on work, getting things done, and making decisions, they have less time to talk about their feelings and their personal needs. Problems aren't solved immediately, resentments aren't aired, and new concerns aren't fully discussed. Couples sometimes feel a pulling apart, a loss of the closeness they used to have. They can feel great disappointment, almost betrayal, about this change in their relationship and wonder whether it's worth the effort to keep the marriage together. They may find that while they are still com-

patible as lovers and even as friends and intimate partners, they don't do well as co-workers. They can't agree on how money should be spent or how jobs in the household should be divided or how they should spend leisure time. The love that seemed so much greater than all these small problems isn't given as much attention as before, and it becomes less and less effective as a foundation for the rest of living. In other words, the success people have as intimate partners may not translate into being good partners for dealing with the external world. Even those who do succeed in being good married partners can expect to feel these stresses. It's hard to tell much about Prince Charles and Princess Diana's private life, but stories in the press indicate that this "fairy-tale couple" has been going through the struggles of adjustment to married life that all couples experience.

When, and if, children come, the pleasure or pain that exists in a marriage can increase sharply. When people have a basically solid marriage and agree well about how to cope with reality's demands as well as each other's needs, they have a good foundation from which to face the challenges of child rearing. In this case the result is usually very positive. The child becomes a source of real joy and satisfaction to the couple, and their relationship can be enhanced. When people have a marriage that is already strained, having a child is likely to strain it even further, probably to the breaking point. This result is an unhappy one for the parents, and especially so for the child. Sometimes whether the child will be a positive or negative addition to the marriage can be forecast before it arrives. Physicians note that women often look their best or their worst during pregnancy (Nevin, 1970). If they are happy and looking forward to the child, there is an unmistakable bloom and look of joy. If they are frightened or resentful about having a baby, they look tired, depressed, and strained. Such women are not in a position to enjoy raising a child, even with an enthusiastic husband.

In sum, living together as married or otherwise strongly committed partners in the struggle with the demands of the world is a challenge. Some people find that meeting the world's challenges is easier in the context of a happy marriage. They also find that solving the problems of living together strengthens their relationship. Others find that coping with life's stresses pulls them apart. They find that their success in dealing with the world is reduced because of worries about their relationship and that worries about their job, home, and children reduce the quality of their relationship. Being successful inside and outside marriage is difficult and requires a great deal of patience and hard work. Genuine caring about oneself and others makes it easier to find the strength to work hard at these challenges and increases the chances for success.

Breaking Up and Getting Divorced

Getting married is an extremely common event in our society today. Approximately 95 percent of the American population gets married at least once. There are some 2 million marriages each year in the United States. Thus institutionalization of relationships happens very frequently. Almost equally frequent, however, is the dissolution of marriages. Nearly 1 million divorces take place each year in the United States. Moreover, the divorce rate has been increasing dramatically over the past several decades. In 1960, 25 percent of all marriages ended in divorce. That figure was up to 33 percent in 1974, and in 1978 there was one divorce for every two marriages, indicating a divorce rate of close to 50 percent. In one recent year there were more divorces than marriages in California, the largest state in the union, though this figure reflects many people who were married in other states, then moved to California and were divorced there. Although many people do get divorced, they are by no means cured of the marriage habit. Eighty percent of people who are divorced get married again within five years.

How can we explain the ever-increasing divorce rate? One thing that makes a difference is that norms have changed over the past several decades. There is much less stigma attached to divorce than there used to be. In many states the laws governing divorce are becoming more liberal, so it's less complicated to end a marriage. Changing ideas about women's rights and about the needs of children have lessened the tendency for people to stay together in an unhappy marriage for the sake of children. All these factors have made it easier for people to get divorced. Still, it appears that marriages are failing now more than ever before, perhaps because of the increased stresses of living in the modern world.

Let's consider what can keep a love relationship alive, how we can nurture companionate love, and the reasons that people in intimate relationships break up or get divorced. We've talked about several key factors in promoting the ease, harmony, and peacefulness of companionate love. It takes successful communication, avoiding the kind of ambiguity and confusion we saw in Chapter 9, and attaining the kind of self-disclosure and honesty we have discussed in this chapter. It also takes equality. There has to be give and take in relationships. Both partners must have times when they are dominant, times when they are submissive, and times when they are on an equal footing. Over time, this alternation in each person being one-up and one-down should make possible an equality in the division of labor and the decision-making power in the relationship. A relationship can become stagnant and sour without such a balance of power.

These kinds of factors—communication, equality, and lots of hard work to keep the communication open and the distribution of effort and satisfaction fair—must overcome strong tendencies for relationships to decline over time. One study comparing arranged marriages to "love" marriages in Japan showed that in both kinds of relationships feelings of well-being, the degree of self-disclosure, sexual satisfaction, and expressions of affection declined dramatically over ten years of marriage (Blood, 1967). For example, the number of expressions of affection fell by nearly 60 percent. The love matches were no better than arranged matches at the start and at the finish, ten years later, but they stayed more positive during the middle years. Charles and Diana's marriage was a love match, but it had elements of arrangement too. The royal family had to scrutinize Charles's choice carefully and give its approval. The data from this study suggest that, no matter what the basis of their marriage was, Charles and Diana will have to fight against the same tendencies for expressions of love and feelings of satisfaction to decline.

So there's a general tendency for the "spark" to go out of marriages over the years. What else contributes to breaking up and getting divorced? One study of breaking up in unmarried college students indicated that there are slightly different reasons for men and women (Hill, Rubin, & Paplau, 1976). Both sexes cite boredom with the relationship as the main cause for breaking up—77 percent for each group—but otherwise men's and women's responses vary somewhat. Women cite different interests and sexual attitudes more than men do, while men cite different backgrounds slightly more than women do. The biggest difference is that women show more concern than men do over different ideas about marriage—43 percent of women to 29 percent of men. But, over all, the desire for something

TABLE 11.1

Reasons for Breaking Up or Getting Divorced

REASONS FOR UNMARRIED COLLEGE STUDENTS TO BREAK UP (HILL, RUBIN, & PAPLAU, 1976)

1. Boredom with the relationship; desire for something new.
2. Different interests.
3. Different attitudes about sex.
4. Different backgrounds.
5. Different ideas about marriage.

REASONS FOR GETTING DIVORCED (MIDDLEBROOK, 1980)

1. Getting married for wrong reasons (family expectations, desire to have children, escape from loneliness, money, pregnancy).
2. Lack of satisfaction of psychological needs.
3. Lack of affection.
4. Attacks on self-esteem.
5. Pressure and stress related to in-laws, money, or work.
6. Poor quality of the relationship: little in common, poor communication.

new dominates both sexes' answers. This shows how important your original choice of a partner is when you get married. Boredom is natural, and to overcome it you have to have committed yourself to someone who can work with you to keep lines of communication open in an equitable relationship.

Studies of the reasons for divorce show that a variety of factors are involved (Middlebrook, 1980). One is that many people get married for the wrong reasons in the first place. Such reasons include getting married because it is expected, to have children, to escape loneliness, for financial security, or because of pregnancy (Tavris & Jayarante, 1976). Another reason for divorce is that the marriage isn't meeting the partners' psychological needs. Married people often feel lonely, misunderstood, and neglected. Lack of affection is common in unsuccessful marriages. Poor communication can also ruin a relationship. If people are misunderstood and their efforts to be helpful

REVIEW QUESTIONS

11. The process in which people in a relationship decide to depend on each other for satisfaction of their needs and to somewhat limit their intimate relationships with other people is called _____.

12. In our society, commitment to an exclusive, intimate relationship is often followed by _____ of the relationship, often in the form of marriage.

13. T or F: Although difficulties in a marriage may strain the relationship, having a child inevitably eases the pressures and enhances the relationship.

14. Which of the following is the most common reason cited by both men and women for the break-up of their relationships?
a. different backgrounds
b. different sexual attitudes
c. boredom
d. conflicting interests

are misinterpreted, unhappiness will almost surely result (Gottman et al., 1976). Highly damaging as well are attacks on self-esteem by ridicule or false accusations (Matthews & Mihanovich, 1963). Intense outside pressures, such as problems with finances, interference from in-laws, and stress on the job, are another factor undermining relationships. The quality of the relationship itself is also important. If couples have little in common and little they enjoy together, divorce is much more likely. Charles and Diana are fortunate to share interests in having a family and in outdoor activities. Although, due to an early fall, Diana doesn't like horses, while Charles is an avid polo player, they do have lots in common. In short, there are a variety of factors that contribute to divorce and the break-up of any committed relationship, but we see again and again that good communication, hard work, flexibility, equality, caring, and willingness to express that caring clearly, are basic to a happy and enduring relationship. Charles and Diana seem to have a strong relationship. We hope you can do as well.

SUMMARY

1. Liking is based on perceived similarity between two people and high regard or respect. Love may include these characteristics, but is also defined by deep emotional attachment, caring, and intimacy.

2. Passionate, romantic love is marked by intense absorption and preoccupation with the loved one, physiological arousal, and feelings of fulfillment and momentary ecstasy. In order to experience romantic passion, people must have a cultural expectation of it, must meet the right person, and must interpret arousal felt while with that person as passionate, romantic love.

3. Companionate love is the affection we feel for those with whom our lives are intertwined. Romantic passion becomes companionate love when a relationship grows and endures over time.

4. Sexual intercourse may be a component of love when people are truly caring and concerned about their partners' needs. It is important to distinguish between love and physical passion. Passion is often a fleeting experience, while love is an emotion that will continue to grow if properly nurtured.

5. People must learn to love. Early family experiences may determine whether or not a person can develop a mature loving relationship. We must love ourselves before we can love others.

6. Love is based on people's ability to accept and respect each other and be concerned for each other's needs. It's important for people to clearly define their own needs and to be aware of the needs of their partners. A loving relationship will grow and develop to the extent that two people engage in open and honest communication with each other.

7. A sense of ambivalence often pervades love relationships. On the one hand, people develop a dependency on the relationship; on the other hand, they want to retain their independence.

8. Problems are apt to arise in relationships if people put on a good front to attract others or display only their faults in order to test the depth of others' interest and acceptance.

9. Relationships move through various stages of development: sampling, bargaining, commitment, and institutionalization.

10. The sampling stage involves a superficial presentation of personal characteristics as people attempt to communicate a positive image to others. The self-presentations of others are seldom challenged. During this initial stage of interaction, people try to cut through the facades and make an accurate forecast of how much potential there is for good relationships with various people.

11. During the bargaining stage, people attempt to build a strong and satisfying relationship. One of the most important aspects of this stage is self-disclosure, opening yourself up to another person and sharing your deepest thoughts and feelings. Telling others about yourself needs to be based on trust. When trust exists and self-disclosure occurs, the quality of your own personal adjustment is enhanced and relationships grow more intimate and satisfying.

12. People evaluate their relationships before making lasting commitments. Satisfaction in a relationship depends first of all on the rewards, or outcomes, of the relationship. People's overall evaluation of their relationship is affected not only by their outcomes, but also by how much satisfaction they expect from the relationship. If a person has a high baseline, or comparison level, he or she will be less satisfied by certain outcomes than will a person who expects less.

13. Satisfaction is often linked to dependence. Dependence on a relationship is determined by the availability of alternatives. When a person has other possibilities that are almost as satisfying as his or her present relationship, the person isn't dependent and thus has more power in the relationship.

14. Equity is another factor that must be considered when evaluating relationships. People are usually disturbed to be in an inequitable relationship and take steps to correct a situation they perceive as unfair. Sometimes they will actually change their inputs or outcomes or those of the other person, but other times they will simply convince themselves that the inequity doesn't exist.

15. During the commitment stage of relationship development, two people agree to begin a relatively long-lasting, more intimate relationship that to some extent excludes other close relationships. This commitment must be made freely by both partners, or the commitment is unlikely to last.

16. A committed relationship becomes institutionalized when the partners decide to formalize and make public their commitment in some way that is sanctioned by the society as a whole. This can, but doesn't have to, involve formal marriage.

17. The vast majority of people in our society get married once they have made a commitment to each other. Nearly half of these marriages end in divorce. People find it easy and exciting to build a positive relationship, but often they aren't able to maintain caring and intimacy when they have to work with their partners to deal with the challenging aspects of everyday living. Common reasons for relationships breaking up include boredom, different interests and sexual attitudes, different backgrounds, and different ideas about marriage. Common reasons for divorce include having been married for the wrong reasons, outside pressures and stresses, poor relationship structures, and the frustration of psychological needs.

KEY TERMS

a. ATTACHMENT
b. BARGAINING
c. CARING
d. COMMITMENT
e. COMPARISON LEVEL
f. COMPARISON LEVEL FOR ALTERNATIVES

g. IDEALIZED PERFORMANCE
h. INSTITUTIONALIZATION
i. INTIMACY
j. OUTCOME LEVEL
k. SAMPLING

1. In Thibaut and Kelley's theory of the stages of relationships, the stage in which people negotiate or work out mutually satisfying ways of interacting while trying to build a relationship

2. In Thibaut and Kelley's theory of the stages of relationships, the stage in which people decide to be special or exclusive partners in a relationship

3. The standard by which the outcome level of interactions in a relationship is evaluated; it is based on all the outcomes a person knows about through his or her own or another's experiences

4. The lowest level of outcomes a person will accept in a relationship, it is the level of outcomes in the next best available relationship

5. In Thibaut and Kelley's theory of the stages of relationships, the stage in which there is some formalization of the commitment

6. The average level of outcomes that is experienced in a relationship

7. In Thibaut and Kelley's theory of the stages of relationships, the process of looking over the possibilities and then deciding on a person with whom to attempt to form a relationship

8. The feeling that another person's satisfactions and well-being are as important as your own

9. The need to be with another person and to be approved of by that person

10. Close and confidential communication along with deep caring

11. Acting as if you support and conform to ideal standards of good conduct more than you actually do

ANSWERS TO REVIEW QUESTIONS

1. Emotional. **2.** Attachment; intimacy. **3.** Physiological arousal. **4.** Companionate. **5.** False.

6. Sampling. **7.** Idealized performances. **8.** False. **9.** Satisfied. **10.** Equitable; distortion.

11. Commitment. **12.** Institutionalization. **13.** False. **14.** c.

HUMAN SEXUALITY

B etty's mother was frantic. Her eighteen-year-old daughter was leaving home and going to Washington, D.C., as part of an acting company to perform the play *Franklin Street*. This was the day that Betty had dreamed about. She had been trying for two years to get an acting part, but had had to settle for modeling clothes. Now she was really going to be an actor. This was also a day her mother had feared and dreaded. Her daughter was going out into the cruel world alone, even if it was for only a short road-trip. As Betty was preparing to leave the house, Mrs. Bacall gave her some parting advice: "Remember: Never give anything away. No man really wants that. Every man wants a wife to be a virgin when he marries her" (Bacall, 1978). This advice meant little to Betty. Men weren't of much concern to her. She had dated very little in high school. The theater was her love, and now she had a chance to act.

Unfortunately, *Franklin Street* wasn't well received by the critics. After the short road-trip, the play closed and Betty was once again looking for work. She got a job as a model for the fashion magazine *Harper's Bazaar*. The publishers were intrigued by her innocent beauty and her seductive look. She posed for a number of pictures, and one was placed on the cover of *Bazaar*.

The picture and "The Look" caught people's attention, and Betty began to get calls from theater and movie producers. Betty knew little about how to choose among these offers, and in desperation she turned to Howard Hank for guidance. Howard felt that Betty was what the American public wanted. He could make her a star, he said, but a number of changes would have to be made. First, Betty had to move to Hollywood. Second, Howard felt that she needed to change her name. "Betty" just didn't seem to fit well with Bacall. It wasn't classy enough. Betty suggested "Sophie," after her grandmother, but Howard quickly put that idea to rest. He finally settled on "Lauren" and instructed Betty to tell everyone it was an old family name. Thus Lauren Bacall was born. Howard instructed the new Lauren Bacall to subdue her natural effervescence, to talk very little, to be "mysterious." Mystery ignited people's fantasies and would increase her appeal, he said.

In February 1944 Lauren Bacall's big chance arrived. She got an important part in the movie *To Have and Have Not* with one of Hollywood's main stars, Humphrey Bogart, whom his friends called Bogie. When Lauren and Bogie met there was no love at first sight, although Bogie made a comment that was certainly prophetic: "I just saw your screen test. We'll have a lot of fun together." The imperceptible beginnings of their attraction took root during the filming. Bogie and Bacall played several love scenes together that were filled with suggestive lines, looks, and leers, including Bacall's famous offer, "If you want anything, just whistle." The producers of the film quickly realized that there were sparks between the two and built in more and more of these tantalizing sequences. In addition to playing love scenes, Lauren and Bogie did a great deal of talking off the set. Both were in transition periods of their lives. Bogie was dealing with an unhappy marriage. Lauren was starting a new career. Both of them were anxious to have someone new and different to discuss ideas and feelings with. They wanted to tell about themselves, to talk over their pasts and their

There was strong physical chemistry between Bogart and Bacall. Bogart was 44 and in the midst of his third marriage while Bacall was 19 and "sexually innocent."

The Bettmann Archive.

futures. In doing so, they discovered great mutual respect and affection, as well as passion.

Many things attracted Bacall and Bogart to each other once they finally became acquainted. Bogart said he liked Lauren's "youth, her animal-like behavior, and don't-give-a-damn attitude" (Hyams, 1966). He also felt that she was unformed and that he could help her become the ideal woman, at least for him. Lauren was an attractive, talented person who seemed capable of strong caring and devotion. Lauren found Bogie to be a man of unusual integrity, honesty, energy, and ability. Everyone who knew him believed he had "class," and Lauren was drawn by his strength of character. And of course there was a strong physical chemistry between them. Lauren remembers: "I was an innocent sexually—Bogie began awakening feelings that were new to me. . . . I knew that physical changes were happening within me—the simplest word, look, or move would bring a gut reaction. It was all so romantic" (Bacall, 1978). She mentions "feelings of physical desire and pain that I had never known—a true awakening. I was beginning to leave girlhood behind, beginning (at last) to move toward womanhood" (Bacall, 1978, p.130).

The Bogart and Bacall, or "B & B," romance had gossip columnists buzzing for months. It was an exciting but unlikely match, and stories about them sold newspapers and magazines. Humphrey Bogart was 44 years old and in the midst of his third marriage. His most recent film, *Casablanca*, had won the Academy Award for best picture, and Bogie commanded one of the highest salaries in Hollywood. Lauren Bacall was single, 19, and, by her own description, a "sexual innocent."

Their affair was a mixture of excitement and guilt. Bogart was drinking heavily. He'd call Lauren at any hour of the day or night, and she'd rush out to meet him. They tried to hide their relationship from the press, Bogart's wife, and Lauren's mother. All eventually found out about it. Lauren's mother was shocked and hurt. She was angry at Bogart and admonished Lauren that "nice Jewish girls" should never get involved in such a situation. Lauren was torn between her guilt and her love for Bogie. Bogie too was pulled between his sense of duty to his wife and his love for Lauren. His drinking increased, and the relationship between Bogart and Bacall suffered. Lauren's career was also in jeopardy; Howard Hawks threatened to fire her if the relationship with Bogie continued.

After a number of bitter fights, Bogart and his wife were divorced and he married Lauren. What seemed like a marriage doomed for failure flourished. Lauren and Bogie were deeply in love. The trials and difficulties of their frantic affair were replaced by the secure caring of marriage. Lauren could finally let go the tight rein she had held on her feelings. The couple had two children. Both of their careers blossomed. They made *Key Largo* together and it was an immediate success.

But just when it seemed as if nothing could go wrong, Bogie developed a constant cough. His coughing seizures became increasingly frequent, and after months of trying to hide his pain he finally visited a doctor. The dreaded news stunned both Bogart and Bacall: Bogie had cancer. Lauren watched Bogie's long, terrible struggle as he slowly wasted away. The end was almost a relief, but Lauren was devastated by the loss of Bogie.

Lauren wanted desperately to recapture the happiness she had experienced with Bogie. She had an on-again-off-again affair with Frank Sinatra. When this abruptly ended, she met Jason Robards. Robards was married at the time, but soon Lauren and Jason were deeply involved. Jason got divorced, but his relationship with Lauren wasn't a smooth one. At times they were wildly happy together, but at other times they were equally unhappy.

As their relationship struggled to survive, Lauren discovered that she was pregnant. This was a bombshell for both Lauren and Jason. Lauren reports that "the idea of an abortion briefly flashed through my mind, but it was too terrible to contemplate and I wanted the baby" (Bacall, 1978, p. 415). After some hesitation, Bacall and Robards were married. The marriage proved no more stable than their earlier relationship; at times it was very good, but at too many other times it wasn't. After years of difficulties, Bacall and Robards were divorced.

Lauren turned her attention to her career. One of her most rewarding moments was when she won a Tony Award for her part in the Broadway play *Applause*. In her book, *By Herself* (1978), Lauren Bacall looks back over her life. "Howard Hawks invented a personality on screen that suited my look and my sound and some of myself—but the projection of worldliness in sex, total independence, the ability to handle any situation had no more relation to me then than it has now. . . . I don't like everything I know about myself, and I'll never be satisfied, but nobody's perfect" (Bacall, 1978, pp. 505–506).

SEXUAL BEHAVIOR: THEN AND NOW

There is a certain irony in the life of Lauren Bacall. The Lauren Bacall who appeared in the magazines and on the screen was a self-assured, worldly young woman who titillated the fantasies of many with her gravel voice and casual seductiveness: "If you want anything, just whistle." This image was created to portray the sensuality that women wanted to project and that men wanted to caress. Lauren Bacall was a symbol of American sexuality in the 1940s and 1950s. Her exploits with stars such as Humphrey Bogart, Frank Sinatra, and Jason Robards added to her allure.

Yet beneath this symbol was the Betty Bacall who grew up in a protected environment in New York City under the watchful eye of her mother. She dated very little during high school. She was admonished that "nice Jewish girls" didn't smoke and "weren't fast." Sexual relationships outside of marriage were wrong: "Every man wants his wife to be a virgin. . . ." It seems odd that one of America's sex symbols knew so little about sex.

Lauren's meeting with Bogie created a clash between her desires and her values. "Nice girls don't" (especially with a married man) was what she'd been taught, but she really wanted to. It was a conflict for which Bacall wasn't prepared. The double standard of the time held that women should look sexy but not encourage actual sexual relationships. Lauren's mother had given her the conventional caution: "Never give anything away." Sex was the prize in a game of hide-and-seek between men and women, a prize men sought to take and women fought to protect.

Sexual behavior wasn't an accepted topic of discussion in those days (except in veiled suggestions in the gossip columns) and certainly wasn't a topic to be taught in schools. Women were expected to be virgins until they got married, when their husbands, who were expected to be sexual experts, would "show them the ropes." The double standard for males' and females' sexual conduct was clear, but the players had very little knowledge about sexual behavior itself. "Learning" occurred through guarded half-informed discussions with same-sex friends or through clumsy experimentation with opposite-sex partners. The hushed nature of the topic was portrayed in movies that were designed to stimulate the imagination through suggestion, but keep the audience ignorant of the behavior itself.

For a number of years now, though, we've been living through what is often called the "Sexual Revolution." The rules about sexual behavior have been changing. The sexual desires of women are acknowledged. Sexual behavior is no longer viewed as the woman "giving away" something to the eager male. Women may now be the hunters. It's recognized that women desire and enjoy sexual behavior as much as men do. Movies today leave little about sex to the imagination.

But, while the rules regarding sexual behavior have changed, people's knowledge of sexual behavior is still woefully lacking. Many people feel that they are now free, or even expected, to get involved in an activity about which they know little. The changing expectations are summed up in the passage presented in Table 12.1.

To a large degree, sex pervades our world. Sex is used by advertisers to sell products. Explicit or implied sexual behavior is portrayed in many, if not most, of our movies and television shows. Magazines are filled with stories about the sexual exploits of movie stars and political figures. Many newspapers carry write-in columns, such as "Dear Abby," that offer advice about sexual behavior. Yet, even with today's more open attitude about sexual behavior, people remain remarkably uninformed about their sexuality. Sex is a private matter; one that is conducted alone or with one other person. Sexual behavior, for the most part, is engaged in at night, often under the sheets. Rarely, except in certain X-rated movies, do we observe other people engaged in sexual activities. And people don't often engage in conversations about sexual behavior. In our society, it's generally assumed that people will naturally "know what to do when the time comes."

TABLE 12.1

The Changing World of Sexual Behavior

Once the goal was orgasm for him (essential for health). For her it was "satisfying him" (to keep him at home and preserve the marriage).

Then the goal was "satisfying her" for him (to prove he was a genuine sexual jock, not a run-of-the-mill athlete). Her goal was reaching orgasm (to prove her femininity). To prove she was also mature, it was necessary for her to reach "vaginal orgasm." That was a change in both rules and goals that unfortunately occurred just after the man had learned to find the clitoris. At first, reaching vaginal orgasm was thought to be her problem. But later, it became his problem, too, as he was expected to keep an erection and keep thrusting (and keep his mind off what he was doing) long enough to bring her to a mature, nonclitoral climax. Otherwise, he wouldn't earn his letter.

The stakes were later raised to a mutual climax, which if you were a real jock would shake the world. . . . Quantity rather than quality became the basis for scoring, with each player pitting himself against vague and varying national averages or healthful weekly requirements.

In the meantime, her performance was to be judged in a new way—as if competing for the Academy Award. She wasn't required to have an orgasm. (She got as much pleasure from pleasuring her partner, the experts said.) But she was required to simulate an orgasm to make his performance look and feel better. To keep either partner from scoring too high, the experts gave him hints to tell if she was faking. Both lost points if her deception was detected.

And then came multiple orgasm (quantity still counts). Now he was able to give her at least three orgasms in the place of one. The first one of several could be clitoral, a pre-intercourse warmup. Then a mature vaginal climax or two after intromission. And finally—back to the mutual orgasm. A truly super performance by two superjocks!

The name of the game is Sexual Freedom, because it has freed sex from the bonds of reproduction, marriage and love. The advertised prizes are health, happiness, and an end to anxiety.

SOURCE: Reprinted from *Intimacy: Sensitivity, Sex and the Art of Love,* © 1971 by Gina Allen and Clement Martin, with the permission of Contemporary Books, Inc., Chicago.

Sex is widely used by advertisers to sell almost every conceivable product.

Ken Karp.

Unfortunately, ignorance is not necessarily bliss when it comes to sexual behavior. As we will see, with proper knowledge and sensitivity, sexual behavior can be a source of great pleasure that enhances our intimacy with ourselves and others. Without this knowledge, it can be a source of constant confusion and anxiety. In any case, our sexuality plays a major role in our personal adjustment process.

THE HUMAN SEXUAL SYSTEM

Curiosity about our bodies begins very early in infancy. Infants spend hours examining their hands and feet. They soon discover their **genitals** and, much to the consternation of some parents, take delight in exploring and manipulating their "new finds." Sigmund Freud

THE MYSTERY OF SEXUAL BEHAVIOR

Of all human behaviors, there is probably more misunderstanding and misinformation about sexual behavior. Most of our knowledge comes through word-of-mouth, rumor, or experimentation. For this reason, there are many myths surrounding sexual behavior. Examine the following statements and rate them as True or False. This chapter will examine these myths and supply you with the correct information. (Adapted from McLary, 1967.)

T F   1. Masturbation is dangerous and causes pimples or acne.
T F   2. Men and women lose their sex drive after age fifty.
T F   3. There is no absolute safe period for sexual intercourse insofar as conception is concerned.
T F   4. Alcohol is a sex stimulant.
T F   5. People are either totally heterosexual or totally homosexual.
T F   6. Women are capable of multiple orgasms.
T F   7. Premature ejaculation is caused by an abnormally sensitive penis.
T F   8. Sterilization diminishes the sex drive.
T F   9. Hormonal imbalance produces homosexuality.
T F 10. Contraception is the responsibility of both the man and woman.

Answers: False, False, True, False, False, True, False, False, False, True

shocked Victorian society when he suggested that children receive sexual gratification through the stimulation of their genitals. Some parents are still so alarmed about this behavior that they go to great lengths to constantly cloth their children so their "private parts" will be inaccessible.

The curiosity of childhood soon gives way to the shyness of adolescence, when people begin to hide their own genitals. People don't just hide their genitals from others; often people hide their genitals from themselves and are ignorant of these "secret" parts of their own bodies. So, as we begin our examination of sexual behavior, a short course in the anatomy of the male and female sexual systems seems in order.

The Male Sexual System

The external organs of the male sexual system include the **penis** and the **scrotum** (Figure 12.1). The average penis is about three to four inches long when relaxed and about six inches long when fully erect. Full erection generally occurs only for a short time before orgasm, so accurate measurement is often difficult to obtain. Externally, the penis consists of a shaft and a head, or **glans.** The glans is the most sensitive area because it contains a large number of nerve endings. At birth, a flabby sheath of skin, called the foreskin, covers the glans. In many cases, for reasons of hygiene or religion, this foreskin is surgically removed soon after birth by a process known as **circumcision.** Internally, the penis contains a **urethra,** which is a tube through which urine and semen pass. In addition, there are three cylinders of spongy tissue inside the penis that are richly laced with blood vessels. When a male is sexually aroused, blood fills the spaces within these cylinders, causing an erection. Thus, contrary to common opinion, it is the flow of blood, rather than muscular action, that causes the erection of the penis.

The **testes** (or testicles) are the main internal organs of the male sexual system. They have two functions: the production of **sperm** and the production of the male sex hormones known as *androgens*. Each testis is made up of

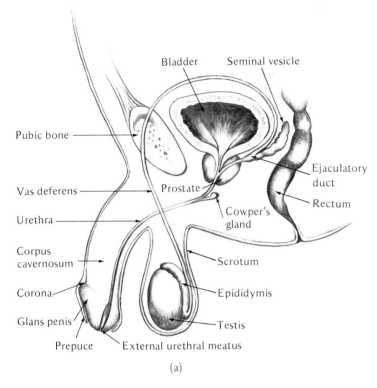

Bladder
Seminal vesicle
Pubic bone
Ejaculatory duct
Vas deferens
Prostate
Rectum
Urethra
Cowper's gland
Corpus cavernosum
Scrotum
Corona
Epididymis
Glans penis
Testis
Prepuce
External urethral meatus

(a)

FIGURE 12.1   THE MALE SEXUAL SYSTEM

about 500 long curled tubes about the width of a thread. Sperm are manufactured within these tubes. The sperm moves through these tubes into a larger tube, the *epididymis,* which is about 20 feet long and lies curled on the top and side of the testis. It generally takes the sperm cell about 70 days from the time it originates until it passes through the epididymis. The sperm then enter another tube which takes them past the *prostate gland.* The prostate gland manufactures a fluid that is mixed with the sperm to make up *semen.* This semen is excreted out the urethra when the male is excited to ejaculation. This may seem like quite a long trip for the sperm cell, but the length of the journey has an important function: The sperm cell requires this time to mature to the point where it is capable of playing its part in the reproductive cycle.

The testes are contained in a loose sack of skin called the **scrotum.** Body temperature would kill the sperm produced by the testes, so the location of the testes in the scrotum allows them to remain three degrees centigrade cooler than body temperature. The scrotum is lined with a muscle that helps control the temperature of the testes. When the outside temperature is hot, the muscle relaxes, allowing the testes to hang away from the body. When the outside temperature is cold, and at times of strong sexual excitement, the muscle contracts, bringing the testes close to the body.

The Female Sexual System

The external parts of the female genitals are collectively called the **vulva.** Most visible is the **mons veneris** (literally "mound of Venus"), which is a fatty pad of tissue, covered with pubic hair, on top of the pubic bone (Figure 12.2). Below this are the **labia majora** ("major lips"), which are made of fleshy folds of tissue rich in

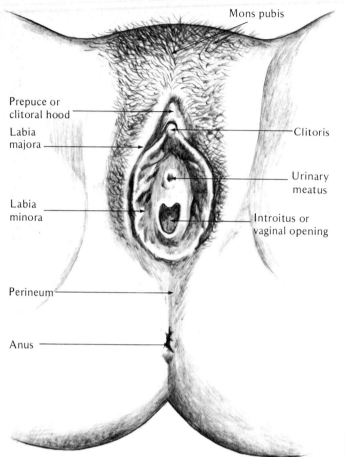

Mons pubis

Prepuce or
clitoral hood

Labia
majora

Labia
minora

Clitoris

Urinary
meatus

Introitus or
vaginal opening

Perineum

Anus

**FIGURE 12.2   THE FEMALE
SEXUAL SYSTEM**

nerve endings. Lying within the labia majora are the **labia minora** ("minor lips"), which contain a large number of blood vessels and nerve endings. The appearance of the labia can vary greatly from woman to woman.

The **clitoris** is situated inside the labia minora. Its sole function is sexual arousal. The clitoris is made up of a shaft and a glans, but only the glans is visible. The clitoris is richly supplied with nerve endings and is the most sexually sensitive part of a woman's body. In some women, the clitoris is so sensitive that they try to avoid having it directly stimulated. During sexual stimulation, the labia majora and minora become engorged with blood and form a protective cushion for the clitoris. The sexually aroused clitoris itself becomes engorged with blood and expands in size.

The internal genitals include the **vagina,**

which is a flexible tube lined with mucous membranes. The labia majora cover and protect the entrance to the vagina. The vagina is 3 to 3 1/2 inches wide at its opening and is controlled by a muscle that can constrict and expand. The lower third of the vagina has more nerve endings than the upper two-thirds and is more sensitive to sexual stimulation. The vagina is connected to the **uterus,** or womb, at an opening called the cervix. The uterus is lined with a layer of blood vessels that form the menstrual flow when shed during menstruation. It is the uterus that houses the fetus during pregnancy. Attached to the uterus are two tubes known as the fallopian tubes. At the end of these tubes are the ovaries. The ovaries contain tiny follicle tubes that house the *ova,* or eggs. Every four weeks (give or take a few days), one of the follicles bursts, releasing its egg into the fallopian tube. If the egg is fertilized by a sperm cell in the fallopian tube, it makes its way into the uterus, where it lodges and begins to form an embryo. In addition to producing mature eggs, the ovaries secrete the female sex hormones.

Other Erogenous Areas

The genitals aren't the only areas of the body whose stimulation results in sexual arousal. In both males and females, light stimulation of the lips, ears, and neck can lead to sexual arousal. Gentle touching of the nipples of the breast also produces sexual arousal in many males and females. In many cultures, including our own, the size and shape of the female breast are associated with attractiveness and sexual arousal (Maier, 1984). The size of the female breast is determined by heredity, and no difference in function of the breasts is associated with size: Small breasts produce as much milk for a nursing baby as do large ones. Nor is breast size related to responsiveness to sexual stimulation.

Another, and in many respects the most important, erogenous zone is the mind. As we will discuss later in this chapter, our minds may conjure up an almost endless variety of sexual fantasies that are capable of arousing us or enhancing sexual arousal we are already experiencing. Females have reported being able to reach orgasm solely through the use of fantasy (Stock & Greer, 1982).

The publishers of *Harper's Bazaar* were clearly aware of the power of sexual fantasy; they were able to skillfully pose Lauren Bacall so that she would arouse the sexual fantasies of the readers. Bacall was able to project a seductive and arousing image while completely clothed in the accepted fashion of the day.

Just as our thoughts can stimulate us to arousal, they can also play a more villianous role of ensuring that almost no amount of stimulation will arouse us or allow us to enjoy sexual experiences. As we will see in the section on sexual dysfunction, feelings of guilt, fear, or embarrassment can turn our sexuality into a nightmare.

Bacall was taught to project a seductive and sexually arousing image. "The Look" was designed to arouse the sexual fantasies of the readers.
The Bettmann Archive.

THE HUMAN SEXUAL RESPONSE

Lauren Bacall was both excited and puzzled by the physical changes that resulted in the intimate moments of her relationship with Humphrey Bogart: "My heart would literally pound. I knew that physical changes were happening within me—the simplest word, look or move would bring a gut reaction" (Bacall, 1978, p. 133). Her innocence or ignorance about her own sexual responses prevented her from understanding what these effects were.

Lauren was clearly not alone in lacking knowledge about the human sexual response. In the 1940s when she met Bogie there had been almost no research on this topic. Indeed, how would anyone study such a private behavior? Many believed that investigators shouldn't conduct research on behavior that was so personal that people wouldn't even talk about the subject.

Not until the early 1960s did laboratory research by William Masters and Virginia Johnson (1966) begin to uncover some of the mystery of the human sexual response. Because of the sensitivity of the issue, Masters and Johnson began their research by recruiting male and female prostitutes. They used instruments that measured blood pressure, heart rate, and breathing, and they developed instruments called **plethysmographs** that could be placed around the penis or inserted inside the vagina to record responses of the genitals. They soon found that the prostitutes weren't good subjects with which to work, and they recruited 694 other subjects from the local population. They took careful readings while the subjects engaged in a wide variety of sexual behaviors, including masturbation and sexual intercourse. The results of their research have presented us with the most complete picture of the human sexual response currently available.

Some people continue to criticize Masters and Johnson for their invasion of a private domain. But there are numerous answers that can be given to the question of why the sexual response should be studied. One is that the results of the research are of great help in diagnosing and developing therapy for sexual dysfunctions; in fact Masters and Johnson developed a therapy technique for treating sexual dysfunctions. The results of research into sexual response also help us better understand our own behavior and responses. No longer must people wonder in ignorance whether a certain physical action or change is unusual; the mystery of the sexual response may provide some excitement, but often it leads to confusion and anxiety.

Before we examine the findings of Masters and Johnson, two cautions should be expressed. First, just as is the case with the size and shape of the genitals, there is a wide variety in people's sexual responsiveness. Research presents a general picture, but it also shows the wonderful variety of people's responses. We aren't machines made from the same mold and programmed to follow the exact same pattern. The second caution is against overanalyzing our own behavior. One of the most maddening experiences is to watch a good movie with a friend (or ex-friend) who insists on analyzing every part of the movie, the acting, and the stage setting. This boorish in-

dividual can suddenly dampen our enjoyment of the movie. So, too, can we ruin our own pleasure of a sexual experience if we become too intent on analyzing every feeling and physical change that occurs. By doing this, we may become inhibited and lose the spontaneity that is so vital for enjoying our sexual experiences. Thus knowledge may remove confusion and misunderstanding, but misuse of this knowledge may have unfortunate consequences.

Masters and Johnson (1966) identified four phases in the sexual response. Interestingly enough, they found that both males and females experience these phases and that their responses during these phases are similar in many cases.

The *excitement phase* of sexual arousal can begin whenever a man or a woman becomes aroused sexually as a result of being caressed by another person or by imagining, reading about, observing, anticipating, or discussing sexual behavior. During this phase the heart rate increases and breathing becomes deeper and faster. In males there is an erection of the penis and in females the breasts and clitoris swell and vaginal lubrication occurs. The vaginal secretions play two important roles. First, they lubricate the vagina to make penetration by the penis easier. Second, they neutralize the vagina's natural acidity, which would kill the sperm (Maier, 1984). This excitement phase can last from slightly more than a minute to several hours, depending on the circumstances.

When arousal increases even more, the *plateau phase* is reached. Even greater swelling of the penis and secretion in the vagina occur. The clitoris retracts under a fold of skin where it can't receive direct stimulation; it is so sensitive during this stage that direct stimulation could be experienced as painful. The male testes also retract, moving up in the scrotum. During this phase, the testes increase in size, sometimes as much as 100 percent. There may be a "sex flush," or reddening of the skin, and an increase in muscle tension throughout the body. As arousal increases, there is a feeling of losing control and of the inevitability of reaching the sexual climax called **orgasm.**

When the **orgasm phase** is reached, people experience very intense pleasure and release from tension. In men there are rhythmic contractions of the muscles in and around the penis and ejaculation of semen. In women there are muscular contractions around the vagina and pulsation of the uterus. In both men and women, the contractions occur every eight-tenths of a second and last for varying lengths of time. For both men and women, the first five or six contractions are the most pleasurable. During orgasm the heart rate may double, muscles may go into intense spasms, and the person may emit uncontrollable cries.

In the *resolution phase,* the body gradually returns to normal. In the female, the vaginal muscles relax and the clitoris re-emerges from its protective fold of skin. Some women begin to perspire during this phase, with the heaviest perspiration being on the forehead and underarms. The amount of perspiration often reflects the intensity of the orgasm. Women may be stimulated back to orgasm at any time during the resolution phase; women often experience the succeeding orgasms more intensely than the initial orgasm. Unlike females, males have a *refractory period* during the resolution phase; during this period they are unresponsive to sexual stimulation. The length of the refractory period varies from male to male and is influenced by a number of factors, including age and health. During the resolution phase, the penis and testes return to their unstimulated state. Both males and females experience the resolution phase as relaxing and pleasant.

Comparing Male and Female Sexual Response

As we have pointed out, there are many similarities between male and female sexual responses. Similar changes occur in breathing, heart rate, and muscle tension. Both males and females may show a sex flush, although it is more common in females. Enlargement of the genitals occurs in both sexes. There is also some evidence that males and females experience, or at least describe, orgasm in similar ways. In an interesting study, Vance and Wagner (1976) asked male and female subjects to write descriptions of their orgasms. These descriptions were then examined by a group of judges (medical students, gynecologists, and clinical psychologists), who were asked to identify which descriptions were written by males and which were written by females. These experts were unable to correctly match the description with the sex of the author.

REVIEW QUESTIONS

1. Match the following terms with their description or function.

_____ the tube through which semen and urine pass

_____ produces male sex hormones

_____ covers the entrance to the vagina and protects the opening

_____ manufactures the fluid that along with the sperm, makes up semen

_____ connected to the uterus

_____ where the egg is fertilized

a. testes
b. fallopian tube
c. scrotum
d. vagina
e. urethra
f. labia majora
g. labia minor
h. prostrate gland
i. uterus

2. Masters and Johnson have identified four phases of sexual arousal. The phase characterized by a "sex flush" and an increase in muscle tension is called the _____ phase.

3. The period of time after orgasm when men are relatively unresponsive to sexual stimulation is called the _____ _____ .

4. T or F: Men and women tend to describe their orgasms in similar ways.

re are many similarities be-
'emale sexual response, there
ences. Males have one orgasm,
...ales show considerable variability.
...en may experience no orgasms, one orgasm, or multiple orgasms during intercourse.
The orgasm for the male is generally similar in
strength and duration from one time to the
next. A woman, on the other hand, may show
considerable variation in strength and duration
of orgasm. While there are many individual differences in the pattern of sexual responses, females show considerably more variability.
Significant variation occurs among women in
the number of orgasms they experience and in
their responses during the resolution phase.
Also, as we will discuss later in the chapter,
there are sex differences in the stimuli that
arouse males and females and in their speed of
arousal. Males generally become aroused more
quickly than females. This latter difference may
account for some of the complaints by females
that their sexual encounters are often too brief
to be fully satisfying (Hite, 1976).

SEXUAL BEHAVIOR: WHAT, WHEN, AND HOW OFTEN

As a child and young woman at home in New
York, Lauren Bacall seemed to completely fit
her mother's definition of a "nice Jewish girl."
She had few dates, didn't "chase men," and
thought little about sex. She shattered this image when she met Humphrey Bogart and began her affair with him at age 19. At one point
in her life when she was married to Bogie, Lauren spent a great deal of time with Adlai Stevenson, who was the Democratic nominee for
president. Some newspapers suggested that she
was having an affair with Stevenson. Bacall's
relationships with Frank Sinatra and Jason Robards also made juicy reading in many newspapers and magazines at the time. Lauren
Bacall was one of America's sex symbols and
many people were curious about her sex life.

But were her sexual exploits unusual? Were her
activities very different from those of other people during the time, or were her sexual relationships simply more in the public eye?

It's difficult to answer this question with
a great deal of certainty, because there was little research on the sexual behavior of Americans. It's somewhat ironic, but until 1948 we
knew more about the sexual behavior of the
Trobriand Islanders and the Samoans than we
did about the sexual activities of people in the
United States. Anthropologists such as Bronis-
law Malinowski and Margaret Mead had studied and published books on the sexual behavior
of tribal and island peoples in far off lands. Not
until 1948 did Alfred Kinsey and his associates
(1948) shock the country by publishing the results of a survey on the sexual behavior of men
in the United States. This book was followed in
1953 by a publication on the sexual behavior
of women. Kinsey and his associates conducted interviews with over 18,000 men and
women, asking them questions about all aspects of their sexual experiences. This work began to give us insight into the sexual behavior
of people during the 1940s and early 1950s.

More recently, other surveys (Hite, 1976;
Hunt, 1974) have been conducted, and it is
now not unusual to see magazines conducting
their own surveys. Results from these surveys
allow us to examine how sexual behavior has
changed (or not changed) in the 30 years since
the pioneering work of Alfred Kinsey. As we review some of these findings, one point will be
particularly striking. While reports about the
frequency of some behaviors show some
change during the period, in many other cases
there seems to have been little change in
sexual behavior during the 30 years. This is despite the obvious change in expressed attitudes. As we review these findings, it is
important to keep in mind that these results rely
on the self-reports of people questioned. It's
difficult to carefully check their accuracy or to
be sure that the people who were interviewed
or completed questionnaires were truly repre-
sentative of the population as a whole. With
this caution in mind, let's examine some specific behaviors.

Sexual Fantasy

One of the most common sexual behaviors is to fantasize about sexual experiences. A **sexual fantasy** is a thought or daydream that is sexually exciting (Schulz, 1984). Kinsey reported that 84 percent of the males and 69 percent of the females in his study reported being sometimes aroused by sexual fantasies.

Sexual fantasies serve many purposes. First, they can excite and arouse a person. One study found that men with active fantasy lives reported the highest level of general sexual arousal (Giambra & Martin, 1977). Men are most likely to use fantasy as a means of becoming aroused, while women tend to fantasize after becoming aroused (Daley, 1975). Second, fantasies can enrich and add excitement to sexual behavior. Third, sexual fantasies may be used to rehearse or plan anticipated sexual contacts. Lauren Bacall reports that during the early period of her relationship she would often daydream about what she and Bogart would do when they were together. Fourth, sexual fantasies may provide relief from boredom. Many people state that they often fantasize during dull situations such as lectures (Maier, 1984). Be-fore you adopt sexual fantasy as a general cure-all, it should be pointed out that some people find that fantasy reduces arousal, either because it arouses guilt and inhibitions or because it distracts their attention from physical arousal (Hensen & Rubin, 1971).

People show a great deal of variety in the topics of their sexual fantasies. Overall, men's fantasies often involve themes of aggression or power, while women's fantasies tend to be more romantic and focused on intimacy. While the specifics of fantasies may vary widely, Hunt (1974) found some common themes. As can be seen in Table 12.2, the most common male fantasies involved having intercourse with a stranger or having sex with more than one opposite sex person at a time. Females most often fantasized about doing things they wouldn't do in reality or about having intercourse with a stranger.

TABLE 12.2

Reports of Fantasies of Men and Women During Masturbation

THEME	PERCENT REPORTING THEME	
	Males	Females
1. Having intercourse with a stranger.	47	21
2. Having sex with more than one person at the same time.	33	18
3. Doing things one would never do in reality.	19	28
4. Being forced to have sex.	10	19
5. Forcing someone to have sex.	13	3
6. Homosexual themes	7	11

SOURCE: Reprinted with permission of PEI Books, Inc. from *Sexual Behavior in the 1970's* by Morton Hunt. Copyright © 1974 by Morton Hunt.

Masturbation

The first and most common sexual experience for most people is **masturbation,** the self-manipulation of one's genitals to orgasm. Kinsey found that more than 90 percent of males and 60 percent of females had masturbated. Males begin masturbating at an earlier age and engage in this behavior more frequently than do females. The frequency of masturbation is greatest during adolescence, although 72 percent of married men and 68 percent of married women over the age of 30 engage in masturbation (Hunt, 1974).

Given these figures, it is somewhat amazing to consider the bad reputation that masturbation has achieved and the great lengths that parents have gone to in trying to prevent their children from masturbating. Kinsey (1948) summed up the conventional horror story about masturbation: "Every conceivable ill, from pimples to insanity, including stooped shoulders, loss of weight, fatigue, insomnia, general weakness, neurasthenia, loss of manly-mindedness, genital cancer, and the rest was ascribed to masturbation" (p. 513). In the early part of the century, the United States Patent Office issued a patent for a device that would ring a bell in the parents' bedroom when the child's bed moved in a pattern suggestive of masturbation (LoPiccolo & Heiman, 1977)! Even today, surveys have found as high as 50 percent of respondents who agree with statements asserting that masturbation is wrong (Levitt & Klassen, 1973). An interesting aside on this result is the finding that people tend to be most disturbed by portrayals of their own sex masturbating; males surveyed were most upset with depictions of males masturbating, while females were most upset with portrayals of females masturbating (Hatfield et al., 1978).

Despite these historical concerns, there is no evidence to suggest any physical harmful effects resulting from masturbation (McMullen & Rosen, 1979). In fact, masturbation may be recommended by sex therapists in treating sexual dysfunctions (Maier, 1984). While masturbation itself isn't harmful, the guilt and anxiety instilled in children by attempts to prevent masturbation may be traumatic. Since masturbation is often the person's first sexual behavior, insensitive attempts to repress and punish it may shape the individual's perception of all sexual behavior; sexual behavior, in general, may come to be viewed as something that is wrong and must be performed in secrecy.

Premarital Intercourse

Lauren Bacall was 19 years old when she met Humphrey Bogart and had her first sexual relationship. To her mother, Lauren was still a child, and it was shocking and painful to think of her little Betty involved in a sexual relationship, especially with an older man like Bogart. Lauren was even somewhat shocked by her own behavior, but she didn't see it as that unusual. She was living in Hollywood, where drinking, drugs, and sexual affairs were relatively commonplace. Although Lauren's behavior made the newspapers and shocked her mother, we may ask whether or not her actions were really that unusual. What sexual experience did most nineteen-year-old women (and men) have at that time? Has the sexual behavior of unmarried men and women changed since the late 1940s?

The Kinsey data collected during the late 1940s and early 1950s suggest that Lauren's decision to engage in a premarital sexual relationship at age 19 was unusual for *women* of that time. Kinsey found that only 20 percent of the women he interviewed had engaged in **coitus** (sexual intercourse) before their twentieth birthdays. On the other hand, over 70 percent of the males reported having coitus before their twentieth birthdays. Kinsey also found differences between males and females when they were asked whether or not they had ever engaged in premarital coitus: More than twice as many men as women answered in the affirmative. As can be seen from these figures, a double standard clearly existed during that time.

Times have changed with regard to the incidence of premarital coitus, especially for women. Table 12.3 shows that two-thirds of the women surveyed by Hunt (1974) in the early 1970s had engaged in premarital intercourse. The rate was also up for men, but not as dramatically. The figures are even more striking when we examine the responses of people between the ages of 18 and 24. Hunt (1974) found that 95 percent of the men and 81 percent of the women had engaged in premarital intercourse. Two conclusions can be drawn from these results: Clearly a greater percentage of people (especially of women) are engaging in premarital sexual intercourse now than was the case 35 years ago; and the double standard seems to be dying, since the difference between the percentage of men and of women engaging in premarital coitus is rapidly decreasing.

TABLE 12.3

Percentage of People Reporting Premarital Intercourse

	AGE GROUP				
	18–24	25–34	35–44	45–54	55 and Over
Men	95	92	86	89	84
Women	81	65	41	36	31

SOURCE: Reprinted with permission of PEI Books, Inc. from *Sexual Behavior in the 1970's* by Morton Hunt. Copyright © 1974 by Morton Hunt.

While a majority of unmarried adults in our society today have had sexual relationships, it isn't true that these people lead wild sexual lives with an endless stream of partners. Quite the contrary is true. Reports indicate that, on the average, women who have engaged in premarital intercourse have done so with two partners; over half of the women reported having done so with only one partner whom they later married (Hunt, 1974). The average male surveyed had had six premarital sex partners.

In addition to a difference in the number of premarital sex partners, there also seems to be a difference in the way males and females react to their first coitus. Males express positive feelings twice as frequently as do females (Sorenson, 1973). Males view their loss of virginity as a triumph, while some females experience guilt and anxiety over having lost their virginity. Women, unlike men, may also experience physical pain associated with their first coitus; one study found that 30 percent of the women surveyed had experienced severe pain, while an additional 50 percent experienced brief or moderate pain (Oliven, 1974). Women's feelings about their first coitus seem to be independent of whether or not they were married at the time; one study (Schofield, 1973) that interviewed a number of women in England found similar responses in women who had experienced their first coitus before and after marriage. In most cases, negative emotional reactions and physical pain disappear quickly, and women express satisfaction with later sexual intercourse.

Before leaving the subject of premarital sexual intercourse, let's examine how this behavior affects, or doesn't affect, a relationship. Lauren Bacall's mother cautioned her that men would lose interest if Lauren became sexually involved with them. A group of investigators (Peplau, Rubin, & Hill, 1977) conducted an in-depth study of 200 dating couples in Boston. Eighty-two percent of the couples had had sexual intercourse with their current partners; approximately half of this group had done so within one month of their first date. Thus we can define three groups based on sexual experience: those who abstained from sexual in-

tercourse, those who experienced it early in the relationship, and those who experienced it later. When the investigators examined the relationships two years later, they found that experience with sexual behavior didn't affect the long-term success of the relationship; overall 20 percent of the couples had married, 34 percent had continued to date, and 46 percent had broken up. Thus engaging in premarital intercourse with one's partner will neither increase the chances of the relationship succeeding nor harm the chances of success.

Marital Intercourse

Western cultures attempt to regulate sexual behavior through the institution of marriage. Sexual intercourse between married people is universally accepted and expected, although some societies have rules governing the nature and frequency of marital intercourse (Schulz, 1984). The association between marriage and intercourse is so strong in our society that, until recently, people could force their marriage partners to have coitus without fear of being prosecuted for rape.

Studies (Kinsey et al., 1948; Hunt, 1974) have found that married couples engage in coitus on the average of two to four times a week. However, Table 12.4 shows that the frequency of marital coitus has changed over the last 30 years and that it is affected by age. Overall,

TABLE 12.4

Frequency of Marital Coitus in the United States, 1938–1949 and 1972

1938–1949		1972	
Age	Median	Age	Median
16–25	2.45	18–24	3.25
26–35	1.95	25–34	2.55
36–45	1.40	35–44	2.00
46–55	0.85	45–54	1.00
56–60	0.50	55 and over	1.00

SOURCE: Reprinted with permission of PEI Books, Inc. from *Sexual Behavior in the 1970's* by Morton Hunt. Copyright © 1974 by Morton Hunt.

married partners now engage in coitus more than they did 30 years ago. This difference is found regardless of the age of the individuals. Surveys (Thornton, 1977; Levin & Levin, 1975) show a positive relationship between frequency of intercourse and satisfaction with the marriage: The more often couples have sexual intercourse, the more likely they are to report being satisfied with their marriages. One study found that only 9 percent of women who reported no sexual relationship in their marriages were happy with their marriages. We can't take these results to mean that frequent coitus makes for better marriages. It may well be the other way around: Satisfaction with a marriage may lead to more frequent intercourse. However, the results do indicate that the two are related.

From Table 12.5 we can also see that the frequency of marital intercourse declines as people become older. This doesn't mean that sexual behavior is not found in the relationships of older people; reports show that men and women in their seventies continue to engage in sexual intercourse and enjoy it as part of their relationships (Maier, 1984). But age does affect people's sexual organs and sexual response. Older men require longer periods of stimulation to achieve erections, and manual stimulation of the penis may be required (Schulz, 1984). The refractory period for older men is usually longer than that for young men. However, older men are typically capable of maintaining their erections for longer periods of time than are young men and hence may engage in coitus for a longer period of time.

Aging women undergo more physiological changes than do aging men. At **menopause,** which generally occurs between the ages of 45 and 55, menstruation ceases, and a woman is no longer capable of reproduction. Menopause is marked by a general hormonal imbalance. The vaginal walls become less elastic and lubrication of the vagina is slower and less complete. Menopause may also be accom-

TABLE 12.5

Methods of Birth Control

METHOD	THEORETICAL FAILURE RATE	MAJOR ADVANTAGES	MAJOR DISADVANTAGES
Withdrawal	9%	No preplanning or artificiality	Frustration or lack of fulfillment
Rhythm	13%	Acceptable to Roman Catholic Church	Anxiety; difficulties with periods of abstinence
Condom	3%	Protection against diseases; ease of use	Reduced sensitivity of penis; interruption of sexual activity
Spermacide	3%	Ease of use; added lubrication	Allergic reactions in some women
Diaphragm	3%	May hold menstrual flow	Allergic reactions in some women; inconvenience
IUD	1–3%	Little attention required after insertion, possible after-the-fact effectiveness	Side effects, including bleeding and possible infections
Oral contraceptive	1%	Ease of use; relief of some menstrual problems	Side effects, especially in very young women, women over thirty-five, and smokers
Female sterilization	Close to 0	Permanent effectiveness	Restoration of fertility not always possible
Male sterilization	Close to 0	Simple procedure, permanent effectiveness	Restoration of fertility unlikely
Induced abortion	—	After-the-fact procedure	Health risks; moral implications

Adapted From Maier, 1984, p. 271.

Although frequency of marital intercourse declines with age, older people often enjoy satisfying sexual relationships.

Mimi Forsyth, Monkmeyer.

panied by headaches, dizziness, and hot flashes, which are sudden waves of heat from the waist up.

Sexual expression among the aged is affected by a number of factors in addition to these physiological changes. One factor is physical health. Not only are the aged more likely to suffer from periodic illnesses that curtail their sexual behavior, but the aged may have a harder time regaining normal sexual functioning after periods of abstinence (Masters & Johnson, 1966). A second important factor is a common notion in our society that sexual behavior in older persons is unusual or even ridiculous. Our society seems to hold the view that sexual behavior is something to be enjoyed only by the young; almost every portrayal of sexual behavior, whether it be movies, magazines, or advertisements, involves younger people. The message is that older people are sexless. Some elderly people accept this propaganda, and even those who don't are often reluctant to discuss their sexual problems, even with doctors. Thus these and

other factors work against the aged engaging in active sex lives, even though they are very capable of doing so.

Extramarital Intercourse

Looking back over her relationships with men, Lauren Bacall observed: "Mentally, I had it straight—it was wrong to become involved, to have anything at all to do with a man who belonged to someone else. . . . With all of that firmly implanted in my brain, I found that with the exception of Frank [Sinatra], every man I was really attracted to had a wife" (1978, p. 405). This statement reflects a conflict that a number of married people face. Extramarital sexual relationships are considered wrong in many societies. One study found that over 61 percent of societies had rules against extramarital sexual relationships; in 16 percent of the societies, these rules applied only to women (Ford & Beach, 1951). A survey of attitudes of people in the United States found that 72 percent of respondents believed that extramarital sex is "always wrong" (Levitt & Klassen, 1973).

Despite these attitudes, Kinsey (1953) found that 50 percent of males and 25 percent of females had experienced extramarital coitus. More recent research (Tavris & Sadd, 1977) found that, while the percentage of males has remained fairly stable, 40 percent of the females reported having extramarital affairs. The frequency of extramarital affairs decreases with age for males but tends to increase up to age 40 for females. Another trend is that wives who hold full-time jobs outside the home are more likely to have affairs than are housewives. One reason for this may be that women who work outside the home have more opportunity to meet a variety of men.

With such strong attitudes against extramarital relationships, we may ask why they occur. In some cases, the cause may be dissatisfaction with marital sex. In other cases, the individual may wish to punish his or her spouse. A third reason is insecurity; the person may feel the need to prove that he or she is still attractive to others. A fourth reason may be a desire to find excitement and escape boredom.

We seem to have a morbid curiosity about extramarital affairs. Lauren Bacall's affairs were widely written about in some newspapers and gossip magazines. Even today, the love lives of movie stars and political figures make the newspapers. Although news items about these affairs may conjure up images of excitement and romance, the facts tend to portray a different picture. People tend to find extramarital affairs less satisfying than marital sex. For example, in one survey two-thirds of husbands rated their marital intercourse as "very pleasurable," while less than 50 percent of the men who had had extramarital affairs rated this intercourse as "very pleasurable" (Hunt, 1974). Guilt, fear of being discovered, and the secretness surrounding extramarital affairs distract from the pleasure and intimacy.

Homosexuality

A great deal of attention has recently been focused on **homosexuality,** which involves sexual relationships between individuals of the same sex. We hear stories today about homosexuals "coming out of the closet" and about fights for "gay rights." The increased attention being given to homosexuality may leave the impression that homosexuality is something new. But homosexual behavior is not a modern-day phenomenon. Homosexual relationships were common among the ancient Greeks; both Plato and Socrates wrote about homosexuality and may have practiced homosexual behavior. The term **lesbian** (female homosexual) originated in ancient Greece. Sappho, one of the great poets of antiquity, ran a school for girls in the sixth century B.C. and fell in love with some of her students. She lived on the Greek island of Lesbos and was therefore called a Lesbian. Homosexuality was also widely accepted by the ancient Romans: Julius Caesar has been described as "every woman's man and every man's woman" (Leiser, 1979). The advent of Christianity was accompanied by condemnation of homosexual behavior. Augustine (354–430 A.D.) described homosexuality as a sin against nature, and by the fourth century A.D. homosexuals were being burned at the stake.

Negative attitudes toward homosexuality continued into recent times. A survey in the United States in 1977 found that 72 percent of white Americans felt that homosexual relations were "always wrong" (Lief, 1977). Another study (Weinberg & Williams, 1974) found that almost half of the people surveyed felt that homosexuality was vulgar and obscene.

While these results paint a very unaccepting picture of homosexuality, there is another side to the coin. For example, the attitudes expressed by Americans aren't found in other Western cultures; only 11.8 percent of a sample of Danes and 5.4 percent of a Dutch sample believed that homosexuality was vulgar and obscene. In 1973, the American Psychiatric Association decided that it was inaccurate to describe homosexuality as a "psychological disorder."

Just as there may be confusion about attitudes toward homosexuality, there is also misunderstanding about "homosexuals" and homosexual behavior. Kinsey argued that there is not a clear line dividing homosexuals and heterosexuals. Rather, sexual orientation should be viewed as a continuum running from exclusively heterosexual to exclusively homosexual (see Figure 12.3). In support of this position, Kinsey found that only about 2 percent of the males and 1 percent of the females he surveyed described themselves as exclusively homosexual in orientation. But almost a quarter of the men and 15 to 20 percent of the females reported some homosexual experience in their lives.

Another misconception about homosexual relationships is that they are solely based on sex. Actually, the frequency of sexual relations is about the same in homosexual relationships as it is in heterosexual relationships (Bell & Weinberg, 1978). Many homosexuals, like heterosexuals, enter relationships in search of mutual love and intimacy; sexual gratification is of secondary importance (Schulz, 1984). The seedy portrayal of the life of homosexuals is partly the result of the need for secrecy; homosexuality is against the law in most states. As a result, meeting other homosexuals may be very difficult, and, because of this fact, the cen-

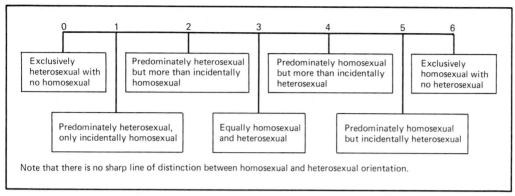

FIGURE 12.3   RANGE OF SEXUAL ORIENTATIONS

SOURCE: Adapted from Kinsey et al., 1948, p. 638, taken from Maier, 1984, p. 361.

tral part of the gay community in many larger cities is the *gay bar*. Gay bars represent places where gay men and lesbians can meet new friends and partners, engage in conversation, enjoy entertainment, and socialize. The bars are places where homosexuals will be accepted.

Numerous theories have attempted to explain the causes of homosexuality. Some theories argue that the cause is genetic or hormonal. Others focus on early family life and socialization. For example, one investigator (Bieber, 1976) found that homosexuals he saw in therapy tended to have dominant mothers and passive fathers. Another recent theory (Storms, 1981) links physiological changes with homosexual social development. According to this theory, a person is more likely to develop a homosexual orientation if his or her sex drive develops at an early stage in life when most friends are of the same sex. At later stages of adolescence, people develop many friendships with opposite-sex others; if the sex drive develops at that stage, sexual desires will be associated with people of the opposite sex.

While there is disagreement about the causes of homosexual orientation, there has been some agreement about the adjustment of homosexuals. At one time, it was common to view homosexuals as emotionally disturbed people who turned to homosexual relationships because they couldn't adjust to the heterosexual world. This doesn't seem to be the case. Most homosexuals tend to have steady relationships and wide circles of friends, to be satisfied with their jobs, and to describe themselves as being "pretty happy" (Bell & Weinberg, 1978). Some, however, report being less accepting of themselves; some have psychosomatic illnesses and have contemplated suicide. It's difficult to know the exact cause of these feelings, but they may well be the result of the stresses experienced by nonheterosexual people in a predominantly heterosexual society.

FACTORS AFFECTING THE JOY OF SEX

The sexual behavior of most animals is controlled by hormones and instinct. The goal of animals' heterosexual intercourse is reproduction. Humans, however, have been freed from the straightjacket of hormones and instinct. We may engage in sexual behavior for pleasure and intimacy, as well as reproduction. Our sexual activities are limited more by our imaginations than by our hormonal attributes. This freedom can add exciting and pleasing dimensions to our lives. For some of us, however, it may create a living hell, dominated by anxiety and insecurity. The choice in most cases is our own, but it can be strongly affected by others. For this reason, it's important that we understand our bodies and our sexual responses and develop a sensitivity to others. A wide variety of factors will influence whether or not we will enjoy our sexuality or dread it.

EXPECTATIONS.   Sex is glorified in our society. Sexual experience supposedly turns girls into women and boys into men. Reading magazines and love novels leads us to expect ecstasy and pure pleasure every time we engage in sexual behavior. In some cases we may even be led to expect drums to beat, fire crackers to shoot into the sky, and bands to play when we engage in sexual activities. Watching movies leads us to believe that people are natural-born lovers; all that is needed for a satisfying sexual encounter is two willing people. The movies rarely show the star having trouble achieving an erection or experiencing pain during intercourse. And, in today's more sexually liberal environment, we may not only assume that everyone knows "how to do it," but also that everyone "should be willing to do it."

These unrealistic expectations may create problems in enjoying our actual sexual experiences. The art of making love is something that must be learned. Each of us is different, and we derive pleasure in different ways. It takes practice and communication with a partner to develop a satisfying relationship. The decision whether or not to engage in any type of sexual behavior must be an individual one. A person can't be expected to experience pleasure or to give pleasure if he or she feels forced into sexual behavior. The pleasure obtained from sexual behavior is affected by a number of factors and may well vary from time to time; expecting pure bliss in every sexual encounter may lead to hurt feelings and confusion.

COMMUNICATION.   Most of us wouldn't hesitate to complain if we were uncomfortable in a room that was too hot or if someone standing on our toes was causing us pain. We are quick to say what movies we enjoyed and what food we don't like. Too often, however, we're reluctant to communicate our feelings about our sexual experiences. Some people are embar-

Open communication and tenderness are important ingredients to a satisfying sexual relationship.
Teri Leigh Stratford.

rassed to discuss the sexual activities that give them pleasure or to tell their partners about the actions that cause pain or discomfort. It's not unusual for a person to fake an orgasm to make his or her partner think a "successful" encounter has occurred. The lack of communication turns sex into a guessing game: Sexual partners must guess what the other person is willing to do and enjoys. Open communication about feelings, both positive and negative, will go a long way toward making sexual behavior more enjoyable for those involved.

EXPLORATION.   Some people approach sexual behavior much as they do their jobs; sexual performance is something to be measured by criteria such as efficiency and speed. Sexual behavior is taken to mean simply sexual intercourse. But coitus is only one of the sexual activities people can enjoy together. Sexual behavior offers people the opportunity to experience a deep sense of intimacy. It's an opportunity to explore another person's body and to experience the exciting sensations that result from touching and being touched. Thus *foreplay,* the activities used to heighten sexual arousal before intercourse, may be as satisfying and enjoyable as intercourse itself. Taking the time to enjoy exploration and experience physical intimacy heightens the pleasure of sexual relationships.

SETTING. Lauren Bacall's early meetings with Humphrey Bogart were rushed and often took place in his car in a dark alley, in hastily arranged motel rooms, and in secret places on film locations. Lauren was excited by her feelings for Bogie, but she felt frustrated at these hurried, secret meetings. She also suggests that these arrangements may have increased her guilt and worry about the relationship.

The setting is important to have a satisfying sexual experience. While variety may instill new excitement in the relationship, both people should be comfortable with the chosen setting. Hurried encounters in unappealing places turn the relationship into a frantic race against time and discovery. They can also result in guilt and in feelings that sex is wrong or something to be hidden.

ALCOHOL AND DRUGS. Humphrey Bogart was a heavy drinker when Lauren Bacall met him. He would often call her after he'd been drinking, and she would rush to meet him. Many people believe that alcohol and drugs enhance sexual pleasure. In one study 60 percent of those surveyed reported that they enjoyed sex more after drinking (Athanasiou et al., 1970). But before you reach for the bottle, consider the following points. First, alcohol is a depressant; it reduces sensation and in large amounts can even result in men's inability to have erections. Given this fact, it has been argued that the positive effects of alcohol on sexual behavior result because alcohol reduces inhibitions and feelings of guilt. It seems, however, that the alcohol itself doesn't accomplish this. Wilson and Lawson (1976) divided male subjects into groups. They gave one group a mixture of vodka and tonic and another group only tonic, although those men were led to believe they were drinking alcohol. A third group was given vodka, but led to believe it was only tonic. The groups were then shown an erotic film, and their arousal was measured. The greatest arousal was found in the men who drank only

Although many people believe alcohol will reduce sexual inhibitions, alcohol is a depressant and reduces sensations.

Rhoda Sidney.

tonic but believed they were drinking vodka. The least arousal resulted in the men who drank vodka but believed it was only tonic. Thus it may be our *belief* that we aren't responsible for behavior when drinking, and not the alcohol itself, that reduces inhibitions and heightens sexual enjoyment.

The effect of drugs on sexual satisfaction hasn't been well studied. There is some indication that heroine decreases sexual desire but that small amounts of cocaine and marijuana increase sensitivity to touch and enjoyment of sex. However, long-term use of even these latter drugs can have negative effects, such as lowered sperm production and retarded ejaculation (Maier, 1984).

BIRTH CONTROL

Lauren Bacall's affair with Jason Robards was a rocky relationship. At times, things were great; they did exciting things together and were very close. At other times, the relationship was terrible; Robards would drink and leave for periods of time without warning. It was during one of these rough times that Lauren discovered she was pregnant. She was somewhat amazed that at thirty-six years old and with her experience she could allow herself to be pregnant and unmarried. In a panic, she considered abortion but decided against it. She eventually married Robards and had the baby, her third child.

There is a certain irony in the fact that one of America's sex symbols didn't have an effective means of birth control. While we may be amused with Lauren Bacall's predicament, some figures related to birth control aren't so amusing. Of the over 3 million births that occur each year in the United States, there are 700,000 unwanted pregnancies in teenaged girls; one out of six teenaged girls will become pregnant before she graduates from high school. Fewer than one-third of college students who acknowledge being sexually active use contraceptives regularly (Byrne, 1982). One recent study found that college women are using less effective contraceptive methods today than they did five years earlier, despite being more sexually active (Gerrard, 1982). These figures are particularly startling given the amount of information on birth control and the ease of obtaining contraceptives today.

While the terms **birth control** and **contraception** are often used interchangeably, there are differences between the two. *Birth control* involves any method used to prevent the birth of children; these include abstinence, contraception, sterilization, and abortion. *Contraception,* on the other hand, refers to methods used to prevent conception. Concern about birth control dates back over 4000 years. Women in ancient Egypt used a contraceptive made of crocodile dung and honey that they inserted into their vaginas before coitus. In earlier times, contraception and birth control were considered by many to be mainly the woman's concern. Today we are coming to realize that contraception and birth control are the responsibility of both the woman and the man. These topics should be discussed openly by both partners and a mutual decision should be reached. Open discussion and satisfactory decisions about contraception and birth control can contribute to a couple's enjoyment of sexual behavior.

Today a wide variety of contraceptives are available. As can be seen in Table 12.5, contraceptives work in a variety of ways. In some cases, the aid of a physician is necessary to obtain or fit the contraceptive, but in other cases the contraceptive can be obtained from birth control centers and drug stores. Table 12.5 also shows that, used properly, many of the contraceptives are highly effective. The difference between the theoretical failure rate and the actual failure rate is the result of improper use of the contraceptive.

Given the availability and effectiveness of contraceptives, it's somewhat surprising to find figures showing that many people don't use contraceptives. It has been suggested (Byrne, 1982) that the decision to use contraceptives occurs in five steps: acquiring information, admitting the likelihood of engaging in sexual intercourse, obtaining contraceptives, discussing contraceptives with the sexual partner, and practicing contraception. A number of factors may break this chain of events and lead people not to use contraceptives.

First, some people have difficulty admitting that they are likely to engage in sexual intercourse. Inserting a diaphragm or buying a condom may seem too "premeditated" to some people. Planning for sexual behavior and obtaining contraceptives may seem to remove the spontaneity and romance from sexual activity. Unfortunately, the romance for people with this attitude may be quickly replaced with the anxiety over an unwanted pregnancy. For other people, admitting ahead of time that they will engage in coitus goes against their self-image; they would rather not think about it, even though they don't refrain from sexual activity.

A second factor is that some people are embarrassed about discussing contraceptives with their sexual partners, doctors, or birth control counselors. As we pointed out earlier, sex for many people is something that may be engaged in but not talked about. This view is often reinforced by movies and novels. After all, how often does a movie portray two people discussing contraceptives before engaging in sexual intercourse? Once again, this failure to communicate may not only inhibit people from obtaining the most pleasure from their sexual activities but also may result in the pain, anxiety, and life upheaval associated with unwanted pregnancies.

Finally, failure to use contraceptives may be an intentional act. People may feel that they can save a dying relationship by an unexpected pregnancy. Indeed, Lauren Bacall and Jason Robards got married soon after Lauren discovered she was pregnant. A relationship that is based solely on an unwanted pregnancy is unlikely to be a stable one, however. Bacall and Robards were divorced within a few years. Thus many factors may inhibit the use of contraceptives. While we may understand these reasons, it is important to see that while some pain, inconvenience, or embarrassment may be avoided in the short run, the price may well be an unwanted pregnancy that will multiply the pain, inconvenience, and embarrassment many times.

Before leaving this topic, let's examine two other means of birth control.

Sterilization is being used with increasing frequency as a means of birth control; in fact, it has become the method most commonly used by married women between the ages of 30 and 44 (Schulz, 1984). New medical techniques allow sterilization to be performed quickly, safely, and with little pain. Male sterilization by vasectomy can be performed in about 15 minutes with a local anesthetic. Although it's possible in some cases to reverse the effects of sterilization, the operation should be considered permanent. For this reason, a decision to undergo sterilization should be accompanied by the decision that the individual doesn't intend to have children in the future.

Another method of birth control is **induced abortion.** Abortion terminates pregnancy by removing the immature fetus from the uterus. Abortions were used by the Chinese over 4000 years ago and have been fairly common in most societies since then. Abortion was legal in the United States until the 1860s. However, during the 1860s laws were passed making abortion illegal. The intent of these laws was largely to protect women from procedures that were dangerous at that time. The laws weren't very effective, however; almost 25 percent of the women interviewed by Kinsey (1953) had had an illegal abortion by the time they reached midlife. In 1973, the United States Supreme

Pro-choice advocates argue that women should have the right to control their own bodies and determine whether or not they want an abortion.

Mimi Forsyth, Monkmeyer.

Court declared that state laws prohibiting abortion were unconstitutional. Women now have the right to have abortions during the first three months of pregnancy; abortions between the third and sixth month are permitted with the consultation of a doctor; abortions after the sixth month (when the fetus has a chance of surviving outside the mother) are permitted only when there is a serious threat to the mother's health.

The issue of abortion is a very emotional one and has been the center of a heated controversy since the Supreme Court's ruling. Pro-abortion, or "pro-choice," advocates argue that women should be able to control their own bodies; a woman should be able to determine whether or not she wishes to carry a fetus. Pro-choice advocates also argue that abortion may be preferable to forcing a mother or a couple to cope with an unwanted child. On the other hand, anti-abortion, or "pro-life," advocates argue that life begins at conception, not at birth. According to this view, abortion is a form of murder, and the rights of the unborn child should be protected. This is clearly a tough issue to deal with, and one that isn't likely to be

Pro-life advocates argue that life begins at conception, and, therefore, abortion should be illegal.

Catholics for a Free Choice.

resolved easily. The question of abortion has become increasingly complicated by advancing medical techniques that can sustain the life of an immature fetus outside the womb. At present, people must rely on their own values and judgments in deciding the role that abortion should play in their own birth control efforts.

REVIEW QUESTIONS

5. Despite its generally taboo reputation, the first and most common sexual experience for most people is _____ .
6. T or F: The long term success of a relationship is decreased for couples who engage in premarital intercourse.
7. Which of the following is(are) true regarding marital intercourse?
   a. Married partners are more likely to engage in coitus than they did 30 years ago.
   b. Frequency of intercourse declines with age.
   c. There is a positive relationship between frequency of marital intercourse and overall satisfaction with the marriage.
   d. Only a and c are true.
   e. All the above are true.
8. T or F: Abstinence, sterilization, and abortion are all forms of contraception.
9. The minor surgical procedure used to sterilize males is called _____ .

SEXUAL DYSFUNCTIONS

Throughout this chapter, we've attempted to dispel the common belief that people are "born lovers." We don't suddenly wake up one morning to discover that we've been transformed into well-functioning sexual machines. A number of factors—including physical health, learning, emotions, and experience—must be combined to teach us the art of love. Even people most experienced with sexual behavior find that their enjoyment and sexual performance vary from time to time. Sometimes sex may be exciting and fulfilling, and at other times nothing seems to go right: It's difficult to get aroused, and when the mind says go, the body simply won't function. Most people experience periodic problems with their sexual behavior. In many cases, these may be caused by fatigue, alcohol, drugs, distractions, or worry. While periodic problems with sexual behavior may be frustrating, they should be expected and not cause great concern.

For some people, however, sexual problems are frequent or long-lasting. In these cases, we refer to the problems as **sexual dysfunctions.** There are numerous causes of these dysfunctions. Some are due to physical or organic problems such as illness, hormonal imbalance, or the side effects of surgery. Some are due to learning, or, more correctly, to the failure to learn satisfying and fulfilling sexual behaviors. Still others are due to emotions associated with sexual behavior such as fear or embarrassment.

Sexual dysfunctions may be particularly devastating to a person for a number of reasons. One is the great emphasis our society places on sexual performance; we can often accept the fact that someone is not a great athlete or musician, but everyone is expected to be able to perform sexually. Therefore sexual dysfunction may destroy a person's self-esteem. Second, the dysfunction affects not only the individual, but also relationships with other people. Frustration over the lack of sexual fulfillment can be at the root of discord and distress between partners. It's also possible that this discord and distress may be the root of the sexual dysfunction. Finally, until recently, people suffering sexual dysfunctions lived in a lonely hell. It was difficult for them to talk about their problem and hard for them to find someone who could effectively treat them. As we will see, this latter problem is quickly changing; there are an increasing number of sex therapists who are trained to diagnose the causes of sexual dysfunction and who can treat them with very high success rates.

ERECTILE DYSFUNCTION (IMPOTENCE). One of the most common sexual dysfunctions in males is **erectile dysfunction,** or impotence. This problem involves the failure to have or maintain an erection long enough to have sexual intercourse. *Primary erectile dysfunction* (which rarely occurs) refers to cases where the man has never had an erection long enough to have sexual intercourse. The more common type is *secondary erectile dysfunction,* which results when a man who has previously functioned normally can no longer maintain an erection.

In some cases, this dysfunction results from the failure to engage in effective foreplay before attempting sexual intercourse. In other cases the problem may stem from emotions such as fear, guilt, shame, or disgust. Unfortunately, the problem often perpetuates itself. For example, a man may experience difficulty maintaining an erection at one time. Although the cause of this failure may be fatigue, he may become very concerned about his ability to perform sexually. At the next opportunity to engage in sexual intercourse, his fear may surface and further inhibit erection. A third cause of secondary impotence is physical. In one study (Spark, White, & Connolly, 1980) physicians examined 105 impotent men and found physical causes in 70 of the cases.

PREMATURE EJACULATION. **Premature ejaculation** involves a man's inability to delay ejaculation long enough "to penetrate and satisfy his partner at least fifty percent of the time" (Masters & Johnson, 1970). Clearly this definition is based not only on the man's behavior, but also on how easily his partner is satisfied. However, in most cases of premature ejaculation, ejaculation occurs as soon as the penis penetrates the vagina (Kaplan, 1974). One of the main causes of this dysfunction is learned behavior. The man's early experience with sexual intercourse may have taught him that sex is a behavior that should be rushed; he may have a history of trying to hurry intercourse in order to avoid being detected or "caught in the act." This habit may have carried over into other situations in which there was no need to hurry sexual behavior. Another cause may be the man's attitude toward women. One study (Masters & Johnson, 1970) found that many premature ejaculators held women in low regard and didn't consider the woman's satisfaction to be of importance in sexual intercourse.

RETARDED EJACULATION. **Retarded ejaculation** is the opposite of premature ejaculation. In this case, the man finds it difficult or impossible to ejaculate during intercourse. In some cases the problem may result from diseases that attack the nervous system or from injury or surgical error that affects the nervous system. But in most cases the problem is psychological. At the extreme of this category is the man's fear that ejaculation is an indication that he is losing control. On the other hand, the most common inhibitions involve the man's fear of impregnating his partner or the loss of feelings of attraction for her. Sometimes hostility toward the partner may result in the man's determination not to "give her part of himself."

ORGASMIC DYSFUNCTION. The inability to experience an orgasm even when there is a normal sexual interest and drive is referred to as **orgasmic dysfunction.** *Primary dysfunction* involves cases where the woman has never experienced an orgasm. According to one survey (Hunt, 1974), about 10 percent of the women who responded stated that they had never had an orgasm. *Secondary,* or *situational, orgasmic dysfunction* involves cases where the woman has had orgasms but is not having them at the present time. The causes of this problem are quite debatable. It could be argued that the man, not the woman, is the cause of the woman's orgasmic dysfunction. The man's lack of tenderness, disinterest in foreplay, or rush to satisfy himself may be the root of this problem for many women. In other cases, the dysfunction may be associated with the woman's inhibitions about experiencing strong sexual feelings. Other feelings that inhibit orgasm include fear of abandonment, hostility or ambivalence toward the partner, and concern about losing control (Kaplan, 1974).

VAGINISMUS. **Vaginismus** is a relatively rare dysfunction that results when the muscles surrounding the vagina involuntarily constrict to inhibit penetration by the penis or to make penetration extremely painful. Like the other dysfunctions, the cause is often psychological. In some cases, the woman may have extreme fear about vaginal penetration. For other women, the cause can be traced to painful experiences associated with penetration, such as rape or an unpleasant pelvic examination.

SEX THERAPY

As we have seen, a wide variety of dysfunctions can interfere with people experiencing fulfilling sexual relationships. Fortunately, a number of techniques have been developed recently to help people overcome these dysfunctions through *sex therapy*. While the specifics of the treatment programs for the different dysfunctions vary, there are many commonalities. One is the assumption that many, if not most, sexual dysfunctions are directly caused or perpetuated by misinformation. People generally have a great deal of misinformation about sexual behavior, which has a particularly devastating effect when they are attempting to cope with dysfunctions. So most sex therapies emphasize education; individuals and couples are taught about sexual behavior (Masters & Johnson, 1970; LoPiccolo, 1978). Their fears and concerns are also explored in discussions that help clear up their misunderstandings and uncertainties about sexuality.

A second assumption underlying many sex therapies is that people must be taught how important touching is in sexual expression and communication. Touching and being touched in caring ways have many functions; they give pleasure, they help people communicate in tender ways, and they help people focus on and learn about their bodies. So in many therapies people are instructed how to touch their partners in ways that give pleasure. They are given help in "letting go" and enjoying the sensations of the experience.

As people's anxiety about sexuality decreases through sex therapy, specific techniques to overcome the various dysfunctions are introduced. In some cases, such as with orgasmic dysfunctions, people may be instructed in masturbation techniques before they're encouraged to attempt intercourse. In other cases, such as with premature ejaculation, the partners may be taught ways to vary their patterns of coitus in order to reduce the problem. In all cases, sex therapy stresses communication between partners. Working together and overcoming the problem often brings the partners closer together and leads to greater appreciation of the relationship. The success rate of many of the sex therapies is very high; in fact, Masters and Johnson (1970) reported a 100 percent success rate in treating clients for vaginismus.

SEXUALLY TRANSMITTED DISEASES

The causes of sexual dysfunctions are largely psychological. On the other hand, a number of diseases that have physical causes are transmitted through sexual contact. These diseases were once known collectively as venereal disease (VD) but are now referred to as **sexually transmitted disease** (STD). These diseases have been recognized for a long time and have in fact had an impact on history. During the late fifteenth century, syphilis became so widespread that it influenced the outcome of some important military battles. It is important to diagnose and treat these diseases as early as possible because they can have disastrous physical effects, including death. Gynecologists specialize in female disease, and urologists often treat male diseases. Although there are a number of different sexually transmitted diseases, we will list some of the most common.

GONORRHEA. **Gonorrhea** is the most prevalent STD today; in fact, of all the communicable diseases, only the common cold is found more frequently in the United States. Gonorrhea is also the oldest known STD; its symptoms are described in the Old Testament. As can be seen in Figure 12.4, the number of cases of gonorrhea has increased dramatically over the last few years. In 1976, there were a million reported cases in the United States, and it is estimated that four times that many cases went unreported.

The cause of gonorrhea is a bacteria transmitted through sexual contact. Ten percent of males and 80 percent of females who have gonorrhea show no symptoms. When symptoms do appear, they are more easily recognizable in males than in females. In males, the symptoms may include a burning sensation when urinating, urine that contains pus or blood, and a mucous discharge that seeps out the tip of the penis. If treatment is neglected, urination becomes more painful, and the penis becomes sore. In extreme cases sterility can result. Females may also discharge pus, but it is often in such small amounts that it is not noticed. If the disease attacks the urethra, urination may be painful. If it isn't treated, the bacteria may move up the uterus during menstruation and settle in the fallopian tubes. When

FIGURE 12.4   NUMBER OF REPORTED GONORRHEA CASES IN THE UNITED STATES, 1950–1978

From Maier, 1984, p. 474

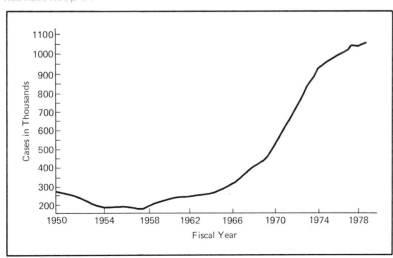

this happens, pelvic pain may result, and in some cases menstruation will become painful and irregular. If not treated, scar tissue will develop in the fallopian tubes, causing sterility.

The treatment of gonorrhea is relatively simple. Two large injections of penicillin will generally cure the disease.

SYPHILIS. Although there are records of **syphilis** dating back well before Columbus, the exact cause of the disease wasn't identified until 1905. Syphilis is caused by spiral-shaped bacteria and can be diagnosed by a blood test. It is the fourth most common communicable disease in the United States. The first sign of syphilis is a chancre—a painless, round sore with hard, raised edges. In males, the chancre appears on the penis or the scrotum. In females, it occurs most frequently on internal sex organs, where it is often unnoticed. The chancre usually appears within two to four weeks of exposure to syphilis and disappears within three to six weeks.

The disappearance of the chancre doesn't mean the disease is cured; it simply means that the bacteria have entered the bloodstream. The next symptoms are usually a rash and a low-grade fever, which begin six months after the appearance of the chancre. These symptoms last anywhere between a few months to a year, and they too disappear on their own. At this point, the disease enters the latent stage, where the bacteria burrow into the blood vessels, central nervous system, and bones. In the last stage of syphilis, which may not develop for several years, cardiovascular or neurological problems may occur and the result can be death or psychosis.

Although syphilis is a terrible disease, the treatment is relatively simple. Antibiotics such as penicillin and tetracycline will kill the bacteria. The longer the individual has had the disease, however, the greater the doses of the antibiotics must be. Therefore early detection and treatment of syphilis are very important.

GENITAL HERPES. **Genital herpes** is caused by a virus similar to the one that causes cold sores in the mouth. This disease was rare in the United States before 1965, but its rate of incidence has increased so rapidly that it is now the second most common sexually transmitted disease. Genital herpes causes small blisters on the genitals that can be quite painful. The disease goes through repeated phases of being active and then dormant. An active phase lasts two to four weeks, and it is during this time that the virus can be transmitted to others. Often an active phase is triggered by fatigue or stress.

The problems associated with herpes are greater than the discomfort resulting in the active stage. In rare cases, the herpes virus can attack the fetus of an infected woman, causing a spontaneous abortion or infecting the brain of the infant after birth. A more likely possibility is that the baby can become infected during birth. For this reason, deliveries are performed

---

REVIEW QUESTIONS

10. The male sexual disorder characterized by an inability to *maintain* an erection once achieved in order to have intercourse is called _____ _____ dysfunction.

11. A female sexual dysfunction that results when the muscles surrounding the vagina involuntarily constrict to prevent penile penetration or to make penetration extremely painful is called _____ .

12. Many, if not most, of the sexual dysfunctions are simply the result of _____ .

13. T or F: Despite the seriousness of sexual dysfunction, the success rate of many of the sex therapies is quite high.

14. Today in the U.S. the most prevalent sexually transmitted disease is _____ .

15. Syphilis and gonorrhea are caused by a bacterium; genital herpes and AIDS are caused by a _____ .

16. The sexually transmitted disease that is most likely to be misdiagnosed as gonorrhea is _____ _____ .

by Caesarean section if the mother is experiencing an active stage of herpes. Recently, there has also been some suggestion that herpes may be associated with cancer (Kessler, 1979).

Unlike the bacterial STDs, there is as yet no cure for herpes. The symptoms may be treated and the pain reduced, but no drug has been discovered that will kill the herpes virus.

NONSPECIFIC URETHRITIS. Nonspecific urethritis (NSU) is an inflammation of the male urethra. It is similar to gonorrhea but is caused by different bacteria and is more difficult to identify than gonorrhea. The symptoms are also similar to gonorrhea: a thin, clear discharge from the penis and pain during urination. The incidence of NSU has been rapidly increasing over the years, and NSU is now more common among college students than gonorrhea is. The disease can be treated with antibiotics or tetracycline, but, unlike with gonorrhea, penicillin is not effective. This makes a correct diagnosis very important.

AIDS. In the last few years, a great deal of publicity has been given to a disease called Acquired Immune Deficiency Syndrome (AIDS). The cause of **AIDS** is unknown, but a virus is generally suspected. The disease attacks the body's natural immune system and makes the person very susceptible to a wide variety of illnesses, especially pneumonia and certain types of cancer. Little is understood about AIDS, but it seems to be transmitted through sexual contact or through contact with the blood of an infected individual. AIDS is most likely to occur in male homosexuals, Haitians, people who use illegal drugs through injection, and hemophiliacs. At this time, there is no known cure for AIDS, and many aspects of it are still not understood.

SUMMARY

1. Despite the more liberal attitudes about sexual behavior today, many people are still very uninformed about sexuality.

2. Sexual systems of both males and females are composed of external and internal parts. The external organs of the male sexual system are the penis and scrotum. The main internal organs are the testes, which produce sperm and androgens. The external parts of the female sexual system are collectively called the vulva. The vulva includes the mons veneris, the labia majora, the labia minora, and the clitoris. The internal organs include the vagina and the uterus. Attached to the uterus are the fallopian tubes containing the ovaries; the ovaries produce the ova (eggs) and female sex hormones.

3. Fantasy is an important part of sexual arousal; many people become sexually aroused by simply fantasizing or imagining sexual events or actions.

4. There are many similarities in the sexual responses of males and females. The first phase is the excitement phase, where sexual arousal may begin by touching, imagining sexual activity, or observing sexual stimuli. The second phase is the plateau phase where physiological responses such as heart rate and breathing increase and swelling occurs in the penis and the vagina. The orgasm phase is experienced as a highly pleasurable release from tension. In men there are rhythmic contractions of the penis and ejaculation of semen. In women there are muscular contractions in the vagina and pulsations of the uterus. In the resolution phase the body gradually returns to normal, muscles relax, and there is often a calm feeling. Women may be stimulated back to orgasm during the resolution phase, but men enter a refractory phase, where they are unresponsive to sexual stimulation.

5. One of the first large surveys on sexual behavior in the United States was published by Alfred Kinsey in 1948.

6. One common sexual behavior is sexual fantasy, which is a thought or daydream that is sexually exciting.

7. The first and most common sexual experience for most people is masturbation, which is the self-manipulation of one's genitals to orgasm. The frequency of masturbation is highest during adolescence but a majority of married people engage in masturbation. Although masturbation has long been considered an evil behavior by many people, there is no evidence that it is harmful, and it is used by many sex therapists in treating sexual dysfunctions.

8. While more people engage in premarital coitus today than 30 years ago, the percentage of women who engage in this behavior has increased most dramatically. The frequency of men and women who have had premarital coitus is becoming more similar, but women typically have had premarital coitus with only two partners, while the average male has had six partners.

9. Married couples engage in coitus on the average of two to four times a week; the frequency of coitus decreases with age, although many older couples continue to have active and satisfying sex lives.

10. Despite a majority of people believing that extramarital sexual relationships are wrong, half of the males and 40 percent of the females in a recent survey reported having had extramarital affairs. While the likelihood of a male having an extramarital affair decreases with age, the likelihood of a female engaging in extramarital sexual behavior increases with age up to age 40.

11. Homosexuality involves a sexual relationship between individuals of the same sex. Although in 1948 only about 2 percent of males and 1 percent of females reported themselves as being exclusively homosexual, Kinsey found that almost 25 percent of males and 20 percent of females reported some homosexual experience in their lives. There are numerous theories about the factors that lead to homosexual preferences; some focus on hormonal and genetic factors; but most argue that family or early childhood experiences influence sexual orientation.

12. Sexual behavior will be enjoyed more fully if people have realistic expectations, openly communicate with their partners, take the time to explore their partner's bodies and experience the sensations of touching, and choosing a comfortable setting.

13. While alcohol and certain drugs may reduce inhibitions, they act as depressants and can work against full enjoyment of sexual behavior.

14. Birth control involves any method used to prevent the birth of children; contraception is one method of birth control. There are numerous types of contraceptives. Despite the easy availability of contraceptives today, there is evidence suggesting that college students are using less effective contraceptive methods today than they did five years ago.

15. Induced abortion has been used as a means of birth control for centuries, but it has become the center of a heated controversy between pro-choice and pro-life advocates in the United States.

16. Sexual dysfunctions refer to sexual difficulties that are frequent or long lasting. There are many causes, including physical or organic problems, failure to learn satisfying sexual behavior, and attitudes or emotions such as guilt. The more common sexual dysfunctions include erectile dysfunction, premature ejaculation, and retarded ejaculation in men and orgasmic dysfunction and vaginismus in women.

17. Sex therapy has developed to treat sexual dysfunctions, and for many sexual problems the therapy has a very high success rate. Therapy emphasizes education, communication between partners, and touching in pleasing and caring ways.

18. Sexually transmitted diseases (STDs) are physical diseases that are transmitted through sexual contact. The most common is gonorrhea. Gonorrhea, syphilis, and nonspecific urethritis are caused by bacteria, while genital herpes is caused by a virus. Early diagnosis of sexually transmitted diseases is important for treatment and to prevent their spread. The bacterial diseases can be treated with antibiotics, but at present, there is no known cure for genital herpes.

KEY TERMS

a. BIRTH CONTROL
b. CLITORIS
c. CONTRACEPTION
d. GENITALS
e. HOMOSEXUALITY
f. MASTURBATION
g. MENOPAUSE
h. ORGASM
i. PENIS
j. SEXUAL DYSFUNCTION
k. SEXUALLY TRANS-
   MITTED DISEASES
l. VAGINA

1. Sex organs
2. An intense physical and emotional experience often experienced at the climax of a sex act such as intercourse or masturbation
3. Most sexually sensitive part of a woman's body including a shaft and glans
4. Method of birth control used to prevent conception
5. Sexual relations between individuals of the same sex
6. Male external sex organ composed of erectile tissue
7. Physical diseases that are transmitted through sexual contact
8. Any method used to prevent the birth of children
9. Time in a woman's life when menstruation ceases and she is no longer capable of reproduction
10. Sexual problems that are frequent or long-lasting
11. Female internal genital comprised of a flexible tube lined with mucus membranes into which the penis is inserted during intercourse
12. Self-manipulation of one's genitals to orgasm

ANSWERS TO REVIEW QUESTIONS

1. e; a; f; h; d; b. **2.** Plateau. **3.** Refractory period. **4.** True.

5. Masturbation. **6.** False. **7.** e. **8.** False. **9.** Vasectomy.

10. Secondary erectile. **11.** Vaginismus. **12.** Misinformation. **13.** True. **14.** Gonorrhea.
15. Virus. **16.** Nonspecific urethritis.

THE INFLUENCE OF GROUPS

F ate sometimes plays strange tricks on people. As a young boy, Cesar Chavez lived on his family's prosperous farm. He saw the migrant workers come into his valley during harvest time and wondered about their lives as nomads. Now Cesar was learning firsthand about the life of a migrant farm worker. A combination of the Great Depression and drought had forced his family to lose the farm. At the age of ten, Cesar joined the hoards of migrant farm workers who moved up and down California searching for work. Picking grapes and lettuce from sunup to sundown was backbreaking labor. Wages ranged from 15 to 40 cents an hour. Shacks, provided by the growers, often had no indoor plumbing.

Cesar learned that the farm workers were completely at the mercy of the growers. They were paid what the growers wanted to pay, they lived where the growers wanted them to live, and they had jobs only when the growers wanted to give them jobs. If a worker complained, he or she would be without a job; there were plenty of migrant laborers anxious for work. A single worker could do little to change the system. And the National Labor Relations Act of 1935, which gave employees in other industries the right to organize, had excluded farm workers.

But the plight of farm workers didn't go unnoticed. Numerous groups tried to organize the migrant laborers to demand their rights. One of these organizers was Fred Ross. One day in 1951 he approached Cesar and outlined a plan to organize the farm workers. Cesar was suspicious of this Anglo, but he agreed to get a group of workers together to meet with Fred Ross. The group of 20 *chicano* workers who gathered at Cesar's house secretly planned to destroy the foolish dreams of Fred Ross. They felt that this Anglo, like the growers, only wanted to use the Mexican-Americans for his own benefit.

To the workers' surprise, Ross greeted the group in Spanish, "Buenas tardes, amigos." He continued to speak in Spanish and drew the workers into the discussion. "Do you know what the largest industry in California is?" After many incorrect guesses, Ross informed the group that agriculture was California's largest industry. Ross outlined how the migrants could influence their own lives if they organized and voted in elections.

Cesar was captured by Ross's ideas. After the meeting Cesar approached Ross and told him, "I want to know more about leadership, Mr. Ross. I want to know how it can come from me, the chicano, and how I can work with you, and the outfit you work for" (Terzian & Cramer, 1970, p. 44). So Cesar became a volunteer. He traveled the agricultural valleys of California helping Mexican-American farm workers register to vote. Cesar began holding meetings with the farm workers who were uneasy about the new ideas Cesar offered. He read many books on the subject of workers' rights and skillfully answered the workers' questions.

Cesar Chavez was successful in getting many of the workers to register to vote. But he saw that more was needed. The workers needed to form a union so the growers would listen to them. As individuals they could do very little to make themselves heard, but together they could have an impact. The law didn't give the farm workers the protection to form a union, but Cesar felt they must organize. In

With Cesar as their leader, the farm workers pushed their demands and finally won many concessions from the large farms.

UPI/Bettmann Archive.

1962 he began to recruit members into the National Farm Workers Association. Each member would have to pay monthly dues of $3.50. Cesar knew this was a large sum of money to the poor migrants, but he believed that "each worker should feel he has a stake in our association." He also knew that people wouldn't join the association unless it met their needs. He put the dues in a bank and set up a credit union from which the workers could borrow during hard times. The NFWA paid for members' funeral expenses so that a death wouldn't force a family into debt and opened a cooperative grocery store and gas station. In these ways, the NFWA offered members something in return for their membership. The symbol of the NFWA was a black Aztec eagle, and it began to be a familiar sight in the farming communities of California.

With the aid of many NFWA members, Cesar began to define goals for the association. One of the first goals was to get a minimum wage of $1.25 an hour for farm workers. A second goal was to improve farm workers' housing. The grape-growing region of the San Joaquin Valley was chosen as the target of a strike protesting unfair wages and poor working conditions. The large grape growers, such as Gallo, Christian Brothers, and Almaden, controlled the valley and the jobs. These powerful corporations saw little reason to negotiate with a group of upstart migrant laborers. The battle lines were now drawn. With harvest time fast approaching, the NFWA set up picket lines in front of the entrances to the vineyards in the valley. The growers answered the threat by importing workers from other areas of California and from Mexico. The growers even paid these new workers higher wages than they had paid the striking farm workers. Tensions were high, and there were a number of violent encounters between the growers and strikers. Cesar worked tirelessly; he had read books about Gandhi and he pushed for a plan of nonviolence.

Cesar quickly realized that there was more to a strike than simply marching in front of the vineyards. The strikers had to be fed, and their needs had to be taken care of. Volunteers from all over the country came to the NFWA's aid; many of the first volunteers were college students. A dairy in Los Angeles donated one hundred dozen eggs a week, and a meat packer delivered 40 pounds of hamburger meat each Saturday to strikers' headquarters in the San Joaquin. A kitchen was set up to feed the workers and their families. People all over the country sent money to the NFWA. Some of the donations were large, but many were small, such as the check for $6.41 sent by a group of Detroit school children. In all, it cost $40,000 a month to keep the strike going.

As the months passed, Cesar made impassioned speeches on television and testified before a Senate subcommittee. The NFWA members worked together to gain support; each member had a job. Some manned the picket lines; some cooked food and carried supplies to the picket lines; some gave speeches and searched for donations.

Despite the organization, the patience of the workers began to wear thin as the strike dragged on for Cesar felt that new action was needed to keep the strike going. Again he borrowed from the techniques of Gandhi. He decided to lead a march from the valley to Sacramento, the state capital, a 300-mile trip. The march would dramatize the demands of the workers and gain national attention. He also used the march to ask people across the country to boycott California grapes until the growers paid fair wages. A group of 200 NFWA members gathered to make the march. As they passed through small towns, they were greeted by groups of well-wishers.

The ranks of the *peregrinacion* grew, then dwindled, and then grew again as the march continued. When the group was 50 miles from Sacramento, the happy news reached them. One of the growers had agreed to negotiate with the NFWA and guarantee minimum wages for the workers. The marchers lept in the air and danced on their sore, blistered feet. They had won. It was only a matter of time before the other growers agreed to the conditions of fair labor practices. Together, the workers had made their point and achieved some very important gains. And just as important as the better wages and working condition was the fact that farm workers had learned they could organize to achieve their goals.

JOINING WITH OTHERS

Cesar Chavez, the individual, could hardly have expected to influence the growers to increase farm workers' wages and improve their working conditions. Had he attempted to fight this battle on his own, the growers wouldn't have paid any attention to him. Cesar Chavez was effective because he influenced others to join with him to bring about reforms. Certainly he deserves credit for organizing and leading the workers, but it was the workers as a group who forced the growers to listen and ultimately to give in to their demands.

The story of the farm workers' crusade raises many interesting questions. How did Cesar Chavez influence the workers to unite when others hadn't been able to do this? Why did the workers stick together and make sacrifices when their chance of success seemed nonexistent? Why did the workers follow Cesar's plan of nonviolence when many secretly wanted to force violent confrontations with the growers? As we attempt to answer these questions, we can also examine our own lives. How are we influenced by other people? Why do we join groups? How do leaders emerge in our groups? How does being a member of a group affect our behavior?

Developing answers to these questions is very important if we are to understand our adjustment to our world. All of us belong to groups, and most of our behavior is conducted in the presence of those groups. We were born into a group (the family), we are educated in groups, we work in groups, and it is very likely that a group will be present when we are placed in our final resting place. One of the most characteristic features of humans is their desire to belong to groups. In fact, at any one time, the average individual will belong to five or six groups (Mills, 1967).

Thus an understanding of groups and how they affect our behavior is important for two reasons. First, such an understanding will allow us to see many of the factors that influence our own behavior. A knowledge of the effects of groups on behavior may help to explain why we wear the kinds of clothes we wear and eat the kinds of food we eat. A second reason for

ARE YOU A GOOD GROUP MEMBER?

Being a constructive member of a group takes work. Groups function well only if each group member takes an active part and uses his or her expertise to help the group move toward a goal. Too often members retire to the sidelines and "go with the flow" rather than working to make the group better. Below are some questions that will help you identify what type of group member you are. Think of your typical behavior in groups and answer the questions. This exercise will help you identify areas where you can improve and make yourself a more valuable group member.

1. *Do I propose new ideas, activities, and procedures?* Or sit and listen?
2. *Do I ask questions?* Or am I shy about admitting that I do not understand?
3. *Do I share my knowledge when it will prove helpful to the problems at hand?* Or do I keep it to myself, fearing I may be wrong?
4. *Do I speak up if I feel strongly about something?* Or am I shy about giving an opinion?
5. *Do I try to bring together our ideas and activities?* Or do I concentrate only on details under immediate discussion and think it's up to the leader to summarize?
6. *Do I understand the goals of the group and try to direct discussion toward them?* Or do I get off the track easily? If I'm not clear about goals do I ask about them?
7. *Do I ever question the practicality or the logic of a project, and do I evaluate afterwards?* Or do I always accept without question the things we do?
8. *Do I encourage my fellow members to do well?* Or am I indifferent to or actually critical of their efforts and achievements?
9. *Do I encourage the group to undertake worthy projects that will accelerate learning?* Or am I satisfied with mediocre projects—"busy work"?
10. *Am I a mediator and a peacemaker?* Or do I allow ill feeling to develop? If it does do I consider it the leader's job to handle it?
11. *Am I willing to compromise in some situations (except where basic issues such as truth and justice are involved)?* Or do I remain inflexible in my point of view?
12. *Do I encourage others to participate and help everyone to have a fair chance to speak?* Or do I sit by while some people hog the floor, and do I sometimes dominate it myself?

studying group dynamics is to allow us to function better in groups. By understanding how groups affect behavior and how the behavior of one member affects the behavior of other members, we may see how we can become more effective group members. Such knowledge will also help us influence the direction taken by a group, so that our own needs can be more clearly met by our membership in it.

WHY JOIN GROUPS?

Joining the National Farm Workers Association had costs for the farm workers. They had to pay dues, they had to spend time attending meetings, they had to give up their jobs to join the strike, and in some cases they suffered verbal and physical abuse for being members of NFWA. If you think about groups you belong to, you'll find that you have also made sacrifices to be a group member. Those sacrifices may be money, time, or forsaking other groups. Given these costs, why do we join groups?

A Sense of Belonging

One of the characteristics of humans is the desire to affiliate with others. The strength of this desire has led many philosophers to postulate that humans have a basic need to belong to a group; in fact, we are often referred to as "social animals." There may be truth in this statement; it's certainly hard to find an individual who doesn't belong to at least one group. As another instance of the strength of our need to belong, consider the fact that in many prisons inmates forfeit their right to affiliate with others as the result of rule infractions. Solitary confinement is considered to be a harsh punishment.

Thus one reason why we belong to groups may be that we have a basic need to affiliate with other people. Nevertheless, this can't explain why we choose the specific groups we do. For example, why do you belong to certain groups, while the student who sits next to you in class belongs to others? To answer these questions, we must examine other reasons for joining groups.

Desire for Information

Cesar Chavez knew that his working conditions weren't good and that he needed more money. But he didn't know the conditions of workers in other areas or what he could do to change his own conditions. When he and a small group of local workers met with Fred Ross, he learned a great deal. He discovered that people in the

One reason for joining a group is to gain information on issues of interest.

Catherine Ursillo, Photo Researchers, Inc.

group shared his dissatisfactions and that other workers in other parts of California were also unhappy with their working conditions. He learned that the growers were dependent on him and other farm workers to plant and harvest their crops. He also learned that the workers could influence their conditions by registering and voting for sympathetic members of Congress. Thus for Cesar Chavez the group of farm workers served as a fountain of information.

Our groups provide us with information in a similar way. You may learn what classes are good and which ones should be avoided from friends in your dorm, people you usually eat lunch with, or sorority or fraternity members. People join professional groups to learn new techniques and where jobs are likely to be found. So our groups provide us with information on a variety of subjects.

Groups also allow for the exchange of information at a personal level. We want to evaluate our personal characteristics and attributes. In many cases we can evaluate a particular characteristic only by comparing it with the characteristics of other people. If you want to determine how well you play tennis, you must compare your play with that of other tennis players. A similar case can be made for attitudes; if you want to evaluate the correctness of your attitude, you must compare your opinion with that of others. Festinger (1950) hypothesized that **social comparison** involves evaluating our attitudes, beliefs, behaviors, or other conditions by comparing them with those of others. In order to make these comparisons, we must seek out other people who are roughly similar to us on the dimension in question. Cesar Chavez couldn't determine whether or not he was making a fair salary by comparing his wages to those of a doctor. He needed to compare his wages and working conditions with those of other workers with similar backgrounds and skills. It became clear that his wages were unfair when he found that other manual laborers were making two or three times as much as he was making. In many cases, we join groups with members similar to

us in order to be able to get information for making such social comparisons. Along these lines, it is interesting to see that when the NFWA did achieve union status in 1972, as the United Farm Workers of America, it affiliated with the AFL-CIO, a federation of unions representing workers in many areas of manual and blue-collar labor.

Receiving Rewards

Although the farm workers had to pay money and sacrifice their time, they received many rewards from the NFWA. The NFWA offered them a credit union, a grocery store, and a gas station, and even paid for necessary funeral expenses. In the end, membership in the farm workers' association paid off with higher wages and better working conditions.

While most groups to which we belong don't provide us with such a range of benefits, many of our groups do provide us with rewards. In some cases, the rewards are material in nature. People join investment groups or business partnerships to obtain monetary rewards.

While some groups directly supply material rewards, most groups provide social rewards. One such social reward is recognition. Individuals often take great pride in belonging to and identifying with a certain group. This pride of recognition is seen in the fact that many groups develop group uniforms, flags, and symbols. The NFWA adopted the black Aztec eagle as its symbol; college students wear the school colors and sing the school songs. In all cases, group members receive recognition by being identified with their group.

Another social reward of group membership is security. Many groups have an unwritten code that the group will come to the aid of a member in need. Street gangs often spring up in areas where individuals fear for their safety. These gangs have clearly stated mutual defense pacts, so that an attack on one is treated as an attack on all. It isn't uncommon to read stories about church groups who help distressed members. Recently, one such church group in

There is safety in numbers. People join groups to gain security.
G. Arvio Peterson, Photo Researchers, Inc.

Lubbock, Texas, helped a member rebuild his home after it had been destroyed by a tornado.

Thus individuals join groups for tangible rewards such as money and for social rewards such as recognition and security. All members need not receive the same type of reward from the group, but each member is generally rewarded in some way. You may belong to a social group for its prestige or recognition, while another member of the same group may be seeking security from it.

Desire to Achieve

Individuals also join groups to help them achieve certain goals. In some cases the importance of a group to a person achieving a goal is obvious. It would be impossible for an individual to play a game of baseball alone. A single farm worker couldn't have forced the growers to pay higher wages. While the necessity of a group to achieve these goals is clear, the importance of the group for goal achievement may be more indirect in other cases. A student may join a medical or law-oriented social club because he or she thinks that being a member of such a group will be a help in being accepted by a medical or law school. A would-be executive may join the local country club so that she or he can meet the "right" people to help one get a start in business. It may be of

interest for you to examine how your goals are facilitated by the groups to which you belong.

THE STRUCTURE OF GROUPS

Given that we all belong to groups and that they have an important influence on our lives, we should understand how groups are structured. A careful look at any group will show that members don't behave in a haphazard or random fashion; their behavior follows prescribed patterns and conforms to identifiable rules.

Norms

The first type of rule applies to everyone. The NFWA adopted the rule of nonviolence in confronting the growers. All members, from leaders such as Cesar Chavez to the newest member, were expected to avoid violent encounters with the growers. Even families have these general rules. For example, many families have a specific time when everyone must gather for dinner.

These general rules are called **norms.** Norms are rules that govern specific behaviors, and they usually apply to all members of the group: "Norms specify what must, or must not, be done when" (Steiner, 1972). Norms are often unwritten, as can be seen in the NFWA and in family settings. It may be interesting for you to consider the groups to which you belong and to list the "unwritten laws" of these groups.

In some cases, however, norms are explicitly written. Laws are an example of written norms. Thus the law setting the speed limit at 55 miles per hour is a norm that applies (or is intended to apply) to everyone in the United States, regardless of age, occupation, sex, or type of automobile driven.

Roles

A second set of guidelines that influences the behavior of group members is **roles.** Roles define the obligations of, and expectations for, an individual in a particular position within a group (Goffman, 1961). In the NFWA, Cesar Chavez had the role of leader. Because he occupied this role he was expected to develop a successful plan for getting higher wages, to take care of the daily needs of the other members, and to represent the united farm workers to the nation. In addition to these expectations, Cesar had benefits the other members didn't have. He could draw a salary from the NFWA. He didn't have to march on the picket lines. These expectations and benefits existed for Cesar only because of his role in the NFWA.

A system of roles can be found in most groups. In families, the roles of father, mother, eldest child, and youngest child can be identified. Each of these positions entails a specific set of privileges, obligations, and expectations. In university and college departments, there are the roles of chairperson, professor, associate professor, assistant professor, lecturer, and teaching assistant. Again, each role has specific obligations and expectations.

Roles and norms are developed so that the group can function in an orderly fashion. A group member who knows the roles and norms of his or her group can predict how other group members will act. If the norms prevail and role expectations are fulfilled, the maintenance of the group is assured. Norms and roles play a vital part in group life: They structure the group,

ensure the predictability of members' behavior, and ensure that the group will be maintained and continue to function.

Role Conflict

Groups develop roles and norms so they can function smoothly. But we must remember that people belong to many groups at once. At times the demands of a person's role in one group may conflict with the demands of his or her role in another group. When this happens we have a situation of **role conflict.** For example, Cesar Chavez was the leader of the National Farm Workers Association; this role demanded that he take care of the association members, and that he travel and gain support for the association. Cesar was also a husband and the father of eight children; his role in the family demanded that he help support his family and spend time with his wife and children. So the roles of NFWA leader and father in a family placed conflicting demands on Cesar.

Another area where the issue of role conflict has been raised involves the role of women in today's world. The traditional role for women has been that of the homemaker who is responsible for keeping the home and raising children. Many women, however, want to apply their skills and abilities in working outside the home. Twenty years ago, women who had this desire faced an uncompromising world which told them the conflict between the roles of mother and working woman couldn't be reconciled. Women were often led to believe that they must choose one role or the other. Today, however, we realize that this isn't the case.

The adaptation that has been made so that women, like men, can have both a family and a career indicates how to deal with potential role conflict. On one hand, adjustments have been made in both family roles and workplace roles. In many families, taking care of the children and keeping house are no longer the sole responsibility of the woman; the requirements of the roles have been changed to allow both the wife and the husband to work outside the home. Sensitive employers have also ad-

Women may face role conflict attempting to fill the demands of the role of wife, mother, and employee outside the home.

United Nations/W. A. Graham   Laimute Druskis

justed job requirements for both men and women to accommodate these changes in the family group. Thus one adjustment made because of role conflict is the change in the requirements of the roles in groups. A second approach to this role conflict concerns how men and women choose partners and jobs. Couples talk about their desires for dual careers, and the choice of a mate is often influenced by considering whether both partners' desires can be met in their relationship. Similarly, decisions about jobs and careers are also influenced by the roles people expect to play in the family. So a second way to deal with potential role conflict is to choose groups that present a minimum of conflict. Finally, many people have accepted the fact that in satisfying their desires they will experience some degree of conflict. Couples expect and openly discuss the conflicts. Adjustments and sacrifices are sometimes made. For example, working couples may realize that the demands of their jobs make it impossible for them to prepare fancy meals at home every night. In such a case, the couple may eat out more often or plan meals that can be cooked more quickly.

Given the number of groups to which we belong, there is probably no way to avoid role conflict completely. But we can attempt to identify the roles that we will be required to fulfill in a certain group and consider whether or not these roles will conflict with the roles required by other groups. We should also explore the possibility that the roles we play in various groups can be modified so that they mesh together more easily. If it's impossible to avoid a role conflict, we will have to decide whether membership in the group is worth the conflict and tension that will be created. While there is no clear formula for making this decision, simply knowing the potential for role conflict should make us better able to choose our groups wisely.

TO INFLUENCE....

With some idea of the structure of groups, we can now begin to examine how groups function. More specifically, we must look at how people behave and interact to influence the behavior of other people and determine the movement of their group. The members of the National Farm Workers Association agreed that they wanted higher wages and better working conditions. But they were divided about how to achieve these goals. Cesar Chavez wanted to use nonviolent methods such as strikes and boycotts. Others such as Emilio Hernandez wanted a more aggressive approach: "What kind of men are we to sit back and wait? Our grandfathers fought with Pancho Villa—they were men, not afraid to fight, not afraid to die. Would they not be ashamed to see us denying our manhood—our *machismo*?" (Terzian & Cramer, 1970, p. 138). Given this split, how was Cesar able to get the members to follow the nonviolent course of action? How was he able to convince them to give up their jobs and suffer the hardships of the long strike? When we examine questions such as these, we are dealing with the issue of **social influence**, the exercise of power or use of reinforcers by a person or group to influence the behavior of others (Worchel & Cooper, 1983).

Social Power

If we examine our lives, we find that our behavior is often influenced by other people.

You may struggle out of bed and hurry to work because your boss has threatened to fire you if you're late. When you get into your car, you buckle your seat belt because you heard a traffic safety official speak about the importance of using seat belts. Despite the strong craving deep in your chest, you resist the temptation to light up a cigarette, because your best friend offered you $50 if you could go a week without smoking. The outfit you're wearing to work is very similar to one your favorite movie star had on in a show you saw last month.

In each of these cases, your behavior has been influenced by others, but the basis for the influence is different in each case. In fact, psychologists have identified six types of **social power** that can be used to influence our behavior (French & Raven, 1959; Aries, 1976).

Coercive Power. One of the most common types of power is coercive power, which involves the use of threats or punishments. Parents use coercive power when they threaten their children with a spanking if they don't go to bed. Coercive power is easy to use and often enhances the self-esteem of the person using it. Many people find a certain satisfaction in feeling that they are strong enough to get others to carry out behaviors simply by threatening them. But there are drawbacks to using threats and punishment to influence others. First, the recipient of the threat or punishment will be motivated to leave the relationship as soon as an opportunity presents itself. Clearly you wouldn't want to be around a person who was always threatening you to get you to change your behavior. Second, coercive power works only as long as the more powerful person is present and watching. Think about the last time you saw a state trooper while you were speeding down the highway. Chances are that you slowed down while in sight of the trooper; but as soon as you saw the trooper off the highway, you probably sped up again. The threat of getting a ticket caused you to slow down as long as you felt the eyes of the law could see you.

Reward Power. Reward power involves giving positive reinforcement to produce change. The reward can be material goods, money, or simple praise or status. The earlier example of the friend offering $50 if you would stop smoking for a week involves the use of reward power. Unlike coercive power, reward power motivates people to stay in relationships that influence their behavior. Although surveillance is required for the effective use of reward power, the degree of surveillance isn't as high as that needed to use coercive power. The disadvantage of reward power is that it may be costly to the person using the power; he or she might have to give up money or other material goods, or expend time and effort, to influence the behavior of others.

Expert Power. People have expert power because we see them as having special knowledge about something. Expert power is generally limited to the area in which the individual has expertise. For example, you may stop smoking or lose weight because your doctor tells you it will be good for your health. But, it's less likely that you'll run down to the store and buy polo shirts because your doctor tells you they're great. The use of expert power doesn't require surveillance by the powerful person. Cesar Chavez tried hard to develop expert power when he formed the National Farm Workers Association. He spent long hours reading books about agricultural activities so that he could answer the workers' questions.

Legitimate Power. As the clear leader of the NFWA, Cesar Chavez had legitimate power because of the role he occupied. Many roles—personnel manager, club president, parent, professor—carry power within the role. People feel that they should follow the demands of people with legitimate power. Like expert power, legitimate power is limited, however. Its domain is only within a single group. For example, your professor has legitimate power to influence your behavior in class, but he or she doesn't have the power to influence your behavior within your family.

Informational Power. There is an old saying that "Knowledge is power." We listen to people we see as having knowledge or special information about something. This power is somewhat different from expert power because the knowledge may not necessarily make the person an expert. If you are on a jury, you will be influenced by someone who has eyewitness information about a crime; this person isn't an expert, but his or her information gives the witness power. The limitation of informational power is that the powerful person loses power once others have the information. In the above case, the witness loses power once he or she has given the jury the information.

Referent Power. Many people in the NFWA admired Cesar Chavez for his courage and ability. One young boy admired him so much he began to dress like Cesar and adopt Cesar's mannerisms. People we like and admire have referent power over us. They can influence our behavior because we want to be like them. Referent power doesn't require surveillance, nor does the powerful person have to change his or her behavior to use this power. Fred Ross understood the importance of referent power; he knew that as an Anglo and a nonfarm worker he couldn't gain the referent power necessary to influence the largely Hispanic agricultural laborers. So he chose Cesar Chavez to organize the workers. Cesar was someone the workers could understand, and they would admire one of their own in the leadership position.

THE CORRUPTING INFLUENCE OF POWER. When we talk of power, the eyes of many people light up. For many of us, the ultimate dream is to have the power to influence others to do whatever we want them to do. What a good life this would be! And this power would make better people of us. Or would it? Another wise old saying holds that "power tends to corrupt, and absolute power tends to corrupt absolutely." History provides many examples that support this statement. It isn't hard to think of the names of dozens of people whose power brought them corruption and ruin.

There are a number of possible explanations for this unfortunate outcome. First, having power and being able to influence others tends to make people think they are better than the nonpowerful others. Power tends to inflate people's self-esteem, and they begin to see themselves as more important than others. Second, people with power often think they can do no wrong. Few people will risk challenging a powerful person. Third, power tends to separate the powerful from the nonpowerful. Powerful people may lose the ability to be sensitive to the needs of less powerful others. Cesar Chavez seemed well aware of this possible outcome; he continued to live with the farm workers, and he refused to take a large salary for his efforts. In this way he continued his close contact with the workers and was able to see the world through their eyes. Cesar's actions provide a valuable lesson in how we can avoid the pitfalls of power. It is important to seek out the company of less powerful people and to invite open communication with them.

Leadership

When we think of power, we also think of leadership. A **leader** is a person who influences other group members (Lord, 1977). In essence, leadership involves the exercise of power. For decades people have questioned what makes a leader. Why did Cesar Chavez, rather than one of the thousands of other farm workers, become the leader of the NFWA?

As it turns out, this is a very difficult question to answer. One set of theories suggests that leaders have some special traits or characteristics that make them leaders. Many businesses and industries have adopted this approach and have developed tests to identify who will be a leader. Unfortunately, hundreds of studies on leadership have failed to clearly identify traits that make a person a leader. There is some indication that leaders tend to be more intelligent, assertive, vocal, and taller than others in the group. However, for the most part, there is often little clear difference between leaders and the people who follow them.

A second set of theories argues that it is the situation that makes a person a leader. In other words, leaders are people who happen to be in the right place at the right time. Using this approach we might argue that Cesar Chavez became a leader of the farm workers movement because he happened to be the person who was approached by Fred Ross to help organize the first meetings. There is some evidence that the situation does influence who will be a leader. For example, studies have shown that people who are seated at the head (as opposed to along the sides) of a rectangular table tend to be more influential (Lecuyer, 1976). Other studies have found that seniority affects leadership; people who have been with the group the longest tend to emerge as leaders (Insko et al., 1980).

The specific needs of the group also help determine who will be its leader. Cesar Chavez

REVIEW QUESTIONS

1. Which of the following is *not* a reason why people join groups?
   a. to gain information about ourselves and others
   b. to satisfy our need to compete
   c. to obtain material and social rewards
   d. to help achieve certain goals
2. General rules that specify appropriate behavior for all group members are called _____ .
3. Particular positions in the group require the individual who holds that position to perform certain behaviors and to fulfill certain obligations. These obligations and expectations define the individual's _____ in the group.
4. Janna Schimler found that the demands of her employer to work overtime and travel were sometimes in competition with her responsibilities as a mother and wife. She is experiencing _____ _____ .
5. The power to influence the behavior of others is derived from different power bases. Match the type of power with the bases from which it is derived.

   _____ coercive power
   _____ reward power
   _____ legitimate power
   _____ informational power
   _____ referent power
   _____ expert power

   a. based on the individual's admired position and the ability to command respect
   b. based on the individual's possession of knowledge unavailable to others
   c. based on the status of the role that the individual plays
   d. based on the individual's ability and willingness to offer positive reinforcement
   e. based on the individual's position that requires him to have special insight or knowledge about a certain area
   f. based on the individual's use of threat and punishment

6. T or F: Studies on leadership have shown that it is the characteristics of the individual that most strongly determine why he or she emerges as a leader.

WHAT TYPE OF LEADER ARE YOU?

Leaders are people who influence the activities of other group members. There are, however, many ways to use this influence. Some leaders tend to be task oriented; their main concern is getting the job done and seeing that a goal is reached. Other leaders tend to be relationship oriented; their main concern is the feelings of other group members. Answer the scale below as instructed. Then add up your score. It has been suggested that low scores represent leaders who are task oriented while high scores identify leaders who tend to be relationship oriented in their approach. Which are you?

Think of the person with whom you can work least well. He or she may be someone you work with now or someone you knew in the past.

This person does not have to be the one you like least well but should be the person with whom you had the most difficulty in getting a job done. Describe this person.

Confident	8	7	6	5	4	3	2	1	Not confident
Distant	8	7	6	5	4	3	2	1	Close
Not hardworking	8	7	6	5	4	3	2	1	Hardworking
Warm	8	7	6	5	4	3	2	1	Cold
Ambitious	8	7	6	5	4	3	2	1	Not ambitious
Happy	8	7	6	5	4	3	2	1	Sad
Productive	8	7	6	5	4	3	2	1	Not productive
Sociable	8	7	6	5	4	3	2	1	Not sociable
Dependable	8	7	6	5	4	3	2	1	Not dependable
Relaxed	8	7	6	5	4	3	2	1	Tense
Creative	8	7	6	5	4	3	2	1	Not creative
Satisfied	8	7	6	5	4	3	2	1	Not satisfied
Intelligent	8	7	6	5	4	3	2	1	Not intelligent
Friendly	8	7	6	5	4	3	2	1	Not friendly
Nervous	8	7	6	5	4	3	2	1	Calm
Pleasant	8	7	6	5	4	3	2	1	Not pleasant

may have become leader of the National Farm Workers Association because the workers needed someone who could organize and give forceful speeches. As the needs of a group change, the person who leads may also change. But even if we accept these situational influences, they don't present the whole picture. Over years of effort, there were many members of the NFWA who had been with the movement for a long time and who could organize and give forceful speeches, yet Cesar Chavez remained their leader.

Thus, neither the trait nor the situational theory can completely explain why some people become leaders. The better answer probably lies somewhere in between these extreme theories (Hollander, 1978). Who will lead a group is a function of personal characteristics of both the leader and the followers and of the specific characteristics of the situation. People with certain traits and abilities will emerge as leaders in certain situations.

This point has been supported by research into what type of person is likely to be an effective leader (Fiedler, 1974, 1978). This work has shown that someone who is very task-oriented and has concerns about getting the job done at all costs will be an effective leader in groups that are either very organized or very disorganized. When the group is only moderately well-organized, a person who has strong concerns about the feelings and well-being of the members will be the most effective leader. The bottom line, therefore, is that both the situation and the characteristics of the people in a group determine who will be the group's leader and how well he or she will lead.

Influencing Other Group Members

We have already examined the bases from which we can influence our groups. Clearly, power comes in many forms, and the skillful leader can effectively use his or her power to influence others. Let's move away from the abstract and see some ways in which power and influence can be wielded to change others' behaviors.

THE POWER OF COMMITMENT.   Cesar Chavez learned a great deal from Fred Ross. One of the most important lessons he learned was to involve his audience in the making of decisions. Cesar always started his meetings by asking the audience questions: "How many of you know how long a *campesino* can expect to live when compared to an Anglo?" Only after the audi-

ence was involved in guessing would Cesar point out that the average Mexican-American migrant worker dies at 49, while the average Anglo lives to be almost 70. After involving the people in the audience, Cesar would help them identify problems and have them suggest solutions. The meetings generally ended with the workers openly committing themselves to take some type of action.

The act of having others openly commit themselves to a position or a course of action is vitally important in getting them to change their behavior. As early as 1943, Kurt Lewin demonstrated that individuals do feel more committed to decisions that result from group interaction than to decisions they arrive at on their own. Lewin became interested in the effects of groups on decisions because of a problem the United States faced during World War II. During the war, a great deal of American beef was sent overseas to feed Allied soldiers. As a result, the supply of beef in the United States decreased, and the price skyrocketed. But there was still no shortage of beef entrails, such as kidneys, brains, liver, and sweetbreads. Americans weren't accustomed to eating these dishes, however, and there was a great deal of resistance to government efforts to increase the use of these foods. Since homemakers were doing most of the grocery shopping and cooking in the United States, Lewin became interested in how the attitudes and behavior of those consumers could be changed to increase compliance with the government requests. He reasoned that many of the housewife's attitudes toward beef entrails were influenced by groups to which she belonged; no self-respecting housewife wanted to be the only person on the block to serve cow brains to her children. Thus Lewin felt that in order to induce change, efforts should be aimed at the group rather than at the individual. He formed groups of 13 to 17 Red Cross volunteers who were also homemakers. Half the groups were given a standard lecture on how serving entrails would help the war effort and shown appetizing ways to prepare these dishes. The other groups were given the opportunity to hold group discussions on the issue; in the presence of a trained leader, the group members expressed their views and heard other group members discuss their feelings. After the meetings, the groups voted publicly on the advisability of serving entrails at least once a week. In all cases the groups accepted this idea. One week later the people in all the groups were interviewed to see how many had complied. The results showed that only 10 percent of the women who were simply given the lecture had served entrails, while over 52 percent of the women in the group-discussion condition had served entrails.

Clearly, individuals who had discussed their views and heard others discuss theirs were more committed to the decision than were individuals who hadn't participated in group discussions. Why did this occur? One possible reason is that women had clearly committed themselves to the decision in the group discussion, while the women who simply listened to a lecture hadn't. Another reason for the effectiveness of the group discussion is that it allowed individuals to see other group members committing themselves to a position. Hence a person could make a commitment with the knowledge that others were doing it also.

Both these processes probably work to increase commitment to decisions made in groups. This information is important in understanding your own behavior: It's very likely that you will feel more compelled to follow through with decisions you've made in groups than with ones you've made alone. Be sure to examine carefully the decisions you make in group discussions; remember that you will later feel quite compelled to stick to them. There will be both internal pressures, urging you to behave just as you want to, and external pressures, as others remind you that "you promised."

THE MAJORITY WINS....MOST OF THE TIME. If you examine your experience in groups, you'll find that group decisions generally reflect what the majority of people want to do. If most of the group members voice a position or support for a particular course of action, the other group members generally go along with them. You probably know how comfortable it is to find your position supported by the majority and remember how uncomfortable you've felt at times when the majority was against you. Clearly there is strength in numbers.

While the strength of the majority may not be surprising, it must be pointed out that there are many times when the minority is able to have a strong influence on a group's decision. You may be able to think of times when a small number of people in your group were able to successfully determine the group's decision. A dramatic portrayal of minority influence was depicted in the classic movie *Twelve Angry Men,* starring Henry Fonda. The movie focused on a jury that had just heard the testimony in a murder trial. After retiring for deliberation and taking a secret ballot, the jurors learned that there were 11 "guilty" votes and 1 "not guilty"; the lone dissenter was the character played by Henry Fonda. The other jurors began to pressure Fonda's character to change his position and side with the majority so that they could get the deliberations over with. But the dissenter remained steadfast and unyielding in his conviction and attempted to explain his position to the others. The pressure continued and nearly erupted into violence, but Fonda's character continued to profess his belief. Then one of the jurors wavered and expressed agreement with the lone dissenter's not-guilty position. As the discussion progressed, the other jurors changed their opinions one by one, until there was unanimous support for acquittal.

In this case, Fonda took a clear position, explained his reasons for holding that position, and refused to yield or compromise. Research indicates that if the minority is to influence the group's opinion, it must take a clear and consistent position and hold steadfastly to it (Moscovici & Nemeth, 1974; Nemeth, 1979). This action will create conflict in the group, which the majority will attempt to reduce by forcing the minority to change its position. Threats and insults may be hurled at the minority to force a change of position. But if the majority finds that it can't influence the minority, it may then incorporate or adopt the minority's position. This of course assumes that the majority can't exclude minority members from the group.

This research suggests that even if you find

yourself in the minority, you may be able to influence the group's position. Certainly there are risks in expressing and maintaining an unpopular position. In some cases these risks are substantial. But they must be weighed against the negative consequences of allowing yourself to adopt a position you oppose. In many cases those negative consequences may be significant compared to the risk of rejection and ridicule. In such situations, you may decide to go along with the group.

There are other situations, however, in which you may feel strongly about the group's decision. In these cases, you have three choices. You can go along with the group and refrain from "making waves." This may make you a popular group member, but you may feel very uncomfortable with yourself. A second choice is to quit the group. You will thereby preserve your personal integrity and beliefs, but you will be giving up membership in a group that you value, and your departure won't help the group make a wiser decision. In many respects, this "abandoning ship" approach is the easy way out, and it is costly both to the group and to you. The third and most valuable choice is to risk group pressures and state your opposing belief. Explain why you feel that your position is correct, and refuse to be moved simply by group pressure. This course of action doesn't mean that you must be deaf to sensible information supplied by the other group members. Rather, you should avoid yielding because of threats or other pressures that don't bear directly on finding the best solution to the problem at hand. By taking this third approach you can make a valuable contribution both to the group and to your own integrity.

FOOT-IN-THE-DOOR: A LITTLE ACTION GOES A LONG WAY.

Cesar Chavez organized his campaign against the growers in an interesting way. First, he held meetings and had farm workers join the NFWA. In order to join the association, workers had to pay $3.50 each month. This was a relatively small step compared to the strike in which the workers had to give up their jobs and march on picket lines. In essence, Cesar had

Door-to-door salesmen often use the foot-in-the-door technique to sell their products. They attempt to get the consumer to make a small commitment (using the product) before trying to make the big sell.

Rhoda Sidney, Monkmeyer.

the workers make a commitment to a small action (joining the NFWA) before he asked them to take the larger step (going out on strike). Anyone who has been a door-to-door salesperson will recognize this technique. The first step is to get the potential buyer to make a small commitment; that commitment may include letting you in the door or trying out the product. Next the buyer is asked to make the larger commitment of buying the product. The technique is called **foot-in-the-door.**

A number of studies (De Jong, 1979; 1981) have found that we are more likely to perform a difficult or major action if we first agree to do a small action. It seems that when people agree to small actions, they change their views of themselves; they now see themselves as people who agree to requests and get involved. Once they have adopted this view of themselves, it becomes easier to influence them to agree to a larger request.

Interestingly enough, the opposite approach can also be successful. That is, we can first make a large request of a person. When he or she refuses this request, we can say, "Well, if you won't do that, at least agree to do this." This technique seems to work because people feel guilty for turning down the first request. Not wishing to hurt the requester, they will try to make amends by agreeing to a smaller request. It is also possible that they see the second request as even smaller when they compare it to the first request. This technique of influence is called **door-in-the-face** (Cann et al., 1975).

It's important to be aware of these types of influences in your daily life. Salespeople often use these techniques to get buyers to commit to purchases. A good salesperson can skillfully manipulate you so that you may find yourself agreeing to a course of action with which you are later uncomfortable.

....OR TO BE INFLUENCED

Thus far we have been examining how we can use power and other techniques to influence the behavior of others in our groups. This discussion should help us better understand how Cesar Chavez was able to successfully organize the farm workers and lead them on strike. There is another factor at work that influences people's behavior in groups. That factor is the effect of being in a group. Being a member of a group tends to bring certain pressures to bear on our behavior.

Deindividuation: Lost in the Group.

The farm workers were a large group. Most were Hispanic and most wore similar types of clothing. When they gathered together at a large rally, it was often hard to distinguish one worker from another. In a sense, the workers lost their individual identities and assumed the identity of the group. A similar thing happens when we attend a football game or a rock concert. In these cases, we become part of a sea of humanity; to the observer, we aren't Bob or Susan, but only an indistinguishable part of the crowd. In psychological terms, we become "deindividuated," losing our personal identity and assuming the group's identity.

Deindividuation occurs in many groups. A similar process occurs in the military, for example. Upon induction, an individual assumes

People in large organizations such as the military often become deindividuated. The use of uniforms and titles strips the individual's identity and submerges him or her into the group.

Marc Anderson.

a group name: private, sergeant, lieutenant, captain. The individual sacrifices more personal identity by wearing a uniform that identifies him or her as a member of the group, rather than as a unique individual. Nurses wear uniforms and are often referred to by both doctors and patients simply as "Nurse." Patients also lose their individuality, wearing hospital uniforms and assuming the identity of "the patient in room 222" or "the gall bladder case." Even in smaller groups such as families deindividuation sometimes occurs. Many women complain that they lose some of their personal identity when they marry; they often assume their husbands' names, and Jane Smith may be referred to as "the wife of Mr. Smith." In response to this deindividuation process, a number of women have elected to retain their maiden names when they marry.

Zimbardo (1970) identified several factors that lead people to feel deindividuated in groups. The larger the group, the more likely it is for an individual to feel deindividuated. People are most likely to lose individuality in groups in which members are relatively anonymous and similarity of dress is required. Deindividuation is most common in groups where individuals don't feel responsible for their actions. In a large crowd, an individual may scream obscenities, knowing that he or she can't be identified or held responsible for these actions. It's very clear that these factors were present in the NFWA meetings and that members felt deindividuated; the NFWA was large, and the members often worked together. The workers were relatively anonymous to outsiders and to the growers, and they felt that "the association" would assume responsibility for many of their actions.

The results of deindividuation are startling. On a personal level, people may lose pride in themselves and their behavior. They receive little personal recognition or credit for outstanding behavior, so why strive for excellence? People also lose concern for social evaluation, and as a result they feel less inhibited— less guilty, ashamed, or fearful—about performing socially unacceptable behaviors.

Zimbardo (1971) presented a frightening demonstration of the effects of deindividuation on an individual's behavior. He set up a mock prison in the basement of the psychology building at Stanford University. The prison contained a number of barred cells with just room enough for three bare beds in each. There was also a guard room where his prison "guards" could observe the inmates. Zimbardo hired 24 carefully selected male students, whom he described as "mature, emotionally stable, normal, intelligent college students from middle-class homes throughout the United States and Canada." Half the students were arbitrarily assigned to the prison group, and the other half were instructed to take the role of guards.

The prisoners were given white dress-like garments to wear and numbers to be used instead of their names. At night each inmate slept with a chain around one leg. The guards were also given uniforms: khaki pants and shirts and dark sunglasses that hid their eyes. These procedures were aimed at deindividuating both groups by effacing individual identities and substituting the class identity of prisoner or guard. Zimbardo expected to observe and record the behavior in his prison over a two-week period. The guards were given complete control of the prison and the "inmates," while Zimbardo served as the prison warden.

What happened as a result of deindividuating these normal college students and placing them in clearly defined groups? Zimbardo reports with disbelief and horror that the deindividuating situation "undid (temporarily) a lifetime of learning; human values were suspended, self-concepts were challenged, and the ugliest, most base, pathologic side of human nature surfaced." The inmates became "servile, dehumanized robots" who thought only of their own survival and hated their guards. Many of the guards became tyrannical and brutalized the inmates. The situation became so bad that the experiement had to be terminated in six days instead of the two weeks originally planned!

Certainly this study shows the extreme. Most of us will never be in a group that deindividuates us to the extent of the Zimbardo prison. The important point, however, is that the factors that led to deindividuation in that experiment exist in many groups. We must therefore be aware of what those factors are and how they are likely to affect our own feelings and behavior. The conditions in many groups invite us to sacrifice our uniqueness and become submerged in the group. Too often we unwittingly accept this invitation and allow ourselves to become deindividuated. The results are often disturbing to us and to observers. An understanding of the deindividuation process should better enable you to determine how much of yourself you will "give" to the group and how much individual identity you will retain. To remain totally aloof from the group is clearly as poor a solution as to become totally submerged in it. A wiser course of action is to understand the forces that push for deindividuation and to be prepared to give into them only to the degree with which you are comfortable.

Conformity: Marching in Step with the Group

News of the grape pickers' strike spread throughout the country. The workers received a great deal of support in the form of money, food, and clothing. They also attracted people from all over the country who wanted to join the strikers. College students, fresh from protest marches against the Vietnam War, arrived in the workers' camps. Members from other labor unions came to join the picket lines. Derelicts, people who were out of work, and curiosity seekers arrived to take part. Some professionals, such as lawyers, also joined forces with the NFWA. This diversity of people also represented diversity of views on how the strike should be conducted. Many agreed with Cesar Chavez's nonviolent approach, but others had different ideas. Some were itching for an open fight with the growers, while others wanted to secretly sabotage the growers. After a time, most of the volunteers adopted the nonviolent

approach, while some who couldn't accept it drifted away from the farm workers.

An interesting question to ponder is why so many of the people who initially disagreed with the nonviolent approach eventually adopted this line of protest. Clearly, some were persuaded by Cesar Chavez's speeches, but others seemed to be swept up by the group and changed their behavior to fit the group standards.

This type of influence occurs many times in everyday situations. It can be clearly seen on any college campus in the country. In the early 1960s, the "dropout look" invaded campuses. Long hair, sandals, ragged jeans, and T-shirts were seen everywhere. Today it is relatively rare to see students sporting this uniform; running shoes, polo shirts and the "preppy look" are "in." Why has this change come about? Did we all suddenly wake up one morning and decide that last year's clothes looked terrible and that this new combination was best?

This is unlikely. A more accurate answer is that people, in the 1960s and now, change their behavior to be accepted by their group. The dissident strikers conformed to the nonviolent approach in order to be accepted by the other strikers. On college campuses, we choose our clothes so that we will be considered "in" and not be laughed at by our peers.

As you consider the groups to which you belong, you can probably think of numerous instances in which you have behaved in accordance with a group's expectations. In some cases, this **conformity** may have involved your beliefs and desires. The other group members may have taken a particular position on an issue or decided on a course of action with which you didn't agree. Rather than express your opposition, you decided to "go along with the group." A common example of this type of conformity is seen when people explain how they started smoking or drinking alcohol. They often state that they hated the taste of cigarettes or alcohol, but "all their friends were doing it," so they felt compelled to go along with the group.

Conformity to group desires or norms is

so commonplace that we often find ourselves succumbing without even being conscious of the compromise. Conformity involves behavior in which people yield to real or imagined group pressure despite a personal feeling that they should act in some other manner. Actual group pressures, such as laws or threats, may be used to force us to conform. But often the pressure may be imagined by the individual. For example, no one on college campuses demands that students wear the current "uniform"—running shoes and polo shirts, say. Students may simply imagine that they will be ridiculed for wearing anything else. These imagined consequences of nonconformity will be enough to motivate students to don a polo shirt with the collar up.

Because the overt signs of all conforming behavior are the same (that is, acting like other group members), we are often prone to overlook an important feature that distinguishes different types of conformity. Conformity, like beauty, can be only skin-deep, or it can operate beneath the surface. In other words, we can conform in our public behavior only, or we can change our private beliefs also, to bring them in line with those of the group. This distinction can be illustrated by the example of smoking. In one case, an individual may decide that he or she hates the taste of cigarettes and should really not be smoking. As a means of being accepted by his or her group, however, the person will smoke in the presence of others. We speak of this type of behavior as **public compliance,** since only the individual's public behavior has changed. Another individual may also smoke in the presence of friends but may convince himself or herself that cigarettes taste good and that smoking is a "good" behavior. In this case we label the conformity **private acceptance,** since both public behavior and private attitudes have changed to support the group's position.

The actions of both individuals are the same when they are in the presence of their friends. But what happens when the group isn't present? In the case of the person whose smoking represented public compliance, we would

not expect him or her to continue smoking. When private acceptance has occurred, however, we would expect the individual to smoke even when alone and away from group scrutiny. Hence the distinction between simple compliance and private acceptance is crucial for predicting how individuals will behave when they are removed from the group.

It may be instructive to compile a list of your own behaviors that fit the definition of conformity. This list could include such things as smoking, drinking, style of dress, driving habits, behavior at parties, or frequency of class attendance. Once you have developed the list, separate the behaviors into those that represent simple compliance and those that represent more ingrained cases of private acceptance. By doing this, you should be able to predict which behaviors will endure even in the absence of the group in which they originated.

WHY CONFORM?   One of the prices of belonging to a group is that we must often give up some of our personal freedom by conforming to the group's norms. In many cases this is a small price; the individual who wears uncomfortable clothing to a party or drives at the speed limit probably suffers very little by conforming to group standards. In other cases, the price of conformity is much larger. In order to be accepted by a group, an individual may engage in behaviors that he or she considers to be morally wrong or personally dangerous. Juvenile deliquents frequently report that they participated in crimes to gain membership in a local gang. Whether we are dealing with small sacrifices or large sacrifices, we have all experienced the power of the group to influence our behavior. What is this power? Where does it come from? Why do we feel so compelled to follow a group's standards?

Many early attempts to answer these questions focused on the characteristics of the individual group members. Investigators tried to identify certain types of personalities that predisposed individuals to yield to group pressures. Crutchfield (1955) reported that the people most likely to conform to group pressures tended to be less intelligent, had greater feelings of inferiority, were more authoritarian, and idolized their parents more than less-conforming individuals. While attempts to identify the personality of the "conformer" are intriguing, they overlook an important point about conformity. Everyone conforms to group standards; some people may conform more than others, but no one is totally free of it. So personality theories can only succeed in identifying people who conform more than others do.

In order to find out why people conform, we need to examine the sources of group power. One of the major sources of a group's power is the information possessed by it. In many cases, an individual may be unsure about how to behave or what to believe. One way to find out how to act is to see what other people are doing. After obtaining the necessary information, one can then follow the example set by others.

In order to understand this **information influence,** consider the college student who joined the farm workers' strike because he or she really wanted to help them achieve their goals. The student may have initially believed that violence was the best way to achieve these goals. However, after observing many of the workers holding nonviolent demonstrations, the student may have become convinced that nonviolence was the best means to win higher wages and better working conditions. In this case, the student changed both behavior and attitude.

Thus one way in which the group influences us is by supplying information that we accept as valid. This is a powerful influence, since we learn as young children that if a majority of people believe something, it must be correct. Even our democratic system of government is based on the premise that the majority should win because it is usually right. Infor-

Groups may influence members to conform by supplying them with information that is accepted by the members.

Suzanne Szasz, Photo Researchers, Inc.

mational influence is most likely to occur in ambiguous situations, where we are unsure about what to believe or how to behave.

A second and usually more potent power of the group is called **normative influence.** As we grow up and interact with groups, we all learn an important and sometimes painful lesson. Groups often reject members who don't conform to group standards. As a child you may have been teased and ridiculed by your classmates for not wearing the "right" clothing or for speaking with a different accent. The "tattletale" who betrays the group's confidence is often thrown out of the group. Thus everyone learns that groups reward loyalty to the group and punish deviance. The punishment for deviance may be mild ridicule, as in the above examples, or it may come in a harsher form, such as physical violence.

In an interesting demonstration of a group's reaction to a deviant, Stanley Schachter (1951) placed three experimental confederates in discussion groups. The group's task was to decide how to handle a young juvenile delinquent named Johnny Rocco. One of the confederates (the "deviant") was instructed to continuously disagree with the group's opinion. A second confederate (the "slider") began the discussion by disagreeing with the group, but adopted the group's position after a while. The third confederate (the "mode") agreed with the group's position from the beginning of the discussion. The reaction of the group to the three confederates was very different. The mode was readily accepted and liked by the group. The slider received a great deal of attention and pressure to change his attitude until he did change his position. Then he was warmly accepted as a valued member of the group. The deviant, on the other hand, received rough treatment. At first, the group laid a great deal of pressure on him to change his position. In groups that were initially cohesive, group members ceased communicating with the deviant when they realized that persuasion was hopeless; they essentially rejected him from the group.

From studies such as this we know that a group can and probably will treat deviance from the norm rather harshly. And it is precisely this fear that motivates us to conform to group norms. The beauty of this normative influence, from the group's standpoint, is that the group need not have an explicit law or rule that deviants will be punished. The individual's past experiences lead him or her to believe that deviance will be punished, and this belief motivates conformity.

In sum, groups influence the individual through the information they can provide and through the threat that they will reject the individual if he or she doesn't conform. In most cases both effects operate simultaneously to pressure the individual to conform. In some cases, however, it's rather easy to identify the relative contribution of informational and normative influences. For example, normative pressures are mainly responsible for behavior in situations in which an individual clearly knows the correct position but takes an incorrect one; the person doesn't need information from the group in such cases. But when the situation is ambiguous, informational pressures are important. When you consider your own behavior in relation to a group, try to identify the influences to which you're reacting. Are you truly trying to obtain information from the group, or are you more concerned with being accepted by it? In most cases, you are more likely to show private acceptance if your conformity is based on informational influence rather than on normative influence.

CONFORMITY: WHO AND WHEN? If you look back over your own history in various groups, you'll find that there were times when you went along with the group and other times when you didn't. Studies examining conformity have indeed found that there are conditions under which people are more likely to give in to group pressures.

If we look first at the characteristics of the individual, we find that people are most likely to conform when they (1) are strongly attracted to the group, (2) have a low status in the group and don't feel completely accepted by it, and

(3) expect future interactions with the group members. Individuals who don't feel competent to perform the group's current task are most prone to conform to group norms. This description fits many of the outsiders who came to California to help the farm workers. These people wanted very much to help the striking workers and believed they would be interacting with the workers for some time. In most cases, these outsiders didn't feel that they belonged in the workers' group; many of the workers were Hispanic, while the outsiders were mostly Anglo. The college students who came to California were well-educated and came mostly from middle-class families; the workers often had little formal schooling and came from poor backgrounds. In addition, the outsiders didn't know what to expect; the situation was strange to them and they didn't know how to act. Thus the outsiders clearly fit the picture of people who are likely to conform to group pressure.

Edwin Hollander (1958; 1960) made an interesting analogy that explains why individuals with the above characteristics are quick to conform. Essentially, Hollander viewed acts of conformity as credits in the group: Each time an individual conforms to the group, he or she receives some credit. This credit (or *idiosyncrasy credit,* as Hollander called it) can be "banked" by the individual. As the individual builds up credits, his or her status increases in the group. The individual can "spend" these credits through acts of nonconformity; each time the individual deviates from the group, he or she loses credits. The group will tolerate nonconformity as long as the individual has credits to "pay" for his or her nonconformity. The group will be rejecting and punishing, however, if the individual doesn't have credits to pay for acts of deviance. As can be seen, new members of a group and members with low status are least likely to have accumulated enough credits to allow them to deviate without incurring the group's wrath. So these individuals must be most careful to conform. It may be interesting to review your own history in groups. You were probably most likely to

conform when you were a new member or had low status in the group.

The characteristics of the group also help determine group members' conformity. Asch (1956) found that people are much more likely to conform to a unanimous group than to one that has dissenters. Even one group member who openly refuses to go along with the group is enough to drastically reduce the amount of conformity. This finding may explain why many groups are quick to punish a person who tries to deviate from the group. You may recall times when you innocently expressed a deviant opinion in a group, only to find that the group's anger was quickly focused at you. The fear in the group may have been that if one person disagreed with the group's opinion *and got away with it,* others might soon be tempted to defect. In history, we find cases like the Spanish Inquisition and the Salem witch trials, where deviants were publicly tortured and killed. Clearly the effect of these punishments was to demonstrate to others that deviation from the norm wouldn't be tolerated. From the group's point of view, allowing one deviant to exist can be very dangerous to the life of the group.

Finally, research has shown that conformity is greater in relation to ambiguous tasks than to tasks where the correct answer is clear. Of course, this doesn't mean that people don't conform even when they know the correct answer; we have already seen that they do. But group members are more likely to conform when they don't know the correct position.

CONFORMITY AS A POSITIVE NECESSITY. An important point that shouldn't be overlooked is that conformity is often a positive behavior. In our society we are taught that conformity is a herd instinct engaged in only by fools and those too weak in character to "hold their own." Even in our commercial advertisements, the hero or heroine is one who "breaks away" from the group and goes his or her "own way." Various singers have made a mint from their recordings of the song "I Did It My Way." "Do your own thing" was the popular slogan of the 1960s and 1970s. Clearly, blind conformity is not a desirable pattern of behavior; but imagine a society where conformity didn't exist. Driving through an intersection, even with a traffic light, would be hazardous; you would never be sure whether or not the oncoming driver would "do his own thing" and run the red light. Coordination in your own family would be almost impossible; at vacation time, your sister might head for the beach, your brother might take off for the mountains, your parents might go to a large city, and your dog would simply stare in confusion and disbelief!

Some conformity is absolutely necessary for the order and survival of the group. Neither blind conformity nor blind deviance is a positive course of action. Rather, you should understand the pressures that motivate you to conform and determine for yourself whether or not a particular situation is one in which conforming feels comfortable. You should also be aware of the possible reaction of the group should you decide not to conform. Taking all this information into account, you will be in a better position to control your own behavior and to make a wise decision about your course of action. Some forethought about your behavior lessens the chances of your making decisions you later regret and of other people's reactions to your behavior taking you by surprise. There will be many behaviors or opinions you will feel you shouldn't conform to. In such cases, it is important for your own integrity that you resist group pressures. But, once you've made a decision to "go your own way," you must be prepared for the reaction of the group and understand why it may respond negatively to you.

Obedience: Follow the Leader

Conformity involves following the example of other group members. **Obedience,** on the other hand, involves following the direct orders of a more powerful person. It is very likely that many outsiders joined the farm workers' strike because they saw others doing it; these people were conforming to the example of the group. On the other hand, it is also likely that many

other farm workers were influenced by orders from Cesar Chavez. These people admired and respected Cesar; they had heard his speeches and watched him work for the NFWA. He was their leader, and they would follow his orders. The outcome in this case was positive; the workers gained higher wages and better working conditions, and there was no widespread violence.

Unfortunately, there are other cases where following the leader has led to tragic results. At the end of World War II, Allied occupying forces in Germany uncovered scores of concentration camps that quickly yielded their grizzly secret. During the war, the Nazis had sent political prisoners and members of persecuted religious and ethnic groups to be "processed." In all, over 6 million men, women, and children were tortured and killed in these camps. How could anyone knowingly send innocent people to such horrible deaths? After the war, many of the Nazis who had operated these camps were put on trial, and the world learned their rationale for their actions. In nearly every case, the executioners argued that they were "merely following orders" and hence were not responsible for their actions.

Such horrible and frightening outcomes of obedience to authority raise a general question about the extent to which group members will blindly follow the orders of their leaders. It was this question that Stanley Milgram (1963; 1965) attempted to answer through a series of controversial experiments. In order to grasp the impact of the procedure, put yourself in the place of a subject who has volunteered for a psychological experiment. When you arrive at the experimental room, you meet a nice middle-aged person who has also signed up for the experiment. You chat until the experimenter arrives and informs you both that the experiment involves the effect of punishment on learning. You draw straws to determine who will be the "learner" and who will be the "teacher": You draw the "teacher" straw. The experimenter then explains that the teacher will ask the learner a series of questions and administer shock each time the learner gives an incorrect answer. The learner expresses some concern about receiving shock, but consents to the procedure. The learner is then led into another room and hooked up with electrodes.

The experimenter returns and shows you the shock machine. There are a series of levers labeled from 15 volts to 450 volts; over the lower levers is the label "SLIGHT SHOCK," and over the upper levers the label reads "DANGER: SEVERE SHOCK." The final 450-volt level is marked "XXX." The experimenter tells you to begin reading the list of questions to the learner and to shock the learner for each incorrect answer given. You are to increase your level of shock by one lever after each incorrect answer; the first shock will be 15 volts, the next will be 30 volts, and so on.

You begin reading the questions, and each time the listener gives an incorrect answer you administer the next level of shock. You begin to get concerned as the level of shock increases. At 90 volts, the learner lets out a cry of pain. At 150 volts, the learner cries out again and begs to be released from the experiment. You turn to the experimenter, who looks unconcerned and instructs you to proceed with the next question. At 180 volts the learner bangs on the wall and cries that he can't stand the pain. You look at the experimenter, who says, "You have no other choice; you must go on." At 300 volts, the learner refuses to answer any more questions and begs to have the experiment stopped. From this point on, there is no further response from the learner, but the experimenter instructs you to continue administering shocks anyhow.

What would you do in this situation? This was the question Milgram wanted to answer by observing the responses of the "teachers" in his study. He was interested in finding out what percentage of his subjects would follow the orders of the experimenter and deliver dangerous levels of shock to a seemingly innocent stranger. What percentage of the subjects do you believe "went all the way" and delivered 450 volts?

In Milgram's study, which was run at Yale University, the subjects were 20 to 50 years old; 40 percent held unskilled jobs, 40 percent held white-collar jobs, and 20 percent were profes-

TABLE 13.1

Maximum Shock Levels in Milgram's Obedience Study

VERBAL DESIGNATION AND VOLTAGE INDICATION	NUMBER OF SUBJECTS FOR WHOM THIS WAS MAXIMUM SHOCK
Slight shock	
15	0
30	0
45	0
60	0
Moderate shock	
75	0
90	0
105	0
120	0
Strong shock	
135	0
150	0
165	0
180	0
Very strong shock	
195	0
210	0
225	0
240	0
Intense shock	
255	0
270	0
285	0
300	5
Extreme-intensity shock	
315	4
330	2
345	1
360	1
Danger—severe shock	
375	1
390	0
405	0
420	0
XXX	
435	0
450	26

SOURCE: Milgram, S. Behavioral study of obedience. *Journal of Abnormal and Social Psychology*, 1963, 67, 376. Copyright © 1963 American Psychological Association. Reproduced by permission.

sionals. Of the 40 subjects in the study, 26 (65 percent) followed orders to the end and administered 450 volts to the learner (see Table 13.1). Amazingly, not a single subject stopped the experiment before delivering 300 volts. Fortunately, the "learner" wasn't really receiving shock, but was actually an experimental accomplice who had been trained to make particular mistakes. The important point, however, is that the subjects thought that the learner was really receiving shock.

The results of the Milgram study are quite disturbing. They suggest that a majority of people are unwilling or unable to resist the orders of someone of higher status. Milgram reports that the subjects didn't enjoy their behavior; as can be seen in Table 13.2, they did suffer and

TABLE 13.2

A Typical Response in the
Milgram Obedience Study

150 volts delivered. You want me to keep going?

165 volts delivered. That guy is hollering in there. There's a lot of them here. He's liable to have a heart condition. You want me to go?

180 volts delivered. He can't stand it! I'm not going to kill that man in there! You hear him hollering? He's hollering. He can't stand it. What if something happens to him? . . . I'm not going to get that man sick in there. He's hollering in there. You know what I mean? I mean I refuse to take responsibility. He's getting hurt in there. He's in there hollering. Too many left here. Geez, if he gets them wrong. There's too many of them left. I mean who is going to take responsibility if anything happens to that gentleman? (The experimenter accepts responsibility.) All right.

195 volts delivered. You see he's hollering. Hear that? Gee, I don't know. (The experimenter says: "The experiment requires that you go on.") I know it does, sir, but I mean—Hugh—he don't know what he's in for. He's up to 195 volts.

210 volts delivered.

225 volts delivered.

240 volts delivered. Aw, no. You mean I've got to keep going up with the scale? No, sir. I'm not going to kill that man! I'm not going to give him 450 volts! (The experimenter says: "The experiment requires that you go on.") I know it does, but that man is hollering there, sir. (Milgram, 1965)

SOURCE: Milgram, S. Behavioral study of obedience. *Journal of Abnormal and Social Psychology,* 1963, 67, 376. Copyright © 1963 American Psychological Association. Reproduced by permission.

protest. Despite this personal suffering, they engaged in behavior they felt was wrong.

The results of this study should make all of us question our ability to refuse to obey the leaders of groups. You may believe that you

REVIEW QUESTIONS

7. People are more likely to agree to a large request if they have previously agreed to a smaller request. This is known as the _____ phenomenon.

8. The psychological state whereby the individual submerges his or her personal identity while assuming the identity of the group is called _____ .

9. Conforming to the position held by the group without private acceptance of the beliefs and attitudes that underlie that position is called _____ .

10. Pressure to conform to group standards at the risk of being rejected by the group is known as _____ influence.

11. Which of the following characterizes the individual who is most likely to conform to group pressure?
   a. the individual who is strongly attracted to the group
   b. the person who has low status in the group
   c. the individual who anticipates future interaction with the group
   d. all the above

12. T or F: Conformity is greater when the group's position is unambiguously stated or on tasks where the correct answer is true.

13. T or F: Private acceptance is a more likely outcome of conformity when the conforming behavior is based on normative pressure rather than informational pressure.

14. Following the direct orders of a more powerful person is called _____ .

would never follow orders that you felt were morally wrong, but are you sure of this? Milgram described his experiment to 14 Yale seniors and to a group of psychiatrists. He then asked them to predict how many of the subjects would follow orders to deliver the 450 volts. They predicted that less than 2 percent would obey orders to the end. Clearly most of us don't believe that we or our friends would blindly follow orders to hurt another person. Yet the results of Milgram's research suggest that we may indeed do just that.

A number of other studies provided striking examples of people's tendency to obey orders. Hofling, Brotzman, Dalrymple, Graves, and Pierce (1966) telephoned nurses in a hospital and ordered them to administer a drug at double the maximum recommended dose to a patient. In their telephone conversations, they used the name of a doctor who was unfamiliar to the nurses. All but one of the 22 nurses who were telephoned followed the order, even though it was against hospital policy and could have been dangerous for the patient. In another series of studies, Orne and Evans (1965) found that subjects would follow an experimenter's orders to perform such personally dangerous tasks as grasping a venomous snake or putting their hands into a jar of acid.

What is this strange power that is contained in a command? Why will people perform behaviors on the basis of a simple order that they would never perform on their own? When Milgram questioned his subjects as to why they followed the experimenter's orders, they reported that they believed the experimenter was taking responsibility for their behavior. Because he gave the orders, the experimenter was responsible for the outcome. This trap of denying responsibility for our actions is a dangerous one, but it is easy to fall into. Our belief that a leader is responsible for our behavior may cause us to perform acts that we later regret and feel ashamed of. It's important to remember that we control our own behavior and that no one else is responsible for our actions. Knowing this should make us less willing to do something blindly because someone has ordered it. Certainly there may be nega-

tive consequences to disobeying an order from a high-status person, but these consequences are usually much less negative than those that follow when we perform a behavior we know to be wrong. For this, we must eventually assume the responsibility.

Group Polarization: The Courting of Extremes

Cesar Chavez's meetings with the farm workers often followed a seemingly strange pattern. When workers entered a meeting Chavez convened to discuss going on strike, many workers were unsure of the action they wanted to follow to confront the growers. As discussion at a meeting progressed, the workers became solid supporters of the strike; even those who had been uneasy about the strike found themselves strongly behind the idea. You may have found a similar pattern in some of your own groups. People may enter a group being only slightly in favor of a certain position or course of action. Then as the group members began to discuss these issues the members begin to adopt increasingly extreme positions.

A great deal of research has examined how decisions are made in groups. A consistent finding (Myers, 1982) is that groups often adopt a more extreme position than the average initial position of the group members. Oftentimes this group position is more extreme in the risky direction. For example, we could picture a situation in which most workers at a meeting felt that they shouldn't strike unless there was at least a 50 percent chance that the strike would succeed in its aims. But it's likely that, after a group discussion, the workers would decide to strike even if there were only a 25 percent chance of the strike succeeding. In essence, groups tend to polarize our views, and few people in group discussions can effectively hold a moderate or uncommitted position.

A number of reasons have been suggested for **group polarization.** First, we often take cautious positions because we're afraid of the consequences of failure. People in groups often feel less responsible for the final group decision and so are more willing to take an extreme position. Their belief that the burden of failure will be shared by the whole group frees them to advocate more extreme and risky positions. Our language can also bolster extreme positions with its tendency toward polarized terminology and rhetoric: "yes or no," "right or wrong," "with it or out of it." People who advocate extreme positions can be very persuasive because our language helps them paint an "either/or" picture in dramatic terms. They can argue "nothing ventured, nothing gained," while chastizing the reluctant group members for being "square" or "sticks in the mud." It's hard to present an exciting case for an uncommitted or moderate position. A third reason involves social comparison. Most of us want to see ourselves as being as willing as anyone else to take a chance. We rarely want to be seen as the most cautious or reluctant person in the group. We also don't want to be seen as the person in the group who can't make up his or her mind. So as we listen to other group members present positions we attempt to adjust our views until ours are at least as extreme as those of other groups members. If everyone in the group does this, the final group decision will be more extreme than the average decision of the group members.

All these processes probably occur in most group discussions, and they often lead people to adopt more extreme, and usually more risky, positions than they would adopt on their own. Many times group discussion leads the group to make a decision that is too extreme for many of the members to feel comfortable with. The group members seem to get "caught up" in the flow of the discussion and find themselves supporting these extreme positions. Often the extreme group decision has positive or, at worst, neutral consequences. But sometimes the consequences of these extreme decisions are tragic.

Be aware of these factors that may influence your own decisions in groups. It is very easy to be lulled into the flow of group discussion and to be led to support a decision that later makes you uncomfortable. Our aim isn't to make you afraid of getting involved in group decision making, but to show you how the group process affects decisions. An awareness of this process should not only give you a better understanding of why groups arrive at certain decisions, but also better prepare you to resist some of the subtle influences that may be working to affect your own decisions and input within a group.

GROUPS: INFLUENCING AND BEING INFLUENCED

Our discussion of groups should indicate that groups are more than a mere collection of people who happen to be together. Groups are complex social organizations in which we attempt to influence others and they attempt to influence us. Groups have structure and form. Pressures arise within the group that influence our behavior and guide our attitudes.

Being a member of a group or many groups is a part of life. We can't survive alone, nor would we wish to. There is no manual or plan that can tell us how to always be a leader in groups or how to avoid the pressures of conformity. No book can give us a foolproof plan about how to be a "good" group member.

We do know, however, that our successful adjustment to our world and to the groups of which we're a part can be aided by understanding the influence process and how group membership is likely to affect our behavior. Knowledge about group processes can be strong medicine to ensure that we aren't swept into mindless and irresponsible behavior by our groups. Understanding group dynamics can prepare us to be effective group members without giving up our uniqueness and individuality. Knowing the possible pressures that groups can bring to bear on us is similar to being able to predict the weather; we can't eliminate the group pressures or change the weather, but we can anticipate them and plan accordingly. By doing this, we can use groups to help us obtain our goals, improve our social interactions, and add excitement and variety to our daily lives. We can also avoid being the unwitting pawn of our groups. In this way, we will not only be valuable resources in our groups, but also feel better about ourselves and our relationships with other people.

SUMMARY

1. The average individual belongs to five or six groups at any one time. People join groups for many reasons. Among these are a sense of belonging, the desire for information, the desire for rewards, and the desire to achieve goals.

2. Groups have definite structure. Norms specify who must do what when. Roles define the obligations and expectations of people in certain positions. Roles and norms help the group function in an orderly manner. Sometimes role conflict can exist; this occurs when the requirements of a person's role in one group conflict with the requirements of his or her role in another group. We can adjust to role conflict by changing the requirements of roles, choosing our groups so that role conflict is minimized, and openly discussing the conflict that exists.

3. Social influence involves the exercise of power or use of reinforcers by a person or group to influence the behavior of others. There are six types of social power: coercive power, reward power, expert power, legitimate power, informational power, and referent power. Coercive power requires the greatest amount of surveillance to use. Referent power is the most general and its use doesn't require surveillance. Power tends to corrupt people because they often become less sensitive to others and begin to see themselves as better than others.

4. A leader is a person who influences other group members; leadership involves the use of social power. There are many theories about what makes a leader. One holds that leaders possess traits different from followers. A second theory argues that the situation makes the leader. Most support has been found for the position that leadership is a function of both personal characteristics and the situation.

5. There are many ways to influence the behavior of group members. One way is to have them openly make a commitment to a particular course of action. The decision made by the group generally reflects what the majority of the members want. The minority may influence the group if it takes a clear and consistent position and holds steadfastly to it. The effectiveness of influence is also determined by how group members are approached. The foot-in-the-door technique involves having people commit themselves to doing a small action and then asking them to perform a larger one. The door-in-the-face technique can also be effective; here people are first asked to perform a large act, and when they refuse they are requested to take a smaller action.

6. Joining a group can lead to deindividuation of the group members. Deindividuation occurs when people lose their personal identity and become submerged into the group. As a result of deindividuation, people feel less responsible for their actions and may perform acts that they wouldn't perform outside the group.

7. Conformity involves behavior in which people yield to the real or imagined pressures of the group. Conformity may involve only overt behavior (public compliance) or

it may include changing attitudes to believe that the new behavior is right (private acceptance). People conform because they look to the group to provide information about the correct ways to behave or believe. They also conform to avoid rejection by their group members. People are most likely to conform when they are strongly attracted to the group, expect future interaction with group members, and have relatively low status in the group. People are more likely to conform to unanimous groups than groups where other dissenters exist. And conformity is highest when the task is difficult or ambiguous.

8. Obedience involves following the direct orders of a higher status person. People who follow the orders of leaders often don't feel responsible for their own actions.

9. Groups tend to polarize people's opinions. One reason for this is that people feel less responsible for the group's position and are more willing to adopt an extreme position. It is also possible that people want to be perceived as decisive and as having definite points of view.

KEY TERMS

a. CONFORMITY
b. DEINDIVIDUATION
c. GROUP POLARIZATION
d. INFORMATIONAL INFLUENCE
e. LEADER
f. NORMATIVE INFLUENCE
g. NORMS
h. OBEDIENCE
i. ROLE CONFLICT
j. ROLES
k. SOCIAL INFLUENCE
l. SOCIAL POWER

1. A set of norms that defines how an individual in a particular position should act
2. The power of the group to influence a member's behavior through the member's desire to obtain information about the "correct" way to believe or behave
3. Conforming to direct orders from a high-status individual
4. The capacity to influence others and to resist influence from others
5. General rules that apply to everyone in a group and specify what must be done when
6. The internal conflict that results when the behavioral expectations of an individual's role in one group contradict the behavioral expectations of another group to which the individual belongs
7. The exercise of power or the use of reinforcers by a person or group to influence the behavior of others
8. An individual who influences the activities of a group
9. A change in behavior or belief toward a group as a result of real or imagined group pressure
10. The power of the group to influence a member's behavior through the member's fear that he or she will be rejected for failing to follow the group's direction.
11. The process whereby group discussion causes an individual to make a more extreme decision than he or she would make alone
12. A condition whereby the individual becomes "submerged into the group" and feels relatively anonymous

ANSWERS TO REVIEW QUESTIONS

1. b. **2.** Norms. **3.** Role. **4.** Role conflict. **5.** f; d; c; b; a; e. **6.** False.

7. Foot-in-the door. **8.** Deindividuation. **9.** Public-compliance. **10.** Normative. **11.** d. **12.** False. **13.** False. **14.** Obedience.

WORKING

The young man shifted uncomfortably as the rickety bus slowly climbed the long hill. The hot July sun made him sweat profusely in his wool suit. He knew it was crazy to wear this suit, but it was his best one. A lot was riding on this interview. It was a bad year for new veterinarians in Great Britain. Farming was in a sad state of affairs in the 1930s, and tractors and other machines were quickly replacing the sturdy draught horses that had been the mainstay of the farm. Had he slaved away for five years in veterinary school only to have to do volunteer work for another few years? His fear about this was justified. There were two or three openings for vets each week and an average of 80 applicants for each opening.

James Herriot got off the bus at Darrowby, a small town in the Yorkshire Dales. He slowly made his way to a large stone house, on which hung an old-fashioned brass sign reading, "S. Farnon, M.R.C.V.S." The housekeeper let James in and offered him a seat. After James had waited for what seemed like a lifetime, the door to the small room burst open, and a tall thin man came in. "Sorry you've had to wait. I'm Siegfried Farnon." Siegfried showed James around the clinic; they examined the operating room, the dispensary, and the living quarters. Siegfried was cheerful and friendly, and James Herriot was immediately attracted to him. James kept waiting for Siegfried to sit down and tell him about the practice, quiz him, and probe for his weaknesses. But after the tour Siegfried smiled, "Rather than talk about the practice, why don't you come on a few calls with me?"

Outside James stared in horror at the battered old Hillman that sat in the driveway; it had treadless tires, a rusted body, and an almost opaque windshield with a network of fine cracks. James got in very carefully, and when the car started up, he suddenly found himself in the back seat. Siegfried had failed to warn him that the passenger seat wasn't fixed to the floor. Determined to redeem himself and regain his dignity, James volunteered to handle one of the cases on their rounds. Mr. Sharpe's cow had a blocked udder. James felt the thickened mass of tissue, and his mind went back to what he had learned in vet school. He reached for the Hudson instrument and began working the thin metal spiral up into the cow's teat. The next thing he knew, he "was sitting gasping in the dung channel with the neat imprint of a cloven hoof on my shirt front, just over the solar plexus" (Herriot, 1972, p. 28). Both Mr. Sharpe and Siegfried tried to contain their laughter, but it was no use. Mr. Sharpe bellowed, "I'm sorry, young man, but I owt to 'ave told you that this is a very friendly cow. She allus likes to shake hands."

On their way home, Siegfried stopped at a pub. Over beer, he told James about the practice. He pointed out the difficulties involved in the work and talked enthusiastically about his plans for the future. Then Siegfried turned to James and said, "Well, you can have the job if you want it. Four quid a week and full board." James almost leapt out of his skin. This was too good to be true. He thought of his many classmates who were so desperate they were offering their services for free. Thus James Herriot became the new veterinarian in Darrowby.

James Herriot's work was varied and interesting. It allowed him to demonstrate his skills while being of help to the farmers in the Dales.

His first few weeks on the job proved to be frustrating. After spending five years in vet school he was ready to take on cases of his own. But Siegfried was cautious; he watched James very closely even on the most minor cases. James felt like he was back in school; he appreciated the guidance, but longed for independence. He wanted to show what he could do on his own.

Finally his chance came. Siegfried was called away one evening, and the telephone rang. The caller demanded Mr. Farnon. When told that Siegfried was out, the caller sounded disappointed. James proudly announced that he was the new vet. The caller answered that he didn't think James could do anything for him. "Do you know anything about colic?" James bristled as he responded, "I'm a veterinary surgeon, so I think I should know something about it!" In the long drive out to the farm, James reviewed what he had been taught about horse colic. The sight that greeted him at the farm was alarming. The beautiful bay horse was obviously in terrible pain. He was staggering around his stall and had already worn out a path in the hay. His head rolled at every step and he gritted his teeth. The gruff attendant ordered James to give him a shot and "get him right." But on careful examination, James knew no shot would help this animal. The horse's intestines were badly twisted, and he was slowly dying. James turned to the attendant and told him that there was no cure: "I suggest you let me put him down immediately." The attendant gave a yell and started cursing. Mr. Farnon could cure the horse, he claimed. Finally he agreed to let James "put the horse down," but he assured James that he would order an autopsy to test the diagnosis. Fortunately, the diagnosis proved James was correct and that he had done the only humane thing.

Life was rarely dull for James Herriot. A steady stream of people carrying an incredible variety of animals visited the clinic every day. At night, James would drag his tired body to bed, only to hear the angry *brreeng-brreeng* of the telephone echo through the house. Regardless of the time, the farmers rarely apologized for calling; farming was a 24-hour-a-day job. The voice on the phone might describe almost any imaginable problem. "I've got a big show 'oss here. He's cut 'isself badly on the hind leg, just above the hock. I want him stitched immediately." Another night, the voice might say, "I've got a heifer calvin' and she's not getting on with t'job. Will you come?"

The working conditions, like the work, varied wildly. James saw some of his "patients" in the surgery clinic; others he saw inside barns; still others he saw on lonely hillsides. He sweated in the heat of the summer; and his fingers went numb as he worked in the bone-chilling cold of a winter's night on a windy slope. Most of the farmers were poor, and Siegfried and James's practice struggled to make ends meet. But the money he received for his services wasn't James's primary concern. His greatest joy came when, after hours of toiling with his arms inside a cow, he delivered a wobbly but healthy calf. James took pride in his ability to perform healing "miracles" and loved to see the relief on a farmer's face when an animal that had been given up for dead staggered to its feet and trotted out into the field. When he went back to his car after a case, James's "prize" was often sitting in the front seat,—perhaps some freshly made sausage or Yorkshire pudding that a grateful family had secretly placed on his seat. It was their way of quietly saying "Thanks."

Life at the clinic was made even more interesting when Siegfried's brother Tristan moved in. Tristan was studying to be a vet, but he just couldn't seem to pass his exams. And, to Siegfried's horror, Tristan seemed to care very little whether he passed or not. Siegfried's serious, concerned view of life was exactly the opposite of Tristan's devil-may-care approach. Siegfried was constantly throwing Tristan out after one disaster after another, but Tristan always came back the next morning. Practicing veterinary medicine didn't only involve dealing with the animals; it also involved refereeing the frequent blow-ups between Siegfried and his brother.

James Herriot's life revolved around the vet practice that was his livelihood. He met an endless variety of people and made many friends through his work. In time the people in the Dale accepted him and would call up and ask for "Mr. Herriot." James learned a great deal from the local people. He met many farmers who were very poor and couldn't read or write, but who took pride in their small farms and had much earthy wisdom that was being forgotten in the modern world. He felt the gloom of failure when he lost an animal he was sure he could have saved but at other times the deep happiness of doing a successful job.

OUR JOBS AND OUR LIVES

James Herriot's books about his life as a veterinarian are fascinating. The appeal of his life story doesn't come from the fact that Herriot was a superman who performed incredible feats that made the front page of the newspaper. His story is similar to what most of us could write about our lives and our work. We would have different experiences to write about and different people to describe. But overall, James Herriot's story is about a person and his day-to-day experiences on his job.

Each incident Herriot describes is a story in itself, but taken together his experiences teach many lessons. One of the most important lessons is the role that people's work plays in their lives. When we think about our jobs, two things usually come to mind: *money* and *time*. Clearly, the money earned from employment plays a major role in our lives: It enables us to feed and clothe ourselves; it helps determine our standard of living—what kind of home we have, the type of car we drive, the number of vacations we take. Holding a job outside the home also influences how we spend much of our time during the day. Most of us will work at least 40 years of our lives at a job. Assuming that we work an average of 40 hours a week, we will spend over 80,000 hours on our jobs. That's a long time, and it's easy to see that our careers will occupy a large part of our attention.

But James Herriot's story shows that our jobs will play a role in our lives even larger than determining how our time is spent and how much money we have. James's job *determined where he lived*. In taking the one job that was open to him, he had to move to a small town in an area he had never even visited. For many of us, our jobs will determine where we live. We may have to leave the place where we now live in order to find the type of work we desire. We may have to move to parts of the country, or to other countries, that we once looked on with disfavor. Some people dread the prospect of moving to New York City to advance their careers, while others wonder how they'll be able to stand living in some small town in the middle of nowhere.

Our jobs may also influence our *daily routine*. Many of us will work the five-days-a-week, nine-to-five schedule, but others won't. James Herriot worked weekends and many nights. Regardless of our particular schedules, the point is that the requirements of our jobs may well determine when we can shop, go out dancing or to the movies, and take our vacations.

Herriot's books are filled with tales about people. The striking part of these stories is that almost all the people he describes he met through his job. They were people who came to the clinic, people whose farms he visited to work on their animals, other vets he met at conventions, or people he met on his way to and from cases he was working on. He even met his future wife when he was called to a farm to work on a sick bull. The same story will hold true for most of us. Our jobs will determine *who we come into contact with* and who will be our friends. As we pointed out in Chapter 10, proximity and similarity are two important factors that influence who will be attractive to us. Thus the job we accept will not only force us to come into contact with certain people, but also will influence who we find with similar interests and experiences.

James Herriot points out another interesting influence of jobs on people's lives. Throughout his books, he mentions the parties and other social events he attended. In almost every case, he was captured by someone who wanted his advice about how to treat a dog, horse or cow, or someone who had just read of a new remedy for this problem or that sickness. As was true in James's case, our occupations will *influence the conversations* we have in settings outside the workplace. The nurse or doctor is invariably approached at a social gathering by someone who wants advice on an illness; the lawyer is asked how he or she feels about the latest court ruling on capital punishment; the psychologist is told about a party-goer's ''odd'' relative; the plumber is asked about how to fix a leaky pipe. The work you perform often influences how others respond to you. Many a spouse dreads going to parties because his or her wife or husband will spend the evening "talking shop" while the spouse is left to look on like a spectator.

The point of this discussion is not to bemoan the evil influences of our jobs or to strike fear into people's hearts because they may become the captive of their jobs. But it is important to recognize the important influence on our lives played by the type of work we choose and the place in which we work. So our personal adjustment process must include adjustment to our work and work setting.

WHY WORK?

Given that a career can "take over" so much of our lives, a natural question to ask is, Why put ourselves through all the effort to have an occupation? Why did James Herriot spend so many years in school learning his profession and then accept a position that required him to work long hours under some very bad conditions? The first answer that comes to mind is money. We work to live. This is certainly true, but it doesn't present the whole picture. Herriot could have taken a job that didn't require college and professional training; he could have found a job that required fewer hours and paid him more money. In a recent study, workers were asked what they would do if they had a million dollars (Rubin, 1979). Although some said they would change their jobs, almost all reported they would continue to work. Thus physical survival is only one of the reasons that we work.

Many years ago, Abraham Maslow (1943, 1954) proposed a theory of *motivation* to explain people's actions. As we saw in Chapter 2, Maslow argued that people act to satisfy their needs, and that these needs are not equal, but are arranged in a hierarchy. The lower needs have to be satisfied before a person tries to satisfy the higher needs. As can be seen from Figure 14.1, Maslow's hierarchy of needs is as follows:

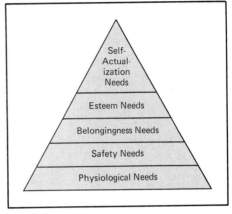

FIGURE 14.1   MASLOW'S HIERARCHY OF NEEDS
Maslow believed that motives at each level must be satisfied before motives at the next higher level will direct behavior.

1. *Physiological Needs.* These are the most basic needs and include the need for food and water.

2. *Safety Needs.* These needs involve acquiring a safe and secure environment, one that is free from continued threats to existence.

3. *Belongingness Needs.* These needs include a desire to belong to a group and to have friends.

4. *Esteem Needs.* These needs are concerned with people's desire to establish an identity, have a positive self-image, and receive recognition from others.

5. *Self-Actualization Needs.* These are the highest-order needs and involve being creative and reaching one's full potential.

There has been a great deal of discussion and argument about the exact nature of needs, whether or not hierarchies exist, and whether needs are learned or innate (see Cofer & Appley, 1964). But whether or not we adopt a specific theory of motivation, need theories of motivation such as Maslow's do give us a clue about some of the reasons people work. The economic benefits of jobs satisfy the physiological and safety needs. What other needs does working satisfy?

INDEPENDENCE.   Working fulfills our need for independence. Having a job and an

People gain self-identity through accomplishments they have worked for.
Rhoda Sidney.

income allows us to achieve independence from our parents. We can support ourselves, set up our own households, and start our own families if we desire. This independence represents freedom; having a job allows us to make basic choices within the limits of our income. We can determine when and what we will eat, where we will live, and how we will spend our free time.

IDENTITY. If someone asked who James Herriot was, people familiar with his books would reply that he was a veterinarian. For many of us, as for Herriot, our occupation becomes a part of our identity. Like our family, hometown, or university, our occupation is one bit of information that makes us unique from many other people and helps define who we are. In fact, some people choose a career based on the identity they want to assume (DuBrin, 1984). For example, someone who wants to be seen as rugged and tough may choose a career that portrays this image, such as truck driving, ranching, or athletics.

SELF-ESTEEM. Despite the fact that he actually earned little money, James Herriot felt that his work was important. Not only was he

helping other people in Darrowby, but each time he cured a sick or injured animal he was demonstrating his skills to himself. His work was like a stage on which he could demonstrate his abilities to others and to himself. Work helps give many of us a sense of self-worth. It bolsters our self-esteem by helping us gain a sense of competency. Our achievements show that we can do things that are valued by others, which gives us a feeling of pride in ourselves.

SELF-ACTUALIZATION. Maslow's concept of *self-actualization* means, in a nutshell, that a person is able to develop his or her potential, to use personal abilities in creative ways. Herriot speaks with pride of one of his most difficult cases. A poor family's prize heifer had an abscess in her throat and was slowly dying. Herriot knew of no technique that had been developed to treat this problem. For days he thought of the problem as the cow became weaker. In desperation he developed a new technique. The technique worked, and the cow was saved! Herriot didn't earn a great deal of money for this operation, nor did his work make the newspaper headlines. But his pride knew no bounds: He had created something new; he had used his skills to the best of his ability. So it is that in many cases our work gives us the opportunity to use our skills, to do the best job we can, and, sometimes, to do it in a new, creative way.

As we can see, though working is crucial to our physical survival, we work to satisfy needs broader than food, clothing, and shelter. We can define **work** as some disciplined activity that gives us a feeling of personal accomplishment and that makes a contribution to our society. An **occupation** or a **job** is the specific form our choice of work takes. You may have chosen educating children as the work you'd like to do, but you could accomplish this work by raising your own children as a full-time occupation or by taking a job as a teacher, writer of children's literature, lobbyist for educational causes, or secretary of your state's department of education. Almost any job will enable us to earn enough money to survive. It is important to choose a form of work that will also enable us to satisfy our desires for independence, identity, self-esteem, and creativity. As we will see later in this chapter, our satisfaction with our jobs can't be measured only in terms of the money we earn. Our satisfaction is determined, to a large degree, by the extent that a job allows us to fulfill these other needs. Because our jobs must do more than simply allow us to survive, it's important that we make a careful decision when choosing a career.

CHOOSING A CAREER

The Decision Process

By the time you entered college, you were probably sick of being asked, "What are you going to be when you grow up?" It seems that in our society we begin asking this question of children almost as soon as they learn to talk. In fact, a child may have an easier time answering this question than a young adult does. When you're at the point of actually choosing a career, the question has real meaning.

Years ago, choosing a career wasn't a difficult question for many people. A son was ex-

pected to "follow in his father's footsteps," taking up his father's occupation or taking over the family business. Women, also had little choice: They would "naturally" get married and raise a family. The only option for them was who they would marry. So the question for women became "What occupation will your husband have?" There is still a tendency for adolescents to aspire to their parents' occupations. But this tendency is not nearly as strong as it was, and it seems to hold only in cases where the parents have prestigious occupations or express pride in their jobs.

On one hand, our present society frees children from the expectation that they will follow in their parents' footsteps. But in today's complex world this freedom of choice about a career may be confusing and frightening, since the word **career** itself usually implies to us a lifelong commitment to a certain type of work. Fortunately, as we will see later in this chapter, the decision you make about your first job isn't as final as it once was. We now have the opportunity to change our occupations at many points in our lives.

Even with this apparent failsafe, the decision about what to be "when we grow up" is a difficult and important one, and not a decision that most of us make overnight. In fact, research suggests that in early childhood we begin laying the groundwork for choosing our careers (Ginsberg, 1966). This research identifies stages we go through in making the decision. The **fantasy stage** begins when we are very young and lasts until approximately the age of 11. During this stage, children assume that they can be whatever they want to be. They spend a great deal of time thinking about various occupations and playing at jobs. You might remember some of the happy moments of your childhood when you "were" a doctor, movie star, firefighter, or astronaut.

Between ages 11 and 17, young people enter the *tentative stage*. During this period they realize that they must soon make a decision about the occupation they will enter. They begin to examine their interests, abilities, and values and search for occupations that will best fit these characteristics.

USING YOUR PAST TO GUIDE FUTURE JOB CHOICES

One of the most difficult questions faced by many people is what type of job they want. Determining what you want involves many steps. Clearly decisions have to be made about where you would like to live and the type of lifestyle you desire. As we have seen, a decision about a job may well affect these aspects of your life. Another important dimension of the decision process is identifying the activities you enjoy. One way to proceed in this area is to look back over your past experiences and identify the activities you enjoyed and the ones which you did not enjoy. Below are some questions that focus on education and work experience that may help you plot the types of jobs you would most likely enjoy.

Education

1. The amount of education and training I now have is . . .
2. The school subjects I enjoyed most were . . .
3. The reasons I enjoyed them are . . .
4. The school subjects I enjoyed least were . . .
5. The reasons I didn't like them were . . .
6. The school subjects I did the best work in and received the highest grades in were . . .
7. The school subjects I did the worst work in and received the lowest grades in were . . .
8. The thing I liked about my favorite teachers were . . .
9. The things offered free at school that I have taken advantage of are . . .
10. The educational and training credentials I hope to obtain are . . .

Work Experience

1. When did you take your first job?
2. What are all the jobs you have had in your past? (List them.)
3. Put a star next to the jobs that were hard work.
4. Put a check next to the jobs that you would not want to do again.
5. Circle the jobs that were fun.
6. What job experience do you hope to get in the near future?

D. W. Johnson, *Human Relations and Your Career: A Guide to Interpersonal Skills,* © 1978, p. 30. Reprinted by permission of Prentice-Hall, Inc. Englewood Cliffs, N.J.

During the *realistic stage* from age 17 on, people begin to realize that no one job may fit all their desires and that their choice may have to be a compromise. People look at the rewards offered by jobs and weigh these against the training required for the job and the effort required in the occupation. Choices become narrowed and more realistic.

Aids to Making an Informed Decision

James Herriot began veterinary school in the early 1930s. Compared to the present, his decision about an occupation was simple. Today the variety in types of jobs is almost unbelievable. In fact, the government publishes the *Dic-*

No decision about occupation is irreversible. With additional education and training, people can change their occupations at any time.

Laimute Druskis.

tionary of Occupational Titles which lists over 20,000 jobs, and new jobs are being added each year. Given the number of possibilities, how can anyone make the "right" choice?

Before examining some of the aids we can use in making a decision, we should stress some important points. First, there is no one "right" job for any of us. Many different occupations could fulfill each of our needs. The aim is to find a job or occupation, not the job, that will make us happy. Second, as we grow older, our needs and desires change. An occupation we choose when we are in our twenties may not fulfill our needs when we are in our forties. So it's important to realize that we will be faced with making decisions about our occupation throughout our lives. No decision is irreversible. But the decision about our first job is a very important one, because it will serve as the foundation for decisions throughout our lives.

COUNSELORS AND TESTS. Many high schools and most colleges and universities have job or **guidance counselors.** These people are trained to help students choose an occupation. Their work doesn't involve telling you what you should be. Rather, the counselors attempt to identify your interests, values, attitudes, and abilities. The counselor will then discuss the wide variety of jobs that are available and help you identify the types of jobs that may be a "good fit" with who you are.

Often counselors will suggest that students take tests aimed at identifying their abilities and interests. A wide variety of tests are available for this purpose (McCormick & Ilgen, 1980). **Ability tests** measure your reasoning, memory, mechanical, math, and psychomotor abilities. Entrance examinations for many professional schools include a wide range of ability questions. For example, a student wishing to enter some dental schools may be given a psychomotor test where he or she is asked to carve a figure out of a block of soap. Other tests, such as the Kuder Interest Inventory and the Strong-Campbell Vocational Interest Inventory, are aimed at identifying a person's interests. These **interest tests** compare the individual's interests with those of successful people in a wide variety of occupations. The assumption behind these tests is that a person is more likely to be happy if his or her basic interests are similar to those of people already in the field.

Armed with the results of the tests and with a record of the person's background, the counselor then conducts an interview with the individual. In the interview, the counselor further pinpoints the person's values and desires and discusses the results of the tests. The counselor and student discuss a number of different occupations, and the counselor outlines what is required to enter each of these professions.

The guidance counselor can be of invaluable help in the process of choosing your profession. In fact, many business organizations employ counselors to help their employees find positions that are most suitable for them or to help retrain employees for new jobs (DuBrin, 1984).

PARENTS. Parents can be either one of the most helpful resources or one of the greatest hindrances for a person attempting to decide on a career. Parents who understand the anxiety and uncertainty that accompany making a decision about a career can supply a supportive environment. They can lend a sympathetic ear and help their children "talk through" their feelings about their career options. They can help arrange interviews with people who work in different professions. They can discourage their children from making premature or uneducated decisions.

Unfortunately, some parents become roadblocks in their children's quest for a career. Parents hold values about what occupations are good and bad, and they may feel that they "know what is best" for their children. They may try to force their children to adopt their values and deny them the independence to make their own choices. Often parents attempt to guide their children because they care about them and want them to have a better life than they themselves had. They have difficulty seeing that their children are capable of making decisions for themselves. In other cases, parents try to live their own lives again through their children. A frustrated father who wanted to be a doctor or an unfulfilled mother who wanted to be a business executive may push his or her children in these directions. If the son or daughter enters the career that was desired by the parent, the parent's disappointment in his or her career choice is reduced.

Attempts by the parents to determine their children's careers can have two disastrous consequences. On the one hand, children may follow the parents' advice, only to find out many years later that they have made a bad decision. Not only will the children be unhappy, but they will resent their parents for causing their misfortune. On the other hand, the children may experience **reactance** (Brehm & Brehm, 1981). Reactance results when a person feels that his or her freedom is being threatened. As a consequence, the threatened freedom becomes more attractive, and the person may engage in the threatened free behavior simply to demonstrate that he or she has freedom. In the case of parental interference, telling children that they must not enter a certain occupation may

boomerang; the forbidden occupation may begin to look more attractive. A child may choose that occupation simply to defy his or her parents and proclaim his or her freedom of choice. The unfortunate result is that choosing an occupation just to defy one's parents is not likely to lead to a wise choice.

As can be seen, parents must walk a thin line in trying to help their children make wise choices, yet giving their children the freedom to make independent decisions. Parents need to be aware that their children may well have needs and aspirations different from their own and that a career that is right for the parents may not be right for the child.

INTERNSHIPS AND SUMMER JOBS. There is an old saying that experience is the best teacher. In the case of career choices, this saying suggests that the more experience you have with different jobs, the better able you'll be to make a wise career choice. You can talk with people or read about jobs, but experience provides further information important for your choice. If you want to be a veterinarian, you can talk with counselors, read books, and talk with veterinarians. These activities will give you a great deal of information about the occupation, but they won't present the complete picture. Herriot's books, for example, offer only sketches of the life of a veterinarian. Herriot rarely talks about the hours of drudgery in mixing medicines and ordering supplies and materials for the practice. The reader doesn't get a feel for the frustration of dealing with customers who refuse to pay their bills. Herriot writes in such a pleasing way that the pain is often eliminated from a dog bite, a horse kick, or the gnawing cold in which he often had to work.

Summer jobs, volunteer work, and internships give you the chance to get first-hand experience with specific jobs before you make a career choice. In many cases, colleges and universities have arrangements with local businesses and agencies that allow students to work on an internship basis during the school year.

REVIEW QUESTIONS

1. T or F: Our jobs are an important aspect of personal adjustment in that jobs influence nearly all other aspects of our lives, even the kinds of conversations we have outside the workplace.

2. Match the needs proposed by Maslow with their description and place both in the appropriate position in his motivation hierarchy.

_____ _____ 1st level (lowest order needs)	a. esteem needs	1. affiliation, be in a group
_____ _____ 2nd level	b. safety needs	2. creativity, reaching one's potential
_____ _____ 3rd level	c. physiological needs	3. establish an identity, receive recognition
_____ _____ 4th level	d. belongingness needs	4. basic needs for food and water
_____ _____ 5th level (highest order needs)	e. self-actualization needs	5. nonthreatening, secure environment

3. The aspect of a job that allows us to support ourself and gives us the freedom of choice is fulfilling our desire for _____.

4. Our occupation often becomes an important part of our identity. Our work achievements may give us a sense of competence and pride, increasing our _____.

5. Research suggests that career choices are made after the individual has passed through three distinct stages. These stages are the _____ period, the _____ stage, and the ____ stage.

6. Guidance counselors attempt to help students choose an occupation by testing the students to determine their _____ and _____.

7. Mr. and Mrs. Bernhardt have forbidden their daughter Sarah to become an actress; in response, Sarah finds that career even more attractive. This may be an example of _____.

These internships may be in the police department, courts, hospitals, law offices, local industries, or even on farms. Students have the opportunity to learn about jobs and can gain course credit for their work. Summer jobs and volunteer work also offer this kind of hands-on experience that allows students to learn about careers. A semester or summer of work clearly won't present the whole picture, but what you learn can be combined with what you've gained from tests and talks with guidance counselors, parents, and people in those professions. With all this information, you'll be prepared to make a wiser choice. Students can often get information about internships, volunteer work, and summer jobs from school placement offices and guidance counselors.

ON THE JOB

James Herriot accepted Siegfried Farnon's offer as soon as it was given. He had known Siegfried for only a few hours, and he didn't know what Siegfried would expect of him. He had heard stories that many of his classmates cleaned house and washed automobiles for their employers. Many left their jobs after a few months. Herriot didn't know if he would be happy with his new job, and he worried about satisfying Siegfried's expectations. The concerns and fears that Herriot experienced are felt by almost everyone who accepts a new job. The concerns generally center around how management treats employees and whether the individual will be satisfied with the job.

Management's Views of Workers

Traditionally, the relationship between employers and employees hasn't been a good one. McGregor (1960) coined the term **Theory X** to characterize management's traditional view. Theory X holds that workers are lazy, dishonest, and dull. They must be made to work and watched carefully. According to Theory X the only way to get workers to work is to pay them a decent wage and to threaten to fire them if they don't perform satisfactorily. This point of view clearly sets management and labor apart from each other; managers are the watchdogs who must constantly be on guard lest workers "get away with something."

A second view is called **Theory Y,** which holds that people want to contribute; the more people become involved in their jobs, the more meaningful the jobs become to them (Steers & Porter, 1979). According to this point of view, workers are quite capable of making decisions that will help both the organization and themselves. The role of management is to create an environment in which employees can fulfill their potential. Under this system employees are given freedom to make decisions that will affect their work. Research has found that employees tend to be more committed to organizations that hold the Theory Y philosophy (Lawler & Hackman, 1969).

Despite the apparent benefits of the Theory Y view and its adoption in many American work situations, there has been some concern recently that American workers aren't as productive or as happy as Japanese workers. After a visit to a number of industries in Japan, Bluestone (1983) characterized the Japanese working organization as being similar to a family. Japanese workers are usually hired at only one time during the year; so they enter the workplace with a "class" of peers. They receive extensive training, in some cases for as long as two years. It is understood that, except under the most unusual circumstances, workers are hired for life. The company often supplies housing for new workers and, after a number of years, loans them the money to buy their own homes. Groups of workers, rather than individuals, are singled out for recognition, and decisions about work and the work environment are also made by groups. The worker's whole life revolves around the organization; in a real sense, workers are adopted into a family rather than hired for a job, as is the case in many American work situations.

Ouchi and Price (1978) have termed this approach **Theory Z.** Siegfried Farnon's approach to James Herriot followed this theory in many respects. James lived in Siegfried's home and in many ways became part of Siegfried's family. Together with Tristan and Siegfried, Herriot participated in making decisions about the practice. There was no specialization of labor; James and Siegfried performed similar tasks.

There has been a great deal of discussion about whether or not Theory Z could be adopted in American companies. Corporations such as Eastman Kodak, Proctor and Gamble, Hewlett-Packard, and IBM have attempted to use certain characteristics of Theory Z (DuBrin, 1984). Their efforts have proven successful to some degree. There have been problems, however. One of the greatest is that employees feel uncomfortable with losing their individuality. There is a sense that they are only part of the organization and that they can't be singled out for exceptional performance. Some also feel that, with its emphasis on group values and beliefs, Theory Z doesn't tolerate deviant views. Although employees have input into making company policies, individuals are not free to "go their own way" once those policies are determined. People brought up in the Japanese culture, which stresses the group, may be more suited to the Theory Z approach than are Americans, whose culture stresses individuality (Bluestone, 1983). Judgments about the effectiveness of Theory Z in the American workplace will have to wait the test of time.

The point of our discussion is to show that there are many different approaches employers can adopt in relation to their employees. The particular approach can greatly affect the way a business is run and the role employees play in the organization. In some cases, the ap-

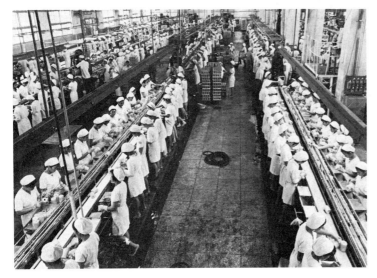

Many Japanese firms have adopted Theory Z which treats workers much like family members. The emphasis is on the group rather than the individual.
United Nations.

proach used by an employer can strongly influence how happy and productive a particular individual will be. Therefore it's in the employee's best interest to determine the employer's general approach to its employees before accepting a position.

Job Satisfaction

Periodically James Herriot would pull the old Hillman to a stop on a hill and look out over the valleys and moors of the Yorkshire Dales thinking about his job. He truly loved the smell of the fresh mowed hay and the clean air; he loved working with the animals and with the people in Yorkshire; he enjoyed being a part of Siegfried's practice and his family. James Herriot was very satisfied with his job.

We can define *job satisfaction* as a pleasurable emotional state that results from feeling that your job is fulfilling. There are some interesting facts and figures about job satisfaction. Older workers report most satisfaction with their jobs. Greatest dissatisfaction is found in workers between the ages of 20 and 29 and in workers in midlife, ages 38 to 45 (Bass & Ryterband, 1979). Similarly, length of service in a job affects satisfaction; job dissatisfaction is greatest shortly after people begin a job (Organ & Hamner, 1978). With occupational level held

constant, there seems to be more dissatisfaction as level of education increases (Korman, 1977). Oftentimes this is not a real problem, because people with higher education levels tend to get higher-status jobs. Again, if we hold job level constant, there doesn't seem to be a difference between men and women or between whites and blacks with regard to job satisfaction. However, as we will see, there is a great deal of discrimination in the workplace, so that job levels of white males are on the average higher than the job levels of females and blacks.

Many questions can be raised about job satisfaction. Since our jobs play such important roles in our lives, it's important to question what factors determine our satisfaction. A second important question is whether or not being satisfied with our jobs has any effect on our behavior. Let's first focus on the factors that influence job satisfaction.

REWARDS. What would make you happier with your job? If we were asked this question, most of us would quickly respond, "More money." But is money really a major factor that determines our satisfaction with our job? It clearly wasn't for James Herriot. He began making four pounds a week (less that $20), and, though his earnings did increase, he could have made a great deal more by moving to a large city practice.

A review of research that asked workers to rate the most important things about their jobs showed that pay was only moderately important (Stagner, 1950). But it would be a mistake to conclude from these data that rewards are not an important factor in determining job satisfaction. Our discussion of rewards so far has been narrowly focused on the material gain of money. Investigators argue that material rewards represent only one of the two motivational processes related to work behavior, extrinsic and intrinsic (Deci, 1975).

Extrinsic motivation comes from factors external to the individual. People can be motivated to work by extrinsic factors such as pay, threats, or pressure from co-workers. Thus our previous focus on "more money" was an extrinsic factor.

But **intrinsic motivation** is also an important factor in work behavior. There are two bases for intrinsic motivation. First, people have a need to see themselves as *controlling their own behavior*. That is, people want to see themselves as deciding when and how they will act. The second base for intrinsic motivation is that people want to see themselves as *being capable and competent*. Intrinsic rewards make workers feel in control and competent. Numerous studies have shown that intrinsic rewards—such as increased choice, opportunity to see the finished results of work, and opportunities to make input into the job process—increase satisfaction with the job (Staw, 1976; Deci, 1971).

The bottom line of this discussion is that rewards do influence satisfaction with a job or career. However, when we speak of rewards we must refer to them in the broadest sense, which includes both extrinsic and intrinsic forms of satisfaction.

Another interesting issue is related to these concepts of rewards. It seems that as extrinsic rewards increase, intrinsic motivation may decrease (Deci, 1975; Lepper, Greene, & Nisbett, 1973).

Consider the situation where you jog because you enjoy running and the feeling you have after a good run (intrinsic rewards). Someone notices that you have the potential to be a world-class runner and offers you $1000 to enter a marathon race. You do well, and the promoter now offers you $10,000 to run in another marathon. What is likely to happen in this case is that you'll find yourself running for the money; extrinsic motivation will now guide your behavior. At the same time your intrinsic motivation may well decrease; you will not enjoy running so much for the good feeling it gives you as for the external rewards it brings. Clearly, the danger here is that an activity you once enjoyed and controlled now controls you. You'll run as long as you receive money.

The loss of intrinsic rewards is a problem faced by people who choose their jobs only for the extrinsic rewards. They may well be satisfied as long as they keep receiving increases in salary and status. But if these rewards are reduced, their satisfaction with their jobs decreases. The task faced by management is to provide workers with enough extrinsic rewards to satisfy their needs and reward performance, while also structuring the job so that there are sufficient intrinsic rewards.

We can see that James Herriot was strongly motivated by the intrinsic rewards of his job. He enjoyed his work because he felt he was helping others, because he was free to try new treatments and operations, and because he had an opportunity to use his skills and demonstrate his competence.

EXPECTATIONS.   The night that James Herriot and Siegfried Farnon had their first discussion in the pub was an important one. James not only got his job offer that night; he also came away with a number of expectations about the veterinary practice. Siegfried was careful to tell James the problems he was having and how difficult it was to make a go of a new practice. But Siegfried couldn't hide his enthusiasm; he told James of his grand plans and the exciting possibilities that existed for the practice. Even though he knew the realities of the situation, James focused on the enthusiastic hopes. The only time James reports being dissatisfied with his job was during the first few weeks. The job simply didn't measure up to what he had expected; it wasn't as exciting as he'd hoped, nor did he have as much freedom as he'd expected.

The expectations we have about people or events are often the standard by which we judge those people or events. For example, you may take a class expecting it to be the best class you ever had. If that class is good, but not the best, it will not meet your expectations, and you will be less satisfied with it than if you had not held such high expectations.

The same process holds true when we judge how satisfied we are with our jobs. It's not an accident that the greatest period of dissatisfaction with a job occurs during the first year and that the young are most dissatisfied. It's at these times that people have the highest expectations about their jobs. Research has found that people get most of their information about their jobs from interviewers (Bray, Campbell, & Grant, 1974). Interviewers generally paint positive pictures of their organizations and the jobs they're offering. They also stress how selective their organizations' hiring practices are. So the newly hired person believes that he or she is special and has chosen a super place to work. But new employees are generally not given a great deal of freedom, nor are they given the most exciting jobs. So what the employee finds often doesn't match his or her expectations. The result is a period of dissatisfaction during the early period on the job. Older employees know the organization better and have more realistic expectations, so they are less often in the position of having their expectations disappointed.

The point is that satisfaction is often determined by the fit between expectations about a job and what the worker finds the job to be. Unrealistically high expectations encourage eventual dissatisfaction.

SOCIAL COMPARISON. Most of us have had the experience of buying something and believing that we got "a good deal." We're delighted with our purchase until a friend informs us that he or she just bought a similar item for 25 per-

According to social comparison theory, this woman's joy with her bonus would quickly diminish if she found that another worker who held a similar job got a bonus twice the size of hers.
Rhoda Sidney.

cent less than we paid. Suddenly our world turns bleak and the cherished purchase becomes an albatross.

We discussed *social comparison theory* (Festinger, 1954; Goethals & Darley, 1977) in Chapter 3. According to the theory, when there is no measurable physical reality to go by, we establish the value or correctness of an ability, characteristic, belief, or condition by comparing what we have to what others have. For example, you may receive an offer as a manager trainee for an annual salary of $15,000. Will you be satisfied with that salary? Chances are that you will be more satisfied with the $15,000 if you find that other trainees earn $12,000 than if you find they earn $20,000.

Social comparison plays an important role in determining job satisfaction. A person often compares his or her own salary, working conditions, office, and vacations with those of other *similar* workers. If your own conditions are better than those of other similar workers, you are likely to be happier than you would be if you find that your working conditions are worse than those of others. We can see this process in practice in the Herriot example. Herriot reports that he was so happy with his new position in part *because* many of his classmates had no jobs or jobs that paid less and offered worse working conditions.

EQUITY.   Another important question to ask in determining job satisfaction is whether or not people are getting from their job what they feel they are worth. **Equity theory** suggests that people determine their satisfaction with relationships or jobs by comparing the *inputs* they contribute with the *outcomes* they receive (Adams, 1965). People are most satisfied when there is equity between the inputs and outcomes—that is, when the inputs equal the outcomes. According to this theory, people also compare their own inputs and outcomes with those of others holding similar jobs. If one's ratio of inputs and outcomes is similar to the ratio of other workers, equity will result. Inputs can be in many forms, including hours worked, education, experience, and skills. Outcomes are also measured in many forms, such as pay, status, recognition, office size and position.

To see how equity theory works consider two women who work for an advertising firm. Woman A has a college degree and four years experience and must travel a great deal because she covers a large territory. Woman B completed two years of business school, has been with the firm for two years, and works mostly out of the main office with a small number of clients. They meet at a convention and find that they have the same title within the company and earn equal salaries. It is very likely that Woman A may feel dissatisfied with her position; her inputs are greater than those of Woman B, yet their outcomes are the same. We might well expect that Woman B would be very satisfied with her position and the company. However, research has shown that inequity can also result when people feel that they are getting more outcomes than they deserve (Adams & Rosenbaum, 1962). Satisfaction should be the highest when people receive

outcomes they feel they deserve, based on their inputs.

THE IMPORTANCE OF JOB SATISFACTION.   We might ask, Why all this interest and concern with job satisfaction? Does it really matter if people are happy with their jobs? One place we might expect to see the effects of job satisfaction is in performance; there is a common saying that "the happy worker is a good worker." While this relationship between happy worker and good work seems to make so much sense, there hasn't been much research to support it (Steers & Porter, 1979). In fact, the reverse relationship is more often found: Good performance often leads to job satisfaction. There are two ways to explain this finding. First, good performance on the job generally results in higher rewards (salary, status), and these rewards increase the worker's satisfaction with his or her job (Porter & Lawler, 1968). A second explanation is that through good performance workers demonstrate their competence, and this feeling of competence enhances their view of their jobs.

While we can't say that satisfaction necessarily leads to better performance, there are many other effects of satisfaction. First, people who are satisfied with their jobs are *less likely to be absent from work or seek other jobs* than are people who are dissatisfied with their jobs (Locke, 1976). This is a very important factor from management's viewpoint, since the training of new employees is very costly and time-consuming. People who are happy with their jobs *tend to be healthier and live longer* than dissatisfied workers (Palmore, 1969). This effect is easy to understand if we imagine the stress (see Chapter 5) placed on workers who must go every day to a job that they dislike. People's satisfaction with their jobs also influences their satisfaction with their lives in general. In a study conducted in Detroit automotive plants, investigators found a strong relationship between job satisfaction and a number of indices of *mental health,* including anxiety, tension, hostility, and personal morale (Kornhauser, 1965).

The examination of job satisfaction brings us back to the point made earlier in this chap-

REVIEW QUESTIONS

8. Match the management philosophy with the appropriate description of workers.

   ____ Theory X   a. workers are part of a "family"; groups of workers make decisions and receive recognition

   ____ Theory Y   b. workers want to contribute; they can be motivated by meaningful jobs

   ____ Theory Z   c. workers are lazy, dishonest, and dull; they are primarily motivated by money

9. The motivation to work is multifaceted. It includes such _____ motivators as pay, praise, and pressure from co-workers, as well as _____ motivators like feelings of competence and opportunities to exercise personal control.

10. T or F: Research has demonstrated that as extrinsic rewards increase, intrinsic motivation may decrease.

11. Dissatisfaction with our job, especially during the first year, is often the result of a mismatch between our prior ____ about the job and the way we find the job to be.

12. One theory applicable to job satisfaction postulates that people are most satisfied when the inputs they contribute to the job equal the outputs they receive. This is called _____ theory.

13. T or F: Despite the importance of job satisfaction, researchers have found few differences in health and longevity between satisfied and nonsatisfied workers.

ter; our jobs influence almost every part of our lives. It's difficult to be happy and healthy if we are unhappy with our jobs.

CRISES IN CAREERS

According to his books, James Herriot's transition into the working world was a smooth one. Although he had periodic doubts about his occupation, he enjoyed his work and, except for service in the Royal Air Force during World War II, spent over 40 years working at the veterinary practice in the Yorkshire Dales with Siegfried and Tristan. While most of us won't work in the same place for 40 years, we can anticipate a comfortable relationship with our careers and jobs. Some of us, however, are likely to experience crises or significant changes in our careers. The career crises include career change, burnout, midlife crisis, and unemployment, and each career crisis involves considerable stress.

Career Change

A variety of factors may lead us to career change. In some cases, a person may feel that his or her present occupation isn't fulfilling important needs. The pay may be too low. The job may not allow opportunities to be creative or may not present new challenges. In other cases, a person may not have been able to get the kind of job he or she most wanted. Statistics show that more than half the workers in dead-end jobs such as bussing dishes and pumping gas will change careers; and 22 percent of people with professional or technical jobs will make career changes (Sommers & Eck, 1977).

As we discussed in Chapter 5, any change in our lives will be stressful. A change as dramatic as a career change will be very stressful even if it is a welcome change. Career changes don't only result in a change in the type of work we perform; they may also mean a change in our daily routine, our friends and acquaintances, and our financial condition. But, despite the stress involved, career changes often have very positive results. People find new challenges and new opportunities to develop and display their skills. Adjustment to a new career can be a very positive experience.

If we look at the human development process, we might expect that a change in career should occur more often than it does. In most cases, people must choose an occupation during their early twenties. The needs and desires of a 20-year-old are very different from those of a person in his or her forties. Thus an interesting question to ask is why people don't change careers more often.

There are many answers to this question. One answer is that the decision to move from the known to the unknown is very difficult to make. Staying with a known job usually provides security, even if the job isn't satisfying. A second answer concerns the committment process that occurs in most jobs and companies (Salancik, 1977). According to *cognitive dissonance* theory, people strive to keep their actions and attitudes consistent (Festinger, 1957). People want to see themselves as acting consistently and rationally. We like to believe that we make good choices, and we like to believe that the things for which we work hard are worth the work. In order to prepare for many careers, a great deal of effort and preparation is required. Four years of college is required for many occupations. In other cases, additional graduate work or specialized training is necessary. After making a career choice and expending a great deal of effort to prepare for that career, it's consistent to believe that our effort was worthwhile—that is, we worked hard to enter a valued occupation. But it's inconsistent to see ourselves as having worked hard to enter a dull, boring career. Thus, for many people, the decision to change careers is to admit that they made an incorrect choice and worked hard to enter an unsatisfying career. This is a difficult confession for many people to make. In addition, by committing employees to their jobs through pay and retirement plans, employers often make it difficult for people to change jobs. Workers often build up incentive pay and credit toward retirement that would be lost if they changed jobs. The result is that some workers are trapped in jobs by their desires to maintain consistency and by the reward structure of the workplace.

Burnout

One of the most satisfying parts of many jobs is working with others. Often our jobs involve working with others toward a common goal or teaching others how to perform their jobs. Jobs in the social welfare and medical fields involve helping people live happier and healthier lives. Being successful in these functions requires that we care about others. While working with others can be rewarding, sometimes it can be very frustrating. We may find people unable to perform as we want them to, or they may not be appreciative of our help. James Herriot relates a number of cases where he labored all night to save a farmer's animal, only to be told by the farmer that he didn't do his job well. These types of experiences may lead to a condition called **burnout.**

Burnout occurs when people lose sympathy for the people with whom or for whom they are working and become exhausted and cynical (Maslach, 1979). The worker experiencing burnout feels fatigued, depressed, and irritable. He or she may experience a wide range of psychosomatic symptoms (see Chapter 4), such as headaches, ulcers, and nausea. Burnout is especially likely to occur in people in the helping professions—teachers, social workers, nurses, doctors, counselors, and psychologists. Managers in business are also prone

Burnout is often accompanied by fatigue, depression, and tension. The treatment of burnout involves reassessing goals and developing new and more realistic ones.
Arthur Tress, Photo Researchers, Inc.

BURN OUT

Burnout occurs when people lose sympathy for the people with whom they work and become exhausted and cynical. It is important to recognize when burnout is developing so that you can reassess your goals and develop new directions and activities. Looking back over your life for the past six months, think about your reactions to your family, friends, work (school), and social situations. Examine each of the questions and assign a number from 1 (indicating no or little change over the last six months) to 5 (indicating a great deal of change over that period) to show the change that has occurred.

1. Do you tire more easily? Feel fatigued rather than energetic?
2. Are people annoying you by telling you, "You don't look so good lately"?
3. Are you working harder and harder and accomplishing less and less?
4. Are you increasingly cynical and disenchanted?
5. Are you often invaded by a sadness you can't explain?
6. Are you forgetting? (appointments, deadlines, personal possessions)
7. Are you increasingly irritable? More short-tempered? More disappointed in the people around you?
8. Are you seeing close friends and family members less frequently?
9. Are you too busy to do even routine things like make phone calls or read reports, or send out your Christmas cards?
10. Are you suffering from physical complaints? (aches, pains, headaches, a lingering cold)
11. Do you feel disoriented when the activity of the day comes to a halt?
12. Is joy elusive?
13. Are you unable to laugh at a joke about yourself?
14. Does sex seem like more trouble than it's worth?
15. Do you have very little to say to people?

The Burn-Out Scale
0–25   You're doing fine.
26–35   There are things you should be watching.
36–50   You're a candidate.
51–65   You are burning out.
over 65   You're in a dangerous place, threatening to your physical and mental well-being.

Excerpt from *Burn-Out: The High Cost of Achievement* by Herbert J. Freudenberger and Geraldine Richelson. Copyright © 1980 by Herbert J. Freudenberger and Geraldine Richelson. Reprinted by permission of Doubleday and Company, Inc.

to burnout. Often it's the conscientious and successful worker who experiences burnout.

It is possible to "treat" burnout. The treatment involves a person in reassessing goals and developing new and more realistic goals (DuBrin, 1982). It is important to examine the positive accomplishments of your work rather than focus on the failures. Altering working conditions and changing work routines is often helpful also. Getting close to friends and talking about the problem may soften the impact of burnout. In some severe cases, a person may simply have to change careers or find a new job.

Midlife Crisis

The concept of midlife crisis has become such a popular topic of conversation that many of us feel that this crisis is unavoidable. In fact, most people do *not* experience a midlife crisis and instead make a smooth transition from youth into middle age. But between their late thirties and middle forties some people do experience an often troubling period of self-questioning. These years can be a time when people look both backward (''What have I done with my life?'') and forward (''What do I want to do with the rest of my life?''). In some cases, this reassessment can be disconcerting. The backward look may result in a person feeling that he or she hasn't been successful or achieved what he or she would have liked. People may feel that their lives and careers have been dull, unrewarding and not at all like their youthful dreams. The forward look can also present a bleak picture. A person may feel that the future has little to offer. In the case of a job or career, there may seem to be no new challenges or possibilities for advancement. To make matters worse, a person may experience panic: Time is quickly passing, you aren't 21 any more, and you may not be able to do the things you would like.

People experiencing midlife crisis may feel bored and trapped in their situation. They may lose the desire to go to work. In some cases, they may react by frantically changing their lives and jobs. They may get divorced, move to a new location, or completely change careers. A more constructive approach is to follow that outlined for burnout—that is, make a *realistic* assessment of your state, set realistic goals, make some changes in routine, develop new hobbies, seek out old friends and make new ones. But remember: Most people don't face serious crises as they enter middle age.

Unemployment

The recession of the 1980s has added the terms *unemployed* and *laid-off* to our everyday vocabularies. Previously, only blue-collar workers were faced with the grim prospects of unemployment. Recently, though, we have seen white-collar workers such as managers, technicians, and professionals suddenly faced with the prospects of unemployment.

Loss of employment has many dramatic effects. The loss of income requires dramatic changes in lifestyle; for some people, it means the loss of homes and other valued possessions. Status and self-esteem are also negatively affected. The unemployed begin to have doubts about their abilities. They must not only ask why they were laid off, but also face the unsettling prospect that they can't easily find other jobs. They may feel that their skills are unwanted. A third result of unemployment is a change in daily pattern of living. No longer does a person get up in the morning with the prospect of spending eight to ten hours at his or her job. New ways of spending time must be found. This problem is often made worse when an unemployed person sees friends and family members going to work. As a result of all these factors, unemployment increases the likelihood of alcoholism and mental and physical disorders (Plant, 1967). Suicide rates increase during periods of high unemployment. Symptoms of these problems are most likely to be observed soon after the person becomes unemployed and after a year of unemployment.

Recently, a number of new ways of combating the problems of unemployment have been attempted. Many employers have hired counselors to help their laid-off employees get new jobs. Government and industry have established retraining programs to help the unemployed train for new occupations where opportunities of employment are higher. Counseling is often offered to the unemployed and their families to help them cope with the stresses of being out of work. In some cases, employers have attempted to forewarn workers of the possibilities of layoff, so they can be better prepared both emotionally and psychologically.

WOMEN AT WORK

James Herriot began practicing veterinary medicine in 1937. At that time, very few women were veterinarians. Women were only about

25 percent of the American workforce, and only one woman in four worked outside the home (Smith, 1979). Forty years later, more than 40 percent of the American workforce was women, and 60 percent of women between the ages of 18 and 64 were working outside the home (U.S. Department of Labor, 1980). It is now predicted that 90 percent of American women will hold jobs outside the home at some period in their lives.

Women's struggle for employment outside the home, and for decent jobs and fair pay, hasn't been an easy one. For centuries the prevailing view has been that "a woman's place is in the home," raising a family and tending to her husband's needs, and that a man's place is out in the "real world," developing a career and supporting his wife and children. Traditional stereotypes long held that the "weaker sex" was incapable of performing much of the work men did. Conventional wisdom said that women were "too emotional" to hold certain jobs. One popular view, still not uncommon, was that women couldn't be as committed to careers as men were because all women really wanted to do was find a man, get married, and stay home.

Of course some women have always held jobs in addition to running households and raising children—because they wanted to or because they had no choice. Not having a job has tended to be a luxury, and a constraint, experienced mainly by middle-class and upper-class women. Working-class women have often had to work and to take any job they could get; their husbands' salaries haven't been enough to support their families or to maintain the standard of living their families would like. There have always been women supporting families by themselves. Even a hundred years ago, when single women were usually considered the wards of their fathers, some single women worked to support themselves, and other women went out into the working world, in spite of the odds against them, simply because they wanted the challenge of a career.

But the jobs women have been able to get have usually paid little and been of low status. For many years, trade schools, professional

schools, and many types of jobs were off-limits to women. These rigid limitations on women's work outside the home placed a straight-jacket on American society well into the 1960s and haven't completely lossened their grip today.

Events in recent decades have shaken the foundations of old stereotypes about "woman's role," however. The civil rights movements of the 1960s inspired many women to rebel against the restrictions on their opportunities. Women began to protest the unfair division of labor that kept them in menial jobs with few rights and low wages. Women had already made great strides in the workplace, but they were still experiencing condescension about their abilities and achievements and still earning much less money than men were. The Women's Movement helped bring women's wide contributions to our culture and economy "out of the closet" and showed that women are as capable as men are of developing careers and sticking to them. The Women's Movement also appealed to the conscience of the nation, demonstrating the unfairness of pigeon-holing women into certain roles and occupations.

At the same time, life in the United States was becoming more and more expensive, and increases in salaries weren't keeping up with the rising cost of living. Many more households than before were faced with the need for two wage-earners. There were also increasing numbers of single-parent households headed by women and more women choosing to remain single. These factors stimulated women's demands for an equal position in the workplace.

For many women, improved work opportunities are bittersweet. Women are still assigned chief responsibility for childcare and housework; working women often have two full-time jobs. There still persist *unfounded* beliefs that children of working mothers suffer because they don't have their mothers' full-time attention (Moore & Hofferth, 1979). Unlike their male counterparts, women often feel that they must choose between having careers or having families (Hoffman, 1974). No such either-or choice is presented to men; the traditional view is that men should have both careers and families. Many women still expect their jobs to be of short duration (Barrett, 1979). As a result, they are often not as well prepared to enter the workforce as are men, who see their careers as long-term commitments. Again, these different expectations are based on the belief that women should sacrifice their careers for the family, while men should develop their careers for the family. Numerous studies have attempted to determine whether women who work outside the home are more satisfied with their lives than are women who do not. The results of these studies don't show a consistent pattern; whether or not a woman works outside the home doesn't necessarily determine her happiness. On the other hand, it does seem clear that women who want to hold jobs outside the home and don't are likely to be dissatisfied with their lives (Tavris, 1976).

Women who want to have careers and/or who must hold jobs outside the home are often faced with some grim options. The jobs open to women are still predominantly low-paying and low-status. Women typically work in service jobs or in assistance positions; 99 percent of secretaries are women, and 98 percent of nurses and childcare workers are women (Greenhouse, 1981). It is true that women are going into professions and technical occupations in increasing numbers, but their average salaries are less than 65 percent of the average salaries for men in the same positions.

The focus on women in the workplace has created an additional problem for many women. The emphasis on women's right to work and efforts to create equal work opportunities for women have sometimes encouraged the view that women *should* work outside the home. Many people place little value on the role of homemaker. Women who choose to be homemakers often find themselves apologizing for this choice. They fear the dreaded reaction when they talk about their work: "Oh, you're just a housewife." The traditional role of women is no longer valued in the way it once was.

Of course condescending treatment of housewives isn't a new phenomenon. The "woman's role" has been applauded, romanticized, and institutionalized for generations; but it has also been taken for granted and looked down upon, as if "women's work" isn't "real work," since it earns no salary. Sometimes the basic goal of the fight for women's equality is overlooked: that women should have the same opportunities as men to choose whatever career will be fulfilling to them and that they should receive equal rewards for their work. Today many supporters of women's rights believe that *all* women's work should receive the respect it deserves, and that homemakers, who play a crucial role in our social life and economy, should receive full social security benefits, if not full salaries, for the work they do.

DISCRIMINATION IN THE WORKPLACE

As we have seen, women must fight discrimination to enter many occupations and professions. In 1977, there were over 180 occupations in the United States in which fewer than 20 percent of the workers were women (Baker et al., 1980). Women's salaries for performing the same jobs as men were on the average much less than those earned by men. Similar cases, and even more extreme cases, of disproportionate representation are true in the case of Americans who are black or members of other ethnic and racial minority groups. In many cases, these startling figures are the result of intentional efforts to keep minorities and women out of certain occupations. In other cases, this unequal distribution of jobs across subgroups is the result of unintentional causes such as word-of-mouth recruitment (McCormick & Ilgen, 1980). In all cases, the result is **job discrimination,** which limits people's job opportunities due to their race, sex, religion, color, or national origin. The people discriminated against aren't the only ones to suffer; society as a whole suffers. The result of job discrimination is that the best talent may not be employed in positions where it is most useful.

The employment picture for women has been changing. Employers are realizing that women are as capable as men at performing jobs that were once reserved "for men only."

Dating back to the post–Civil War era, there has been legislation aimed at combatting discrimination. The most vigorous efforts to correct discrimination in the workplace didn't take place until the 1960s with the passage of the Equal Pay Act and the Age Discrimination in Employment Act, which were aimed at defining fair employment practices. But the law that stands out as the boldest attempt to correct job discrimination is Title VII of the Civil Rights Act of 1964, amended by the Equal Employment Acts of 1972. The aim of these laws was twofold. First and most important, they were aimed at protecting minority group members and women from unfair discrimination in the workplace (McCormick & Ilgen, 1980). The laws described what was fair business practices and outlined appeal procedures that could be followed by someone who felt that he or she was being unjustly treated. The second aim of the laws was to correct the effects of past discrimination in the workplace against minorities and women. It was realized that discrimination would not be eliminated by passive efforts to open more doors for members of groups who had previously been the objects of discrimination; therefore, efforts to actively attract minorities and women into certain occupations were spelled out in programs such as Affirmative Action.

The backbone of today's laws against discrimination can be found in Title VII:

It shall be an unlawful employment practice for an employer—
(1) to fail or refuse to hire or to discharge any individual or otherwise to discriminate against any individual with respect to his compensation, terms, conditions, or privileges of employment, because of such individual's *race, color, religion, sex, or national origin;* or
(2) to limit, segregate, or classify his employees or applicants for employment in any way which would deprive or tend to deprive any individual of employment opportunities or otherwise adversely affect his status as an employee because of such individual's race, color, religion, sex, or national origin.

Title VII also established the Equal Employment Opportunity Commission to enforce the law. The commission conducts investigations on its own initiative or when a complaint is brought to it by an individual or by a group. The enormous size of its job can be seen in the fact that the commission was processing almost 70,000 cases a year by the mid-1970s (Ash & Kroeker, 1975).

Despite antidiscrimination efforts such as Title VII, the task of reducing discrimination and its effects remains of major importance today. Minorities and women are still underrepresented in many occupations and overrepresented in unemployment statistics. The task of reducing discrimination doesn't simply mean opening up job opportunities to minorities and women. It involves training minorities and women for the jobs. It involves changing the self-images of women and members of minority groups, who for years have been told that they don't have the ability, much less the opportunity, to perform certain jobs and who have been denied admission to the training programs that would give them the skills they need. The devastating effects of this propaganda and prejudice must be reduced, so that members of these groups will have not only the job opportunities they deserve as much as any other American, but also the skills, self-confidence, and community support other workers have long taken for granted.

RETIREMENT

As James Herriot approached the age where it was physically more difficult for him to climb a wind-swept hill in the dead of winter to tend to a sick calf, he had to face the possibility of retirement. His response was to reduce his involvement in his vet practice and to engage in a new activity, writing. He loved to write, and he loved the practice of veterinary medicine, so his choice of writing about his experiences as a vet was a natural and satisfying activity for him.

For many workers, the mere mention of the word **retirement** sends shivers up their spines. Many people don't look forward to retirement. For one thing, they view it as a period when they will have to give up something they enjoy and that gives them a sense of accomplishment and of contributing to society, their work. More likely, however, many of the negative feelings about retirement are the result of it being associated with old age and

REVIEW QUESTIONS

14. Three major crises in a person's career that can have profound effects on a person's adjustment and well-being are _____, _____, and _____.

15. T or F: A career change, and the concommitant changes that occur in routine, friends, and finances, will be very stressful even if it is a *positive* change.

16. T or F: Research by Moore and Hofferth (1979) has shown that children of working mothers are likely to show detrimental effects as a result of the decreased time spent with their mothers.

17. Within the last twenty years, laws have been written to redress discriminatory practices in the work setting. The agency established by Title VII of the Civil Rights Act of 1964 and charged with the task of enforcing fair employment practices is called the _____.

18. T or F: Retirement issues are less important in today's society, because improvements in medical care are allowing people to remain on the job long past the traditional retirement age of sixty-five.

The key to successful retirement is to find enjoyable activities for the time previously spent at work.

George S. Zimbel, Monkmeyer.

eventual death (Streib & Schneider, 1971). Despite these pessimistic views, however, research suggests that retirement is not experienced as negatively as people anticipate. Streib and Schneider (1971) interviewed 4,000 people before and after they retired. Almost one-third of them found retirement more enjoyable than they had expected, and only 5 percent found it to be worse.

The key to successful retirement is substituting enjoyable activities for the time previously spent at work (Lowenthal, 1972). Interestingly enough, women often adjust better to retirement than men do because the role of homemaker is an acceptable activity for women to take on after they've quit their jobs. Men adjust better if they share in the housework, but unfortunately some men, especially blue-collar workers, feel that housework is demeaning. Well-planned leisure activities such as travel or gardening also help make retirement enjoyable. A third popular substitution is another job more suited to the individual's physical and psychological needs. James Herriot followed this latter route when he chose to write books. Research has found that 73 percent of people who consider work to be a major source of satisfaction in their lives find another job after retirement (Streib & Schneider, 1971).

One of the issues that is hotly debated today is whether or not retirement should be mandatory at a certain age. On one hand, it seems senseless to deny job opportunities to someone who is capable and willing to work. On the other hand, it has been argued that having a mandatory retirement age allows people to better plan for retirement (Botwinick, 1977). Issues such as this and others related to retirement are becoming of increasing importance in today's society. A process referred to as the "graying of society" is taking place: The proportion of older people in American society is rapidly increasing. For example, in 1978 there were 24 million people aged 65 years and older. By the year 2000, there will be 32 million people in this category. One reason for this change is the declining birth rate in America. A second reason is that there have been major advances in health care; the health of today's 55-year-old compares favorably with that of people who were 40 or 45 in 1970 (Rosow & Zager, 1980). In addition, people often stay on their jobs longer; recent federal laws allow workers to stay on their jobs until age 70 if they wish. The result of these changes is that we will see an increasingly large number of people entering retirement over the next decade. It is becoming more important for us to understand the stresses and the changes people undergo when they retire. Research is now being conducted on how to make the transition into retirement a happy and satisfying one.

SUMMARY

1. People's jobs have a number of influences on their lives. The money they make determines their standard of living. The job also influences how they will spend much of their time, since most people work eight to ten hours a day. Jobs also influence where people will live, who they will associate with, the nature of their daily routine, and even the topics of their social conversations.

2. People are motivated to work for a number of reasons. In addition to working to survive, people hold jobs to establish their independence and personal identity, to enhance their self-esteem, and to strive toward self-actualization.

3. The decision about a person's occupation occurs in stages beginning in early childhood. These stages include the fantasy stage, the tentative stage, and the realistic stage.

4. In order to make an informed decision about an occupation, a person can seek advice from counselors, take ability and interest tests, and engage in internships or sum-

mer work programs. Parents who provide a supportive and understanding environment can greatly help their children make informed choices about their careers. Some parents, however, hinder the decision-making process by trying to determine the occupations their children enter.

5. Management may hold a number of views of employees. The traditional view, Theory X, is that workers are lazy, dishonest, and dull and must be forced to work with pay or threats. Theory Y holds that workers want to contribute and that they are capable of making decisions that will help both the organization and themselves. Theory Z is based on the Japanese approach to relations between employer and employee, which perceives workers as part of a family and in which workers are rewarded as groups and make decisions as groups.

6. Job satisfaction is influenced by rewards (extrinsic and intrinsic), the fit between expectations and actual job conditions, the comparison between working conditions of people holding similar jobs, and perceptions of fairness (equity). Good performance often leads to increased satisfaction in one's job. People who are satisfied with their jobs are less likely to be absent from work or to look for other jobs. They are also more likely to be physiologically and psychologically healthy.

7. Some workers face important crises in their working lives. Career change due to job satisfaction is stressful for some people because it is often difficult to abandon one's desire for consistency and security. The reward structures established by many employers also make it difficult for a person to leave a job without sustaining significant losses in terms of pay and pensions. Burnout occurs when people lose sympathy for the people with whom or for whom they are working and become exhausted and cynical. The treatment for burnout involves reassessing goals, focusing on positive accomplishments, altering daily routine, and talking the problem over with friends. Some people experience a difficult transition period between their late thirties and mid-forties where they feel that their lives haven't amounted to much and that the future holds no new challenges. The treatment of this midlife crisis is similar to that for burnout; in some cases, a career change may be helpful. People in any occupation may face unemployment. The wide-ranging effects of unemployment include economic loss, loss of status and self-esteem, change in daily pattern of living, and increased likelihood of mental and physical illness.

8. Woman now make up 40 percent of the workforce but often are forced to accept low-status and low-paying jobs. Women who work outside the home must overcome traditional stereotypes about "women's place" and deal with discriminatory attitudes that undervalue their abilities, achievements, and commitment. Unlike men, women are often forced to make an unfair choice between career and family, since they are still assigned the chief responsibility for housework and childcare.

9. Job discrimination results when members of minority groups and women are underrepresented in a particular occupation due to prejudice against people on the basis of race, sex, religion, color, or national origin. Title VII of the Civil Rights Act of 1964 has been the most important law aimed at combatting job discrimination. Efforts to protect the rights of women and minorities to open job opportunities and fair pay must also correct the effects of past discrimination in the workplace.

10. Retirement is often viewed negatively because it is a sign of old age and involves giving up the work that people enjoy and that gives them fulfillment and status in our society. Many people, however, don't find retirement to be as bad as they'd expected. Successful retirement can be achieved by finding enjoyable substitutes for work, becoming involved in well-planned leisure activities, or engaging in new types of work suitable to a retired person's stage of life.

KEY TERMS

a. BURNOUT   f. SELF-ACTUALIZATION
b. CAREER   g. THEORY X
c. EXTRINSIC MOTIVATION   h. THEORY Y
d. INTRINSIC MOTIVATION   i. THEORY Z
e. JOB DISCRIMINATION   j. WORK

1. The traditional theory of management that holds that workers are lazy and dishonest and must be watched carefully

2. The desire to perform work based on external factors such as pay or threats

3. The desire to perform based on internal factors of wishing to control one's behavior and demonstrate competence

4. The theory of management that states that workers want to contribute and achieve and that the role of management is to create a positive work environment

5. Some disciplined activity that gives us a feeling of personal accomplishment and that makes a contribution to society

6. The progress or general course of work activity through a person's life or through some phase of it

7. Limiting people's job opportunities because of their race, sex, religion, color, or national origin

8. The state that results when a person loses sympathy for others with whom he or she works and becomes exhausted and fatigued

9. Striving to reach personal potential and using abilities in a creative way

10. The management theory followed by Japanese companies that views workers as being adopted into a family rather than simply as being hired to do a specific job

ANSWERS TO REVIEW QUESTIONS

1. True. **2.** c,4; b,5; d,1; a,3; e,2. **3.** Independence. **4.** Self-esteem. **5.** Fantasy, tentative, realistic. **6.** Interests, abilities. **7.** Reactance.

8. c, b, a. **9.** Extrinsic, intrinsic. **10.** True. **11.** Expectations. **12.** Equity. **13.** False.

14. Burnout, midlife crisis, unemployment. **15.** True. **16.** False. **17.** Equal Employment Opportunity Commission. **18.** False.

15

ENVIRONMENT AND BEHAVIOR

O
n a warm day in May 1870, 11-year-old Herman Lehmann, his brother, and two sisters ran into the fields to scare the birds away from the new wheat. Herman's family had just recently moved to that farm in Mason County, Texas, and they were hoping for a good harvest. The Lehmanns were fairly typical of the Germans who immigrated to Texas in the nineteenth century. They spoke only German and saw few other people because the farm was located several miles off the main road.

Herman was happy on the farm, but his life was to change suddenly and completely on that May day. After the children had dispatched the birds, they began playing in the field. They were completely absorbed in their games when, all at once, they were surrounded by Indians with frightening painted faces. The children screamed and ran, but Herman never made it to the house. The chief of the Apache raiding party, Carnoviste, grabbed him by the hair and forced him to the ground. Other Apaches quickly bound him, and the raiding party made a hasty retreat, dragging Herman with them, as gunfire sounded from the house. Herman was now a captive of the Apaches.

As the raiding party headed north, the country became increasingly barren. For four days of traveling day and night they found no food or water. Finally, on the fourth day, they came to a small creek, and the whole party drank. On that day they also found a herd of antelope and shot several. A fire was quickly built, and Herman reports that everyone was so hungry they took no time to butcher the antelope; the Apaches simply threw the animals whole, and in some cases alive, onto the fire for a short while, then devoured them (Greene, 1972). The remainder of the trip went on in a similar fashion; they ate and drank only when the plains provided food and water.

Finally they arrived at the Apache village, which was located near a large lake somewhere in New Mexico. The village contained nearly 2,500 people. Such a large concentration of people occurred only where water was abundant. In most cases the environment allowed only a few hundred people to camp together.

Herman became the property of Chief Carnoviste; he waited on the chief, cooked much of his food, and was responsible for catching lice for him to eat. In return, the chief taught the boy Apache ways. Herman learned to ride; to shoot a bow; to make poison arrows from a concoction of rattlesnake venom, skunk musk, and a prickly weed; and to make shields from buffalo hide. Carnoviste taught him how to read the signs of his surroundings. He learned how to forecast the weather by looking at spider webs. In dry weather the webs were thin, long, and high, while before a rain the webs were low, short, and thick.

Herman also learned Apache "manners." He wouldn't enter another Indian's camp area without being invited. He learned that even though there was only one "room" in a tepee, certain areas were used for specific purposes; there were private areas that a visitor didn't enter.

Despite the fact that the Apache village contained more people than Herman had ever seen in one place, he felt bitterly lonely. He reports never crying "while I

The Apache lived in harmony with their environment. They were nomads whose life was controlled by their environment.

The Bettmann Archive, Inc.

was being tortured, nor when I ran the gauntlet, nor when I nearly drowned. In those times I gave a yell of defiance or a snarl of vengeance, but . . . in my loneliness and desolation, I wept'' (Greene, 1972, p. 18).

Thus Herman Lehmann became an Apache named Enda. In less than a year Herman had completely adapted to his new social and physical environment. He became part of a small band of Apaches that raided, stole horses, and killed and scalped whites in Texas, New Mexico, Kansas, and Mexico. Herman himself proudly displayed many scalps on his tepee pole. After a number of years, he became a subchief and led numerous raids on white settlers and soldiers.

The Apache raiders led a nomadic life, always traveling in search of water and food. Summers they followed the game into the Rocky Mountains. As winter began to set in, they moved south. The size of the band was determined by the availability of food; when game was abundant, large concentrations of Apaches gathered together. As the years passed, the number of white settlers increased, and game became increasingly scarce. With the settlers came large numbers of soldiers and rangers who relentlessly hunted the roving nomads. Many of the Indians were killed or herded onto reservations; the number of Indians who roamed the frontier dwindled.

Five years after Herman's capture, Carnoviste was killed, and Herman had to flee from the Apaches so as not to be killed and buried with his master. By this time, his last thought was to return to the whites; he hated them and had spent the last five years killing them. For six months after his flight from the Apaches, Herman wandered the plains, living on whatever food his environment provided him. Soon he began to yearn for human companionship and started searching for another band of Indians he could join. He had to avoid the Apaches, but he was able to locate a small Comanche hunting party. Although the Comanches regarded him with some suspicion in the beginning, they soon accepted him, and Herman assumed the Comanche name Montechena. The Comanches lived a life similar to that of the Apaches and traveled a similar territory. Herman quickly adjusted to his new people and proved his bravery many times.

The great white net, however, began to draw tighter, and Herman's group of Comanches was finally captured and sent to the Fort Sill reservation. Herman concealed himself among his Indian brothers so that the soldiers wouldn't see that he was a white captive and send him back to a white settlement. At Fort Sill, Herman was adopted and hidden by the great Comanche chief Quanah Parker.

Herman was soon discovered by his captors nevertheless. After some inquiry, the whites identified Herman and located his white family. The Lehmanns had moved to Loyal Valley, Texas, but they had never given up hope of finding Herman alive. There was a great deal of rejoicing when they learned that Herman had been found; he had been among the Indians for almost nine years.

Herman returned to Loyal Valley to assume the way of the white man. He was now 20 years old and totally unprepared for what he found. The customs of the whites were strange to him. The whites owned land and grew their own food. They didn't move from place to place like the Indians had. Permanent settlements had sprung up, where the whites lived with hardly any breathing room between them. White people lived in houses with many rooms rather than in one-room tepees. The ''iron horse''—the steam locomotive—ran on steel tracks and connected the communities. The telegraph allowed people to communicate with each other even though they were many miles apart.

All these things were strange to Herman, and he worked hard to adjust to his new environment. In the beginning he found it terribly difficult. He wandered from one job to another. He got married, but his wife proved unfaithful, and he was soon divorced. During this time, he made numerous trips to visit Quanah Parker at the Comanche reservation in Oklahoma. Slowly, Herman adapted to his white environment. He bought a ranch and raised cattle. He remarried and had five children. Despite all this, he continued to return to the Indian reservation to see his Comanche comrades.

Herman Lehmann was the last white captive to be released by the Comanche Indians, ''but more than that, he remained a voluntary captive to their way of life for the remainder of his years'' (Greene, 1972, p. 160). The Indian way of life in close relationship with the natural environment was always a part of Herman Lehmann.

THE ENVIRONMENT AND HUMAN BEHAVIOR

While the story of Herman Lehmann has many fascinating aspects, one of the most interesting is its illustration of the relationship between physical environment and human behavior. The life of Herman, the Apache Indian, was ruled by the environment. What and when Herman drank and ate were determined by the environment. If he came upon a stream or river, Herman drank his fill of water; if he didn't find a stream, he would roam for many days without drinking. Herman's diet in the desert consisted of snakes, lizards, and small rodents. The grassy plains provided Herman with a diet of antelope, mustang, and buffalo. In the mountains, Herman often feasted on grizzly bear. The environment determined where Herman made camp and how many others camped with him. The weather also determined Herman's home, as the Indians often moved into mountainous areas during the spring and summer and into the flatlands as the cold of winter blew into the mountains. For the Indian, the environment was master, and Indians acknowledged this in their ceremonies and religion.

The situation for Herman, the white man, was very different. At the end of the nineteenth century and into the twentieth, white people thought they had nature pretty much under their control. Strong houses were built to withstand the weather and allow the inhabitants to live in one place, regardless of the whims of the environment. Through agriculture and the domestication of animals, the settlers determined their diet, rather than depending on the environment for their menu. If the land didn't readily supply water, a deep well could be dug to extract water from the reluctant earth. As more settlers moved onto the frontier, cities and towns were built, and roads were carved through the wilderness. If a forest stood where the settlers wanted a town, the forest would be eliminated.

As technology improved and widened its sphere of influence, so did human mastery over the physical environment. Lakes and canals were constructed; irrigation allowed farming in many desert areas. Mountains were leveled or moved to make way for new towns. Bridges were built over rivers that once stymied travel, and those rivers became the sewers and garbage dumps for the refuse of cities and industries. Much of this drastic change happened in the lifetime of Herman Lehmann.

People had truly become the rulers of the natural environment—or had they? In recent years, this "people rule nature" view has changed; the natural environment has shown that it isn't willing to live as a servant of humans; it may settle for an equal partnership, but it will slave no longer. Many of the destroyed forests have become sites of erosion and desolation. Many of the artificial lakes have burst their dikes and inflicted terrible destruction and loss of life on the human population. Houses built in nature's flood plains have been washed away, and mountainside homes have slid into oblivion. The air in many cities has become hazardous to breathe, and the once-harnessed atom has caused many to question whether human or atom is truly master.

Herman never lived to see this "revenge" of the environment. But during the first decade of the 1900s he reported concern about the disregard that was being shown the natural world. He wrote that people should try harder to understand and live in harmony with nature.

Herman's concerns have become our concerns in today's world. With each new environmental disaster and each new threatened shortage of food, water, or energy, we are waking up and realizing that, despite our technology, every aspect of our lives is closely tied to, and affected by, the environment in which we live. And we are realizing that we must understand this environment and the effect it has on us if we are to have a happy existence. Just as we must adjust to our social world, so too must we adjust to our physical world. And just as we are both affected by and have an effect on our social world, so too do we exist in a give-and-take relationship with our environment.

Sounding the doom alarm is not our aim in this chapter. But we do hope to show how much our behavior is influenced by the environment in which we live. We often overlook these environmental influences because they are subtle and do not visibly boast of their influence on us. A clearer understanding of the relationship between environment and behavior gives us greater ability to perceive the reasons for our behavior, and, because the environment is to a certain degree flexible, this understanding also allows us to create situations in which we can behave happily and effectively.

PERCEIVING OUR ENVIRONMENT

When we talk about our physical environment, we might believe that we are discussing a physical entity that is seen by everyone in the same way and has the same effects on everyone. Indeed, this is not the case. Our responses to the environment are not determined solely by its physical characteristics, but by our perceptions of the environment.

For example, when you drive home from school this afternoon, you may get caught in a traffic jam that turns your normal 15-minute trip into a 20-minute trip. If you come from a small town, you may perceive the traffic to be terrible and begin to think that this town is becoming very crowded. But if you're from a large city, your perceptions of this trip home will be very different. You may be amazed at how quickly the traffic is moving and begin to wonder where everyone has gone. Thus we evaluate our present environment by comparing it to our expectations and to previous environments we have known (Fisher, Bell, & Baum, 1984).

A second important feature of perceiving our environment is that we are selective in our attention. Our environment contains more information than we could possibly comprehend at one time, so we narrow down our focus by paying attention only to certain aspects. If you looked at the desert where Herman Lehmann lived as an Indian, you might focus on the lack of people, trees, and houses; to some eyes, it might have been a desolate, barren place. Herman, whose concern was survival, focused on the places that could provide protection and on parts of the desert that might be hiding game or water. A third person who was a naturalist would see the varied types of trees and plants that dotted the desert.

The point is that although each of us may be faced with the same physical environment, we may well focus on different features of the world around us and react to that environment and interpret it differently. For this reason, it is important for us to examine not only the physical features of our environment, but also to pay heed to the factors that affect our interpretations of it.

Isolation and Privacy

An interesting example of the importance of environmental perceptions can be found when we consider isolation and privacy. Both of these conditions result in a lack of social interaction, yet one is experienced negatively and avoided and the other is viewed positively and sought out.

When Herman was 16, his master Car-

noviste was killed. When an Apache warrior was killed, he was buried with all his possessions. A warrior's horse and servants were killed and sent to the "happy hunting grounds" with him, along with his weapons. Thus Herman knew that Carnoviste's death meant that he too would be killed and buried with the chief. Rather than suffer this fate, Herman gathered his belongings and fled from the Apaches. After many days of travel, he found a narrow canyon that offered shelter and plenty of food and water. All his physical needs were satisfied in this place, and he was safe from the Apaches and from wild animals. But he soon found that he wasn't safe from the effects of an environment void of social stimulation. He began to miss being with other people. He worked hard to overcome this feeling; he set about doing small jobs such as making arrows, and he even began to draw pictures in the sand. As his longing for other people grew, he found himself talking to his horse and to wolves that visited the canyon. His dreams were constantly filled with other people. Finally he moved from his canyon home in search of other people. At first he just wanted to see people and would secretly follow groups of whites and Indians. Eventually he joined the Comanches.

Herman's account of his solitude is very similar to the accounts given by hermits, prisoners of war, and others who have spent long periods of time away from other people. After receiving reports from isolated individuals and conducting experiments by isolating subjects in a room for varying periods of time, Stanley Schachter (1959) made three conclusions about the effects of **social isolation.** First, he found that the effects of social isolation are most dramatic early in the isolation and begin to decline slowly as time passes. After long periods of isolation, the individual may enter a schizophrenic-like state of apathy where little matters. Second, socially isolated individuals often become preoccupied with thoughts of other people; they think, dream, and even hallucinate about other human beings. Third, isolated individuals who are able to occupy themselves with physical or mental activities suffer less than individuals who are unable to occupy them-

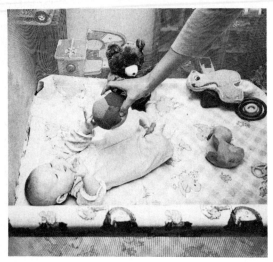

The environment that is both physically and socially stimulating is important for healthy development.

Freda Leinwand, Monkmeyer.

selves. Clearly a person who lives in a socially deprived environment experiences a significant degree of suffering.

The studies on social deprivation point up the significance of our environment for our adjustment. A varied environment that includes other people is important for our psychological well-being. Such variety is especially important for children, since their psychological development is strongly affected by their social milieu. But variety and richness in our environment is important for us even as adults. In most cases, people enjoy a relatively rich environment throughout most of their lives. Unfortunately, as individuals get older, they are often forced to sacrifice environmental richness for the sake of convenience. Many elderly people, who may be ill and lack mobility, are placed in "homes for the aged." In some cases these homes present a sterile environment; the resident lives in a simply furnished room, is guided by a rigid schedule, and associates with the same few people day in and day out. The monotony doesn't utilize the elderly person's full potential, nor does it promote the person's healthy adjustment to this last stage in his or her life and development as a human being. Thus, regardless of age, a person should seek out an environment that presents a degree of

social variety that will stimulate his or her continued growth and participation in the world and guard against stagnation.

Turning to the other side of the same coin we find that there are times when isolation from others is both desired and beneficial. Simply "getting away" can give us the opportunity to reflect and relax. This "getting away" is often referred to as a search for **privacy.**

As we discussed in Chapter 10, the difference between the positive situation of privacy and the negative situation of social isolation or loneliness involves the perception of choice (Altman, 1975). In fact, Ittelson et al. (1974) define privacy as "an individual's freedom to choose what he will communicate about himself and to whom he will communicate it in a given circumstance." Thus privacy involves the perception that social isolation is chosen rather than forced upon us. Some elderly people may choose to live in "old folks' homes" because their physical and economic circumstances require it; they may experience their relative isolation as a worthwhile "retreat" from the cares of formerly busy lives and a peaceful opportunity to meditate on their life experiences. Forced social isolation, on the other hand, is a condition in which we have no control over our environment or feelings. In these cases, isolation exists despite our desire for interpersonal interaction. Old people who are simply "dumped" in nursing homes may suffer greatly from the loss of their power of choice, as well as from their undesired isolation.

While social isolation and the resulting loneliness can have a destructive effect on us, privacy has a very constructive effect. Westin (1967) describes four beneficial effects of privacy. First, it allows us personal autonomy by providing us with the opportunity to control the environment. Second, it allows us to evaluate ourselves by providing the chance to withdraw from others. Third, it gives us a chance to release emotional tensions that are caused by everyday life. Most of us have had the desire to scream or cry to release our tensions. In most cases we are reluctant to do this in front of other people. In private, however, we feel freer to "let it all hang out." Finally, Westin suggests that privacy allows us limited and protected communication by giving the choice of when and with whom we will share our thoughts.

Privacy, then, is a natural and important condition. The fact that you wish to be alone should not be construed as an unnatural desire. The important point is that the perception of choice determines our reaction to an environment that lacks social stimulation and the effects this experience has on us.

PHYSICAL SPACE AND BEHAVIOR

Territoriality

While Herman Lehmann was with the Apaches, he spent most of his time searching for game with small hunting parties of 10 to 15 people. They didn't choose their hunting grounds haphazardly. Their first consideration was to find areas where game would most likely be found. Their second consideration was whether other Apache groups had staked out the area as theirs. If there were signs that another band had already claimed an area, Herman's band would move on to hunt elsewhere.

When Herman returned to the whites, he found a different custom of territorial behavior. The white settlers claimed personal ownership over land. Their claim gave them not only the right to farm, hunt, and live on a piece of land, but also the right to sell it or pass it on as a gift. At first, the settlers marked their territory by placing stakes or piles of rocks at the boundaries. As more settlers moved into the area, barbed wire fences and "NO TRESPASSING" signs marked an individual's borders.

Almost every type of animal, two-legged or four-legged, exhibits territorial behavior. **Territoriality** involves claiming exclusive use of areas or objects (Porteous, 1976). Such exclusiveness is usually intraspecific: Only members of the same species are restricted from a claimed piece of territory. (So a person who

owns a piece of ground usually won't object if birds stake their own claims on the property.) Once a territory is claimed, the "owner" will defend it even if he or she must resort to aggression.

While animals usually claim a single circumscribed area as their own, human territorial behavior is often more complex. For example, we may claim ownership over several nonadjacent pieces of property: home, office, beach home, mountain retreat. Humans often show territorial behavior over a wide range of objects as well: stereos, clothes, jewelry, furniture, tools, cars, boats, houses, land—even friends, lovers, and spouses are sometimes treated as "owned objects." It might be interesting for you to list the number of objects over which you display territorial behavior—things you would defend if someone tried to claim them. No doubt the list will be quite long.

Another aspect of human territorial behavior is the number of types of territories involved. Altman (1975) suggests that humans have three types of territories. **Primary territories** are exclusively owned and controlled by individuals and groups. These primary territories are central to the lives of those individuals. For example, your home would be your primary territory. Of all their territories, individuals are most attached to and protective of their primary territory.

Secondary territories include properties that are less central; the individual can't claim ownership over them. Individuals often become very emotionally attached to these territories nevertheless and attempt to control them. Your "regular" seat in a classroom may be your secondary territory; even though you don't own it, you feel entitled to occupy it and may become disturbed if someone else takes it. A similar case may be made for your seat at the dinner table; in many families, individuals have their own seats at the table.

The third type of territory is **public territory;** this includes property over which individuals do not feel ownership. They do, however, feel that they have control over the territory while they are occupying it. A spot on the beach, for example, may be viewed as public

"Your" regular seat in a classroom is an example of secondary territory; you don't own it but you feel entitled to occupy it during the class.

Miami-Dade Community College.

territory. Individuals often claim a spot for themselves and feel that no one should intrude on it while they are occupying it. When they leave, however, the territory goes "up for grabs," and others may occupy it.

It is important to understand the various types of territories because people respond differently to invasions of each type. Uninvited trespassing on primary territories such as one's home or bedroom is likely to be met with stern rebukes and angry words. As the territory becomes less central, the responses to invasion will be less severe. Territorial behavior is so ingrained in us that we often don't recognize it directly. For example, you may have a feeling of growing irritation at a guest who, while visiting your room, sits down on your bed and begins to chat. This person may be friendly enough, but you still find yourself feeling increasingly tense and upset without understanding the basis for your reactions. It is very possible that these feelings are a response to the guest's invasion of your primary territory, your bed.

THE FUNCTIONS OF TERRITORIALITY. When the white settlers arrived in the Texas plains area, they were constantly baffled by the Indians. Despite their superior weapons and, in most cases, superior numbers, the settlers and cav-alry had a very difficult time beating the Indians in combat or capturing them. The Indians used hit-and-run tactics, and they seemed to know which spots were advantageous for encounters and which were not. Herman Lehmann reports that he was amazed at how the Apaches could "disappear" into the environment, while the white settlers seemed to stand out against the land. One clear difference between the Indians and the settlers was that the Indians were fighting on their own territory; they had lived and hunted the plains area for years and were very familiar with it. The settlers, on the other hand, were newcomers, and they were not as familiar with the land.

This example shows that one of the functions of territoriality is *protection;* individuals are better able to protect themselves on their own territory than on foreign territory. A large part of this may be a function of familiarity. Herman states that the Apaches knew every rock and crevice in their hunting area. Because of this, they knew not only when and where to fight and hide, but also the most likely places to find game and water. Thus possessing and knowing a territory has a protective function.

Being on one's own territory also seems to provide a *psychological advantage.* Observations of animal behavior show that in most cases animals fighting in their own territory defeat an intruder (Carpenter, 1958). The knowledge that you are in your own home seems to increase your motivation to protect what is yours. In an effort to study the psychological advantage of the home territory, Edney (1975) had pairs of subjects complete a number of tasks, such as moving furniture and clearing floor space in a room. The experiment was conducted in the dormitory room of one of the subjects, who was termed the resident. Edney found that the resident generally took the leadership role, while the visiting subject reported feeling uncomfortable and was willing to take a more submissive role. Finally, Martindale (1971) found that people argued more aggressively and persuasively in their home territories than in foreign areas. Thus being in your own territory is likely to increase your sense of security and your motivation to defend yourself and your position. The result is that you have a psychological advantage over a visitor.

Another important aspect of territoriality is that it *increases social order*. Having a clear division of property should reduce friction and misunderstanding between individuals; you know what is yours and have marked it, and your neighbor has done the same. Thus you are less likely to argue over who can plant a tree on a particular piece of property or who has control over an object such as a lawn mower or an automobile. In an interesting study, Rosenblatt and Budd (1977) found that married couples showed more territorial behavior than did unmarried couples who were living together. Presumably married couples knew they would be together for a long time and attempted to reduce the areas of possible conflict by arriving at a clear agreement about territories. The study showed that married couples were more likely than cohabiting couples to have a clear understanding about who slept on what side of the bed, who sat at a particular place at the dinner table, and to whom a particular side of the closet belonged.

Having territory also helps us achieve *privacy*. We can escape from others when we have the exclusive control of an area. You can see this function when you think about how relaxed you felt when you finally were inside the safe confines of your home or room after a particularly hectic day.

Territoriality also helps *control aggression*.

The poet Robert Frost wrote that "good fences make good neighbors." When individuals or groups have clear agreement about boundaries, they can avoid conflict by "staying on their side." Unfortunately, while territorial boundaries often control aggression, they can be the source of aggression when the parties disagree over where the boundaries should be drawn. Numerous wars have been started when countries disagreed about where boundaries should be drawn; in some cases the disagreement involved only a few miles of land. Recently, the world witnessed with horror the Russians destroying a Korean passenger airplane filled with people; the sole reason was that the airline violated Russian territory and flew into that country's air space.

SOME PRACTICAL EFFECTS OF TERRITORIAL BEHAVIOR. Some interesting studies have been made of the everyday effects of territorial behavior. One study found that a home was less likely to be burglarized if it displayed clear signs of being someone's territory (Brown, 1979). As Figure 15.1 shows, the home that had a fense marking its boundary and separating it from the street, clear indications of ownership (name plate and address signs), and indications of occupancy was less likely to be the target of a burglary than the home that didn't have these territorial markings. Territorial signals probably increase burglars' fears of being caught. Burglaries may also have been thwarted by peo-

FIGURE 15.1   THE APPEARANCE OF A HOME CAN INFLUENCE ITS CHANCES OF BEING BURGLARIZED (LEFT, NONBURGLARIZED; RIGHT, BURGLARIZED).

(From Brown, 1979; reprinted by permission.)

ple's natural reluctance to invade another's territory.

In another study Worchel and Lollis (1982) found that residents in both the United States and Greece were more likely to pick up litter that was in their primary territory than litter that was in public territory. This effect was found even when the litter in the public territory was unsightly and detracted from the

---

REVIEW QUESTIONS

1. Understanding the relationship between the environment and behavior involves realizing that our behavior is influenced by our _____ of the environment as well as by its physical characteristics.
2. Social interactions can be characterized by our willingness to engage in them and the opportunities for interaction that are presented. Choosing not to engage in social interactions is called _____, while not being allowed the opportunity to interact is called _____.
3. _____ involves claiming exclusive use of areas or objects and defending that area or object from other members of the same species.
4. Territories can be defined by the degree to which individuals own and control them. _____ territories, such as homes, are exclusively owned and controlled by individuals. Territories which individuals do not own, but which they control while occupying them, are _____ territories.
5. Which of the following can be thought of as resulting from territoriality?
   a. protection   c. psychological
   b. privacy   advantage
                    d. all the above
6. T or F: People are just as likely to pick up litter in a public territory if the litter detracts from the attractiveness of their private territory.

---

beauty of the people's own territory. Worchel and Lollis suggested that an effective way to control litter would be to change people's perceptions and make them believe that they controlled public places. For example, people in a neighborhood could be given control over a local park and told that they were responsible for its maintenance.

These findings show that an understanding of territorial behavior can be used to foster positive social interactions and make our environment a more enjoyable place.

Personal Space

Herman Lehmann probably noticed many similarities in the behavior of the whites and the Indians, despite their wide differences in life style and habitat. As we pointed out earlier, both had customs involving the ownership of fixed pieces of property. Though the specifics of the behavior differed, both whites and Indians often used a mark or sign to claim control of a piece of ground.

In addition to similarities in territorial behavior, it is likely that Herman also noticed similarities between the Indians and the whites in the treatment of "mobile territory," or the space immediately surrounding the individual. Some years ago, Edward Hall (1959, 1966), an anthropologist, observed people from many different cultures interacting in numerous situations. He noticed patterns in the way people utilized space when interacting. Within each culture there seemed to be unwritten customs regulating how close individuals approached each other. As we will see later, the degree of distance varied from culture to culture and was influenced by the nature of the interaction. It seemed to Hall, however, that all individuals felt a certain sense of ownership of the space immediately surrounding them and that others avoided trespassing upon this space. Hall coined the term **personal space** to denote these "bubbles of space" that people keep around them when they are interacting.

Hall identified four sizes of interaction distance, or bubbles of space, each with a close and far phase. The size of one's personal space

TABLE 15.1

Keeping Your Distance: Hall's
Spatial Zones for Different Types
of Interpersonal Relationships

DISTANCE	APPROPRIATE RELATIONSHIPS AND ACTIVITIES
Intimate distance (0 to 1½ feet)	Intimate contacts (e.g., making love, comforting) and physical sports (e.g., wrestling)
Personal distance (1½ to 4 feet)	Contacts between close friends, as well as every-day interactions with acquaintances
Social distance (4 to 12 feet)	Impersonal and business-like contacts
Public distance (more than 12 feet)	Formal contacts between an individual (e.g., actor, politician) and the public

SOURCE: Based on Hall, 1963. (Reproduced by permission of American Anthropological Association, *American Anthropologist*, 65, 5:1003–1026, 1963.)

is determined by the type of interaction taking place. As can be seen in Table 15.1, the *intimate distance* (0 to 18 inches) is generally used by close friends for comforting, making love, and telling secrets. On the other hand, the *public distance* (12 feet and more) is used by people in very formal gatherings and is the distance accorded important public figures. It might be very instructive for you to make note of the distances at which you interact with various people. Usually we are not conscious of the different distances we keep, since our spacing occurs almost reflexively. But if you make a conscious effort to observe your own behavior and that of others, you should be able to observe the uniformity of spacing behavior in interactions.

FUNCTIONS OF PERSONAL SPACE. One of the interesting aspects of much of our territorial behavior is that it has important survival and adjustment functions. For example, territoriality influences species survival by spacing individuals and allowing them intimate knowledge of a defined area. It has been argued (Ardrey,

1966) that spacing behavior also plays a role in personal survival. As you can see, the distance kept in most interactions involves a space that keeps the other at "arm's length" and allows for observation of the other's arms and legs. In an earlier time, when arms and legs were the main weapons available, this spacing served a protective function.

Another important function of personal space behavior is *communication*. Our spacing behavior is related to communication in two ways. First, we can communicate specific messages, such as attraction, through our use of space. It has been shown repeatedly that we stand closer to people we like than to those we dislike. Thus we can "tell" others how much we like them and how comfortable we are with them by how close we place ourselves when interacting. You may observe how sensitive others are to the communication aspect of personal space. Simply place a greater than usual interaction distance between yourself and an intimate friend. Chances are that the friend will not directly ask why you are using this larger distance. But it is likely that this spacing will make your friend uncomfortable, and he or she may soon ask: "What's wrong? Are you angry?"

Space also has a more indirect effect on communication. In Chapter 9, we discussed the wide range of messages that can be communicated nonverbally through the use of eye contact, body posture, and hand movements. Hall (1966) pointed out that spacing behavior determines which of these nonverbal channels can be used in communication. For example, if you are communicating with someone at the public distance (greater than 12 feet), you may hear his or her voice and see hand movements, but you will have difficulty determining if that person is making eye contact, leaning slightly forward or backward, frowning or smiling, sweating or remaining calm. On the other hand, when you communicate at the intimate distance (0 to 18 inches), you should have no trouble picking up messages communicated through facial expression and eye contact, but you may be too close to notice arm and hand movements.

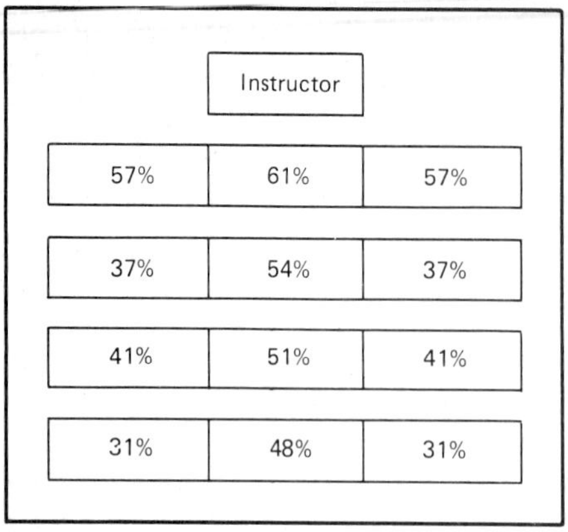

	Instructor	
57%	61%	57%
37%	54%	37%
41%	51%	41%
31%	48%	31%

FIGURE 15.2   THE PARTICIPATORS: RELATION BETWEEN CLASS SEATING AND PARTICIPATION

(From Sommer, R. Classroom ecology, *Journal of Applied Behavioral Science*, 1967, 3, 500. Copyright 1967 by NTL Institute Publications.)

Another interesting way to look at the communication effects of interpersonal spacing is to examine the classroom. A number of studies have focused on how seating position affected students' participation in classroom discussions and their grades (Stires, 1980; Kinarthy, 1975; Sommer, 1967). As can be seen from Figure 15.2, students seated in the front and middle rows of seats in classrooms are most likely to actively participate in class discussions. In these positions, students are most likely to be able to hold eye contact with the instructor and see his or her face clearly. (It has also been found that students who choose the middle seats in the classroom are most likely to get the best grades in class.) As you can guess, there are two ways to interpret these results. On one hand, good students may simply choose the middle rows of seats. On the other hand, it could be argued that students who are in the middle rows feel more a part of the class and receive more visual and verbal contact with the instructor than do students at the back of the class.

FACTORS INFLUENCING PERSONAL SPACE. We have already pointed out that the type of interaction and the type of relationship between people affect the size of personal space. A number of other factors influence the size of personal space. It is important to understand these, since they will make you aware of why others may be using spacing that is not comfortable for you.

Race and culture have strong effects on the amount of personal space an individual will require to be comfortable. Numerous investigators have observed that Latin Americans, Arabs, Greeks, and the French have closer personal spaces than do Americans, Germans, the English, and the Swiss (e.g., Hall, 1966; Willis, 1966; Watson & Graves, 1966). In order to see the potential importance of this difference, consider the intriguing story about a Latin American and a North American who were conversing at a party. After exchanging a few pleasantries, the Latin American moved closer and closer to the North American. As the conversation progressed, the North American became uncomfortable with this distance and moved backward to restore a North American personal space limit. The Latin American countered these backward movements by continually moving closer to the North American. The result was the "Latin Waltz": The Latin American moved closer each time the North American moved backward. During the course of conversation, the two "waltzed" across the room, even though they were unaware of their behavior. This action was not the result of either party being impolite or rude. Rather, the Latin American had a closer personal space norm than the North American did, and each time the Latin American tried to establish a comfortable spacing, the North American moved back in an effort to conform to a different personal space norm.

This story may be amusing, but Worchel and Cooper (1983) point out that cultural variations in personal space can have serious implications. In many cities, individuals from different cultures interact. Clearly, there are differences in language and customs that may make these interactions difficult. It is also possible that differences in personal space requirements add to the stress associated with these interactions. For example, an individual from a German background may find it very uncomfortable to interact with a Latin American because they have difficulty establishing satisfactory interpersonal spacing. The Latin American wants to interact at a close range, while the German desires a great deal of space. Friction is likely to develop between the two, since each may view the other as rude. Actually they are both attempting to establish spacing that is comfortable and acceptable to individuals from their different cultures. This type of conflict is more likely to be found in cities such as New York and San Francisco, which have a great deal of cultural heterogeneity, than it is in cities such as Berlin and Tokyo where there is more cultural homogeneity.

Even within our own society, there are differences in personal space norms. Hispanic-Americans interact more closely than do Anglo-Americans. An interesting picture emerges when we compare black and white Americans. At young ages blacks interact more closely than do whites. But adolescent blacks interact at greater distances than do adolescent whites (Aiello & Thompson, 1980). There is also evidence that people in mixed-racial pairs keep greater distances from each other than do pairs of people of the same race.

The *sex* of the individual affects not only the size of personal space but also the shape of it. Females have smaller personal space zones than males (Heckel & Hiers, 1977). The distance between people in male-female pairs tends to be smaller than the distance between same-sexed pairs. There has been a great deal of speculation about the reason for this size difference. Worchel and Cooper (1979) point out that in Western culture there are strong taboos against homosexuality, especially male homosexuality. Young boys are taught very early that they should not caress each other. There is a great deal less touching between a father and a son than between a mother and a daughter. This early training may instill in young children the belief that males should not interact at close distances, while such close interaction is permissible between females or between members of the opposite sex.

Men's discomfort with physical closeness is also seen when we compare the spatial behavior of people who are attracted to each other. Females interact at closer distances with other females they like than with other females they dislike. But attraction doesn't influence the distance at which males interact with other males. Most men in our culture usually don't feel comfortable being physically close to other men, except in "permissible" situations such as football games. It is also interesting that in mixed-sex pairs, women are more likely than men to move closer to a person they like; men are less likely to "make the first move" and move physically close to women who attract them. Overall, women are more likely than men are to respond to attraction by moving physically to the other person (Fisher et al., 1984).

Another interesting finding regarding sex differences in spatial behavior is that males seem most concerned with protecting their frontal space, while females are most sensitive about the space at their sides. Byrne, Baskett, and Hodges (1971) found, that given a choice, males prefer to position themselves across from friends, while females choose to position themselves next to friends. In a later study, Fisher and Byrne (1975) observed students in a library setting. They found that males generally placed their books and personal effects between themselves and facing seats. This prevented invasions from the front. Females, on the other hand, placed their materials between themselves and adjacent seats, thus blocking others from coming too close on the side.

The *age* of a person also influences personal space behavior. Research by Eberts and Lepper (1975) and Aiello and Aiello (1974) shows that children begin to develop consistent spatial behavior around the age of four or five, and that the size of the child's personal space increases as he or she grows older. Adultlike spatial norms generally develop as the child reaches puberty (Altman, 1975). It is of further interest to note that while adults generally respect the spatial rights of other adults, they don't show the same respect for a child's space. Surely you've witnessed a stranger walking over to a child and rubbing his hair or pinching her cheeks while saying, "Aren't you cute!'' Adults also don't seem to be bothered by invasions of their personal space by children under the age of ten (Fry & Willis, 1971). But children over the age of ten who invade an adult's personal space make the adult uncomfortable.

This discussion should alert you to the fact that spatial behavior is often complex and influenced by many variables. We can't flatly state that a certain distance is proper in a certain type of relationship. The appropriate distance is influenced by factors such as the age, sex, and culture of the people involved in the interaction. While we can't supply a table of proper distances, we can alert you to the fact that these variables influence spacing behavior.

RESPONSES TO VIOLATIONS OF PERSONAL SPACE. Since Herman Lehmann spent many of his formative years with the Indians, he was probably unfamiliar with the white norms of personal space. As a result, it is likely that he violated many of these customs when he returned to the white world. Recent research has shown that such violations would have been met with a variety of responses.

One of the most common responses to violations of personal space is *stress*. People whose personal space is violated report feeling tense and anxious (Worchel & Teddlie, 1976). Physiological functions such as galvanic skin response, heart rate, and blood pressure also increase when personal space is violated.

People also attempt *nonverbal compensations* for these violations. Argyle and Dean (1965) had subjects converse with an experimental confederate at distances of two, six, and ten feet. They observed the subject's response behind a one-way mirror. As can be seen in Figure 15.3, the closer the confederate stood, the less eye contact the subject kept. Other research has shown that people respond to spatial violations by leaning backward or turning their shoulder toward the violator (Patterson, 1977). All these responses communicate discomfort to the violator and serve to reduce the intensity of interaction. If the violation continues, people take flight and completely avoid the other person.

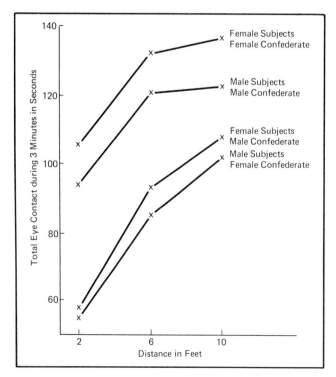

FIGURE 15.3   EYE-CONTACT AS A FUNCTION OF DISEASE
The closer the experimental confederate stood, the less eye contact the subject maintained.

SOURCE: Michael Argyle and Janet Dean, ''Eye Contact, Distance and Affiliation,'' Sociometry, Vol. 28, 1965, 289–304. Reproduced by permission.

Another reaction to violations of personal space is that individuals simply *do not like the invaders.* Worchel and Yohai (1979) found that subjects rated a person as less attractive and likable when he or she violated their personal space. In another interesting study showing the consequences of this effect, Konečni et al. (1975) had a confederate violate the personal space of a subject. Next, the confederate dropped some personal objects. If the confederate had violated the subjects' personal space, subjects were less likely to help pick up the dropped objects than they were if the confederate hadn't violated their personal space.

In some cases, the violation of personal space can lead to increased attraction to the intruder, if we see the intruder as making a friendly overture. But in general violating people's personal space is not likely to win their friendship. People react negatively when their personal space is trespassed upon, even if the trespasser acts unknowingly. Hence it is important that we understand people's norms regarding spatial behavior. Such an awareness will not only help us win and keep friends, but also allows us to better understand our reactions to others.

Density and Crowding

Herman Lehmann spent his early days on an isolated farm or roaming the plains with the Apaches and Comanches. Even after returning to the white world, he spent his remaining days in the sparsely populated area of Mason County, Texas. He never lived in a densely populated area or experienced prolonged feelings of crowding. This is not the case, however, for a large number of people throughout the world. With the coming of the industrial age, people began to flock to centralized areas to reap the fruits of the amazing new technological inventions and to partake of the readily available employment opportunities. At the same time, the world's population began to grow tremendously, and today this rate of growth is both staggering and frightening. Ehrlich (1968) points out that in 1650 the world's population was about 500 million. By the time of Herman's birth in the late 1850s, over 1 billion people inhabited the earth; it took 200 years for the world's population to double. Herman died in 1932, and at that time there were 2 billion people in the world; the population had doubled in just 80 years. Ehrlich estimated that it now takes only 35 years for the world's population to double. If this estimate is correct, it means that the number of people living on earth will double twice during our lifetimes.

Given these figures and the fact that the size of the earth is constant, the amount of space available to the average person is shrinking and will continue to shrink. In recent years psychologists, biologists, and sociologists have begun to ask how this diminishing availability

Density is a physical measure of the amount of space available to a person in a given environment. Crowding, on the other hand, is a psychological state that is affected by social, physical, and personal variables.

Bettye Lane, Photo Researchers, Inc.

of space will affect human behavior and adjustment. Two major but related concepts have been developed to characterize and categorize the effects of limited space on behavior.

The first term is **density,** which is a simple physical measure of the amount of space available to a person. The density of a room can be found by dividing the number of square feet contained in the room by the number of people occupying the room. For example, there may be 50 students in your classroom of 500 square feet. So the density is 10 square feet per person.

The second term is **crowding.** Crowding is not a physical measure. Rather, it describes the psychological state of a person. We feel crowded to a greater or lesser degree; we don't feel density. Crowding and density are often related, but this isn't always the case.

When we think of crowding on a world level, our concerns probably focus on shortages; too many people means too little food, energy, housing, and other resources that make our lives comfortable. These are important concerns, but psychologists have examined a somewhat different issue related to crowding: How does crowding influence our behavior? Some of the earliest research on this question looked at animals, not at people. One investigator (Calhoun, 1962) observed a colony of rats that were confined to a pen for a long period of time. The animals had sufficient food, water, and nesting material, and they rapidly reproduced. But as the density in the pen increased, gross distortions in the rats' behavior occurred. Nest-building behavior was severely disrupted. The females failed to take proper care of their young, and many of the offspring died of neglect. Abnormal sexual behavior developed, as male rats would attempt copulation with immature rats or engage in homosexual behavior. Aggression increased until "it was impossible to enter the room without observing fresh blood spattered about the room from tail wounds" (Calhoun, 1962). Females had complications with pregnancies, and many developed cancer of the sex organs and mammary glands. The death rate among females was 3½ times greater than that for males.

Sociologists have examined statistics of human behavior in high-density urban areas. A number of these studies seem to indicate that as the density of an area increases, negative effects such as crime, infant mortality, disease, mental illness, and juvenile delinquency also increase (Schmitt, 1957, 1966). These data are certainly alarming, and they suggest that high density can have devastating effects on human adjustment to the environment.

Concern about such possibilities has motivated a number of investigators to study the effects of density on human behavior. The results of these studies, however, cast some doubt on the premise that high density alone leads to adjustment problems. For example, Schmitt (1963) compared Hong Kong, the most densely populated city in the world, with 2,000 people per acre, with New York City, which has a density of less than 450 people per acre. He found that the mortality rate in New York was twice as large as that in Hong Kong, hospitalization for mental illness was ten times greater in New York than in Hong Kong, and the number of murders and manslaughter cases in New York was six times greater than in Hong Kong. Even some of the early laboratory studies, in which groups of people were often packed into rooms so that their reactions and performance of tasks could be observed, suggested that high density didn't always cause people to feel uncomfortable or to perform poorly.

CONDITIONS THAT LEAD TO CROWDING. All this presents quite a confusing picture; sometimes people (and animals) react very negatively to high density, and other times they don't. This situation has the makings of a good mystery story; the challenge is to discover the critical ingredients that make people feel crowded and uncomfortable. The research we have discussed shows that the answer can't be only the amount of space.

In order to begin to solve this mystery, consider the following common situations. In the first situation, you are going to the library to study for an important exam coming up the next morning. You arrive rather early, spread your materials out, and begin to thumb through some books. Soon others arrive, and you find yourself sandwiched between two other people; you are forced to place your belongings under your chair. Even though the library is not completely filled and the density is not particularly high, you may feel cramped and crowded and have trouble concentrating. Now place yourself at a football game. The stadium is filled and people are jammed around you; the density is many times greater than in the library. The game has started and the score is very close. On each critical play, the fans erupt with cheering; you even find yourself hugging the stranger sitting next to you. Do you feel as crowded in this situation as in the library? Probably not. You are likely to report feeling excited and exhilarated at the football game and unlikely to report feeling terribly crowded. So high density doesn't always lead us to feel crowded. What, then, are the other differences in these two situations that could determine when people will feel crowded?

One difference is the *focus of your attention*. In the library, you are focusing on the other people, while at the football game you are watching the action on the field. It has been found that we are more likely to feel crowded and uncomfortable when we are paying attention to other people being too close to us (Worchel & Brown, 1984).

A second difference revolves around the issue of *control*. At the library, you expect to be able to control the space at your table. Control in this situation is important to accomplishing your task of studying. At the football game, you don't expect to have control over more space than your own seat, and as long as you can see the game, control of space is not important.

Judith Rodin and her colleagues (Rodin & Baum, 1978; Baron & Rodin, 1978) suggest that high density will make us feel crowded only when the situation causes us to feel that we have no control over the environment or have less control than we want. In order to demonstrate this effect, Rodin et al. (1977) had four people wait until they spotted a single individual waiting for an elevator at the Yale University library. When the doors opened, the four people in the experiment and the unaware subject entered the elevator. In some cases, the four people positioned themselves so that the subject was standing next to the control panel and could control the elevator. In other cases, they stood so that the subject couldn't reach the controls. When the elevator stopped and the four people had departed, the experimenter asked the subject how crowded he or she had felt during the ride. Subjects who had had no control (were not near the control panel) reported feeling more crowded and perceived the elevator as being smaller than subjects who had had control over the movement of the elevator. Thus it seems that you are more likely to feel crowded in a situation that limits your control than in one in which you can still influence your environment.

A third difference involves desire for *privacy*. At the library you want privacy, but privacy wasn't one of your goals when you go to a football game. As we can see, our need for privacy and solitude varies according to the situation. Crowding results when our desired level of privacy is greater than the level of privacy we have in a given situation (Altman, 1975).

As you can see, crowding and high density are not always related; the experience of crowding is affected by more factors than high density. In order to determine the validity of these arguments, you may wish to pay particular attention to your feelings under conditions of varying density. You should find that you don't always feel crowded in high-density situations. This exercise may also reveal clearly the various conditions that are most likely to cause you to feel crowded.

THE EFFECTS OF CROWDING.   Given that we know some of the conditions that cause us to feel crowded, we can now ask how crowding affects our behavior. If we ask ourselves this question, the first point that comes to mind is that when we feel crowded we are also likely to feel uncomfortable. In fact, the most consistent finding in research on this subject is that conditions that lead to crowding also cause us to feel uncomfortable and anxious; people do not like feeling crowded (Sundstrom, 1978). Interestingly enough, one study found that even the anticipation of feeling crowded elicits a negative mood (Baum & Greenberg, 1975).

Numerous studies have shown that we are likely to perform more poorly on tasks when we feel crowded. These studies examined tasks such as working puzzles, mazes, and anagrams and solving problems in human relations. Two results are especially striking. First, crowding seems to have the most negative influence on complex tasks and relatively little influence on simpler tasks. This suggests clearly that if you are going to work on a complex problem, such as one that requires reasoning or intense concentration, you should be careful to seek an environment in which you will not feel crowded. A second finding is that males are more affected by crowding than females (Stokols et al., 1973). The research indicates that whereas the performance and emotional state of males is negatively affected by crowding, these effects are not reliably found with females. The specific reason for this puzzling finding is not clear. Worchel (1978) has postulated that because females have smaller personal space requirements, they may not feel crowded in a density that causes males to experience crowding.

Another consistent finding is that crowding leads to a deterioration in interpersonal relationships, especially with males. People who are crowded don't like each other as much as do uncrowded people. One research project asked dormitory residents how much they liked their roommates (Baron et al., 1976). Half the subjects were living under crowded conditions (three students in a room built for two), while the other half were living two to a room and were less likely to experience crowding. The "triples" liked their roommates less than the students living in pairs did. Other research (e.g., Hutt & Vaizey, 1966) found that aggression was greater from subjects who were crowded than from uncrowded subjects.

Overall, the research shows that our behavior may be strongly affected by environmental conditions that make us feel crowded. Crowding seems to be an irritant that makes us less social and hinders our concentration. It is

REVIEW QUESTIONS

7. According to Edward Hall, people will avoid trespassing upon the area immediately surrounding another person. This area is called _____.

8. Hall identified different interaction distances which are determined by the type of interaction occurring. Provide the term used by Hall to describe the distances under which the following interactions are likely to occur.
   a. telling secrets; making love; wrestling _____ distance
   b. conversational distance at casual social gatherings; conducting business _____ distance
   c. distance for formal interactions and for important public figures _____ distance
   d. the distance for ordinary social interactions between close friends _____ distance

9. Personal space requirements are not universal. Three factors related to the determination of interactional distances are _____ (including race), _____, and _____ .

10. T or F: Although women in general interact at closer distances than men, men interact at closer distances when they are with other men whom they like.

11. One way to counteract the stress caused by personal space violations is to reduce eye contact and to turn one's shoulder toward the violator. These maneuvers are called _____ .

important to understand this relationship because we are often unaware of the range of factors that influence us. After a long ride on a crowded bus, we may be surprised at how quickly we become annoyed with other people or how difficult it is to perform tasks we normally handle well. At other times we may be the recipient of the short temper of a person who is experiencing crowding. When we understand the influence of crowding on human behavior, we may understand more easily why people respond as they do. This knowledge may also help guide our own choice of environments.

OTHER ENVIRONMENTAL INFLUENCES

Noise

Herman Lehmann spent his life on the Texas plains. He rarely had to experience the high-density situations that many of us face on a daily basis. Another feature of Herman's environment was quiet. The noises that Herman heard were, for the most part, those made by nature: the sound of animals, the whisper of the breezes, the crackle of fire, and the boom of thunder. The one exception to this was Herman's encounter with the "iron horse." He reports that a raiding party of which he was part came upon two ribbons of steel running across the plains. They puzzled over this discovery until they were startled by a loud noise. The noise pierced their ears and frightened them. Their fright increased when they looked up and saw "a huge one-eyed iron devil breathing fire and smoke" rushing down the tracks after them. Thereafter, they avoided that spot and told stories about the screeching, fire-breathing devil.

If Herman considered the noise of the oncoming train to be deafening and painful, we can only imagine his response to rush hour in the center of a large city! In recent years, we have become concerned with the noise pollution in our environment. Our technology had advanced to the point where we can make bigger and faster vehicles and larger machines to do our work, but an increase in noise has accompanied this achievement. Our world is becoming more crowded and more noisy. In many of our factories, workers are able to per-

form their jobs only by wearing earplugs that dampen the noise. Major protests have been staged in many large cities to prohibit the landing of supersonic airplanes, which can create deafening sonic booms. It is interesting and somewhat disturbing to note that almost all the noise we hear today is the by-product of humans and their machines; only a small part of the noise most of us hear is caused by the natural environment.

The **sounds** of our world are created by changes in air pressure. These changes in pressure affect a small membrane in our ears. The changes in the membrane caused by these pressures are transmitted to our brains through a series of three small bones, a hollow canal filled with fluid, and the auditory nerve. A sound becomes a **noise** when it is unwanted by the listener because it is unpleasant, bothersome, and interferes with activities (Cohen & Weinstein, 1981). Thus, while the latest rock song may seem like music to one person, it may be noise to another.

Given that humans have created noise and that the amount of noise in our environment is steadily increasing, it is important for us to determine how humans are affected by their own creation. One of the most easily measurable effects of noise is hearing loss. In 1972 the United States Environmental Protection Agency (EPA) estimated that close to 3 million Americans suffer hearing loss caused by loud noises. The EPA conducted hearing tests for high-frequency sounds on a youthful population and found that 3.8 percent of sixth graders, 10 percent of ninth and tenth graders, and a staggering 61 percent of college freshmen failed the test. It is possible that some of this hearing loss was caused by listening to loud rock music; individuals often expose themselves to music that reaches 110 to 120 decibels for hours on end, and research indicates that exposure to this loud noise for only 30 minutes a day may have serious consequences for hearing. In a shocking testimony to the effects of noise, one group of researchers (Rosen, Bergman, Plestor, El-Mofty, & Satti, 1962) found that 70-year-olds in quiet Sudanese villages have the hearing abilities of 20-year-olds in the

Our world is becoming more crowded and more noisy. Noise can have physical, psychological, and social effects on us.

Ian Lukas, Photo Researchers, Inc.

United States. Some recent evidence shows that taking drugs such as antibiotics may result in increased effects of noise and cause greater hearing loss (Kaloff, 1982). Thus one effect of loud noise is that it can damage our hearing.

Another area of concern has been the effects of noise on people's performance of various tasks. A number of carefully controlled studies have been conducted to determine the influence of noise on task performance (Glass & Singer, 1972). The initial results were quite surprising; noise, even fairly loud noise, didn't significantly impair a subject's performance. People seemed to adapt very quickly to the noise, and after a while even their psychological functioning was unaffected by it. You may be familiar with this adaptation response (often called *habituation*) if you live close to a busy street or a railroad track. At first you are very bothered by the noise and may have some trouble functioning. But after some time you adapt and become almost unaware of it. You don't "hear" it again until a friend visits and questions how you can "stand all this noise."

While initial studies suggested that noise may not have serious effects on human perfor-

mance, further research has presented a different picture. In these studies, investigators manipulated the predictability and controllability of the noise. They also examined its *aftereffects,* that is, how well people performed in a quiet setting after they had been exposed to noise. The results of this research again showed that individuals can adapt very quickly to noise, even uncontrollable or unpredictable noise. People who were forced to work while a loud noise was sounded made only slightly more mistakes than people working in a quiet setting. However, people who were first exposed to noise and then worked under quiet conditions showed large decreases in the quality of their performance. These decreases were especially large when the noise had been both unpredictable and uncontrollable. Thus the aftereffects of the noise were more serious than the immediate effects. Glass and Singer (1972) suggest that people expended so much "psychic energy" adapting to the noise that they were unable to cope with subsequent environmental demands or frustrations.

While we may be able to adapt to loud noises on a short-term basis, the price we pay for this adaptation is the impairment of our subsequent actions. Another demonstration of the insidious effects of noise is seen in a study that examined the reading ability of children living in a large high-rise apartment complex situated over a highway in New York City (Cohen, Glass, & Singer, 1973). The children on the lower floors were exposed to more noise than the children on the upper floors. The researchers found that the children living on the lower floors had more hearing problems and poorer reading ability than the children living on the upper floors. Despite the fact that noise often doesn't have an immediate effect on our performance, the long-term aftereffects of noise can seriously impair our ability to perform tasks.

Noise also influences how we interact with other people. Consider the last time you were at a party where loud music was playing and many people were talking. How did you interact with other people? The noise probably affected your conversations, for one thing. Because it's difficult to hear when loud music is playing, we practically have to yell to be heard, so we avoid talking about important or intimate subjects, and our conversations tend to be short. Also, because the noise is irritating, we may take out our discomfort on other people. It has been shown that noise, especially unpredictable and uncontrollable noise, leads people to be more aggressive (Geen & O'Neal, 1969). Along these same lines, research shows that we are less likely to offer help to others in a noisy environment. In one study an accomplice dropped an armload of books in front of an unsuspecting person (Matthews & Cannon, 1975). In half the cases, a loud lawnmower was running and in the other half it was not. People were much more likely to help in the quiet environment than in the noisy one.

So the loud noises we've created in our environment can have profound effects on us. Prolonged loud noise can impair our hearing. It can also influence our ability to perform tasks and to interact in a satisfying manner with others. Remember these effects when you have the opportunity to choose where you will live or work. Certainly we can't eliminate noise-producing phenomena, but we can use our knowledge of the effects of noise to guide the design and placement of our highways, airports, factories, and machines.

Weather

Herman Lehmann's Apache and Comanche bands ranged the plains and deserts of Texas, New Mexico, and Mexico, where it's not un-common for daytime temperatures to remain well above 90°F for weeks on end. The Apaches and Comanches were considered to be the bravest and most hostile warriors. They were among the last tribes to be conquered by the whites. Numerous factors certainly contribute to the aggressiveness of a people, and there is some evidence that temperature may be one of them.

Heat has been the one most widely studied weather variable related to human behavior. When most of us think of heat, we focus only on temperature; we can imagine the sweltering temperatures that Herman endured in the desert. But temperature isn't the only factor that influences how hot we feel. As can be seen from Table 15.2, **relative humidity**—the percentage of moisture in the air—also affects how hot we feel. The desert where Herman roamed had low humidity, so while the above-90° temperatures were hot, they weren't as uncomfortable as would have been the case in areas that have high humidity. Wind, on the other hand, tends to reduce the discomfort of heat.

Heat is a weather variable worth study because the environments in which many of us live are becoming hotter. Cities are generally 10° to 20°F hotter than rural areas because of high concentration of automobiles, asphalt, buildings, and air conditioning units. One investigator (Hurt, 1975) concluded that air conditioners in downtown Houston, Texas, put out enough waste heat (heat blown out of buildings) in eight hours to boil ten pots of water the size of the Astrodome!

TABLE 15.2

Effect of Relative Humidity on Experienced Temperature

RELATIVE HUMIDITY (%)	THERMOMETER READING (°F)					
	41°	50°	59°	68°	77°	86°
	Effective Temperature					
0	41	50	59	68	77	86
20	41	50	60	70	81	91
40	40	51	61	72	83	96
60	40	51	62	73	86	102
80	39	52	63	75	90	111
100	39	52	64	79	96	120

Much of the concern with heat has focused on its effects on aggression. The United States Riot Commission (1968) reported that most riots occur during the summer months; in fact, the Commission found that in the riot-plagued year of 1967 all but one riot started when daytime temperatures were over 80°F. We can explain the relationship between heat and aggression by viewing heat as a frustration. Hot temperatures cause people to feel uncomfortable and irritable, and they react to little frustrations by striking out at people and things around them. Additional research shows that, up to a point, aggression increases as temperature increases (Baron & Bell, 1976; Carlsmith & Anderson, 1979). There is some disagreement about the point at which it becomes so hot that aggression decreases. We can imagine, however, that at very hot temperatures, people don't want to interact with each other; their attention in these very hot environments turns to keeping cool.

Very hot temperatures also affect our performance of tasks. Some evidence indicates that our ability to perform mental tasks is reduced if we spend over two hours in temperatures over 90°F, and our ability to do moderate physical work is reduced if we spend over an hour in those same temperatures (Fisher et al., 1984). On the other hand, performance of many tasks is also negatively affected in temperatures below 55°F. Interestingly enough, people seem to be able to adapt to extreme temperatures over time so that the effects are reduced (Fox, 1967). Thus, if you had lived in a warm southern climate for a long period of time and were suddenly transported to Greenland, you would have greater difficulty performing tasks in that very cold climate than would someone who had been living in Greenland since birth.

Other weather conditions have also been linked to human behavior in some interesting ways. While the validity of this research is yet to be demonstrated, some of the findings are fascinating. For example, Dexter (1900) reported a positive correlation between wind speed and suicide; the windier the day, the more suicides. Lieber and Sherin (1972) examined the relationship between lunar cycles and homicide in Ohio and Florida. They found that the greatest number of murders occurred after the new and full phases of the moon. Other research has found that suicide and depression are highest on cloudy days. Seattle, Washington, has one of the highest suicide rates and also one of the highest frequencies of cloudy days for all major cities in the United States.

While some may question the validity of these findings, these studies do call our attention to another environmental influence on human interaction. We often acknowledge this relationship in our everyday language. We refer to cloudy and rainy days as "depressing" and describe happy, cheerful people as having "sunny dispositions."

Thus the weather may indeed influence our behavior in various ways, and an understanding of this influence may allow us to more accurately predict our own behavior and that of others. It may, in fact, be interesting for you to keep a day-to-day chart of your behavior and the weather conditions. Does your own behavior show noticeable changes that could correlate with the weather?

THE CONSTRUCTED ENVIRONMENT

As an Indian, Herman Lehmann spent most of his days and nights in the open. When he traveled with the Apaches and Comanches, he slept under the stars. His home while in the villages usually consisted of a one-room teepee or hogan. The Apaches and Comanches didn't build permanent buildings, and the temporary structures they did build were made from materials available in the immediate environment. They weren't encumbered by bulky furniture; they ate, sat, and slept on the ground.

This is quite different from our own environment, with its wide variety of houses and towering buildings. Within these structures one can find rooms of almost every size, shape, and color, and the variety of furniture design and arrangement seems limitless. Just as other aspects of the environment influence our behavior, so too does the design of our buildings and rooms. In fact, it seems as if almost every detail of the constructed environment can guide our actions and interactions.

One of the clearest examples of this influence occurred in St. Louis in the late 1950s. In 1954, 43 11-story high-rise apartment buildings were erected on a 57-acre tract as a governmentally assisted public housing project. The buildings of the Pruitt-Igoe project were beautiful, and they received awards for their architectural design. Each apartment had the most modern facilities, and the nearly 12,000 residents were assured adequate space. All signs suggested that the project should be a huge success and could revolutionize the building of

housing projects. But the high hopes for the Pruitt-Igoe project were shattered before long. In a few years, the complex resembled a battlefield; windows in many of the apartments were broken or boarded; the elevators became piled with human waste; gang warfare broke out, and residents were afraid to leave their apartments after dark; rape and robbery were common. An exodus from the complex began, and officials couldn't find people willing to move into the apartments. By 1970 only 16 of the 43 buildings were occupied, and in April 1972 city officials ordered demolition of the entire project.

How could this monument once praised as the greatest advancement in subsidized housing end in such utter failure? The general answer is that even though the project looked

The Pruitt-Igoe complex was hailed as an architectural wonder and a great advance in low-income housing when it was built.
UPI/Bettmann Archive.

However, a few years after it was built, Pruitt-Igoe resembled a battlefield. It did not fit the needs of the people who lived there, and it was eventually demolished.
UPI/Bettmann Archive.

beautiful and was well designed from an architectural standpoint, it didn't fit the needs of the people who lived there. Residents complained that the long hallways in the building didn't foster interaction between neighbors and, consequently, the residents often felt lonely. Parents pointed out that the high-rise nature of the buildings made it impossible to easily supervise their children in the playgrounds. Imagine a parent trying to watch out of a window on the eleventh floor as his or her child plays below. Newman (1972) also argued that there was too much *indefensible territory* in the project. Indefensible space includes areas that can't easily be marked or observed; consequently people fear entering them. Residents of the Pruitt-Igoe project were afraid to enter the elevators because they often couldn't see who was in them, and once the doors closed they were at the mercy of other passengers. The Pruitt-Igoe story shows that we must design our environments to meet the needs of the people who will inhabit them.

On a smaller scale, research has shown that physical aspects of a single room can affect our emotions and behaviors. Desor (1972) found that subjects perceived a rectangular room to be more spacious than a square room, although the actual number of square feet in the two rooms was the same. A number of investigators compared "open offices," where workers are separated only by low partitions, to the small, closed office design, where each worker has his or her own office. The results of this research suggested that whereas workers in the open offices interacted with more people, workers in the smaller offices formed closer friendships with a small number of people. Workers in the open offices felt less crowded and perceived the area to be more spacious than workers in the small offices (Wells, 1972; Sommer, 1974). But the open-office workers felt they had less privacy and noisier conditions than workers in the smaller, closed offices. Even the color of a room may affect our behavior (Bennett, 1977). People associate various moods with various colors, as Table 15.3 demonstrates (Wexner, 1954). In one study, people became more physiologically aroused (higher

TABLE 15.3

Relation between Moods and Colors

Blue:	secure, comfortable, tender, soothing, calm, serene
Red:	exciting, protective, defending, defiant
Orange:	distressed, upset
Black:	despondent, powerful
Purple:	dignified
Yellow:	cheerful

SOURCE: Wexner, 1954.

galvanic skin response) when watching red slides than when watching green slides (Wilson, 1966).

Moving closer to home, we can point out that the type of dormitory in which students live affects their behavior in a number of ways. Generally, students live in one of two types of dormitories. In the **corridor dormitory** bedrooms are arranged along a hallway (see Figure 15.4). Residents share a bathroom and a common lounge. A second type, the **suite dormitory,** is arranged more like a typical apartment, with three or four bedrooms arranged around a lounge or living area and students in the suite sharing a bathroom (see Figure 15.4). Although the amount of space students have is the same in both types of dormitories, the effects on the residents are very different. Suite residents both feel and exercise more control over their environment than corridor residents do (Baum & Valins, 1977). They can decide who enters their lounge and bedrooms better than corridor residents can. Students in the corridor dorms feel more crowded than suite residents do, have more unwanted social encounters, and feel less control over their living situations. Their response is to withdraw into their rooms and not try to improve common areas such as bathrooms and lounges.

Thus the type of building, the shape of a room, and the color of an office can influence our emotional states and behaviors. In the past, too many mistakes have been made by designing buildings and rooms to look pleasing to the

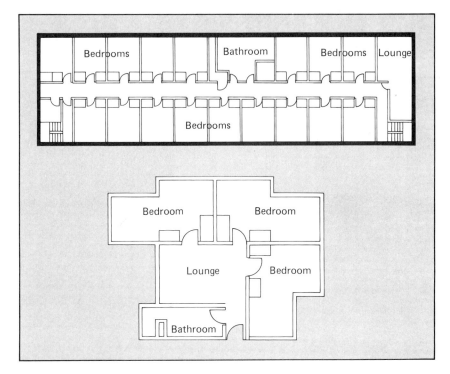

FIGURE 15.4   FLOOR PLAN OF (A) A CORRIDOR-STYLE DORMITORY AND (B) A
SUITE-STYLE DORMITORY

SOURCE: Baum, A. & Valins, S. (1977). *Architecture and social behavior: Psychological studies in social density.* Hillsdale, N.J.: Erlbaum. Reproduced by permission.

eye with little attention given to making the de-sign fit people's needs and behavior. The ne-cessity of fitting design to behavior should be kept in mind when you choose a home or an apartment. A wise choice will facilitate your adjustment to your new environment and should make your life more enjoyable and carefree. A poor choice will add complication and annoyance.

The Arrangement of Furniture

It may be difficult, if not impossible, for many of us to change the size, shape, or color of the room in which we live. However, in most cases, we can influence the arrangement of furniture in our living and working space. As you will see, seemingly simple changes in the arrange-ment of furniture can have a noticeable effect on behavior.

Sommer and Ross (1958) describe how the supervisors in a geriatric ward of a Cana-dian hospital carpeted and painted the day-room and installed new furniture in an effort to facilitate greater interaction among the pa-tients. These efforts were unsuccessful, how-ever, as the patients sat in the dayroom "like strangers in a train station waiting for a train that never came" (Sommer & Ross, 1958). The new furniture had been lined up in rows so that the patients could only sit side-by-side or back to back. Sommer and Ross felt that the arrange-ment of furniture inhibited interaction, and they placed groups of chairs in a circular fashion around tables instead. After a few weeks, in-teraction among patients had doubled, and use of the dayroom had greatly increased.

Furniture can be arranged so that inter-action is either fostered or inhibited. Chairs that are placed close together in a circular or other "facing" manner invite social interaction. Peo-ple are much less likely to interact when they occupy chairs that are spread out or placed side

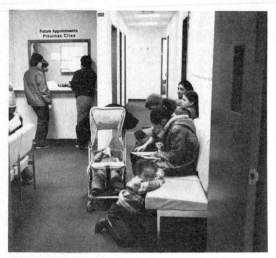

The arrangement of furniture affects our social interactions. Seating in long rows tends to limit the amount of social interaction people have.

Ken Karp.

by side. You can see the effect of this arrangement by watching strangers in a waiting room or airport lounge. The side-by-side arrangement eliminates most eye contact, and people spend much of their time reading or staring straight ahead. Just as the design of a room or building should fit the needs of the inhabitants, so too should the arrangement of furniture. If the room is one in which social interaction is likely to take place or is desired, the furniture should be placed so that individuals can conduct conversations and hold eye contact. On the other hand, if the desire is to reduce social interactions (such as in a library), chairs should be arranged in a side-by-side or back-to-back fashion.

Obviously, the constructed environment in general can have a great influence on your feelings and behavior, and there are many ways you can shape your environment to facilitate your adjustment.

THE URBAN ENVIRONMENT

A discussion of the relationship between environment and human behavior wouldn't be complete without an examination of the most visible human contribution to the environment: the city. Herman Lehmann probably never saw a city. While living with the Apaches and Comanches, he rarely saw concentrations of more than a thousand people. Even when these groups gathered, they rarely left permanent effects on the earth's surface. Even after returning to the whites, Herman avoided large crowds. Thus he never experienced the phenomenon of life in a large city.

Many discussions of urban life often deteriorate into an argument about whether it is "good" or "bad." This type of argument is futile; urban centers have both positive and negative influences on human behavior. Instead of arguing the merits of the city, we need to understand its effects on human behavior and how these effects are perpetrated.

One word that can be used to describe the urban environment is "diversity." Large cities boast almost every type of architecture, person, entertainment, work, vehicle, neon sign, and noise known to humans. This variety offers nearly unlimited opportunities for cultural stimulation, learning, shopping, and eating. In addition, the city offers a certain type of freedom not found elsewhere. The immense size of cities gives the individual a degree of anonymity, and in this lies freedom. An unwritten code in many cities is "I won't bother you if you don't bother me." Thus an individual can practice his or her trade, openly express his or her opinion, and wear whatever he or she chooses, so long as the practice doesn't directly interfere with others. A visit to a large city will quickly show that this freedom is extensively exercised by city dwellers!

While this freedom has many positive effects, unfortunate consequences result when the freedom changes into disregard and lack of concern for others. In most cities, some people are forced to live in woefully inadequate conditions. Harris and Lindsay (1972) reported that 24 percent of urban welfare families in the United States had no running water, and 22.4 percent had no private use of a bathroom with a shower. Incidence of disease such as tuberculosis, heart disease, and syphilis is higher in inner-city areas than in suburbs.

Visitors to large cities are often prone to describe city dwellers as cold and unfriendly. Many of us have read newspaper accounts of someone who was in need of help but whose cries were ignored by passing city dwellers. Can we blame the urban environment for these behaviors? Stanley Milgram (1970) suggests that, yes, the urban environment may indeed be responsible for these responses. He points out that the city is an immensely complex environment; the urbanite is confronted with a huge array of sounds, people, and sights. According to Milgram, humans can cope with only a limited amount of stimulation. When the stimulation becomes too great, the individual must protect himself or herself by filtering some of it out. This filtering simply involves not paying attention to many of the people or activities in the environment.

For the individual, this filtering is necessary in order to adjust to the complex city environment. To the observer, it makes the individual appear unconcerned and uncaring about others in the environment. Thus an action that is necessary for personal adjustment to the environment may hinder social interaction.

In order to experience the dilemma of the city dweller, first imagine yourself living in a small town. You see a few hundred or even a thousand people in a typical day. You can't begin to personally acknowledge all these people. Now imagine yourself working in midtown Manhattan where 220,000 people are within a ten-minute radius of your office. Imagine trying to say "hello" to each of these people, or even trying to pay attention to each one!

At the risk of sounding too anti-city, we must mention some of the problems posed by city life. First, cities are noisier than rural areas. An EPA study showed that even the quietest times in an inner-city apartment are noisier than the noisiest times in small towns. The large concentration of motor vehicles, machines, and people add to the pollution of cities. One investigator has reported that just living in New York City is equivalent to smoking 38 cigarettes a day (Rotton, 1978). And cities tend to be more stressful than other environments. Stress results

because movement is often impaired by traffic and other people, there is a great deal of contact with strangers, it is often difficult to find your way around, and the environment is often unpredictable and uncontrollable.

Some cities are easier to live in than others are, however. One difference between cities involves the ease of navigation and locating where one is. Research suggests that clear visible landmarks help people navigate in cities (Porteous, 1977). These landmarks are often tall buildings, like the Empire State Building in New

REVIEW QUESTIONS

12. T or F: The most accurate measure of the psychological state of crowding is the density of people in an area.
13. The experience of the psychological state of crowding is determined by a number of different environmental and cognitive factors. Three such factors are focus of _____, issues of _____, and desire for _____.
14. T or F: Males are more affected by crowding than females.
15. T or F: Although noise often has an immediate detrimental effect on performance, its aftereffects are negligible.
16. Although the evidence is equivocal, there is some indication that hot temperatures may increase _____ and decrease _____ on complex tasks.
17. Students who live in suite dormitories feel less crowded than students who live in corridor dorms even though the amount of space is the same. According to Baum and Valins (1977) this occurs because suite residents feel more _____ over their environment.
18. The mental images that we form of our environment help us to reduce the confusion and anxiety that occurs when we find ourself in totally unfamiliar surroundings. Psychologists call these mental images _____.

York. No matter where you are in New York, you can usually see the Empire State Building and roughly determine your location. Streets that are laid out in identifiable squares and have an easily understood pattern of names (such as numbers or names of presidents) help people find their way. Cities that have clear boundaries such as rivers, oceans, or high walls also help people locate themselves. All of these factors help us form **cognitive maps,** or mental images, of a city. When we have these clear cognitive maps we are less likely to be confused or feel lost. These maps help us feel more in control and better able to guide our actions in the city. Newcomers to large cities are often struck with panic because they don't have these mental images; they feel lost in a gulf of confusion until they can orient themselves.

Thus coping in the city requires a different pattern of behavior than coping in a smaller town does. Each environment influences behavior, but the type of influence is very different. Each environment presents a set of opportunities that must be dealt with, and a behavior that's an appropriate reaction in one environment wouldn't be helpful in the other. Hence, just as we must plan our environment to fit our behavioral needs, so must we be able to vary our behavior to fit the requirements of the environment.

SUMMARY

1. The relationship between people and their environment has changed to the point where people are realizing that they must live in partnership with their environment.

2. We are influenced not only by the physical aspects of our environment, but also by how we perceive and interpret the environment.

3. Isolation results when our environment forces us into a monotonous situation where we cannot interact with other people. Isolation is experienced negatively and causes stress. Privacy, on the other hand, is chosen isolation; we seek privacy and it is a necessary part of adjusting to our environment.

4. Territoriality involves claiming exclusive use of something. Humans generally have three types of territory: primary, secondary, and public. Territoriality gives us protection, helps establish social order, allows us to have privacy, and controls aggression.

5. Personal space is the space immediately around each of us that we feel is ours. The size of personal space is influenced by our age, race, sex, and the type of interaction we are having with others. Personal space controls aggression and determines the channels of communication we can use when interacting with others. Violations of personal space cause stress. People may attempt to reestablish their space by moving backwards or use other compensations such as avoiding eye contact. People don't like others who violate their space, unless they see them as making a friendly overture by the violation.

6. Density is a physical measure of the amount of space available to an individual in a given setting. Crowding is a negative psychological state that is influenced by spatial, psychological, and personal factors. Crowding is influenced by the individual's focus of attention, the amount of control he or she has in the setting, and the person's need for privacy at the particular time. Crowding causes people to feel uncomfortable and can reduce the effective performance of tasks.

7. A sound becomes noise when it is unwanted by the listener because it is unpleasant, bothersome, and interferes with activities. Loud noise can damage our hearing. Noise that is unpredictable and uncontrollable can also negatively affect our performance of tasks. Noise reduces the quality of our social interactions. Noise's aftereffects on task performance may be more dramatic than the immediate effects.

8. Heat has been found to increase the likelihood of aggression. Very hot temperatures also inhibit task performance. On the other hand, performance is also affected by cold temperatures.

9. The type of environment we construct can affect our behavior. For example, students generally feel more in control and less crowded in suite dormitories than in corridor dormitories, even though the amount of space is the same. Furniture can be arranged to increase or decrease social interaction.

10. Cities offer a variety of experiences. Cities tend to be hotter, noisier, more polluted, and more stressful than small towns. Some cities are easier to adjust to than are others. Those cities that have clear landmarks and well-defined boundaries help people form cognitive maps. These maps that we carry around in our heads affect how comfortable we feel in a city by helping us not become lost in a complex urban environment.

KEY TERMS

a. COGNITIVE MAPS	g. PRIMARY TERRITORY
b. CROWDING	h. PRIVACY
c. DENSITY	i. PUBLIC TERRITORY
d. INDEFENSIBLE TERRITORY	j. SECONDARY TERRITORY
e. NOISE	k. TERRITORIALITY
f. PERSONAL SPACE	

1. Areas or objects that are exclusively owned or controlled by individuals and are of central importance in their lives
2. A sound that is unwanted by the listener because it is unpleasant, bothersome, and interferes with activities
3. Mental images of a city or other area
4. A psychological state of stress that results when people are too close physically
5. The behavior involving the claim of exclusive use of areas or objects
6. The space individuals keep when interacting with others; there is often a feeling of ownership of the space directly around an individual, and uninvited intrusions are met with retreat or hostility
7. Areas or objects to which individuals are emotionally attached and which they feel they control exclusively; they do not, however, own these territories or objects
8. A physical measure of the space available to an individual in a certain area
9. Chosen social isolation
10. An area that individuals control only while occupying it
11. An area that cannot be easily marked or observed

ANSWERS TO REVIEW QUESTIONS

1. Perceptions. **2.** Privacy; social isolation. **3.** Territoriality. **4.** Primary; public. **5.** d. **6.** False.

7. Personal space. **8.** Intimate; social; public; personal. **9.** Culture; sex; age. **10.** False. **11.** Nonverbal compensations.

12. False. **13.** Attention; control; privacy. **14.** True. **15.** False. **16.** Aggression; performance. **17.** Control. **18.** Cognitive maps.

GLOSSARY

Ability test test designed to examine an individual's reasoning, memory, mechanical, math, or psychomotor skills

Acceptance the final stage in the dying process where people feel at peace and able to accept the fact that they are dying

Adjustment complex personal process that involves learning about one's self, setting goals, and coping with social and situational demands

Affect feeling or emotion

Affiliation being close or interacting with other people

AIDS Acquired Immune Deficiency Syndrome resulting from a virus that attacks the body's immune system and makes the individual very susceptible to a wide variety of diseases

Amnesia complete or partial loss of memory

Anal stage Freud's second stage of development, discussed by Erikson, beginning around the age of 18 months with toilet training

Anger and resentment the second stage in the dying process where people feel unfairly stricken and say "Why me?"

Anorexia nervosa an eating disorder in which the person, usually a woman, loses a great deal of weight, often to the point of endangering her health, but still feels that she must lose more

Anxiety generalized feelings of fear and apprehension

Anxiety disorder psychological disorders including anxiety states, phobias, and obsessive-compulsive disorders characterized by intense fear the individual cannot manage

Anxiety state a psychological disorder characterized by constant feelings of extreme anxiety and worry interspersed with short periods of intense panic

Assertiveness training a behavior modification technique in which a person is trained to act appropriately assertive in interpersonal situations

Asthma psychological disorder in which breathing becomes difficult

Attachment the need to be with another person and to be approved of by that person

Attribution the process of labeling physiological arousal as a particular emotional state

Autogenic training reducing muscle tension by focusing on your own suggestions that your muscles and limbs are getting warm and heavy and that your breathing is becoming regular

Bargaining the third stage in the dying process where people strive to stay alive to reach a particular event

Behavior therapy a form of therapy based on the principles of reinforcement which focuses on changing behavior rather than analyzing feelings

Being motive the motivation to grow and develop

Beneffectance the ego's tendency to take credit for success but deny responsibility for failure

Birth control any method used to prevent the birth of children

Body language nonverbal communication of emotions by posture, positioning, and facial expressions

Bulimia an eating disorder characterized by binges of eating followed by purging through self-induced vomiting or laxatives

Burnout state that results when a person loses sympathy for others with whom he or she works and becomes exhausted and fatigued

Career progress or general course of work activity through a person's life or through some phase of it

Caring the feeling that another person's satisfactions and well-being are as important as your own

Catharsis the process whereby an act of aggression reduces the desire for further aggression

Circumcision an operation, often performed shortly after birth, that removes the foreskin from the penis

Classical conditioning a form of conditioning in which a formerly neutral stimulus is paired with a stimulus that elicits a response, so that the neutral stimulus acquires the capacity to elicit the response

Clitoris the most sexually sensitive part of a woman's body including a shaft and glans

Coercive power capacity to deliver threats and punishments to force compliance from another individual

Cognitive conservatism the ego's tendency to maintain its beliefs and to perceive the beliefs it currently holds as the ones that it has held for a long time

Cognitive dissonance theory (1) a relationship among cognitions such that one cognition follows from the opposite of another; or (2) a feeling of discomfort resulting from inconsistent thoughts

Cognitive maps mental images of a city or other area

Coitus the act of sexual intercourse

Collaboration in Sullivan's theory, the process by which two adolescents, usually of the same sex, both having the need and capacity for intimacy, form a close bond, pursue similar satisfactions, and adapt to each other's behavior

Commitment in Thibaut and Kelley's theory of the stages of relationships, the stage in which people decide to be special or exclusive partners in a relationship

Comparison level the standard by which the outcome level of interactions in a relationship is evaluated; it is based on all the outcomes a person knows about through his or her own or another's experiences

Comparison level for alternatives the lowest level of outcomes a person will accept in a relationship; it is the level of outcomes in the next available relationship

Complementarity having opposite but congruent needs

Compulsion recurring, ritualistic behavior pattern experienced as irresistible

Conditions of worth in Rogers's theory of personality, the standards that a child must live up to in order to get approval from parents and in order to feel worthy

Conflict theory the theory that prior to a decision the choices spread in value so that the person can make a decision between them

Conformity a change in behavior or belief toward a group as a result of real or imagined group pressure

Congruence in psychotherapy, the matching of a therapist's inner feelings with what he or she expresses overtly

Conscience in Freudian theory, that part of the superego containing prohibitions and restrictions

Contraception method of birth control used to prevent conception

Coping mechanism conscious and deliberate efforts to manage stressful situations

Corridor dormitory dormitory in which bedrooms are arranged along a long hallway

Crowding a psychological state of stress that results when people are too close

Cultural orientation at midlife, an interest in spiritual and cultural matters as opposed to the gratification of instincts and gaining more experience

Deficiency motive a motive instigated by some psychological deficit experienced as an inner drive to obtain what is missing

Deindividuation a condition whereby the individual becomes "submerged into the group" and feels relatively anonymous

Delusion a false belief held by a person without any objective evidence

Denial an ego-defense mechanism in which an individual refuses to acknowledge an external source of threat

Density a physical measure of the space available to an individual in a certain area

Depression the fourth stage in the dying process where people feel extremely unhappy and depressed

Diffuse anxiety the experience of dread without being able to identify the reason for the feeling

Disparagement a mode of enhancing one's self-esteem by derogating and criticizing others

Displaced aggression an angered individual's attack on a target that was not responsible for the frustration

Displacement an ego-defense mechanism in which anger felt toward a powerful person is expressed in the form of aggression against a person who cannot retaliate

Dissociated states psychological disorders in which there is loss of memory and recognitions of one's past behavior and experience

Dissonance theory the theory that people are made uncomfortable by inconsistent cognitions and have a drive to reduce the discomfort by changing a cognition

Door-in-the-face effect a persuasion technique in which a target is more likely to comply with a request after refusing to comply with an excessively large request

Double-bind a situation characterized by paradoxical communication, dependence on the communicator, and inability to meta-communicate

Dream in Levinson's theory, the goal that one sets one's life toward in early adulthood

Ego the structure of the psyche that notices, perceives, remembers, and helps the individual cope with reality

Egocentricity the ego's tendency to see one-self as the center of action and as the cause of one's own and others' behavior

Ego-ideal in Freudian theory, that part of the superego containing aspirations and values

Ego-identity a positive sense of self and of the role one can play in society

Emotion a complex state of feeling involving conscious experience, internal and overt physical responses, and motivation to action

Empathic understanding in psychotherapy, the therapist's capacity to view the world from the client's point of view and to understand his or her feelings

Encounter group therapeutic groups emphasizing personal growth through authentic communication and through the expression of personal feelings about one's self and others

Equity state that results when one person's ratio of inputs and outcomes is the same as that of another worker

Erectile dysfunction often called impotence, refers to a dysfunction involving males' failure to have or maintain erection long enough to have sexual intercourse

Expert power power an individual derives by being seen as possessing special insight or knowledge about a particular area

Extinction the process by which a conditioned response gradually disappears when the unconditioned stimulus or reinforcer is removed

Extrinsic motivation desire to perform work based on external factors such as pay or threats

Family therapy therapy involving a couple, parents and a child, or a whole family, in which the established interactional system is analyzed

Feedback in encounter groups, other people's reactions, expressed in terms of their own feelings, to one's behavior or statements

Foot-in-the-door effect a persuasion technique in which a target is more likely to comply with a large request after agreeing to a small request

Free association a psychoanalytic technique in which the patient verbalizes whatever thoughts or feelings come to mind without censoring

General adaptation syndrome (GAS) the body's reaction to threat in Selye's theory, consisting of (1) an alarm stage marked by a mobilization of the body's resources, (2) a resistance stage marked by the organism's attempts to protect itself, and (3) an exhaustion stage in which the organism can no longer resist the threat

Generalization a process by which a person comes to fear other stimuli that are associated with an original fearful event

Generativity a concern for establishing and guiding the next generation

Genital herpes sexually transmitted disease caused by a virus that during its active phase results in small blisters on the genitals

Genitals sex organs

Gestalt therapy a form of humanistic group or individual psychotherapy emphasizing personal integration and taking responsibility for one's own life

Goal object or condition that a person desires to obtain

Gonorrhea sexually transmitted disease caused by a bacteria that results in pain during urination and a discharge of pus or blood

Group polarization process whereby group discussion causes an individual to make a more extreme decision than he or she would make alone

Guidance counselor person trained to help students choose occupations to fit their interests and abilities

Hallucination a perception or mental image occurring without any external stimulus to cause it

Hierarchy a ranked list of anxiety-provoking situations ranging from terrifying to minimally threatening

Homosexuality sexual relations between individuals of the same sex

Hypochondriasis constant worrying about physical symptoms caused by anxiety

Hysteria a disorder marked by physical symptoms, such as paralysis, mutism, or tics, that have no organic or physical basis

Id the structure of the psyche that instinctively and unconsciously seeks pleasure and satisfaction of bodily needs

Idealized performance acting as if you support and conform to ideal standards of good conduct more than you actually do

Identification (1) a process by which a person adopts a pattern of behavior in an attempt to be like someone he or she admires; (2) an ego-defense mechanism in which anxiety is reduced by identifying with a high status individual or institution

Identity confusion lack of a clear sense of self and what one is capable of accomplishing in society

Implosive therapy a behavior therapy in which the client is asked to imagine as vividly as possible the most frightening situation possible; gradually, the anxiety response to these situations extinguishes

Incubation a period of time in which a phobic reaction intensifies as a person avoids the original stimulus

Indefensible territory area that cannot be easily marked or observed

Induced abortion termination of pregnancy by removing the immature fetus from the uterus

Informational influence the power of the group to influence a member's behavior through the member's desire to obtain information about the "correct" way to believe or behave

Informational power power derived by the possession of a specific piece of information

Ingratiation attempts by an individual to enhance his or her image in the eyes of another by expressing attitudes that he or she thinks the other person wants to hear

Instinct innate program that determines an organism's behavior in a given situation

Intellectualization an ego-defense mechanism in which the individual reacts to a stressful situation in a detached and analytical manner

Interest test test designed to compare an individual's interest with those of successful people in a wide variety of occupations

Interpersonal distance the distance people keep between themselves and others when interacting

Intimacy a close emotional relationship characterized by deep caring for another person

Intrinsic motivation desire to perform based on internal factors of the wish to control one's own behavior and to demonstrate competence

Job discrimination limiting people's job opportunities because of their race, sex, religion, color, or national origin

Kinesis the study of communication through body movements

Labia majora "major lips" made up of fleshy folds of tissue protecting the entrance to the vagina

Labia minora "minor lips" made up of tissue rich in blood vessels and nerve endings lying within the labia majora

Latency period according to Freud and Erikson, a long stage during middle and late childhood in which children attempt to develop intellectual, athletic, artistic, and social skills

Leader individual who influences the activities of a group

Legitimate power power an individual derives from occupying a particular role or position

Lesbian female homosexual

Logotherapy Frankl's therapy, which emphasized helping clients find meaning in their lives

Loneliness a state of mental stress and anxiety that results when people either erect mental barriers to wall themselves off from others or are afraid to break down existing barriers

Love (1) mature love, a positive emotion about another person involving caring, attachment, and the desire for intimacy; (2) romantic love, a strong, often fleeting positive feeling about another person that has a physiological arousal component

Mania an extreme mood of elation, well-being, and euphoria

Mask the attempt by an individual to hide one emotion by displaying another

Masturbation self-manipulation of one's genitals to orgasm

Menopause time in a woman's life where menstruation ceases and she is no longer capable of reproduction

Metacommunication a communication about another communication

Micromomentary expressions barely visible facial expressions that show emotions one is attempting to control during interaction with another

Model in social learning theory, a person who performs or models a behavior that can be observed and learned by another person

Mons veneris most visible part of female sexual system, composed of a pad of tissue covered with pubic hair

Moral realism in Piaget's theory of moral development, the strict and literal application of rules with no thought of intentions and possible mitigating circumstances

Moral relativism in Piaget's theory of moral development, the considering of intentions in evaluating the morality of behavior

Mutism an inability to speak associated with hysteria

Neurasthenia chronic tiredness, exhaustion, or fatigue

Neutralize to attempt to conceal an emotion from another

Noise sound that is unwanted by the listener because it is unpleasant, bothersome, and interferes with activities

Nonspecific urethritis an inflammation of the male urethra similar to gonorrhea but cannot be treated with penicillin

Nonverbal communication sending messages through body language without talking

Normative influence the power of the group to influence a member's behavior through the member's fear that he or she will be rejected for failing to follow the group's direction

Norms general rules that apply to everyone in a group and specify what must be done when

Obedience conforming to direct orders from a high-status individual

Observational learning learning that takes place when a person observes a model performing a behavior

Obsession recurring thought or image experienced as uncontrollable intrusions into consciousness

Occupation the specific form our choice of work takes

Operant a behavior that has been acquired on the basis of reinforcement

Operant conditioning the process of learning in which a response or change in behavior is strengthened with a reinforcer

Oral stage Freud's first stage of development, discussed by Erikson, spanning approximately the first year of life, in which the child primarily needs nourishment and physical comfort

Orgasm an intense physical and emotional experience often occurring at the climax of a sex act such as intercourse or masturbation

Orgasmic dysfunction female's inability to experience an orgasm even when there is normal sex interest and drive

Ostracism in Sullivan's theory, the rejection of an individual by a group that finds him or her different and undesirable

Outcome level the average level of outcomes that is experienced in a relationship

Ovaries female sex glands which produce ova and female sex hormone

Overcompensation effect a tendency to overcorrect for an initial incorrect impression and overemphasize the most recent information

Paradoxical communication a message that contradicts itself

Paralanguage aspects of speaking, such as pace of speech and tone of voice, which qualify the meaning of what is stated

Paranoia a psychosis in which people have delusions of persecution and conspiracy but no overall breakdown in thought

Penis male external sex organ composed of erectile tissue

Personal space the space individuals keep when interacting with others; there is often a feeling of ownership of the space directly around an individual, and uninvited intrusions are met with retreat or hostility

Personification in Sullivan's theory, young children's vague images about themselves that contain both "good me" and "bad me" elements

Person perception the process of forming impressions of other people

Phallic stage Freud's third stage of development, discussed by Erikson, spanning ages three to four, when the child is interested in his or her sexual organs and develops strong attachments to the opposite sex parent

Phobia an intense fear of a particular behavior, object, or place that poses no immediate threat to the individual

Plethysmograph instrument that can record responses of the penis or vagina

Polygraph a machine, often called a lie detector, which records changes in heart rate, blood pressure, and galvanic skin responses

Power-expressive rapes rapes in which men attempt to assert and show their power and dominance over women

Power-reassurance rapes rapes in which men who feel insecure about their power and worth attempt to make themselves feel better by overcoming uncertainty about their power

Preadolescence in Sullivan's theory of development, the years just before adolescence, starting at about age 9, when children first establish intimate relationships with same sex peers

Premature ejaculation male's inability to delay ejaculation long enough to penetrate and satisfy his partner at least 50 percent of the time

Primacy effect an impression of another that is most heavily influenced by the earliest information received about the person

Primary process in Freudian theory, the imagining of objects or behaviors that will gratify the id

Primary territory areas or objects that are exclusively owned or controlled by individuals and are of central importance in their lives

Privacy chosen social isolation

Private acceptance changing both attitudes and behavior to be more congruent with group norms

Projection an ego-defense mechanism in which an individual's unacceptable thoughts or impulses are attributed to others

Proxemics studies concerned with how people position themselves in social interaction

Proximity one person's geographical closeness to another person; an important factor in influencing interpersonal attraction

Psychophysiological disorder a disorder in which the individual shows physical symptoms that have psychological causes

Psychosis more severe form of psychological disorder marked by severe disturbances in thought and loss of ability to function in society

Public compliance conformity in which an individual changes only overt behavior to follow the group

Public territory an area that individuals control only while occupying it

Radical behaviorism B. F. Skinner's philosophy that psychologists should only discuss behavior and not thoughts and feelings, because behavior is all that they can observe

Rational-emotive therapy the process of learning that our beliefs that we have to live up to other people's expectations of us are debilitating and irrational

Rationalization an ego-defense mechanism by which people convince themselves and others that their behavior was performed for socially desirable reasons

Reactance theory psychological motivational state that results when a person feels his or her freedom has been threatened or eliminated

Reaction formation an ego-defense mechanism in which anxiety is reduced by repressing one set of feelings and over-emphasizing an opposite set of feelings

Recency effect the heavy influence of the most recent information about another person in the creation of one's impression of that person

Recovery the final stage in the grieving process where one begins to put suffering behind and tries to continue an active life

Referent power power an individual derives from being admired and liked

Regression an ego-defense mechanism in which an individual reacts to a stressful situation by reverting to childish or juvenile behavior

Reinforcer a desired stimulus that strengthens a behavior, a reward

Relative humidity percent of moisture in the air

Relaxation a response marked by tensionless muscles and breathing which is used in systematic desensitization; relaxation is incompatible with feeling anxiety

Repression an ego-defense mechanism in which unwanted thoughts or impulses are driven from one's consciousness

Resistance in Freudian psychoanalysis, the patient's avoidance of thinking about or discussing anxiety-provoking thoughts or feelings

Retarded ejaculation male finds it difficult or impossible to ejaculate during intercourse

Reward power capacity to give positive reinforcements to achieve compliance from another person

Role conflict the internal conflict that results when the behavioral expectations of an individual's role in one group contradict the behavioral expectations of another group to which the individual belongs

Roles a set of norms that defines how an individual in a particular position should act

Sampling in Thibaut and Kelley's theory of the stages of relationships, the process of looking over the possibilities and then deciding on a person with whom to attempt to form a relationship

Scapegoat a person or group that people blame for their troubles and toward whom they displace aggression

Scheme/(pl.)schemata an organization of knowledge, such as a belief, derived from past experience that we use to interpret new experience or information

Schizophrenia a psychosis marked by disintegration of normal thought processes

Scrotum sack composed of loose skin containing the testes

Secondary territory areas of objects to which individuals are emotionally attached, which they feel they control exclusively; they do not, however, own these territories or objects

Self-actualization striving to reach personal potential and using abilities in a creative way

Self-appraisal self-examination aimed at identifying one's abilities, values, and goals

Self-concept one's perceptions of one's abilities, goals, and aspirations and one's overall feeling of worth

Self-esteem the degree to which one likes and respects oneself

Self-fulfilling prophecy a prophecy or prediction that may not be inevitable but that leads to certain behaviors which make it come true

Self-schema a belief about the kind of person one is

Sense of autonomy a sense of control over one's body and a feeling one is free to act independently

Sense of basic mistrust in Erikson's theory, the child's feeling that the world cannot be counted on and that he or she is inadequate to meet its demands

Sense of basic trust a basic feeling of trust in one's self and the environment, and the feeling of adequacy in meeting external demands

Sense of guilt in Erikson's theory, the child's sense that his or her wishes, desires, and actions are inappropriate and immoral

Sense of industry the child's sense of control, power, and competence in achieving desired goals

Sense of inferiority in Erikson's theory, the child's feeling that he or she has little worth and is inferior to others

Sense of initiative the child's sense of having some control over objects and other people, along with the ability to act creatively

Sense of integrity a sense of peace with one's self and others, and the acceptance of responsibility for one's life

Sense of isolation in Erikson's theory, a feeling of distance from others and alienated and cynical attitude toward humanity

Sense of shame and doubt in Erikson's theory, a child's feeling that he or she may not have the capacity to control bodily functions and act autonomously

Sexual dysfunction sexual problems that are frequent or long-lasting

Sexual fantasy thought or daydream that is sexually stimulating

Sexually transmitted diseases physical diseases that are transmitted through sexual contact

Shock the stage in the grieving process where the person tries to deal with the surprise and finality of another person's death

Similarity-attraction finding that people are attractive to others who have attitudes, appearance, background, or desires in common

Simulate to attempt to display emotions that

seem appropriate to the situation but are not genuinely felt

Social accommodation in Sullivan's theory, a process of learning to perceive others realistically and make the necessary accommodations for secure and satisfying interactions with others

Social exchange theory theory that views social relationships in economic terms such as inputs, costs, and outcomes

Social influence the exercise of power or the use of reinforcers by a person or group to influence the behavior of others

Social interaction relating to or interacting with other people

Social isolation a condition in which other people are not present in the environment

Social judgment in Sullivan's theory, a juvenile's categorization of his or her peers as popular, average, stupid, pretty, ugly, etc.

Social learning theory a theory of personality and behavior emphasizing observational learning during social interaction

Social power capacity to influence others and resist influence from others

Social subordination in Sullivan's theory, a process of learning to deal appropriately with authority figures

Sound changes in air pressure that affect the membrane in the ear and are perceived by the person

Sperm male reproductive cells

Stereotypes (1) rigidly held beliefs about people's characteristics based on their membership in ethnic groups; (2) implicit personality theories that are widely shared in a culture

Sterilization method of birth control which makes the individual incapable of reproduction

Stress a condition that results when one perceives that one's well-being or integrity is threatened, and one must devote all one's resources to coping with that threat

Sublimation an ego-defense mechanism in which sexual and aggressive urges are channeled into socially acceptable behavior

Suffering the stage in the grieving process following shock where the greatest suffering and loneliness are experienced

Suite dormitory dormitory arranged like an apartment in which a small number of bedrooms are placed around a common living area

Superego the structure of the psyche that contains the parents' morals, ideals, and values

Syphilis sexually transmitted disease caused by a spiral-shaped bacteria that causes chancres on external or internal sex organs

Systemic desensitization a behavior therapy in which the client is taught to relax, is presented with a hierarchy of anxiety-arousing situations, and learns to relax even when contemplating the most threatening situation

Systemic stress stress whose effects can be seen throughout the body in the form of damaged organs

Territoriality the behavior involving claiming exclusive use of areas or objects

Testes main male internal sex organ which produces androgens and sperm

Theory systematic statement that explains why events occur

Theory X traditional theory of management that holds that workers are lazy and dishonest and must be watched carefully

Theory Y theory of management that states that workers want to contribute and achieve, and the role of management is to create a positive work environment

Theory Z management theory adopted by Japanese companies which views workers as being adopted into a family rather than simply hired to do a specific job

Tics spasmodic jerking or involuntary twitches associated with hysteria

Token economy a form of behavior therapy in which desired behavior is rewarded with tokens which can be used to purchase reinforcers

Transactional analysis a form of group therapy analyzing transactions between the Parent, Adult, and Child ego states

Transference in psychoanalytic therapy, the process by which the patient projects the attitudes of significant others onto the therapist and acts toward the therapist as he or she may have acted toward those significant others

Unconditional positive regard in psychotherapy, complete acceptance of the client by the therapist along with the therapist's warm caring for the client as a human being, with no conditions attached

Urethra tube which extends from the bladder to the exterior through which urine (and semen, in males) passes

Uterus often called the womb, it is an organ which houses the fetus during pregnancy

Vagina female internal genital comprised of a flexible tube lined with mucus membranes into which the penis is inserted during intercourse

Vaginismus dysfunction resulting when the muscles surrounding the vagina involuntarily constrict to inhibit penetration by the penis during intercourse

Voice stress analyzer a machine that records tremors in speech which reflect stress and tension

Vulva external parts of the female genitals

Work some disciplined activity that gives us a feeling of personal accomplishment and that makes a contribution to society

REFERENCES

ADAMS, J. S. (1965). Inequality in social exchange. In L. Berkowitz (Ed.), *Advances in experimental psychology* (Vol. 2). New York: Academic Press.

ADAMS, J. S., & ROSENBAUM, W. E. (1962). The relationship of worker productivity to cognitive dissonance about inequities. *Journal of Applied Psychology, 46*, 161–164.

ADAMS, P. R., & ADAMS, G. R. (1984). Mount St. Helens Ashfall: Evidence for a disaster response. *American Psychologist, 39*, 252–260.

ADLER, J. (1984, April 23). The fight to conquer fear. *Newsweek*, pp. 66–72.

ADORNO, T. W., FENKEL-BRUNSWICK, E., LEVINSON, D. L., & SANFORD, R. N. (1950). *The authoritarian personality*. New York: Harper & Row.

AIELLO, J. R., & AIELLO, T. (1974). The development of personal space: Proxemic behavior of children 6 through 16. *Human Ecology, 2* (3), 177–189.

AIELLO, J. R., & THOMPSON, D. E. (1980). Personal space, crowding and spatial behavior in a cultural context. In I. Altman, J. F. Wohlwill, & A. Rapoport (Eds.), *Human behavior and environment* (Vol. 4). New York: Plenum.

ALEXANDER, F. (1950). *Psychosomatic medicine*. New York: Norton.

ALI, M. (1975). *The greatest: My own story*. New York: Random House.

ALTMAN, I. (1975). *The environment and social behavior*. Monterey, Calif.: Brooks/Cole.

ALTMAN, I., & HAYTHORN, W. W. (1965). Interpersonal exchange in isolation. *Sociometry, 28*, 411–426.

ARDREY, R. (1966). *The territorial imperative*. New York: Atheneum.

ARGYLE, M., & DEAN, J. (1965). Eye-contact, distance and affiliation. *Sociometry, 18*, 289–304.

ARIES, D. (1976). Interaction patterns and themes of male, female and mixed groups. *Small Group Behavior, 7*, 7–18.

ARONSON, E. (1976). *The social animal* (2nd ed.). San Francisco: W. H. Freeman.

ARONSON, E., & LINDER, D. E. (1965). Gain and loss of esteem as determinants of interpersonal attractiveness. *Journal of Experimental Social Psychology, 1*, 156–171.

ASCH, S. (1951). Effects of group pressure upon the modification and distortion of judgement. In H. Guezkow (Ed.), *Groups, leadership and men*. Pittsburgh: Carnegie Press.

ASCH, S. (1952). *Social psychology*. Englewood Cliffs, N. J.: Prentice-Hall.

ASCHER, L. M., & EFRAN, J. S. (1978). Use of paradoxical intention in a behavioral program for sleep onset insomnia. *Journal of Consulting and Clinical Psychology, 46*, 547–550.

ASH, P., & KROEKER, L. P. (1975). Personnel selections, classification and placement. *Annual Review of Psychology, 26*, 481–508.

ASH, S. (1956). Studies of independence and conformity: I. A minority of one against a unanimous majority. *Psychological Monographs: General and Applied, 40*, 1–70.

ATHANASIOU, R., SHAVER, P., & TAVRIS, C. (1970, July). *Psychology Today*, pp. 39–52.

AUSTIN, W. G., & WORCHEL, S. (1979). *The social psychology of intergroup relations*. Monterey, Calif.: Brooks/Cole.

BACALL, L. (1978). *By myself*. New York: Knopf.

BACH, G., & WYDEN, P. (1968). *The intimate enemy: How to fight fair in love and marriage*. New York: Avon.

BAKER, M. A., BERHEIDE, C. W., GRECKEL, F. R., GUGIN, L. C., LIPETZ, M. J., & SEGAL, M. T. (1980). *Women today: An interdisciplinary approach to women's studies*. Monterey, Calif.: Brooks/Cole.

BANDURA, A. (1965). Behavior modification through modeling procedures. In L. Krasner & L. P. Ullman (Eds.), *Research in behavior modification*. New York: Holt, Rinehart and Winston.

BANDURA, A. (1977). *Social learning theory*. Englewood Cliffs, N. J.: Prentice-Hall.

BANDURA, A. (1982). Self-efficacy mechanism in human agency. *American Psychologist, 37*, 122–147.

BARKER, J. P., DEMBO, T., & LEWIN, K. (1941). Frustration and regression: An experiment with young children. *University of Iowa Studies of Child Welfare, 18* (1), 1–314.

BARON, R. A., & BELL, P. (1976). Aggression and heat: The influence of ambient temperature, negative affect, and a cooling drink on physical aggression. *Journal of Personality and Social Psychology, 33*, 245–255.

BARON, R. A., MANDEL, D., ADAMS, C., & GRIFFIN, L. (1976). Effects of social density in university residential environments. *Journal of Personality and Social Psychology, 3*, 434–446.

BARON, R. A., & RODIN, J. (1978). Perceived control and crowding stress. In A. Baum, J. Singer, & S. Valins (Eds.), *Advances in environmental psychology* (Vol. 1). Hillsdale, N. J.: Lawrence Erlbaum.

BARRETT, N. S. (1979). Women in the job market: Occupations, earnings, and career opportunities. In R. E. Smith (Ed.), *The subtle revolution: Women at work*. Washington, D. C.: The Urban Institute.

BASS, B. M., & RYTERBAND, E. C. (1979). *Organizational psychology*. Boston: Allyn and Bacon.

BATESON, G., JACKSON, D., HALEY, J., & WEAKLAND, J. (1956). Toward a theory of schizophrenia. *Behavioral Science, 1*, 251–264.

BAUM, A., & GREENBERG, C. (1975). Waiting for a crowd: The behavioral and perceptual effects of anticipated crowding. *Journal of Personality and Social Psychology, 32*, 667–671.

BAUM, A., & VALINS, S. (1977). *Architecture and social behavior: Psychological studies in social density*. Hillsdale, N. J.: Lawrence Erlbaum.

BECKER, J. V., ABEL, G. G., & SKINNER, L. J. (1979). The impact of a sexual assault on the victim's sexual life. *Victimology: An International Journal, 4*, 229–235.

BELL, A. P., & WEINBERG, M. S. (1978). *Homosexualities: A study of diversity among men and women*. New York: Simon & Schuster.

BEM, D. J. (1970). *Beliefs, attitudes and human affairs*. Belmont, Calif.: Wadsworth.

BEM, S. L. (1975). Sex-role adaptability: One consequence of psychological androgyny. *Journal of Personality and Social Psychology, 31*, 634–643.

BEM, S. L., & BEM, D. J. (1970). Case study of a nonconscious ideology: Training the woman to know her place. In D. J. Bem, *Beliefs, attitudes and human affairs*. Belmont, Calif.: Wadsworth.

BEMIS, K. M. (1978). Current approaches to the etiology and treatment of anorexia nervosa. *Psychological Bulletin, 85*, 593–617.

445

BENGLESDORF, I. S. (1970, March 5). Alcohol, morphine addictions believed similar. *Los Angeles Times, Part II,* p. 7.

BENNETT, C. (1977). *Spaces for people.* Englewood Cliffs, N. J.: Prentice-Hall.

BENSON, H. (1975). *The relaxation response.* New York: Morrow.

BERGIN, A. E. (1966). Some implications of psychotherapy research for therapeutic practice. *Journal of Abnormal Psychology, 71,* 235–246.

BERNE, E. (1964). *Games people play.* New York: Grove Press.

BERSCHEID, E. (1983). Emotion. In H. H. Kelley et al. (Eds.), *Close relationships.* San Francisco: W. H. Freeman and Company.

BERSCHEID, E., DION, K., WALSTER, E., & WALSTER, G. W. (1971). Physical attractiveness and dating choice: A test of the matching hypothesis. *Journal of Experimental Social Psychology, 7,* 173–189.

BERSCHEID, E., & WALSTER, E. (1974). A little bit about love. In T. L. Houston (Ed.), *Perspectives on interpersonal attraction.* New York: Academic Press.

BERSCHEID, E., & WALSTER, E. (1978). *Interpersonal attraction.* Reading, Mass.: Addison-Wesley.

BETTELHEIM, B. (1958). Individual and mass behavior in extreme situations. In E. E. Maccoby, T. M. Newcomb, & E. L. Hartley (Eds.), *Readings in social psychology.* New York: Holt, Rinehart and Winston.

BIEBER, I. (1976). A discussion of homosexuality: The ethical challenge. *Journal of Consulting and Clinical Psychology, 44,* 163–166.

BIGGERS, T., & PRYOR, B. (1982). Attitude change: A function of emotion-eliciting qualities of environment. *Personality and Social Psychology Bulletin, 8,* 94–99.

BILLINGS, A. G., & MOSS, R. H. (1984). Coping, stress and social resources among adults with unipolar depression. *Journal of Personality and Social Psychology, 46,* 877–891.

BIRDWHISTELL, R. L. (1952). *Introduction to kinesics.* Louisville, Ky.: University of Louisville Press.

BLOOD, R. A. (1967). *Love match and arranged marriage.* New York: Free Press.

BLUESTONE, I. (1983). Labor and management relations. Presentation at Texas A & M University.

BLUMSTEIN, P., & SCHWARTZ, P. (1983). *American couples: Money, work, sex.* New York: Morrow.

BORYSENKO, J. (1984, March 12). Ways to control stress and make it work for you. *U. S. News and World Report,* pp. 69–70.

BOSTON WOMEN'S HEALTH BOOK COLLECTIVE. (1979). *Our bodies, our selves.* New York: Simon & Schuster.

BOTWINICK, J. (1977). Intellectual abilities. In J. E. Birren & K. W. Schaie (Eds.), *Handbook of the psychology of aging.* New York: Van Nostrand.

BOWER, G., & COHEN, P. (1982). Emotional influences in memory and thinking: Data and theory. In M. Clark & S. Fiske (Eds.), *Affect and cognition.* Hillsdale, N. J.: Lawrence Erlbaum.

BRAY, D. W., CAMPBELL, R. J., & GRANT, D. L. (1974). *Formative years in business: A long-term AT&T study of management lives.* New York: Wiley-Interscience.

BREHM, J. W. (1966). *A theory of psychological reactance.* New York: Academic Press.

BREHM, S. S., & BREHM, J. W. (1981). *Psychological reactance: A theory of freedom and control.* New York: Academic Press.

BROADBENT, D. E. (1978). The current state of noise research: Reply to Poulton. *Psychological Bulletin, 85* (5), 1052–1067.

BRODY, J. E. (1984, April 25). *New York Times News Service.* Pittsfield, Mass.: The Berkshire Eagle.

BROWN, B. B. (1979, August). *Territoriality and residential burglary.* Paper presented at the meeting of the American Psychological Association, New York.

BROWN, R. (1965). *Social psychology.* New York: Free Press.

BROWNMILLER, S. (1975). *Against our will: Men, women, and rape.* New York: Simon & Schuster.

BYRNE, D. (1982). Sex without contraception. In D. Byrne & W. A. Fisher (Eds.), *Adolescents, sex and contraception.* Hillsdale, N. J.: Lawrence Erlbaum.

BYRNE, D., BASKETT, C. D., & HODGES, L. (1971). Behavioral indicators of interpersonal attraction. *Journal of Abnormal and Social Psychology, 1,* 137–149.

CALHOUN, J. F. (1962). Population density and social pathology. *Scientific American, 206,* 139–148.

CALHOUN, J. F. (1977). *Abnormal psychology.* New York: Random House.

CALHOUN, J. F., & ACOCELLA, J. R. (1978). *Psychology of adjustment and human relationships.* New York: Random House.

CAMPBELL, A. (1947). Factors associated with attitudes toward Jews. In R. M. Newcomb & E. L. Hartley (Eds.), *Readings in social psychology.* New York: Holt, Rinehart and Winston.

CANN, A., SHERMAN, S. J., & ELKES, R. (1975). Effects of initial request size and timing of a second request on compliance: The foot in the door and the door in the face. *Journal of Personality and Social Psychology, 32,* 774–782.

CANTRIL, H. (1940). *The invasion from Mars.* Princeton, N. J.: Princeton University Press.

CARLSMITH, J., & ANDERSON, C. (1979). Ambient temperature and the occurrence of collective violence: A new analysis. *Journal of Personality and Social Psychology, 37,* 337–344.

CARPENTER, C. R. (1958). Territoriality: A review of concepts and problems. In A. Roe & G. G. Simpson (Eds.), *Behavior and evolution.* New Haven, Conn.: Yale University Press.

CASH, J. (1975). *Man in black.* Grand Rapids, Mich.: Zondervan.

CHAIKIN, A. L., & DERLEGA, V. J. (1976). Self-disclosure. In J. W. Thibaut, J. T. Spence, & R. C. Carson (Eds.), *Contemporary topics in social psychology.* Morristown, N. J.: General Learning Press.

CHRISTIE, R., & GEIS, F. L. (1970). *Studies in Machiavellianism.* New York: Academic Press.

CLARK, M. (1982). A role for arousal in the link between feeling states, judgements, and behavior. In M. Clark & S. Fiske (Eds.), *Affect and cognition.* Hillsdale, N. J.: Lawrence Erlbaum.

CLARK, M., GOSNELL, M., SHAPIRO, D., & HAGER, M. (1981, July 13). The mystery of sleep. *Newsweek,* pp. 48–55.

CLARKE, A. (1952). An examination of the operation of residual propinquity as a factor of mate selection. *American Sociological Review, 27,* 17–22.

COCKS, J. (1981, August 3). Magic in the daylight. *Time,* pp. 20–28.

COFER, C. N., & APPLEY, M. H. (1964). *Motivation: Theory and research.* New York: Wiley.

COHEN, S., GLASS, D., & SINGER, J. (1973). Apartment noise, auditory discrimination and reading ability in children. *Journal of Experimental Social Psychology, 9,* 407–422.

COHEN, S., & WEINSTEIN, N. (1981).

Nonauditory effects of noise on behavior and health. *Journal of Social Issues, 37* (1), 36–70.

COLEMAN, J. C., BUTCHER, J. N., & CARSON, R. C. (1980). *Abnormal psychology in modern life* (6th ed.). Glenview, Ill.: Scott Foresman.

COOLEY, C. H. (1902). *Human nature and the social order.* New York: Scribner.

COZBY, P. C. (1972). Self-disclosure, reciprocity, and liking. *Sociometry, 35,* 151–160.

COZBY, P. C. (1973). Self-disclosure: A literature review. *Psychological Bulletin, 79,* 73–91.

CRIDER, A. (1979). *Schizophrenia: A biopsychological perspective.* Hillsdale, N. J.: Lawrence Erlbaum.

CRIDER, A. B., GOETHALS, G. R., KAVANAUGH, R. D., & SOLOMON, P. R. (1983). *Psychology.* Glenview, Ill: Scott Foresman.

CRUTCHFIELD, R. A. (1955). Conformity and characters. *American Psychologist, 10,* 191–198.

DALEY, P. (1975). *The fantasy game: How male and female sexual fantasies affect our lives.* New York: Stein and Day.

DARLEY, S. A., & COOPER, J. (1972). Cognitive consequences of forced noncompliance. *Journal of Personality and Social Psychology, 24,* 321–326.

DARWIN, C. (1872). *The expression of the emotions in man and animals.* London: J. Murray.

DAVIS, W. L., & PHARES, E. J. (1967). Internal-external control as a determinant of information-seeking in a social influence situation. *Journal of Personality, 35,* 547–561.

DAVITZ, J. P. (1964). *The communication of emotional meaning.* New York: McGraw-Hill.

DEAUX, K. (1976). *The behavior of women and men.* Monterey, Calif.: Brooks/Cole.

DECI, E. L. (1971). Effects of externally mediated rewards on intrinsic motivation. *Journal of Personality and Social Psychology, 18,* 105–115.

DECI, E. L. (1975). *Intrinsic motivation.* New York: Plenum.

DE JONG, W. (1979). An examination of self-perception mediation of the foot-in-the-door effect. *Journal of Personality and Social Psychology, 37,* 2221–2239.

DE JONG, W. (1981). Consensus information and the foot-in-the-door effect. *Personality and Social Psychology Bulletin, 7,* 423–430.

DEMING, A. (1981, March 9). Prince Charles finds his lady. *Newsweek,* pp. 40–44.

DERLEGA, V., & MARGULIS, S. (1982). Why loneliness occurs: The interrelationship of social-psychological and privacy concepts. In L. Peplau & D. Perlman (Eds.), *Loneliness.* New York: Wiley.

DESOR, J. A. (1972). Toward a psychological theory of crowding. *Journal of Personality and Social Psychology, 21,* 79–83.

DEXTER, E. (1900). *Popular Science Monograph, 58,* 604.

DIAMOND, M. (1976). Human sexual development: Biological foundations for social development. In F. A. Beach, *Human sexuality in four perspectives.* Baltimore, Md.: Johns Hopkins University Press.

DION, K. K., BERSCHEID, E., & WALSTER, E. (1972). What is beautiful is good. *Journal of Personality and Social Psychology, 24,* 285–290.

DIPBOYE, R., ARVEY, R., & TERPSTRA, D. (1977). Sex and physical attractiveness of raters and applicants as determinants of resumé evaluations. *Journal of Applied Psychology, 62,* 288–294.

DOLLARD, J., DOOB, L. W., MILLER, N. E., MOWRER, O. H., & SEARS, R. R. (1939). *Frustration and aggression.* New Haven, Conn.: Yale University Press.

DU BRIN, A. J. (1982). *Contemporary applied management.* Plano, Tex.: Business Publications.

DU BRIN, A. J. (1984). *Foundations of organizational behavior.* Englewood Cliffs, N. J.: Prentice-Hall.

DUTTON, D., & ARON, A. (1974). Some evidence for heightened sexual attraction under conditions of high anxiety. *Journal of Personality and Social Psychology, 30,* 510–517.

EBERTS, E. H., & LEPPER, M. R. (1975). Individual consistency in the problemic behavior of preschool children. *Journal of Personality and Social Psychology, 32,* 841–849.

ECKENRODE, J. (1984). Impact of chronic and acute stressors on daily reports of mood. *Journal of Personality and Social Psychology, 46,* 907–918.

EDNEY, J. J. (1975). Territoriality and control: A field experiment. *Journal of Personality and Social Psychology, 31,* 1108–1115.

EFRAN, M. G. (1974). The effect of physical appearance on the judgment of guilt, interpersonal attraction, and severity of recommended

punishment in a simulated jury task. *Journal of Experimental Research in Personality, 8,* 45–54.

EHRLICH, P. (1968). *The population boom.* New York: Ballantine.

EKMAN, P., & FRIESEN, W. V. (1968). Nonverbal behavior in psychotherapy research. In J. N. Schlien (Ed.), *Research in psychotherapy.* Washington, D. C.: American Psychological Association.

EKMAN, P., & FRIESEN, W. V. (1971). Constants across cultures in the face and emotion. *Journal of Personality and Social Psychology, 17,* 124–129.

EKMAN, P., & FRIESEN, W. V. (1975). *Unmasking the face.* Englewood Cliffs, N. J.: Prentice-Hall.

EKMAN, P., FRIESEN, W. V., & ELLSWORTH, P. (1972). *Emotion in the human face.* New York: Pergamon Press.

EKMAN, P., FRIESEN, W. V., & ELLSWORTH, P. (1973). *Emotion in the human face: Guidelines for research and an integration of findings.* New York: Pergamon Press.

EKMAN, P., SORENSON, E., & FRIESEN, W. (1969). Pan-cultural elements in facial displays of emotion. *Science, 164,* 86–88.

ELLIS, A. (1962). *Reason and emotion in psychotherapy.* New York: Lyle Stuart.

ELLSWORTH, P., & CARLSMITH, J. (1968). Effects of eye contact and verbal content on affective response to a dyadic interaction. *Journal of Personality and Social Psychology, 10,* 15–20.

EPSTEIN, S. (1973). The self-concept revisited: Or a theory of a theory. *American Psychologist, 28,* 404–416.

ERIKSON, E. H. (1968). *Identity: Youth and crisis.* New York: Norton.

EXLINE, R., & WINTERS, L. (1965). Affective relations and mutual glances in dyads. In S. Tompkins & C. Izard (Eds.), *Affect, cognition and personality.* New York: Springer.

EYSENCK, H. J. (1961). The effects of psychotherapy. In H. J. Eysenck (Ed.), *Handbook of abnormal psychology.* New York: Basic Books.

EYSENCK, H. J. (1964). The outcome problem in psychotherapy: A reply. *Psychotherapy, 1,* 97–100.

FAGOT, B. I., & PATTERSON, G. R. (1969). An "in vivo" analysis of reinforcing contingencies for sex-role behavior in the pre-school child. *Developmental Psychology, 1,* 563–568.

FESTINGER, L. (1950). Informal social

communication. *Psychological Review, 57,* 271–282.

FESTINGER, L. (1954). A theory of social comparison processes. *Human Relations, 7,* 117–140.

FESTINGER, L. (1957). *A theory of cognitive dissonance.* Evanston, Ill.: Row Paterson.

FESTINGER, L. (1964). *Conflict, decision and dissonance.* Stanford, Calif.: Stanford University Press.

FESTINGER, L., RIECKEN, H., & SCHACHTER, S. (1956). *When prophecy fails.* Minneapolis: University of Minnesota Press.

FESTINGER, L., SCHACHTER, S., & BACK, K. (1950). *Social pressures in informal groups: A study of a housing community.* Stanford, Calif.: Stanford University Press.

FIEDLER, F. E. (1978). Recent developments in research on the contingency model. In L. Berkowitz (Ed.), *Group process.* New York: Academic Press.

FISHER, J., BELL, P., & BAUM, A. (1984). *Environmental psychology.* New York: Holt, Rinehart and Winston.

FISHER, J., & BYRNE, D. (1975). Too close for comfort: Sex differences in response to invasions of personal space. *Journal of Personality and Social Psychology, 32,* 15–21.

FORD, C., & BEACH, F. A. (1951). *Patterns of sexual behavior.* New York: Paul Hoeber.

FOX, W. F. (1967). Human performance in the cold. *Human Factors, 9,* 203–220.

FRANKL, V. E. (1963). *Man's search for meaning.* Boston: Beacon Press.

FRENCH, J. R. P., JR., & RAVEN, B. H. (1959). The bases of social power. In D. Cartwright (Ed.), *Studies in social power.* Ann Arbor: University of Michigan.

FREUD, A. (1946). *The ego and the mechanisms of defense.* New York: International Universities Press. (First German Edition, 1936.)

FREUD, S. (1953). Fragment of an analysis of a case of hysteria. In J. Strachey (Ed.), *The standard edition of the complete psychological works of Sigmund Freud* (Vol. 7). London: Hogarth Press. (Originally Published in 1905.)

FREUDENBERGER, H., & RICHELSON, G. (1980). *Burnout: The high cost of high achievement.* New York: Anchor Doubleday.

FROMM, E. (1956). *The art of loving.* New York: Harper & Row.

FRY, A. M., & WILLIS, F. N. (1971). Invasion of personal space as a function of the age of the invader. *Psychological Record, 21,* 383–389.

GEEN, R. G., & O'NEAL, E. C. (1969). Activation of cue-elicited aggression by general arousal. *Journal of Personality and Social Psychology, 11,* 289–292.

GEEN, R. G., & QUANTY, M. (1977). The catharsis of aggression: An evaluation of a hypothesis. In L. Berkowitz (Ed.), *Advances in experimental social psychology* (Vol. 10). New York: Academic Press.

GELLES, R. J., & STRAUS, M. A. (1979). Violence in the American family. *Journal of Social Issues, 35,* 15–39.

GERGEN, K. J. (1971). *The concept of self.* New York: Holt, Rinehart and Winston.

GERRARD, M. (1982). Sex, sex guilt, and contraceptive use. *Journal of Personality and Social Psychology, 42,* 153–158.

GIAMBRA, L. M., & MARTIN, C. E. (1977). Sexual daydreams and quantitative aspects of sexual activity: Some relations for males across adulthood. *Archives of Sexual Behavior, 6,* 497–505.

GINZBERG, E. (1966). *The development of human resources.* New York: McGraw-Hill.

GLASS, D. C. (1976). Stress, competition and heart attacks. *Psychology Today, 10,* 54–57, 134.

GLASS, D. C., & SINGER, J. (1972). *Urban stress: Experiments on noise and social stressors.* New York: Academic Press.

GLASSER, W. (1965). *Reality therapy.* New York: Harper & Row.

GOETHALS, G. R., & DARLEY, J. M. (1977). Social comparison theory: An attributional approach. In J. M. Suls & R. L. Miller (Eds.), *Social comparison process: Theoretical and empirical perspectives.* Washington, D.C.: Hemisphere/Halsted.

GOFFMAN, E. (1959). *The presentation of self in everyday life.* Garden City, N. Y.: Anchor Books.

GOFFMAN, E. (1961). *Asylums: Essays on the social situation of mental patients and other inmates.* Garden City, N. Y.: Anchor Books.

GOFFMAN, E. (1967). *Interaction ritual: Essays on face-to-face behavior.* Garden City, N. Y.: Doubleday.

GOLDMAN, W. (1957). *The temple of gold.* New York: Knopf.

GOLEMAN, D. (1978). Special abilities of the sexes: Do they begin in the brain? *Psychology Today, 12,* 48–59.

GOTTMAN, J., NOTARIUS, C., MARKMAN,

H., BANK, S., YOPPI, B., & RUBIN, M. (1976). Behavior exchange theory and marital decision making. *Journal of Personality and Social Psychology, 34,* 14–23.

GREENE, A. C. (1964). *The last captive.* Austin, Tex.: Encino Press.

GREENHOUSE, L. (1981, March 22). Equal pay debate now shifts to a far wider concept. New York: *The New York Times,* Section 4, p. 20.

GREENWALD, A. G. (1980). The totalitarian ego: Fabrication and revision of personal history. *American Psychologist, 35,* 603–613.

GRIFFITT, W., & GRAY, P. (1969). "Object" evaluation and conditioned affect. *Journal of Experimental Research in Personality, 4,* 1–8.

GROTH, A. N., & BIRNBAUM, H. J. (1979). *Men who rape: The psychology of the offender.* New York: Plenum Press.

GROTH, A. N., BURGESS, A. W., & HOLMSTROM, L. L. (1977). Rape: Power, anger, and sexuality. *American Journal of Psychiatry, 134,* 1239–1243.

GRUSEC, J., & BRINKER, H. (1972). Reinforcement for imitation as a social learning determinant with implications for sex-role development. *Journal of Personality and Social Psychology, 21,* 149–158.

GUILES, F. (1969). *Norma Jean: The life of Marilyn Monroe.* New York: McGraw-Hill.

GUNTHER, J. (1949). *Death be not proud: A memoir.* New York: Harper & Row.

HAGGARD, E. A., & ISAACS, K. S. (1966). Micromomentary facial expressions as indicators of ego mechanisms in psychotherapy. In L. A. Gottschank & A. H. Auerback (Eds.), *Methods of research in psychotherapy.* New York: Meredith.

HALL, E. T. (1959). *The silent language.* New York: Fawcett.

HALL, E. T. (1966). *The hidden dimension.* New York: Doubleday.

HARLOW, H. (1971). *Learning to love.* New York: Albion.

HARRIS, R. F., & LINDSAY, D. (1972). *The state of cities.* New York: Praeger.

HARRIS, T. (1969). *I'm O.K.— you're O.K.: A practical guide to transactional analysis.* New York: Harper & Row.

HARTUP, W. W., MOORE, S., & SAGER, G. (1963). Avoidance of inappropriate sex-typing by young children. *Journal of Consulting Psychology, 27,* 467–473.

HASTORF, A. H., & CANTRIL, H. (1954). They saw a game: A case study. *Journal of Abnormal and Social Psychology, 49,* 129–134.

HATFIELD, E., & SPRECHER, S. (1984). *Mirror, mirror on the wall.* Unpublished manuscript cited in Watson, D., deBortali-Tregerthan, R., & Frank, J., *Social psychology.* Glenview, Ill.: Scott Foresman.

HATFIELD, E., SPRECHER, S., & TRAUPMANN, J. (1978). Men's and women's reactions to sexually explicit films: A serendipitous finding. *Archives of Sexual Behavior, 7,* 583–592.

HECKEL, R. V., & HIERS, J. M. (1977), Social distance and locus of control. *Journal of Clinical Psychology, 33,* 469–471.

HEIDER, F. (1944). Social perception and phenomenal causality. *Psychological Review, 51,* 358–374.

HEIDER, F. (1958). *The psychology of interpersonal relations.* New York: Wiley.

HENDRICK, C., & HENDRICK, S. (1983). *Liking, loving and relating.* Monterey, Calif.: Brooks/Cole.

HENLEY, N. M. (1977). *Body politics.* Englewood Cliffs, N. J.: Prentice-Hall.

HENSEN, D. E., & RUBIN, H. B. (1971). Voluntary control of eroticism. *Journal of Applied Behavior Analysis, 4,* 37–44.

HERRIOT, J. (1972). *All creatures great and small.* New York: Bantam Books.

HERSHER, L. (Ed.). (1970). *Four psychotherapies.* New York: Appleton-Century-Crofts.

HESS, E. H. (1965). The pupil responds to changes in attitude as well as to changes in illumination. *Scientific American, 212,* 46–54.

HESS, E. H., & POLT, J. M. (1960). Pupil size as related to interest value of visual stimuli. *Science, 132,* 349–350.

HEW (1974). Chafetz, M. (Chairman of the Task Force). *Alcohol and health.* Washington, D. C.: U. S. Government Printing Office.

HEW (1978). The alcoholism report: The authoritative newsletter for professionals. Washington, D. C.: U.S. Government Printing Office, 7(3), 2.

HILL, C., RUBIN, Z., & PEPLAU, L. (1976). Breakups before marriage: The end of 103 affairs. *Journal of Social Issues, 32,* 147–168.

HITE, S. (1976). *The Hite report: A na-*tionwide study of female sexuality. New York: Macmillan.

HOBART, C. W. (1958, May). The incidence of romanticism during courtship. *Social Forces, 36,* 363–367.

HOFFMAN, L. W. (1974). Effects of maternal employment on the child: A review of the research. *Developmental Psychology, 10,* 204–228.

HOFLING, C. K., BROTZMAN, E., DALRYMPLE, S., GRAVES, N., & PIERCE, C. M. (1966). An experimental study in nurse-physician relationships. *The Journal of Nervous and Mental Disease, 143(2),* 171–180.

HOKANSON, J. E., BURGESS, M., & COHEN, M. F. (1963). Effect of displaced aggression on systolic blood pressure. *Journal of Abnormal and Social Psychology, 67,* 214–218.

HOLDEN, C. (1975). Lie detectors: PSE gains audience despite critics' doubts. *Science, 190,* 359–362.

HOLLANDER, E.P. (1958). Conformity, status and idiosyncrasy credit. *Psychological Review, 65,* 117–127.

HOLLANDER, E. P. (1960). Competence and conformity in the acceptance of influence. *Journal of Abnormal and Social Psychology, 61,* 361–365.

HOLLANDER, E. P. (1978). *Leadership dynamics: A practical guide to effective relationships.* New York: Free Press/Macmillan.

HOLMES, T. H., & RAHE, R. H. (1967). The social readjustment rating scale. *Journal of Psychosomatic Research, 11,* 213–218.

HORNEY, K. (1945). *Our inner conflicts.* New York: Norton.

HORTON, R. L. (1973). An empirical investigation of variation in students' premarital sex standards and behavior. *Dissertation Abstracts International, 34 (3-A),* 1385–1386.

HOVLAND, C., & SEARS, R. R. (1940). Minor studies in aggression: VI correlations of lynchings with economic indices. *Journal of Psychology, 9,* 301–310.

HULL, C. W. (1943). *Principles of behavior.* New York: Appleton-Century-Crofts.

HUNT, M. (1974). *Sexual behavior in the 1970's.* Chicago: Playboy Press.

HURT, H. (1975). The hottest place in the whole U.S.A. *Texas Monthly, 3,* 50 ff.

HUTT, C., & VAIZEY, M. J. (1966). Differential effects of group density on social behavior. *Nature, 209,* 1371–1372.

HYAMS, J. (1966). *Bogie: A biography* of Humphrey Bogart. New York: New American Library.

INSKO, C. A., THIBAUT, J., MOEHLE, D., WILSON, M., DIAMOND, W. D., GILMORE, R., SOLOMAN, M. K., & LIPSITZ, A. (1980). Social evolution and the emergence of leadership. *Journal of Personality and Social Psychology, 39,* 431–449.

ISMAIL, A. H., & TRACHTMAN, E. (1973). Jogging the imagination. *Psychology Today, 6,* 78–82.

ITARD, J. M. (1932). *The wild boy of Averyron.* New York: Appleton-Century-Crofts.

ITTLESON, W. H., PROSHANSKY, H. M., RIVLIN, L. G., & WINKEL, G. (1974). *An introduction to environmental psychology.* New York: Holt, Rinehart and Winston.

IZARD, C. E. (1977). *Human emotions.* New York: Plenum Press.

IZARD, C. E. (1982). Comments on emotion and cognition: Can there be a working relationship? In M. Clark & S. Fiske (Eds.), *Affect and cognition.* Hillsdale, N. J.: Lawrence Erlbaum.

JACKSON, E. (1975). On the wise management of grief. In D. Dempsey (Ed.), *The way we die.* New York: Macmillan.

JAHODA, M. (1958). *Current concepts of positive mental health.* Joint Commision on Mental Illness and Health. New York: Basic Books, No. 1.

JAMES, W. (1884). What is emotion? *Mind, 9,* 188–204.

JAMES, W. (1908). *The principles of psychology.* New York: Holt.

JANIS, I. L., & MANN, L. (1977). *Decision making.* New York: Free Press.

JECKER, J., & LANDY, D. (1969). Liking a person as a function of doing him a favor. *Human Relations, 22,* 371–378.

JEFFREY, D. B., & KATZ, R. C. (1977). *Take it off and keep it off: A behavioral program for weight loss and healthy living.* Englewood Cliffs, N.J.: Prentice-Hall.

JOHNSON, D. W. (1978). *Human relations and your career: A guide to interpersonal skills.* Englewood Cliffs, N.J.: Prentice-Hall.

JONES, C., & ARONSON, E. (1973). Attribution of fault to a rape victim as a function of respectability of the victim. *Journal of Personality and Social Psychology, 26,* 415–419.

JONES, E. E. (1964). *Ingratiation.* New York: Appleton-Century-Crofts.

JONES, E. E., & BERGLAS, S. (1978). Control of attributions about the self through self-handicapping strategies: The appeal of alcohol and the role of underachievement. *Personality and Social Psychology Bulletin, 4*(2), 200–206.

JONES, E. E., & NISBETT, R. E. (1971). *The actor and the observer: Divergent perceptions of the causes of behavior.* Morristown, N. J.: General Learning Press.

JONES, E. E., ROCK, L., SHAVER, K. G., GOETHALS, G. R., & WARD, L. M. (1968). Pattern performance and ability attribution: An unexpected primary effect. *Journal of Personality and Social Psychology, 10,* 317–341.

JOURARD, S. M. (1966). An exploratory study of body-accessibility. *British Journal of Social and Clinical Psychology, 5,* 221–231.

JOURARD, S. M. (1971). *Self-disclosure: An experimental analysis of the transparent self.* New York: Wiley.

JOURARD, S. M., & FRIEDMAN, R. (1970). Experimenter-subject distance and self-disclosure. *Journal of Personality and Social Psychology, 25,* 278–282.

JUNG, C. G. (1960). The structure and dynamics of the psyche. In *The Collected Works* (Vol. 8). New York: Pantheon.

KAPLAN, H. S. (1974). *The new sex therapy.* New York: Bruner/Mazel.

KAVANAUGH, R. E. (1974). *Facing death.* Baltimore: Penguin.

KELLEY, H. H. (1950). The warm-cold variable in first impressions of persons. *Journal of Personality, 18,* 431–439.

KELLEY, H. H., & THIBAUT, J. W. (1978). *Interpersonal relations: A theory of interdependence.* New York: Wiley Interscience.

KENNEDY, C. (1981, March 9). Our next queen. *Maclean's,* pp. 25–29.

KERNIS, M., & WHEELER, L. (1981). Beautiful friends and ugly strangers: Radiation and contrast effects in perception of same-sex pairs. *Personality and Social Psychology Bulletin, 7,* 617–620.

KESSLER, I. I. (1979). On the etiology and prevention of cervical cancer. A status report. *Obstetrics and Gynecological Survey, 34,* 790–794.

KIERNAN, T. (1982). *Jane Fonda: Heroine of our time.* New York: Delilah.

KINARTHY, E. L. (1975). *The effect of seating position on performance and personality in a college classroom.* Doctoral dissertation.

KINSEY, A. C., POMEROY, W. B., & MAR-

TIN, C. E. (1948). *Sexual behavior in the human male.* Philadelphia: W. B. Saunders.

KINSEY, A. C., POMEROY, W. B., MARTIN, C. E., & GEBHARD, P. H. (1953). *Sexual behavior in the human female.* Philadelphia: W. B. Saunders.

KLEINKE, C. L. (1975). *First impressions.* Englewood Cliffs, N. J.: Prentice-Hall.

KLEINKE, C. L. (1978). *Self-perception.* San Francisco: W. H. Freeman.

KLEMESRUD, J. (1983, December 19). *Appearing in The Berkshire Eagle.* Pittsfield, Mass.: New York Times News Service.

KLONOFF, H. (1974). Marijuana and driving in real-life situations. *Science, 186,* 317–323.

KOHLBERG, L. (1976). Moral stages and moralization: The cognitive-developmental approach. In T. Lickona (Ed.), *Moral development and behavior: Theory, research and social issues.* New York: Holt, Rinehart and Winston.

KONEČNI, V. J. (1975). The mediation of aggressive behavior: Arousal level versus anger and cognitive labeling. *Journal of Personality and Social Psychology, 32,* 706–712.

KONEČNI, V. J. (1979). The role of adverse events in the development of intergroup conflict. In W. G. Austin & S. Worchel (Eds.), *The social psychology of intergroup relations.* Monterey, Calif.: Brooks/Cole.

KONEČNI, V. J., & DOOB, A. N. (1972). Catharsis through displacement of aggression. *Journal of Personality and Social Psychology, 23,* 379–387.

KORMAN, A. K. (1977). *Organizational behavior.* Englewood Cliffs, N. J.: Prentice-Hall.

KORNHAUSER, A. (1965). *Mental health of the industrial worker.* New York: Wiley.

KREIS, B. (1969). *Up from grief.* New York: The Seabury Press.

KROEBER, T. C. (1963). The coping functions of the ego mechanisms. In R. W. White (Ed.), *The study of lives.* New York: Atherton Press.

KÜBLER-ROSS, E. (1969). *On death and dying.* New York: Macmillan.

LAING, R. D. (1967). *The politics of experience.* New York: Pantheon.

LANDY, D., & ARONSON, E. (1969). The influence of the character of the criminal and his victim on the decisions of simulated jurors. *Journal of Experimental Social Psychology, 5,* 141–152.

LANDY, D., & SIGALL, H. (1974). Beauty

is talent: Task evaluation as a function of the performer's physical attractiveness. *Journal of Personality and Social Psychology, 30,* 299–304.

LATANÉ, B., & DARLEY, J. M. (1970). *The unresponsive bystander: Why doesn't he help?* Englewood Cliffs, N. J.: Prentice-Hall.

LAWLER, E. E., III, & HACKMAN, J. R. (1969). Impact of employee participation in the development of pay incentive plans: A field experiment. *Journal of Applied Psychology, 53,* 467–471.

LAZARUS, R. S. (1966). *Psychological stress and the coping process.* New York: McGraw-Hill.

LAZARUS, R. S. (1976). *Patterns of adjustment.* New York: McGraw-Hill.

LAZARUS, R. S. (1982). Thoughts on the relations between emotion and cognition. *American Psychologist, 37,* 1019–1024.

LEARY, T. (1957). *Interpersonal diagnosis of personality.* New York: Ronald Press.

LECUYER, R. (1976). Man's accommodation to space, man's accommodation of space. *Travail Humain, 39,* 195–206.

LEISOR, B. M. (1979). *Liberty, justice and morals: Contemporary value conflicts* (2nd ed.). New York: Macmillan.

LEPPER, M. R., GREENE, D., & NISBETT, R. E. (1973). Undermining children's intrinsic interest with extrinsic rewards: A test of the "overjustification" hypothesis. *Journal of Personality and Social Psychology, 28,* 129–137.

LERNER, M. J. (1970). The desire for justice and reactions to victims. In J. Macauley & L. Berkowitz (Eds.), *Altruism and helping behavior.* New York: Academic Press.

LEVENTHAL, H. (1982). The integration of emotion and cognition: A view from the perceptual-motor theory of emotion. In M. Clark & S. Fiske (Eds.), *Affect and cognition.* Hillsdale, N. J.: Lawrence Erlbaum.

LEVIN, R. J., & LEVIN, A. (1975, September). Sexual pleasure: The surprising preferences of 100,000 women. *Redbook,* pp. 51–58.

LEVINGER, G. (1983). Development and change. In H. Kelley et al., *Close relationships.* San Francisco: Freeman, 1983.

LEVINSON, D. J. (1978). *The seasons of a man's life.* New York: Knopf.

LEVITT, E. E., & KLASSEN, A. D., JR. (1973). *Public attitudes toward sexual behaviors: The latest investiga-*

tion of the institute for sex research. Bloomington: Indiana University Press.

LEWIN, K. (1935). *A dynamic theory of personality.* New York: McGraw-Hill.

LEWIN, K. (1943). Forces behind food habits and methods of change. *Bulletin of the National Research Council, 108,* 35–65.

LIEBER, A. L., & SHERIN, C. R. (1972). Homicides and the lunar cycle: Toward a theory of lunar influence on human emotional disturbance. *American Journal of Psychiatry, 129,* 69–74.

LIEBERMAN, M. A., YALOM, I. D., & MILES, M. B. (1973). *Encounter groups: First facts.* New York: Basic Books.

LINDER, D. E., & CRANE, K. A. (1970). Reactance theory analysis of predecisional cognitive processes. *Journal of Personality and Social Psychology, 15,* 258–264.

LOCKE, E. A. (1976). The nature and causes of job satisfaction. In M. D. Dunnette (Ed.), *Handbook of industrial and organizational psychology.* Chicago: Rand McNally.

LOPICCOLO, J. (1978). Direct treatment of sexual dysfunctions. In J. LoPiccolo & L. LoPiccolo (Eds.), *Handbook of sex therapy.* New York: Plenum.

LOPICCOLO, J., & HEIMAN, J. (1977). Cultural values and the therapeutic definition of sexual function and dysfunction. *Journal of Social Issues, 33*(2), 166–183.

LORD, R. G. (1977). Functional leadership, behavior measurement and relation to social power and leadership perceptions. *Administrative Science Quarterly, 22,* 114–133.

LOTT, A. J., & LOTT, B. E. (1974). The role of reward in the formation of positive interpersonal attitudes. In T. Huston (Ed.), *Foundations of interpersonal attraction.* New York: Academic Press.

LOWENTHAL, M. F. (1972). Some potentialities of a life-cycle approach to the study of retirement. In F. M. Carp (Ed.), *Retirement.* New York: Behavior Publications.

LUBORSKY, L., & SPENCE, D. P. (1971). Quantitative research on psychoanalytic therapy. In A. E. Bergin & S. L. Garfield (Eds.), *Handbook of psychotherapy and behavior change: An empirical analysis.* New York: Wiley.

LUCHINS, A. S. (1957). Primacy-recency in impression formation. In C. Hovland (Ed.), *The order of presen-*

tation in persuasion. New Haven, Conn.: Yale University Press.

LUFT, J. (1969). *Of human interaction.* Palo Alto, Calif.: National Press Books.

MACCOBY, E., & JACKLIN, C. (1974). *The psychology of sex differences.* Stanford, Calif.: Stanford University Press.

MAIER, N. R. F. (1949). *Frustration: The study of behavior without a goal.* New York: McGraw-Hill.

MAIER, R. A. (1984). *Human sexuality in perspective.* Chicago: Nelson-Hall.

MAILER, N. (1975). *Marilyn.* New York: Warner.

MARCUS, M. G. (1976). Cancer and character. *Psychology Today, 10,* 53–54, 59, 85.

MARKS, G., MILLER, N., & MARUYAMA, G. (1981). Effect of targets' physical attractiveness on assumptions of similarity. *Journal of Personality and Social Psychology, 41* (1), 198–206.

MARTINDALE, D. (1971). Territorial dominance behavior in dyadic verbal interaction. *Proceedings of the 79th Annual Convention of the American Psychological Association, 6,* 305–306.

MASLACH, C. (1979). Negative emotional biasing of unexplained arousal. *Journal of Personality and Social Psychology, 37,* 953–969.

MASLOW, A. H. (1943). A theory of human motivation. *Psychological Review, 50,* 370–396.

MASLOW, A. H. (1954). *Motivation and personality.* New York: Harper & Row.

MASLOW, A. H. (1970). *Motivation and personality* (2nd ed.). New York: Harper & Row.

MASTERS, W. H., & JOHNSON, V. E. (1966). *Human sexual response.* Boston: Little, Brown.

MASTERS, W. H., & JOHNSON, V. E. (1970). *Human sexual inadequacy.* Boston: Little, Brown.

MATHEWS, K. E., & CANNON, L. K. (1975). Environmental noise level as a determinant of helping behavior. *Journal of Personality and Social Psychology, 32,* 571–577.

MATTHEWS, V., & MIHANOVICH, C. (1963). New orientations on marital adjustment. *Marriage and Family Living, 25,* 300–304.

MAY, R., ANGEL, E., & ELLENBERGER, H. F. (Eds.). (1958). *Existence: A new dimension in psychiatry and psychology.* New York: Basic Books.

MCCORMICK, E. J., & ILGEN, D. R. (1980).

Industrial psychology (7th ed.). Englewood Cliffs, N. J.: Prentice-Hall, Inc.

MCGREGOR, D. (1960). *The human side of enterprise.* New York: McGraw-Hill.

MCMULLEN, S., & ROSEN, R. C. (1979). Self-administered masturbation training in the treatment of primary orgasmic dysfunction. *Journal of Consulting and Clinical Psychology, 47,* 912–918.

MEAD, G. H. (1934). *Mind, self and society.* Chicago: University of Chicago Press.

MEAD, M. (1935). *Sex and temperament in three primitive societies.* New York: Morrow.

MEHRABIAN, A. (1971). Nonverbal betrayal of feeling. *Journal of Experimental Research in Personality, 5,* 64–73.

MERTON, R. K. (1957). *Social theory and social structure.* New York: Free Press.

MIDDLEBROOK, P. N. (1980). *Social psychology and modern life.* New York: Knopf.

MILGRAM, S. (1963). Behavioral study of obedience. *Journal of Abnormal and Social Psychology, 67,* 376.

MILGRAM, S. (1965). Some conditions of obedience and disobedience to authority. *Human Relations, 18,* 57–76.

MILGRAM, S. (1970). The experience of living in cities. *Science, 167,* 1461–1468.

MILLER, N. E. (1944). Experimental studies of conflict. In J. McV. Hunt (Ed.), *Personality and the behavior disorders* (Vol. 1). New York: Ronald Press.

MILLER, N. E., & BUGELSKI, R. (1948). Minor studies of aggression: II. The influence of frustrations imposed by the in-group on attitudes expressed toward the out-group. *Journal of Psychology, 25,* 437–453.

MILLER, W. R. (1978). Behavioral treatment of problem drinkers: A comparative outcome study of three controlled drinking therapies. *Journal of Consulting and Clinical Psychology. 46,* 74–86.

MILLS, T. M. (1967). *The sociology of social groups.* Englewood Cliffs, N.J.: Prentice-Hall.

MIRA, E. (1943). *Psychiatry in war.* New York: Norton.

MISCHEL, W. (1973). Toward a cognitive social reconceptualization of personality. *Psychological Review, 80,* 252–283.

MONEY, J., & EHRHARDT, A. (1972). *Man*

and woman, boy and girl: The differentiation and dimorphism of gender identity from conception to maturity. Baltimore: Johns Hopkins University Press.

MOORE, K. A., & HOFFERTH, S. L. (1979). Women and their children. In R. E. Smith (Ed.), *The subtle revolution: Women at work*. Washington, D. C.: The Urban Institute.

MORELAND, R., & ZAJONC, R. (1982). Exposure effects in person perception: Familiarity, similarity and attraction. *Journal of Experimental Social Psychology, 43*, 395–415.

MORRIS, W., WORCHEL, S., BOIS, J., PEARSON, J., ROUNDTREE, C., SAMAHA, G., WACHTLER, J., & WRIGHT, S. (1976). Collective coping with stress: Group reactions to fear, anxiety, and ambiguity. *Journal of Personality and Social Psychology, 13*, 131–140.

MORSE, S. J., & GERGEN, K. J. (1970). Social comparison, self-consistency and the concept of self. *Journal of Personality and Social Psychology, 16*, 148–156.

MORTENSEN, C. (1972). *Communication: The study of human interaction*. New York: McGraw-Hill.

MOSCOVICI, S., & NEWMETH, C. (1974). Social influence II: Minority influence. In C. Nemeth (Ed.), *Social psychology: Classic and contemporary integration*. Chicago: Rand McNally College.

MOSS, H. A. (1967). Sex, age and state as determinants of mother-infant interaction. *Merrill-Palmer Quarterly, 13*, 19–36.

MOWRER, O. H. (1971). Freudianism, behavior therapy and self-disclosure. In E. Southwell & M. Merbaum (Eds.), *Personality: Readings in theory and research* (2nd ed.). Monterey, Calif.: Brooks/Cole.

NAPOLITAN, D. A., & GOETHALS, G. R. (1979). The attribution of friendliness. *Journal of Experimental Social Psychology, 15*, 105–113.

NATIONAL COMMISSION ON THE CAUSES AND PREVENTION OF VIOLENCE. (1969). *Report*. New York: Bantam.

NEMETH, C. J. (1979). The role of an active minority in intergroup relations. In W. Austin & S. Worchel (Eds.), *The social psychology of intergroup relations*. Monterey, Calif.: Brooks/Cole.

NEVIN, R. W. (1970). *Pregnancy and emotional state*. Edgartown, Mass.: School Street Press.

NEWCOMB, T. M. (1961). *The acquaintance process*. New York: Holt, Rinehart and Winston.

NEWMAN, O. (1972). *Defensible space*. New York: Macmillan.

NGUYEN, T., HESLIN, R., & NGUYEN, M. (1975). The meaning of touch: Sex differences. *Journal of Communication, 25*, 92–103.

NICASSIO, P., & BOOTZIN, R. A. (1974). A comparison of progressive relaxation and autogenic training as treatments for insomnia. *Journal of Abnormal Psychology, 83*, 253–260.

NISBETT, R. E., CAPUTO, C., LEGANT, P., & MARECEK, J. (1973). Behavior as seen by the actor and as seen by the observer. *Journal of Personality and Social Psychology, 27*, 154–164.

OLIVEN, J. F. (1974). *Clinical sexuality*. Philadelphia: J. B. Lippincott.

ORGAN, D. W., & HAMNER, W. C. (1978). *Organizational behavior: An applied psychological approach*. Plano, Tex.: Business Publications.

ORNE, M. T., & EVANS, F. J. (1965). Social control in the psychological experiment: Antisocial behavior and hypnosis. *Journal of Personality and Social Psychology, 1*, 189–200.

OUCHI, W. G., & PRICE, R. L. (1978, Autumn). Hierarchies, clans, and theory Z: A new perspective on organizational development. *Organizational Dynamics*, pp. 24–44.

PACKARD, V. (1972). *A nation of strangers*. New York: McKay.

PALMORE, E. (1969, Winter). Predicting longevity: A follow-up controlling for age. *The Gerontologist*, pp. 247–250.

PARKE, D., BERKOWITZ, L., LEYENS, J. P., WEST, S. G., & SEBASTIAN, R. J. (1970). Some effects of violent and nonviolent movies on the behavior of juvenile delinquents. *Advances in Experimental Social Psychology, 10*, 139–169.

PATTERSON, M. L. (1977). Interpersonal distance, affect and equilibrium theory. *Journal of Social Psychology, 101*, 205–214.

PEPLAU, L. A., & PERLMAN, D. (1982). *Loneliness: A source book of current theory, research and therapy*. New York: Wiley.

PEPLAU, L. A., RUBIN, Z., & HILL, C. T. (1977). Sexual intimacy in dating relationships. *Journal of Social Issues, 33* (2), 86–109.

PERLS, F. S. (1969). *Gestalt therapy ver-*

batim. Lafayette, Calif.: Real People Press.

PERLS, F. S. (1970). Four lectures. In J. Fagan & I. L. Shepherd (Eds.), *Gestalt therapy now: Therapy, techniques, applications*. Palo Alto, Calif.: Science and Behavior Books.

PERLS, F. S., HEFFERLINE, R. R., & GOODMAN, P. (1951). *Gestalt therapy: Excitement and growth in the human personality*. New York: Julian Press.

PHARES, E. J. (1976). *Locus of control in personality*. Morristown, N. J.: General Learning Press.

PIAGET, J. (1965). *The moral judgment of the child*. New York: Free Press. (Original American Edition, 1932.)

PIZER, S. A., & TRAVERS, J. R. (1975). *Psychology and social change*. New York: McGraw-Hill.

PLAUT, T. F. A. (1967). *Alcohol problems: A report to the nation by the cooperative commission on the study of alcoholism*. New York: Oxford University Press.

PORTEOUS, J. D. (1977). *Environment and behavior*. Reading, Mass.: Addison-Wesley.

PORTER, L. W., & LAWLER, E. E., III. (1968). *Managerial attitudes and performances*. Homeweed, Ill.: Dorsey Press.

PRINCE, M. (1905). *The dissociation of personality*. New York: Longmans.

RAHE, R. H., & LIND, E. (1971). Psychosocial factors and sudden cardiac death: A pilot study. *Journal of Psychosomatic Research, 15* (1), 19–24.

Random House Dictionary. (1969). New York: Random House.

RICE, B. (1978, June). The new truth machine. *Psychology Today*, pp. 61–74.

ROBBINS, T. W., & FRAY, P. J. (1980). Stress induced eating: Fact, fiction, or misunderstanding? *Appetite, 1*, 103–133.

RODIN, J., & BAUM, A. (1978). Crowding and helplessness: Potential consequences of density and loss of control. In A. Baum & Y. Epstein (Eds.), *Human response to crowding*. Hillsdale, N. J.: Lawrence Erlbaum.

RODIN, J., & SLOCHOWER, J. (1976). Externality in the obese: The effects of environmental responsiveness on weight. *Journal of Personality and Social Psychology, 33*, 338–344.

RODIN, J., SOLOMAN, S., & METCALF, J. (1978). Role of control in mediating perceptions of density. *Journal of*

Personality and Social Psychology, 36, 988–999.

ROGERS, C. (1951). Client-centered therapy: Its current practice, implications and theory. Boston: Houghton-Mifflin.

ROGERS, C. (1959). A theory of therapy, personality and interpersonal relationship, as developed in the client-centered framework. In S. Koch (Ed.), Psychology: A study of science. New York: McGraw-Hill.

ROGERS, C. (1961). On becoming a person: A therapist's view of psychotherapy. Boston: Houghton-Mifflin.

ROGERS, C., & STEVENS, B. (1967). Person to person: The problem of being human. New York: Pocket Books.

ROGERS, C. (1970). Carl Rogers on encounter groups. New York: Harper & Row.

ROHSENOW, D. J., & O'LEARY, M. R. (1978). Locus of control research on alcoholic populations: A review. I. Development, scales, and treatment. International Journal of the Addictions, 13, 55–78.

ROSEN, S., BERGMAN, M., PLESTOR, D., EL-MOFTY, A., & SATTI, M. (1962). Presbycusis study of a relatively noise-free population in the Sudan. Annals of Otology, Rhinology, and Laryngology, 71, 727–743.

ROSENBLATT, P. C., & BUDD, L. (1977). Territoriality and privacy in married and unmarried couples. Journal of Social Psychology, 44, 112–118.

ROSENFELD, H. M. (1965). The effect of an approval-seeking induction on interpersonal proximity. Psychological Reports, 17, 120–122.

ROSENTHAL, R. (1973). The Pygmalion effect lives. Psychology Today, 7, 56–63.

ROSENTHAL, R., & JACOBSON, L. (1968). Pygmalion in the classroom: Teacher expectation and pupil's intellectual development. New York: Holt, Rinehart and Winston.

ROTTER, J. B. (1966). Generalized expectancies for internal vs. external control of reinforcement. Psychological Monographs, 80 (Whole No. 609).

ROTTON, J. (1978). Air pollution is no choke. Unpublished manuscript, University of Dayton.

ROWLAND, N. E., & ANTELMAN, S. M. (1976). Stress induced hyperphagia and obesity in rats: A possible model for understanding human obesity. Science, 191, 310–312.

RUBIN, J. L., PROVENZANO, F. J., & LURIA, Z. (1974). The eye of the beholder: Parents on sex of newborns. American Journal of Orthopsychiatry, 44, 512–519.

RUBIN, Z. (1970). Measurement of romantic love. Journal of Personality and Social Psychology, 16, 265–273.

RUBIN, Z. (1973). Liking and loving: An invitation to social psychology. New York: Holt, Rinehart and Winston.

RYAN, W. (1971). Blaming the victim. New York: Vintage.

SALANCIK, G. R. (1977). Commitment is too easy! Organization Dynamics, 6, 62–80.

SCHACTER, S. (1951). Deviation, rejection and communication. Journal of Abnormal and Social Psychology, 46, 190–207.

SCHACTER, S. (1959). The psychology of affiliation. Stanford, Calif.: Stanford University Press.

SCHACTER, S. (1971). Some extraordinary facts about obese humans and rats. American Psychologist, 26, 129–144.

SCHACTER, S. (1971). Emotion, obesity, and crime. New York: Academic Press.

SCHACTER, S., & SINGER, J. (1962). Cognitive, social and psychological determinants of emotional state. Psychological Review, 69, 379–399.

SCHMECK, H. M., JR. (1974, May 11). Wives' emotions linked to cancer. New York: The New York Times.

SCHMITT, R. C. (1957). Density, delinquency and crime in Honolulu. Sociology and Social Research, 41, 274–276.

SCHMITT, R. C. (1963). Implications of density in Hong Kong. Journal of the American Institute of Planners, 29, 210–217.

SCHMITT, R. C. (1966). Density, health and social disorganization. Journal of the American Institute of Planners, 32, 38–40.

SCHNEIDER, D. J. (1973). Implicit personality theory: A review. Psychological Bulletin, 79, 294–309.

SCHOFIELD, M. (1973). The sexual behavior of young adults. Boston: Little, Brown.

SCHROEDER, D. H., & COSTA, P. T. (1984). Influence of life event stress on physical illness: Substantive effects or methodological flaws? Journal of Personality and Social Psychology, 46, 853–863.

SCHULBERG, B. (1971). Loser and still champion: Muhammad Ali. New York: Popular Library.

SCHULTZ, W. C. (1973). Elements of encounter. Big Sur, Calif.: Joy Press.

SCHULZ, D. A. (1984). Human sexuality (2nd. ed.). Englewood Cliffs, N. J.: Prentice-Hall.

SCHUMER, F. (1983). Abnormal psychology. Lexington, Mass.: D. C. Heath.

SEEMAN, M., & EVANS, J. W. (1962). Alienation and learning in a hospital setting. American Psychological Review, 27, 772–783.

SEGAL, M. W. (1974). Alphabet and attraction: An unobtrusive measure of the effect of propinquity in a field study. Journal of Personality and Social Psychology, 30, 645–657.

SELIGMAN, M. E. P. (1974). Depression and learned helplessness. In R. J. Friedman and M. M. Katz (Eds.), The psychology of depression: Contemporary theory and research. New York: Halsted Press.

SELYE, H. (1956). The stress of life. New York: McGraw-Hill.

SHAVER, K. G. (1970). Defensive attribution: Effects of severity and relevance on the responsibility assigned for an accident. Journal of Personality and Social Psychology, 14, 101–113.

SHAVER, K. G. (1975). An introduction to attribution processes. Cambridge, Mass.: Winthrop.

SHAW, J. I., & SKOLNICK, P. (1971). Attribution of responsibility for a happy accident. Journal of Personality and Social Psychology, 18, 380–383.

SHEEHEY, G. (1976). Passages: Predictable crises of adult life. New York: Dutton.

SHERIF, M., HARVEY, O. J., WHITE, B. J., HOOD, W. R., & SHERIF, C. W. (1961). Intergroup conflict and cooperation: The robbers' cave experiment. Norman, Okla.: University of Oklahoma Press.

SIMMEL, G. (1950). The stranger. In K. H. Wolff (Ed.), The sociology of Georg Simmel. Glencoe, Ill.: Free Press.

SIMON, G. T., & FRIENDS. (1979). The best of the music makers. Garden City, New York: Doubleday.

SINGER, J. (1975). The inner world of day dreaming. New York: Harper & Row.

SIZEMORE, C. C., & PITTILLO, E. S. (1978). I'm Eve. New York: Doubleday.

SKINNER, B. F. (1938). The behavior of organisms. New York: Appleton.

SKINNER, B. F. (1971). Beyond freedom and dignity. New York: Knopf.

SMITH, R. E. (1979). The movement of women into the labor force. In R. E. Smith (Ed.), The subtle revolution:

Women at work. Washington, D. C.: The Urban Institute.

SOBELL, M. B., & SOBELL, L. C. (1978). *Behavioral treatment of alcohol problems: Individualized therapy and controlled drinking*. New York: Plenum.

SOMMER, R. (1967). Small group ecology. *Psychological Bulletin, 67*, 145–152.

SOMMER, R. (1974). *Tight spaces: Hard architecture and how to humanize it*. Englewood Cliffs, N. J.: Prentice-Hall.

SOMMER, R., & ROSS, H. (1958). Social interaction on a geriatric ward. *International Journal of Social Psychiatry, 4*, 128–133.

SOMMERS, D., & ECK, A. (1977, January). Occupational mobility in the American labor force. *Monthly Labor Review*, pp. 3–19.

SORENSON, R. C. (1973). *Adolescent sexuality in contemporary America*. New York: World Publishing.

SPARK, R. F., WHITE, R. A., & CONNOLLY, P. B. (1980, October 3). Impotence is not always psychogenic. *Journal of the American Medical Association, 243* (8), 1558.

STAGNER, R. (1950). Psychological aspects of industrial conflict. II. Motivation. *Personnel Psychology, 3*, 1–16.

STAMPFL, T. G. (1961). *Implosive therapy: A learning-theory derived psychodynamic therapeutic technique*. Paper presented at a colloquium of the University of Illinois. Champagne-Urbana, Ill.

STAW, B. M. (1976). *Intrinsic and extrinsic motivation*. Morristown, N. J.: General Learning Press.

STEERS, R. M., & PORTER, L. W. (1979). *Motivation and work behavior*. New York: McGraw-Hill.

STEINER, I. D. (1972). *Group process and productivity*. New York: Academic Press.

STIRES, L. (1980). Classroom seating location, student grades, and attitudes: Environment or selection? *Environment and Behavior, 12*, 241–254.

STOCK, W. E., & GREER, J. H. (1982). A study of fantasy-based sexual arousal in women. *Archives of Sexual Behavior, 11*, 33–47.

STOKOLS, D., RALL, M., PINNER, B., & SCHOPLER, J. (1973). Physical, social and personal determinants of the perception of crowding. *Environment and Behavior, 5*, 87–110.

STORMS, M., & NISBETT, R. E. (1970). Insomnia and the attribution process. *Journal of Personality and Social Psychology, 16*, 319–328.

STORMS, M. D. (1981). A theory of erotic orientation development. *Psychological Review, 88*, 340–353.

STREIF, G. F., & SCHNEIDER, G. J. (1971). *Retirement in American society: Impact and process*. Ithaca, New York: Cornell University Press.

STRONGMAN, K. T. (1973). *The psychology of emotion*. London: Wiley.

STUART, R. B. (1967). A three dimensional program for the treatment of obesity. *Behavioral Research and Therapy, 5*, 357–365.

STUNKARD, A., D'AQUILL, E., FOX, S., & FILLION, R. D. L. (1972). Influence of social class on obesity and thinness in children. *JAMA, 221*, 579–584.

SULLIVAN, H. S. (1953). *The interpersonal theory of psychiatry*. New York: Norton.

SUNDSTROM, E. (1978). Crowding as a sequential process: Review of research on the effects of population density on humans. In A. Baum & Y. Epstein (Eds.), *Human response to crowding*. Hillsdale, N. J.: Lawrence Erlbaum.

SWENSON, C. H. (1973). *Introduction to interpersonal relations*. Glenview, Ill.: Scott, Foresman.

SZASZ, T. S. (1974). *The myth of mental illness: Foundations of a theory of personal conduct*. New York: Harper & Row.

TAVRIS, C. (1976). Women: Work isn't always the answer. *Psychology Today, 10* (4), 78.

TAVRIS, C., & JAYARANTE, T. E. (1976, June), How happy is your marriage? What 75,000 wives say about their most intimate relationship. *Redbook*, pp. 90–92, 132, 134.

TAVRIS, C., & SADD, S. (1977). *The Redbook report on female sexuality*. New York: Delacorte Press.

TAYLOR, D. A. (1968). The development of interpersonal relations: Social penetration processes. *Journal of Social Psychology, 75*, 79–90.

TERZIAN, J., & CRAMER, K. (1970). *Mighty hard road: The story of Cesar Chavez*. New York: Doubleday.

THIBAUT, J. W., & KELLEY, H. H. (1959). *The social psychology of groups*. New York: Wiley.

THIEL, H., PARKER, D., & BRUCE, T. A. (1973). Stress factors and the risk of myocardial infarction. *Journal of Psychosomatic Research, 17*, 43–57.

THIGPEN, C. H., & CLECKLEY, H. (1954). A case of multiple personality. *Journal of Abnormal and Social Psychology, 49*, 135–151.

THIGPEN, C. H., & CLECKLEY, H. (1957). *The three faces of Eve*. New York: McGraw-Hill.

THOMAS, M., HORTON, R., LIPPINCOTT, E., & DRABMAN, R. (1977). Desensitization to portrayals of real-life aggression as a function of exposure to television violence. *Journal of Personality and Social Psychology, 35*, 450–458.

THOMPSON, J. K. (1984). Personal communication.

THORNDIKE, E. L. (1898). Animal intelligence: An experimental study of the associative process in animals. *Psychological Review Monograph Supplement, 2* (4, Whole No. 8).

THORNTON, B. (1977). Toward a linear prediction model of marital happiness. *Personality and Social Psychology Bulletin. 3*, 674–676.

TOFFLER, A. (1970). *Future shock*. New York: Random House.

TOMPKINS, S. S., & McCARTER, R. (1964). What and where are the primary affects? Some evidence for a theory. *Perceptual and Motor Skills, 18*, 119–158.

TOUHEY, J. C. (1972). Comparison of two dimensions of attitude similarity on heterosexual attraction. *Journal of Personality and Social Psychology, 23*, 8–10.

TREADWAY, J. (1984, April 25). United Press International. Pittsfield, Mass.: *The Berkshire Eagle*.

UNITED STATES DEPARTMENT OF LABOR. (1980). Office of the Secretary, Women's Bureau. *Facts on working women*. Washington, D. C.: Government Printing Office.

UNITED STATES RIOT COMMISSION. (1968). *Report of the National Advisory Commission on Civil Disorders*. New York: Bantam.

VALINS, S., & NISBETT, R. E. (1972). Attribution processes in the development and treatment of emotional disorders. In E. Jones, D. Kanouse, H. Kelley, R. Nisbett, S. Valins, & B. Weiner (Eds.), *Attribution: Perceiving the causes of behavior modification*. Morristown, N. J.: General Learning Press.

VANCE, E. B., & WAGNER, N. N. (1976). Written descriptions of orgasm: A study of sex differences. *Archives of Sexual Behavior, 5*, 87–98.

VIDEBECK, R. (1960). Self-conception and the reactions of others. *Sociometry, 23*, 351–362.

WALLIS, C. (1981, March 9). Prince Charles picks a bride. *Time*, pp. 66–67.

WALSTER, E. (1965). The effect of self-esteem on romantic liking. *Journal of Experimental Social Psychology, 1,* 184–197.

WALSTER, E., ARONSON, V., ABRAHAMS, D., & ROTTMANN, L. (1966). Importance of physical attractiveness in dating behavior. *Journal of Personality and Social Psychology, 4,* 508–516.

WALSTER, E., & BERSCHEID, E. (1971). Adrenaline makes the heart grow fonder. *Psychology Today, 5,* 47–62.

WALSTER, E., & PRESTHOLDT, P. (1966). The effect of misjudging another: Over-compensation or dissonance reduction? *Journal of Experimental Social Psychology, 2,* 85–97.

WALSTER, E., WALSTER, B., ABRAHAM, D., & BROWN, A. (1966). The effect on liking of underrating or overrating another. *Journal of Experimental Social Psychology, 2,* 70–84.

WALSTER, E., & WALSTER, G. W. (1978). *A new look at love.* Reading, Mass.: Addison-Wesley.

WALSTER, E., WALSTER, G. W., & BERSCHEID, E. (1978). *Equity: Theory and research.* Boston: Allyn and Bacon.

WALSTER, E., WALSTER, G. W., PILIAVIN, J., & SCHMITT, L. (1973). Playing hard to get: Understanding an elusive phenomenon. *Journal of Personality and Social Psychology, 26,* 113–121.

WALTERS, B. (1970). *How to talk with practically anybody about practically anything.* New York: Dell.

WALTERS, H., & MALAMUD, P. (1975). "Drop that gun, Captain Video." *Newsweek, 85* (10), 81–82.

WATSON, J. B. (1925). *Behaviorism.* New York: Norton.

WATSON, J. B., & RAYNER, R. (1920). Conditioned emotional reactions. *Journal of Experimental Social Psychology, 3,* 1–4.

WATSON, O. M., & GRAVES, T. D. (1966). Quantitative research in proxemic behavior. *American Anthropologist, 68,* 971–985.

WATZLAWICK, P., BEAVIN, J. H., & JACKSON, D. D. (1967). *Pragmatics of human communication.* New York: Norton.

WECHSLER, H. (1980). Epidemiology of male/female drinking over the last half century. In *Alcoholism and alcohol abuse and women: Research issues.* Research Monograph No. 1. National Institute on Alcohol Abuse and Alcoholism, U. S. Department of Health, Education and Welfare.

WEINBERG, M. S., & WILLIAMS, C. (1974). *Male homosexuals: Their problems and adaptations.* New York: Oxford University Press.

WEINER, B., FREIZE, J., KUKLA, A., REED, L., REST, S., & ROSENBAUM, R. M. (1971). *Perceiving the causes of success and failure.* Morristown, N. J.: General Learning Press.

WELLS, B. (1972). The psycho-social influence of building environment: Sociometric findings in large and small office spaces. In R. Gutman (Ed.), *People and buildings.* New York: Basic Books.

WESTIN, A. F. (1967). *Privacy and freedom.* New York: Atheneum.

WEXNER, L. B. (1954). The degree to which colors (hues) are associated with mood tones. *Journal of Applied Psychology, 38,* 432–435.

WHITE, R. W. (1964). *The abnormal personality.* New York: Ronald Press.

WHITE, R. W. (1976). *The enterprise of living.* New York: Holt, Rinehart and Winston.

WILLIAMS, F., & SUNDENE, B. (1965). Dimensions of recognition: Visual vs. vocal expression of emotion. *AV Communication Review, 13,* 44–52.

WILLIAMS, L. (1984, March 15). *New York Times News Service.* Pittsfield, Mass.: *The Berkshire Eagle.*

WILLIS, F. (1966). Initial speaking distance as a function of the speaker's relationship. *Psychonomic Science, 5,* 221–222.

WILSON, G. D. (1966). Arousal properties of red versus green. *Perceptual and Motor Skills, 23,* 947–979.

WILSON, G. T., & LAWSON, D. W. (1978). Expectancies, alcohol and sexual arousal in women. *Journal of Abnormal Psychology, 87,* 358–367.

WOLFF, S., & WOLFF, H. G. (1947). *Human gastric functions.* New York: Oxford University Press.

WOLPE, J. (1958). *Psychotherapy by reciprocal inhibition.* Stanford, Calif.: Stanford University Press.

WOLPE, J. (1974). *The practice of behavior therapy.* New York: Pergamon Press.

WORCHEL, S. (1978). The experience of crowding: An attributional analysis. In A. Baum & Y. Epstein (Eds.), *Human response to crowding.* Hillsdale, N. J.: Lawrence Erlbaum.

WORCHEL, S., AXSOM, D., FERRIS, F., SAMAHA, G., & SCHWEITZER, S. (1978). Determinants of the effects of intergroup cooperation on intergroup attraction. *Journal of Conflict Resolution, xxii,* 429–439.

WORCHEL, S., & BROWN, E. H. (1984). The role of plausibility in influencing environmental attributions. *Journal of Experimental Social Psychology, 20,* 86–96.

WORCHEL, S., & COOPER, J. (1979). *Understanding social psychology.* Homewood, Ill.: Dorsey Press.

WORCHEL, S., & COOPER, J. (1983). *Understanding social psychology.* Homewood, Ill.: Dorsey Press.

WORCHEL, S., & LOLLIS, M. (1982). Reactions to territorial contamination as a function of culture. *Personality and Social Psychology Bulletin, 8,* 365–370.

WORCHEL, S., & SHEBILSKE, W. (1983). *Psychology: Principles and applications.* Englewood Cliffs, N. J.: Prentice-Hall.

WORCHEL, S., & TEDDLIE, C. (1976). The experience of crowding: A two-factor theory. *Journal of Personality and Social Psychology, 34,* 30–40.

WORCHEL, S., & YOHAI, S. M. L. (1979). The role of attribution in the experience of crowding. *Journal of Experimental Social Psychology, 15,* 91–104.

ZAJONC, R. (1968). Attitudinal effects of mere exposure. *Journal of Personality and Social Psychology, 9,* 1–27.

ZIMBARDO, P. (1970). The human choice: Individuation, reason and order versus deindividuation, impulse and chaos. In W. J. Arnold & D. Levine (Eds.), *Nebraska Symposium on Motivation.* Lincoln, Neb.: University of Nebraska Press.

ZIMBARDO, P. (1971). *The psychological power and pathology of imprisonment.* Statement prepared for the U.S. House of Representatives Committee on the Judiciary (Subcommittee No. 3, Robert Kastemeyer, Chairman, hearings on prison reform). Unpublished paper, Stanford University, Stanford, Calif.

ZIMBARDO, P. (1977). *Shyness.* Reading, Mass.: Addison-Wesley.

NAME INDEX

SUBJECT INDEX

ABOUT THE AUTHORS

Stephen Worchel

George R. Goethals

Stephen Worchel is a professor of psychology and head of the Psychology Department at Texas A&M University. He received a B.A. degree from the University of Texas and a Ph.D. from Duke University. Before coming to Texas A&M he taught at the University of Virginia, University of North Carolina, and North Carolina Central University. Steve was a Senior Fullbright Research scholar in Athens, Greece, during 1979–1980. He has held several editor posts including associate editor of the *Personality and Social Psychology Bulletin,* Advisory Editor to *Psychological Abstracts,* and Editorial Consultant to *Basic and Applied Social Psychology* and the *Journal of Environmental Psychology and Nonverbal Behavior.* He has been a Series Editor for books in psychology for D. Van Nostrand Company and Nelson-Hall Company. Steve has published more than 50 research articles in a wide variety of journals and has co-authored *Understanding Social Psychology* (3 editions), *Adjustment and Human Relations, Clinical Psychology: A Social Psychological Approach,* and the *Social Psychology of Intergroup Relations* (2 editions). He is a Fellow in the American Psychological Association. Steve's areas of research include intergroup relations, conflict and conflict resolution, human aggression, group dynamics, effects of environment on human behavior, and attitude change. When not teaching or writing, Steve escapes to his ranch outside of College Station where he raises cattle and horses.

George R. Goethals is Professor of Psychology and Chairman of the Psychology Department at Williams College in Williamstown, Massachusetts. He received his A.B. from Harvard and his Ph.D. from Duke. Goethals spent a year as a visiting scholar at Princeton and one at the University of Virginia. His research has focused on self-evaluation through social comparison, attribution, and the perception of other people, and attitude change. He is co-author of *Psychology* with Crider, Kavanaugh, and Solomon. He is Associate Editor of the *Journal of Experimental Social Psychology.*